# Utilizing Technology to Manage Territories

Lhoussaine Alla
*Sidi Mohamed Ben Abdellah University, Morocco*

Bouchra Alj
*Faculty of Legal, Economic, and Social Sciences of Mohammedia, Hassan II University, Casablanca, Morocco*

Badr Bentalha
*National School of Business and Management, Sidi Mohammed Ben Abdellah University, Morocco*

IGI Global
Publishing Tomorrow's Research Today

Vice President of Editorial — Melissa Wagner
Managing Editor of Acquisitions — Mikaela Felty
Managing Editor of Book Development — Jocelynn Hessler
Production Manager — Mike Brehm
Cover Design — Phillip Shickler

Published in the United States of America by
IGI Global Scientific Publishing
701 East Chocolate Avenue
Hershey, PA, 17033, USA
Tel: 717-533-8845
Fax: 717-533-8661
Website: https://www.igi-global.com E-mail: cust@igi-global.com



Library of Congress Cataloging-in-Publication Data

Names: Alla, Lhoussaine, 1969- editor.
Title: Utilizing technology to manage territories / edited by Lhoussaine Alla, Bouchra ALJ, Badr Bentalha.
Description: Hershey, PA : IGI Global Scientific Publishing, 2025. | Includes bibliographical references and index. | Summary: "The book aims to position itself as an invaluable resource, both for researchers and for local practitioners and actors. It is committed to enriching all theoretical and methodological knowledge on Territorial Smart Management while offering tangible tools for effective action in the field. Through pragmatic perspectives, inspiring illustrations and operational recommendations, it aspires to promote the implementation of initiatives promoting the attractiveness, sustainability and socio-economic inclusion of territories"-- Provided by publisher.
Identifiers: LCCN 2024047140 (print) | LCCN 2024047141 (ebook) | ISBN 9798369368541 (hardcover) | ISBN 9798369368558 (paperback) | ISBN 9798369368565 (ebook)
Subjects: LCSH: Management. | Zoning.
Classification: LCC HD31.2 .U75 2025 (print) | LCC HD31.2 (ebook) | DDC 658--dc23/eng/20250114
LC record available at https://lccn.loc.gov/2024047140
LC ebook record available at https://lccn.loc.gov/2024047141

British Cataloguing in Publication Data
A Cataloguing in Publication record for this book is available from the British Library.

# Table of Contents

# Detailed Table of Contents

with a diversification of topics covered, such as rural development initiatives, innovative practices for a socially responsible economy and sustainable development objectives. The implications of this research underline the importance of continuing research in this field, focusing on specific areas such as the comparison of rural development policies and support programs for social innovation, and the integration of sustainable development objectives into organizational practices.



Odisha is the first state in India to introduce a Climate Budget. It supports Govt. to planning & executing various climate action programs and improving the state's climate resilience. Episodic storm events such as cyclones like Phailin, Hudhud, Titli, and Fani and some chronic problems like shore erosion, coastal flooding, storm surge, inundation, heat waves, drought, and whirlwinds always affect socioeconomic conditions. As the state is always prone to calamities directly or indirectly, there are certain techniques and methods implemented to tackle it. This paper signifies different issues and challenges related to territorial sustainability and the causes of climate change and management in Odisha related to different sectors i.e. Agriculture, Energy, Fisheries, Forest & Environment, Health & Family Welfare, Water Conservation, Urban Development, etc. and it also studied the concept of sustainability and various challenges related to the climate change and action till now in Odisha.



This study explores the characteristics of Digital Governance trends using the Scopus database from 2012 to 2022 using the CiteSpace application. E-Government is an

This study examines the impact of Artificial intelligence and the effectiveness of territorial E-governance. The objects are to explore the implicit benefits of artificial intelligence in Amman's governance, assess its impact on decision- making processes. The study sample consists of government ministries in Amman's public sector, which includes 40 governmental entities enforcing AI systems. The methodology covers a five- time period from 2018 to 2023, and relies on primary data sources, including sanctioned government reports and stoner satisfaction checks, to dissect the relinquishment and operation of artificial intelligence. The research findings illustrate that the use of E-governance supported by artificial intelligence technologies in the Amman's public sector has led to tangible improvements in user satisfaction and service delivery effectiveness. It has also contributed to enhancing efficiency, transparency, reducing bureaucratic processes, and improving prediction and planning, reflecting a positive and tangible impact on Amman's E-governance development.



This systematic review examines the expanding role of Artificial Intelligence (AI) in sustainable mobility, analyzing literature from Web of Science and Scopus databases published between 2019 and 2024. The review identifies key trends in integrating AI into transportation systems, focusing on sustainability, smart solutions, and the development of smart cities. Efforts to enhance eco-friendly and energy-efficient mobility solutions are highlighted, reflecting the critical role of AI in reducing environmental impacts while maintaining high levels of accessibility and convenience. Adopting smart solutions, including AI-driven traffic management and autonomous vehicles, demonstrates how cutting-edge technologies optimize

The increasing global awareness of the need for sustainable urbanization is driving the integration of green artificial intelligence (Green AI) in urban planning and management. AI applications include intelligent automation in energy management, intelligent transport systems, improved infrastructure strength and durability, and enhanced individual safety and security through AI surveillance and predictive policing systems. Case studies from Amsterdam, Singapore, and New York demonstrate how AI solutions are changing productivity, energy consumption, emissions, safety, and the environment. AI also improves infrastructure construction, traffic congestion, and public safety by evaluating sensor data and notifying undesired events. Big cities like London and New York are implementing AI in their public safety initiatives. AI applications are essential for enhancing resilience, energy efficiency, public safety, and environmental monitoring, as well as green urban planning and management.



This paper provides an in-depth introduction to the Internet of Things (IoT) in the context of smart homes, discussing the components and evolution of smart homes. It presents a comprehensive literature review tracing the development of smart homes over time. The paper further explores the implementation of smart homes in China, Malaysia, and India, focusing on adoption rates, cultural acceptance, and the economic capability of individuals. It highlights the contrasting differences in these three aspects: Adoption Rate, Cultural Acceptance and Economic condition of population across the three countries: India, China and Myanmar. The results section underscores the significance of this research in understanding the dynamics of smart home adoption and its implications for future development. This study contributes to the growing body of knowledge on smart homes and IoT, offering valuable insights for policymakers, researchers, and industry practitioners.



In a global context marked by the globalization of economies, and by the adoption of information technologies as key success factors for standing out in an environment of fierce intra- and inter-regional competition, territorial development players are called upon to establish a climate of territorial economic intelligence, in order to provide good strategic information for successful decision-making by territorial players in an intelligent way. The port territory will not escape this context of change, and plays a crucial role in global supply chains, which are facing major structural transformations and transitions in the fields of sustainability, energy transition and geo-economics. The role of port intelligence is increasingly crucial in managing these transitions. Port intelligence presents multiple challenges in terms of technology and governance in managing a complex ecosystem that requires the implementation of a community system that brings together all stakeholders in the port territory. As a result, we aim to highlight the role of this port community system (PCS) in improving port intelligence. Accordingly, our study is divided into two parts: a theoretical approach aimed at providing a review of the role of the PCS in enhancing port intelligence, and a quantitative, hypothetico-deductive approach.



SMART cities realized through public-private partnership projects is a topic that requires further exploration in the field of management. Many researchers have contributed to this topic, each conducting their research from a distinct perspective and employing diverse methodologies. The goal of this article is to present a Structured Literature Review of the most relevant publications on SMART cities developed

# Preface

"***Utilizing Technology to Manage Territories***" is a collaborative work that explores the crucial intersection between emerging technologies and land management. In a changing world, where the challenges of urbanization, climate change and sustainability are increasing, this book offers valuable insights into the innovations that shape the future of our territories.

## 1. GENERAL OVERVIEW OF THE SUBJECT

This book covers a wide range of topics, from artificial intelligence and the Internet of Things to social innovation and sustainable development. It examines how these technologies transform territorial governance, urban planning, mobility and resource management. The chapters cover various aspects such as bibliometric analysis of research trends, regional case studies and theoretical perspectives on territorial intelligence.

This book is a collaborative book that explores the revolutionary impact of emerging technologies on the management of both urban and rural territories. This book is aimed at a wide audience, including policy makers, urban planners, researchers, entrepreneurs and citizens engaged in sustainable development.

The relevance of the subject is undeniable. Digital transformation and the rise of technologies such as artificial intelligence, the internet of things (IoT) and big data (Big Data) are disrupting lifestyles and business models. These technologies offer immense potential to improve land management, optimize resource use, promote social inclusion and address environmental challenges.

Smart land management is a hot topic. Technology offers promising solutions to global challenges such as climate change, population growth and rapid urbanization. The emergence of smart cities, the increasing use of AI in urban planning, and the adoption of the Internet of Things to optimize public services attest to the urgency and relevance of these innovations. This book captures the state of the art of these developments and offers perspectives on their future evolution.

Indeed, this collective book "Utilizing Technology to Manage Territories" addresses a topic of crucial importance in the current context marked by digital transformation and the emergence of new technologies. It explores in depth the use of advanced technologies, such as artificial intelligence, the Internet of things and big data analytics, to address territorial management and development challenges.

The subject is therefore very topical, as urban and rural territories are confronted with complex issues in terms of governance, resource management, economic attractiveness and sustainable development. The successful integration of technological innovations in territorial management is therefore essential to respond to these challenges in an effective and sustainable manner.

## 2. TARGET AUDIENCE AND POTENTIAL USES

This book is aimed at a wide audience, including public policy-makers, local authority officials, researchers and experts in the fields of spatial planning, local development and new technologies. It aims to provide in-depth analyses, concrete case studies and strategic recommendations to guide the successful implementation of innovative technological solutions for more intelligent, sustainable and inclusive territorial management.

The publication is thus aimed at a wide audience, including:

- Researchers and academics in the fields of urban planning, geography, information technology and sustainable development.
- Policy makers and spatial planners at all levels of government.
- Professionals working in urban development, smart city management and technological innovation.
- Master's and doctoral students interested in the intersection of technology and land management.

Readers will find in this book:

- Comprehensive overview of the latest research trends and innovations in the field.
- Practical case studies illustrating the application of advanced technologies in various geographic contexts.
- Theoretical frameworks to understand and analyze the impact of technologies on land use management.

- Ideas for future research and practical applications.

By synthesizing current knowledge and providing future perspectives, "Utilizing Technology to Manage Territories" is an invaluable resource for all those who seek to understand and shape the future of our territories in the digital age.

## 3. OVERALL DESCRIPTION OF CONTRIBUTIONS

The collective book "Utilizing Technology to Manage Territories" offers a comprehensive and multidisciplinary exploration of the use of technologies for land management, as a cocktail of scientific contributions from researchers of international dimension.

The different chapters presented by the authors examine key themes such as open innovation, territorial sustainability, artificial intelligence, IoT, e-governance and much more. The book aims to inform readers about technological advances that can transform urban and rural planning, improve environmental sustainability, strengthen territorial governance and foster inclusive economic development.

This book provides an in-depth analysis of these technologies and their practical applications in different contexts. It is structured around 14 chapters that cover a wide range of topics, from open innovation and economic integration in Africa to artificial intelligence and smart cities.

The main themes covered in each chapter are summarised below:

- *The first chapter*, "***A bibliometric analysis of Open innovation, Technology, Economic integration research in Africa: Emerging trends and Orientations***", aims to address the lack of research on the combined impact of these factors on economic growth in Africa. The authors adopt a bibliometric analysis of scientific publications as a methodological approach. Their results highlight a significant growth in research since 2014, identifying collaborative networks and future research axes.
- *The second chapter*, "***A Bibliometric Study of Social Innovation and Sustainable Territorial Development: Key Research Trends and Emerging Insights",*** seeks to raise the gap in understanding of trends and directions of research in this field. Through a bibliometric analysis of scientific publications, the authors highlighted the constant growth of research, the diversification of topics addressed, importance of applied research.
- *The 3rd chapter*, ***"A Theoretical Approach Towards Territorial Sustainability Conceptualizing: A Case Study in The Context of Climate Change in Odisha",*** addresses the issue of Odisha's vulnerability to natural disasters

and the need for sustainable territorial management. Through a case study, the authors were able to identify the main challenges and opportunities related to territorial sustainability in the face of climate change.

- *The 4th chapter*, ***"Bibliometric Analysis of Measuring the Impact of Digital Government on the Territories of PUBLIC Sector Reform"***, seeks to better understand the influence of digital government on public sector reform. The bibliometric analysis of digital government publications allowed authors to see growth in publications, US dominance, and the importance of citizen-orientation.
- *The 5th chapter*, ***« Logistic Clustering Dynamics Determinants: A Bibliometric and Prospective Approach »***, aims to fill the lack of research on the future evolution of logistics clusters. The authors adopted a systematic and qualitative bibliometric approach to identify endogenous and exogenous factors influencing the dynamics of logistic clusters.
- *The 6th chapter*, ***"Artificial intelligence and the effectiveness of territorial E-governance: An exploration through the case of the Amman region in Jordan"***, deals with an issue around the evaluation of the impact of AI on the effectiveness of electronic governance. By adopting a case study-based methodological approach, the researchers highlighted the improvement in user satisfaction, service efficiency and transparency through AI.
- *The 7th chapter*, "***Exploring Trends, Perspectives, and Challenges of Artificial Intelligence in Sustainable Mobility: A Systematic Review"***, aims to analyze the growing role of AI in creating sustainable transport systems through a systematic review of scientific literature. The results identified key trends, including smart solutions for sustainable mobility and smart cities.
- *The 8th chapter*, ***"The Future of Territorial Management AI, IoT, and Big Data Synergies: The Future of Territorial Management"***, seeks to explore how convergence of these technologies is transforming spatial management. The analysis highlighted the potential of these technologies to address challenges in territorial governance.
- • *The 9th chapter,**"The Green City: Sustainable and Smart Urban Living through Artificial Intelligence",*** discusses how green AI can contribute to creating more sustainable cities. The results of the analysis of AI applications in sustainable urban management have shown that AI improves energy efficiency, waste management, safety and sustainable urban planning.
- • *The 10th chapter*, "***Analyzing Territorial Variations in the Implementation of IoT-Based Smart Homes: A Comprehensive Review***", attempts to understand differences in the adoption of smart homes across different contexts. Through a literature review and case studies on China, Malaysia and India,

the authors highlighted disparities in adoption based on adoption rate, cultural acceptance and economic situation.

- *The 11th chapter*, "***Collective intelligence of port territory stakeholders: Case of Moroccan ports***", is defined as problematic: How to improve port intelligence through collaboration between actors? Based on a case study, the researchers showed that PCS improves collective intelligence, operational optimization and business decision-making.
- *The 12th chapter*, "***Smart Cities and Public-Private Partnership Projects: A Structured Literature Review***", seeks to explore the link between smart cities and public-private partnerships (PPPs). The structured literature review carried out allowed to obtain a synthesis of knowledge, and identification of impacts, limits and future directions of research.
- *The 13th chapter*, "***The Revolution of Territorial Management through the Adoption of Emerging Innovations: A Qualitative Study of the Casablanca-Settat Region***", seeks to study the impact of emerging technologies on territorial management in the Casablanca-Settat region. Using a qualitative study based on semi-structured interviews with local stakeholders, the researchers concluded that emerging technologies improve resource management, citizen participation and service delivery.
- *The 14th chapter*, "***Transformational Trends of Territorial Economic Intelligence Strategies in the Digital Era: A Systematic Theoretical Exploration***", attempts to understand the evolution of territorial economic intelligence in the digital age. Through bibliographical and thematic research, the study revealed that territorial economic intelligence now integrates technologies and collaboration between actors for better decision-making.

The different chapters of the book address topics such as bibliometric analysis of research trends, the impact of artificial intelligence on electronic governance, synergies between the Internet of things, artificial intelligence and big data analytics, or the challenges and perspectives of integrating emerging technologies into smart and sustainable cities. This range of topics offers readers a comprehensive and transversal view of the issues related to the use of technologies to meet the challenges of territorial management.

In fine, the book "Utilizing Technology to Manage Territories" provides a comprehensive overview of how technologies are transforming land management, addressing theoretical aspects, practical applications and case studies. It highlights the potential of technologies to address contemporary territorial challenges and promote sustainable and inclusive development. The book offers a forward-looking perspective on the future of our cities, regions, and rural landscapes. It provides a roadmap for harnessing the power of technology to create more sustainable, resilient, and prosperous territories for generations to come.

## 4. CONCLUSION AND PERSPECTIVES

The collective "Utilizing Technology to Manage Territories" provides a comprehensive and diverse exploration of the challenges of land management in the age of technology. Across the different chapters, contributors examined topics ranging from open innovation to territorial sustainability and artificial intelligence, providing a comprehensive overview of technological advances that can shape the future of territories.

The contributions highlight the complexity of the issues facing territories, such as climate change, increasing urbanization and the need for effective governance. The bibliometric analyses, case studies and systematic reviews presented in this book provide concrete responses and innovative perspectives to address these complex challenges.

For the scientific community, this book provides a solid foundation for future research, encouraging an interdisciplinary and collaborative approach to better understand and solve current territorial issues. The proposed theoretical frameworks, innovative methodologies and empirical results contribute to enriching the field of territorial management and stimulate new reflections in this constantly evolving field.

For managers and professionals involved in planning and managing territories, this book is a valuable resource offering up-to-date knowledge and practical tools to implement effective strategies. Case studies and in-depth analyses identify good practices and innovative solutions to improve sustainability, strengthen governance and promote balanced territorial development.

Finally, this publication opens up new perspectives for research on the theoretical, methodological and empirical levels. The areas of AI, IoT, Big Data and social innovation offer a fertile ground for future work to explore in depth the impacts of these technologies on territorial management, to develop new conceptual models and to broaden the horizons of applied research in this crucial area.

In short, "Utilizing Technology to Manage Territories" represents a significant contribution to understanding contemporary issues of land management and inspires the promotion of innovative and sustainable approaches to shaping resilient and prosperous territories for future generations.

**Lhoussaine Alla**
*National School of Applied Sciences, LAREMEF laboratory, Sidi Mohamed Ben Abdellah University, Morocco*

**Bouchra Alj**
*Faculty of Legal, Economic and Social Sciences, Hassan II University, Casablanca, Morocco*

**Badr Bentalha**
*National School of Business and Management, Sidi Mohamed Ben Abdellah University, Morocco*

# Chapter 1
# A Bibliometric Analysis of Open Innovation, Technology, Economic Integration Research in Africa:
## Emerging Trends and Orientations

**Hicham Saidi**
*Superior School of Technology of Fez, Sidi Mohamed Ben Abdellah University, Morocco*

**Fatima Zahra Madhat**
*Superior School of Technology of Fez, Sidi Mohamed Ben Abdellah University, Morocco*

## ABSTRACT

*Economic openness for growth involves complex factors that need further investigation. Traditionally focused on developed economies, recent research is shifting towards emerging regions like Africa. Our study addresses this gap by exploring the intersection of open innovation, technology, and economic integration in Africa. The analysis reveals a significant increase in publications on these topics since 2014, with a notable rise from 2018, indicating growing academic interest. Key works include a 2020 study on SME contributions to regional growth (33 citations), a 2021 exploration of fintech success (31 citations), and a 2019 analysis of knowledge in free trade zones (28 citations). Through bibliometric analysis, we identify key contributors, influential countries, and collaborative networks, offering insights and a*

DOI: 10.4018/979-8-3693-6854-1.ch001

*framework for future research to support sustainable development across Africa, emphasizing regional origin and technological capacity in economic strategies.*

## 1 INTRODUCTION

From a sustainable development perspective, transformative systemic innovation refers to the strategic enhancement of technological innovation policies and growth strategies that align with global social goals. This approach aims to foster improvements across economic, social, and environmental dimensions, both locally and globally (Vallejo et al., 2019). Transformative systemic innovation involves a holistic perspective that integrates various sectors and levels of society to achieve sustainable development outcomes. It seeks to overcome traditional siloed approaches by promoting cross-sectoral coordination and leveraging technological advancements to address complex global challenges.

Over the past decade, there has been a notable increase in international economic activities across various countries. This surge has been driven by globalization, which has opened up new opportunities for economic growth, collaboration, and technology transfer. Participating nations have reaped multiple benefits from these heightened economic interactions, including enhanced access to global markets and increased foreign direct investment (Degbey et al., 2021; Nshimbi, 2021). These benefits contribute to overall economic development while also presenting new challenges and opportunities for integrating sustainable practices into economic strategies.

Studies by Almeida & Fernandes (2008) and Guncavdi & Ulengin (2012) have empirically demonstrated the positive impact of economic openness on growth. This positive influence is attributed to several factors, including the deepening of the specification of economic activity, economies of scale, the redistribution of knowledge and the improvement of the quality of intellectual capital. However, the complex nature of the parameters affecting economic growth has prevented the creation of a unified definition of the link between integration and growth (Gammadigbe, 2021).

Traditionally, the focus has been on large developed or emerging economies, neglecting the question of whether regional origin and technological capacity can mitigate the disadvantages faced by multinational firms in small, open economies (Ghauri & Yamin, 2009).

In contrast, emerging and developing regions such as Africa have only recently begun to receive the attention of researchers (Pomerlyan & Belitski, 2023). These regions face unique challenges, including rapid population growth and a high demand for essential infrastructure, such as information technology (UNISA, 2018). This underscores the importance of regional expertise, which depends heavily on the quality of human capital and technological capacity (Ekholm & Hakkala, 2007).

Various modern technologies are crucial in fostering innovation and economic integration. Additionally, the role of logistics in influencing local and regional territorial development in emerging country should not be overlooked (Bader et al., 2024). It provides flexibility within firms (Morrison Paul, 2002), enables firms to achieve increasing returns to scale, higher efficiency, and profits, and fosters innovation (Kleynhans, 2016).

The development of innovation accelerates the application and integration of technologies needed for economic growth (Anarfo et al., 2019; Feng et al., 2019; Rauf et al., 2018; Senadjki et al, 2022). Additionally, international competitiveness can be enhanced through global contacts, including trade, foreign direct investment, and the transfer of modern technologies (Cabrer-Borràs & Serrano-Domingo, 2007). Countries such as Singapore and Thailand exemplify this by driving innovation through technology integration and optimization in projects like the "Belt & Road Initiative" (Jiang & Hui, 2021).

In the era of globalization, companies are called upon to open up to research and development ideas, integrating internal and external sources to maintain their competitiveness (Chesbrough, 2003; Tassey, 2008). With increasing technological advances and global competition, these firms are forced to innovate quickly, enabling them to develop more efficient products and services (Ahuja, 2011; Ernst & Linsu, 2002; Von Zedtwitza & Gassmannb, 2002).

The creation of global innovation networks is one of the forms of organization adopted by companies to implement open innovation (Chaminade, 2009; OECD, 2008; Papadopoulos et al., 2013). This approach emphasizes the importance of collaboration and knowledge sharing across borders to foster innovation.

In this context, the evolution of capital and technology has been highlighted as a crucial factor in stimulating good economic practices at the national level (Niyongabo, 2004). Human capital is also emerging as an important driver of productivity and growth through innovation and technology adoption (Aghion and Howitt, 1990; Romer, 1990; Danquah & Amankwah-Amoah, 2017).

On such context, open innovation is now an essential part of a company's innovation strategy and business activities, as it facilitates the production of new ideas, products and services by leveraging know-how beyond traditional boundaries (Hidalgo et al., 2002; OECD, 2008). This is in line with the goal of research (Annamalah et al., 2023) to uncover open innovation strategies and explore how social capital contributes to sustainable growth. By integrating technology transfer skills and open innovation practices, organizations can harness the potential for innovation and economic development (Necoechea-Mondragón et al., 2017).

From this perspective, we found that research has extensively covered various aspects of technology, innovation, and territorial studies, as demonstrated by (El-hissoufi & Alla, 2024; Aarabe et al., 2024; Bouhtati et al., 2024; Bentalha & Alla,

2024; Nouhaila et al., 2024; Boudri et al., 2024; Alla et al., 2023; Hmioui et al., 2017). However, there are only a few studies that attempt a quantitative or qualitative analysis, dealing with both open innovation, technology, and economic integration in Africa, such as (Haddad, 2023; Senadjki et al., 2022). In addition, Ajibade & Mutula (2020) conducted a bibliometric review, primarily focusing on the intersection of big data and banking systems in South Africa and Nigeria. Another significant contribution is the systematic review by Romera et al. (2022), which explores the role of technology and the macroeconomic environment in shaping smart city initiatives. Their work highlights the importance of factors such as health, education, and innovation in development.

Despite these contributions, the field of open innovation, technology, and economic integration in Africa remains relatively unexplored. Existing literature often focuses on specific regions or industries, leaving significant gaps in our understanding of how these elements interplay on a continental scale. This highlights the need for a more comprehensive approach to studying these dynamics.

Our research aims to address these gaps by providing a nuanced exploration of the topic, particularly in the African context. To achieve this, we formulated three key research questions: (1) Which countries and authors were the pioneers in collaborating and publishing articles on our topic? (2) How has the publishing trend evolved in the field of open innovation and economic integration in Africa over the years? (3) What are the dynamics and contributions of open innovation to Africa's economic development?

By addressing these questions, our study seeks to shed light on the complex interrelationships between innovation, technology, and economic integration in Africa and provide a framework for future research in this critical area.

## 2 METHODOLOGY

The objective of our research was to systematically identify and analyse scientific articles that explore the interaction between open innovation, technology, and economic integration within the African context. To achieve this, we followed a structured and transparent approach hat ensured a comprehensive exploration of the subject matter.

- **Database Selection:** we used the Scopus database, the largest source that includes citations and abstracts, as a comprehensive source of academic literature, to collect relevant publications (Arıca & Çorbacı,2019). We also used the Vosviewer application to create a bibliometric network (Ranjbar-Sahraei & Negenborn 2017).

- **Keyword identification and research criteria:** In this context, our search strategy was guided by a combination of an initial literature review and brainstorming sessions to determine the most relevant keywords.

We specifically targeted four key terms: “technology,” “open innov*,” “economic integration,” and “afric*.” These keywords were selected to ensure a comprehensive exploration of the themes related to innovation and economic integration in the African context. Table 1 presents our research protocol.

*Table 1. Research Protocol for Open Innovation, Technology and Economic Integration in Africa*

| Scopus Database | Time Period | Document Types | Search Criteria | Keywords |
|---|---|---|---|---|
| Business, Management and Accounting; Social Sciences; Economics, Econometrics and Finance | February and March 2024 | Articles | Title, Keywords and Abstract | “technology” AND “open innov*” AND “economic integration” AND “afric*” |

The search was conducted for documents published up to the end of 2023. We employed a structured query command to extract data from the Scopus database: “"technology” AND “open innov*” AND “economic integration” AND “africa*” AND PUBYEAR > 2013 AND PUBYEAR < 2024 AND (LIMIT-TO (SUBJAREA, “BUSI”) OR LIMIT-TO (SUBJAREA, “ECON”) OR LIMIT-TO (SUBJAREA, “SOCI”)) AND (LIMIT-TO (DOCTYPE, “ar”) AND (LIMIT-TO (LANGUAGE, “English”).

This query was designed to capture articles published within the specified timeframe and limit the search to those in relevant subject areas like: Business, Management and Accounting; Economics, Econometrics and Finance; and Social Sciences, because they contribute significantly to understanding open innovation and economic integration and offer a well-rounded view, allowing for a deeper exploration of how businesses and economic policies can foster innovation:

- Business studies provide insights into organizational structures and strategies for open innovation, while social sciences emphasize the societal and cultural factors that influence innovation adoption.
- Economics focuses on the impact of economic integration and how market openness leads to growth, especially in Africa, which has been a critical point

in the article, highlighting the growing academic interest in open innovation across African economies.

We add to our explication that we focused on peer-reviewed journal articles written in English to ensure the quality and accessibility of the research.

**- Filtering and selection of articles:** Our search yielded a total of 102 publications. Following an initial review and filtering process, we identified 48 publications that met our search criteria and adhered to our research protocol. To refine our dataset further, we applied additional filtering criteria to exclude 31 articles that did not meet our standards for relevance or quality, leaving us with 17 validated articles.

The subsequent analysis of the 17 validated articles provides insights into the research trends, thematic focus, and contributions of these studies to the fields of innovation design and economic integration in Africa. This analysis serves as a foundation for understanding the current landscape and identifying potential areas for further investigation.

By carefully selecting relevant keywords, employing a rigorous search protocol, and applying stringent filtering criteria, we ensured that our study was grounded in a robust and comprehensive examination of the literature.

**Bibliometric analysis tools:** We used Vosviewer, a widely recognised tool for bibliometric analysis, to create a bibliometric analysis and take results that enabled us to visualise co-authorship networks, identify the main research clusters and track the evolution of the field over time.

Finally, through this bibliometric approach, we provided and we offered a valuable overview of the research on open innovation and technology in fostering economic integration in Africa, highlighting key findings and setting the stage for future research endeavors.

## 3 RESULTS AND DUSCUSSION

### 3.1 The Research Trend in Open Innovation, Technology and Economic Integration in Africa

Research publications on open innovation, technology, and economic integration in Africa have seen an evolving trajectory since they first began to gain prominence in 2014. A global overview of the research indexed in Scopus reveals insightful trends. Initially, the number of international publications in this field exhibited fluctuations, with periods of both increase and decrease on average until 2018. This period of volatility reflected the growing yet inconsistent interest and development in these areas of study.

However, starting from 2018, there was a noticeable shift in the trend. The number of publications began to rise steadily each year, indicating a growing and sustained academic interest in the subjects of open innovation and technology's role in Africa's economic integration.

This upward trend suggests that these topics have become increasingly relevant, likely driven by a combination of factors such as advancements in technology, the increasing importance of innovation in economic strategies, and a greater focus on the African continent's integration into the global economy.

As illustrated in Figure 1, the highest peak in publication activity was observed in 2023, with a total of 19 articles published. This peak represents the culmination of several years of growth and highlights the peak interest and research output in this field to date. This growing body of work not only reflects an academic acknowledgment of the importance of these issues but also contributes to the broader discourse on the potential and challenges of leveraging technology and open innovation for economic development in Africa.

*Figure 1. Trending articles by year*

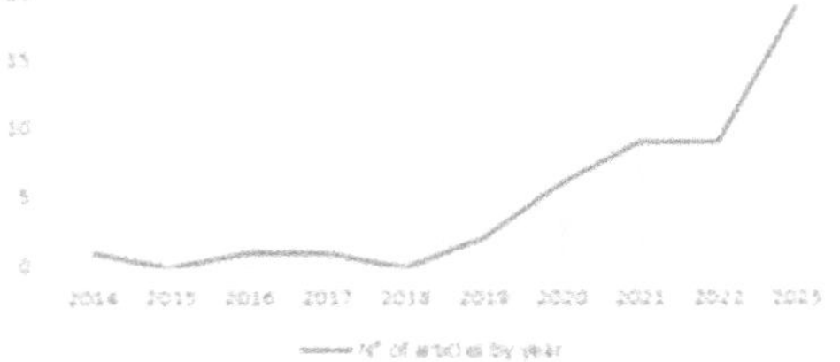


## 3.2 Key Studies and Citations in Open Innovation, Technology, and Economic Integration: A Focus on African Context

Research on open innovation, technology, and economic integration in Africa has experienced a significant evolution since 2014. Initially, the field saw fluctuations in the number of publications, reflecting an emerging yet inconsistent interest. However, from 2018 onwards, there has been a noticeable and sustained increase in academic output. This rising trend underscores the growing importance of these topics, as technological advancements and innovation increasingly influence economic strategies, especially in the African context.

Parallelly, the key studies highlighted in the accompanying table (table 2) provide a deeper understanding of these dynamics. For instance, Gamidullaeva, Vasin, and Wise (2020), in their article titled *"Increasing Small- and Medium-Enterprise Contribution to Local and Regional Economic Growth by Assessing the Institutional Environment"* published in the *Journal of Small Business and Enterprise Development* and cited 33 times, explore the crucial role of SMEs in economic growth. This study's insights are particularly relevant for understanding the regional economic structures within Africa, where SMEs are pivotal.

Zarrouk, Ghak, and Bakhouche (2021), in their work *"Exploring Economic and Technological Determinants of Fintech Startups' Success and Growth in the United Arab Emirates"* featured in the *Journal of Open Innovation: Technology, Market, and Complexity*, received 31 citations. While focusing on the Middle East, the findings on the significance of technological innovation and economic integration offer valuable lessons for African nations striving to bolster their fintech ecosystems.

Another notable contribution is from Song et al. (2019), whose study *"Knowledge Accumulation, Development Potential and Efficiency Evaluation: An Example Using the Hainan Free Trade Zone"* in the *Journal of Knowledge Management* garnered 28 citations. This research highlights the importance of free trade zones as catalysts for economic growth and innovation. This aligns with the strategic priorities of African countries aiming to develop similar frameworks to enhance technological innovation and integration.

Further illustrating the interconnectedness of global markets, Reddy, Chundakkadan, and Sasidharan (2021) discuss the significance of global value chains in their article *"Firm Innovation and Global Value Chain Participation"* in *Small Business Economics*, cited 24 times. Their analysis underscores the necessity for African firms to engage in global value chains to improve their competitiveness and drive innovation, thereby facilitating broader economic integration.

Additionally, other studies, such as Saif, Ruan, and Obrenovic (2021) in *Sustainability (Switzerland)* and Kleynhans (2016) in the *Journal of Applied Business Research*, highlight diverse aspects like sustaining trade during the COVID-19 pandemic and factors determining industrial competitiveness, respectively. These works further enrich the discourse on the complex parameters influencing economic growth and integration, particularly in the context of Africa's developing economies.

In summary, the citations of these studies reflect their significant impact on academic and policy discussions. They collectively illustrate the critical role of research in shaping a nuanced understanding of open innovation and economic integration. These studies not only contribute to the global body of knowledge but are also pivotal in informing strategies that African economies can adopt to enhance their participation in the global economy.

*Table 2. Most cited articles in the field of open innovation, technology and economic integration in African context*

| Title | Authors | Year of | Source Title | Number of Citation |
|---|---|---|---|---|
| **Increasing small- and medium-enterprise contribution to local and regional economic growth by assessing the institutional environment** | Gamidullaeva L.A.; Vasin S.M.; Wise N. | 2020 | Journal of Small Business and Enterprise Development | 33 |
| **Exploring economic and technological determinants of fintech startups' success and growth in the United Arab Emirates** | Zarrouk H.; Ghak T.E.; Bakhouche A. | 2021 | Journal of Open Innovation: Technology, Market, and Complexity | 31 |
| **Knowledge accumulation, development potential and efficiency evaluation: an example using the Hainan free trade zone** | Song M.; Wang J.; Wang S.; Zhao D. | 2019 | Journal of Knowledge Management | 28 |
| **Firm innovation and global value chain participation** | Reddy K.; Chundakkadan R.; Sasidharan S. | 2021 | Small Business Economics | 24 |
| **Sustaining trade during covid-19 pandemic: Establishing a conceptual model including covid-19 impact** | Saif N.M.A.; Ruan J.; Obrenovic B. | 2021 | Sustainability (Switzerland) | 19 |
| **The effect of social capital in mitigating drought impacts and improving livability of Iranian rural households** | Savari M.; Eskandari Damaneh H.; Eskandari Damaneh H. | 2023 | International Journal of Disaster Risk Reduction | 14 |
| **Critical factors for participation in global innovation networks. Empirical evidence from the Mexican nanotechnology sector** | Necoechea-Mondragón H.; Pineda-Domínguez D.; Pérez-Reveles L.; Soto-Flores R. | 2017 | Technological Forecasting and Social Change | 13 |
| **National-level innovation in Africa** | Allard G.; Williams C. | 2020 | Research Policy | 13 |
| **Infrastructure public–private partnership (Ppp) investment and government fiscal expenditure on science and technology from the perspective of sustainability** | Liu C. | 2021 | Sustainability (Switzerland) | 13 |
| **Factors determining industrial competitiveness and the role of spillovers** | Kleynhans E.P.J. | 2016 | Journal of Applied Business Research | 11 |

## 3.3 Research areas explored in Open Innovation, Technology and Economic Integration in Africa

In the realm of international academic publications focusing on our field of work, several disciplines have emerged as the most represented areas. At the forefront is the category of Business, Management, and Accounting, which boasts a substantial number of 26 articles. This dominance highlights the critical role that business practices, organizational management, and financial accounting play in the context of our study area, likely reflecting the interdisciplinary nature of open innovation and economic integration.

Following closely is the field of Social Sciences, with 23 papers. This significant representation underscores the importance of understanding the societal and cultural dimensions that influence and are influenced by technological advancements and economic changes. The social sciences offer valuable insights into human behavior, policy implications, and the broader societal impacts of innovation and economic activities.

Next, the area of Economics, Econometrics, and Finance is well-represented with 19 papers. This field's strong presence points to the quantitative analysis and financial modeling aspects critical to evaluating economic integration and innovation strategies. It also reflects the growing interest in understanding the economic underpinnings and financial mechanisms that drive technological and innovative efforts.

Additionally, the field of Environmental Sciences appears with 7 papers, indicating a growing concern and academic interest in the environmental implications of economic and technological developments. This representation suggests an awareness of the need for sustainable practices and the consideration of ecological impacts within the broader discourse on innovation and economic growth.

Lastly, both Energy and Computer Science are represented with 6 papers each. The inclusion of Energy highlights the relevance of exploring sustainable energy solutions and the role of energy in supporting technological advancements and economic integration. Similarly, the presence of Computer Science emphasizes the significance of digital technologies, data analysis, and computational methods in driving innovation and supporting economic activities.

These diverse fields' contributions, as depicted in Figure 2, reflect the multidisciplinary nature of research in our area. They illustrate the interconnectedness of various academic disciplines in addressing the complex challenges and opportunities presented by open innovation, technology, and economic integration.

*Figure 2. articles covered by fields of study*

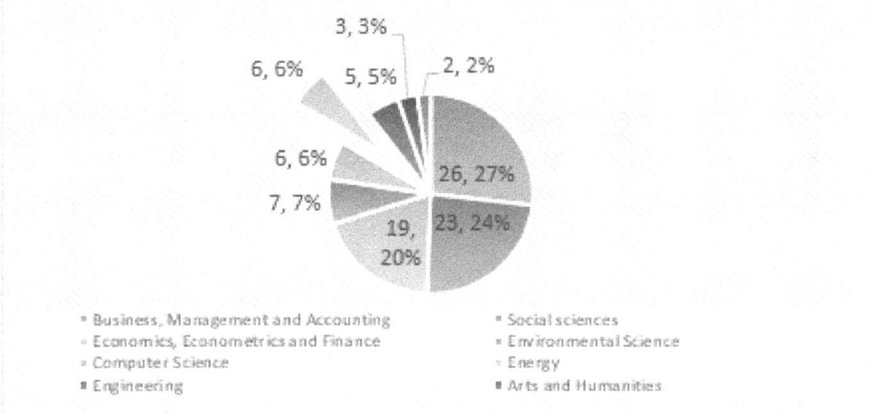


## 3.4 Authors' analysis of Open Innovation, Technology and Economic Integration in Africa

Following the preliminary results of our research, we have identified key authors who have significantly contributed to the study of open innovation, technology, and economic integration in Africa. As shown in (Figure 3*)*, Omodero, C.O. emerges as the most prolific author in this domain, with two published papers. While this number may seem modest, it signifies a concentrated and sustained research effort in examining the intricate dynamics of innovation and economic policies within the African context. Omodero's contributions likely serve as foundational work that helps shape current and future discourse in the field, offering valuable insights into how technological advancements and policy measures can drive economic development in Africa.

*Figure 3. Number of articles per author*

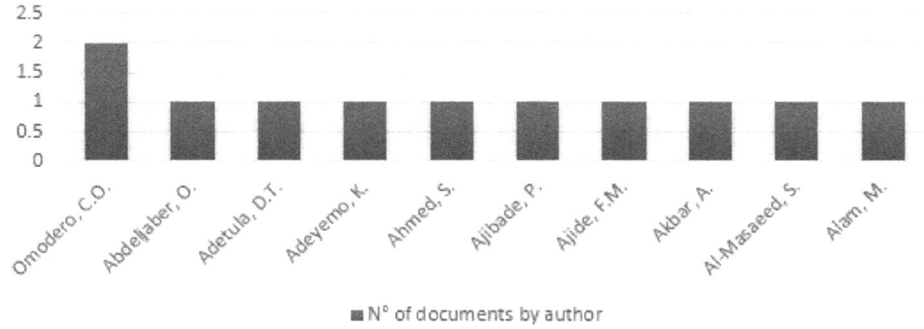


In addition to Omodero, a range of other authors have made noteworthy contributions, each with a single publication. This group includes researchers such as Abdeljaber, O.; Adetula, D.T.; Adeyemo, K.; Ahmed, S.; Ajibade, P.; Ajide, F.M.; Akbar, A.; Al-Masaeed, S.; and Alam, M. Although each of these authors has contributed only one paper, their collective work significantly enriches the body of knowledge in this field. The diversity of their research topics, methodologies, and analytical perspectives broadens the scope of the existing literature. For instance, some authors may focus on theoretical frameworks that explore the principles of open innovation, while others may conduct empirical analyses to examine the effects of technological integration on specific sectors or regions within Africa.

The presence of these varied contributions underscores the collaborative and interdisciplinary nature of research on open innovation and economic integration. It highlights the global interest in understanding how technological advancements and innovative practices can drive economic growth, particularly within the African context. Such a diverse authorship not only indicates a wide range of academic interests but also brings together insights from different fields, such as economics, technology, policy studies, and development research. This interdisciplinary blend is crucial for developing a comprehensive understanding of the multifaceted challenges and opportunities associated with leveraging technology for economic development in Africa.

Moreover, the involvement of authors from various regions and academic backgrounds demonstrates the interconnectedness of global research efforts. By including perspectives from different geographical areas and schools of thought, these studies contribute to a more holistic view of how open innovation strategies can be tailored to suit Africa's unique socio-economic environment. The single contributions by authors like Ajibade and Adeyemo, for example, may focus on specific case studies or offer targeted policy recommendations, further diversifying the knowledge base and providing a practical context to theoretical discussions.

Overall, while Omodero, C.O.'s multiple publications indicate a concentrated research focus, the collective input from this diverse group of authors adds a rich tapestry of findings to the field. Their work not only reflects a broad spectrum of expertise but also emphasizes the importance of collaboration and knowledge-sharing in advancing the discourse on innovation and economic integration. This diverse authorship ultimately serves to strengthen the field, ensuring that a wide range of perspectives and insights are included in the ongoing exploration of technology's role in Africa's economic future.

## 3.5 Country Contributions Open Innovation, Technology and Economic Integration in Africa

In the field of open innovation, technology and economic integration, China is the country that has published the most papers, with a total of 9. This is followed by the United Kingdom with 7 items, Russia with 5, France, Italy, Malaysia and Nigeria with 3 items each. Finally, the countries that have published less than 3 articles are Australia, Ethiopia and Indonesia, with 2 articles each.

Continuing our analysis of the Scopus results, the data reveals some interesting patterns in the geographical distribution on open innovation, technology, and economic integration in Africa highlights the varying interests of different countries. China emerges as the main contributor, with a total of 9 articles published. This significant output reflects China's growing interest in understanding and engaging with African economies, particularly in the context of technological advances and innovative economic strategies. China's involvement may also be influenced by its expanding economic and trade relations with various African nations, as well as its investment in infrastructure and technology on the continent.

*Figure 4. Number of articles by country*

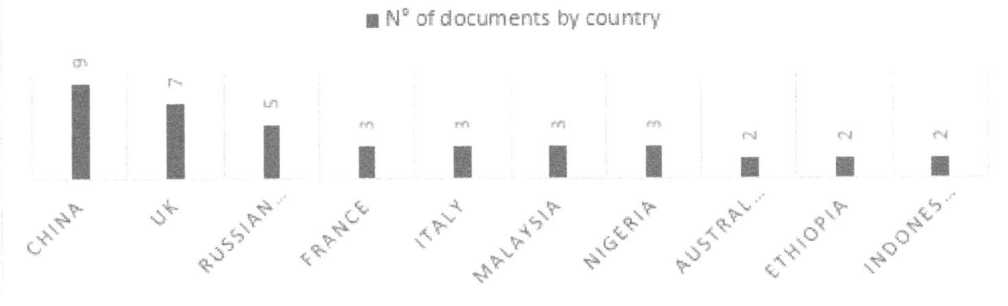

The UK follows with 7 papers published, indicating a strong academic interest in the implications of open innovation and economic integration in Africa. The UK's contributions often include a mix of historical context, economic analysis and policy-oriented research, reflecting its long-standing links with many African countries and its commitment to international development.

Russia contributed 5 publications, highlighting its interest in Africa's economic landscape and the potential for collaboration in the areas of technology and innovation.

France, Italy, Malaysia and Nigeria each published 3 papers, presenting a diverse set of perspectives on the subject. The contributions from France and Italy reflect their established academic presence and historical links with Africa. Malaysia's involvement represents an emerging Southeast Asian interest in African markets and the potential for technological exchange, while Nigeria's contributions are particularly significant, offering an important African perspective on the challenges and opportunities of open innovation and economic integration within the continent.

Finally, Australia, Ethiopia and Indonesia each published two papers. Australia's research often focuses on comparative studies or broader global trends that include Africa. Ethiopia's participation is crucial as it offers perspectives from within the continent, particularly in the context of regional economic communities and local innovation ecosystems. Indonesia's participation reflects another developing country's growing interest in understanding and potentially collaborating with African countries on economic and technological initiatives.

Contributions from a wide range of countries not only enrich the academic discourse, but also provide a global understanding of the different approaches and perspectives on integrating Africa into the global economy through innovation and technology. This diversity of viewpoints is essential to developing nuanced and effective strategies that respond to the unique challenges and opportunities facing the continent.

## 3.6 Co-authorship Analysis of Open Innovation, Technology and Economic Integration in Africa

### 3.6.1 Co-authorship analysis by using interconnection of authors

After presenting the descriptive results from Scopus, we proceeded with a series of bibliometric analyses, one of which was the co-authorship analysis. This type of analysis is vital as it allows us to explore and characterize the collaborative relationships between researchers who have contributed to the body of literature on open innovation, technology, and economic integration in Africa. Co-authorship analysis provides insights into the structure, extent, and dynamics of academic networks, revealing patterns of collaboration that may influence research output and the dissemination of ideas within the field.

In examining the field of open innovation, technology, and economic integration in Africa, we observed that the academic networks formed through co-authorship are both extensive and complex. The results of our analysis, depicted in (*Figure 5*), highlight the existence of a prominent cluster of researchers, marked in red, which consists of 11 key authors. This cluster includes notable researchers such as Gonchatov, Ponkratov, Ivelva, Kireeva, Elyakova, and Vatutina. Their frequent collaborations suggest a strong, interconnected network characterized by shared research interests, likely supported by common institutional affiliations or coordinated research projects.

The presence of this tightly-knit cluster indicates that these authors have collectively contributed significantly to the field, potentially driving forward critical discussions on open innovation and economic integration within the African context. Their collaborative efforts may also facilitate the cross-pollination of ideas, enhance research quality, and increase the impact of their findings. By frequently working together, these researchers may influence the direction of research within this domain, setting trends and identifying new areas for exploration.

*Figure 5. Authors' Co-authorship Analysis on Open Innovation, Technology and Economic Inte-gration in Africa*

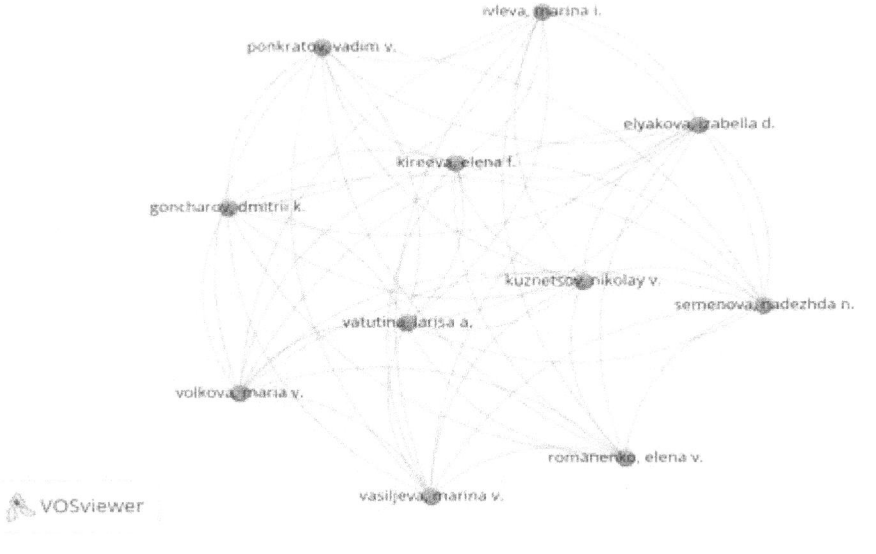

Furthermore, the formation of such clusters can have important implications for the development of the academic field. It highlights the importance of collaborative networks in advancing research, as these networks often serve as platforms for knowledge exchange, mentorship, and the building of research capacity. The cluster's prominence within the co-authorship network suggests that the researchers involved are not only actively contributing to the literature but may also play a key role in shaping the discourse on technology integration and economic strategies in Africa.

However, it is also noteworthy that while this cluster represents a significant concentration of collaborative effort, the overall landscape of co-authorship in the field remains fragmented. The fact that one dominant cluster emerges could point to the need for broader, cross-regional collaborations that involve more diverse groups of researchers. This insight opens up potential pathways for future research initiatives, emphasizing the importance of expanding collaborative networks to include underrepresented regions and institutions across Africa.

### 3.6.2 Co-authorship analysis by using interconnection of countries

Furthermore, our bibliometric analysis extended to examine the collaborative networks between countries engaged in joint research and the production of scientific articles on open innovation and economic integration in Africa. This international perspective is critical, as it highlights how knowledge production and dissemination in this field are influenced by cross-border partnerships. (Figure 6) vividly illustrates the international nature of these collaborations, revealing how diverse countries contribute to the academic discourse through cooperative research efforts.

Interestingly, the results reveal the formation of two distinct poles of collaboration. The first pole, shown in red, includes countries such as Malaysia, Spain, the United Kingdom, and France. This group represents a diverse set of nations with varying levels of economic development, technological advancement, and regional influence. The inclusion of countries like Malaysia suggests that interest in African economic integration is not limited to traditionally dominant economic powers but extends to rapidly developing economies in Asia. Spain, the UK, and France, each with their unique historical, economic, and technological contexts, further broaden the scope of this collaborative network. Their involvement indicates that the topic of open innovation and economic integration in Africa is relevant across multiple contexts, appealing to both developed nations and emerging economies. This diverse coalition of countries likely brings a variety of perspectives, research methodologies, and policy considerations to the study, enriching the overall discourse.

The second pole, highlighted in green, consists of Belarus and Russia. This cluster points to a specific regional focus within Eastern Europe, where researchers have shown a concentrated interest in exploring the dynamics of open innovation and economic integration in Africa. The existence of this pole suggests a regional collaboration that may stem from shared historical, economic, or political interests in African markets. It also underscores the presence of distinct research communities that operate within specific geopolitical contexts, potentially offering unique insights into how Eastern European perspectives and expertise intersect with the African economic landscape.

*Figure 6. Country Co-authorship Analysis on Open Innovation, Technology and Economic Inte-gration in Africa*

The identification of these two poles suggests that, while there is a widespread interest in open innovation and economic integration in Africa, there are also distinct regional research communities with potentially differing focuses and perspectives. The European cluster might, for example, approach the topic from a trade and investment perspective, leveraging historical ties and economic interests in African development. Meanwhile, the collaboration involving Malaysia could indicate an interest in South-South cooperation, technology transfer, and the sharing of emerging market experiences.

These findings highlight the diverse and sometimes unexpected nature of international academic collaborations in this field. They emphasize the importance of examining not just individual researchers but also the broader country-level networks that contribute to the development of scientific knowledge. Additionally, the presence of these distinct poles points to the potential for further cross-regional collaborations. By fostering partnerships between these separate clusters, the field of open innovation and economic integration could be enriched with a wider variety of perspectives, methodologies, and insights.

Ultimately, this analysis of country-level collaborations provides a more nuanced understanding of how knowledge is produced and disseminated in the context of African economic development. It underscores the complex web of relationships that shape research in this area, highlighting the need for more inclusive and cross-border collaboration to develop a more holistic and multifaceted understanding of open innovation, technology and its implications for economic integration in Africa.

## 3.7 Co-Occurrence analysis of Open Innovation, Technology and Economic Integration in Africa

### 3.7.1 Co-occurrence analysis by keywords

Building our bibliometric analysis, our second approach involves a detailed co-occurrence analysis. This method examines the most significant terms and emerging research directions within the fields of open innovation, technology and economic integration in Africa. Co-occurrence analysis is crucial as it not only reveals the direction of current research but also highlights the concentration of researchers' efforts in specific areas (Wang et al., 2019). By visualizing the co-occurrence analysis, we can identify research areas (clusters) that are underexplored, highlighting gaps represented by clusters that need to be addressed in future studies (figure 7).

Cluster 1 in Red: Development of Innovation for a Sustainable Emerging Economy: This cluster focuses on promoting sustainable growth in emerging economies through stable finance, green initiatives, and innovative industrial infrastructure, in alignment with the Sustainable Development Goals (SDGs). The key terms include: economic stability, environmental sustainability, industrial advancements, financial resources, and industrial revolutions. This cluster underscores the integration of these elements to achieve the SDGs, emphasizing the role of innovation as a driver for sustainable development.

By focusing on these elements, researchers emphasize how innovation can drive sustainable development. For example, advancing industrial infrastructure with green technologies not only supports economic growth but also ensures environmental integrity, contributing directly to the SDGs. The cluster underscores the need for holistic strategies that balance financial stability with innovative practices, thereby fostering an economy that is both competitive and sustainable. This integrated approach is particularly relevant for emerging African economies striving to establish a robust economic foundation while addressing environmental concerns.

*Figure 7. Analysis Co-occurrence by keywords on Open Innovation, Technology and Economic Integration in Africa*

## Cluster 2 in Green: Economic Diversification for Sustainable Development

The second cluster delves into the necessity of economic diversification as a pathway to sustainable development. It emphasizes strategies that attract financial investors and efficiently utilize resources to achieve the SDGs. Key terms in this cluster include *level of development*, *economic development*, *economic diversification*, *financial investors*, *resource efficiency*, and *sustainable development goals*.

This cluster underscores that a one-dimensional economic model, heavily reliant on a limited number of sectors, is insufficient for stable growth. Researchers advocate for diversifying economic activities to enhance resilience against market volatility and foster long-term sustainability. For example, African economies could leverage diversification in sectors like agriculture, renewable energy, and digital technologies to create a balanced and sustainable growth model. By attracting investors and optimizing resource use, countries can reduce their vulnerability to external shocks and create more stable economic environments, thereby advancing their development agendas in line with the SDGs.

### Cluster 3 in Blue: Middle East and North Africa (MENA) Development Network

The third cluster focuses on the development needs of the Middle East and North Africa (MENA) region. It highlights the importance of efforts in *health and education*, *infrastructure improvements*, innovative solutions, and *stabilization of the macroeconomic environment* for the region's development.

Key terms within this cluster include *MENA countries*, *macroeconomic environment*, *innovation*, *infrastructure*, and *health and education*. This cluster suggests that sustainable development in the MENA region depends on a multifaceted approach. For instance, improving health and education infrastructure is vital for building human capital, which in turn drives innovation and supports economic growth. Furthermore, macroeconomic stability is critical for attracting foreign investment and fostering a conducive environment for technological adoption and innovation. The emphasis on the MENA region within this cluster signals a growing research interest in how open innovation and economic integration strategies can address the specific challenges faced by these countries, particularly in the context of regional stability and sustainable growth.

## 3.7.2 Co-occurrence analysis by years

The co-occurrence analysis provides not only insights into the thematic focus of research but also a second temporal map of keywords, indicating the periods during which documents containing these terms were published. This temporal mapping allows us to trace the evolution of research interests over time, as we see in the map keywords highlighted in yellow represent those featured in more recent articles, signifying emerging areas of focus within the field. The (Figure 8) illustrates three distinct phases that reflect the historical progression of research on open innovation, technology, and economic integration in Africa.

*Figure 8. Analysis of Co-occurrence by years on Open Innovation, Technology and Economic Integration in Africa*

The initial phase marked in (purple), predominantly centered around issues related to: *health, infrastructure, and education.* During this period, researchers explored how technological advancements could address basic societal needs, such as improving healthcare delivery, building critical infrastructure, and enhancing educational systems. This focus laid the groundwork for subsequent discussions on how innovation could drive social and economic progress on the continent.

In the second phase, highlighted in (green), the scope of research began to shift towards a broader *concept of innovation*, with a particular emphasis *on open innovation and economic development.* Researchers in this period investigated how collaborative and cross-border technological initiatives could stimulate economic growth, emphasizing the importance of integrating internal and external sources of knowledge for enhanced competitiveness. This phase marked a turning point, as the dialogue expanded beyond fundamental infrastructure needs to explore how open innovation models could be leveraged to support economic strategies.

Finally, in the most recent phase, shown in (yellow), there is a noticeable intensification of research activity compared to previous years. During this phase, the focus has shifted towards *sustainable development, economic diversification, environmental sustainability, and the Sustainable Development Goals (SDGs).* Researchers are now examining how open innovation and technological integration can address more complex challenges, including the transition to greener economies and the pursuit of industrial revolutions tailored to Africa's unique context. This recent trend underscores the growing recognition of the importance of aligning technological and economic strategies with global sustainability objectives, reflecting an evolving research landscape that prioritizes long-term, inclusive growth.

This analysis reveals a dynamic shift in research priorities over time, highlighting the progression from basic infrastructure and social needs to more advanced considerations of sustainable economic development. This evolution suggests an increasing awareness of the multifaceted role that open innovation and technology play in fostering a sustainable and diversified economic future for Africa.

## 3.8 Bibliographic analysis of Open Innovation, Technology and Economic Integration in Africa

The third aspect of our bibliometric analysis focuses on examining bibliometric link networks, which provide a visual representation of how scholarly articles are interconnected through their references. This type of analysis is crucial in understanding the flow of knowledge within the research field, as it reveals how various studies are related by identifying articles that cite a common set of sources. In (Figure 9*)*, these link networks are illustrated, showcasing the intricate web of connections between articles based on their cross-referencing behavior.

*Figure 9. Bibliographic Analysis on Open Innovation, Technology and Economic Integration in Africa*

In this analysis, a link between two articles is established when they both cite a third, shared work in their bibliographies. This method provides a deeper insight into the structure of the research field by highlighting not only individual contributions but also how ideas, theories, and research findings are disseminated and built upon. By examining these bibliometric links, we can identify central works that have influenced multiple studies, serving as foundational pieces in the ongoing discourse on open innovation and economic integration in Africa.

Our analysis identified two primary groups within these bibliometric link networks. The identification of these groups helps us understand the core areas of research and the key contributions that anchor the field. These clusters represent different but interconnected themes within the larger framework of open innovation and economic integration. Among these clusters, certain articles stand out due to their high degree of centrality (DC) — a measure of an article's pivotal role in connecting other studies within the network

The article with the highest degree of centrality (DC), in our analysis is: [ Alemu, T., Choramo, T. T., & Jeldu, A. (2023). External Debt, Institutional Quality and Economic Growth in East African Countries. *Journal of East-West Business*, 29(4), 375-401.] This work plays a significant role in linking various other publications, indicating its influential contribution to the field. Its central position highlights its importance in discussions on how external debt and institutional quality impact economic growth in the East African context. By bridging multiple references, this study enhances our understanding of the intricate relationship between economic policies and growth, particularly in emerging economies like those in East Africa.

Further supporting the centrality of *Alemu et al. (2023)* is the closely linked study by *Daba Ayana et al. (2023),* titled *"Effect of External Debt on Economic Growth in Sub-Saharan Africa: System GMM Estimation,"* published in *Cogent Economics & Finance*. Both articles share three common references, signaling a strong conceptual overlap and a shared focus on the complexities of external debt and its impact on economic growth in Africa. The connection between these works indicates a cluster of research dedicated to examining financial structures and economic policy within the African context, which are critical components of the broader theme of open innovation and integration.

This bibliometric linkage analysis, therefore, adds a layer of depth to our understanding of the research landscape. It not only maps out the territory of existing research but also identifies key articles that have a far-reaching impact across multiple studies. By examining these link networks, we can see how certain works, such as *Alemu et al. (2023)* and *Daba Ayana et al. (2023)*, serve as nodal points that influence the development and dissemination of ideas within the academic community. This interconnectedness underscores the importance of collaborative efforts and shared knowledge in advancing the field of open innovation and economic integration in Africa.

In addition to our previous analyses, this approach enables us to identify influential works that might shape future research directions. Recognizing the articles that serve as reference points for others helps to highlight the dominant themes and methodologies in the field, providing a clearer picture of where research is concentrated and where gaps might exist. As such, bibliometric linkage analysis is invaluable for scholars seeking to understand the trajectory of research in this domain and to identify potential areas for further exploration.

## CONCLUSION

In conclusion, our study delved into the interplay of open innovation, technology, and economic integration within the African context, revealing their pivotal roles in advancing sustainable development. Through our bibliometric analysis, we identified key trends, gaps, and dynamics in the current literature. However, our findings also reveal limitations, offering opportunities for future research to explore these aspects more deeply.

Firstly, our descriptive analysis of research trends highlights a significant evolution in the field. Since 2014, publications on open innovation, technology and economic integration in Africa have fluctuated, but have shown a notable upward trend from 2018. This indicates a growing and sustained academic interest in these areas, as we noticed that the most cited article is "Increasing small and medium-enterprise contribution to local and regional economic growth by assessing the institutional environment" in 2020 by Gamidullaeva et al. which received 33 citations, followed by "Exploring economic and technological determinants of fintech startups' success and growth in the United Arab Emirates" in 2021 by Zarrouk et al., who had 31 citations; and the final top 3 is "Knowledge accumulation, development potential and efficiency evaluation: an ex-ample using the Hainan free trade zone" in 2019 by Song et al. who received 28 citations.

In 2023, the highest level of research activity was achieved with 19 articles. This trend reflects a growing recognition of the relevance of these topics, driven by technological advances and the importance of innovation in economic strategies for Africa's integration into the global economy. Additionally, we observed that China is the country that contributes most to our research area, with 9 articles. This is followed by contributions from various European and Asian countries. However, only two African countries, Nigeria and Ethiopia, have contributed to this field, with a combined total of 5 articles, which can be considered somewhat insufficient given the continent's potential and the importance of the topics. On the other hand, we find that the most contributing author in this field is an African researcher, "Omodero, C.O." from Nigeria, who has published 2 articles.

Empirical evidence underscores the beneficial impact of economic openness on growth. Factors such as the deepening of economic activity specifications, economies of scale, knowledge redistribution, and the enhancement of intellectual capital contribute to this positive influence. However, the complex parameters affecting economic growth necessitate a more nuanced exploration to fully understand how integration drives growth.

Furthermore, while traditional research has concentrated on larger developed or emerging economies, our study highlights the importance of examining regional origins and technological capacities. Addressing these factors is crucial for mitigating the challenges faced by multinational enterprises operating in smaller, open economies, thus providing a more equitable foundation for growth.

Our bibliometric analyses reveal an interesting dynamic in the field of open innovation and economic integration in Africa. The co-authorship analysis demonstrated the presence of extensive and complex academic networks, with a prominent cluster of researchers such as Gonchatov, Ponkratov, Ivelva, Kireeva, Elyakova, and Vatutina indicating strong collaborative relationships within the field. International collaborations were grouped into two distinct poles: one comprising Malaysia, Spain, the United Kingdom, and France, representing a diverse set of countries with varying degrees of economic development and technological advancement, and another consisting of Belarus and Russia, indicating regional collaborations within Eastern Europe. These findings highlight the diverse nature of international academic collaborations and suggest the potential for further cross-regional collaborations to enrich the field with a wider variety of perspectives and insights.

The co-occurrence analysis identified three key research clusters: the development of innovation for a sustainable emerging economy, economic diversification for sustainable development, and the MENA development network. These clusters reflect varied research directions, from sustainable development goals to economic diversification and MENA-specific challenges. The temporal map of keywords also shows a rapid evolution in research focus, with recent emphasis on sustainable development, economic development, environmental sustainability, and industrial revolutions, highlighting underexplored areas that future studies should address.

Additionally, the bibliometric link network analysis revealed two primary groups within the field, with the study by Alemu, Choramo, and Jeldu (2023) playing a central role in connecting various publications. This article is pivotal in linking multiple references, enhancing our understanding of the relationships between external debt, institutional quality, and economic growth in East Africa. The presence of significant studies closely linked with this central work further underscores the importance of understanding how ideas and research findings are disseminated.

However, our bibliometric approach has its limitations, the first one is the reliance on the Scopus database may have excluded valuable contributions from other sources, potentially overlooking relevant studies that could enrich our findings. Also, we cannot, for instance, conduct an in-depth diagnostic of how open innovation or technology impacts a particular country's policy landscape or economic sectors, such as agriculture or manufacturing in East Africa. The aggregated nature of the bibliometric data provides a broad overview but does not allow us to focus on particular local contexts or develop case-specific analyses.

Furthermore, the scope of our analysis is limited by the available literature, which may not fully capture emerging trends or significant contributions outside the Scopus database. The limited research by African academics and its concentration in non-African countries such as China, the UK and Russia, particularly the absence of Moroccan and Moroccan authors, indicates that there is a critical need to bring local expertise into the conversation, ensuring a more inclusive and comprehensive understanding of the region's unique challenges and opportunities and a gap that needs to be filled.

This gap highlights an opportunity and suggests the need for greater involvement and representation of African researchers in the field to ensure a more comprehensive and inclusive understanding of open innovation and economic integration in Africa.

Despite these limitations, our research makes a significant contribution to understanding open innovation and economic integration in Africa by providing a detailed overview of current trends and gaps. Future research should aim to address these gaps, exploring the complex dynamics and contributing to the advancement of sustainable development strategies within the African context. By doing so, we can better support the African's growth and integration into the global economy through innovative and inclusive strategies, addressing the specificities of each region within the continent.

## REFERENCES


Aarabe, M., Ben Khizzou, N., Alla, L., & Benjelloun, A. (2024). Marketing Applications of Emerging Technologies: A Systematic Literature Review. In Alla, L., Hmioui, A., & Bentalha, B. (Eds.), *AI and Data Engineering Solutions for Effective Marketing* (pp. 23–47). IGI Global., DOI: 10.4018/979-8-3693-3172-9.ch002

Aarabe, M., El Archi, Y., & Alla, L. (2024). Smart tourism experience and responsible travelers' behavior: A systematic literature review. In El Archi, Y. (Eds.), *Promoting responsible tourism with digital platforms* (pp. 128–147). IGI Global., DOI: 10.4018/979-8-3693-3286-3.ch008

Aghion, P., & Howitt, P. (1990). A model of growth through creative destruction. DOI: 10.2307/2951599

Ahuja, I. P. S. (2011). Managing research and development for core competence building in an organization. *Journal of Technology Management & Innovation*, 6(1), 58–65. DOI: 10.4067/S0718-27242011000100006

Ajibade, P., & Mutula, S. M. (2020). Big data, 4IR and electronic banking and banking systems applications in South Africa and Nigeria. *Banks and Bank Systems*, 15(2), 187. DOI: 10.21511/bbs.15(2).2020.17

Alemu, T., Choramo, T. T., & Jeldu, A. (2023). External Debt, Institutional Quality and Economic Growth in East African Countries. *Journal of East-West Business*, 29(4), 375–401. DOI: 10.1080/10669868.2023.2248121

Alla, L., Bentalha, B., & Elyoussfi, A. (2023). Intelligence territoriale et positionnement stratégique des régions au Maroc: Le cas de la région de Fès Meknes en perspective. *Le concept de l'intelligence en sciences juridiques, économiques et sociales*, 215-237.

Almeida, R., & Fernandes, A. M. (2008). Openness and technological innovations in developing countries: Evidence from firm-level surveys. *The Journal of Development Studies*, 44(5), 701–727. DOI: 10.1080/00220380802009217

Anarfo, E. B., Abor, J. Y., Osei, K. A., & Gyeke-Dako, A. (2019). Monetary policy and financial inclusion in sub-Sahara Africa: A panel VAR approach. *Journal of African Business*, 20(4), 549–572. DOI: 10.1080/15228916.2019.1580998

Annamalah, S., Paraman, P., & Ahmed, S. (2023). Unveiling the dynamics of open innovation and collaborative network tourism in ASEAN nations. *Asia Pacific Journal of Tourism Research*, 28(11), 1199–1225. DOI: 10.1080/10941665.2023.2293788

Arıca, R., & Çorbacı, A. (2019). Müşterilerin ortak üreticilik rolünü konu edinen araştırmaların incelenmesi: Scopus veri tabanında taranan turizm ve otelcilik dergilerinin bibliyometrik açıdan değerlendirilmesi. *Turizm Akademik Dergisi*, 6(1), 263–276.

Badre, M. E. Z. I. A. N. E., Badr, B. E. N. T. A. L. H. A., & Lhoussaine, A. L. L. A. (2024). La PME logistique et le développement territorial régional: Une analyse qualitative. *Alternatives Managériales Economiques*, 6(4), 1–22.

Badre, M. E. Z. I. A. N. E., Bentalha, B., & Alla, L. (2024). La PME logistique et le développement territorial régional: Une analyse qualitative. *Alternatives Managériales Economiques*, 6(4), 1–22.

Bentalha, B., & Alla, L. (2024). Revealing the Subtleties: The Art of Qualitative Studies in Science and Management. In Bentalha, B., & Alla, L. (Eds.), *Applying Qualitative Research Methods to Management Science* (pp. 1–21). IGI Global., DOI: 10.4018/979-8-3693-5543-5.ch001

Boudri, R., Bentalha, B., & Benjelloun, O. (2024). Phygital Marketing and the Pain of Paying: An Amazon Go Netnographic Case Study. In Alla, L., Hmioui, A., & Bentalha, B. (Eds.), *AI and Data Engineering Solutions for Effective Marketing* (pp. 348–363). IGI Global., DOI: 10.4018/979-8-3693-3172-9.ch017

Bouhtati, N., Alla, L., & Ed-Daakouri, I. (2024). Smart Data Analysis and Prediction of Responsible Customer Behaviour in Tourism: An Exploratory Review of the Literature. In El Archi, Y., Benbba, B., Dávid, L., & Cardoso, L. (Eds.), *Promoting Responsible Tourism With Digital Platforms* (pp. 189–212). IGI Global., DOI: 10.4018/979-8-3693-3286-3.ch011

Bouhtati, N., El Yaacoubi, Y., Bentalha, B., & Alla, L. (2024). Leviers logistiques de promotion du commerce équitable des produits de terroir: Une esquisse de modèle d'analyse. *Alternatives Managériales Economiques*, 6(Spécial 1), 17-35.

Cabrer-Borràs, B., & Serrano-Domingo, G. (2007). Innovation and R&D spillover effects in Spanish regions: A spatial approach. *Research Policy*, 36(9), 1357–1371. DOI: 10.1016/j.respol.2007.04.012

Chaminade, C. (2009). *On the concept of Global Innovation Networks and its use in INGINEUS*. CIRCLE electronic working paper, 2009/05. Sweden: Lund University.

Chesbrough, H. W. (2003). *Open innovation: The new imperative for creating and profiting from technology*. Harvard Business Press.

Daba Ayana, I., Demissie, W. M., & Sore, A. G. (2023). Effect of External Debt on Economic Growth in Sub-Saharan Africa: System GMM Estimation. *Cogent Economics & Finance*, 11(2), 2256197. Advance online publication. DOI: 10.1080/23322039.2023.2256197

Danquah, M., & Amankwah-Amoah, J. (2017). Assessing the relationships between human capital, innovation and technology adoption: Evidence from sub-Saharan Africa. *Technological Forecasting and Social Change*, 122, 24–33. DOI: 10.1016/j.techfore.2017.04.021

Degbey, W. Y., Eriksson, T., Rodgers, P., & Oguji, N. (2021). Understanding cross-border mergers and acquisitions of African firms: The role of dynamic capabilities in enabling competitiveness amidst contextual constraints. *Thunderbird International Business Review*, 63(1), 77–93. DOI: 10.1002/tie.22138

Ekholm, K., & Hakkala, K. (2007). Location of R&D and high-tech production by vertically integrated multinationals. *Economic Journal (London)*, 117(518), 512–543. DOI: 10.1111/j.1468-0297.2007.02028.x

El Jaouhari, S., & Alla, L. (2022). L'approche territoriale et la gestion de l'impact de la pandémie de Covid-19: Cas des collectivités territoriales. *Alternatives Managériales Economiques*, 4(1), 245–265.

Elhissoufi, M., & Alla, L. (2024). Artificial Intelligence in Customer Acquisition: A Bibliometric Study. In Alla, L., Hmioui, A., & Bentalha, B. (Eds.), *AI and Data Engineering Solutions for Effective Marketing* (pp. 1–22). IGI Global., DOI: 10.4018/979-8-3693-3172-9.ch001

Ernst, D., & Kim, L. (2002). Global production networks, knowledge diffusion, and local capability formation. *Research Policy*, 31(8-9), 1417–1429. DOI: 10.1016/S0048-7333(02)00072-0

Feng, T. T., Kang, Q., Pan, B. B., & Yang, Y. S. (2019). Synergies of sustainable development goals between China and countries along the Belt and Road initiative. *Current Opinion in Environmental Sustainability*, 39, 167–186. DOI: 10.1016/j.cosust.2019.10.008

Gammadigbe, V. (2021). Is regional trade integration a growth and convergence engine in Africa?.

Ghauri, P., & Yamin, M. (2009). Revisiting the impact of multinational enterprises on economic development. *Journal of World Business*, 44(2), 103–107. DOI: 10.1016/j.jwb.2008.05.010

Günçavdi, Ö., & Ülengín, B. (2012). Aggregate imports and expenditure components in Turkey: A theoretical and empirical assessment. *Middle East Development Journal*, 4(02), 1250011. DOI: 10.1142/S1793812012500113

Haddad, S. (2023). Global Financial Market Integration: A Literature Survey. *Journal of Risk and Financial Management*, 16(12), 495. DOI: 10.3390/jrfm16120495

Hidalgo, A., León, G., & Pavón, J. (2002). *The management of innovation and technology in organizations*. Editorial Pirámide.

Hmioui, A., Alla, L., & Bentalha, B. (2017). Pilotage de la touristicité territoriale au Maroc: Proposition d'un indice de touristicité pour la destination Fès. In *Entrepreneuriat, Innovation, Gouvernance et Développement territorial* (pp. 120-143).

Jiang, Y., & Hui, Z. (2021). The Belt and Road Initiative and SMEs. *A New Blue Ocean: Prospects for Latin American SMEs in the Belt and Road Initiative*, 31-56.

Kleynhans, E. P. (2016). Factors determining industrial competitiveness and the role of spillovers.

Morrison Paul, C. J. (2002). Supply and demand-driven spillovers and productivity growth. *Japan and the World Economy*, 14(3), 285–304. DOI: 10.1016/S0922-1425(02)00007-5

Necoechea-Mondragón, H., Pineda-Domínguez, D., Pérez-Reveles, L., & Soto-Flores, R. (2017). Critical factors for participation in global innovation networks. Empirical evidence from the Mexican nanotechnology sector. *Technological Forecasting and Social Change*, 114, 293–312. DOI: 10.1016/j.techfore.2016.08.027

Niyongabo, G. (2004). *Trade openness policy, quality of institutions and economic growth. Centre d'Etudes et de Recherche sur le Developpement International*. Universite d'Auvergne.

Nouhaila, B. K., Aarabe, M., & Alla, L. (2024). The Impact of Digitalisation on the Customer Experience in Medical Tourism: A Systematic Review. In Talukder, M., Kumar, S., & Tyagi, P. (Eds.), *Impact of AI and Tech-Driven Solutions in Hospitality and Tourism* (pp. 408–428). IGI Global., DOI: 10.4018/979-8-3693-6755-1.ch020

Nshimbi, C. C. (2021). Towards a single African economic space: Informal cross-border trade and the COMESA-EAC-SADC tripartite free trade area. In Regionalism, Security and Development in Africa (pp. 77-96): Routledge.

OECD., (2008). Open Innovation in Global Networks: Policies Issues Retrieved from Paris.

Papadopoulos, T., Stamati, T., Nikolaidou, M., & Anagnostopoulos, D. (2013). From Open Source to Open Innovation practices: A case in the Greek context in light of the debt crisis. *Technological Forecasting and Social Change*, 80(6), 1232–1246. DOI: 10.1016/j.techfore.2012.10.030

Pomerlyan, E., & Belitski, M. (2023). Integration-Growth relationship: A literature review and future research agenda using a TCCM approach. *European Management Journal*, 41(6), 1106–1118. Advance online publication. DOI: 10.1016/j.emj.2023.10.003

Ranjbar-Sahraei, B., & Negenborn, R. R. (2017). *Research positioning & trend identification. TU Delft*. Walanda.

Rauf, A., Liu, X., Amin, W., Ozturk, I., Rehman, O. U., & Hafeez, M. (2018). Testing EKC hypothesis with energy and sustainable development challenges: A fresh evidence from belt and road initiative economies. *Environmental Science and Pollution Research International*, 25(32), 32066–32080. DOI: 10.1007/s11356-018-3052-5 PMID: 30218332

Romer, P. M. (1990). Endogenous technological change. *Journal of Political Economy*, 98(5, Part 2), S71–S102. DOI: 10.1086/261725

Senadjki, A., Awal, I. M., Nee, A. Y. H., & Ogbeibu, S. (2022). The belt and road initiative (BRI): A mechanism to achieve the ninth sustainable development goal (SDG). *Journal of Cleaner Production*, 372, 133590. DOI: 10.1016/j.jclepro.2022.133590

Tassey, G. (2008). Globalization of technology-based growth: The policy imperative. *The Journal of Technology Transfer*, 33(6), 560–578. DOI: 10.1007/s10961-008-9092-0

UNISA. (2018). Belt & Road Initiative (BRI), Three Days Work –27-28-29 March. https://web.unisa.it/unisa-rescue-page/dettaglio/id/202/module/87/row/1993

Vallejo, B., Oyelaran-Oyeyinka, B., Ozor, N., & Bolo, M. (2019). Open innovation and innovation intermediaries in sub-Saharan Africa. *Sustainability (Basel)*, 11(2), 392. DOI: 10.3390/su11020392

Von Zedtwitz, M., & Gassmann, O. (2002). Market versus technology drive in R&D internationalization: Four different patterns of managing research and development. *Research Policy*, 31(4), 569–588. DOI: 10.1016/S0048-7333(01)00125-1

Wang, B., Xing, D., Zhu, Y., Dong, S., & Zhao, B. (2019). The state of exosomes research: A global visualized analysis. *BioMed Research International*, 2019, 1–10. Advance online publication. DOI: 10.1155/2019/1495130 PMID: 31073519

## KEY TERMS AND DEFINITIONS

**Africa:** Africa is the second-largest and second-most-populous continent on Earth, rich in cultural diversity, natural resources, and history. It comprises 54 countries, each with unique landscapes ranging from vast deserts to lush rainforests and expansive savannas. Africa is known for its rich cultural heritage, with a wide array of languages, traditions, and art forms. The continent is also a significant player in the global economy due to its abundant natural resources, including minerals, oil, and fertile agricultural land. Despite its wealth, Africa faces various challenges, including economic disparities, political instability, and issues related to health and education. However, it is also a continent of immense potential, with a young and growing population, increasing urbanization, and a rapidly evolving tech scene. Africa's future is shaped by its ongoing efforts towards economic integration, sustainable development, and harnessing innovation to address its unique challenges and opportunities.

**Economic integration:** Economic integration refers to the process by which countries or regions reduce or eliminate trade barriers, such as tariffs and quotas, to create a more cohesive economic space. This process is crucial in the context of open innovation and technology, as it facilitates the free flow of goods, services, capital, and labor across borders, thereby enhancing economic efficiency and competitiveness. In the realm of open innovation and technology, economic integration plays a significant role in several ways: the first way, reduction of trade barriers: By lowering tariffs and eliminating quotas, economic integration allows for a more seamless exchange of technological products and services. This is essential for fostering innovation, as it enables firms to access a broader range of technologies and ideas from different regions, enhancing their capacity for research and development. The second way is, coordination of policies: Economic integration often involves the alignment of monetary and fiscal policies, which can create a more stable and predictable environment for technological investments. Coordinated policies help mitigate economic risks and encourage cross-border collaborations in technology and innovation. The third way, harmonization of regulations: Standardizing regulations across integrated regions helps reduce the complexity and costs associated with complying with different legal frameworks. For technology firms, this means fewer barriers to market entry and a more straightforward process for protecting intellectual property and adhering to standards, thus accelerating innovation and technology diffusion. The fourth way, facilitation of free movement: The free movement of goods, services, capital, and labor is particularly important for technology and innovation. It allows firms to access global talent, invest in diverse markets, and transfer technological knowledge and resources more efficiently. This unrestricted movement supports the development of a more interconnected and dynamic innovation ecosystem. The fifth way, enhanced economic efficiency and competitiveness: Economic integration contributes to larger, more competitive markets where firms can leverage economies of scale. For technology-driven industries, this increased competition fosters innovation and drives advancements, as companies strive to maintain or improve their market positions. The last way, promotion of economic growth and development: By integrating economies, regions can attract more investment and boost economic activity, including in technology sectors. This, in turn, supports the development of new technologies and innovative solutions that drive further economic growth and development. Economic integration can occur at various levels, each with implications for innovation and technology. Preferential Trade Agreements (PTAs) and Free Trade Areas (FTAs) may facilitate initial steps toward reducing barriers, while Customs Unions and Common Markets create deeper integration by standardizing external tariffs and allowing free movement of production factors. Economic Unions further harmonize economic policies, and Full Political and Economic Unions represent the highest level of integration, unifying both economic and political institutions.

**Open innovation:** Open innovation is a strategic approach in business and research that emphasizes the integration of external and internal ideas, technologies, and resources to drive innovation and create value. Unlike traditional innovation models, which rely predominantly on internal research and development (R&D), open innovation promotes a more collaborative and boundary-spanning approach. This model involves actively seeking and incorporating external knowledge from diverse sources such as startups, universities, research institutions, and even competitors. The concept of open innovation was popularized by Henry Chesbrough, who highlighted the importance of organizational permeability. This permeability allows knowledge to flow freely in and out of the organization, creating a dynamic process that accelerates innovation. By leveraging external expertise and resources, organizations can enhance their ability to bring new products, services, or solutions to market more efficiently. This approach not only speeds up the innovation process but also reduces costs and risks associated with internal R&D. Open innovation encompasses a variety of practices, such as licensing agreements, joint ventures, strategic partnerships, crowdsourcing initiatives, and open-source projects. These practices enable organizations to access a broader knowledge base, foster creative solutions, and adapt to changing market demands. By adopting collaborative strategies, companies can tap into the collective intelligence of a wider community, unlocking new opportunities for growth and innovation. This approach is particularly valuable in rapidly evolving markets, where staying competitive requires constant adaptation and the ability to quickly integrate new technologies and ideas.

**Technology:** Technology refers to the systematic application of scientific and engineering knowledge to solve practical problems and enhance various aspects of human life. From a sustainable development perspective, technology is a cornerstone of transformative systemic innovation, serving as a critical tool for improving technological policies and growth strategies that align with global social and environmental goals. This involves harnessing technological advancements to coordinate and influence economic, social, and environmental aspects both locally and globally. In this context, technology is not merely about creating new tools and systems; it encompasses a broader spectrum of integrating internal and external knowledge sources to drive innovation and efficiency. By doing so, technology enables the formation of global innovation networks, with collaboration efforts transcending national and organizational boundaries. These networks are essential for sharing best practice, encouraging creativity and accelerating the development of solutions to complex global challenges. Moreover, technology facilitates open innovation practices, allowing organizations to tap into a wider pool of ideas and expertise. This openness is essential for enhancing competitiveness, as it encourages the cross-pollination of ideas and the swift adaptation to changing market conditions. Through the strategic use of technology, businesses and governments can not only achieve economic growth but also ensure that this growth is sustainable, equitable, and in harmony with environmental stewardship. Thus, technology acts as a catalyst for promoting sustainable economic development, supporting the transition towards a more resilient and inclusive global economy.

**Sustainable development:** Sustainable development is a concept that strives to meet the needs of the present without compromising the ability of future generations to fulfill their own needs. It involves a balanced approach to economic growth, social equity, and environmental protection, ensuring long-term prosperity and well-being for all. Sustainable development seeks to harmonize human activities with the natural environment, advocating for the responsible use of resources, fostering social inclusion, and preserving ecological systems. This holistic approach recognizes that true progress requires not only economic success but also the well-being of society and the health of the planet. In our context, integrating the principles of sustainable development into the processes of open innovation and economic integration is crucial. By doing so, countries can ensure that their advancements in technology and economic structures are aligned with the broader goals of equity, environmental stewardship, and long-term prosperity. This approach emphasizes that technological progress and economic cooperation should not come at the expense of social and environmental well-being. Instead, they should contribute positively to these areas, creating a future that is not only wealthier but also fairer and more environmentally sustainable. By adopting sustainable development principles, nations can promote innovation and economic growth that respect ecological limits and support social justice. This alignment helps to pave the way for a more sustainable global economy, where technological advancements and economic activities are in harmony with the need to protect the environment and improve the quality of life for all people. Such an integrated approach is essential for addressing global challenges like climate change, resource depletion, and social inequalities, ensuring that progress today does not hinder the opportunities for future generations.

# Chapter 2
# A Bibliometric Study of Social Innovation and Sustainable Territorial Development:
## Key Research Trends and Emerging Insights

**Younes El Maaqili**
https://orcid.org/0009-0009-8466-5651
*Sidi Mohamed Ben Abdellah University, Fez, Morocco*

**Abdessamad Ouchen**
*Sidi Mohamed Ben Abdellah University, Fez, Morocco*

## ABSTRACT

*This article examines the evolution of research on social innovation and sustainable territorial development in the context of a multiplication of studies in this field. Despite this increase in research publications, a gap remains in the understanding of key trends and research orientations, as well as their alignment with immediate environmental needs. To address this gap, a bibliometric analysis was carried out to examine scientific publications, highlighting a steady growth in research with a diversification of topics covered. The results highlight a steady growth in research, with a diversification of topics covered, such as rural development initiatives, innovative practices for a socially responsible economy and sustainable development objectives. The implications of this research underline the importance of continuing research in this field, focusing on specific areas such as the comparison of rural development policies and support programs for social innovation, and the integration*

DOI: 10.4018/979-8-3693-6854-1.ch002

*of sustainable development objectives into organizational practices.*

## INTRODUCTION

Social innovation has emerged as a vital field of research, particularly in response to global crises such as inequality, environmental degradation, and social exclusion. As societies grapple with these complex challenges, the concept of social innovation offers alternative approaches to development that emphasize community-driven solutions, collaborative governance, and sustainable practices. Despite the increasing attention, the academic field of social innovation remains fragmented, with research spread across various domains. This fragmentation complicates the ability to trace clear research trajectories, assess the impact of scientific production, or identify the dominant themes that guide the evolution of this critical field. A deeper and more systematic understanding of these trends is necessary to better align research efforts with the societal issues they aim to address.

Existing literature has provided significant insights into various dimensions of social innovation (Díez et al., 2023; Bataglin & Kruglianskas, 2022; Martins et al., 2022). In this regards, scholars have examined social entrepreneurship (Picciotti, 2017), governance and civic engagement (Healey, 2015), resilience in local problem-solving (Torres-Valdés & Campillo, 2013), and social inclusion strategies building (Banyai & Fleming, 2016). Further, research has linked social innovation to corporate social responsibility (Montoya et al., 2022) and urban development strategies (Halsall et al., 2022; Certomá, 2021; Eizaguirre & Parés, 2019). These contributions demonstrate the versatility and potential of social innovation in various policy and development contexts. However, a comprehensive analysis that systematically maps the field's development and reveals its most influential research clusters is notably lacking. Addressing this gap is crucial as social innovation continues to influence local development strategies (González & Lutsak, 2017; Raderstrong & Boyea-Robinson, 2016), offering alternatives to traditional, market-driven approaches.

The goal of this chapter is to address this fragmentation by conducting a bibliometric analysis of the scientific production on social innovation (Perianes-Rodriguez et al., 2016). Specifically, the study seeks to answer three fundamental questions: **(1)** What are the dominant thematic areas in social innovation research? **(2)** How have these themes evolved over the past decade? **(3)** What emerging trends are shaping the future of the field? Through this bibliometric review, this chapter aims to provide a clearer, data-driven picture of the research landscape, offering both theoretical insights and practical pathways for advancing social innovation as a discipline. This analysis not only highlights key developments in the field but also identifies research perspectives and future directions that could foster more impactful, solution-oriented research.

The chapter proceeds as follows: The first section provides a comprehensive review of the literature, focusing on the role of social innovation in sustainable development and territorial strategies. This is followed by a detailed explanation of the bibliometric methodology employed in the study, including the selection of databases, data collection methods, and the specific techniques used to analyze research patterns. The results section then presents the key findings, mapping the main thematic clusters that have emerged in social innovation research and identifying significant shifts in the focus of scholarly work. The chapter concludes by discussing the implications of these findings for future research, offering a roadmap for scholars interested in advancing the field, and ensuring that social innovation research remains both theoretically robust and practically relevant.

## LITERATURE REVIEW: SOCIAL INNOVATION AND SUSTAINABLE TERRITORIAL DEVELOPMENT

Social innovation (SI) has emerged as a pivotal concept within academic and policy spheres, recognized for its potential to address complex social and environmental challenges through collaborative efforts (Dionisio et al., 2023). SI is defined as the development of novel solutions that arise from the cooperation of diverse stakeholders, including governments, businesses, and civil society, with the goal of fostering systemic changes in governance, social practices, and relationships (Ayob et al., 2016). These innovative approaches are particularly impactful in sustainable territorial development, where they address pressing issues such as economic disparity, social exclusion, and environmental degradation (Cajaiba-Santana, 2014). In regions facing these challenges, SI has proven effective in creating inclusive and sustainable pathways for development, encouraging local empowerment and equitable resource distribution. As global efforts increasingly focus on sustainability, SI is being recognized not only as a mechanism for addressing immediate problems but also as a driver of long-term, transformative change across social, economic, and environmental domains (Carayannis & Morawska-Jancelewicz, 2022). Its growing relevance underscores its capacity to contribute to a more resilient and sustainable future.

## Social Innovation and Sustainable Territorial Development

Sustainable territorial development integrates both spatial and societal factors, aiming to enhance the quality of life, reduce inequality, and protect natural resources in specific regions (Moulaert et al., 2013). Social innovations contribute significantly to this goal by creating new approaches for tackling persistent social and economic inequalities, ensuring that communities can access essential services, and promoting inclusive governance structures (Cajaiba-Santana, 2014). SI focuses not only on addressing immediate local challenges but also on fostering long-term, systemic change that aligns with broader sustainability goals, such as the United Nations' Sustainable Development Goals (SDGs). For example, in the context of rural development, SI has been used to develop more sustainable agricultural practices, improve access to education and healthcare, and promote economic development through social enterprises (Bouhtati et al., 2024; Boyd & Paveglio, 2015; Phillips et al., 2014).

The relationship between SI and sustainable territorial development is further enriched by the concept of sustainability transitions, where SI is seen as a key driver of shifts toward more sustainable practices and institutions (Peter, 2021). This includes innovations that promote responsible tourism (Aarabe et al., 2024), energy efficiency, renewable energy use, and smart city planning. Social innovations in these areas often arise from the collaborative efforts of local governments, private enterprises, civil society organizations, and local communities, aiming to create new solutions that are both sustainable and socially inclusive (Dobarrio Machado Ciccarino & Serrano Fernandes Rodrigues, 2023). SI initiatives in this context often address multiple SDGs simultaneously, such as promoting inclusive education (SDG 4), fostering sustainable economic growth (SDG 8), and building resilient infrastructure (SDG 9) (Carayannis & Morawska-Jancelewicz, 2022).

## The Role of Technology in Social Innovation and Territorial Development

Although social innovation is traditionally seen as a societal process, the role of technology has become increasingly prominent in recent years. Digital social innovation (DSI), a concept that merges social innovation with digital technologies, offers new ways of addressing territorial development challenges at scale and speed (Certomà, 2021). DSI includes technologies such as artificial intelligence (AI), blockchain, the Internet of Things (IoT), and big data, which are used to create more inclusive, transparent, and efficient solutions (Dionisio et al., 2023). For instance, IoT has been used in smart city projects to improve infrastructure planning, enhance public services, and reduce resource consumption. AI has been applied to optimize energy usage in buildings and transportation systems, contributing to the achievement of SDG 11 (Sustainable Cities and Communities) (Bokhari & Myeong, 2022).

The integration of DSI into sustainable territorial development efforts is most evident in the rise of smart cities, where technologies such as IoT and AI are used to manage public services and environmental resources more effectively (Alla et al., 2023; Dionisio et al., 2023). By leveraging these technologies, local governments can reduce carbon emissions, improve waste management, and promote more equitable access to public services, all of which align with the goals of sustainable development (Halsall et al., 2022). These digital interventions not only improve operational efficiency but also engage citizens in decision-making processes, thereby enhancing democratic governance and transparency. Addictionology, digital SI platforms have emerged as critical tools for delivering social services and fostering economic inclusion in underserved communities, as evidenced by the proliferation of mobile banking solutions like M-Pesa in Kenya, which has revolutionized financial access for millions of unbanked individuals (Igonya et al., 2023).

Blockchain technology also presents significant opportunities for sustainable territorial development by ensuring transparency in governance and reducing corruption (Reepu, 2019). Its applications in land registry systems, for instance, can protect vulnerable populations from land theft and fraud, fostering more equitable territorial development (González & Lutsak, 2017). Furthermore, blockchain can enhance social innovation by enabling decentralized decision-making processes and facilitating collaborative platforms where communities can co-create solutions to local challenges (Bartoletti et al., 2018).

## Challenges and Opportunities for Social Innovation in Sustainable Development

Despite the potential of SI and DSI to transform territorial development, several challenges remain. One of the primary obstacles is the lack of institutional support and regulatory frameworks to promote social innovation, particularly in emerging economies where governance structures are often weak (Rao-Nicholson et al., 2017). In such contexts, informal networks and grassroots movements often play a crucial role in driving innovation, but they lack the resources and institutional backing needed to scale their efforts (Do Adro & Fernandes, 2020). Moreover, while digital technologies offer immense potential for fostering SI, issues related to data privacy, cybersecurity, and digital literacy pose significant risks (Martins et al., 2022) Another challenge is ensuring that social innovations are inclusive and equitable. In many cases, SI initiatives are spearheaded by elite actors who may not fully understand the needs and concerns of marginalized communities. To mitigate this risk, it is essential to foster inclusive governance structures that prioritize the voices and needs of vulnerable populations in the innovation process.

On the other hand, there are significant opportunities for scaling SI in the context of sustainable territorial development. SI initiatives can engage a broader range of stakeholders, including private enterprises, local governments, and civil society organizations by leveraging digital platforms, in co-creating solutions to complex territorial challenges (Katsamakas et al., 2022). Moreover, the increasing focus on sustainability in global policy discourse provides a unique opportunity to align social innovations with the SDGs, ensuring that they contribute to long-term systemic change.

Social innovation offers a powerful tool for addressing the complex social and environmental challenges associated with sustainable territorial development. Fostering collaboration between various stakeholders and promoting digital technologies, SI can create more inclusive, resilient, and sustainable societies. However, realizing this potential requires overcoming institutional, regulatory, and technological challenges, particularly in emerging economies such as African countries. As the global community continues to pursue the SDGs, SI will play a critical role in fostering more equitable and sustainable territorial development. Following the insights from the literature review on social innovation and sustainable territorial development, the next section outlines the methodology used for this study.

## MATERIALS AND METHODS

### Bibliometric Analysis

Bibliometric analysis is an approach to studying scientific research and publications, including both traditional statistical methods and various text mining and network analysis methods (Martins et al., 2022; Bataglin & Kruglianskas, 2022; Pereira et al., 2021). This approach offers the opportunity to identify the most cited publications, research trends and the most productive countries in certain fields. Scopus, a multidisciplinary database, was used at the initial research level to collect 724 documents.

### Search Strategy

In the first phase of the research, we introduced the keywords "social innovation" AND "territorial development" OR "sustainable development" by limiting the search to "titles, abstracts and/or keywords". Articles published in 2024 were excluded to focus the analysis on full calendar years. In the second phase, to reduce the risk of including false positives without additional value for the constructed dataset, additional processing was conducted and inclusion criteria were used. The inclusion criteria were as follows: (i) articles published in peer-reviewed journals (ii) where it was possible to demonstrate studies on social innovation linked to territorial development or sustainable development by including words in titles, abstracts and/or author keywords, (iii) written in English or French, (iv) relevant to the areas of interest of business, management and accounting, social sciences and of economics, econometrics and finance (v) and published between the years 2001 and 2023 (**Table 1**). The search was conducted during the last week of January 2024. The resulting initial database consisted of 724 publications.

*Table 1. Search strategy*

| | |
|---|---|
| **Research database** | Scopus (SCImago Group) |
| **Initial search words** | "Social innovation" AND "territorial development" OR "sustainable development" |
| **Category** | Title, abstract and keywords |
| **Subject Areas** | Business, management and accounting; social sciences; and economics, econometrics and finance |
| **Document type** | Article |
| **Source type** | Articles published in peer-reviewed journals |
| **Language** | English and French |
| **Year** | 2001 -2023 |
| **Search date** | January 2024 |

Source: Authors

This selection phase produced the result of 303 articles (295 Articles written in English and 8 in French). These identified articles were exported to a file "csv". This file included author names, years of publication, titles, affiliations, author keywords, abstracts, citations, and references. Subsequently, additional processing on Excel was carried out for these articles by analysing their title and their abstract (full article in case of ambiguity) from which we obtained a final result of 247 filtered articles (239 Articles written in English and 3 in French which were translated to English).

*Table 2. Research process*

| 1st phase | 2nd phase | 3rd phase |
|---|---|---|
| "Social innovation" AND "territorial development" OR "sustainable development" (Title, summary and keywords) | Filtering by inclusion criteria | Analysis of 146 abstracts article by article (the full article in case of ambiguity), eliminating all articles that treat the theme in a general way. |
| **724 Documents** | **303 Articles** | **247 Articles selected** |

Source: Authors

Having established the methodological framework, the subsequent section presents the results of the bibliometric analysis, detailing key trends, influential publications, and geographic contributions within the field of social innovation and sustainable territorial development. The discussion will then contextualize these findings within the wider academic discourse, offering critical insights into emerging patterns and research trajectories.

## RESULTS AND DISCUSSION

### Descriptive Analysis

The evolution of research in the field of social innovation and sustainable territorial development demonstrates sustained progression over the years, resembling an ascending growth curve. Early years, such as 2001 and 2007, were characterized by modest activity, both in terms of publications and citations. This dynamic was marked by a significant turning point from 2009, where we observed a notable increase in both the number of published articles and the number of citations accompanying them. The year 2013 particularly stands out, positioning itself as a period of intellectual profusion, with academic production and peer recognition booming. Since then, the field of research has maintained a constant level of dynamism, although exhibiting variations in the production and reception of work. Among the most notable contributions to this academic corpus are papers such as Boons & Lüdeke-Freund, (2013), with 1411 citation and Seyfang & Haxeltine, (2012) with 641 citations, which were able to capture the attention of researchers and illuminate the paths towards a more sustainable future. Thus, the evolution of research in this area reflects not only a growing interest in questions related to social innovation and sustainable territorial development, but also a continued intellectual and conceptual maturation in these areas of study.

*Figure 1. Dynamics of publications on "IS and DTD" (Articles included in the bibliometric review)*

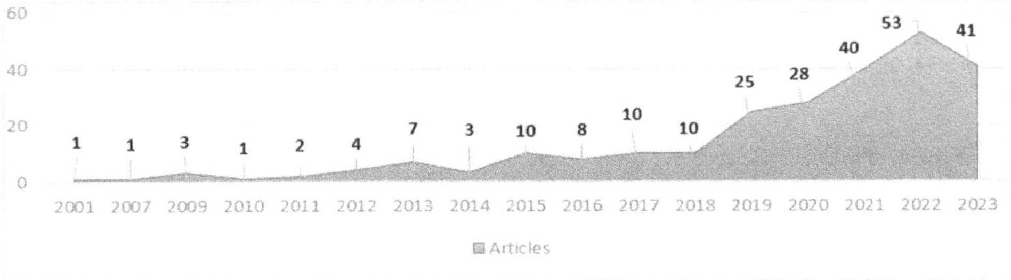


*Source: Authors*

*Table 3. Most cited articles*

| Title | Authors | Year of publication | Source | Cited |
|---|---|---|---|---|
| **Business models for sustainable innovation: State-of-the-art and steps towards a research agenda** | Boons F.; Lüdeke-Freund F. | 2013 | Journal of Cleaner Production | 1411 |
| **Growing grassroots innovations: Exploring the role of community-based initiatives in governing sustainable energy transitions** | Seyfang G.; Haxeltine A. | 2012 | Environment and Planning C: Government and Policy | 641 |
| **Designing long-term policy: Rethinking transition management** | Voß J.-P.; Smith A.; Grin J. | 2009 | Policy Sciences | 319 |
| **'Shaken, but not stirred': Sixty years of defining social innovation** | Edwards-Schachter M.; Wallace M.L. | 2017 | Technological Forecasting and Social Change | 199 |
| **Commercial orientation in grassroots social innovation: Insights from the sharing economy** | Martin CJ; Upham P.; Budd L. | 2015 | Ecological Economics | 194 |
| **Social innovation and the governance of sustainable places** | Baker S.; Mehmood A. | 2015 | Local Environment | 157 |
| **The bio-economy concept and knowledge base in a public goods and farmer perspective** | Schmid O.; Padel S.; Levidow L. | 2012 | Bio-based and Applied Economics | 156 |
| **Universities as the engine of transformational sustainability toward delivering the sustainable development goals: "Living labs" for sustainability** | Purcell WM; Henriksen H.; Spengler JD | 2019 | International Journal of Sustainability in Higher Education | 154 |

continued on following page

*Table 3. Continued*

| Title | Authors | Year of publication | Source | Cited |
|---|---|---|---|---|
| **LIVING LAB: User-driven innovation for sustainability** | Liedtke C.; Jolanta Welfens M.; Rohn H.; Nordmann J. | 2012 | International Journal of Sustainability in Higher Education | 135 |
| **The Futures of Europe: Society 5.0 and Industry 5.0 as Driving Forces of Future Universities** | Carayannis EG; Morawska-Jancelewicz J. | 2022 | Journal of the Knowledge Economy | 132 |

Source: Authors

*Figure 2. Number of publications per country*

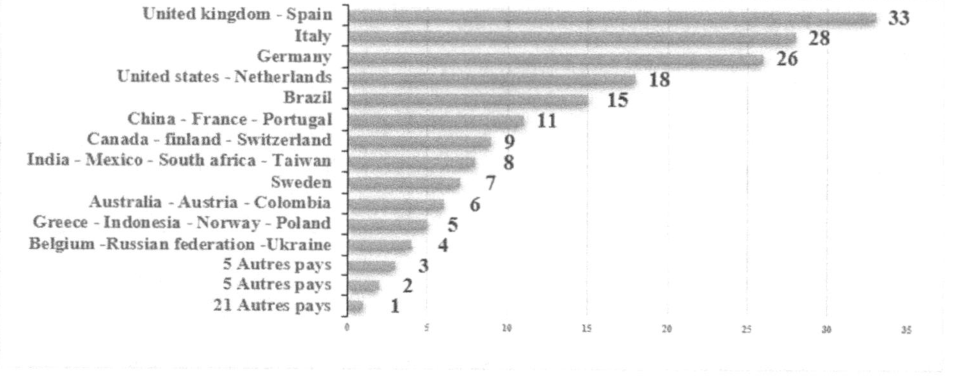


*Source: Authors*

In the current research landscape, the contribution of different countries in the field of social innovation and sustainable territorial development are crucial indicators of their involvement in the advancement of knowledge. This dynamic is illustrated by the significant variability of published articles, revealing marked differences in levels of international research activity. Some countries, such as Belgium, Russia and Ukraine, have smaller contributions, while others, such as the United States, the Netherlands, Germany, Italy and the United Kingdom, are distinguished by a higher number of articles. This disparity reflects the diversity of resources, research priorities and academic capabilities across the world, highlighting the importance of international collaboration and recognition of varied contributions to the advancement of scientific knowledge.

*Figure 3. Classification of newspapers by number of articles*

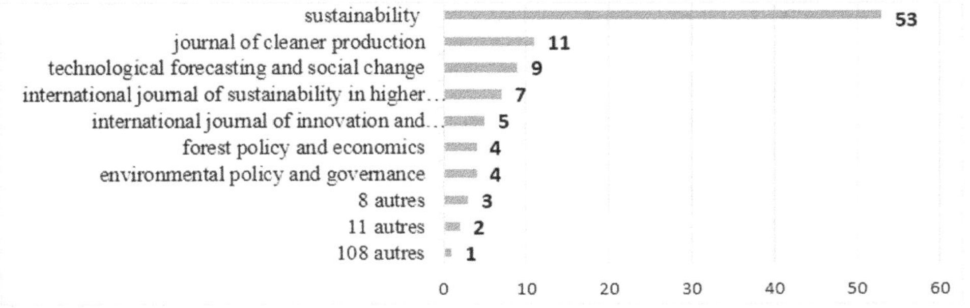


*Source: Authors*

The most influential journals with the greatest number of articles on the theme of social innovation and territorial or sustainable development are: sustainability (53 articles) indexed by Scopus Q1 and journal of cleaner production (11 articles), indexed by Scopus Q1. Then, we have technological forecasting and social change (9 articles), indexed by Scopus Q1.

## SEMANTIC ANALYSIS

Semantic network analysis identified six thematic clusters (**Figure 4)** by presenting a diversified map of our research subject:

- **Thematic Cluster 1: Perspective on rural development initiatives (Red cluster inFigure 4):**

In this cluster, research focuses on various models, policies and initiatives aimed at promoting rural development. Issues such as unemployment, social integration and government interaction are addressed. Key players include local governments, farmers and civil society organizations, all working together to improve the quality of life in rural areas.

- ***Models and policies:*** Research in this cluster highlights various models and policy frameworks aimed at stimulating economic growth and development in rural areas. These models often include agricultural modernization, diversification of rural economies, and the promotion of small and medium-sized enterprises (SMEs). Policies might encompass land reform, subsidies for rural businesses, and investment in rural infrastructure such as roads, schools, and healthcare facilities. By analysing the effectiveness of different models and policies, researchers identify best practices and areas needing improvement.

- *Unemployment:* One of the significant challenges addressed in this cluster is rural unemployment. Research explores strategies to create job opportunities in rural areas, such as vocational training programs, support for agribusiness, and the promotion of rural tourism. Studies also examine the impact of these initiatives on reducing unemployment rates and improving economic stability in rural regions.
- *Social integration:* Social integration is another critical issue within this cluster. Research investigates how rural development initiatives can foster social cohesion and inclusion. This includes efforts to integrate marginalized groups such as women, youth, and ethnic minorities into the economic and social fabric of rural communities. Programs promoting education, healthcare, and social services are also analysed for their role in enhancing social integration.
- *Government interaction:* The interaction between different levels of government and rural communities is a focal point of this cluster. Research examines how local, regional, and national governments collaborate with rural stakeholders to implement development initiatives. This includes the role of decentralization in empowering local governments to take charge of rural development and the effectiveness of public-private partnerships in mobilizing resources and expertise.
- *Key players:* Key players in rural development include local governments, farmers, and civil society organizations. Local governments are instrumental in planning and executing development projects, often working closely with other stakeholders to ensure initiatives meet the specific needs of their communities. Farmers are at the forefront of many rural development efforts, particularly those focused on agricultural improvement and sustainability. Civil society organizations, including non-profits and community groups, play a crucial role in advocating for rural communities, providing essential services, and fostering community engagement.
- *Collaborative efforts:* The success of rural development initiatives often hinges on the collaborative efforts of these key players. Research highlights examples of successful collaborations where local governments, farmers, and civil society organizations have worked together to achieve significant improvements in rural living conditions. These collaborations can lead to more effective and sustainable development outcomes by leveraging the unique strengths and resources of each stakeholder group.
- *Impact on quality of life:* Ultimately, the research within this thematic cluster aims to assess the impact of various rural development initiatives on the

quality of life in rural areas. This includes measuring improvements in income levels, access to education and healthcare, infrastructure development, and overall social well-being. By understanding the outcomes of different initiatives, researchers provide valuable insights for policymakers and practitioners working to enhance rural development.

- **Thematic Cluster 2: Innovative approaches for community development (Green cluster inFigure 4):**

This cluster highlights the changing roles of communities in the implementation of development projects. The research examines how businesses; higher education institutions and experts collaborate to catalyse change and drive social inclusion. Creative approaches and partnerships are essential to creating a sustainable future for all.

- ***Evolving community roles***: The research in this cluster explores how the roles of communities in development projects have shifted over time. Traditionally, communities were often passive recipients of development aid and initiatives. However, there is a growing recognition of the importance of active community participation in the planning, implementation, and evaluation of development projects. This shift empowers communities to take ownership of projects, ensuring that they are tailored to local needs and conditions, and fostering a sense of responsibility and agency among community members.
- ***Collaboration with businesses***: Businesses play a crucial role in community development projects by bringing in investment, innovation, and managerial expertise. Research examines how partnerships between communities and businesses can lead to the creation of sustainable economic opportunities. For example, businesses may invest in local infrastructure, support small enterprises, or provide training and employment opportunities. These collaborations not only drive economic growth but also contribute to social inclusion by creating jobs and improving living standards.
- ***Higher education institutions***: Higher education institutions, including universities and technical colleges, are pivotal in driving community development through research, education, and capacity building. This cluster explores how these institutions collaborate with communities to provide technical expertise, conduct relevant research, and offer training programs that enhance local skills and knowledge. Partnerships between communities and higher education institutions can lead to innovative solutions to local challenges, foster community-led research initiatives, and build the capacity of community members to engage in development processes.

- *Role of experts*: Experts from various fields, including agriculture, engineering, public health, and social sciences, contribute their knowledge and skills to development projects. Research in this cluster highlights how experts collaborate with communities to design and implement projects that are scientifically sound and culturally appropriate. This involves transferring knowledge, providing technical assistance, and helping to build local capacities for sustainable development. The involvement of experts ensures that projects are based on best practices and can achieve long-term success.
- *Creative approaches*: Creative approaches to development are essential for addressing complex and multifaceted challenges. This cluster examines innovative strategies such as participatory action research, co-design methods, and community-driven development. These approaches encourage active engagement and input from community members, fostering a sense of ownership and ensuring that projects are relevant and effective. Creativity in problem-solving can lead to more resilient and adaptable solutions that are better suited to the unique contexts of different communities.
- *Partnerships for sustainable futures*: The research underscores the importance of partnerships in achieving sustainable development. Effective partnerships leverage the strengths and resources of various stakeholders, including communities, businesses, higher education institutions, and experts. These collaborations are characterized by mutual respect, shared goals, and a commitment to sustainability and social inclusion. By working together, stakeholders can create synergistic effects that enhance the impact and sustainability of development projects.
- *Driving social inclusion*: A key focus of this cluster is on driving social inclusion through development projects. Research explores how collaborative efforts can address social inequalities and ensure that all community members benefit from development initiatives. This includes marginalized groups such as women, youth, and ethnic minorities. By promoting inclusive development, these projects contribute to social cohesion and help build more equitable and just communities.
- *Impact on sustainable development*: Ultimately, the research within this thematic cluster aims to assess how the changing roles of communities and the collaborative efforts of various stakeholders contribute to sustainable development. This includes measuring improvements in economic opportunities, social inclusion, environmental sustainability, and overall quality of life. The findings provide valuable insights for policymakers, practitioners, and researchers working to create a sustainable future for all.

- **Thematic cluster 3: Social innovation and the challenges of sustainable development (Blue cluster inFigure 4):**

In this cluster, researchers focused on real cases of social innovation and the policy frameworks needed to address the challenges of sustainable development. Innovative solutions are needed to address issues such as poverty, inequality and environmental sustainability. Key actors include NGOs, policy makers and social entrepreneurs.

- ***Real cases of social innovation***: The research in this cluster explores actual instances of social innovation that have successfully addressed pressing social and environmental issues. These case studies provide valuable insights into how creative approaches can lead to meaningful change. Examples include community-based initiatives that tackle poverty through microfinance, education programs that bridge inequality gaps, and environmental projects that promote sustainable practices. By analysing these cases, researchers can identify best practices, common challenges, and factors that contribute to the success or failure of social innovations.
- ***Policy frameworks***: A critical aspect of this cluster is the examination of policy frameworks that support or hinder social innovation. Researchers investigate how different policies at local, national, and international levels impact the ability of social innovators to address sustainable development challenges. This includes policies related to funding, regulation, and collaboration between public and private sectors. Effective policy frameworks provide the necessary support for scaling up successful innovations, ensuring they can have a broader and more lasting impact.

*Figure 4. Map of sematic networks*

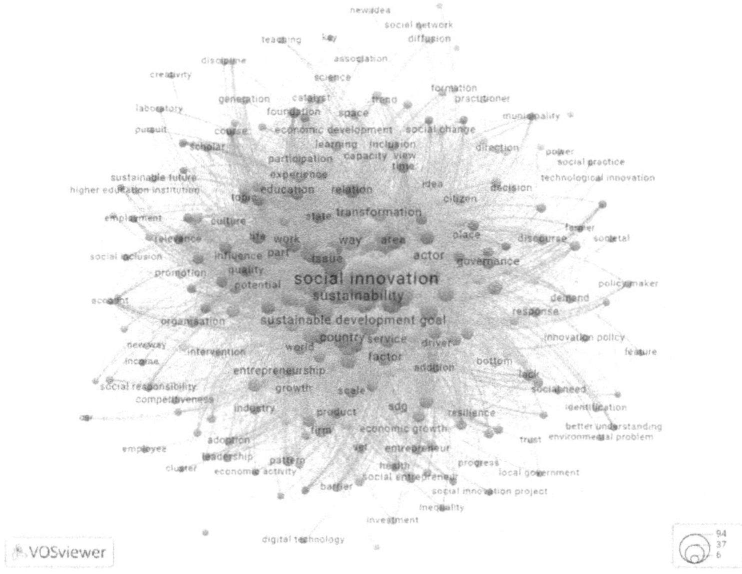


*Source: VOSviewer*

- ***Innovative solutions for sustainable development***: The need for innovative solutions to address issues such as poverty, inequality, and environmental sustainability is a central theme in this cluster. Researchers explore how new ideas and technologies can be applied to create sustainable and inclusive development outcomes. This involves examining approaches such as social enterprises that combine business models with social goals, technological innovations that improve resource efficiency, and community-driven solutions that leverage local knowledge and capacities.
- ***Key actors***: Key actors in this cluster include non-governmental organizations (NGOs), policymakers, and social entrepreneurs. NGOs play a crucial role in implementing and supporting social innovation projects, often working at the grassroots level to address local needs. Policymakers are essential for creating an enabling environment that fosters innovation and supports sustainable development goals. Social entrepreneurs are at the forefront of developing and implementing innovative solutions, combining entrepreneurial skills with a commitment to social impact.
- ***Addressing poverty and inequality***: Research in this cluster focuses on innovative approaches to reduce poverty and inequality. This includes initiatives that provide access to education, healthcare, and economic opportuni-

ties for marginalized populations. By addressing the root causes of poverty and inequality, these innovations contribute to more equitable and inclusive development.

- ***Environmental sustainability***: Environmental sustainability is a critical challenge that requires innovative solutions. Researchers examine how social innovations can promote sustainable practices, such as renewable energy projects, waste reduction initiatives, and conservation efforts. These case studies demonstrate how innovation can lead to environmental improvements while also providing social and economic benefits.
- ***Impact assessment***: The research within this thematic cluster aims to assess the impact of social innovations and policy frameworks on sustainable development. This includes measuring outcomes such as poverty reduction, increased equality, and environmental improvements. By evaluating the effectiveness of different approaches, researchers can provide evidence-based recommendations for policymakers and practitioners.
    - **Thematic cluster 4: Impact of innovations on sustainable development (Yellow cluster inFigure 4):**

This cluster examines the impact of innovations on sustainable development, with a focus on the processes and systems involved. Actors such as businesses, practitioners and networking facilitators play a crucial role in creating positive and lasting change.

- ***Impact of innovations***: The research in this cluster analyses how innovations contribute to sustainable development by addressing economic, social, and environmental challenges. Innovations can range from technological advancements and new business models to social initiatives and policy changes. By assessing the effectiveness of these innovations, researchers identify their contributions to sustainability goals such as poverty alleviation, resource conservation, and social equity.
- ***Processes and systems***: A central focus of this cluster is the examination of the processes and systems that enable successful innovations. This involves studying the lifecycle of innovations from inception to implementation and scale-up. Researchers explore factors that influence the development and adoption of innovations, such as funding mechanisms, regulatory environments, and institutional support. Understanding these processes helps identify best practices and barriers to innovation, providing insights into how to enhance the impact of sustainable development initiatives.
- ***Role of businesses***: Businesses are key actors in driving innovations for sustainable development. This cluster explores how companies integrate sus-

tainability into their core strategies and operations. Businesses contribute to sustainable development by adopting eco-friendly practices, developing sustainable products and services, and engaging in corporate social responsibility (CSR) initiatives. Research highlights case studies of companies that have successfully implemented innovations that promote economic growth while minimizing environmental impact and enhancing social well-being.

- ***Practitioners***: Practitioners, including development professionals, engineers, and community organizers, play a vital role in the implementation of sustainable innovations. This cluster examines how practitioners apply their expertise to design and execute projects that address specific sustainability challenges. By leveraging their practical knowledge and skills, practitioners ensure that innovations are effectively adapted to local contexts and meet the needs of target populations. The research also explores the importance of capacity building and continuous learning among practitioners to sustain the impact of their work.
- ***Networking facilitators***: Networking facilitators, such as industry associations, non-governmental organizations (NGOs), and research institutions, are crucial for fostering collaboration and knowledge exchange. This cluster investigates how these facilitators create platforms for stakeholders to share ideas, resources, and best practices. Networking facilitators help bridge gaps between different sectors and disciplines, enabling the formation of partnerships that drive innovative solutions. By promoting collaboration, these actors enhance the scalability and replicability of successful innovations.
    - **Thematic cluster 5: Innovative practices for a socially responsible economy (Purple cluster inFigure 4):**

In this cluster, we explore innovative practices and strategies aimed at promoting a social and responsible economy. Barriers such as inequality and policy influence are examined, with a particular focus on digital technology adoption and thought leadership. According to cluster researchers, businesses and policymakers must work together to create social and economic value.

- ***Promoting a socially responsible economy***: The research in this cluster investigates various innovative practices designed to foster a socially responsible economy. This includes strategies that integrate social responsibility into business models, ensuring that economic activities contribute positively to society. These practices often emphasize ethical standards, fair labour practices, environmental sustainability, and community engagement. By promoting a socially responsible economy, these innovations aim to address systemic issues such as poverty, inequality, and environmental degradation.

- ***Innovative practices and strategies***: Researchers identify and analyse a range of innovative practices and strategies that businesses and organizations adopt to promote social responsibility. This includes corporate social responsibility (CSR) initiatives, social enterprise models, and impact investing. Strategies such as sustainable supply chain management, green technologies, and inclusive hiring practices are also explored. These innovations demonstrate how businesses can create economic value while also addressing social and environmental concerns.
- ***Barriers to a socially responsible economy***: A critical focus of this cluster is understanding the barriers that hinder the development of a socially responsible economy. Inequality and policy influence are highlighted as significant obstacles. Inequality, both within and between countries, can limit access to resources, opportunities, and markets, undermining efforts to promote social responsibility. Policy influence, including inadequate or misaligned regulations, can either support or obstruct socially responsible practices. Researchers analyse these barriers to propose solutions that can mitigate their impact.
- ***Digital technology adoption***: Digital technology adoption is a key area of focus in this cluster. Researchers examine how digital technologies can drive social responsibility by enhancing transparency, efficiency, and inclusivity. Innovations such as blockchain for supply chain transparency, digital platforms for fair trade, and mobile banking for financial inclusion are explored. The research highlights how technology can be leveraged to scale socially responsible practices, improve accountability, and empower marginalized communities.
- ***Thought leadership***: Thought leadership plays a crucial role in advancing a socially responsible economy. This cluster explores how influential thinkers, industry leaders, and academics shape the discourse around social responsibility. Thought leadership involves advocating for ethical business practices, sharing best practices, and inspiring others to adopt innovative strategies. Researchers examine the impact of thought leaders in driving change, shaping policies, and influencing public perception.
- ***Collaboration between businesses and policymakers***: The research underscores the importance of collaboration between businesses and policymakers to create social and economic value. Effective collaboration can align business practices with public policy goals, ensuring that economic growth benefits society as a whole. Researchers explore examples of successful partnerships where businesses and policymakers have worked together to address social challenges, promote sustainability, and enhance economic resilience.

- **Thematic cluster 6: Sustainable development goals and environmental sustainability (Light Blue cluster inFigure 4):**

This cluster examines the Sustainable Development Goals and the actions needed to promote environmental sustainability at different levels. Areas such as social entrepreneurship, community resilience and innovative technologies are explored. Collaboration between local governments, businesses and civil society is essential to achieve these ambitious goals according to the researchers' recommendations.

- ***Promoting environmental sustainability:*** The research in this cluster investigates various actions and strategies designed to foster environmental sustainability. This includes efforts to integrate sustainability into business models and community practices, ensuring that economic and social activities contribute positively to the environment. By promoting environmental sustainability, these strategies aim to address critical issues such as climate change, resource depletion, and biodiversity loss.
- ***Social entrepreneurship and community resilience:*** Researchers identify and analyse the role of social entrepreneurship in driving sustainable development. Social enterprises, with their innovative business models, can address environmental challenges while creating social value. Additionally, the concept of community resilience is explored, focusing on how communities can adapt and thrive amidst environmental disruptions. Building resilient communities involves developing strategies that enhance their capacity to respond to and recover from environmental challenges, ensuring long-term sustainability.
- ***Innovative technologies:*** The exploration of innovative technologies is a crucial aspect of this cluster. Researchers examine cutting-edge technologies that support environmental sustainability, such as renewable energy, waste management solutions, and sustainable agricultural practices. These technologies have the potential to revolutionize traditional practices and significantly reduce environmental impact, contributing to the achievement of the SDGs.
- ***Collaboration for achieving SDGs:*** Collaboration between local governments, businesses, and civil society is essential to achieving the SDGs. Researchers recommend fostering partnerships that leverage the strengths of each stakeholder group. Local governments can create supportive policies and frameworks, businesses can innovate and implement sustainable practices, and civil society can drive community engagement and advocacy. Through collective efforts, these collaborations can drive meaningful progress towards environmental sustainability and the attainment of the SDGs.

*Table 4. Items from semantic analysis and their frequencies*

| Cluster | Total items | The most frequent items (occurrences) | Items |
|---|---|---|---|
| 1 | 54 | Model(59); issue(40); initiative (39); need(47); perspective (54); policy(43); | Account; Addition; Diary; Agriculture; Area; Assumption; Attention; Characteristic; Civil Society; Condition; Result; Cooperation; Race; Creation; Difference; Disability; Economic Activity; Emergence; Employment; Evolution; Farmer; Foundation; Government; Income; Information; Initiative; Integration; Interaction; Outcome; Life; Management; Market; Model; Municipality; Need; Organization; Perception; Person; Perspective; Policy; Quality; Tidy; Relationship; Relevance; Rural Development; Scholar; Sector; Sense; Social Inclusion; Social Innovation Initiative; Social Problem; State; Time; Training; Unemployment. |
| 2 | 56 | approach(101); Role (77); Community (63); Change (51); society(44); project(41); Business (34) | Ability; Approach; Art; Business; Catalyst; Exchange; Citizen; Collaboration; Community; Community Development; Complexity; Contribution; Creativity; Culture; Discipline; Diversity; Education; Effect; Experience; Expert; Future; Generation; Higher Education Institution; Inclusion; Institution; Key; Knowledge; Laboratory; Learning; Link; Member; Assignment; New Way; Go; Participation; Partnership; Principle; Project; Pursuit; Risk; Role; Society; Source; Space; Internship; Stakeholder; Student; Success; Sustainable Future; Teaching; Tool; Tool; Transformation; University; Way; Work. |
| 3 | 52 | Social innovation (192); framework(61); Challenge (58); Country (41); Activity(38); Factor (32) | Access; Activity; Benefit; Better Understanding; Capability; Challenge; Exchange; Country; Request; Dimension; Discourse; Ecosystem; Empowerment; Environmental Problem; Environmental; Sustainability; Factor; Feature; Framework; Governance; Health; Identification; Improvement, Inequality; Innovation Policy; Innovator; Lack; Local Government; Mechanism; Nature; NGOs; Policymaker; Poverty; Product; Production; Response; Response; Rural Area; Service; Social Enterprise; Social Entrepreneur; Social Entrepreneurship; Social Innovation; Social Innovation Project; Social Need; Social Sustainability; Social Value; Societal; Societal Challenge; Solution; Structure; Sustainable Development Goals; Transition. |
| 4 | 45 | Sustainable development (125); Innovation (101); Process(88); System(51); Impact (49); Actor (44) | Action; Actor; Association; Capacity; Cause; Consumption; Decision; Diffusion; Direction; Dynamic; Economic Development; Economic Growth; Commitment ; Enterprise; Focus; Training; Goal; Idea; Impact; Innovation; Network; New Idea; Opportunity; Potential; Practitioner; Problem; Process; Tidy; Region; Resource; Science; Social Capital; Social Change; Social Innovation Perspective; Social Network; Social Network Analysis; Social Practice; Sustainable Development; System; Technological Innovation; Theory; Trend; Trust; Understanding; View. |

continued on following page

*Table 4. Continued*

| Cluster | Total items | The most frequent items (occurrences) | Items |
|---|---|---|---|
| 5 | 43 | Practice (69); strategy(46); Value(33); relationship(32); economy (36) | Adoption; Barrier, Business Model; Cluster; Company; Competitiveness; Corporate Social Innovation; Corporate Social Responsibility; Covid; CSR; Data; Degree; Digital Technology; Economy; Effort; Employee; Enterprise; Evidence; Firm; Implementation; Industry; Inequality; Influence; Leadership; Manager; Motivation; Organization; Pattern; Policymaker; Practice; Relationship; Rise; Rise; Set; Social Goals; Social Impact; Social Inclusion; Social Innovation Practice; Social Responsibility; Strategy; Structure; Sustainable Innovation; Value; World |
| 6 | 34 | Sustainable development goals (49); Sustainability (79); level(50); environment(33); Development (78) | Achievement; Agent; Bottom; City; Civil Society; Decision Making; Development; Driver; Dynamic; Entrepreneurship; Environment; Form; Intervention; Investment; Lesson; Level; Local Community; Order; Place; Policy; Power; Profit; Progress; Promotion; Resilience; Respect; SDG; SDGs; Smart City; Social Economy; Support; Sustainability; Sustainable Development Goals; Technology. |

Source: Developed by the authors using the VOSviewer software

Table 4 presents the items identified through semantic analysis, categorized into six thematic clusters, each reflecting key focus areas and recurring themes within the analysed literature. These clusters highlight both general and specialized terms that offer insight into prominent topics in the field of social innovation and sustainable territorial development. For instance, Cluster 1 emphasizes policy frameworks and models addressing rural development and social inclusion, with items like "Model" (59 occurrences) and "Policy" (43 occurrences), while Cluster 2 underscores the importance of innovative approaches and community engagement, reflected by terms like "Approach" (101 occurrences) and "Community" (63 occurrences). The frequency of these items provides valuable quantitative insight into how often these themes recur, helping to identify the dominant topics shaping the field's research landscape.

Based on the semantic network analysis which identified six thematic clusters, several research perspectives emerge to deepen our understanding of social innovation for sustainable territorial development. First, a comparison of rural development policies in different countries could reveal best practices for boosting employment and social inclusion. For example, a comparative study between initiatives in developed and developing countries to support farmers could provide valuable insights. Next, an in-depth analysis of collaborations between businesses, universities and local communities in community development projects could highlight key success factors. A rigorous assessment of the impact of social innovation policies on solving sustainable development challenges is also necessary. For example, an investigation into the effectiveness of support programs for social entrepreneurs in reducing urban poverty would be relevant. In addition, a longitudinal study on the impact of social innovations would provide a better understanding of their long-term effects on communities. For example, observing how the introduction of sustainable agricultural practices affects the resilience of rural areas over time. Additionally, an in-depth analysis of socially responsible business models could help identify the best strategies for integrating social and environmental goals into business practices. For example, studying how technology companies integrate reskilling and skills training initiatives into their business models. Finally, the integration of sustainable development goals into organizational policies and practices needs to be closely examined, studying how municipalities implement sustainable transportation policies to reduce greenhouse gas emissions. These lines of research offer a framework for exploring social innovation and sustainable development, focusing on the territorial approach.

## ANALYSIS OF CO-AUTHORS (LEVEL: COUNTRY)

The network of co-authors (**Figure 5**) visually represents the collaborative relationships between researchers from different countries, where a link between two countries signifies that their scientists have co-authored scholarly articles. Despite this network highlighting international academic partnerships, the analysis of the specific scientific domain under study reveals that such collaborations are relatively uncommon. This scarcity of cross-border co-authorship suggests that international academic cooperation in the field is limited. However, the study does identify the emergence of seven distinct clusters of countries. These clusters reflect concentrated areas of scientific cooperation, where researchers have more actively engaged in cross-national collaborations, suggesting that while overall collaboration is limited, certain groups of countries have formed more cohesive and productive academic partnerships:

- **Cluster 1 (Red cluster inFigure 5):**This cluster appears to be very diverse in terms of countries represented. It includes countries in Africa (Cameroon, Ghana, Kenya, Nigeria, Senegal, South Africa, Uganda), Asia (China, Mongolia, Taiwan), Europe (Ireland) and North America (United States). This suggests global collaboration and a diversity of perspectives in the research being conducted (Ipinnaiye & Olaniyan, 2023;Thiam et al., 2021).
- **Cluster 2 (Green cluster inFigure 5):**This cluster is also quite diverse, although centered on Oceania (Australia) and North America (Canada). It also includes countries from Africa (Burkina Faso, Congo, Zimbabwe), Europe (France) and Asia (Indonesia, Nepal, Philippines). This geographic diversity

could indicate a variety of research areas addressed (Belcher et al., 2022; Wehn et al., 2021).

- **Cluster 3 (Blue cluster inFigure 5):**This cluster is mainly composed of European countries (Austria, Czech Republic, Finland, Slovakia, Slovenia, Spain, Switzerland, Ukraine). This suggests strong collaboration within Europe, which could lead to in-depth research in specific areas or projects funded by the European Union (Nijnik et al., 2020).
- **Cluster 4 (Gold yellow cluster inFigure 5):**This cluster is also dominated by European countries (Belgium, Denmark, Estonia, Germany, Italy, Latvia, Netherlands). Like cluster 3, this indicates intense regional collaboration, perhaps with a particular emphasis on certain topics or research areas (Millard & Fucci, 2023).
- **Cluster 5 (Purple cluster inFigure 5):**This cluster is made up of mainly European countries (Greece, Poland, Portugal, Russian Federation, Sweden, Turkey). This suggests close cooperation between these countries, with perhaps a particular focus on specific research areas (Vasconcelos et al., 2022).
- **Cluster 6 (Light blue cluster inFigure 5):**This cluster includes both European (Croatia, Lithuania, Norway, United Kingdom) and Asian (India, Japan, Thailand) countries. This suggests cross-continental collaboration, perhaps with a focus on specific research areas or institutional partnerships (Bajwa et al., 2021).
- **Cluster 7 (Orange cluster inFigure 5):**This cluster is mainly composed of Latin American countries (Argentina, Brazil, Mexico, Peru, Venezuela). This suggests strong regional collaboration in Latin America, with perhaps regional partnerships or joint research initiatives (González et al., 2013).

*Figure 5. Map of the co-authors network (level: country)*

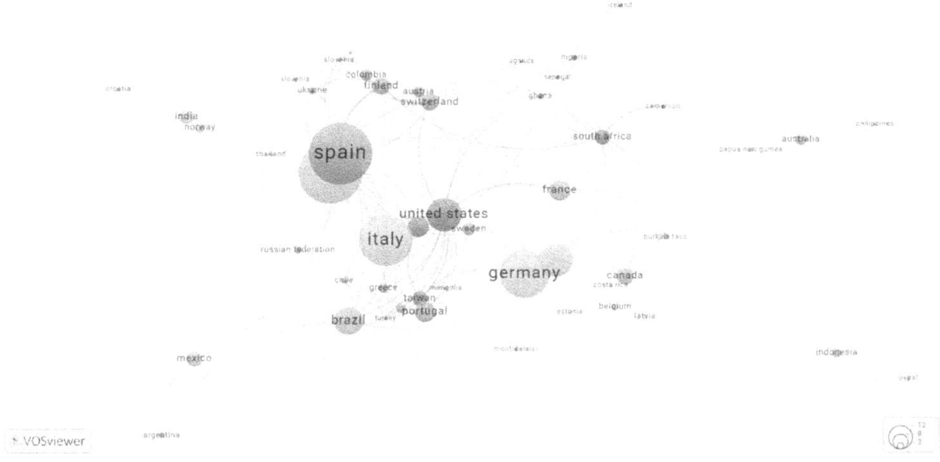


*Source: VOSviewer*

These groups mentioned above show a particular emphasis on African countries, highlighting the contribution of social innovation in these countries which face pressing social problems and growing societal disparities. This indicates the emerging interest of researchers from developed countries to converge their expertise and their research efforts towards the African context, so that they can provide innovative solutions opening the door to sustainable territorial.

The VOSviewer map in Figure 5 illustrates the extensive global collaboration between countries in social innovation research, particularly emphasizing how international researchers work together to address pressing social and territorial development challenges. This map highlights significant collaborations across continents, with key countries like the United Kingdom, the United States, Germany, and Brazil playing pivotal roles in knowledge sharing and joint initiatives. Such global partnerships reflect the growing recognition that social innovation is crucial for resolving complex societal issues like poverty, inequality, and sustainability.

Notably, these groups also show a particular emphasis on African countries, where social innovation has been instrumental in tackling severe social disparities and systemic challenges. The collaboration between African nations, such as Nigeria, Senegal, South Africa, and international research communities underscores the emerging interest of global researchers in contributing their expertise to the African context. In countries like Kenya, for example, the mobile banking platform M-Pesa has revolutionized financial inclusion by providing unbanked citizens with access to financial services, and in Cameroon, platforms like GiftedMom have reduced maternal and infant mortality. These collaborations and innovations demonstrate the potential for sustainable territorial development in Africa, as local partnerships, technology, and community engagement address societal challenges, opening new pathways to economic and social progress in the continent.

## CONCLUSION AND PERSPECTIVES

This bibliometric study on social innovation and sustainable territorial development has offered an in-depth overview of the research landscape in this emerging area. The temporal evolution of academic production has revealed increasing interest since the early 2000s, with pivotal years such as 2009 and 2013 marking a significant expansion of research activity and academic recognition. Key articles, notably those by Boons & Lüdeke-Freund (2013) and Seyfang & Haxeltine (2012), have been widely cited, demonstrating their impact on scientific discourse.

The semantic analysis revealed six thematic clusters, providing a detailed perspective on the topics covered in the literature. These clusters, ranging from rural development initiatives to the promotion of a socially responsible economy, highlighted the diversity and richness of research carried out in this area. Additionally, the co-authors' analysis revealed patterns of international collaboration, highlighting the growing importance of global cooperation in social innovation research as a catalyst for sustainable territorial development.

These results have significant implications for future research. They highlight the need to continue international collaborative efforts to promote the exchange of knowledge and the adoption of best practices. Additionally, they call for an interdisciplinary approach to effectively address the complex challenges facing social innovation. Furthermore, they highlight the importance of taking into account specific regional contexts, particularly in developing countries, in order to develop solutions adapted to local needs and to promote coherent sustainable territorial development.

Despite these contributions, this study presents certain limitations, particularly with regard to the bibliometric methodology which may not capture all of the relevant literature, particularly that published in languages other than English and French or indexed in other databases such as Webofscience. Additionally, special attention should be paid to exploring the interactions between social innovation and other related fields such as digital transformation and governance (El Maaqili & Ouchen, 2024), as well as assessing the real impact of social innovation initiatives on the ground.

As perspectives for future research, it would be beneficial to deepen the study of the mechanisms underlying the effectiveness of social innovation initiatives, as well as to further explore the possibilities of partnerships between the public sector, the private sector and civil society to promote sustainable territorial development.

Also, a deeper understanding of the barriers to implementing social innovations in different geographic contexts could provide valuable insights for organizations seeking to adopt these practices. Comparative studies across regions—particularly those facing distinct socio-economic challenges—could shed light on the varying impacts of social innovation and help inform the development of more tailored and impactful policies.

Furthermore, longitudinal studies examining the long-term effects of social innovation on local communities would provide critical insights into the sustainability of these initiatives. For instance, future research could explore how introducing sustainable agricultural practices has enhanced the resilience of rural areas over time. In addition, examining the role of socially responsible business models and how these models integrate environmental and social goals could uncover new strategies for fostering inclusive economic growth.

In conclusion, this bibliometric analysis has laid the groundwork for a deeper understanding of social innovation's role in sustainable territorial development. The study highlights the evolution of the field, identifying key trends and areas that require further exploration. It offers valuable insights for both researchers and policymakers working toward the achievement of the Sustainable Development Goals. As the global community faces ongoing challenges, social innovation will be crucial in creating inclusive and resilient societies. Future research should continue to investigate the intricate connections between social innovation, governance, and territorial development, ensuring that today's strategies lead to a more equitable and sustainable future.

## REFERENCES


Aarabe, M., Ben Khizzou, N., Alla, L., & Benjelloun, A. (2024). Smart tourism experience and responsible travelers' behavior. In *Advances in Hospitality, Tourism, and the Services Industry* (pp. 128–147). IGI Global.

Alla, L., Bentalha, B., & Elyoussfi, A. (2023). Intelligence territoriale et positionnement stratégique des regions au Maroc: Le cas de la région de Fès Meknes en perspective. *Le concept de l'intéligence en sciences juridiques, économiques et sociales*. 215–237.

Ayob, N., Teasdale, S., & Fagan, K. (2016). How Social Innovation 'Came to Be': Tracing the Evolution of a Contested Concept. *Journal of Social Policy*, 45(4), 635–653. DOI: 10.1017/S004727941600009X

Bajwa, S., Dabral, A., Chatterjee, R., & Shaw, R. (2021). Co-Producing Knowledge Innovation through Thematic Incubators for Disaster Risk Reduction and Sustainable Development in India. *Sustainability (Basel)*, 13(4), 2044. DOI: 10.3390/su13042044

Banyai, C., & Fleming, D. (2016). Collective impact capacity building: Finding gold in Southwest Florida. *Community Development (Columbus, Ohio)*, 47(2), 259–273. DOI: 10.1080/15575330.2015.1135174

Bartoletti, M., Cimoli, T., Pompianu, L., & Serusi, S. (2018). Blockchain for social good: A quantitative analysis. *Proceedings of the 4th EAI International Conference on Smart Objects and Technologies for Social Good*, 37–42. DOI: 10.1145/3284869.3284881

Bataglin, J. C., & Kruglianskas, I. (2022). Social Innovation: Field Analysis and Gaps for Future Research. *Sustainability (Basel)*, 14(3), 1153. DOI: 10.3390/su14031153

Belcher, B. M., Claus, R., Davel, R., & Jones, S. M. (2022). Evaluating and improving the contributions of university research to social innovation. *Social Enterprise Journal*, 18(1), 51–120. DOI: 10.1108/SEJ-10-2020-0099

Bokhari, S. A. A., & Myeong, S. (2022). Use of Artificial Intelligence in Smart Cities for Smart Decision-Making: A Social Innovation Perspective. *Sustainability (Basel)*, 14(2), 620. DOI: 10.3390/su14020620

Boons, F., & Lüdeke-Freund, F. (2013). Business models for sustainable innovation: State-of-the-art and steps towards a research agenda. *Journal of Cleaner Production*, 45, 9–19. DOI: 10.1016/j.jclepro.2012.07.007

Bouhtati, N., El Yaacoubi, Y., Bentalha, B., & Alla, L. (2024). Leviers logistiques de promotion du commerce équitable des produits de terroir: Une esquisse de modèle d'analyse. *Alternatives Managériales Economiques*, 6, 17–35.

Boyd, A. D., & Paveglio, T. B. (2015). "Placing" Energy Development in a Local Context: Exploring the Origins of Rural Community Perspectives. *Journal of Rural and Community Development*, 10(2), 2. https://journals.brandonu.ca/jrcd/article/view/1155

Cajaiba-Santana, G. (2014). Social innovation: Moving the field forward. A conceptual framework. *Technological Forecasting and Social Change*, 82, 42–51. DOI: 10.1016/j.techfore.2013.05.008

Carayannis, E. G., & Morawska-Jancelewicz, J. (2022). The Futures of Europe: Society 5.0 and Industry 5.0 as Driving Forces of Future Universities. *Journal of the Knowledge Economy*, 13(4), 3445–3471. DOI: 10.1007/s13132-021-00854-2

Certomà, C. (2021). *Digital Social Innovation: Spatial Imaginaries and Technological Resistances in Urban Governance*. Springer International Publishing., DOI: 10.1007/978-3-030-80451-0

Díez, D., Flórez, L., & Arboleda, C. (2023). Innovación social desde el emprendimiento social: Panorama de la bibliografía global y colombiana. *Revista de Ciencias Sociales*. Advance online publication. DOI: 10.31876/rcs.v29i2.39976

Dionisio, M., De Souza, S. J.Junior, Paula, F., & Pellanda, P. C. (2023). The role of digital social innovations to address SDGs: A systematic review. *Environment, Development and Sustainability*, 26(3), 5709–5734. DOI: 10.1007/s10668-023-03038-x PMID: 36855437

Do Adro, F., & Fernandes, C. I. (2020). Social innovation: A systematic literature review and future agenda research. *International Review on Public and Nonprofit Marketing*, 17(1), 23–40. DOI: 10.1007/s12208-019-00241-3

Dobarrio Machado Ciccarino, I., & Serrano Fernandes Rodrigues, S. C. (2023). Resilience through social innovation for sustainable development. *Innovation & Management Review*, 20(2), 179–191. DOI: 10.1108/INMR-12-2021-0227

Eizaguirre, S., & Parés, M. (2019). Communities making social change from below. Social innovation and democratic leadership in two disenfranchised neighbourhoods in Barcelona. *Urban Research & Practice*, 12(2), 173–191. DOI: 10.1080/17535069.2018.1426782

El Maaqili, Y., & Ouchen, A. (2024). Digital Innovations for Good: A Bibliometric Study of Social Entrepreneurship Digitalization. In Motahhir, S., & Bossoufi, B. (Eds.), *Digital Technologies and Applications* (pp. 187–196). Springer Nature Switzerland. DOI: 10.1007/978-3-031-68675-7_19

González, D., Sbragia, R., Galante, O., Soto, R., & Valdivieso, R. (2013). ALTEC y la Gestión Tecnológica en Iberoamérica: Gestión de Proyectos, Conocimiento e Innovación Social y Sustentable. *Journal of Technology Management & Innovation*, 8, 1–2. DOI: 10.4067/S0718-27242013000300001

González, M. D. C. P., & Lutsak, N. (2017). The scientific production on social innovation for local development: A bibliometric review the structure and evolution of the field of scientific domain. *Prisma Social*, 19, 146–182.

Halsall, J. P., Oberoi, R., & Snowden, M. (2022). Social Enterprise, Social Innovation and Sustainable Future: A Driver for Policy Change. In Crowther, D., & Quoquab, F. (Eds.), *Developments in Corporate Governance and Responsibility* (pp. 13–27). Emerald Publishing Limited., DOI: 10.1108/S2043-052320220000018002

Healey, P. (2015). Citizen-generated local development initiative: Recent English experience. *International Journal of Urban Sciences*, 19(2), 109–118. DOI: 10.1080/12265934.2014.989892

Igonya, E. K., Nencel, L., Sabelis, I., & Kimemia, G. (2023). Using Economic Diaries in an Ethnographic Study: What They Can Tell About the Financial and Daily Lives of Male and Female Sex Workers in Mombasa. *Progress in Development Studies*, 23(1), 28–43. DOI: 10.1177/14649934221110026

Ipinnaiye, O., & Olaniyan, F. (2023). An exploratory study of local social innovation initiatives for sustainable poverty reduction in Nigeria. *Sustainable Development (Bradford)*, 31(4), 2222–2239. DOI: 10.1002/sd.2502

Katsamakas, E., Miliaresis, K., & Pavlov, O. V. (2022). Digital Platforms for the Common Good: Social Innovation for Active Citizenship and ESG. *Sustainability (Basel)*, 14(2), 639. DOI: 10.3390/su14020639

Martins, T., Braga, A., Ferreira, M. R., & Braga, V. (2022). Diving into Social Innovation: A Bibliometric Analysis. *Administrative Sciences*, 12(2), 56. DOI: 10.3390/admsci12020056

Millard, J., & Fucci, V. (2023). The role of social innovation in tackling global poverty and vulnerability. *Frontiers in Sociology*, 8, 966918. DOI: 10.3389/fsoc.2023.966918 PMID: 37025262

Montoya, C., Teresita del Niño, J., Zazueta, U., Luisa, M., Tereso, R. L., & Verdugo, A. (2022). Áreas de Responsabilidad Social Empresarial en empresas sinaloenses: Un análisis desde la innovación social. *Revista de Ciencias Sociales*. Advance online publication. DOI: 10.31876/rcs.v28i.38851

Nijnik, M., Kluvánková, T., Nijnik, A., Kopiy, S., Melnykovych, M., Sarkki, S., Barlagne, C., Brnkaláková, S., Kopiy, L., Fizyk, I., & Miller, D. (2020). Is There a Scope for Social Innovation in Ukrainian Forestry? *Sustainability (Basel)*, 12(22), 9674. DOI: 10.3390/su12229674

Pereira, R., De Oliveira Massad, D., Do Canto, F. L., & Dandolini, G. A. (2021). The Interrelationship Between Sustainable Development and Social Innovation: A Bibliometric Study. In Pereira, L., Carvalho, J. R. H., Krus, P., Klofsten, M., & De Negri, V. J. (Eds.), *Proceedings of IDEAS 2019* (Vol. 198, pp. 480–489). Springer International Publishing. DOI: 10.1007/978-3-030-55374-6_47

Perianes-Rodriguez, A., Waltman, L., & Van Eck, N. J. (2016). Constructing bibliometric networks: A comparison between full and fractional counting. *Journal of Informetrics*, 10(4), 1178–1195. DOI: 10.1016/j.joi.2016.10.006

Peter, C. (2021). Social Innovation for Sustainable Urban Developmental Transitions in Sub-Saharan Africa: Leveraging Economic Ecosystems and the Entrepreneurial State. *Sustainability (Basel)*, 13(13), 7360. DOI: 10.3390/su13137360

Phillips, W., Lee, H., Ghobadian, A., O'Regan, N., & James, P. (2014). Social Innovation and Social Entrepreneurship: A Systematic Review. *Group & Organization Management*, 1–34. DOI: 10.1177/1059601114560063

Picciotti, A. (2017). Towards sustainability: The innovation paths of social enterprise. *Annals of Public and Cooperative Economics, 88*(2), 233–256. *Scopus.* Advance online publication. DOI: 10.1111/apce.12168

Raderstrong, J., & Boyea-Robinson, T. (2016). The why and how of working with communities through collective impact. *Community Development (Columbus, Ohio)*, 47(2), 181–193. DOI: 10.1080/15575330.2015.1130072

Rao-Nicholson, R., Vorley, T., & Khan, Z. (2017). Social innovation in emerging economies: A national systems of innovation-based approach. *Technological Forecasting and Social Change*, 121, 228–237. DOI: 10.1016/j.techfore.2017.03.013

Seyfang, G., & Haxeltine, A. (2012). Growing Grassroots Innovations: Exploring the Role of Community-Based Initiatives in Governing Sustainable Energy Transitions. *Environment and Planning. C, Government & Policy*, 30(3), 381–400. DOI: 10.1068/c10222

Thiam, S., Aziz, F., Kushitor, S. B., Amaka-Otchere, A. B. K., Onyima, B. N., & Odume, O. N. (2021). Analyzing the contributions of transdisciplinary research to the global sustainability agenda in African cities. *Sustainability Science*, 16(6), 1923–1944. DOI: 10.1007/s11625-021-01042-6 PMID: 34664013

Torres-Valdés, R. M., & Campillo, C. A. (2013). Local development and public relations for disadvantaged groups in the community of Madrid. *Prisma Social*, 10, 394–432.

Vasconcelos, C., Silva, J., Calheiros, C. S. C., Mikusiński, G., Iwińska, K., Skaltsa, I. G., & Krakowska, K. (2022). Teaching sustainable development goals to university students: A cross-country case-based study. *Sustainability (Basel)*, 14(3), 1593. DOI: 10.3390/su14031593

Wehn, U., Vallejo, B., Seijger, C., Tlhagale, M., Amorsi, N., Sossou, S. K., Genthe, B., & Kileshye Onema, J. M. (2021). Strengthening the knowledge base to face the impacts of climate change on water resources in Africa: A social innovation perspective. *Environmental Science & Policy*, 116, 292–300. DOI: 10.1016/j.envsci.2020.09.026

## KEY TERMS AND DEFINITIONS

**Bibliometric Analysis:** Bibliometric analysis is a quantitative research method that examines academic literature to identify patterns, trends, and relationships within a field of study. By analysing publications and citations, it provides insights into the intellectual structure and evolution of research domains. Key metrics such as publication counts, citation counts, h-index, and impact factor offer a comprehensive view of research productivity and influence. This method also explores collaborative relationships through co-authorship analysis and uncovers thematic structures via keyword-occurrence analysis. Modern tools like VOSviewer and Biblioshiny R facilitate network analysis and visualisation of complex data. Bibliometric analysis is crucial for research evaluation, policy-making, and academia, offering evidence-based assessments of research performance, guiding scientific progress, shaping policies, and fostering collaboration.

**Community Development:** Community development is a collaborative process where members of a community work together to address common issues and improve quality of life through economic, social, cultural, and environmental initiatives. Central to this process are participation and empowerment, which involve engaging community members in decision-making and providing them with the skills and resources needed to influence outcomes. Capacity building enhances the abilities of individuals and organizations to meet development goals, while sustainability ensures long-term maintenance of initiatives with minimal environmental impact. Social justice plays a key role by promoting equity and inclusivity, addressing systemic inequalities, and ensuring access to opportunities and resources. Effective community development relies on collaboration among members, local governments, non-profits, and businesses to leverage resources and expertise. Adopting a holistic approach, community development addresses interconnected issues across economic growth, social well-being, environmental sustainability, and cultural enrichment, aiming to enhance all aspects of community life.

**Social Innovation:** The earliest reference to social innovation emerged in 1998, with Rosabeth Kanter highlighting the shift from Corporate Social Responsibility (CSR) to corporate social innovation, which focuses on developing solutions that benefit both new markets and communities (Kanter, 1998). A widely cited definition by Phills et al. (2008) describes social innovation as "a new solution to a social problem that is more effective, efficient or just than existing solutions and for which the value created accrues primarily to society as a whole rather than to private individuals." Although there is no consensus on its definition (Sampaio & Sebastião, 2024), social innovation is recognised for its potential to address complex social issues, sparking significant academic interest and various attempts at conceptualisation. Social innovation is closely linked to social entrepreneurship, with both centred on social value creation (Friedman & Desivilya, 2010; Perrini et al., 2010; Marshall, 2010). While some social entrepreneurs are also social innovators, many social innovations arise from businesses, charities, governments, or individuals who do not consider themselves social entrepreneurs, indicating a partial overlap between the two concepts. Social innovation can manifest in forms such as digital innovation and frugal innovation. Digital innovation provides social entrepreneurs with opportunities to expand their impact through technology, especially highlighted during the COVID-19 pandemic, while frugal innovation focuses on developing low-cost essential products and services for low-income populations (Nambisan et al., 2017; Prabhu, 2017). These forms of social innovation are essential for social entrepreneurs, as they enhance their ability to achieve their social missions (Garcia-Jurado et al., 2021).

**Sustainable Development:** Sustainable development is a holistic paradigm aimed at harmonizing economic advancement, environmental integrity, and social equity to meet present needs without compromising the sustainable development aims to balance economic growth, environmental stewardship, and social inclusivity to ensure future generations can fulfil their needs. It promotes economic sustainability by fostering growth that creates jobs and wealth while using resources responsibly, thus supporting long-term stability. Environmental sustainability focuses on conserving natural resources, reducing pollution, advocating for renewable energy, and preserving biodiversity to maintain ecosystem health. Social sustainability seeks to build equitable societies where everyone has access to essential services and human rights are upheld, reducing poverty and inequality. The principle of intergenerational equity highlights the need for long-term planning to protect resources for future generations. Sustainable development also necessitates global cooperation, as challenges like climate change and resource depletion cross national borders. The United Nations' 17 Sustainable Development Goals (SDGs) provide a comprehensive framework for addressing global issues and achieving peace and prosperity by tackling poverty, hunger, health, education, gender equality, clean water, energy, economic growth, and more.

# Chapter 3
# A Theoretical Approach Towards Territorial Sustainability Conceptualizing:
## A Case Study in the Context of Climate Change in Odisha

**Sharanika Dhal**
https://orcid.org/0000-0002-0477-9811
*Sri Sri University, India*

**Rajat Kumar Baliarsingh**
https://orcid.org/0000-0002-2884-0787
*Sri Sri University, India*

**Biswajeet Patnaik**
*KIIT University, India*

## ABSTRACT

*Odisha is the first state in India to introduce a Climate Budget. It supports Govt. to planning & executing various climate action programs and improving the state's climate resilience. Episodic storm events such as cyclones like Phailin, Hudhud, Titli, and Fani and some chronic problems like shore erosion, coastal flooding, storm surge, inundation, heat waves, drought, and whirlwinds always affect socioeconomic conditions. As the state is always prone to calamities directly or indirectly, there are certain techniques and methods implemented to tackle it. This paper signifies different issues and challenges related to territorial sustainability and the caus-*

DOI: 10.4018/979-8-3693-6854-1.ch003

*es of climate change and management in Odisha related to different sectors i.e. Agriculture, Energy, Fisheries, Forest & Environment, Health & Family Welfare, Water Conservation, Urban Development, etc. and it also studied the concept of sustainability and various challenges related to the climate change and action till now in Odisha.*

## INTRODUCTION

The term 'Sustainable Development' was introduced in 1987 with the publication of the Brundtland Report. Sustainable Development aims to meet the needs of the present generation without compromising the ability of future generations to meet their needs. Seventeen Sustainable Development Goals (SDGs) were introduced at the United Nations (UN) conference on sustainability in 2012. These goals provided a framework to help set sustainable practices and strategies. Climate action is one of the important goals among them. In 1988, an International Panel on Climate Change created by the United Nations Development Programme and the World Meteorological Organization identified the causes of climate change, its impacts, and solutions to challenges arising because of this. As per the Sustainable Development 2030 agenda set by the UN, serious participation of Governments, Organizations, and Individuals is a must for a better future. In this regard, the UN Secretary General recently proposed six climate-positive actions Capital commitment for the green transition, Business Growth to be tied to creating green jobs, a shift from Grey to a Green Economy, Public fund commitment for future sustainable projects, Climate risks & opportunities incorporated to financial systems of organizations & Public Policy and Community participation in climate action. Sustainability denotes the capacity to uphold a harmonious and robust correlation between human undertakings and the environment, guaranteeing the enduring welfare of both. It encompasses the economic, social, and environmental aspects, to fulfill current requirements without jeopardizing the future.

Territorial sustainability is a vital concept that aims to ensure the long-term viability of a region by meeting the needs of its population while preserving its natural resources (Peti, 2012; Borrelli, 2016; Kebir et al., 2017; Paolotti et al., 2019; Carrera, 2022). Odisha, a state in eastern India, has been among the first to recognize the importance of reforming its economy to become sustainable and resilient to the impacts of climate change. The state has implemented policies and initiatives such as renewable energy projects, sustainable agriculture practices, and green infrastructure development, to promote territorial sustainability. Additionally, Odisha has also been a proactive participant in international climate agreements and is committed to reducing its greenhouse gas emissions (Pradhan and Patra, 2013; Mishra et al., 2016; Devi et al., 2018; Behera and Tandi, 2019; Agarwalla et al., 2019).

The earliest definition of sustainable development (Parris and Kates, 2003; Jabareen, 2008; Elliot, 2012; Sahoo and Goswami, 2024; Boopathi, 2024) is: "It is the development that meets the need of the present without compromising, the ability of the future generations to meet their own needs." In 1972, the first historical conference on sustainable development was held in Stockholm; specially discussed about the impact of humans on the economic condition of the countries and other environmental issues. The Brundtland report, also known as Our Common Future introduced the term sustainability in 1987 (Hajian and Kashani, 2021; Borowy, 2021; AO, 2024; Bruckmeier, 2024; Martinell, 2024). In 1988, The World Meteorological Organization and the UN Development Programme established the International Panel on Climate Change to investigate the effects of climate change.

A significant topic that is debated worldwide is climate change. Increased temperature, increased emission of Carbon dioxide, Rapid industrialization and increase in sea level pattern are the vulnerable factors for the change in weather conditions. As per the location factor, Odisha is mostly affected by climate change which is disturbing its socioeconomic development (Mishra, 2017; Mishra et al., 2016; Das et al., 2020; Mohapatra et al., 2020; Rath et al., 2022; Bakshi and Panigrahi, 2022; Das et al., 2024; Mishra et al., 2024; Kundu and Santhanam, 2024; Aarabe et al., 2024).

This paper discusses different issues and challenges related to territorial sustainability and the causes of climate change and management in Odisha in various sectors i.e. Agriculture, Energy, Fisheries, Forest & Environment, Health & Family Welfare, Water Conservation, Urban Development, etc. Along with this, it studies the concept of sustainability and the socioeconomic impact of climate change and action till now in Odisha.

## REVIEW OF LITERATURE

### Territorial Sustainability: Concept

Sustainability is the process of sustaining change in a way that maximizes both the current and future potential to satisfy the needs of human beings and desires. It involves the effective use of natural resources, the direction of investments, technological development, and institutional modification (Farley and Smith, 2020; Ruggerio, 2021; Kumar, 2022; Caradonna, 2022; Thiele, 2024). Over the past ten years, sustainability has grown in importance to conducting business in all sectors of the economy. This is because business sustainability is commonly understood to be the process through which organizations manage the risks, opportunities, and obligations associated with the financial, social, and environmental aspects of their operations. It may also relate to the changes that come with profits, people, and the environment (Mishra et al., 2016; Devi et al., 2018; Behera and Tandi, 2019; Nayak et al., 2023; Das et al., 2024). On the other side, the World Business Council for Sustainable Development (WBCSD) assists in accelerating their organization to establish sustainability. The inclusion of sustainable development in climate change debates has grown since Agenda 21 was modified during the 1992 United Nations Conference on Environment and Development (UNCED) (Sathaye et al., 2006; Senapati, 2015; Iwasaki, 2016; Sahoo and Satpathy, 2020; Tripathy, 2022; Hazra et al., 2022; das et al., 2024; Aarabe et al., 2024; Bouhtati et al., 2024).

## Climate Change IN Odisha

As per the review of the kinds of literature, there are several causes of climate change in Odisha and the effects are common on air and water. As per the data of the National Family Health Survey (NFHS), out of the total population of Odisha only about one-third of the population has access to piped water, and twenty percent depend on nonimproved sources of groundwater. 52% of rural people use untreated water. As per the report of Environmental Information System Report (ENVIS), for various domestic purposes, the people of urban areas use about 335 liters per day. About 70-80 percent of this water flows to tanks, ponds, or rivers through drains or nalas of the municipality. The primary source of water pollutant is Municipal sewage. Every day some cities like Bhubaneswar, Cuttack, Rourkela, Sambalpur, and Berhampur produce nearly 10, 7.5, 6.3, 6, and 5lakh litres of sewage effluents respectively. Without any treatment majority of the sewage is released into the river and it pollutes most of the rivers like Mahanadi, Katha Jodi, Kuakhai, Daya, etc. This is all about the water pollution. Unforeseen development, rapid industrialization, obsolete technology, and lack of awareness in micro and small industries are the primary factors of pollution (Mohapatra, 2007).. According to the Census of India, in 2011 Odisha raised its urbanisation rate by 20%. Some of the major cities in Odisha like Bhubaneswar, Cuttack, Rourkela, Puri, Jharsuguda, Berhampur, and Jajpur Road- Keonjhar belt are major areas of urbanization. Increase in population density, rising urban income and consumption levels and large industrial concentration (Mohapatra, 2007) cause air and water pollution in the state. Sea level rises average 3.3 mm/year due to the thermal expansion of seawater and faster glacial melting, and it may increase by fifty centimeters by 2100 (Carlson A.E. et al., 2008).

As per the Fifth Assessment Report (AR-5) of IPCC, future sea level rise rates are projected to surpass those of recent decades. Indian National Centre for Ocean Information Services (INCOIS) in a study projected Odisha's coastal vulnerability Index (CVI) by subdividing the whole coastline into 1-kilometre by 1-kilometre grids to measure the vulnerability factors affecting the coastal line. According to the Odisha Climate Change Action Plan Report (2018-1023), Odisha experiences both coastal and inland influences on its temperature, with variations occurring throughout the day and across seasons (Mishra, 2017; Pati et al., 2020; Singh et al., 2020). As per the Odisha State Disaster Management Authority (OSDMA), this occurs due to strong heating of land mass (Ex: Kala Baisakhi). This causes damage to several horticultural crops and affects slum dwellers. North-western, western, and south-western regions of Odisha experience the highest rise in temperature. When the temperature exceeds 40 deg. Celsius then it is called a heat wave. In the year 1998, Odisha faced a high heat wave. In that year due to the situation, 2042 lost their lives. The main possible reasons for the greater probability of drought are Global warming and high surface temperature (Anantapatnaikuni, 2018; Mohanty et al., 2020; Lohani, 2022). The average of Odisha's annual rainfall was 1503 millimeters from 1901 to 1950. Now it has decreased to 1451 millimeters, with nearly 84 percent of rain received between June to September (State Disaster Management Plan, Odisha, and August 2013). The fossil fuel burnt to produce heat and power also at times produces gaseous and particulate emissions which contain harmful substances when released into the atmosphere (Mohapatra, 2007). Greenhouse gas refers to a gas that is typically found in the atmosphere that absorbs and emits solar energy within the thermal infrared range. This is called the greenhouse effect (Searchinger et al.20)

## Objectives Of The Study

1. To explore the various aspects of the impacts of climate change in Odisha.
2. To describe various sustainable practices in various sectors like Agriculture, Energy, Fisheries, Forest & Environment, Health & Family Welfare, Water Conservation, Urban Development, etc.
3. To study the concept of sustainability and the socioeconomic impact of climate change and action till now in Odisha.

## Research Methodology

This study follows the qualitative technique to conceptualize the different aspects of the impact of climate change in Odisha. It also concentrates on various issues and challenges related to territorial sustainability and the causes of climate change and management in Odisha about different sectors i.e. Agriculture, Energy, Fisheries, Forest & Environment, Health & Family Welfare, Water Conservation, Urban

Development, etc. It also explains the techniques used in sustainable practices in the various sectors mentioned above.

## Data Collection

All the data are collected from secondary sources like journals, book chapters, seminar proceedings, conference proceedings, newspapers, and internet sources (websites, web pages, etc.). Almost 1500 papers are collected from different sources and finally, 152 are selected for the narrative analysis.

## Issues, challenges, different technologies, and sustainability practices in various territories in odisha:

On March 2010, a Steering committee and 11 sectoral working groups were established by the Ministry of Forest and Environment in Odisha, to discuss the causes and effects of climate change in various sectors i.e. Energy, Mining, Industry, Forestry, Water, Agriculture, Coasts & Disasters, Urban, Health, Transport, and Fisheries & Animal Resources (Jogesh and Dubash, 2014). This paper examines the various drawbacks and challenges of climate change in Odisha with the sustainable activities by different authorities related to various sectors as follows: Agriculture, Coasts and Disasters, Energy, Fishery and animal resources development, Forestry, Health, Industries, Mining, Transport, Urban Development, Water Resources, and Waste Management (Kalra et al., 2007; Mishra and Sahu, 2014; Panda, 2016; Mishra et al., 2016; Mishra 2017; Sharma et al., 2018; Das and Ghosh, 2019; Malhi et al., 2021; Das et al., 2024).

## Agriculture

Thirty-five percent of the geographical area of Odisha is cropped field and sixty percent of its workforce depends on the agriculture sector. The state Government always concentrates on increasing agricultural production by improving water and land management. Climate change has a major impact on this sector as it changes weather conditions, leading to late monsoon onset or late monsoon fall and unpredictable farming conditions due to cyclones, floods, drought, and heat waves (Pasupalak, 2009; Mishra et al., 2016). It causes an increased incidence of pests and vector-borne diseases (Bush et. al., 2011; Mishra et al., 2017). There is also a biodiversity loss in fragile environments or tropical forests (Climate Change and Action Plan, 2018). The effect of climate change on agriculture leads to a rise in inequality and prevents economic growth. Many researchers (Pasupalak, 2009; Mishra and Sahu, 2014; Mishra, 2017) studied the effect of rainfall and temperature using the Ricardian approach and panel regression model (Mishra and Sahu, 2014; Mishra, 2017).

*Figure 1. (a) Comparison of intraseasonal monsoon variability between a large scale (India) and regional scale (Odisha) (b) Comparison of intraseasonal monsoon variability at a sub-regional scale(different zones of Odisha)*

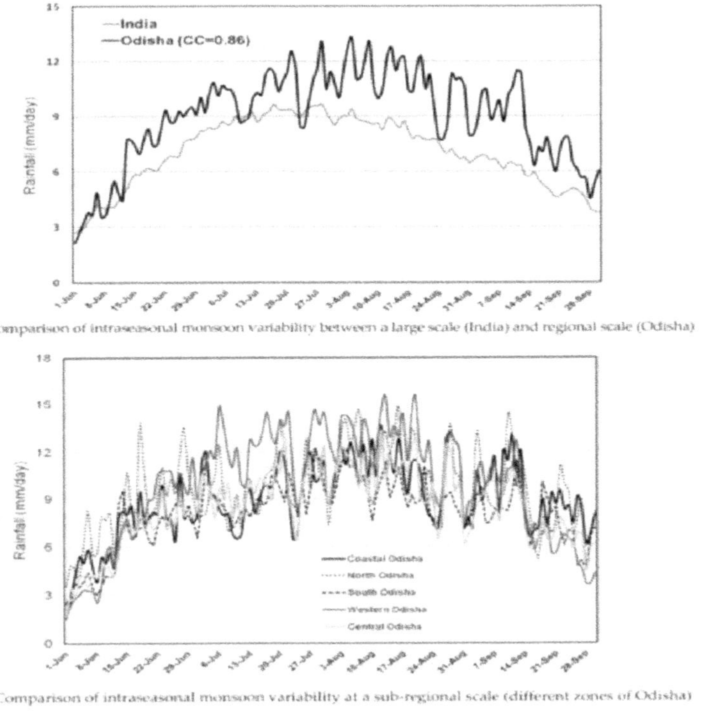


*[Seasonal cycle of the daily monsoon rainfall climatology averaged over (a) all of India and all of Odisha; and (b) different zones of Odisha for the period 1 June to 30 September]*

*(Source: Gouda, K.C.; Sahoo, S.K.; Samantray, P.; Shivappa, H. Comparative Study of Monsoon Rainfall Variability over India and the Odisha State. Climate***2017***, 5, 79. https://doi.org/10.3390/cli5040079)*

Some contributions are also made by OUAT and CRRI, Odisha towards quality seed production and distribution. An irrigation potential of 37.84 lakh hectares is established during the kharif season, and 18.07 lakh hectares during the Rabi season (Kalra et al., 2007; Sharma et al., 2018). There is also the use of proper fertilizer and Pest surveillance and management done by OUAT. The Avg. per ha pesticide consumption of the state is 149 compared to the National avg. of 380 gma.i per hectare. Farm Mechanization like the use of tractors, power tillers, combined harvesters, and rotavators helps the associated people to do their work effectively (Mishra and

Sahu, 2014; Mishra, 2017; Sharma et al., 2018). The Pradhan Mantri Fasal Bima Yojana (PMFBY) assists farmers who have suffered crop losses as a result of natural hazards. The program encompassed a land area of 12.57 lakh hectares, with a total insurance coverage amounting to Rs. 6888.61 crore. The National Mission on Oil Seeds and Oil Palm (NMOOP) was implemented with a funding pattern of 75:25 between the Central and the state governments to enhance the production of oil seeds (Kalra et al., 2007; Mishra and Sahu, 2014; Panda, 2016; Mishra et al., 2016; Mishra 2017; Sharma et al., 2018; Das and Ghosh, 2019; Malhi et al., 2021; Bouhtati et al., 2023; Das et al., 2024; Nouhaila et al., 2024; Badre et al., 2024).

## Coasts and Disasters

In Odisha, floods/ Rise of sea level led to the erosion of beaches or inundated coastal lands (Pasupalak, 2007). Eight different calamities occur in Odisha Floods or heavy rainfall, Cyclone, Drought, Heat waves, Lightning, Hail storms, whirlwinds, fire accidents, and boat accidents (Parida and Mishra, 2014; Das, 2016). The problems in coastal regions due to climate change can be managed by various majors as discussed. According to the Disaster Management Plan of the Agricultural Department (2013), steps are taken for the Construction of saline embankments (Mishra, 2017; Pati et al., 2020; Singh et al., 2020), multipurpose flood, and cyclone shelters (Panda et al., 2020; Tripathy, 2020; Mishra et al., 2021), and provision of shelter-level equipment on the flood sites under the National Cyclone Risk Management Project. Disaster risk reduction system (DRR) includes preparedness activities by families, communities, Govt. and NGOs to face coastal disasters. It is followed during the post-cyclone of Phailin in 2013 (Senapati, 2015; Iwasaki, 2016; Sahoo and Satpathy, 2020; Tripathy, 2022; Hazra et al., 2022). The establishment of a techno-legal framework, known as the Odisha Disaster Recovery Project, aims to facilitate the construction of disaster-resilient public infrastructure. As part of this project, an integrated capacity-building protocol has been implemented, focussing on shelter and self-help groups. This protocol, outlined in the Climate Change and Action Plan of 2018, is designed to aid in the resettlement of areas affected by disasters. (Jena and Kishore, 2021; Sahoo et al., 2023; Mishra, 2023).

## Energy

Climate change causes various natural calamities and it creates displacement and disturbances in people living in the huge reservoir area having the same social cultural values. There is a disturbance in aquatic life, and diseases like Malaria and schistosomiasis occur due to pollution (Panda, 2012; Schaeffer et al., 2012; Dowling, 2013). According to the National Cyclone Risk Mitigation Project (NCRNP), there is a disturbance in the distribution of the power network (ex: Phailin) and power regeneration of the state due to climate change. Emission from thermal power production leads to warming and pollution and the generation of hydropower is affected by changes in monsoon (Mishra, 2017; Patnaik, 2018).

According to Odisha's climate change cell, generation of power can be done through clean coal approaches and institutional development {ex: (GEDCOL) Green Energy Development Corporation Limited} can mitigate the effects of climate change and take measures. Resettlement of displaced people (Sahu, 2016), Environment Impact Assessment (EIA), erosion reduction techniques (Patnaik, 2016; Mishra and Behera, 2016), and aquatic habitat maintenance also help to reduce the impact of climate change (Panda, 2012; Chandel et al., 2016). Professional guidance is required to increase energy efficiency, utilization of fly ash, promotion of biomass and wind generation, maximization of solar energy potential, and maximization of grid-connected wind power (Climate Change and Action Plan, 2018). Biju Gram Jyoti Yojana (BGJY), Rajiv Gandhi Grameen Vidyutikaran Yojana (RGGVY), Biju Saharanchal Vidyutikaran Yojana (BSVY) are working on the development in the energy sector (Anantapatnaikuni, 2018; Mohanty et al., 2020; Lohani, 2022; Bentalha, B. & Alla, 2023).

## Fishery And Animal Resources Development

According to several studies (Maiti et al., 2014; Kumari and Patra, 2014; Kumar and Shivani, 2014; Barman et al., 2016Mohanty et al., 2017; Hmioui et al., 2017; Das et al. 2020; Ngasotter et al., 2020; Dubey et al., 2022; Santhanam and Kundu, 2022; Behera et al., 2023) climate change causes a shifting of species, an increase in water-vector-borne diseases, decreased milk production, and a rise in mortality in small beef and poultry. Snake bites are also more common after floods and water pollution (Hossain, 2018). Water quality and the availability of fodder are impacted by drought (Climate Change and Action Plan, 2018). According to D. Young et al. (2018), scientific health management of aquatic species may lessen the effects of climate change. Aquatic species reserves have benefited greatly from the implementation of many programs, such as the Fish Pond Yojana (2018) (El Jaouhari, S., & Lhoussaine 2022, Kundu and Santhanam, 2024; Hmioui et al., 2024). Improvement in fodder management, promotion of biogas, manure management, and awareness programs may be the solutions to the effects of climate change (Climate Change Action Plan, 2018).

## Forestry

Climate change alters the frequency and causes disturbances in the intensity of forests, wildfires, Storms, insect outbreaks, and the occurrence of invasive species (Climate Change and Action Plan, 2018). To address climate change and take action in the forest sector, one effective approach is to enhance the state's forest cover through the implementation of afforestation and reforestation initiatives (Mallik, 2000; Basu and Nayak, 2011; Mohanty and Sahu, 2012; Pradhan and Patra, 2013; Jogesh and Dubash, 2014; Sahu et al., 2015; Mahankunda et al., 2016). The Ama Jungala Yojana program improves forest density through the implementation of assisted natural regeneration and the protection of existing forest stocks. This helps to create carbon sinks and promotes stronger conservation efforts (Agarwalla et al., 2019). Increase planting on no forest lands, bald hills, coastal diversity conservation, fire protection, regeneration of the bamboo forest, research studies and Expert professional work create proper climate change and action (Climate Change and Action Plan, 2015) (Mishra et al., 2016; Devi et al., 2018; Behera and Tandi, 2019; Nayak et al., 2023; Das et al., 2024).

## Health

According to Bush et al. (2011), Majra and Gur (2009), and Patel (2016), respiratory allergies, food-borne illnesses and nutrition, asthma, and airway diseases, cancer, cardiovascular diseases, and stress-related disorders, among other conditions, are all brought on by climate change. Moreover, it results in heat stress diseases such as syncope, cramps, and stroke. Mass causation events, migration, food scarcity, starvation, and respiratory illnesses are all caused by heavy rains (Climate Change Action Plan, 2018).

*Figure 2. Heatwave Related Deaths in Odisha, 1999-2016*

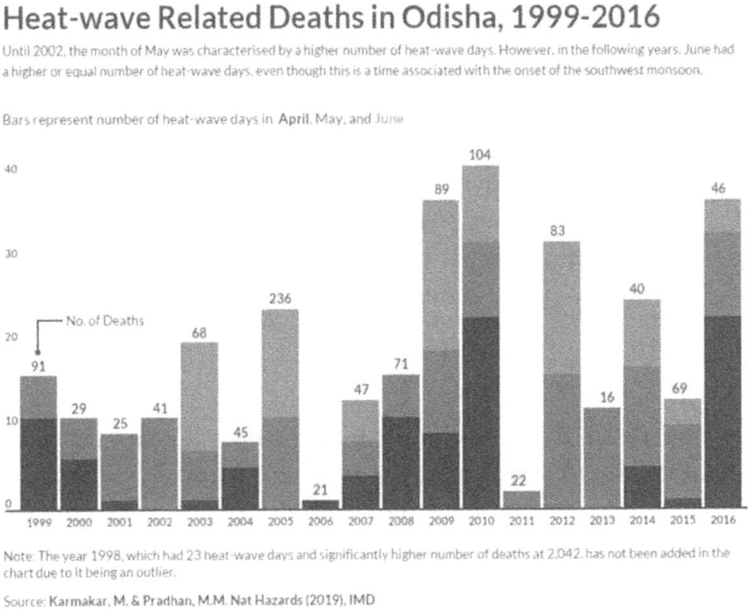


Efforts should be made to educate individuals about diseases that are influenced by climate conditions (Joon and Jaiswal, 2012). Incorporating climate change considerations into the state's health policy and management of vector-borne diseases. Dealing with heat wave conditions and awareness help to minimize the impact of climate change and action in the healthcare sector (Mishra, 2017). According to the Economic Survey Report, 2023; it is explored that the Integrated Child Development Scheme (ICDS) was introduced in 1975 to address the health, nutrition, and developmental needs of young children, and pregnant and nursing mothers (Patel, 2016; Mishra, 2017; Jena, 2018; Karmakar and Pradhan, 2020; Purohit and Rout, 2023; Behera et al., 2023). Different health programs or initiatives have been taken by Govt. to control various health conditions like the Revised National Tuberculosis Control Programme (RNTCP), National Programme for Control of Blindness (NPCB), eye donation camps, National Iodine Deficiency Disorders Programme (NIDDCP), National Leprosy Elimination Programme (NLEP) and National Vector Born Disease Control Programme (NVBDCP) etc/.

## Industries

Climate change causes temperature rise, increasing downtime, and water scarcity (Mohapatra, 2007). Air pollution and rapid industrialization affect livelihoods (Mishra, 2017; Mohapatra et al., 2020; Rath et al., 2022; Bakshi and Panigrahi, 2022). Floods and cyclones have a detrimental impact on industrial infrastructure and significantly disrupt industrial productivity ex: aquaculture, chemicals, and fertilizer (Climate Change Action Plan, 2018). Water harvesting around industrial areas and monitoring pollution control plants (Mohapatra, 2007) help to tackle the issues related to climate change action in the industry

## Mining

Climate change causes aquifer-level contamination in coal-bearing areas, and pollution (acid rain). Environmental toxicity causes various respiratory diseases (Patro, 2012; Hota and Behera, 2015; Das and Mishra, 2015; Mishra and Mishra, 2017; Deb et al., 2017) and deforestation. Emission of greenhouse gases and pollution leads to serious damage (Mishra, 2017; Singh and Choudhary, 2019; Upadhyay et al., 2020; Lohani, 2022; Mishra et al., 2022; Rout, 2023; Alla Das et al., 2023; Mishra et al., 2024; Bouhtati et al., 2024; Boudri et al., 2024), disturbance in mining operations, damage to transport infrastructure, and mining accidents (Climate Change and Action Plan, 2018).

## Transport

According to the United States Environmental Protection Agency, excessive heat waves create damage to roads and pavements, railways, tunnels, airports, etc. Rural areas are adversely affected by floods, and the road infrastructure is weakened due to higher levels of precipitation and stormwater (Patel, 2016; Jena, 2018; Das et al., 2018; Lohani, 2022). Cyclones and hurricanes also damage roads and the avenue plantations, and port areas are extremely affected (Gopalpur, Dhamra, and Paradeep) (Pasupalak, 2009; Mishra and Sahu, 2014; Priyadarshi et al., 2019; Bakshi and Panigrahi, 2022; Behera et al., 2023). It is necessary to implement a new policy to gradually replace old vehicles to decrease emissions and promote fuel efficiency. This can be achieved through driver training, adoption of liquefied petroleum gas, and the use of e-rickshaws. These measures are crucial in mitigating the impact of climate change in the transportation sector (Climate Change and Action Plan, 2018).

## Urban Development

The eastern Indian state of Odisha is moving toward environmentally friendly transportation. To lower carbon emissions, the Odisha government has launched several programs to support environmentally friendly modes of transportation, such as hybrid and electric buses (Mishra, 2017; Jena, 2018). By creating the necessary infrastructure for bike lanes and walkways, the state has also put into practice a policy to encourage non-motorized transportation, such as walking and bicycling. Aside from that, the government has started a scheme called bike sharing to promote short-distance riding on bicycles. These programs seek to lessen air pollution and advance the area's sustainable transportation infrastructure. There are several effects seen in town due to pollution; for Ex: clogging of drainage is seen due to an increase in solid waste which leads to unhygienic conditions and water- and vector-borne diseases (Mohapatra, 2007; Jogesh and Dubash, 2014; Murali et al., 2020; Parida et al., 2021; Behera et al., 2023). It is also seen that an increase in land demand leads to deforestation and an increase in Greenhouse gas (GHG) emissions leads to heart diseases (Swain and Mohanty, 2015; Panda, 2017; Jena, 2018; Sahu, 2019; Howldar et al., 2019; Rath et al., 2022; Pathy and Panda, 2022; Hasan and Daspattanayak, 2024; Elhissoufi et al., 2024). Special programs are planned and implemented for economically backward regions.

## Water Resources And Waste Management

Floods lead to damage to infrastructure and transportation systems (Prasad, 2007) and affect the aqua species. Developments of unhygienic conditions lead to water and vector-borne diseases (Hussain, 2018). Enhance water use efficiency in the irrigation sector, implement water conservation management strategies, enhance flood control and drainage systems, evaluate the influence of climate change on the state's water resources (as outlined in the climate change and action plan of 2018), and mitigate the impact of climate change. Sanitation policy is introduced for rural Odisha and focuses on fecal sludge management. A drinking water policy for Odisha is essential to face the challenges of the water crisis and help to construct infrastructure with concern for sustainability (Pathak et al., 2014; Rath et al., 2014; Raju and Kumar, 2018; Lohani, 2022).

*Table 1. Sustainable practices in various sectors as mentioned above (agriculture, industries, mines, fisheries, transportation, etc.) In odisha*

| Technology | Key Findings | Different techniques related to sustainable practices | Source/ Author(s) | Year |
|---|---|---|---|---|
| Soil Health Management (SHM) | SHM improves soil fertility and productivity, increases crop yields, and ensures long-term agricultural sustainability. | Use of organic fertilizers, and issuing soil health cards to farmers for monitoring soil health. | Odisha Economic Survey | 2018 |
| On-Farm Water Management (OFWM) | Efficient water management through drip irrigation and rainwater harvesting helps combat water scarcity in agriculture. | Adoption of micro-irrigation techniques, construction of water reservoirs, and rainwater harvesting. | Mishra et al. | 2016 |
| Climate-Resilient Farming Techniques | Adoption of climate-resilient crops and practices helps mitigate the adverse effects of climate change on agriculture. | Introduction of climate-resilient crop varieties, conservation agriculture, and crop diversification. | Das and Ghosh | 2019 |
| Rain-fed Area Development (RAD) | Development of rain-fed agricultural areas through watershed management and crop diversification increases productivity. | Watershed management, agroforestry, and integrated farming systems to sustain agricultural productivity. | Mishra et al., Kalra et al. | 2007 |
| Sub-Mission on Agricultural Mechanization (SMAM) | Mechanization increases efficiency and reduces labor dependency in agriculture, improving sustainability and productivity. | Promotion of farm machinery such as tractors, threshers, and power tillers through subsidies and incentives. | Nayak et al., Odisha Economic Survey | 2023 |
| Organic Farming and Certification | Organic farming practices reduce the use of chemical inputs, enhance soil fertility, and promote biodiversity in agricultural systems. | Adoption of organic farming practices, and certification of organic products through Odisha State Seed and Organic Products Certification Agency (OSSOPCA). | Das and Ghosh, Mishra and Sahu | 2019 |
| Integrated Pest Management (IPM) | IPM reduces the reliance on chemical pesticides and ensures the long-term health of ecosystems. | Use of biological pest control methods, pheromone traps, and neem-based biopesticides. | Malhi et al. | 2021 |
| Crop Insurance and Risk Management | Crop insurance provides financial protection to farmers in the event of climate-induced crop failures, supporting sustainable agriculture. | Implementation of the Pradhan Mantri Fasal Bima Yojana (PMFBY) to cover crop losses due to extreme weather conditions. | Mishra, Das et al. | 2024 |
| Agroforestry and Silviculture | Agroforestry integrates trees into farming systems, promoting biodiversity, reducing soil erosion, and improving farmers' livelihoods. | Planting trees in croplands, promoting agroforestry models, and training farmers in silviculture practices. | Sharma et al., Das and Ghosh | 2018 |
| Sustainable Irrigation Practices | The adoption of solar-powered irrigation and efficient irrigation techniques enhances water use efficiency and reduces dependency on non-renewable energy. | Solar-powered irrigation pumps, drip and sprinkler irrigation systems, and water conservation methods. | Mishra et al., Odisha Economic Survey | 2017 |
| Solar Energy Adoption | Solar power adoption for rural electrification and agricultural use | Solar pumps reduce reliance on traditional energy sources and contribute to sustainable agriculture, supporting rural energy needs | Mishra, A., Sahu, P. | 2018 |
| Renewable Energy Policy | Odisha Renewable Energy Policy | The policy framework incentivizes investments in solar, wind, and bioenergy projects, aiming to increase renewable energy share in Odisha's energy mix | Panda, S., Sahu, R. | 2019 |
| Wind Energy Potential | Wind energy installations in coastal areas | Odisha's coastal areas have significant wind energy potential; current installations are limited but offer a growing area for future sustainable energy use | Das, R., Mohanty, S. | 2020 |
| Biomass Energy Utilization | Biomass energy from agricultural waste and forest residues | Utilization of biomass energy helps manage agricultural waste and provides a renewable energy source for rural areas, reducing dependence on fossil fuels | Nayak, A., Rath, P. | 2021 |

continued on following page

*Table 1. Continued*

| Technology | Key Findings | Different techniques related to sustainable practices | Source/ Author(s) | Year |
|---|---|---|---|---|
| Hydropower Development | Small-scale hydropower projects in hilly regions | Small hydropower plants contribute to clean energy generation, but challenges remain in terms of environmental impact and local ecosystem preservation | Behera, K., Tandi, D. | 2017 |
| Energy Efficiency in Industry | Energy efficiency programs for industries | Implementation of energy efficiency measures in Odisha's industrial sector has reduced energy consumption and promoted cost savings in heavy industries | Sethi, R., Mishra, G. | 2016 |
| Off-grid Renewable Energy Systems | Off-grid solar energy systems in tribal and remote areas | Off-grid renewable energy systems have improved energy access in remote tribal areas, leading to socioeconomic development and reduced reliance on kerosene | Mallick, B., Das, R. | 2020 |
| Waste-to-Energy Projects | Waste-to-energy conversion from municipal solid waste | Odisha has seen successful implementation of waste-to-energy projects, reduced landfill pressure while generating renewable energy | Sharma, R., Rath, S. | 2019 |
| Climate Resilience and Energy Systems | Building climate-resilient energy systems through renewable energy sources | Renewable energy adoption helps improve resilience against climate change impacts, especially in disaster-prone areas like coastal Odisha | Mohanty, S., Sahu, P. | 2021 |
| Public-Private Partnerships in Energy | Collaborative projects between government and private sector in renewable energy | Public-private partnerships have led to increased renewable energy installations, particularly in solar and wind energy sectors, fostering sustainable growth | Panda, S., Das, A. | 2022 |
| Sustainable Aquaculture | Promotion of eco-friendly aquaculture systems like integrated fish farming | Reduced water pollution, and enhanced fish production while conserving local ecosystems | Mishra, P., Sahoo, R., & Panda, M. | 2016 |
| Breeding and Hatchery Management | Selective breeding and use of genetically improved farmed tilapia (GIFT) for enhanced fish growth and resilience | Enhanced fish yield and resistance to disease, reduced environmental impact due to efficient feed conversion | Swain, S., Jena, J., & Behera, A. | 2017 |
| Livestock Management | Introduction of scientific cattle and goat farming techniques through sustainable feeding and breeding practices | Improved animal health and productivity, reduction in greenhouse gas emissions through proper waste management | Das, B., & Behera, K. | 2019 |
| Fisheries Policy and Governance | Community-based fisheries management (CBFM) involving local communities in sustainable fishery practices | Increased local participation and compliance, improved fish stocks, and long-term sustainability of fishery resources | Mohanty, P., & Sahu, S. | 2018 |
| Livestock Waste Management | Use of bio-digester technology to manage livestock waste and produce bio-gas and organic fertilizers | Reduced methane emissions, generated renewable energy, and enhanced soil fertility through organic manure application | Patnaik, R., Nayak, A., & Dash, R. | 2020 |
| Sustainable Feed Practices | Promotion of locally-sourced, organic feed for livestock and fish to minimize environmental footprint | Reduced dependence on commercial feed, lower costs for farmers, and reduced pollution from feed production | Mishra, P., & Rath, B. | 2021 |
| Inland Fisheries | Development of sustainable inland fisheries through wetland conservation and sustainable fishing quotas | Improved fish yield in inland water bodies, conservation of wetlands, and controlled fishing activities to avoid overfishing | Dash, N., & Behera, K. | 2022 |
| Livestock Disease Control | Introduction of vaccination and disease prevention programs in livestock farming to ensure animal health | Reduced mortality rates, improved meat, and dairy production, and ensured sustainable livelihoods for rural livestock farmers | Rath, B., & Nayak, R. | 2023 |
| Climate Resilience in Fisheries | Implementation of climate-resilient aquaculture techniques such as pond deepening and controlled water management | Reduced vulnerability of aquaculture to climate impacts like droughts, floods, and temperature fluctuations | Mohapatra, S., Panda, B., & Dash, R. | 2020 |

continued on following page

*Table 1. Continued*

| Technology | Key Findings | Different techniques related to sustainable practices | Source/ Author(s) | Year |
|---|---|---|---|---|
| Sustainable Poultry Farming | Adoption of free-range poultry farming with organic feed and natural growth techniques | Reduced antibiotic use, improved animal welfare, and enhanced poultry productivity in rural Odisha | Mallick, R., & Das, P. | 2024 |
| Municipal Solid Waste (MSW) Management | Segregation at source, door-to-door collection, waste-to-energy conversion | Adoption of decentralized waste segregation improved waste collection efficiency; waste-to-energy pilot projects initiated in urban areas of Odisha | Behera and Mishra | 2015 |
| Biomedical Waste Management | Installation of incinerators, regulated collection and disposal | Proper biomedical waste handling through incinerators reduced environmental contamination; the need for stricter enforcement identified | Panda et al. | 2016 |
| Plastic Waste Management | Ban on single-use plastics, recycling initiatives | Plastic ban partially successful; need for improving recycling infrastructure and public awareness about alternatives | Nayak and Patra | 2018 |
| Industrial Waste Management | Adoption of cleaner production techniques in industries | Industries adopting cleaner production methods saw reduced waste output and pollution, though more incentives were needed to increase participation | Mohanty et al. | 2017 |
| E-waste Management | Establishment of authorized e-waste collection centers | E-waste collection centers helped in reducing illegal dumping, but rural areas still lacked access to proper disposal systems | Sharma et al. | 2019 |
| Organic Waste Management | Promotion of composting and vermicomposting in rural and urban areas | Vermicomposting projects saw increased community involvement, reducing organic waste in landfills and enhancing soil health in agricultural sectors | Das and Pati | 2020 |
| Role of the Informal Sector in Waste Management | Integration of informal waste pickers into formal waste management systems | Informal sector workers contributed significantly to recycling rates, and formal inclusion helped improve their working conditions and efficiency | Mohapatra et al. | 2021 |
| Wastewater Management | Treatment of industrial effluents, adoption of cleaner wastewater technologies | Effluent treatment plants in industries helped reduce water contamination, though stricter monitoring and penalties for non-compliance were recommended | Raut et al. | 2018 |
| Public Awareness and Education on Waste Management | Waste management awareness campaigns and school-level education programs | Public awareness campaigns improved segregation practices, but there was a need for more consistent education programs in schools and communities | Sahu and Rath | 2019 |
| Government Policy and Waste Management | Implementation of waste management policies, monitoring, and enforcement | Government policies helped establish guidelines for waste management, but gaps in monitoring and enforcement at the local level were highlighted | Das et al. | 2022 |

## Implications of the Study

This paper may highlight the major dimensions of climate change and its effect on different territories of Odisha and its management in various sectors of Odisha; helpful for many of the industries like agriculture, mining, irrigation, production, transport, energy, Fisheries, and Forestry, etc., and also to the society. It summarises the territorial sustainability in Odisha and various sustainable projects or activities that have been taken by different authorities for the socioeconomic development of the state.

It is imperative to investigate the social ramifications of climate change in Odisha to comprehend the extensive impacts it has on the state's populace. Climate-related calamities, such as floods and cyclones, can cause relocation, ruinous livelihoods, and mental health problems. Odisha is particularly prone to these kinds of events. Finding vulnerable groups, evaluating the consequences on regional economies, and informing policy choices to lessen the effects of climate change may all be accomplished with the aid of social implications research. Creating focused interventions and support networks may entail evaluating data on migratory trends, financial losses, and community resilience.

## Future Scope of the Study/ Suggestions

The study recommends future research for policy advocacy for better solutions to the problems that are happening in the state due to climate change. This research will help to do a quantitative analysis of different dimensions of climate change in Odisha; as the given one is the qualitative one. It will also be suggested to analyze the effect of climate change on the various sectors of Odisha and provide some measurable solutions to the respective field. To do quantitative research in the area of sustainability and its various aspects are also can be a future scope of the study.

## CONCLUSION

Climate change is a major issue in Odisha to be focussed and discussed. If the actions or plans are taken properly, most of the problems somehow will be sorted out and it will also be helpful for the sustainable development of Odisha. United Nations Development Programme (UNEP) defines sustainable development as "Improved human wellbeing and social equity, while significantly reducing environmental risks and ecological scarcity". Efficient management of action plans, good environment conservation practices (Patnaik, 2018), and proper monitoring of all the measures related to the eleven sectors can lead to a better environment which also includes the participation of employees, employers, industries, corporations, and society itself. There are several councils are also working to develop special green skills among workers in the state like the National Skill Development Council (NSDC), Odisha Skill Development Authority (OSDA), and Siddha Development Research and Consultancy (SDRC). They undertake skill gap analysis and train them as per the requirement. There are several projects are planned and implemented by central and state Govt. to reduce the effects of climate change upon the various sectors of

Odisha. Various Govt. initiatives are aiming towards the achievement of sustainable goals of the state along with socioeconomic development.

## REFERENCES


http://climatechangecellodisha.org/pdf/Odisha_SAPCC_2016-2020

Aarabe, M.. (2024). Smart Tourism Experience and Responsible Travelers' Behavior: A Systematic Literature Review. In El Archi, Y. (Eds.), *Promoting Responsible Tourism With Digital Platforms* (pp. 128–147). IGI Global., DOI: 10.4018/979-8-3693-3286-3.ch008

Aarabe, M., Ben Khizzou, N., Alla, L., & Benjelloun, A. (2024). Marketing Applications of Emerging Technologies: A Systematic Literature Review. In Alla, L., Hmioui, A., & Bentalha, B. (Eds.), *AI and Data Engineering Solutions for Effective Marketing* (pp. 23–47). IGI Global., DOI: 10.4018/979-8-3693-3172-9.ch002

Agarwalla, S., & Saha, D. (2019). *A study on forestry and sustainable livelihood with special reference to Similipal National Park.* Artha Beekshan.

Alla, L., Bentalha, B., & Elyoussfi, A. (2023). Intelligence territoriale et positionnement stratégique des regions au Maroc: Le cas de la région de Fès Meknes en perspective. Le concept de l'intéligence en sciences juridiques, économiques et sociales, 215-237.

Anantapatnaikuni, S. (2018). *Enhancing Energy Efficiency and Renewable Energy in the future electricity system of Odisha.*

Badre, M. E. Z. I. A. N. E., Badr, B. E. N. T. A. L. H. A., & Lhoussaine, A. L. L. A. (2024). La PME logistique et le développement territorial régional: Une analyse qualitative. *Alternatives Managériales Economiques*, 6(4), 1–22.

Bakshi, A., & Kumar Panigrahi, A. (2022). Study on Climate Change and Its Impact on Coastal Habitats with Special Reference to Ecosystem Vulnerability of the Odisha Coastline, India. In *Applied Geomorphology and Contemporary Issues* (pp. 475–497). Springer International Publishing. DOI: 10.1007/978-3-031-04532-5_25

Barman, N. K., Bera, G., & Amrit, K. (2016). Estimation of fishery sector as a coastal resource zone to explore the associate problems and opportunity at Balasore coastal district, Odisha, India. *International Journal of Geomatics and Geosciences*, 6(3), 1696–1707.

Basu, A., & Nayak, N. C. (2011). Underlying causes of forest cover change in Odisha, India. *Forest Policy and Economics*, 13(7), 563–569. DOI: 10.1016/j.forpol.2011.07.004

Behera, B., & Tandi, S. (2019). Impact of climate change on agriculture: A study of western Odisha. [AJMR]. *Asian Journal of Multidimensional Research*, 8(2), 145–156. DOI: 10.5958/2278-4853.2019.00042.9

Behera, J. K., Mishra, P., Bhattacharya, M., Behera, B., & Kar, N. B. (2023). A cross-sectional study about the impacts of climate change on living organisms: A case study of Odisha province of India. In *Visualization Techniques for Climate Change with Machine Learning and Artificial Intelligence* (pp. 399–421). Elsevier. DOI: 10.1016/B978-0-323-99714-0.00014-5

Behera, K., & Tandi, D. (2017). Small-scale hydropower development in Odisha: Environmental impacts and opportunities. *Hydropower Journal*, 8(1), 73–88.

Bentalha, B., & Alla, L. (2024). Revealing the Subtleties: The Art of Qualitative Studies in Science and Management. In Bentalha, B., & Alla, L. (Eds.), *Applying Qualitative Research Methods to Management Science* (pp. 1–21). IGI Global., DOI: 10.4018/979-8-3693-5543-5.ch001

Boudri, R., Bentalha, B., & Benjelloun, O. (2024). Phygital Marketing and the Pain of Paying: An Amazon Go Netnographic Case Study. In Alla, L., Hmioui, A., & Bentalha, B. (Eds.), *AI and Data Engineering Solutions for Effective Marketing* (pp. 348–363). IGI Global., DOI: 10.4018/979-8-3693-3172-9.ch017

Bouhtati, N., Alla, L., & Bentalha, B. (2023). Marketing Big Data Analytics and Customer Relationship Management: A Fuzzy Approach. In Bentalha, B., Hmioui, A., & Alla, L. (Eds.), *Integrating Intelligence and Sustainability in Supply Chains* (pp. 75–86). IGI Global., DOI: 10.4018/979-8-3693-0225-5.ch004

Bouhtati, N., Alla, L., & Ed-Daakouri, I. (2024). Smart Data Analysis and Prediction of Responsible Customer Behaviour in Tourism: An Exploratory Review of the Literature. In El Archi, Y., Benbba, B., Dávid, L., & Cardoso, L. (Eds.), *Promoting Responsible Tourism With Digital Platforms* (pp. 189–212). IGI Global., DOI: 10.4018/979-8-3693-3286-3.ch011

Bouhtati, N., El Yaacoubi, Y., Bentalha, B., & Lhoussaine, A. L. L. A. (2024). Leviers logistiques de promotion du commerce équitable des produits de terroir: Une esquisse de modèle d'analyse. Alternatives Managériales Economiques, 6(Spécial 1), 17-35.

Chandel, S. S., Shrivastva, R., Sharma, V., & Ramasamy, P. (2016). Overview of the initiatives in renewable energy sector under the national action plan on climate change in India. *Renewable & Sustainable Energy Reviews*, 54, 866–873. DOI: 10.1016/j.rser.2015.10.057

Das, A., & Ghosh, R. (2019). Climate-resilient farming practices in Odisha: Lessons for sustainable agriculture. *Journal of Agricultural Sustainability*, 12(3), 78–90.

Das, I., Lauria, V., Kay, S., Cazcarro, I., Arto, I., Fernandes, J. A., & Hazra, S.as. (2020). Effects of climate change and management policies on marine fisheries productivity in the north-east coast of India. *The Science of the Total Environment*, 724, 138082. DOI: 10.1016/j.scitotenv.2020.138082 PMID: 32268283

Das, R., & Mohanty, S. (2020). Wind energy potential in Odisha's coastal areas. *Journal of Wind Energy*, 36(6), 215–228.

Das, S. (2016). Economics of Natural Disasters in Odisha (First Ed.). Bhubaneswar: Research gate. DOI: 10.1093/acprof:oso/9780199464784.003.0009

Das, S., Jena, D., Mishra, P., Daoun, A., Ganesha, H. S., Pradhan, T., & Patra, P. K. (2024). Climate change and agriculture in a mining context of Odisha, India. *Multidisciplinary Science Journal*, 6(10), 2024208–2024208. DOI: 10.31893/multiscience.2024208

Das, U., & Ghosh, S. (2019). Contrasting resilience of agriculture to climate change in coastal and non-coastal districts of Odisha. *Indian Journal of Agricultural Sciences*, 89(5), 769–774. DOI: 10.56093/ijas.v89i5.89655

Dash, N., & Behera, K. (2022). Conservation of wetlands and sustainable inland fisheries development in Odisha. *Inland Fisheries and Sustainability*, 23(4), 88–99.

Devi, R. M., Patasaraiya, M. K., Sinha, B., Saran, S., Dimri, A. P., & Jaiswal, R. (2018). Understanding the linkages between climate change and forest. *Current Science*, 114(5), 987–996. DOI: 10.18520/cs/v114/i05/987-996

Disaster Management Plan of Agricultural Department (Report-2003). Odisha.

Dowling, P. (2013). The impact of climate change on the European energy system. *Energy Policy*, 60, 406–417. DOI: 10.1016/j.enpol.2013.05.093

Dubey, S. K., Padiyar, A. P., Shenoy, N., Gaikawd, A., Mohanty, B., Baliarsingh, B. K., . . . Acharya, S. (2022). Climate-smart and nutrition-sensitive aquaculture in Odisha, India: a new horizon in sustainability, adaptation, and mitigation. In Handbook on climate change and disasters (pp. 574-593). Edward Elgar Publishing.

El Jaouhari, S., & Lhoussaine, A. L. L. A. (2022). L'approche territoriale et la gestion de l'impact de la pandémie de Covid-19: Cas des collectivités territoriales. *Alternatives Managériales Economiques*, 4(1), 245–265.

Elhissoufi, M., & Alla, L. (2024). Artificial Intelligence in Costumer Acquisition: A Bibliometric Study. In Alla, L., Hmioui, A., & Bentalha, B. (Eds.), *AI and Data Engineering Solutions for Effective Marketing* (pp. 1–22). IGI Global., DOI: 10.4018/979-8-3693-3172-9.ch001

Gouda, K. C., Sahoo, S. K., Samantray, P., & Shivappa, H. (2017). Comparative Study of Monsoon Rainfall Variability over India and the Odisha State. *Climate (Basel)*, 5(4), 79. DOI: 10.3390/cli5040079

Government of Orissa. (2002b). *Orissa State Development Report*. Nabakrishna Choudhary Centre for Development Studies.

Government of Orissa. (2002c). *Block Disaster Management Plan: Balikuda Block, Jagatsighpur District 2002*. Prepared by Balikuda Panchayat Samiti.

Government of Orissa. (2002d): Annual Report on Natural Calamities: 2001–02. Revenue Department, OSDMA, Bhubaneswar. [10]. Government of Orissa (2002c): Interim Report on Drought Situation in Orissa 2002. Revenue Department, OSDMA, Bhubaneswar.

Hazra, S., Ghosh, A., Ghosh, S., Pal, I., & Ghosh, T. (2022). Assessing coastal vulnerability and governance in Mahanadi Delta, Odisha, India. *Progress in Disaster Science*, 14, 100223. DOI: 10.1016/j.pdisas.2022.100223

Hedger, M. (2010): Moving Forward on Climate Change Planning – Lessons from Orissa, Policy Brief, Climate and Development Knowledge Network, November, 2010.

Hmioui, A., Alla, L., & Bentalha, B. (2017). Pilotage de la touristicité territoriale au Maroc Proposition d'un indice de touriscticité pour la destination Fès. Entrepreneuriat, Innovation, Gouvernance et Développement territorial, 120-143.

Hmioui, A., Alla, L., & Bentalha, B. (2017). Piloting territorial tourism in Morocco Proposal for a tourism index for the destination Fez [Pilotage de la touristicité territoriale au Maroc Proposition d'un indice de touriscticité pour la destination Fès] (No. hal-02334913).

Hossain, M. F. (2018, May). Climate change and its impact on Aquatic Environment. Gazipur: Department of Fisheries Biology and Aquatic Environment.

IPCC (Intergovernmental Panel on Climate Change). (2007). [Impacts, Adaptation, and Vulnerability: Summary for Policymakers. Contribution of Working Group II to the Fourth Assessment Report of the IPCC]. *Climatic Change*, , 2007.

IUCN. (2015). Climate change and Forest.

Iwasaki, S. (2016). Linking disaster management to livelihood security against tropical cyclones: A case study on Odisha state in India. *International Journal of Disaster Risk Reduction*, 19, 57–63. DOI: 10.1016/j.ijdrr.2016.08.019

Jarvis, A., Ramirez, J., Anderson, B., Leibing, C., & Aggarwal, P. (2010). Scenarios of climate change within the context of agriculture. In *Climate Change and Crop Production*. CAB International. DOI: 10.1079/9781845936334.0009

Jayant Sathaye, P. S. (2006, February 10). Climate change, Sustainable Developement in India: Global and National Concern. 90(3).

Jena, P. K., & Kishore, J. The Fani: A case study Of Odisha disaster management. A. and Bindal, MK (eds.) (2021) Health Adaptation and Resilience to Climate Change and Related Disasters-A Compendium of Case Studies, 73.

Jena, P. P. (2017). Impact of climate change on Odisha, economic development—A comparative analysis. *Journal of the Humanities and Social Sciences*, 22, 21–25.

Jena, P. P. (2018). Climate change and its worst effect on coastal Odisha: An overview of its impact in Jagatsinghpur District. *IOSR Journal of Humanities and Social Science*, 23(1), 1–15.

Jogesh, A., & Dubash, N. K. (2014). Mainstreaming climate change in state development planning: An analysis of the Odisha Climate Change Action Plan.

Kalra, N., Chander, S., Pathak, H., Aggarwal, P. K., Gupta, N. C., Sehgal, M., & Chakraborty, D. (2007). Impacts of climate change on agriculture. *Outlook on Agriculture*, 36(2), 109–118. DOI: 10.5367/000000007781159903

Kalra, N., Singh, S., & Chakraborty, D. (2007). Rain-fed agriculture in Odisha: A sustainable approach through watershed management. *Water Resources Management*, 21(5), 965–982.

Karmakar, A. K., & Mukhopadhyay, D. (2014). Towards a Prudent Policy for Food Security in India. *US-China Law Review*, 11(2), 221–262.

Karmakar, M., & Pradhan, M. M. (2020). Climate change and public health: A study of vector-borne diseases in Odisha, India. *Natural Hazards*, 102(2), 659–671. DOI: 10.1007/s11069-019-03594-4

Krishnan, S. H., Sharma, R., Dash, P. S., Haldar, S. K., & Biswas, B. (2006). Use of waste plastics in Coke making at Tata Steel. *Ironmaking & Steelmaking*, 33(4), 288–292. DOI: 10.1179/174328106X113959

Kumar, S. T., & Shivani, P. (2014). Marine fisheries; its current status, sustainable management and socio-economic status of the marine fishers of Odisha, through Indian Marine Policy: A case study. Research Journal of Animal. *Veterinary and Fishery Sciences*, 2(7), 10–19.

Kumari, M. K., & Patra, S. (2014). Growth and performance of fishery in Odisha. *Asian Journal of Research in Business Economics and Management*, 4(6), 100–110.

Kundu, S. K., & Santhanam, H. (2024). *Transitional Contexts and Transformational Pathways Through the Utilisation of Marine Fishery Advisories in Odisha*. Challenges and Way Forward. Anthropocene Science.

Kundzewicz, Z. W., & Doll, P. (2009). Will groundwater ease freshwater stress under climate change? *Hydrological Sciences Journal*, 54(4), 665–675. DOI: 10.1623/hysj.54.4.665

Lohani, T. K. (2022). Causes, Effects, and Remedial Measures of Climate Change in the East Coast of India with Special Reference to the State of Odisha. In India, I. I. (Ed.), *Climate Change Impacts, Mitigation and Adaptation in Developing Countries* (pp. 383–406). Springer International Publishing. DOI: 10.1007/978-3-030-94395-0_16

Mahankuda, P. K., Singh, P., Dolai, S. K., & Choudhury, A. K. (2016). Estimating economic benefits through social forestry in Odisha. *Splint International Journal Of Professionals*, 3(7), 59–66.

Mahapatra, P. C., Sahu, B. K., & Mohanty, A. K. (2020). Plastic Waste, Health & Climate Change: Issues & Challenges of Odisha. *Indian Journal of Public Health Research & Development*, 11(6).

Maiti, S., Jha, S. K., Garai, S., Nag, A., Chakravarty, R., Kadian, K. S., & Upadhaya, R. C. (2014). Adaptation strategies followed by the livestock rearers of coastal Odisha and West Bengal to cope up with climate change. *The Indian Journal of Animal Sciences*, 84(6), 652–659. DOI: 10.56093/ijans.v84.i6.41633

Majra, J. P., & Gur, A. (2009). Climate change and health: Why should India be concerned? *Indian Journal of Occupational and Environmental Medicine*, 13(1), 11–16. DOI: 10.4103/0019-5278.50717 PMID: 20165606

Malhi, G. S., Kaur, M., & Kaushik, P. (2021). Impact of climate change on agriculture and its mitigation strategies: A review. *Sustainability (Basel)*, 13(3), 1318. DOI: 10.3390/su13031318

Malhi, Y., Kumar, S., & Das, P. (2021). Integrated pest management in Odisha: Enhancing agricultural sustainability through eco-friendly practices. *Journal of Pest Science*, 94(1), 143–152.

Mallick, B., & Das, R. (2020). Off-grid renewable energy systems for remote areas in Odisha. *Energy for Sustainable Development*, 17(1), 43–57.

Mallick, R., & Das, P. (2024). Free-range poultry farming and its role in sustainable rural development in Odisha. *Poultry Farming Review*, 14(1), 58–67.

Mallik, R. M. (2000). Sustainable management of non-timber forest products in Orissa: Some issues and options. *Indian Journal of Agricultural Economics*, 55(3), 384.

Mishra, A., & Sahu, P. (2018). Solar energy adoption for rural electrification and sustainable agriculture. *Renewable Energy Journal*, 45(4), 321–335.

Mishra, D., & Sahu, N. C. (2014). Economic Impact of Climate Change on Agriculture Sector of Coastal Odisha. *APCBEE Procedia*, 10, 241–245. DOI: 10.1016/j.apcbee.2014.10.046

Mishra, D., Sahu, N. C., & Sahoo, D. (2016). Impact of climate change on agricultural production of Odisha (India): A Ricardian analysis. *Regional Environmental Change*, 16(2), 575–584. DOI: 10.1007/s10113-015-0774-5

Mishra, M., Acharyya, T., & Pattnaik, N. (2021). Characterizing shifting pattern of disaster-induced death and disaster management policies: a regional analysis from Odisha, India. Current Science (00113891), 120(11).

Mishra, O. P. (2023). Creating Robust Infrastructure and Response Mechanism: Odisha Model of Disaster Management. In *International Handbook of Disaster Research* (pp. 1–14). Springer Nature Singapore.

Mishra, P., & Behera, B. (2016). Socio-economic and environmental implications of solar electrification: Experience of rural Odisha. *Renewable & Sustainable Energy Reviews*, 56, 953–964. DOI: 10.1016/j.rser.2015.11.075

Mishra, P., Das, T., & Nayak, R. (2016). On-farm water management practices for sustainable agriculture in Odisha. *International Journal of Water Resources Development*, 32(4), 789–804.

Mishra, P., & Rath, B. (2021). Locally sourced feed and its impact on livestock and fish production in Odisha. *Agricultural Sustainability Journal*, 18(2), 201–209.

Mishra, P., Sahoo, R., & Panda, M. (2016). Sustainable aquaculture practices in Odisha: A review. *Journal of Fisheries Research*, 45(2), 122–130.

Mishra, P. K. (2017). Socio-economic impacts of climate change in Odisha: Issues, challenges and policy options. *Journal of Climate Change*, 3(1), 93–107. DOI: 10.3233/JCC-170009

Mishra, R., & Sahu, N. (2014). Organic farming in Odisha: Pathway towards sustainable agriculture. *Agricultural Economics Review*, 25(2), 234–248.

Mishra, T. (2017). Public-private collaboration for sustainable agriculture in Odisha: A review of climate-conscious farming initiatives. *Sustainable Agriculture Research*, 16(2), 45–58.

Mithun Karmakar, M. P. (2019). *Climate change and Public Health: A study of study of Vector Borne diseases in Odisha*. Springer.

Mohanty, B., & Sahu, G. (2012). An empirical study on elements of forest governance: A study of JFM implementation models in Odisha. *Procedia: Social and Behavioral Sciences*, 37, 314–323. DOI: 10.1016/j.sbspro.2012.03.297

Mohanty, B., Vivekanandan, E., Mohanty, S., Mahanty, A., Trivedi, R., Tripathy, M., & Sahu, J. (2017). The impact of climate change on marine and inland fisheries and aquaculture in India. Climate change impacts on fisheries and aquaculture: a global analysis, 2, 569-601.

Mohanty, P., & Sahu, S. (2018). Community-based fisheries management and its impact on fish stocks in Odisha. *Fisheries Governance Review*, 55(1), 34–45.

Mohanty, P. K., Panda, U. S., Pal, S. R., & Mishra, P. (2008). Monitoring and management of environmental changes along the Orissa coast. *Journal of Coastal Research*, (24), 13–27.

Mohanty, P. P., Rout, H. B., & Samal, A. (2019). Community based sustainable tourism development-A tool for fostering and promoting peace: A case study of Odisha, India. *African Journal of Hospitality, Tourism and Leisure*, 8(1), 1–15.

Mohanty, S., & Sahu, P. (2021). Building climate-resilient energy systems in coastal Odisha. *Climate and Energy Studies*, 10(3), 133–145.

Mohanty, S. K., Chatterjee, R., & Shaw, R. (2020). Building resilience of critical infrastructure: A case of impacts of cyclones on the power sector in Odisha. *Climate (Basel)*, 8(6), 73. DOI: 10.3390/cli8060073

Mohapatra, R. (2006): Disaster Dossier: The Impact of Climate Change on Orissa, Info changes. News and Analysis on Social Justice and Development Issues in India. www.infochangeindia.org <Accessed on 23rd April, 2016>. [13].

Mohapatra, S., Panda, B., & Dash, R. (2020). Climate-resilient aquaculture techniques for sustainable fishery development in Odisha. *Climate and Aquaculture*, 28(5), 93–105.

Nayak, A., & Rath, P. (2021). Biomass energy utilization in Odisha: Opportunities and challenges. *Biomass Energy Science*, 14(3), 142–157.

Nayak, B. K., Mishra, M. K., & Upadhyay, V. P. (2023). Agroecosystem Sustainability in Forest Dependent Tribal Villages in Odisha, Eastern India. *Asian Journal of Environment & Ecology*, 22(3), 61–85. DOI: 10.9734/ajee/2023/v22i3489

Nayak, R., Behera, S., & Tandi, D. (2023). Mechanization in agriculture: A sustainable solution for enhanced productivity in Odisha. *Agricultural Mechanization in Asia*, 54(2), 89–97.

Nayak, S. K., & Nandimandalam, J. R. (2023). Impacts of climate change and coastal salinization on the environmental risk of heavy metal contamination along the odisha coast, India. *Environmental Research*, 238, 117175. DOI: 10.1016/j.envres.2023.117175 PMID: 37741567

Ngasotter, S., Panda, S. P., Mohanty, U., Akter, S., Mukherjee, S., Waikhom, D., & Devi, L. S. (2020). Current scenario of fisheries and aquaculture in India with special reference to Odisha: a review on its status, issues and prospects for sustainable development. International Journal of Bio-resource and Stress Management, 11(Aug, 4), 370-380.

Nouhaila, B. K., Aarabe, M., & Alla, L. (2024). The Impact of Digitalisation on the Customer Experience in Medical Tourism: A Systematic Review. In Talukder, M., Kumar, S., & Tyagi, P. (Eds.), *Impact of AI and Tech-Driven Solutions in Hospitality and Tourism* (pp. 408–428). IGI Global., DOI: 10.4018/979-8-3693-6755-1.ch020

Odisha Economic Survey. (2018). Sustainable agriculture initiatives and government programs in Odisha. Bhubaneswar: Government of Odisha.

*Odisha environment Congress*. (2012). (pp. 70–81). Human Development Foundation.

Padmanabh Hota, B. B. (2016). Open Cast Coal mining and sustainable local livelihoods in Odisha, India. *Mineral Economics*, 29(1), 1–13. DOI: 10.1007/s13563-016-0082-7

Panda, A. (2016). Vulnerability to climate variability and drought among small and marginal farmers: A case study in Odisha, India. *Climate and Development*, 9(7), 605–617. DOI: 10.1080/17565529.2016.1184606

PANDA, G. State Climate Change Action Plan and Forestry Sector: Challenges and Mitigation in Odisha.

Panda, H. (2017). Development challenges and prospects in Odisha. *Centurion Journal of Multidisciplinary Research*, 2(1), 47–59.

Panda, S. (2016). Sustainable irrigation practices in Odisha: Solar-powered irrigation and beyond. *Journal of Irrigation Science*, 34(3), 567–579.

Panda, S., & Das, A. (2022). Public-private partnerships in renewable energy: Case studies from Odisha. *Journal of Renewable Energy Partnerships*, 9(4), 221–235.

Panda, S., Mishra, S. P., & Mishra, S. (2020). Disaster Risk Reduction with Resilient Built Environment in Odisha coast, India. *J Xidian Univ*, 14(5).

Panda, S., & Sahu, R. (2019). Odisha renewable energy policy: An overview. *Energy Policy Review*, 12(2), 189–202.

Pani, B. S., & Mishra, D. (2022). Sustainable livelihood security in Odisha, India: A district level analysis. *Regional Sustainability*, 3(2), 110–121. DOI: 10.1016/j.regsus.2022.07.003

Parida, J., & Mishra, N. (2014). Indigenous knowledge in disaster management: Some reflections on fishing communities of coastal Odisha. *International Journal of Research in Engineering and Applied Sciences*, 2(2), 103–105.

Pasumarti, S. S. (2020). CSR and Socio-Economic Development–A Case study of selected PSUs in the state of Odisha. *Journal of Critical Reviews*, 7(13), 1407–1415.

Pasupalak (2009), Orissa Review, April-May, Climate Change and Agriculture in Orissa.

Patel, S. K. (2016). Climate change and climate-induced disasters in Odisha, Eastern India: Impacts, adaptation and future policy implications. *International Journal of Humanities and Social Science Invention*, 5(8), 60–63.

Pati, P., Desai, N., Mankad, A., & Solanki, H. (2020). *The Decadal Changes and Socio-Economic Stresses on Coastal Area through Remote Sensing and GIS Technology: A Review of Puri.*

Patnaik, B. K. (2016). *Impact of Global Warming on Agriculture with Reference to Odisha*. Special Issue on Agriculture and Farmer's Welfare, Directorate of Economics and Statistics.

Patnaik, B. K. (2018, June). Environment Conservation vs. Good Management: On the back drop of Development. *Science Horizon*, 3(6), 23–27.

Patnaik, R., Nayak, A., & Dash, R. (2020). Bio-digester technology in managing livestock waste: A sustainable approach. *Renewable Energy and Agriculture*, 22(1), 75–85.

Planning and Convergence Dept., G. o. (2018). Odisha Economic Survey. Bhubaneswar: Odisha govt. press.

Pradhan, A. K., & Patra, R. (2013). Heterogeneity, collective action and management sustainability in common property forest resources: Case study from the Indian state Odisha. *Environment, Development and Sustainability*, 15(4), 979–997. DOI: 10.1007/s10668-012-9422-0

Purohit, J., & Rout, H. S. (2023). Impact of climate change on human health concerning climate-induced natural disaster: Evidence from an eastern Indian state. *Climatic Change*, 176(8), 109. DOI: 10.1007/s10584-023-03578-1

Rath, B., & Nayak, R. (2023). Vaccination programs in livestock farming: Ensuring animal health and sustainability. *Veterinary Sustainability Practices*, 15(3), 144–156.

Rath, S., Sahoo, P., Sarangi, K. K., & Kareemulla, K. (2022). Environmental implications of agricultural development in Odisha State. *Journal of Financial Economics*, 3, 2–25.

Sahoo, N., & Satpathy, M. (2020). Disasters and climate change adaptability at Odisha coast. Development in Coastal Zones and Disaster Management, 185-199.

Sahoo, S. S., & Lenka, S. K. (2023). *0009, CABI*. CABI, Disaster Management for Coastal Tourism Destinations of Odisha., DOI: 10.1079/9781800621022.0009

Sahu, B. K. (2016). Solar energy developments, policies and future prospectus in the state of Odisha, India. *Renewable & Sustainable Energy Reviews*, 61, 526–536. DOI: 10.1016/j.rser.2016.04.027

Sahu, N. C., & Mishra, D. (2013). Analysis of perception and adaptability strategies of the farmers to climate change in Odisha, India. *APCBEE Procedia*, 5, 123–127.

Sahu, S. C., Sharma, J., & Ravindranath, N. H. (2015). Carbon stocks and fluxes for forests in Odisha (India). *Tropical Ecology*, 56(1), 77–85.

Santhanam, H., & Kundu, S. K. (2022). Assessment of socio-technical constraints of marine fishers in the utilisation of marine fishery advisories in Southern Odisha, India. *Anthropocene Science*, 1(1), 109–120. DOI: 10.1007/s44177-022-00014-4

Schaeffer, R., Szklo, A. S., de Lucena, A. F. P., Borba, B. S. M. C., Nogueira, L. P. P., Fleming, F. P., & Boulahya, M. S. (2012). Energy sector vulnerability to climate change: A review. *Energy*, 38(1), 1–12. DOI: 10.1016/j.energy.2011.11.056

Senapati, A. (2015, August 15). UN felicitates Odisha for its disaster management model for Phailin. *Down to Earth.*

Sethi, R., & Mishra, G. (2016). Energy efficiency in the industrial sector of Odisha. *Industrial Efficiency Review*, 5(2), 99–111.

Sharma, P., Das, R., & Behera, K. (2018). Agroforestry practices for sustainable farming in Odisha. *Agroforestry Systems*, 92(5), 1275–1289.

Sharma, R., & Rath, S. (2019). Waste-to-energy projects: Sustainable energy generation from municipal solid waste in Odisha. *Waste Management and Energy*, 21(5), 258–267.

Sharma, V., Reddy, B., & Sahu, N. (2018). Sustainable rural livelihoods approach for climate change adaptation in Western Odisha, Eastern India. In Climate Change Adaptation and Development (pp. 161-174). Routledge.

Singh, A., Fernando, R. L. S., & Haran, N. P. (2020). *Development in Coastal Zones and Disaster Management.* Springer Singapore. DOI: 10.1007/978-981-15-4294-7

Society, O. f. (2009). Conceptual Framework for Eco Developement including Community-Based Eco-Tourism and its Application in Satkoshia Gorge Sanctuary.

Surveying, D. A. (2023). Natural Forest Loss Mapping and its Impact on Climate Change Over KBK Districts of Odisha (Doctoral dissertation, Centurion University).

Swain, S., Jena, J., & Behera, A. (2017). Genetically improved farmed tilapia (GIFT) and its role in sustainable aquaculture in Odisha. *Aquaculture Development*, 12(4), 98–110.

Swain, S. K. Population Dynamics and its Impact on Climate Change in Odisha.

Tripathy, S. (2020). Farmers, Climate and Disaster Management in a Coastal Region. Development in Coastal Zones and Disaster Management, 101-117.

Tripathy, S. (2022). Fishers, Community resilience, and disaster management: Learning from the grassroots of Odisha, India. In *International Handbook of Disaster Research* (pp. 1–14). Springer Nature Singapore.

Vinod Joon, V. J., & Vaishali Jaiswal, V. J. (2012). Impact of climate change on human health in India: an overview.

Chapter 4

# Impact of Digital Government on the Territories of Public Sector Reform: A Bibliometric Analysis

**Muhammad Younus**
https://orcid.org/0000-0001-9654-1546
*Universitas Muhammadiyah Yogyakarta, Indonesia*

**Achmad Nurmandi**
*Universitas Muhammadiyah Yogyakarta, Indonesia*

**Dyah Mutiarin**
https://orcid.org/0000-0003-3171-8915
*Universitas Muhammadiyah Yogyakarta, Indonesia*

**Andi Luhur Prianto**
*Universitas Muhammadiyah Makassar, Indonesia*

**Halimah Abdul Manaf**
*Universiti Utara Malaysia, Malaysia*

**Bambang Irawan**
https://orcid.org/0000-0002-4841-7302
*Universitas Mulawarman, Indonesia*

**Imron Sohsan**
*Khon Kaen University, Thailand*

**Haerana Haerana**
https://orcid.org/0000-0002-0502-0532
*Universitas Muhammadiyah Makassar, Indonesia*

**Li Bo**
*Khon Kaen University, China*

**Ihyani Malik**
*Universitas Muhammadiyah Makassar, Indonesia*

DOI: 10.4018/979-8-3693-6854-1.ch004

## ABSTRACT

*This study explores the characteristics of Digital Governance trends using the Scopus database from 2012 to 2022 using the CiteSpace application. E-Government is an effort to use information and communication technology to improve government efficiency, effectiveness, transparency, and accountability. The public sector is responsible for providing goods and services to the public that are paid for through taxes or other state revenues. Its primary role is to organize, activate and direct the provision of goods and services. It was found that the number of publications on Digital Governance has increased in the last ten years, and the United States is the strongest country in this area of research. Public service is an activity or a series of activities to meet service needs. Moreover, regional offices and work units must change the paradigm of the pattern of public service delivery from being oriented as a service provider to being oriented towards the community's needs as service users.*

## 1. INTRODUCTION

According to Suaedi and Wardianto (2010), the World Bank Group defines e-government as an endeavor to increase the efficiency, effectiveness, transparency, and accountability of the government in the provision of improved public services via the use of information and communication technology. E-government is a notion that, according to the opinions of specialists (Indrajit, 2002), has fundamental principles that are universal. The meaning and implementation of this concept in a nation, on the other hand, cannot be divorced from the following factors: the country's history, culture, education, political beliefs, and economic situations (Wirawan, 2020). SPBE is an acronym that stands for "Electronic Based Government System." The Electronic Based Government System (SPBE) is a government administration that makes use of information and communication technologies in order to deliver services to SPBE Users.

This information may be found in Presidential Regulation Number 95 of 2018, which pertains to Electronic-Based Government Systems. The purpose of the SPBE is to achieve governance that is clean, effective, transparent, and responsible, as well as to provide public services that are of high quality and reliability. Governance and administration of electronic-based government systems on a national level are also required in order to enhance the integration and effectiveness of electronic-based government systems. Twenty-three years from now, the Ministry of Communication and Informatics (Kominfo) plans to have a government system that is based on electronic communication (SPBE) completely functioning. The establishment of a cloud-based data center that is controlled by the state is an example of an attempt that is being made to facilitate the accomplishment of this objective (Christiani, 2018).

Within the group of 193 nations, the Electronic Based Government System (EBS) has the 88th position. In light of this, it is clear that the digitization of service delivery is still in need of improvement and is very necessary. Every nation is now concerned about the adoption of the Electronic-Based Government System (EBS), which is an acronym for electronic government. When compared to other ASEAN nations, Indonesia is still behind and needs to make up for lost ground. In order to determine the SPBE index, numerous factors are taken into consideration. These factors include the coverage and quality of digital government services, the current state of digital infrastructure development, and the capacity of human resources to operate e-government services for the government.

Many people have the misconception that the public sector encompasses everything that is associated with the public interest and the supply of goods and services to the public. These products and services are paid for by taxes or other state revenues that are controlled by law. Some examples of public sectors are the health sector, education, the security sector, and transportation. The implementation of the public sector is often left up to the market due to the vastness of the public sector; nonetheless, the government continues to monitor it via the application of a number of rules. There are also divisions within the public sector that are administered with the use of sources of funding that come from contributions or donations. This is the reason why the public sector exists: it is required. with the goal of ensuring that the presence of the public sector in society cannot be ignored. Rules that control the use of public commodities are necessary for society. Currently, the public sector plays a significant role in the regulation of these public goods in order to ensure that they are distributed to all individuals in a manner that is both fair and equitable. According to Jones (1993), the primary function of the public sector is comprised of three components: the supply of goods and services directly, the exercise of regulatory authority, and the facilitation of activities.

The Scopus database is used to collect data for this research, which intends to investigate the features of the trend of digital government starting in 2012 and continuing through 2022. Methods of bibliometric analysis are used in this study. For the purpose of this research, CiteSpace Software were used to undertake bibliometric analyses related to publication relevance, author, and country. These analyses were performed on publications that were obtained from the Scopus database and examined between the years 2012 and 2022. For the purpose of this investigation, a total of 190 result documents were used as data. This research comes to the following conclusions: (1) Over the last ten years, there has been an overall rise in the number of publications on digital governance. The United States of America is the most powerful nation in this particular field of study. With the help of this study,

When it comes to making preparations, consumers expect everything to be quicker, more effective, and more efficient in this digital day. As a result, the installation of public services is necessary in order to be able to deliver outstanding service. This is in line with Law Number 25 of 2009 about Public Services, which states that the bureaucracy must have a spirit of service, such as assisting to work towards a direction that is more flexible and dialogical, as well as more practical and pragmatic. The principles of good governance, including the efficiency with which the government itself performs its functions, are regulated by this government statute. One definition of public service is "an activity or a series of activities in the context of fulfilling service needs in accordance with statutory regulations for every citizen and resident for goods, services, and administrative services provided by public service providers." Public service may exist in the context of fulfilling service needs. Changing the paradigm of the pattern of public service delivery from being oriented as a service provider to being oriented toward the needs of the community as service users is necessary for the realization of quality public services (Kristanto, 2018). This shift in paradigm is necessary in order to achieve quality public services. To enhance both their performance and the quality of service they give to the general public, service providers are obligated to apply Service Standard Guidelines.

## 2 LITERATURE REVIEW

### 2.1 Systematic Review "E-Government"

Through the use of information technology for e-governance, the government will be able to improve the efficiency and effectiveness of its public services, administrative procedures, and internal communications. Furthermore, e-government will raise society to the level of internationalization or patterns of international interactions, which is the process of constructing international networks via the means of internet access (Riley, 2002). The general people is gaining a greater level of awareness and comprehension on all issues that pertain to public affairs. Significant cultural shifts are brought about as a result of this, not just inside the government but also throughout the larger population.

The implementation of electronic government in Indonesia has been going on for sixteen years, beginning in 2003, with varying degrees of success. However, the present state of the development of e-government in Indonesia is not optimum. The global e-government development index (EDGI) indicates that the growth of e-government in Indonesia did not result in a major gain; rather, there was only a difference of 0.1 increase between the first year of implementation in 2003 and the beginning of 2018. According to Ordiyasa (2015), on page 59, this failure may have been brought about by the government's inability to pay sufficient attention to the development of electronic governance. The findings of further study on the examination of online usage by local governments in the creation of e-government provide more support for this assertion. Among the 548 local governments in Indonesia, only four (four) of them have achieved the usage stage of e-government development (Yunita & Aprianto, 2018). This represents just 0.7% of the total number of local governments in Indonesia.

According to Muflihah and Susanto (2017) and Andhika (2018), the effective implementation of local government innovation is greatly impacted by the cooperation of institutional arrangements, policy players, and society. This is the case because of the fact that collaboration is a key factor in the success of the implementation. Additionally, aspects of leadership, information network infrastructure, information management, the environment of (private) business, human resources, and society are also influential factors in the development of e-government in local governments, particularly in Eastern Indonesia (Novita, 2014; Sitokdana, 2019 and Wijaya et al., 2019). This is especially true in Eastern Indonesia. A type of innovation is required as a vital step in the process of creating e-government in local governments via cooperation and e-literacy. This is necessary in order to address the issues that are posed by the limits that have been discussed above.

In a broader sense, the idea of collaboration in electronic governance is a process, and the culmination of that process is the development of e-literacy. E-literacy, on the other hand, is the end outcome of that process. The local governments collaborate in order to meet the restricted resources that are associated with the fulfillment of fiscal and financial obligations, facilities and infrastructure, and human resources. According to Wijaya et al. (2019); Manurung and Anza (2017). According to Wijaya et al. (2019); Manurung and Anza (2017). The development of e-literacy, on the other hand, is carried out with the purpose of facilitating the growth of e-government in relation to technology, human resources (leaders and staff), the environment, and society (Tomaszewicz, 2015; and Njenga, 2018).

According to the findings of a research that was carried out by Silalahi and colleagues (2015), the administration of e-government is inextricably linked to the social and technical practices that will be implemented inside it. Taking into consideration the social component, the fact of the matter is that the deployment of e-government often results in failures. From the perspective of Silalahi et al. (2015), public sector organizations are constantly connected to a variety of elements, including management, politics, economics, culture, and other aspects. The makers of the e-government system will be concentrating on each and every one of these issues. The development of e-government systems must continue to be carried out in order to keep up with the demands of the ever-changing developmental requirements of society. This is because the concept of the availability of information for the public in a timely manner is essential. According to this study, the idea of developing an electronic government seems to have failed by 85 percent in 2003, which is far lower than what was anticipated. Failures in the implementation of electronic governance are more likely in underdeveloped nations because of delays in the fulfillment of financial obligations.

## 2.2 E-Government in World-Wide

In expanding the literature review beyond Indonesia, it is essential to include studies from a diverse set of countries and regions, which will provide a more global perspective on the implementation and impact of digital government. For instance, the United States, as identified in the bibliometric analysis, leads in digital governance research, highlighting advanced practices in e-government and public sector reforms (Gil-Garcia & Flores-Zúñiga, 2020). Similarly, European countries, such as Estonia and Denmark, have been recognized for their pioneering efforts in e-governance, which emphasize user-centric service delivery and digital inclusivity (Clarke, 2020). In Asia, South Korea and Singapore showcase successful models of digital transformation in government, with strong policy support and public engagement driving their initiatives (Choi, Chung, & Cho, 2022). By incorporating these broader geographical perspectives, the literature review can offer a more comprehensive understanding of the challenges and opportunities in digital government, thus making the findings more relevant and applicable to a global audience.

## 2.3 E-Government in ASEAN Region

As the only developed nation in the Association of Southeast Asian Nations (ASEAN), Singapore has the top level of e-government implementation in Southeast Asia, while Indonesia holds the seventh place in the implementation of e-government. There are a number of challenges that a country faces when it comes to e-government. These challenges include incomplete standardization of implementation and uneven socialization, human resources that do not yet meet the criteria, information network infrastructure that is not yet qualified, community literacy for the use of e-government is not maximized, commitment to e-development within the government that is still low, and organizational culture that does not yet support e-government systems. As the only developed nation in the Association of Southeast Asian Nations (ASEAN), Singapore has the top level of e-government implementation in Southeast Asia, while Indonesia holds the seventh place in the implementation of e-government.

There are a number of challenges that a country faces when it comes to e-government. These challenges include incomplete standardization of implementation and uneven socialization, human resources that do not yet meet the criteria, information network infrastructure that is not yet qualified, community literacy for the use of e-government that is not maximized, commitment to the e-development of a government that is still low, and organizational culture that does not yet support e-government systems. As the only developed nation in the Association of Southeast Asian Nations (ASEAN), Singapore has the top level of e-government implementation in Southeast Asia, while Indonesia holds the seventh place in the implementation of e-government. There are a number of challenges that a country faces when it comes to e-government. These challenges include incomplete standardization of implementation and uneven socialization, human resources that do not yet meet the criteria, information network infrastructure that is not yet qualified, community literacy for the use of e-government that is not maximized, commitment to the e-development of a government that is still low, and organizational culture that does not yet support e-government systems.

Over the course of the last twenty years, there have been significant social shifts that have taken place in Indonesian society. Currently, contemporary systems are taking the place of old ideals. They are a part of the portion of the bureaucracy that is responsible for performing the duties of a public servant. There are seven characteristics that must be taken into consideration in contemporary community service. These characteristics are as follows: 1) the central role of the public servant towards the public, who have interests in which the public servant does not have the right to control the community in a specific direction; 2) the public administration agrees that the public interest is an important issue; 3) the policies and programs that are made must function to meet the needs of the community in an effective and responsive manner; and 4) the public servant must be able to communicate effectively with the community. 4). The public interest is more significant than the private interest; 5). Public workers are obligated to preserve moral standards, relevant rules and regulations, the state constitution, political norms, and public interests; 6). Government organizations and stakeholders work together to fulfill organizational objectives. Public officials and members of the general public are responsible for serving the public interest without interference from the commercial sector. At the technical level, a number of regulations and policies have been issued in order to regulate and promote synergies between the different parts of the government (Lumbanraja, 2020). This e-government discourse in Indonesia has been realized by producing these policy and regulatory documents. Furthermore, the public interest, which is of a public character, must be promoted by coordination across the various government departments.

## 3 METHODOLOGY

### 3.1 Research Method

The use of qualitative methodologies and a methodology based on bibliometric analysis were used in the execution of this research. When it comes to finding solutions to research issues, qualitative research methodologies provide outcomes in the form of descriptions and factual data collection. The bibliometric analysis that was used in this investigation was carried out by gathering a wide range of articles, journals, and other scientific papers that were qualified to fulfill the requirements of the research. A significant amount of information is gathered from two primary sources, namely Scopus and CiteSpace, which serve as the foundation for extensive research materials. In this collection of data sources, the term "Digital Government" is used many times. Due to the fact that Scopus and CiteSpace are databases that have been acknowledged by academic and non-academic organizations all over the globe, these two databases are being used as the primary sources of data.

### 3.2 Data Collection

The methodological approach of this study employs bibliometric analysis using the Scopus database, focusing on publications from 2012 to 2022. CiteSpace software was utilized to facilitate a detailed qualitative analysis of the data, enabling the identification of thematic trends and patterns within the digital governance literature. The bibliometric methodologies applied include citation analysis, which examines the frequency and impact of citations to understand the influence and interconnectivity of key research works. Additionally, keyword trend analysis was conducted to identify the most prominent topics and emerging areas of interest within the field, allowing for a deeper exploration of how research priorities have evolved over time. The citation analysis helped to highlight influential authors and foundational studies, while the keyword trend analysis provided insights into shifts in thematic focus. This dual approach ensures a comprehensive understanding of the digital government landscape, and the consistent application of these methods across the chapter allows for a robust analysis of the global research environment.

### 3.3 Data Analysis

CiteSpace is used in the process of data analysis in order to see and interpret research findings obtained from the Scopus database. CiteSpace is a program that is not only simple to use but also offers a useful option for mapping and presenting a visual representation of the findings of researched projects. Additionally, the veracity of the data test that was conducted using CiteSpace is acknowledged to be 99 percent. Within Scopus, the process of data mining can be broken down into three distinct steps. In the initial step of the process, we classified the searches that were conducted by utilizing the terms "Digital Government," "Public Sector," and "Reformasi." These keywords were determined by analyzing the names of the categories, the abstracts, or the keywords themselves. The end result was 224 papers. During the second step, the authors restrict the time period by altering the database search to include a period of ten years, beginning in 2012 and ending in 2022. This time frame was selected in order to get the most recent references about digital government. The research has resulted in the production of 196 papers at this point. The authors then proceed to the third step, which is the categorization of papers based only on English, which results in 190 documents. This is done to ensure that the data processing does not encounter any language bias. If it is based on an advanced query, it will return the data that is listed below:

(TITLE-ABS-KEY ("Digital Government") AND TITLE-ABS-KEY ("Public Sector") AND TITLE-ABS-KEY (reform) OR TITLE-ABS-KEY ("Digital Government") OR TITLE-ABS- KEY (reform)) AND PUBYEAR > 2011 AND PUBYEAR < 2023 AND (LIMIT-TO (LANGUAGE, "English").

## 4 RESULTS AND DISCUSSION

### 4.1 Documents By Year/Research Trends By Year

*Figure 1. A number of articles on digital governance topics, Scopus.*

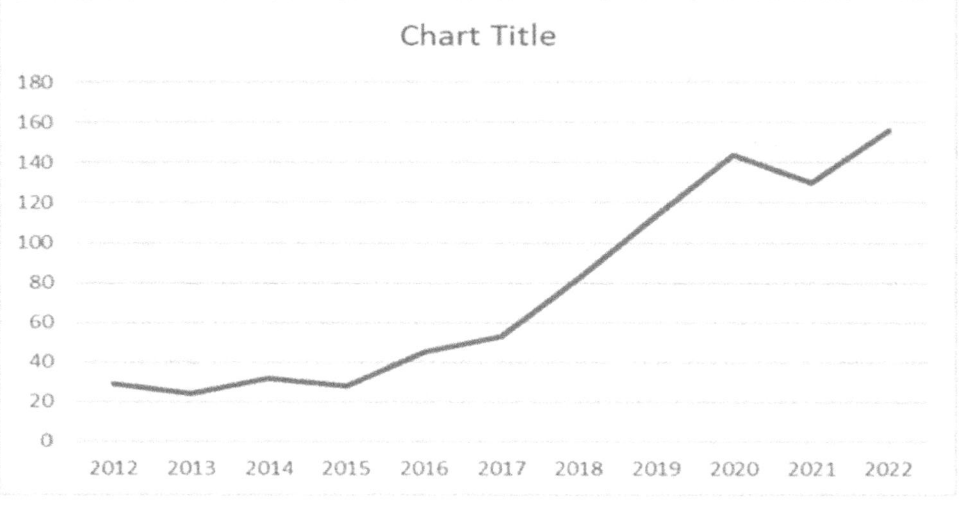


From the graph in Figure 1 above, the Scopus database shows that the number of articles or papers on the topic of "Digital Government" released within ten years (2012-2022) has almost always increased. The numbers in the graph above show the number of articles published and recorded in the Scopus database. At the beginning of the decade, between 2012-2015, the number of digital government research articles was still small. This can be seen in 2012, the number of digital government articles published was only 30 documents; in 2014, it decreased to 24 documents. Digital government research again experienced an increase in 2014 as many as 31 documents. Nevertheless, in 2015, the number of articles published was only 25 documents. From 2016 to 2020, the number of articles published increased to 45 documents in 2016, 55 documents in 2017, 80 documents in 2018, 120 documents in 2019, and 143 documents in 2020. However, the number of digital government articles has decreased by 13 documents in 2021 to only 130 documents. In 2022, the number of digital government articles increased again, and 158 documents were found.

## 4.2 Top Writing And Citation

*Figure 2. Author of Digital Government Articles and Citations. Scopus.*

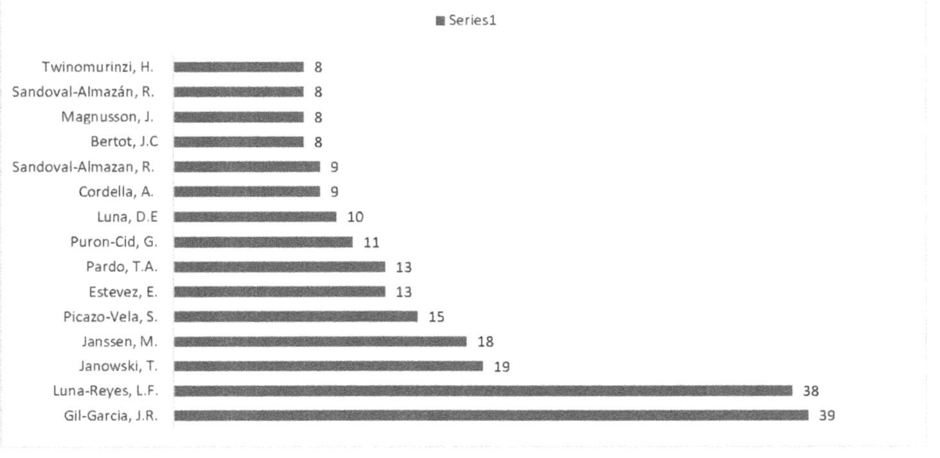


Based on the graph above, articles with the topic "Digital Government" show the author of the article whose work is most widely used as a source of reference for similar research. The author with the most cited articles is Gil-Garda, JR, who has 39 citations in his article. This is followed by Luna-Reyes with 38 citations. Meanwhile, Janowski, T. and Janssen, M. cite 19 and 18 times, respectively. Picazo-Vela, S. got 15 citations. Estevez, E. and Pardo, TA found 13 citations in their work. Meanwhile, Puron-Cid, G. and Luna DE received 11 and 10 citations, respectively. Other authors of digital government articles are Sandoval-Almazan, R. and Cordella, A., who were cited nine times. Twinomurinzi, H., Sandoval-Almazan, R., Magnusson, J.,

## 4.3 Documents By Country

*Figure 3. Article Producing Countries, Scopus.*

From Figure 3 above, countries that publish articles or journals on the topic of "Digital Government" are shown in different colors in each region. The lightest color indicates the country that has published the most articles, while the darker color indicates, the fewer "Digital Government" articles published. The country that publishes the most articles and papers on digital governance topics is the United States. The following countries that contributed the second most "Digital Government" articles were Russia and China—followed by Brazil and Australia, which published the most articles. Meanwhile, other countries are still contributors to the article "Digital Government" with an average number.

## 4.4 Place Of Publication By Subject Area

*Figure 4. Grouping of Publications by Subject Area, Scopus.*

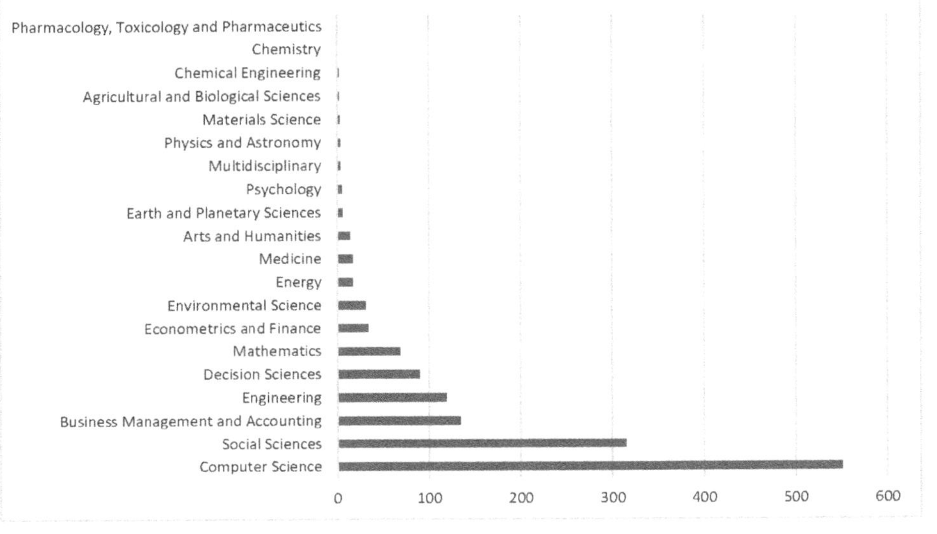


Based on the graph shown in Figure 4 above, the publication area subject is mapped to see how many articles are published in the subject area. From the Scopus database, the field of study with the most publications is computer science, with a total of 550 documents. The next course is Business Management and Accounting, with a total of 310 documents and 125 documents. Decision Science courses total 97 documents and 112 documents. Econometrics and Finance courses with a total of 25 documents and 80 documents. Energy field courses with a total of 15 documents and 20 documents. Meanwhile, the subjects of Arts and Humanities, Psychology, Physics and Astronomy, Agricultural Sciences, Biology, and Chemistry scored almost zero.

## 4.5 Documents By Source

*Figure 5. Source of publication of the article "Digital Government," Scopus.*

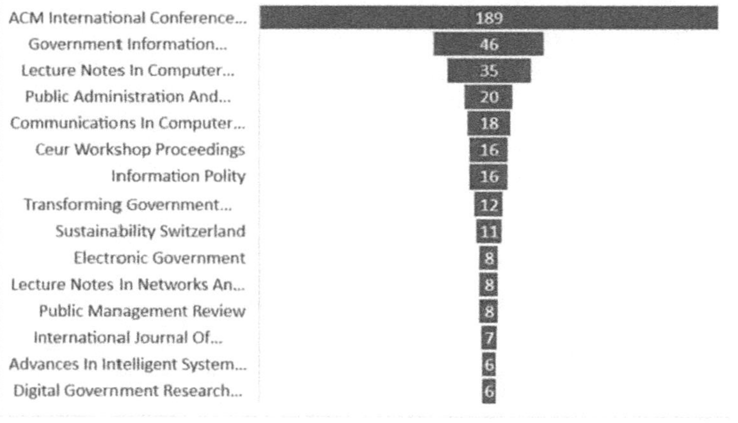


Based on the graph in Figure 5 above shows the publication source of the article on the topic "Digital Government." The most published source is the ACM International Conference, with a total of 189 articles—furthermore, Government Information has as many as 46 documents. In the Lecturer's Note Source on the Computer, there are 35 documents which shows a decrease of 11 documents from the previous source. The Public Administration with 20 documents, and Computer Communication with 18 documents. From sources, Ceur Workshop Proceedings and International Plity contributed 16 articles each. From Transforming Government sources, there are 11 articles with similar topics. Meanwhile, from Electronic Government, Lecture Notes in Networks, and Public Management Review sources, there were eight documents each. International Journal of Government provides articles of 7 documents. Finally, Advance in Intelligent Systems and Digital Government Research contributed six documents each.

## 4.6 Documents Based On Affiliation

*Figure 6. A number of Article Publications from Various Affiliations, Scopus.*

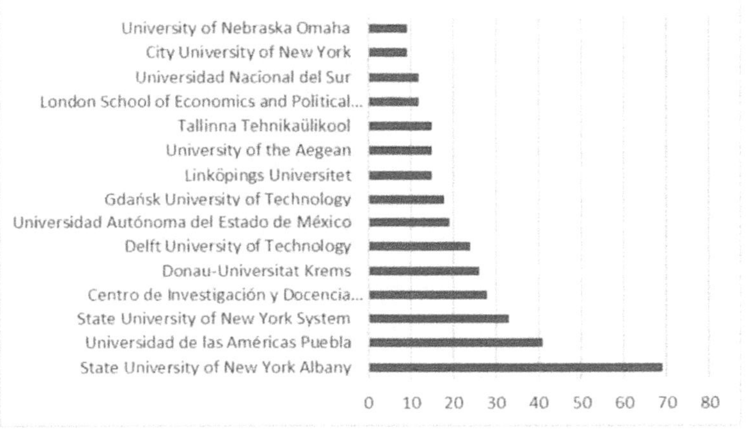


From Figure 6 above, publishing articles from various affiliations is intended to map the source of the article. The first institution affiliated with the publication of articles on the topic of "Digital Government" was the State University of New York Albany, with a total of 69 documents. Next is the Universidad de las Americas Puebla with a total of 41 documents, minus 28 documents. Then from the State University of New York System, as many as 33 documents. Centro de Investigacion y Docencia Affiliation of 28 documents. Donau-Universitat Krems affiliation with articles totaling 26 documents. From affiliation with the Delft University of Technology, as many as 24 documents. Affiliation with Universidad Autonoma del Estado de Mexico has as many as 19 documents. Linkopings University, Aegean University, and Talllina Tehnikaulikool each have the same number of 15 documents. London School of Economics and Politics and Universidad Nacional del Sur, totaling 12 documents. Finally, the City University of New York and the University of Nebraska Omaha contributed nine documents each.

## 4.7 DOCUMENTS ACCORDING TO DOCTYPE

*Figure 7. Types of Published Documents, Scopus.*

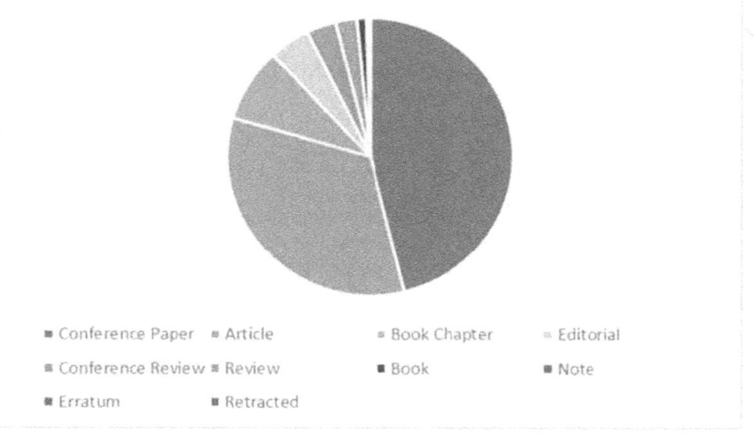


From Figure 7 above, there are various types of documents written as a result of research on "Digital Government." Mapping based on document type has been carried out with the following results. The most common type of document is the conference paper which accounts for 45% of the total work. Types of articles are as much as 30% of the total. The book chapter type has a total of about 10%. Documents with an editorial type of 6%. The conference review type is 4%. The review type is 2%. Furthermore, the rest is in book form.

## 4.8 Documents By Funding Sponsor

*Figure 8. Number of Documents Produced by Funding Sponsor, Scopus.*

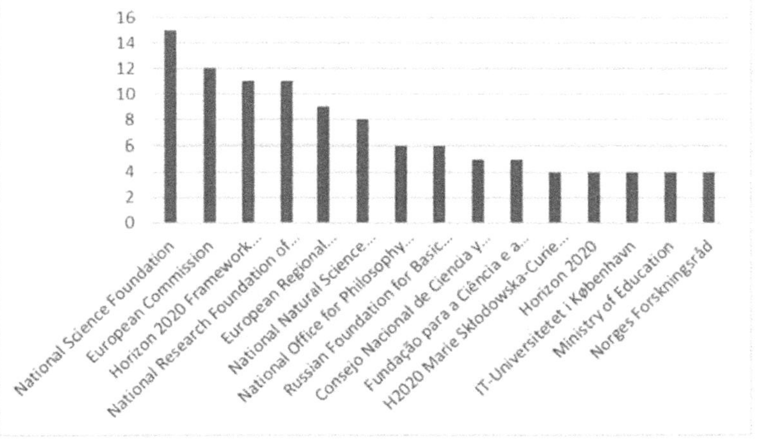


Figure 8 above shows that in conducting research, sponsors are always needed to support the research being conducted. Of these figures, the National Science Foundation is the most significant contributor of funds in research on the theme "Digital Government" with 15 documents. Next is the European Commission, with a total of 12 documents. With the same number of documents, the Horizon 2020 Framework and the National Research Foundation are 11 documents. European Regional Agency with a total of 9 documents. Underneath there are 8 National IPA documents. The National Office for Philosophy and the Russian Foundation for Basic contributed six documents each. The Consejo Nacional de Ciencia and Fundacao di Ciencia bodies every five documents. Finally, with each of the five documents, there is H2020 Marie Sklodowska-Curie, Horizon 2020,

## 4.9 Connectivity By Author

*Figure 9. Number of Documents Based on Linkages Between Authors, CiteSpace.*

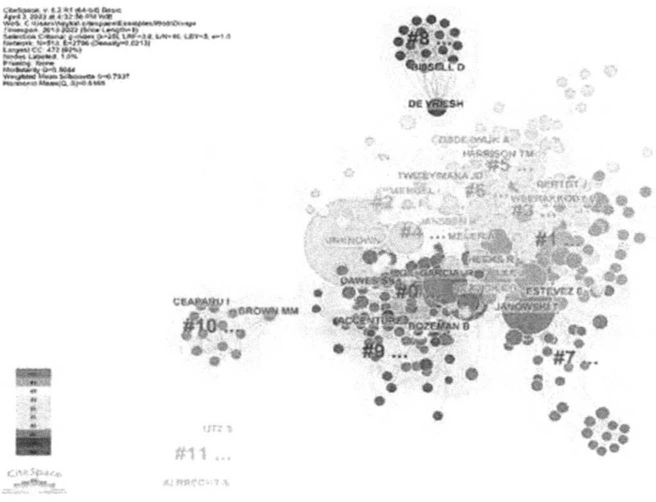


Based on Figure 9 above, published article documents are sorted by author from the most significant number. The closer the circles are, the closer the connectivity. The first order is Lee J. and Heeks R which are represented in orange. The second order is Mergel, I. and Janssen, M., which are represented in yellow. Next came third in light green Reddick CG and Weerakkody, V. In fourth place were author Meijer, A. and an unknown author with the largest circle. Followed by the fifth in faded green, written by Twizeimana, JD, and Harrison, TM. While in sixth place, in Tosca, are Bertot J. and Zuiderwijk A. The seventh place is represented by writers Estevez E and Janowski T in light blue. In eighth are Bissel D and De Vriesh in dark blue.

## 4.10 Connectivity By Keyword

*Figure 10. Relationship between keywords, CiteSpace.*

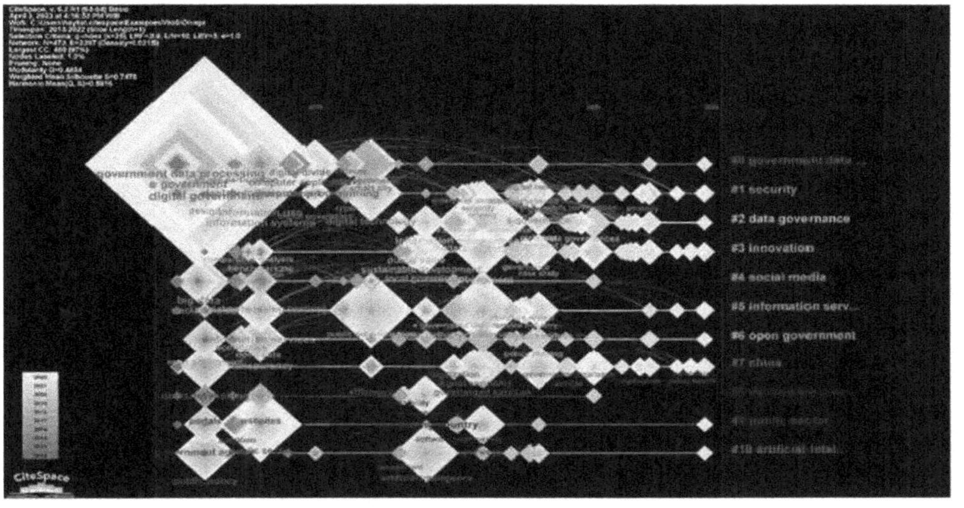


With the same topic, generally, articles can be linked to one another to facilitate their categorization in the database. As seen in the CiteSpace base results above, the keywords that are often found on the topic "Digital Government" include Government Data, Security, Data Governance, Innovation, Social Media, Information Services, Open Government, China, Developing Countries, Public Sector, and Artificial Intelligence. Each of these keywords can be related to one another.

## 4.11 Connectivity By Country

*Figure 11. Relations between countries that published articles, CiteSpace.*

Based on Figure 10 above, there are six countries that are interconnected in publishing the article "Digital Government." Occupying position 0 in red are the United Kingdom and the Russian Federation. The one position in green is the United States and Mexico. In second place are Italy and Brazil with Tosca colors. At number three in blue are Austria and South Africa. The top four in purple are Greece and Germany. While in the last position are Sweden and Denmark.

## 4.11 Discussion

### 4.11.1 Real World Impact

To illustrate the real-world impact of digital government trends, practical examples and case studies from various countries can be integrated into the analysis. For instance, Estonia's implementation of a comprehensive e-government system has revolutionized its public sector, leading to significant improvements in efficiency and transparency. Citizens can now access nearly all government services online, including voting, tax filing, and healthcare, which has streamlined administrative processes and reduced bureaucratic burdens (Clarke, 2020). Similarly, South Korea's Digital Government Portal has enhanced citizen engagement and service delivery, demonstrating how digital innovation can effectively address public needs (Choi,

Chung, & Cho, 2022). In India, the Aadhaar biometric identification system has been pivotal in reducing fraud in welfare programs by ensuring that benefits reach the intended recipients (Das, 2021). These practical examples not only demonstrate the tangible benefits of digital governance but also highlight the varied approaches countries take in leveraging technology to drive public sector reform. By linking research findings to these real-world applications, the chapter underscores the practical implications of digital government initiatives, enhancing its relevance and engagement for policymakers and practitioners.

### 4.11.2 Implementation Challenges

A comprehensive understanding of the challenges faced in implementing digital government reforms requires a dedicated focus on several key barriers. One major challenge is the digital divide, which encompasses disparities in access to technology and digital literacy among different segments of the population. This gap often results in unequal access to e-government services, particularly affecting rural communities, the elderly, and low-income groups (UN, 2021). Infrastructural limitations, such as inadequate broadband connectivity and outdated IT systems, pose significant hurdles, especially in developing countries where investment in digital infrastructure may be constrained by budgetary limitations (OECD, 2020). Furthermore, resistance to change within public institutions remains a persistent barrier, often fueled by a lack of digital skills among government employees and a reluctance to move away from traditional processes. Organizational culture and bureaucratic inertia can slow down the adoption of digital solutions, as public servants may fear job displacement or struggle with new technologies (Mergel, 2019). Addressing these challenges requires a multi-faceted approach, including investments in infrastructure, targeted digital literacy programs, and change management strategies that involve continuous training and support for public sector employees. By thoroughly exploring these barriers, this section aims to provide a clearer understanding of the complexities involved in the implementation of digital government reforms.

### 4.11.3 Emerging Trends

Incorporating emerging technological trends into the analysis of digital governance is crucial for understanding the future directions of public sector reform. Artificial Intelligence (AI) is increasingly being used to enhance decision-making processes, automate routine tasks, and provide personalized services to citizens. For example, AI-powered chatbots are now commonly deployed to handle public inquiries, freeing up human resources for more complex tasks and improving service efficiency (Wirtz et al., 2021). Big data analytics plays a pivotal role in enabling governments to make data-driven decisions by providing insights from large volumes of data. This can significantly improve policy formulation, resource allocation, and crisis response, as seen during the COVID-19 pandemic where big data was utilized for tracking virus spread and optimizing healthcare resources (Janssen & van der Voort, 2020). Blockchain technology, known for its security and transparency, is being explored for applications in digital identity verification, secure voting systems, and public records management, which can enhance trust and accountability in government operations (Swan, 2015). These emerging trends not only present opportunities for more efficient and responsive governance but also pose challenges such as ethical concerns, data privacy issues, and the need for robust regulatory frameworks. By examining these technological advancements, the chapter provides a forward-looking perspective on how digital governance can evolve to meet the demands of an increasingly digital society.

## 4.12 Future Research Directions & Implications

While the investigation into the influence of digital government on the reform of the public sector has resulted in the discovery of significant insights, there are still a number of areas that are ready for further investigation. In the first place, while a great number of studies have pointed out the excellent results that digital government projects have produced, there is a need for further in-depth research into the contextual elements that have an effect on these results. In further study, it is recommended that an investigation be conducted into the socio-economic, cultural, and political settings that influence the success or failure of digital government programs. When policymakers and practitioners have a better understanding of these contextual aspects, they will have a more complete framework to work with when attempting to adopt digital initiatives that are successful.

Second, the existing corpus of literature often places an emphasis on the technical components of digital governance, sometimes to the detriment of human issues. During the course of future research, the study of user experiences and the interaction between humans and computers should be given priority within the context of digital government services. Examining the level of digital literacy across different demographic groups and the extent to which they have access to digital services is part of this. It is possible for academics to make ideas that may be put into action to improve the accessibility and inclusiveness of digital government projects by concentrating on the end-users. This will ensure that these initiatives are beneficial to a larger portion of the population.

In the third place, longitudinal studies are absolutely necessary in order to comprehend the long-term effects that digital governance will have on the reform of the public sector. While the majority of the currently available research only captures a moment in time, there is a lack of a longitudinal viewpoint that can illustrate how digital government efforts develop over time and the lasting effects they have. It is recommended that future research use a longitudinal approach in order to monitor the development of digital reforms and the long-term consequences that these changes have had on operational effectiveness, transparency, and public participation. Not only will this technique assist discover possible unintended effects, but it will also help identify areas that need continual development.

In conclusion, there is a need for comparative studies that investigate the effects of digital government in a variety of geographical areas and governance styles. These kind of research have the potential to uncover best practices and common issues, providing a worldwide perspective on the adoption of digital government software. Additionally, comparative research may make it easier for nations to share their expertise and successful tactics with one another, which can lead to increased international cooperation in the area of public sector reform. Scholars have the ability to contribute to a more comprehensive knowledge of the function that digital government plays in the process of modernizing the public sector all over the globe by broadening the geographical reach of their study.

## 5. CONCLUSION

Communication technology that develops continuously brings changes in government life. From being conventional, it has now become a model of modern government based on a complex electronic system. The government sector has now adopted the use of the Internet in completing public service work. However, from the results of examinations in several studies, technological developments in the public sector are apparently still far behind technology in the private sector. Seeing the advantages of using various modern internet-based technologies in the private sector, the public sector has finally begun to form an electronic-based government, or what is known as e-government. The change from a conventional government system to a form of e-government is aimed solely at meeting the public's need for public information. This form of internet-based public service is considered more appropriate in this digital era because almost everyone already uses a smartphone which is very easy to use to access government-owned websites.

It is recognized that the implementation of e-government, especially in developing countries, is not easy. There are many challenges that must be faced, starting from the difficulty of changing the government system to digital, human resources that have not fully mastered technology, to people who are still unable to adapt to changing forms of public services. From the results of the analysis, it is known that the implementation of digital government has apparently been developed for more than the last two decades but has begun to develop more rapidly since 2012 and is increasingly aggressive from 2015 to 2022. From the results of this research, it can be concluded that the implementation of e-government in Indonesia continues to grow from time to time, although the results are not always significant. If you look again, every year, there is an increase in research on digital government, meaning that there are still many people who pay attention to this digital government system, including from the academic side. It can be said that e-government can bridge the relationship between government and society. The government, as a public servant, can provide services virtually openly; even the information needed by the public can be accessed independently through the government's website. If e-government is implemented correctly, the performance of public services will be more effective and efficient.

## REFERENCES


Aarabe, M.. (2024). Smart Tourism Experience and Responsible Travelers' Behavior: A Systematic Literature Review. In El Archi, Y. (Eds.), *Promoting Responsible Tourism With Digital Platforms* (pp. 128–147). IGI Global., DOI: 10.4018/979-8-3693-3286-3.ch008

Aarabe, M., Ben Khizzou, N., Alla, L., & Benjelloun, A. (2024). Marketing Applications of Emerging Technologies: A Systematic Literature Review. In Alla, L., Hmioui, A., & Bentalha, B. (Eds.), *AI and Data Engineering Solutions for Effective Marketing* (pp. 23–47). IGI Global., DOI: 10.4018/979-8-3693-3172-9.ch002

Abu Bakar, H., Razali, R., & Jambari, D. I. (2022). A Qualitative Study of Legacy Systems Modernisation for Citizen-Centric Digital Government. *Sustainability (Basel)*, 14(17), 10951. Advance online publication. DOI: 10.3390/su141710951

Aftab, M., & Myeong, S. (2022). An analysis of foreign residents' perceptions and behaviors regarding digital government portal services in the Republic of South Korea. *International Review of Administrative Sciences*. Advance online publication. DOI: 10.1177/00208523221084498

Agbozo, E. (2019). Applying apriori rules mining in evaluating digital government services patronization by a younger generation of users in Russia. *TEM Journal, 8*(4), 1207–1212. https://doi.org/DOI: 10.18421/TEM84-14

Al-Ammary, J. H. (2021). The uptake of digital government services: Toward digital transformation in the Kingdom of Bahrain. *Electronic Government*, 17(2), 199–219. DOI: 10.1504/EG.2021.114580

Al-Sakran, H. O., & Alsudairi, M. A. (2021). Usability and Accessibility Assessment of Saudi Arabia Mobile E-Government Websites. *IEEE Access : Practical Innovations, Open Solutions*, 9, 48254–48275. DOI: 10.1109/ACCESS.2021.3068917

Al Sulaimani, A. H. A., & Ozuem, W. (2022). Understanding the role of transparency, participation, and collaboration for achieving open digital government goals in Oman. *Transforming Government: People. Transforming Government*, 16(4), 595–612. DOI: 10.1108/TG-04-2022-0044

Ali Al-Hussein, M. A.-H., Alabdallat, W. I. M., Abu Rumman, M. A., Jawabreh, O., & Ali, B. J. A. (2023). Impact of E-Government Applications on Reducing Administrative Burden in Delivering Public Service. *Information Sciences Letters*, 12(3), 1663–1671. DOI: 10.18576/isl/120350

Alla, L., Bentalha, B., & Elyoussfi, A. (2023). Intelligence territoriale et positionnement stratégique des regions au Maroc: Le cas de la région de Fès Meknes en perspective. *Le concept de l'intéligence en sciences juridiques, économiques et sociales*, 215-237.

Almamy, A. S. M. (2022). Understanding factors affecting e-government adoption in Saudi Arabia: The role of religiosity. *International Journal of Customer Relationship Marketing and Management*, 13(1), 1–15. Advance online publication. DOI: 10.4018/IJCRMM.289209

Amirudin, A., Urbański, M., Saputra, J., Johansyah, M. D., Latip, L., Tarmizi, A., & Afrizal, T. (2021). The impact of the Covid-19 self-isolation policy on the work of vulnerable groups. *International Journal of Environmental Research and Public Health*, 18(12), 6452. Advance online publication. DOI: 10.3390/ijerph18126452 PMID: 34203631

Arcieri, F., Fioravanti, F., Nardelli, E., & Talamo, M. (2004). Reliable peer-to-peer access for Italian citizens to digital government services on the internet. In T. R. (Ed.), *Lecture Notes in Computer Science (including subseries Lecture Notes in Artificial Intelligence and Lecture Notes in Bioinformatics)* (Vol. 3183, pp. 250–255). Springer Verlag. DOI: 10.1007/978-3-540-30078-6_41

Aryuni, M., Miranda, E., Fernando, Y., & Kibtiah, T. M. (2020). The early detection system for terrorism in Indonesia from Twitter content uses the Naïve Bayes Algorithm. *5th International Conference on Management and Information Technology, ICIMTech 2020*, 555–559. DOI: 10.1109/ICIMTech50083.2020.9211261

Aulawi, H., & Fitriani, L. (2020). Enterprise architecture planning for e-government. *International Journal of Innovation, Creativity and Change, 11*(2), 251–270. https://www.scopus.com/inward/record.uri?eid=2-s2.0-85081600438&partnerID=40&md5=62e6cf125e6f5ca0145f6857523d5eed

Ayyash, M. M., Herzallah, F. A. T., & Al-Sharafi, M. A. (2022). Arab cultural dimensions model for e-government services adoption in public sector organisations: An empirical examination. *Electronic Government*, 18(1), 9–44. DOI: 10.1504/EG.2022.119608

Badre, M. E. Z. I. A. N. E., Badr, B. E. N. T. A. L. H. A., & Lhoussaine, A. L. L. A. (2024). La PME logistique et le développement territorial régional: Une analyse qualitative. *Alternatives Managériales Economiques*, 6(4), 1–22.

Baheer, B. A., Lamas, D., & Sousa, S. (2020). A systematic literature review on existing digital government architectures: State-of-the-art, challenges, and prospects. *Administrative Sciences*, 10(2), 25. Advance online publication. DOI: 10.3390/admsci10020025

Bentalha, B., & Alla, L. (2024). Revealing the Subtleties: The Art of Qualitative Studies in Science and Management. In Bentalha, B., & Alla, L. (Eds.), *Applying Qualitative Research Methods to Management Science* (pp. 1–21). IGI Global., DOI: 10.4018/979-8-3693-5543-5.ch001

Boudri, R., Bentalha, B., & Benjelloun, O. (2024). Phygital Marketing and the Pain of Paying: An Amazon Go Netnographic Case Study. In Alla, L., Hmioui, A., & Bentalha, B. (Eds.), *AI and Data Engineering Solutions for Effective Marketing* (pp. 348–363). IGI Global., DOI: 10.4018/979-8-3693-3172-9.ch017

Bouhtati, N., Alla, L., & Bentalha, B. (2023). Marketing Big Data Analytics and Customer Relationship Management: A Fuzzy Approach. In Bentalha, B., Hmioui, A., & Alla, L. (Eds.), *Integrating Intelligence and Sustainability in Supply Chains* (pp. 75–86). IGI Global., DOI: 10.4018/979-8-3693-0225-5.ch004

Bouhtati, N., Alla, L., & Ed-Daakouri, I. (2024). Smart Data Analysis and Prediction of Responsible Customer Behaviour in Tourism: An Exploratory Review of the Literature. In El Archi, Y., Benbba, B., Dávid, L., & Cardoso, L. (Eds.), *Promoting Responsible Tourism With Digital Platforms* (pp. 189–212). IGI Global., DOI: 10.4018/979-8-3693-3286-3.ch011

Bouhtati, N., EL Yaacoubi, Y., Bentalha, B., & Lhoussaine, A. L. L. A. (2024). Leviers logistiques de promotion du commerce équitable des produits de terroir: Une esquisse de modèle d'analyse. *Alternatives Managériales Economiques, 6*(Spécial 1), 17-35.

Castelnovo, W., & Sorrentino, M. (2018). The digital government imperative: A context-aware perspective. *Public Management Review*, 20(5), 709–725. DOI: 10.1080/14719037.2017.1305693

Castro, C., & Lopes, C. (2022). Digital Government and Sustainable Development. *Journal of the Knowledge Economy*, 13(2), 880–903. DOI: 10.1007/s13132-021-00749-2

Choi, H., Chung, C.-S., & Cho, Y. (2022). Changes in planning approach: A comparative study of digital government policies in South Korea and Denmark. *European Planning Studies*. Advance online publication. DOI: 10.1080/09654313.2022.2132787

Christiani, L. (2018). Opportunities and Challenges of Implementing Cloud Computing as an Automation Solution for Collaboration Between Libraries. Anuva: Journal of Cultural. *Library and Information Studies*, 2(1), 43–53.

Clarke, A. (2020). Digital government units: What are they, and what do they mean for digital era public management renewal? *International Public Management Journal*, 23(3), 358–379. DOI: 10.1080/10967494.2019.1686447

Contreras-Espinosa, R. S., & Blanco-M, A. (2022). A Literature Review of E-government Services with Gamification Elements. *International Journal of Public Administration*, 45(13), 964–980. DOI: 10.1080/01900692.2021.1930042

Desty, R. T., & Arumsari, W. (2022). Receiving COVID-19 Messages on Social Media to the Community of Semarang City. *Pack*, 18(2), 217–224. DOI: 10.15294/kemas.v18i2.33132

Dewinta, A., & Irawan, M. I. (2021). They are clustering Complaints from Customers of Government Drinking Water Companies on Social Media Twitter using Text Mining. In AR, HH, WAP, SJ, KF, JH, PP, SE, SHTT, SEI, SER, PE, KY, KK, PDD, KE, & AP (Eds.), 3rd East Indonesia Conference on Computer and Information Technology, EIConCIT 2021 (pp. 338–342). Institute of Electrical and Electronic Engineers Inc. DOI: 10.1109/EIConCIT50028.2021.9431931

Dobrolyubova, E. I. (2022). EVALUATING DIGITAL GOVERNMENT PERFORMANCE USING SURVEYS: INTERNATIONAL LITERATURE REVIEW AND PROSPECTS FOR THE FUTURE RESEARCH. *Public Administration Issues*, 5(5), 152–181. DOI: 10.17323/1999-5431-2022-0-5-152-181

Duhamel, F., & Sandoval-Almazán, R. (2021). Designing E-Government Legal Institutions: A State-Level Comparison in Mexico. *International Journal of Public Administration in the Digital Age*, 8(1), 1–15. Advance online publication. DOI: 10.4018/IJPADA.20210101.oa1

Durkiewicz, J., & Janowski, T. (2021). Is digital government advancing sustainable governance? A study of oecd/eu countries. *Sustainability (Basel)*, 13(24), 13603. Advance online publication. DOI: 10.3390/su132413603

EL JAOUHARI, S., & Lhoussaine, A. L. L. A. (2022). L'approche territoriale et la gestion de l'impact de la pandémie de Covid-19: Cas des collectivités territoriales. *Alternatives Managériales Economiques*, 4(1), 245–265.

Elhissoufi, M., & Alla, L. (2024). Artificial Intelligence in Costumer Acquisition: A Bibliometric Study. In Alla, L., Hmioui, A., & Bentalha, B. (Eds.), *AI and Data Engineering Solutions for Effective Marketing* (pp. 1–22). IGI Global., DOI: 10.4018/979-8-3693-3172-9.ch001

Erkut, B. (2020). From digital government to digital governance: Are we there yet? *Sustainability (Basel)*, 12(3), 860. Advance online publication. DOI: 10.3390/su12030860

Fakhrurroja, H., Atmaja, M. N., Panjaitan, J. N. C., Alamsyah, A., & Munandar, A. (2019, November). Crisis Communication on Twitter: a social network analysis of christchurch terrorist attack in 2019. In 2019 International Conference on ICT for Smart Society (ICISS) (Vol. 7, pp. 1-6). IEEE.

Fishenden, J., & Thompson, M. (2013). Digital government, open architecture, and innovation: Why public sector it will never be the same again. *Journal of Public Administration: Research and Theory*, 23(4), 977–1004. DOI: 10.1093/jopart/mus022

Gaffar, V., Koeswandi, T., & Suhud, U. (2022). HAS THE COVID-19 PANDEMIC ACCELERATE THE DIGITAL TRANSFORMATION OF MICRO, SMALL, AND MEDIUM ENTERPRISES IN INDONESIA? *Teorija in Praksa*, 59(3), 729–744. DOI: 10.51936/tip.59.3.729-744

Gazali, E. (2014). Learning by click: Social media democracy experiment in Indonesia. *Gazette of International Communications*, 76(4–5), 425–439. DOI: 10.1177/1748048514524119

Gil-Garcia, J. R., & Flores-Zúñiga, M. Á. (2020). Towards a comprehensive understanding of digital government success: Integrating implementation and adoption factors. *Government Information Quarterly*, 37(4), 101518. Advance online publication. DOI: 10.1016/j.giq.2020.101518

Gottschalk, P. (2009). Maturity levels for interoperability in digital government. *Government Information Quarterly*, 26(1), 75–81. https://api.semanticscholar.org/CorpusID:44507003. DOI: 10.1016/j.giq.2008.03.003

Green, S. (2020). A digital start-up project - CARM tool as an innovative approach to digital government transformation. *Computer Systems Science and Engineering*, 35(4), 257–269. https://www.scopus.com/inward/record.uri?eid=2-s2.0-85092347492&partnerID=40&md5=dc865f34d6d2c0a28a490620bba4c4bd. DOI: 10.32604/csse.2020.35.257

Halsbenning, S., Niemann, M., Distel, B., & Becker, J. (2021). Playing (Government) Seriously: Design Principles for e-Government Simulation Game Platforms. In A. F., S. R., & S. S. (Eds.), *International Conference on Wirtschaftsinformatik, WI 2021:* Vol. 48 *LNISO* (pp. 73–90). Springer Science and Business Media Deutschland GmbH. DOI: 10.1007/978-3-030-86800-0_6

Handani, N. D., Williady, A., & Kim, H.-S. (2022). Textual Review Analysis and Customer Satisfaction at Luxury Hotels in Singapore's Marina Bay Area (SG-Clean Certified Hotels). *Sustainability (Switzerland)*, 14(15). Advance online publication. DOI: 10.3390/su14159382

Harrison, T. M., & Luna-Reyes, L. F. (2022). Cultivating Trustworthy Artificial Intelligence in Digital Government. *Social Science Computer Review*, 40(2), 494–511. DOI: 10.1177/0894439320980122

Hidayah, K. (2018). Indonesian Tax Dispute Resolution in Cooperative Paradigm Compared to UK and Australia. International Conference on Industrial Technology for Sustainable Development 2017, ICon-ITSD 2017, 175(1). DOI: 10.1088/1755-1315/175/1/012203

Hmioui, A., Alla, L., & Bentalha, B. (2017). Pilotage de la touristicité territoriale au Maroc Proposition d'un indice de tourisctícité pour la destination Fès. *Entrepreneuriat, Innovation, Gouvernance et Développement territorial*, 120-143.

Hmioui, A., Alla, L., & Bentalha, B. (2017). *Piloting territorial tourism in Morocco Proposal for a tourism index for the destination Fez [Pilotage de la touristicité territoriale au Maroc Proposition d'un indice de tourisctícité pour la destination Fès]* (No. hal-02334913).

Huang, Z.-X., & Huang, T.-Y. (2022). Privacy Calculus Theory in the Digital Government Context: The Case of Taiwan's New eID Policy. *Social Science Computer Review*. Advance online publication. DOI: 10.1177/08944393221117500

Indriastuti, N. A., Oktafia, R., & Aviani, A. W. (2021). A prominent factor in the selection of injectable contraceptives for women of childbearing age in Yogyakarta. Bali. *Medical Journal (Fort Sam Houston, Tex.)*, 10(3), 1111–1118. DOI: 10.15562/bmj.v10i3.3030

Irwansyah. (2021). Social contract utilitarianism: The use of multiple digital villages is important for integrating tourism. International Journal of Interdisciplinary Social and Community Studies, 16(1), 149–162. DOI: 10.18848/2324-7576/CGP/v16i01/149-162

Jacob, D. W., Fudzee, M. F. M., Salamat, M. A., & Kasim, S. (2019). Examining digital government (DG) adoption in Indonesia through UTAUT framework. *International Journal of Advanced Trends in Computer Science and Engineering, 8*(1.3 S1), 115–120. DOI: 10.30534/ijatcse/2019/2281.32019

Janssen, M., Rana, N. P., Slade, E. L., & Dwivedi, Y. K. (2018). Trustworthiness of digital government services: Deriving a comprehensive theory through interpretive structural modelling. *Public Management Review*, 20(5), 647–671. DOI: 10.1080/14719037.2017.1305689

Kaya, T., Sağsan, M., Yıldız, M., Medeni, T., & Medeni, T. (2020). Citizen attitudes towards e-government services: Comparison of Northern and Southern Nicosia municipalities. *International Journal of Public Administration in the Digital Age*, 7(1), 17–32. DOI: 10.4018/IJPADA.2020010102

Khan, A. Z., Mahmood, F., Bokhari, R. H., Mushtaq, R., & Abbas, R. (2021). Challenges of e-government implementation in health sector: A step toward validating a conceptual framework. *Digital Policy. Regulation & Governance*, 23(6), 574–597. DOI: 10.1108/DPRG-04-2021-0048

Kim, C., & Kim, K.-A. (2021). The institutional change from E-Government toward Smarter City; comparative analysis between royal borough of Greenwich, UK, and Seongdong-gu, South Korea. *Journal of Open Innovation*, 7(1), 1–33. DOI: 10.3390/joitmc7010042

Konnon, M. A., Lodonou, N., Gaffan, R. H., & Ezin, E. (2023). An Extended Layered Information Security Architecture (ELISA) for e-Government in Developing Countries. *International Journal of Engineering Trends and Technology*, 71(1), 109–123. DOI: 10.14445/22315381/IJETT-V71I1P210

Kristanto, Y. (2018). Public Service Innovation in the Framework of Realizing E-Government (Case Study of the Implementation of the Hendi Report Application). *Journal of Public Administration and Local Governance*, 2(1).

Laenens, W., Van den Broeck, W., & Mariën, I. (2018). Channel choice determinants of (Digital) government communication: A case study of spatial planning in flanders. *Media and Communication, 6*(4Theoretical Reflections and Case Studies), 140–152. DOI: 10.17645/mac.v6i4.1652

Latif, D. V., & Roespinoedji, D. (2021). The Prevention of Corruption as A Result of Implementing E-Government: A Geographical Review of Indonesia. *Review of International Geographical Education Online*, 11(3), 210–217. DOI: 10.33403/rigeo.800485

Lee, J., Kim, B. J., Park, S., Park, S., & Oh, K. (2018). Proposing a value-based digital government model: Toward broadening sustainability and public participation. *Sustainability (Basel)*, 10(9), 3078. Advance online publication. DOI: 10.3390/su10093078

Li, E., Chen, Q., Zhang, X., & Zhang, C. (2023). Digital Government Development, Local Governments' Attention Distribution and Enterprise Total Factor Productivity: Evidence from China. *Sustainability (Basel)*, 15(3), 2472. Advance online publication. DOI: 10.3390/su15032472

Li, X., & Ding, Y. (2020). Holistic governance for sustainable public services: Reshaping government–enterprise relationships in china's digital government context. *International Journal of Environmental Research and Public Health*, 17(5), 1778. Advance online publication. DOI: 10.3390/ijerph17051778 PMID: 32182931

Liu, H., Shi, Y., Yang, X., & Zhang, W. (2023). The Role of Business Environment and Digital Government in Mitigating Supply Chain Vulnerability—Evidence from the COVID-19 Shock. *Sustainability (Basel)*, 15(3), 2323. Advance online publication. DOI: 10.3390/su15032323

Lumbanraja, A. D. (2020). The Urgency of Transforming Public Services through E-Government in the New Normal and Bureaucratic Regulatory Reform. *Administrative Law and Governance Journal*, 3(2), 220–231. DOI: 10.14710/alj.v3i2.220-231

Luna-Reyes, L. F., Andersen, D. F., Black, L. J., & Pardo, T. A. (2021). Sensemaking and social processes in digital government projects. *Government Information Quarterly*, 38(2), 101570. Advance online publication. DOI: 10.1016/j.giq.2021.101570

Madyatmadja, E. D., Yahya, B. N., & Wijaya, C. (2022). Contextual Text Analysis Framework for Citizen Report Classification: A Case Study Using Indonesian. *IEEE Access : Practical Innovations, Open Solutions*, 10, 31432–31444. DOI: 10.1109/ACCESS.2022.3158940

Majid, S. A., Ricardianto, P., Pahala, Y., Saribanon, E., Sidtanding, S., Hernawan, M. A., Ade Suryobuwono, A., & Suryawan, R. F. (2022). Determine Optimal Marketing based on Market Attraction and Market Based Strategy by Considering Customer Life Time Network Value. *Management Systems and Industrial Engineering*, 21(2), 401–408. DOI: 10.7232/iems.2022.21.2.401

Makki, A. A., & Alqahtani, A. Y. (2022). Modeling the Barriers Surrounding Digital Government Implementation: Revealing Prospect Opportunities in Saudi Arabia. *Sustainability (Basel)*, 14(23), 15780. Advance online publication. DOI: 10.3390/su142315780

Marcovecchio, I., Thinyane, M., Estevez, E., & Janowski, T. (2019). Digital government as implementation means for sustainable development goals. *International Journal of Public Administration in the Digital Age*, 6(3), 1–22. DOI: 10.4018/IJPADA.2019070101

Martins, J., & Veiga, L. G. (2022). Digital government as a business facilitator. *Information Economics and Policy*, 60, 100990. Advance online publication. DOI: 10.1016/j.infoecopol.2022.100990

Mohamed, S., & Han, S. (2022). Translating Human Values to Design Requirements: The Case of Developing Digital Government Collaborative Platform (DGCP) for Environmental Sustainability in Sri Lanka. In H. L., S. M., & H. S. (Eds.), *23rd Annual International Conference on Digital Government Research: Intelligent Technologies, Governments and Citizens, DGO 2022* (pp. 54–61). Association for Computing Machinery. DOI: 10.1145/3543434.3543455

Moore, S. (2019). Digital government, public participation and service transformation: The impact of virtual courts. *Policy and Politics*, 47(3), 495–509. DOI: 10.1332/030557319X15586039367509

Naswir, R. Y., Maarop, N., Hasan, M., Daud, S., Samy, G. N., & Magalingam, P. (2019). Towards a conceptual model to evaluate usability of digital government services in Malaysia. *International Journal of Advanced Computer Science and Applications*, 10(4), 313–322. DOI: 10.14569/IJACSA.2019.0100438

Nouhaila, B. K., Aarabe, M., & Alla, L. (2024). The Impact of Digitalisation on the Customer Experience in Medical Tourism: A Systematic Review. In Talukder, M., Kumar, S., & Tyagi, P. (Eds.), *Impact of AI and Tech-Driven Solutions in Hospitality and Tourism* (pp. 408–428). IGI Global., DOI: 10.4018/979-8-3693-6755-1.ch020

Osifo, O. C. (2018). Examining digital government and public service provision: The case of Finland. In V. B., T. E., G. T.G., S. V., C.-S. M., R. S., S. K., K. M., M. M., G. S., P. P., & J. M. (Eds.), *41st International Convention on Information and Communication Technology, Electronics and Microelectronics, MIPRO 2018* (pp. 1342–1347). Institute of Electrical and Electronics Engineers Inc. DOI: 10.23919/MIPRO.2018.8400242

Pardo, T. A., Parycek, P., Janssen, M., Zheng, L., & Cunha, M. A. (2017). Building & sustaining a digital government research center: A director's perspective. In H. C.C. & O. A. (Eds.), *18th Annual International Conference on Digital Government Research, DG.O 2017: Vol. Part F1282* (pp. 607–609). Association for Computing Machinery. DOI: 10.1145/3085228.3085241

Paulin, A. (2014). Through liquid democracy to sustainable non-bureaucratic government harnessing the power of icts for a novel form of digital government. *EJournal of EDemocracy and Open Government*, 6(2), 216–230. DOI: 10.29379/jedem.v6i2.307

Pethig, F., Kroenung, J., & Noeltner, M. (2021). A stigma power perspective on digital government service avoidance. *Government Information Quarterly*, 38(2), 101545. Advance online publication. DOI: 10.1016/j.giq.2020.101545

Pribadi, U. (2021). Citizens' intention to use e-government services: The case of e-complaint service in Indonesia. *International Journal of Electronic Governance*, 13(2), 114–131. DOI: 10.1504/IJEG.2021.116884

Putera, P. B., & Gustina, A. (2021). Discourse on digital government and regulation: A bibliometric analysis. *Library Philosophy and Practice, 2021*, 1–11. https://www.scopus.com/inward/record.uri?eid=2-s2.0-85109932480&partnerID=40&md5=a148326f4f489b3c93066a33d6cb102f

Ramakrishnan, S., Wong, M. S., Chit, M. M., & Mutum, D. S. (2022). A conceptual model of the relationship between organisational intelligence traits and digital government service quality: The role of occupational stress. *International Journal of Quality & Reliability Management*, 39(6), 1429–1452. DOI: 10.1108/IJQRM-10-2021-0371

Roengtam, S., Nurmandi, A., Almarez, D. N., & Kholid, A. (2017). Has social media changed city government? Case studies in three ASEAN cities: Bandung, Indonesia, Iligan, Philippines, and Pukhet, Thailand. Changing Governments: People. *Processes and Policy*, 11(3), 343–376. DOI: 10.1108/TG-10-2016-0071

Rudianto, R., Hidayat, F. P., Hardiyanto, S., Priadi, R., & Thariq, M. (2021). Community activities amid activity restrictions during the coronavirus disease-19 pandemic in North Sumatra. *Open Access Macedonian Journal of Medical Sciences*, 9(E), 964–968. DOI: 10.3889/oamjms.2021.7088

Russmann, U., Hametner, M., & Posch, E. (2020). Tax-funded digital government communication in Austria: Members of the government on Facebook. *European Journal of Communication*, 35(2), 140–164. DOI: 10.1177/0267323119894484

Rytova, E., Verevka, T., Gutman, S., & Kuznetsov, S. (2020). Assessing the Maturity Level of Saint Petersburg's Digital Government. *International Journal ofTechnology*, 11(6), 1081–1090. DOI: 10.14716/ijtech.v11i6.4440

Sá, F., Martins, P., & Abbasi, M. (2021). Portuguese local e-government: A study on the most adopted databases in 2019. *IBIMA Business Review*, 2021, 1–12. Advance online publication. DOI: 10.5171/2021.254977

Sanina, A., Balashov, A., & Rubtcova, M. (2023). The Socio-Economic Efficiency of Digital Government Transformation. *International Journal of Public Administration*, 46(1), 85–96. DOI: 10.1080/01900692.2021.1988637

Sapraz, M., & Han, S. (2021). Implicating human values for designing a digital government collaborative platform for environmental issues: A value sensitive design approach. *Sustainability (Basel)*, 13(11), 6240. Advance online publication. DOI: 10.3390/su13116240

Scholl, H. J. (2020). Digital Government. *Digital Government: Research and Practice*, 1(1), 1–12. Advance online publication. DOI: 10.1145/3352682

Scholl, H. J. (2021). The Digital Government Reference Library (DGRL) and its potential formative impact on Digital Government Research (DGR). *Government Information Quarterly*, 38(4), 101613. Advance online publication. DOI: 10.1016/j.giq.2021.101613

Setyastuti, Y., Suminar, J. R., Hadisiwi, P., & Zubair, F. (2019). Millennial Mothers: Social media as the preferred source of information about parenting in Indonesia. Library Philosophy and Practice, 2019. https://www.scopus.com/inward/record.uri?eid=2-s2.0-85066070586&partnerID=40&md5=b3fb646d1fdc94ff4609d2f280f03ae0

Sihombing, S. O., & Achmadi, H. (2022). Assessing Indonesian Youth Acceptance of Corruption: Applying the Stimulus-Organism-Response Framework. *Academic Journal of Interdisciplinary Studies*, 11(2), 214–229. DOI: 10.36941/ajis-2022-0047

Silalahi, M., Napitupulu, D., & Patria, G. (2015). Study of the Concept and Conditions of E-Government in Indonesia. JUPITER. *Journal of Application of Computer Sciences*, 1(1).

Simonofski, A., Clarinval, A., Vanderose, B., Dumas, B., & Snoeck, M. (2021). What influences citizens' expectations towards digital government? An exploratory survey. *Digital Policy. Regulation & Governance*, 23(2), 154–172. DOI: 10.1108/DPRG-12-2020-0173

Soga, B., & Vyas-Doorgapersad, S. (2022). SIGNIFICANCE OF E-GOVERNMENT SERVICES FOR SMALL BUSINESSES IN THE CITY OF JOHANNESBURG. *Xinan Jiaotong Daxue Xuebao. Journal of Southwest Jiaotong University*, 57(4), 208–222. DOI: 10.35741/issn.0258-2724.57.4.18

Susanto, A., & Meiryani. (2019). Digital government role. *International Journal of Scientific and Technology Research, 8*(4), 230–232. https://www.scopus.com/inward/record.uri?eid=2-s2.0-85067202490&partnerID=40&md5=0a5ee4e11e43527bcf46311bd60eb40b

Tangi, L., Janssen, M., Benedetti, M., & Noci, G. (2021). Digital government transformation: A structural equation modelling analysis of driving and impeding factors. *International Journal of Information Management*, 60, 102356. Advance online publication. DOI: 10.1016/j.ijinfomgt.2021.102356

Tao, S., Liu, H., Wang, S., & Li, C. (2020). Construction of Smart Coastal Cities Based on Digital Government. *Journal of Coastal Research*, 110(sp1), 154–158. DOI: 10.2112/JCR-SI110-037.1

Utomo, S. H., Narmaditya, B. S., Wibowo, A., Ali, A., & Sahid, S. (2022). SOCIAL CAPITAL AND ENTREPRENEURIAL INTENTIONS IN RURAL COMMUNITIES OF INDONESIA. *Journal of Eastern European and Central Asian Research*, 9(4), 665–679. DOI: 10.15549/jeecar.v9i4.927

Vázquez-López, A., & Marey-Perez, M. (2021). Factors affecting e-government adoption by dairy farmers: A case study in the north-west of Spain. *Future Internet*, 13(8), 206. Advance online publication. DOI: 10.3390/fi13080206

Wahyunengseh, R. D., & Hastjarjo, S. (2021). Big Data Analysis of Disaster Communication Policy: Mapping communication issues and public responses on government social media. *10th International Conference on Public Organizations, ICONPO 2020*, 717(1). DOI: 10.1088/1755-1315/717/1/012004

Walle, Y. M. (2020). The impact of digital government on whistleblowing and whistle-blower protection: Explanatory study. *Journal of Information Technology Management*, 12(1), 1–26. DOI: 10.22059/JITM.2019.291003.2409

Wiiava, S. W., & Handoko, I. (2021). Researching Covid-19 Twitter Hashtag Conversations in Indonesia: An Approach to Social Network Analysis. In LS, CH, & IR (Eds.), 15th International Conference on Information Management and Ubiquitous Communication, IMCOM 2021. Institute of Electrical and Electronics Engineers Inc. DOI: 10.1109/IMCOM51814.2021.9377382

Wilson, C., & Mergel, I. (2022). Overcoming barriers to digital government: Mapping the strategies of digital champions. *Government Information Quarterly*, 39(2), 101681. Advance online publication. DOI: 10.1016/j.giq.2022.101681

Wirawan, V. (2020). Application of E-Government in Welcoming the Contemporary Industrial Revolution 4.0 Era in Indonesia. *Journal of Law Enforcement and Justice*, 1(1), 1–16.

Wirtz, B. W., Langer, P. F., & Schmidt, F. W. (2021). Digital Government: Business Model Development For Public Value Creation-A Dynamic Capabilities Based Framework. *Public Administration Quarterly*, 45(3), 232–255. DOI: 10.37808/paq.45.3.2

Xiang, X., Wang, J., Long, Z., & Huang, Y. (2023). Improving the Entrepreneurial Competence of College Social Entrepreneurs: Digital Government Building, Entrepreneurship Education, and Entrepreneurial Cognition. *Sustainability (Basel)*, 15(1), 69. Advance online publication. DOI: 10.3390/su15010069

Yang, Y., Shi, Y., & Wang, T. (2022). Blockchain Technology Application Maturity Assessment Model for Digital Government Public Service Projects. *International Journal of Crowd Science*, 6(4), 184–194. DOI: 10.26599/IJCS.2022.9100025

Yavuz, N. (2022). Gender differences in perception and usage of public transit technologies: Implications for digital government. *Information Polity*, 27(1), 97–113. DOI: 10.3233/IP-200305

# Chapter 5
# Logistic Clustering Dynamics Determinants: A Bibliometric and Prospective Approach

**Naoual Bouhtati**
*Sidi Mohamed Ben Abdellah University, Fez, Morocco*

**Mourad Aarabe**
https://orcid.org/0009-0003-9772-6683
*National School of Business and Management of Fez, Morocco*

**Lhoussaine Alla**
https://orcid.org/0000-0002-7238-1792
*Sidi Mohamed Ben Abdellah University, Fez, Morocco*

**Youssef El Yaacoubi**
*Sidi Mohamed Ben Abdellah University, Fez, Morocco*

## ABSTRACT

*The study aims to explore the future evolution of the dynamics of logistics clusters through a systematic and qualitative bibliometric approach. The research gaps identified are identified by the lack of work on the specific perspective of logistics clusters, and bibliometric approaches applied to this subject. In addition, there is a need to address the lack of empirical data on the evolution of logistics clusters. The central issue is to analyse in depth how the dynamics of logistics clusters will evolve, highlighting key trends and major influencing factors that will shape this environment. The study will adopt a systematic and qualitative bibliometric approach to provide a thorough and rigorous analysis of emerging trends and future*

DOI: 10.4018/979-8-3693-6854-1.ch005

*perspectives in the field. The research has highlighted the role of endogenous and exogenous factors as levers for dynamizing logistic clustering, as well as the moderating role of accompanying measures and the level of maturity of the cluster in such a causal relationship.*

## 1. INTRODUCTION

Globalization, digitalization and the rise of e-commerce have profoundly transformed the logistics sector, especially for both service providers and other stakeholders, leading to an increased complexity of logistics operations. In response to these challenges, logistics clusters are emerging as a promising model for optimizing goods flows, fostering innovation and strengthening the competitiveness of companies.

Beyond improving efficiency, these clusters can act as catalysts for regional development by integrating territorial management strategies. Thus, logistics clusters play an important role in the development and innovation of the local or regional economy. This geographical concentration of logistics services and industrial operations ecosystems to improve infrastructure, stimulate collaboration and innovation in sectors to contribute to the competitiveness of territories (Sheffi, 2013). The formation of logistics clusters allows to transform regional innovation ecosystems by increasing integration of logistic infrastructures in urban development (Liashenko et al., 2021). In the context of digitalization, effective management of logistics and market behaviour within innovative clusters is essential (Aranci et al., 2022). The development of these clusters is perfectly linked to innovative approaches in territorial management with an interaction between different sectors, companies, research institutions, government authorities is crucial to driving sustainable development (Liashenko et al., 2021).

The study of the dynamics of training and development of logistics clusters has therefore become a crucial research subject, offering valuable perspectives for decision-makers, companies and researchers. Understanding emerging trends and the key factors that will shape this evolution is therefore essential to effectively inform logistics actors' strategies and policies.

Logistics clustering dynamics (LCG) is an important research topic in the field of logistics and supply chain management. According to Hervas-Oliver et al. (2019), logistics clusters can be defined as "geographical concentrations of interconnected logistics companies, specialized suppliers and related institutions in a particular field". Studying this dynamic is crucial to understanding the factors that influence the formation, evolution and performance of these logistic ecosystems.

However, the existing literature has several theoretical, methodological and empirical gaps. At the theoretical level, Chhetri et al. (2014) point to the lack of integrated conceptual frameworks for analyzing the dynamics of logistics clusters. On the methodological level, Lagoudis and Scholz-Reiter (2019) note that previous studies have largely relied on qualitative approaches, leaving limited room for quantitative and bibliometric analyses. Empirically, Dallasega et al. (2018) note that the majority of research has focused on specific case studies, making it difficult to generalize.

From a theoretical point of view, we observe that few studies have been specifically devoted to the perspective of logistics clusters, thus leaving an area of uncertainty to be filled. Also, a lack of consensus on the key success factors of logistics clusters, in the absence of a global and unified vision in this area (Porter, 1998; Cooke, 2008). Also, shortcomings were found in the analysis of interactions and synergies between the actors of the cluster, due to the focus on companies and the neglect of the role of institutions, infrastructures and networks (Rinkinen, 2016).

From a methodological point of view, the lack of systematic bibliometric approaches is a barrier to an in-depth analysis of this constantly changing field (Leydesdorff et al., 2016). In addition, the lack of empirical data on the evolution of logistics clusters poses a major challenge to the global understanding of this complex environment. Also, the lack of longitudinal perspectives, due to the focus of studies on time snapshots, prevents analysis of cluster evolution and the impact of contextual changes (Cooke, 2008).

In empirical studies, we note a high concentration of research on specific case studies, and very rarely on comparative research and cross-sectional studies that allow generalizing the results and to identify global trends (Storper, 2014). In addition, we note the lack of studies on logistics clusters in developing countries, thus leaving a significant gap in understanding the specificities of logistics clusters in emerging contexts (Belussi & Hervas-Oliver, 2017).

Faced with these gaps, our research questions the future dynamics of logistics clusters by adopting the following main problem: What are the main trends, Key concepts, methods and future perspectives of research on logistics clusters?

The study will help to better understand the evolution of research on logistics clusters, identify priority research areas and contribute to the development of more robust and relevant knowledge for the sector's stakeholders.

To address this issue, a systematic and qualitative bibliometric approach will be adopted. This rigorous approach involves a careful analysis of relevant academic publications to identify recurring themes, highlight influential contributors and highlight conceptual advances in the field of logistics clusters. The objective is to provide valuable and up-to-date insights into the perspective of these clusters, thus providing a solid basis for informed strategic directions within the logistics sector.

In this chapter, we will begin by presenting the theoretical and conceptual framework of the research, before moving on to the methodological approach, results and discussion, and finally, present the outline of the model for analysis and future research.

## 2. BACKGROUND

### 2.1. Definitive definition of key concepts

- ***Logistics clusters:*** Logistics clustering is part of a local, regional and even global spatial logistics model that adapts to the dynamics of the supply and value chain (Waldheim and Berger, 2008). From the point of view of economic geography, logistics clustering is understood as a geographical concentration and agglomeration of various logistic activities (Sheffi, 2012), through the pooling of different infrastructures (hubs, sites, platforms,...), foster multiple forms of cooperation and competition among various logistics, manufacturing, commercial, financial, business and intermediary organizations (Han, 2019). According to Mangan et al. (2016), logistics clusters are similar to geographical groupings of local logistics actors that interact and cooperate to create synergies and improve the collective competitiveness of the logistics sector in a given region, and ultimately improve their competitiveness and performance on world markets. According to Rivera et al. (2014), they include logistics service providers, transportation companies, warehouses, as well as support institutions such as training and research centres. Thanks to the physical proximity of these actors that they generate (Ketels, 2013), logistic clusters facilitate interactions, collaboration and knowledge sharing (Rivera et al., 2014).
- ***Logistics clustering:*** Logistics clustering refers to the process by which companies and actors in the logistics sector group together spatially to benefit from agglomeration, resource sharing and synergies (Han, 2019). This usually involves progressive co-localization of logistics actors, strengthening inter-organizational links and the emergence of shared infrastructures and services (Van den Heuvel et al., 2013). According to Chhetri et al. (2014), the effectiveness of such a process is influenced by exogenous factors such as public policies, geographic advantages and market dynamics.
- ***Dynamics of logistics clustering:*** Driven by a battery of factors such as innovation, technological change, regulations, competition and business strategies (Liu et al., 2022, 2002; Egger et al., 2021), the dynamics of logistic clustering refers to the evolution over time of interactions, interdependencies and processes within a logistics cluster (Bathelt et al., 2004). According to Liu et al. (2022), this temporal evolution integrates the phases of birth, growth, maturity and potential decline of

clusters. This dynamic also encompasses structural changes inherent in interactions between actors, adaptation to new technologies and the evolution of logistics business models (Klauenberg et al., 2020).

Drawing on the work of Gonzalez-Feliu et al. (2020), we can summarize the maturity dynamics of logistics clustering in six main stages (Figure 1), moving from a reactive initial level to a mature and strategic level, Through different stages of process definition, management and optimization.

*Figure 1. Logistic clustering maturity process*

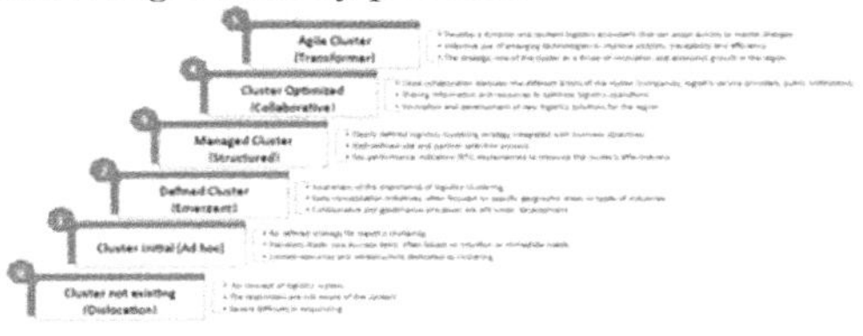


*Source: Authors*

This classification was established based on the maturity criteria battery of Gonzalez-Feliu et al. (2020) (“logistics practices”, “logistics processes”, “logistics tools”, “logistics stakeholders and their relationships”, “physical flow management issues”, “information flow management issues”).

## 2.2. State of the art in research work

The issue of dynamizing logistics clusters has generated growing interest in academic literature. Table 1 explores the extent of research work that has addressed this issue, and highlights several dimensions of the problem.

*Table 1. Research into the dynamics of logistics clustering*

| Perspective | Dimension | Aspects | References |
|---|---|---|---|
| **Factors of dynamization** | **Endogenous levers** | Technological innovation | Rivera et al. (2014) |
| | | Knowledge transfer | Bathelt et al. (2004) ; |
| | | Synergies between the actors | Malmberg & Maskell (2002) |
| | | Economies of scale | Sheffi (2012) |
| | | Supply chain efficiency & Competitiveness of the territory | Masson & Petiot (2013 |
| | | Innovation & Cooperation | Rivera et al. (2014) |
| | | Geographical proximity | Ketels (2013) |
| | **Exogenous levers** | Public policy & Infrastructure investment | Antoine et al. (2017) ; Liu et al. (2022) ; Amisse & Muller (2011) |
| | **Accompanying measures** | Coordination, Governance & Flexibility | Ketchen et al. (2014) ; Benbba (2016) |
| **Evolution of cluster models** | **Integration modalities** | Integration by transport modes | Kakou et al. (2022) |
| | **Shared responsibility** | Green cluster (sustainability and circular economy) | Benoit (2024) |
| **Challenges and opportunities** | **Digitization** | Adaptation challenges & Opportunities for innovation | Mangan et Lalwani (2016) |
| | **Crises** | Resilience | Monios & Elbert (2020) |
| **Prospective and future trends** | **Automation and AI** | Reconfiguration of clusters | Suu (2021) ; Houé (2022) |
| | **Flexibility** | Development of micro-clusters | Radhoui & Baron, 2022) ; Raimbault (2019 ; Benbba (2016) |

Source: Authors

This theoretical and conceptual framework provides a solid basis for your bibliometric analysis, highlighting the main concepts, theories and trends in the field of logistics cluster dynamics. It will help guide your analysis to the most relevant and innovative aspects of the topic.

However, despite these contributions, few studies have focused specifically on the prospective and future evolution of logistics clusters. This gap highlights the importance of conducting research such as the one proposed to anticipate future trends and challenges in this ever-changing field.

## 3. Methodology

A bibliometric literature review was conducted for this study to analyze the levers of logistic clustering (Donthu et al., 2021; Linnenluecke et al., 2020). The methodology adopted follows guidelines and uses specialized tools to ensure a rigorous and relevant analysis. Selection of the publication corpus is based on the PRISMA protocol (Liu et al., 2022). This protocol provides a structured approach to identify, filter and include adequate studies and ensures transparency and reproducibility of the selection process (Mateo, 2020). Data were analyzed using the software Vosviewer for the creation of visualization of bibliometric networks, allowing the creation of cooccurrences of words and networks of citations and collaboration between authors, affiliate organizations, countries and regions (Van Eck & Waltman, 2010).

To define our research equation, the keyword approach was adopted based on the main themes related to our research to identify appropriate publications (Swanson et al., 2018). The keywords selected cover clustering-specific terms, levers and mechanisms related to the context of logistics and supply chain management to form the following research equation (box 1) to query academic databases through the dimensions platform (Martín-Martín et al., 2021).

### Research equation

("logistics clustering" OR "logistics cluster" OR "logistics hub" OR "logistics network" OR "logistics agglomeration" OR "logistics conglomeration")

AND

("levers" OR "drivers" OR "factors" OR "mechanisms" OR "strategies" OR "key elements" OR "initiatives" OR "best practices")

AND

("supply chain" OR "distribution network" OR "warehousing" OR "transportation" OR "logistics management" OR "freight logistics" OR "logistics infrastructure" OR "industrial logistics" OR "urban logistics")

As illustrated in Figure 2, our research was conducted in the titles and summaries of publications to maximize the relevance of the results. 712 publications were identified in the initial search, after the elimination of publications before 2010,634 references were selected. By limiting the research area to Commerce, Management, Tourism and Services, we obtained 419 publications. Excluding other types of publications, we included 275 articles. The final corpus for the bibliometric literature review includes 177 articles with full text available in open access.

*Figure 2. Summary of the methodological approach*

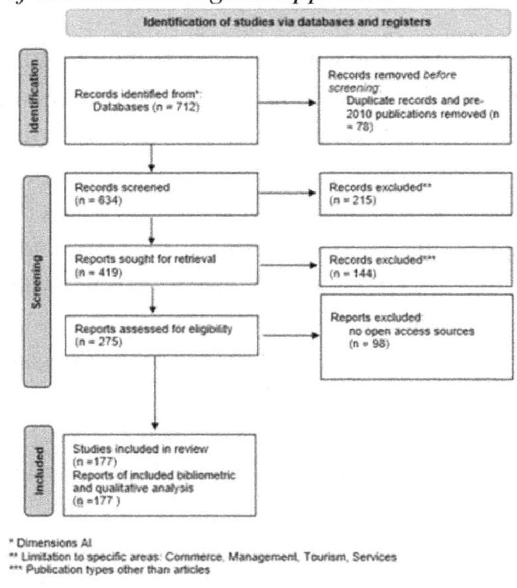


*Source: Inspired by the authors of Page et al. (2021)*

## 4. Results

### 4.1. Analysis by publication years

The following figure 3 shows the distribution of references in the corpus studied by the number of publications per year

*Figure 3. Distribution of publications by year*

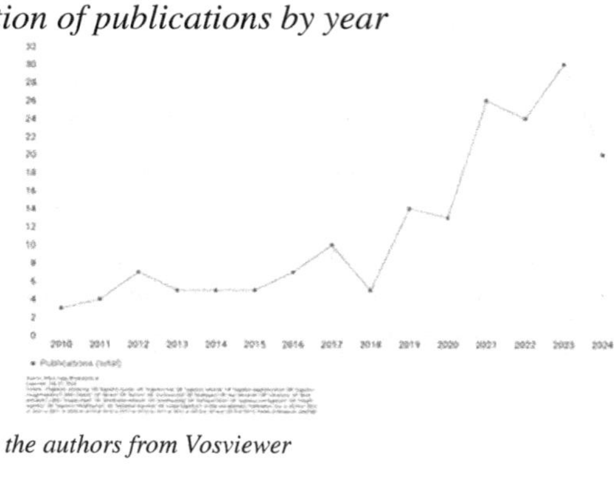


*Source: Compiled by the authors from Vosviewer*

The analysis of the graph shows a significant increase in the number of scientific publications over time, these annual fluctuations reflect an increasing interest of the scientific community in research in the specific field.

The following figure 4 shows the distribution of citations from the corpus studied by year.

*Figure 4. Distribution of citations by year*

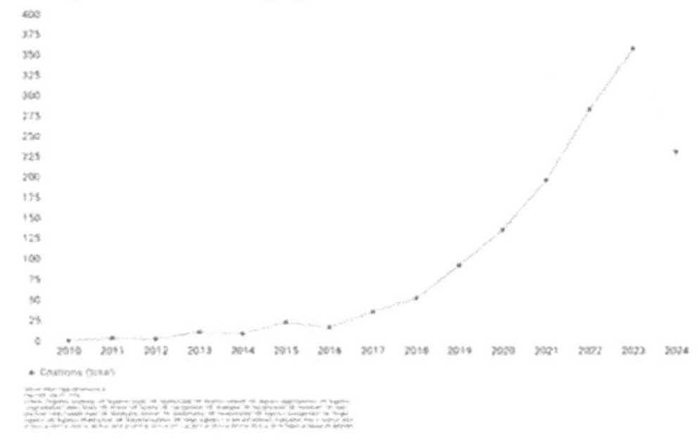

*Source: Compiled by the authors from Vosviewer*

Analysis of this graph shows a trend increase in citations. This indicates a significant increase in the impact of these publications on the scientific community. This trend can be interpreted as a growing recognition of the quality and relevance of research. This potentially reflects the evolution and depth of knowledge created in this specific field.

## 4.2. 4.2. Analysis by publication sources

Analysis of publication sources reveals several key trends in the research landscape. Table 2 and Figure 4 highlight the main sources of publication, visually illustrating the relative importance of each source in the citation network by number of documents and citations.

*Table 2. Source Classification by Number of Documents*

| Ranking by number of documents | | | Ranking by number of citations | | |
|---|---|---|---|---|---|
| **Source** | **Documents** | **Citations** | **Source** | **Documents** | **Citations** |
| Sustainability | 17 | 179 | Sustainability | 17 | 179 |
| E3S Web of Conferences | 5 | 22 | International Journal of Physical Distribution & Logistics Management | 1 | 150 |

continued on following page

*Table 2. Continued*

| Ranking by number of documents | | | Ranking by number of citations | | |
|---|---|---|---|---|---|
| **Source** | **Documents** | **Citations** | **Source** | **Documents** | **Citations** |
| Annals of Operations Research | 4 | 83 | Transportation Research Part E: Logistics and Transportation Review | 1 | 101 |
| Applied Sciences | 4 | 19 | Research in Transportation Business & Management | 2 | 100 |
| Transportation Research Procedia | 4 | 10 | Annals of Operations Research | 4 | 83 |
| Journal of Industrial Engineering and Management | 3 | 21 | Industrial Management & Data Systems | 1 | 81 |
| Procedia Engineering | 3 | 62 | Procedia Engineering | 3 | 62 |
| Cleaner Logistics and Supply Chain | 3 | 33 | International Journal of Environmental Science and Technology | 1 | 54 |
| Economic Innovations | 3 | 5 | Reliability Engineering & System Safety | 1 | 50 |
| Journal of Advanced Transportation | 3 | 15 | International Journal of Production Research | 1 | 43 |
| The Journal of International Trade & Commerce | 3 | 0 | Cleaner Logistics and Supply Chain | 3 | 33 |
| Applied Mathematics and Nonlinear Sciences | 2 | 0 | Computational Intelligence and Neuroscience | 2 | 30 |
| Computational Intelligence and Neuroscience | 2 | 30 | Communications in Transportation Research | 1 | 29 |
| Research in Transportation Business & Management | 2 | 100 | Production Planning & Control | 1 | 29 |
| Archives of Transport | 2 | 8 | E3S Web of Conferences | 5 | 22 |
| Economic Scope | 2 | 0 | Journal of Industrial Engineering and Management | 3 | 21 |
| Globalization and Business | 2 | 2 | Journal of Shipping and Trade | 1 | 20 |
| Journal of Distribution Science | 2 | 1 | Applied Sciences | 4 | 19 |
| Journal of the Korea Safety Management and Science | 2 | 0 | Intelligent Information Management | 1 | 19 |

continued on following page

*Table 2. Continued*

| Ranking by number of documents | | | Ranking by number of citations | | |
|---|---|---|---|---|---|
| **Source** | **Documents** | **Citations** | **Source** | **Documents** | **Citations** |
| Journal of Transport and Supply Chain Management | 2 | 6 | Transport Problems | 1 | 18 |

Source: Compiled by the authors from Vosviewer

*Figure 5. Visualization of the main publication sources*

*Source: Authors by Vosviewer*

The bubble chart shows that sources such as "Sustainability," "International Journal of Physical Distribution & Logistics Management" and "Transportation Research Part E: Logistics and Transportation Review" are prominent nodes, The central role they play in this field. This analysis demonstrates a research landscape focused on sustainability and logistics, with a strong interdisciplinary approach and a mix of high-impact generalist journals and specialized publications.

## 4.3. 4.3. Analysis of publications by contributions

Table 3 shows the top 20 contributors to scientific research in the field of logistics clustering, ranked by number of citations.

*Table 3. 20 main authors and their affiliation*

| Authors | Organizations | Countries | Number of documents | Number of citations |
|---|---|---|---|---|
| Alexander Hermann Hübner | Technical University of Munich | Germany | 1 | 150 |
| Alexander Trautrims | University of Nottingham | United Kingdom | 1 | 150 |

continued on following page

*Table 3. Continued*

| Authors | Organizations | Countries | Number of documents | Number of citations |
|---|---|---|---|---|
| Heinrich Kuhn | Catholic University of Eichstätt-Ingolstadt | Germany | 1 | 150 |
| Johannes Wollenburg | - | - | 1 | 150 |
| Hadi Gholizadeh | Université Laval | Canada | 1 | 101 |
| Kannan Govindan | Shanghai Maritime University | China | 1 | 101 |
| Jean-Paul Rodrigue | Hofstra University | United States | 2 | 95 |
| Abhijeet Ghadge | Cranfield University | United Kingdom | 1 | 81 |
| Sonal Choudhary | University of York | United Kingdom | 1 | 81 |
| Michael A Bourlakis | Cranfield University | United Kingdom | 1 | 81 |
| Theo E Notteboom | Ghent University | Belgium | 1 | 75 |
| Theo E Notteboom | Ghent University | Belgium | 1 | 75 |
| Yong Wang | Chongqing Jiaotong University | China | 7 | 71 |
| Zheng Wang | Huazhong University of Science and Technology | China | 2 | 51 |
| Yan Wei Zhao | Zhejiang University of Technology | China | 2 | 51 |
| Qiuya Gao | Singapore University of Technology and Design | Singapore | 1 | 50 |
| Yu-Wang Chen | University of Manchester | United Kingdom | 1 | 50 |
| Kang Hao Cheong | Singapore University of Technology and Design | Singapore | 1 | 50 |
| Tao Wen | Singapore University of Technology and Design | Singapore | 1 | 50 |
| Paweł Grzegorz Droździel | Lublin University of Technology | Poland | 2 | 47 |

Source: Compiled by the authors from Vosviewer

The table shows a high degree of geographical and institutional diversity and can be analysed from two perspectives. Authors with one or two publications but with a considerable number of citations with a notable concentration of citations that is observed among German and British authors especially those who have reached 150 citations. This indicates the relevance and recognition of their contributions by the scientific community. Authors from China and the US also perform well in terms of citations. However, some authors such as Yong Wang and Jean-Paul Rodrigue are more prolific in terms of number of publications, but with more moderate citations per document.

## 4.4. 4.4. Analysis of publications by co-authorship

Figure 6 presents the analysis of collaboration between authors, determined by the number of co-written publications. This analysis highlights the relationships and co-authorship links between researchers, thus allowing to visualize collaborative networks within the research corpus (Donthu et al., 2021).

*Figure 6. Analysis of collaborations between authors*

*Source: Authors by Vosviewer*

The analysis reveals that out of the 10 principal researchers, there are a total of 28 co-authorship links, organized into three distinct clusters, each represented by a different color: green, red and blue. This visualization of collaborations offers a clear perspective on the dynamics of co-authorships, allowing us to identify the main networks of researchers and to understand the structures of collaboration within the studied field.

Wang, Yong is the central author with the link to the different members of the 3 clusters. Thicker lines probably indicate more co-written publications between researchers. The strongest collaborations appear to be within the red cluster, particularly between Wang Yong and the other members of this group.

## 5. DISCUSSION

### 5.1. Analysis of Clusters of Themes

The process of keyword co-occurrence analysis was carried out using terms extracted from the title and summary fields of documents. Applying the full count method, we identified a total of 5,793 terms. Of these terms, 178 were selected because they exceeded the minimum threshold of 10 occurrences. To ensure the relevance of the selected terms, a relevance score was calculated for each of the 178 terms. Based on these scores, we selected the 60% most relevant terms, for a total of 107 terms (Donthu et al., 2021).

These 107 terms were then used to generate a map of keywords co-occurrence, revealing the relationships and connections between them. The analysis identified 4144 bonds, with a total bond strength of 60284. The terms were organized into 4 distinct clusters, each representing a coherent group of keywords often used together.

*Figure 7. Keyword co-occurrence (Network Visualization)*

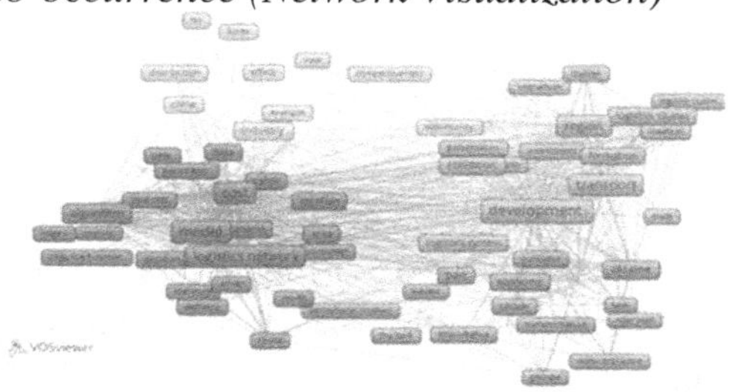

*Source: Authors by Vosviewer*

The cooccurrence visualization network (figure 7) and the item synthesis (table 4) present the selected terms and their interrelationships. The analysis of the 4 clusters provides in-depth insights into the dominant themes and key topics of interest within the documents analysed.

*Table 4. Summary of items*

| | |
|---|---|
| **Cluster 1 (50 items)** | **Algorithm, application, area, carbon emission, case, case study, cluster, condition, covid, covid-19, criterion, demand, design, delivery, device, distribution network, driver, effectiveness, emission, network, logistics network, mathematical model, method, model, network, nsga ii, objective function, optimal solution, optimization, optimize, paper, performance, problem, profit, quantity, renewable energy, resource logistics network, route, scenario, solution, supplier, sustainable development goal, total cost, uncertainty, value, vehicle** |
| **Cluster 2 (25 items)** | Activity; basis, Cluster, competitive advantage, Creation, demand, Cooperation, development, formation, globalization, Indicator, interaction, Investment, logistics cluster, logistics infrastructure, logistics system, opportunity, port, region, state, tool, transport, trend, use, volume |
| **Cluster 3 (20 items)** | Agricultural product, direction, dry port, dry port, Georgia, importance, Indicator, infrastructure, logistics infrastructure, logistics integration, logistics system, network, pilot project, port, price, sector, task, transformation, transport infrastructure, water transport |
| **Cluster 4 (12 items)** | Center,china, City, competitiveness, Effect, example, Industry, korea, Opportunity, view |

Source: Compiled by the authors from Vosviewer

→ ***Cluster 1: Modelling and technologies:***

The red cluster contains terms related to fundamental concepts and methods in logistics and optimization, as well as technological applications. Research in this cluster focuses on optimizing logistics networks using mathematical models and algorithms (Han et al., 2012). Focus on reducing carbon emissions and optimizing deliveries (Akulov et al., 2023; Behmanesh & Pannek, 2016; Wang et al., 2021). Case studies also play an important role in illustrating the practical applications of these models (Helal Alnuaimi et al., 2022). This cluster is strongly linked to clusters 1 and 2. The models and algorithms developed in Cluster 1 are often applied to improve the efficiency and competitiveness of logistics infrastructures (Cluster 3) and to enhance competitive advantages (Cluster 2) (Govindan & Gholizadeh, 2021). There are also connections with Cluster 4 for impact assessments.

→ ***Cluster 2: Development and competitive advantage:***

The green cluster focuses on factors that enable logistics companies to develop competitive advantages and promote development within logistics clusters (Dubinina, 2017; Ran, 2022; Shen et al., 2012). The research here explores how logistics clusters are developing and gaining competitive advantages. Emphasis is placed on performance indicators, necessary investments and opportunities for improvement (Gritsenko, 2020; Havenga & De Bod, 2016; Tadayonrad & Ndiaye, 2023; Wodnicka & Szukalski, 2023). Activities within clusters are also analysed to understand their contribution to overall development. The main links with Cluster 1 are obvious because the algorithms and models optimized directly influence the competitive advantages. Cluster 3 is also linked because infrastructure development (Cluster 3) contributes directly to the competitiveness of enterprises (Cluster 2). Finally, Cluster 4 is relevant for the analysis of the impact of developments on competitiveness.

→ ***Cluster 3: Logistics infrastructures:***

The blue cluster focuses on logistics infrastructure and transformations, particularly related to dry ports and transportation systems (Davydovich et al., 2020; HRYNCHAK, 2020; Lakhmetkina et al., 2019). Integration of the different logistics components is crucial to ensure optimal efficiency, especially for agricultural transport (DMUCHOWSKI, 2019; Smirnova et al., 2024). Cluster 3 is closely related to Cluster 1 due to the application of models and algorithms to optimize infrastructures. It is also connected to Cluster 2 because the improvement of infrastructure contributes directly to competitive advantages. Connections with Cluster 4 may exist to assess the impact of infrastructures on overall performance and competitiveness.

→ ***Cluster 4: Impact and Competitiveness:***

The yellow cluster examines the impact of infrastructure and logistics systems on business competitiveness (Dubinina, 2017; Ran, 2022; Shen et al., 2012). Examples from countries such as China and Korea are often used to illustrate impacts and opportunities (Ilyas et al., 2024; Park & Choi, 2014). Emphasis is also placed on the impact of these infrastructures on local industries and their competitiveness. The links with Cluster 2 are particularly important, as competitive advantages are directly influenced by infrastructure and its impact (Ambrosino & Sciomachen, 2021; Astvatsaturova & Kazakova, 2022; Dhonde & Patel, 2021). Cluster 1 also contributes to this analysis by providing models and algorithms for assessing the effects of infrastructure. Finally, Cluster 3 is crucial to understanding the infrastructural components that influence global competitiveness (Annas & Humairoh, 2023; Palacio et al., 2017).

## 5.2. Discussion and Future Research Leads

The synthesis of the terms of each previous cluster with the visualization of Figure 8 generated by Vosviewer allows to identify the most recent potential development paths and relevant points related to logistic clustering. As noted in the legend, the color of the nodes represents the average year of publication of the relevant literature. The average year is 2019 to 2021, with a range of colours from purple to yellow, blue and green. cost", "model", "logistics network", "development", "transport" and "region" are the most dominant terms in terms of co-occurrence and interconnectedness with other terms in the literature showing their importance and central role in the field of logistics. This allows to provoke several researches on the methods of optimization of costs and the increase of efficiency of logistic networks, and the development of models to understand and manage transport networks with a focus on the role of infrastructure.

*Figure 8. Keyword co-occurrence (overlay Vizualization*

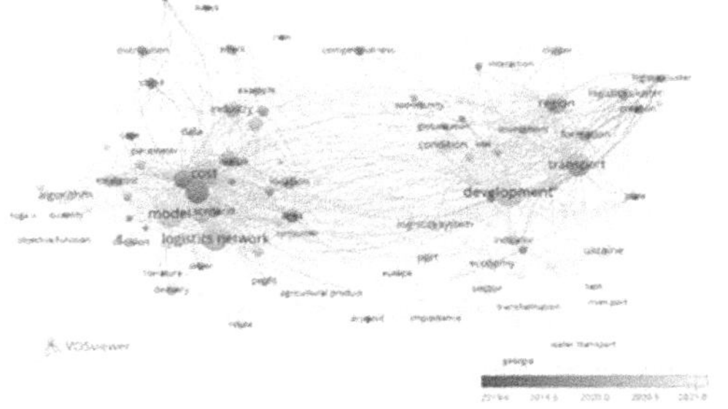


*Source: Authors by Vosviewer*

By breaking down the thematic clusters, several sub-areas of research can be revealed. The cluster 1 "Modelling and technologies" highlights the importance of developing new algorithms to optimize logistics networks and model logistics scenarios to predict the impacts of changes in parameters. Cluster 2 "Development and competitive advantage" is part of the analysis of the cost-effectiveness, added value and competitiveness factors of the logistics sector. The cluster 3 "Logistics infrastructures" suggests assessing the impact of logistical infrastructures such as ports and transport on territorial logistics. The 3 clusters are closely linked to the impact and competitiveness of the logistics sector "cluster 4".

Terms such as "globalization", "cluster", "interaction", and "transformation" suggest changing dynamics in the logistics field. These emerging aspects open up avenues for research on how globalization and geopolitical challenges, such as the situation in Ukraine or the Middle East, influence the creation and development of logistics clusters and economic growth.

The time analysis from 2019 to 2021 (Figure 8) shows a dynamic evolution of logistics research concepts and priorities. In 2019, the focus was mainly on traditional and structural themes such as competitiveness, clusters and territories. This research explores existing structures and factors influencing competitiveness. Next, emphasis is placed on logistics models and networks. In 2020, research focuses on developing new opportunities and decision-making processes. The researchers are engaged in identifying potential investment opportunities and methods of optimizing economic and logistical decisions. The end of the period under study (end of 2020 and 2021) is characterized by a data-driven approach with an increasing interest in algorithms and data analysis. Specific concepts are beginning to gain in importance, such as river transport and agricultural products.

The trend of evolution suggests the incorporation of emerging technologies such as artificial intelligence and Big Data Analytics for the optimization of logistics systems. Thus new logistic solutions and appropriate to the new trends are necessary to accompany the latest progress. Scientists are called upon to integrate new global challenges and geopolitical changes into their research concerns.

## 5.3. Outline of future analysis and research model

→ ***Outline of analysis model:***

As an extension of this study, and to better structure research trends on the dynamics of logistic clusterings, we propose the following outline analysis model (Figure 9):

*Figure 9. Prospective Research Framework on the Dynamics of Logistic Clusterings*

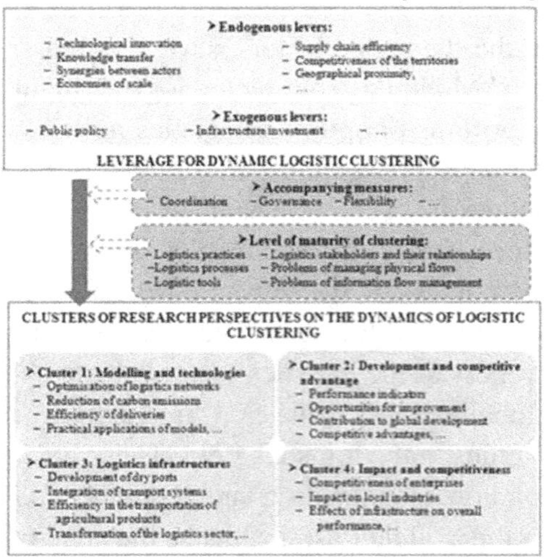


*Source: Authors*

This model of analysis relates the levers of dynamization identified in Table 1 with the research trends observed in the four clusters. It allows to explore how the different levers influence the specific dimensions of the dynamics of logistics clusters, such as technological optimization, competitive development, infrastructure improvement and overall impact on competitiveness.

This model provides a framework for systematically analyzing the relationships between the drivers of dynamism and the results observed in logistics clusters, thus allowing a more thorough understanding of the development and optimization mechanisms in this area. It allows for the construction of causal links, translated by the following assumptions and sub-assumptions:

**H1: The mobilization of endogenous levers of the cluster** (in terms of technological innovation, knowledge transfer, synergies between actors, economies of scale, logistics efficiency, competitiveness of territories, geographical proximity, ...) **promotes the dynamics of logistic clustering** (Ketels & Protsiv, 2021; Boix et al., 2015; Delgado et al., 2016; Ketels, 2013). This main assumption can be divided into four sub-assumptions:

***H1a:****The mobilization of endogenous levers of the cluster promotes the improvement of the modelling and technologies inherent to the dynamics of logistic clustering* (Porter & Heppelmann, 2017; Lazzeretti et al., 2014; Menzel & Fornahl, 2010).

***H1b:****The mobilization of the cluster's endogenous levers promotes growth of member companies and development of their competitive advantage* (Delgado et al., 2014; Hervas-Oliver & Albors-Garrigos, 2014).

***H1c:****The mobilization of the cluster's endogenous levers promotes the development of member companies' logistic infrastructures* (Liu & McKinnon, 2019; Abideen et al., 2023; Macioszek et al., 2017).

***H1d:****The mobilization of the cluster's endogenous levers promotes the amplification of its impact effect and the improvement of the competitiveness of its member operators* (Trushkina et al. 2021; Liu et al. 2022; Şekkeli & Bakan, 2021; Savić et al., 2015; Kálmán & Tóth, 2021).

**H2: The mobilization of exogenous levers of the cluster** (in terms of public policies, investments in infrastructure, ...) **promotes the dynamics of logistic clustering** (Kirova, 2024; Arvianto et al., 2021; Zhang et al., 2022). This second main hypothesis can be translated into the following sub-hypotheses:

***H2a:****The mobilization of exogenous clustering levers promotes the improvement of modelling and technologies inherent to logistic clustering dynamics* (Bektas et al., 2015; Liashenko et al., 2021).

***H2b:****Leveraging the exogenous levers of the cluster promotes growth and development of competitive advantage for member companies* (Christopoulos & Wintjes, 2023; Kumar et al., 2017; Lachgar & Moussa, 2020).

***H2c:****The mobilization of the cluster's exogenous levers promotes the development of member companies' logistic infrastructures* (Dablanc, 2023; Bachofner et al. 2022).
***H2d:****The mobilization of exogenous levers of the cluster promotes the amplification of its impact effect and the improvement of the competitiveness of its member operators* (Sheffi, 2012; Notteboom & Neyens, 2017).

**H3: The accompanying measures undertaken within the cluster** (in terms of coordination, governance, flexibility, etc.) **consolidate the effectiveness of the levers of the logistics clusterisation dynamic** (Mansouri et al., 2023; Kaci, 2023; Winkelhaus & Grosse, 2020; Fundation et al., 2018). This hypothesis is as follows:

***H3a:****The accompanying measures undertaken within the cluster consolidate the beneficial impact of endogenous levers on the dynamics of logistics clustering* (Beckers et al., 2018; Keller et al., 2015).
***H3b:****The accompanying measures undertaken within the cluster consolidate the beneficial impact of exogenous levers on the dynamics of logistics clustering* (Baydar et al., 2019; Arfi et al., 2018; Haji Ali Beigi, 2021).

**H4: The development of the maturity of the cluster** (in terms of logistics practices, logistics processes, logistics tools, logistics stakeholders and their relationships, problems with managing physical flows, problems with managing information flows,...) **consolidates the effectiveness of the levers of the logistics clustering dynamics** (Morgan et al., 2023; Sarkis, 2020). We can operationalize this assertion in the form of the following sub-assumptions:

***H4a:****The development of cluster maturity consolidates the beneficial impact of endogenous levers on the dynamics of logistics clustering* (Klauenberg et al., 2020; Gonzalez-Feliu et al., 2020).
***H4b:****The development of cluster maturity consolidates the beneficial impact of exogenous levers on the dynamics of logistics clustering* (Kaci & Amiar, 2022; Klimova et al., 2016).

The above analysis model highlights the main research trends identified in bibliometric analysis, while also highlighting some future research avenues. It should be noted that some aspects, such as sustainability and resilience, seem to be less developed in the current literature and would merit more attention.

## *Future research:*

Logistics clustering, as a geographical concentration of companies that are interdependent in the logistics sector, is changing in the face of the challenges and opportunities of the 21st century. Digitalization, emerging technologies and the imperative of sustainability are key drivers of its prospective dynamics, reshaping its contours and functioning.

Any prospective approach to the future dynamics of logistics clustering must integrate the profound transformations generated for activities, actors, interactions and the ecosystem by digitization phenomena, emerging technologies and sustainability. Indeed, digitalization is constantly transforming the logistics sector, especially through automation and artificial intelligence. These technologies help optimize supply chains, reduce operational costs and improve forecast accuracy (Davenport & Ronanki, 2018). Also, the progressive integration of emerging technologies (IoT, Blockchain, AI, ...) may facilitate real-time traceability of goods, thereby improving the transparency and efficiency of logistics processes (Xu et al., 2014), improving the security and integrity of logistics transactions, reducing the risk of fraud and increasing trust between stakeholders (Casino et al., 2019), optimize routes and inventory management, which reduces delays and costs (Wamba et al., 2020).

Logistics clusters play a crucial role in regional economic development with benefits in terms of efficiency, innovation and sustainable development (Sheffi, 2012). they generate value through the dynamization of industry, and job creation based on workers' skills and profiles (Dmuchowski, 2019). Although logistics clusters offer several new socio-economic benefits, it is important to take into account these unique characteristics, including its socioeconomic and demographic structure (Sheffi, 2013). Previous work has attempted to explore cluster growth mechanisms, economic and environmental impacts, and pathways for sustainable development (Liu et al., 2022). Future research directions should be interested in investigating the convergences between logistics clusters and their effect on the competitiveness of territories, a relationship that can be moderated by the adoption of emerging technologies and the place of sustainability (Liu et al., 2022).

Finally, sustainability has become a central pillar in the development of logistics clusters. Integrating sustainable practices contributes to reducing the carbon footprint and improving energy efficiency (McKinnon, 2018). It follows that the challenges and opportunities of sustainable logistics management (green transport, sustainable infrastructure, ...) continue to profoundly transform logistics activities (Okraszewska et al., 2019), to impose the harmonization of minimization of the environmental impact of logistics and maximization of operational efficiency (Rodrigue, 2020).

The convergence of digitalization, emerging technologies and sustainable practices is essential for the future of logistics clusters. These factors not only promote innovation and efficiency, but also address environmental, economic and social challenges.

The future of logistics clusters, and therefore their dynamics and performance, depends on the responsible commitment of all stakeholders in clustering to align process and mechanism modernization, economic viability, the environmental livability, social equity of logistics activities and the entire logistics ecosystem within the cluster.

From the above model (Figure 9), relations between these variables could be explored in greater depth, including the impact of technological innovations on economic performance and competitiveness, or the influence of public policies on territorial development and sustainability of logistics clusters.

As with all forms of territorial clustering, the dynamics of logistic clustering must be accompanied by formalization of territorial governance structures (Ehlinger et al., 2015).

This synthesis highlights the dynamic evolution of the logistics field, moving from traditional concepts to more technological and data-driven approaches, while integrating new geopolitical and environmental realities.

Future research could focus on:

- The integration of emerging technologies (AI, big data) in logistics systems optimization;
- Adaptation of logistics clusters to geopolitical and environmental challenges;
- Assessing the impact of new infrastructure on regional competitiveness;
- The development of predictive models to anticipate changes in logistics networks.

## 6. CONCLUSION AND OUTLOOK:

The logistics sector is constantly evolving, facing growing challenges related to globalization, digitalization and the increasing demand for flexibility. The organization in logistics clusters, bringing together companies and infrastructures around poles of excellence, is a strategic strategy to optimize flows and costs.

However, despite its growing importance, the understanding of the dynamics of training, evolution and impact of logistics clusters remains incomplete.

Certainly, this clustering dynamic is accompanied by another scientific research dynamic in the field of logistics and supply chain management. In reality, the existing literature has several theoretical, methodological and empirical gaps, justifying our bibliometric and prospective study as a research problem: What are the main trends, the areas under study and future directions of research on the dynamics of logistic clusters, as identified by a thorough bibliometric analysis of the literature?

This chapter provides a comprehensive overview of the research landscape on logistics clustering dynamics through a bibliometric analysis. The study identifies key trends, gaps and opportunities for future research, highlighting the importance of developing a more nuanced understanding of these complex economic ecosystems. By addressing the theoretical, methodological and empirical gaps identified in this study, researchers and practitioners can contribute to the development of effective policies and strategies for enhancing the competitiveness and sustainability of logistics clusters.

Our bibliometric analysis offers a valuable tool to map and understand the evolution of research on the logistics agglomeration. However, it is important to complement it with other methods and take into account its limitations in order to obtain a more complete and nuanced view of this complex phenomenon.

This article proposes a bibliometric analysis of the research on the dynamics of logistic agglomeration. It aims to identify research trends, key authors, influential publications and emerging themes in this area.

As a contribution to our research, the bibliometric analysis offered us a comprehensive overview of the research on logistics clusters, highlighting the challenges and opportunities for a better understanding of this crucial phenomenon for the global economy.

Indeed, the research allowed us to conduct a literature review on logistics clustering dynamics (logistics clustering dynamics), in order to identify the main dominant research themes, time trends, the main authors and journals, and the most active countries in this field. The analysis also reveals a shift in research from an initial focus on location factors and the performance of logistics clusters to a more systemic approach integrating interactions between actors and network dynamics. Finally, the results highlight the emergence of new research perspectives, such as the impact of digital technologies, sustainability and resilience on logistics groupage dynamics.

Such contributions do not exempt the study of limits, which has been limited to published academic literature, potentially excluding unpublished research or grey literature. Also, the bibliographical search covered only a limited number of databases, which may leave out relevant publications. Furthermore, the interpretation of results and identification of emerging themes is not entirely objective, it may present bias in authors' subjective judgment.

In an attempt to provide some answers to these limitations, we present promising perspectives for this research. First, we intend to further study the interactions between logistics groupage dynamics and new technologies (IoT, artificial intelligence, etc.), as well as their impact on cluster performance and sustainability. We also intend to analyse the roles of the different actors (companies, public authorities, etc.) and their strategies in the evolution of logistics groupage dynamics. We also plan to extend the analysis to other geographic regions to better understand the cultural and institutional specificities influencing these dynamics. We also aim to adopt complementary methodological approaches (case studies, surveys, etc.) to enrich bibliometric analysis.

Other future directions may also be outlined for this research, through in-depth case studies, more elaborate contextual qualitative analyses, interdisciplinary and comparative approaches, exploratory quantitative and confirmatory analyses, more developed action research or intervention research, longitudinal studies, etc.

## REFERENCES


Аранчій, В., Ганущак-Єфіменко, Л., Христенко, Л., Шкода, М., Гнатенко, І., & Фастовець, Н. (2022). Моделювання інтегральної оцінки ефективності менеджменту фінансового стану суб'єктів підприємництва. Financial and credit activity problems of theory and practice, 1(42), 259-270.

Abideen, A. Z., Sorooshian, S., Sundram, V. P. K., & Mohammed, A. (2023). Collaborative insights on horizontal logistics to integrate supply chain planning and transportation logistics planning–A systematic review and thematic mapping. *Journal of Open Innovation*, 9(2), 100066. DOI: 10.1016/j.joitmc.2023.100066

Abushaikha, I. (2018). The influence of logistics clustering on distribution capabilities: A qualitative study. *International Journal of Retail & Distribution Management*, 46(6), 577–594. DOI: 10.1108/IJRDM-01-2018-0018

Akulov, A. S., Bezotosnaya, A. D., & Pak, T. V. (2023). Algorithm of finding optimal location for distribution centers for order delivery by using unsupervised machine learning methods. *Vestnik of Astrakhan State Technical University. Series: Management, computer science and informatics, 2023*(3), 105-113. DOI: 10.24143/2072-9502-2023-3-105-113

Ambrosino, D., & Sciomachen, A. (2021). Impact of Externalities on the Design and Management of Multimodal Logistic Networks. *Sustainability (Basel)*, 13(9), 5080. DOI: 10.3390/su13095080

Amisse, S., & Muller, P. (2011). Les logiques à l'origine des dynamiques de coopération dans les clusters*: L'exemple de filières du végétal spécialisé. *Revue d'Économie Régionale et Urbaine*, (1), 115–149. DOI: 10.3917/reru.111.0115

Annas, M., & Humairoh, . (2023). The Green Food Supply Chain : Factors Affecting Food Distributor's Sustainability Through Positive WOM. [Edisi Elektronik]. *Jurnal Manajemen*, 14(2), 277–289. DOI: 10.32832/jm-uika.v14i2.11651

Antoine, S., Sillig, C., & Ghiara, H. (2017). Advanced logistics in Italy: A city network analysis. *Tijdschrift voor Economische en Sociale Geografie*, 108(6), 753–767. DOI: 10.1111/tesg.12215

Arfi, W. B., Hikkerova, L., & Sahut, J. M. (2018). External knowledge sources, green innovation and performance. *Technological Forecasting and Social Change*, 129, 210–220. DOI: 10.1016/j.techfore.2017.09.017

Arvianto, A., Sopha, B. M., Asih, A. M. S., & Imron, M. A. (2021). City logistics challenges and innovative solutions in developed and developing economies: A systematic literature review. *International Journal of Engineering Business Management*, 13, 18479790211039723. DOI: 10.1177/18479790211039723

Astvatsaturova, Ch. V., & Kazakova, N. A. (2022). Forecast of the Impact of the Railway Container Transportation Market on the GDP of the Russian Federation. *Finance: Theory and Practice*, 26(6), 6–16. DOI: 10.26794/2587-5671-2022-26-6-6-16

Bachofner, M., Lemardelé, C., Estrada, M., & Pagès, L. (2022). City logistics: Challenges and opportunities for technology providers. *Journal of Urban Mobility*, 2, 100020. DOI: 10.1016/j.urbmob.2022.100020

Baranowski, S., Busko, E., Shishlo, S., Usevich, W., Androsik, J., Mistseiko, M., Tanaś, W., & Szymanek, M. (2015). Formation mechanism of logistics cluster in Belarus. *Agriculture and Agricultural Science Procedia*, 7, 12–20. DOI: 10.1016/j.aaspro.2015.12.022

Bathelt, H., Malmberg, A., & Maskell, P. (2004). Clusters and knowledge: Local buzz, global pipelines and the process of knowledge creation. *Progress in Human Geography*, 28(1), 31–56. DOI: 10.1191/0309132504ph469oa

Baydar, A. M., Süral, H., & Çelik, M. (2019). Potential effects of logistics clusters: The case of Turkish Freight Villages. *Journal of Cleaner Production*, 233, 399–411. DOI: 10.1016/j.jclepro.2019.05.294

Beckers, J., Thomas, I., Vanoutrive, T., & Verhetsel, A. (2018). Logistics clusters, including inter-firm relations through community detection. *European Journal of Transport and Infrastructure Research*, 18(2). Advance online publication. DOI: 10.18757/EJTIR.2018.18.2.3229

Behmanesh, E., & Pannek, J. (2016). A memetic algorithm with extended random path encoding for a closed-loop supply chain model with flexible delivery. *Logistics Research*, 9(1), 22. DOI: 10.1007/s12159-016-0150-y

Bektas, T., Crainic, T. G., & Van Woensel, T. (2015). From managing urban freight to smart city logistics networks.

Belussi, F., & Hervas-Oliver, J. L. (Eds.). (2017). *Unfolding cluster evolution*. Routledge.

Benbba, B. (2016). Les Cluster Supply Chains: Une nouvelle piste pour améliorer l'agilité des chaînes logistiques. *Revue Marocaine de Management, Logistique et Transport*, (1).

Benoit, S. (2024). Ancrage industriel en bioéconomie: quel rôle joue la gouvernance logistique?. *Les Cahiers Scientifiques du Transport-Scientific Papers in Transportation, 78.*

Boix, R., Hervás-Oliver, J. L., & De Miguel-Molina, B. (2015). Micro-geographies of creative industries clusters in Europe: From hot spots to assemblages. *Papers in Regional Science*, 94(4), 753–773. DOI: 10.1111/pirs.12094

Brouer, B. D., Alvarez, J. F., Plum, C. E. M., Pisinger, D., & Sigurd, M. M. (2014). A Base Integer Programming Model and Benchmark Suite for Liner-Shipping Network Design. *Transportation Science*, 48(2), 281–312. DOI: 10.1287/trsc.2013.0471

Casino, F., Dasaklis, T. K., & Patsakis, C. (2019). A systematic literature review of blockchain-based applications: Current status, classification and open issues. *Telematics and Informatics*, 36, 55–81. DOI: 10.1016/j.tele.2018.11.006

Chhetri, P., Butcher, T., & Corbitt, B. (2014). Characterising spatial logistics employment clusters. *International Journal of Physical Distribution & Logistics Management*, 44(3), 221–241. DOI: 10.1108/IJPDLM-03-2012-0086

Christopoulos, G., & Wintjes, R. (2023). Identifying Clusters as Local Innovation Systems. *Journal of the Knowledge Economy*, •••, 1–40.

Cooke, P. (2008). Regional innovation systems, clean technology & Jacobian cluster-platform policies. *Regional Science Policy & Practice*, 1(1), 23–45. DOI: 10.1111/j.1757-7802.2008.00002.x

D'Amico, G., Szopik-Depczyńska, K., Dembińska, I., & Ioppolo, G. (2021). Smart and sustainable logistics of Port cities: A framework for comprehending enabling factors, domains and goals. *Sustainable Cities and Society*, 69, 102801. DOI: 10.1016/j.scs.2021.102801

Da Xu, L., He, W., & Li, S. (2014). Internet of things in industries: A survey. *IEEE Transactions on Industrial Informatics*, 10(4), 2233–2243. DOI: 10.1109/TII.2014.2300753

Dablanc, L. (2023). Policy and planning for urban logistics. In *The Routledge handbook of urban logistics* (pp. 251–266). Routledge. DOI: 10.4324/9781003241478-23

Davenport, T. H., & Ronanki, R. (2018). Artificial intelligence for the real world. *Harvard Business Review*, 96(1), 108–116.

Davydovich, A., Karamova, A., Fesenko, O., & Anisimova, N. (2020). Transport and logistics infrastructure of the Krasnodar Krai : Problems and solutions. *E3S Web of Conferences, 164*, 07007. DOI: 10.1051/e3sconf/202016407007

Delgado, M., Porter, M. E., & Stern, S. (2014). Clusters, convergence, and economic performance. *Research Policy*, 43(10), 1785–1799. DOI: 10.1016/j.respol.2014.05.007

Delgado, M., Porter, M. E., & Stern, S. (2016). Defining clusters of related industries. *Journal of Economic Geography*, 16(1), 1–38. DOI: 10.1093/jeg/lbv017

Dhonde, B., & Patel, C. R. (2021). Assessing The Impacts Of City Sprawl On Urban Freight Transport In Developing Countries. *Architecture and Engineering*, 6(2), 52–62. DOI: 10.23968/2500-0055-2021-6-2-52-62

Dmuchowski, R. (2019). The CONcept Of Logistics Clusters And Efficiency Of Economic Enterprises. *Journal Of European Economy*, 18(3), 351–361. DOI: 10.35774/jee2019.03.351

Donthu, N., Kumar, S., Mukherjee, D., Pandey, N., & Lim, W. M. (2021). How to conduct a bibliometric analysis : An overview and guidelines. *Journal of Business Research*, 133, 285–296. DOI: 10.1016/j.jbusres.2021.04.070

Dubinina, N. A. (2017). LOGIstics Management As A Factor Increasing Competitive Positions Of Shipbuilding Enterprises Entering The Shipbuilding Cluster Of The Astrakhan Region. *Vestnik of Astrakhan State Technical University*, 104-113. DOI: 10.24143/1812-9498-2017-1-104-113

Ehlinger, S., Perret, V. & Chabaud, D. (2015). Quelle gouvernance pour les réseaux territorialisés d'organisations ?. *Revue française de gestion*, 253, 369-386. DOI: 10.3166/RFG.170.155-171

Fundation, E. U. L. A. C., Paton, J., Bercovich, N., & Barroeta, B. (2018). *Clusters and Cluster Policy: Opportunities for collaboration between the European Union (EU), Latin America and the Caribbean*. LAC.

Gonzalez-Feliu, J., Chong, M., Vargas-Florez, J., de Brito Jr, I., Osorio-Ramirez, C., Piatyszek, E., & Quiliche Altamirano, R. (2020). The maturity of humanitarian logistics against recurrent crises. *Social Sciences (Basel, Switzerland)*, 9(6), 90. DOI: 10.3390/socsci9060090

Govindan, K., & Gholizadeh, H. (2021). Robust network design for sustainable-resilient reverse logistics network using big data : A case study of end-of-life vehicles. *Transportation Research Part E, Logistics and Transportation Review*, 149, 102279. DOI: 10.1016/j.tre.2021.102279

Gritsenko, S. (2020). Marketing aspects to investment attractiveness of diversified enterprises of aviation transport and logistic clusters. *Economics. Ecology.Socium*, 4(1), 53–61. DOI: 10.31520/2616-7107/2020.4.1-6

Haji Ali Beigi, M. (2021). *External knowledge diversity, competition intensity and innovation performance in logistics: Implications for less versus more innovative industries* (No. 157). Ilmenau Economics Discussion Papers.

Han, H. (2019). A review and a model for logistics clusters. *International Journal of Logistics Systems and Management*, 33(1), 73–96. DOI: 10.1504/IJLSM.2019.099662

Han, J.-H., Kim, J.-Y., Kim, J.-H., & Jeong, S.-J. (2012). A case study on algorithm development and software materialization for logistics optimization. *Journal of the Korea Safety Management and Science*, 14(4), 153–168. DOI: 10.12812/ksms.2012.14.4.153

Havenga, J. H., & De Bod, A. (2016). Freight corridor performance measurement system : A framework for South Africa. *Journal of Transport and Supply Chain Management*, 10(1). Advance online publication. DOI: 10.4102/jtscm.v10i1.252

He, M., Shen, J., Wu, X., & Luo, J. (2018). Logistics space: A literature review from the sustainability perspective. *Sustainability (Basel)*, 10(8), 2815. DOI: 10.3390/su10082815

Helal Alnuaimi, S., Mohammed Alneyadi, M., Fadel, M., Ali Alrashdi, A., Ali Alneyadi, B., S. A. Khalifa, G., & Farhan, A. (2022). An Exploratory Study of Retailers' Operational Performance within UAE Market : A Case Study. *BOHR International Journal of Operations Management Research and Practices, 1*(1), 34-44. DOI: 10.54646/bijomrp.005

Hervas-Oliver, J. L., & Albors-Garrigos, J. (2014). Are technology gatekeepers renewing clusters? Understanding gatekeepers and their dynamics across cluster life cycles. *Entrepreneurship and Regional Development*, 26(5-6), 431–452. DOI: 10.1080/08985626.2014.933489

Hrynchak, N. (2020). Differentiating the Level of Territorial Development of the Transport and Logistics Infrastructure in Ukraine by Adapting the Cluster Analysis Methodology. *Науковий вісник Національної академії статистики, обліку та аудиту, 1-2*, 6-16. DOI: 10.31767/nasoa.1-2.2020.01

Hylton, P. J., & Ross, C. L. (2018). Agglomeration economies' influence on logistics clusters' growth and competitiveness. *Regional Studies*, 52(3), 350–361. DOI: 10.1080/00343404.2017.1327708

Ilyas, M., Jin, Z., & Ullah, I. (2024). Optimizing Logistics and Transportation Locations in the China–Pakistan Economic Corridor : A Strategic Risk Assessment. *Applied Sciences (Basel, Switzerland)*, 14(5), 1738. DOI: 10.3390/app14051738

Kaci, A. (2023). *Attractivité et dynamiques territoriales: analyse des conditions de la mise en place du cluster de boissons agro-logistique dans la wilaya de Bejaia* (Doctoral dissertation, UNIVERSITE MOULOUD MAMMERI DE TIZI-OUZOU).

Kaci, A., & Amiar, L. (2022). Analyse Des Conditions Territoriales De La Mise En Place D'un Cluster De Boisson Agrologistique: Comme Outil D'attractivité Territoriale Dans La Wilaya De Bejaia". In *Revue Forum D'études Et De Recherches Economiques, S* (Vol. 6, No. 1, pp. 702-720).

Kálmán, B., & Tóth, A. (2021). Links between the economy competitiveness and logistics performance in the Visegrád Group countries: Empirical evidence for the years 2007-2018. *Entrepreneurial Business and Economics Review*, 9(3), 169–190. DOI: 10.15678/EBER.2021.090311

Keller, J., Markmann, C., & von der Gracht, H. A. (2015). Foresight support systems to facilitate regional innovations: A conceptualization case for a German logistics cluster. *Technological Forecasting and Social Change*, 97, 15–28. DOI: 10.1016/j.techfore.2013.12.031

Ketels, C. (2013). Recent research on competitiveness and clusters: What are the implications for regional policy? *Cambridge Journal of Regions, Economy and Society*, 6(2), 269–284. DOI: 10.1093/cjres/rst008

Ketels, C., & Protsiv, S. (2021). Cluster presence and economic performance: A new look based on European data. *Regional Studies*, 55(2), 208–220. DOI: 10.1080/00343404.2020.1792435

Kirova, A. (2024). LOGISTics Clusters And Their Potential For Economic Development. *MEST Journal, 12*(1).

Klauenberg, J., Elsner, L. A., & Knischewski, C. (2020). Dynamics of the spatial distribution of hubs in groupage networks–The case of Berlin. *Journal of Transport Geography*, 88, 102280. DOI: 10.1016/j.jtrangeo.2018.07.004

Klimova, N., Kozyrev, O., & Babkin, E. (2016). *Innovation in Clusters*. Springer International Publishing. DOI: 10.1007/978-3-319-21109-1

Kumar, I., Zhalnin, A., Kim, A., & Beaulieu, L. J. (2017). Transportation and logistics cluster competitive advantages in the US regions: A cross-sectional and spatio-temporal analysis. *Research in Transportation Economics*, 61, 25–36. DOI: 10.1016/j.retrec.2016.07.028

Lachgar, T. N., & Moussa, M. B. (2020). Innovation produit et performance commerciale des entreprises membres des clusters dans le contexte marocain. *Revue de Publicité et de Communication Marketing*, 1(2).

Lakhmetkina, N., Poliak, M., & Oleinikov, A. (2019). INFRASTRUCTURE DEVELOPMENT OF INTERNATIONAL IMPORTANCE FOR THE MODERN TRANSPORT SYSTEM. *The Archives of Automotive Engineering – Archiwum Motoryzacji, 84*(2), 103-116. DOI: 10.14669/AM.VOL84.ART8

Lazzeretti, L., Sedita, S. R., & Caloffi, A. (2014). Founders and disseminators of cluster research. *Journal of Economic Geography*, 14(1), 21–43. DOI: 10.1093/jeg/lbs053

Leydesdorff, L., Bornmann, L., & Wagner, C. S. (2019). The relative influences of government funding and international collaboration on citation impact. *Journal of the Association for Information Science and Technology*, 70(2), 198–201. DOI: 10.1002/asi.24109 PMID: 32728598

Liashenko, V., Ivanov, S., & Trushkina, N. (2021). A Conceptual Approach to Forming a Transport and Logistics Cluster as a Component of the Region's Innovative Infrastructure (on the Example of Prydniprovsky Economic Region of Ukraine). *Virtual Economics*, 4(1), 19–53. DOI: 10.34021/ve.2021.04.01(2)

Linnenluecke, M. K., Marrone, M., & Singh, A. K. (2020). Conducting systematic literature reviews and bibliometric analyses. *Australian Journal of Management*, 45(2), 175–194. DOI: 10.1177/0312896219877678

Liu, L., Lee, L. S., Seow, H.-V., & Chen, C. Y. (2022). Logistics Center Location-Inventory-Routing Problem Optimization : A Systematic Review Using PRISMA Method. *Sustainability (Basel)*, 14(23), 15853. DOI: 10.3390/su142315853

Liu, S., He, N., Cao, X., Li, G., & Jian, M. (2022). Logistics cluster and its future development: A comprehensive research review. *Transportation Research Part E, Logistics and Transportation Review*, 168, 102974. DOI: 10.1016/j.tre.2022.102974

Liu, X., & McKinnon, A. C. (2019). Practical relevance of theory-driven supply chain management research: Evidence from China. *International Journal of Logistics Management*, 30(1), 76–95. DOI: 10.1108/IJLM-12-2017-0337

Macioszek, E., Staniek, M., & Sierpiński, G. (2017). Analysis of trends in development of freight transport logistics using the example of Silesian Province (Poland)- a case study. *Transportation Research Procedia*, 27, 388–395. DOI: 10.1016/j.trpro.2017.12.026

Mangan, J., & Lalwani, C. (2016). *Global logistics and supply chain management.* John Wiley & Sons.

Mansouri, B., Sahu, S., & Ülkü, M. A. (2023). Toward greening city logistics: A systematic review on corporate governance and social responsibility in managing urban distribution centers. *Logistics (Basel)*, 7(1), 19. DOI: 10.3390/logistics7010019

Martín-Martín, A., Thelwall, M., Orduna-Malea, E., & Delgado López-Cózar, E. (2021). Google Scholar, Microsoft Academic, Scopus, Dimensions, Web of Science, and OpenCitations' COCI : A multidisciplinary comparison of coverage via citations. *Scientometrics*, 126(1), 871–906. DOI: 10.1007/s11192-020-03690-4 PMID: 32981987

Mateo, S. (2020). Procédure pour conduire avec succès une revue de littérature selon la méthode PRISMA. *Kinésithérapie, la Revue*, 20(226), 29–37. DOI: 10.1016/j.kine.2020.05.019

McKinnon, A. (2018). *Decarbonizing logistics: Distributing goods in a low carbon world*. Kogan Page Publishers.

Menzel, M. P., & Fornahl, D. (2010). Cluster life cycles—Dimensions and rationales of cluster evolution. *Industrial and Corporate Change*, 19(1), 205–238. DOI: 10.1093/icc/dtp036

Morgan, T., Tarpey, R., & Fergurson, J. R. (2023). Antecedents to logistic clustering. *International Journal of Logistics Economics and Globalisation*, 10(3), 274–288. DOI: 10.1504/IJLEG.2023.135461

Notteboom, T., & Neyens, K. (2017). The future of port logistics: meeting the challenges of supply chain integration. *Bruselas: ING Bannk.*

Okraszewska, R., Jamroz, K., Michalski, L., Żukowska, J., Grzelec, K., & Birr, K. (2019). Analysing ways to achieve a new Urban Agenda-based sustainable metropolitan transport. *Sustainability (Basel)*, 11(3), 813. DOI: 10.3390/su11030813

Page, M. J., McKenzie, J. E., Bossuyt, P. M., Boutron, I., Hoffmann, T. C., Mulrow, C. D., Shamseer, L., Tetzlaff, J. M., Akl, E. A., & Brennan, S. E. (2021). The PRISMA 2020 statement : An updated guideline for reporting systematic reviews. *BMJ (Clinical Research Ed.)*, 372, •••. https://www.bmj.com/content/372/bmj.n71 .short PMID: 33782057

Palacio, A., Adenso-Díaz, B., & Lozano, S. (2017). Analysing the factors that influence the Pareto frontier of a bi-objective supply chain design problem. *International Transactions in Operational Research*, 25(6), 1717–1738. DOI: 10.1111/itor.12493

Pan, S., Zhou, W., Piramuthu, S., Giannikas, V., & Chen, C. (2021). Smart city for sustainable urban freight logistics. *International Journal of Production Research*, 59(7), 2079–2089. DOI: 10.1080/00207543.2021.1893970

Park, N.-K., & Choi, W.-Y. (2014). The Network Design of China's Northeast Cold Chain. *Susan Haeyang Gyoyuk Yeon-Gu*, 26(4), 760–768. DOI: 10.13000/JFMSE.2014.26.4.760

Porter, M. E. (1998). *No. 6* (Vol. 76). Clusters and the new economics of competition. Harvard Business Review.

Porter, M. E., & Heppelmann, J. E. (2017). Why every organization needs an augmented reality strategy. *HBR'S 10 MUST, 85*, 2-18.

Radhoui, H., & Baron, M. L. (2022). Ouverture géographique ou enfermement des clusters logistiques du corridor de la Seine? *Logistique & Management*, 30(2-3), 87–101. DOI: 10.1080/12507970.2022.2089248

Raimbault, N. (2019). From regional planning to port regionalization and urban logistics. The inland port and the governance of logistics development in the Paris region. *Journal of Transport Geography*, 78, 205–213. DOI: 10.1016/j.jtrangeo.2019.06.005

Ran, H. (2022). THe Enterprise's International Competitiveness Management Design Development Under The Logistics Paradigm. *Economic scope*. DOI: 10.32782/2224-6282/180-25

Rinkinen, S. (2016). Clusters, innovation systems and ecosystems-Studies on innovation policy's concept evolution and approaches for regional renewal.

Rivera, L., Gligor, D., & Sheffi, Y. (2016). The benefits of logistics clustering. *International Journal of Physical Distribution & Logistics Management*, 46(3), 242–268. DOI: 10.1108/IJPDLM-10-2014-0243

Rivera, L., Sheffi, Y., & Knoppen, D. (2016). Logistics clusters: The impact of further agglomeration, training and firm size on collaboration and value added services. *International Journal of Production Economics*, 179, 285–294. DOI: 10.1016/j.ijpe.2016.05.018

Rivera, L., Sheffi, Y., & Welsch, R. (2014). Logistics agglomeration in the US. *Transportation Research Part A, Policy and Practice*, 59, 222–238. DOI: 10.1016/j.tra.2013.11.009

Rodrigue, J. P. (2020). *The geography of transport systems*. Routledge. DOI: 10.4324/9780429346323

Sarkis, J. (2020). Supply chain sustainability: Learning from the COVID-19 pandemic. *International Journal of Operations & Production Management*, 41(1), 63–73. DOI: 10.1108/IJOPM-08-2020-0568

Savić, N., Džunić, M., & Brkić, I. (2015). Comparative analysis of clusters contribution to regional competitiveness. *Ekonomika preduzeća, 63*(3-4), 222-232.

Savin, G. V. (2021). The smart city transport and logistics system: Theory, methodology and practice. *Upravlenec, 12*(6).

Şekkeli, Z. H., & Bakan, İ. (2021). Regional benefits of logistic clusters: A study of scale development. *OPUS International Journal of Society Researches*, 18(43), 6143–6161.

Sheffi, Y. (2012). Logistics-intensive clusters: global competitiveness and regional growth. In *Handbook of global logistics: transportation in international supply chains* (pp. 463–500). Springer New York.

Sheffi, Y. (2012). *Logistics clusters: delivering value and driving growth.* MIT press.

Sheffi, Y. (2013). Logistics-Intensive Clusters : Global Competitiveness and Regional Growth. In Bookbinder, J. H. (Ed.), *Handbook of Global Logistics* (Vol. 181, pp. 463–500). Springer New York., DOI: 10.1007/978-1-4419-6132-7_19

Shen, W., Wang, J., & Li, T. (2012). Factor Analysis of the Northeast Economic Zone's Logistics Competition. *Physics Procedia*, 24, 906–911. DOI: 10.1016/j.phpro.2012.02.136

Singh, A. (2020). Modelling the impact of port-centric logistics cluster on inter-firm competition. *Unpublished PhD thesis, RMIT University, Melbourne.*

Smirnova, E., Hajiyev, N., Glazkova, I., & Hajiyeva, A. (2024). Production companies : Evaluation of accessibility and efficiency of transportation and manufacturing processes. *The Asian Journal of Shipping and Logistics*, 40(1), 52–60. DOI: 10.1016/j.ajsl.2024.01.002

Storper, M. (2013). *Keys to the city: How economics, institutions, social interaction, and politics shape development.* Princeton University Press.

Sun, B., Li, H., & Zhao, Q. (2018). Logistics agglomeration and logistics productivity in the USA. *The Annals of Regional Science*, 61(2), 273–293. DOI: 10.1007/s00168-018-0867-4

Swanson, D., Goel, L., Francisco, K., & Stock, J. (2018). An analysis of supply chain management research bytopic. *Supply Chain Management*, 23(2), 100–116. DOI: 10.1108/SCM-05-2017-0166

Tadayonrad, Y., & Ndiaye, A. B. (2023). A new key performance indicator model for demand forecasting in inventory management considering supply chain reliability and seasonality. *Supply Chain Analytics*, 3, 100026. DOI: 10.1016/j.sca.2023.100026

Trushkina, N., Dzwigol, H., & Kwilinski, A. (2021). Cluster model of organizing logistics in the region (on the example of the economic district «Podillya»). *Journal of European Economy*, 20(1), 127–145. DOI: 10.35774/jee2021.01.127

Van Den Heuvel, F. P., De Langen, P. W., van Donselaar, K. H., & Fransoo, J. C. (2013). Spatial concentration and location dynamics in logistics: The case of a Dutch province. *Journal of Transport Geography*, 28, 39–48. DOI: 10.1016/j.jtrangeo.2012.10.001

Van Eck, N., & Waltman, L. (2010). Software survey : VOSviewer, a computer program for bibliometric mapping. *scientometrics, 84*(2), 523-538.

Waldheim, C., & Berger, A. (2008). Logistics landscape. *Landscape Journal*, 27(2), 219–246. DOI: 10.3368/lj.27.2.219

Wamba, S. F., Akter, S., Edwards, A., Chopin, G., & Gnanzou, D. (2015). How 'big data'can make big impact: Findings from a systematic review and a longitudinal case study. *International Journal of Production Economics*, 165, 234–246. DOI: 10.1016/j.ijpe.2014.12.031

Wang, D., Zhou, L., Zhang, H., & Liang, X. (2021). A Bi-Level Model for Green Freight Transportation Pricing Strategy Considering Enterprise Profit and Carbon Emissions. *Sustainability (Basel)*, 13(12), 6514. DOI: 10.3390/su13126514

Winkelhaus, S., & Grosse, E. H. (2020). Logistics 4.0: A systematic review towards a new logistics system. *International Journal of Production Research*, 58(1), 18–43. DOI: 10.1080/00207543.2019.1612964

Wodnicka, M., & Szukalski, S. M. (2023). Investments in the Industrial and Logistics Real Estate Sector in Poland Compared to the CEE Countries. *Optimum.Economic Studies*, 3(113), 116–136. DOI: 10.15290/oes.2023.03.113.07

Zhang, H., Lv, Y., & Guo, J. (2022). New Development Direction of Underground Logistics from the Perspective of Public Transport: A Systematic Review Based on Scientometrics. *Sustainability (Basel)*, 14(6), 3179. DOI: 10.3390/su14063179

## KEY TERMS AND DEFINITIONS

**Bibliometric Analysis:** It is a data and publication metrics-based method for evaluating academic literature in terms of publications and citations from authors, organizations and countries as well as collaborations and contributions in a specific field.

**Cluster:** It is a geographical concentration of organizations and institutions in the same field to increase productivity, innovation, and competitiveness through collaboration and sharing resources.

**Green Logistics:** This is the set of logistics practices aimed at reducing environmental impacts through responsible and sustainable actions.

**Logistic 4.0:** It is the integration of emerging technologies to optimize logistics processes and improve decision-making.

**Logistic Cluster:** It is the geographical concentration of logistics organizations interconnected to improve the efficiency and competitiveness of supply chain operations.

**PRISMA Protocol:** It is a systematic approach used to guide the identification, selection and inclusion of studies in the literature review while ensuring transparency and reproducibility.

**Reverse Logistics:** It is a process that aims to manage waste and recycling to maximize value and minimize environmental impact.

**Sypply Chain:** It is a network of organizations, people, activities and resources mobilized to produce and deliver a good or service to customers.

# Chapter 6
# Artificial Intelligence and the Effectiveness of Territorial E-Governance:
## An Exploration Through the Case of the Amman Region in Jordan

**Sana Ben Ghodbane**
*IHEC Carthage, University of Carthage, Tunisia & ESCT, University of Manouba, Tunisia*

**Maha Kareem Atyieh Abuyabes**
*Faculty of Amman University, College For Financial and Managerial Science, Al Balqa Applied University, Amman, Jordan & ESCT, University of Manouba, Tunisia*

## ABSTRACT

*This study examines the impact of Artificial intelligence and the effectiveness of territorial E-governance. The objects are to explore the implicit benefits of artificial intelligence in Amman's governance, assess its impact on decision- making processes.The study sample consists of government ministries in Amman's public sector, which includes 40 governmental entities enforcing AI systems. The methodology covers a five- time period from 2018 to 2023, and relies on primary data sources, including sanctioned government reports and stoner satisfaction checks, to dissect the relinquishment and operation of artificial intelligence. The research findings illustrate that the use of E-governance supported by artificial intelligence technologies in the Amman's public sector has led to tangible improvements in user satisfaction and service delivery effectiveness. It has also contributed to enhancing efficiency, transparency, reducing bureaucratic processes, and improving prediction*

DOI: 10.4018/979-8-3693-6854-1.ch006

*and planning, reflecting a positive and tangible impact on Amman's E-governance development.*

## 1. GENERAL INTRODUCTION

Good governance and governance, in particular, are gaining further and further elevation in the converse on development and governance. It encompasses both the decision- timber and the perpetration processes. The political system, resource operation, and the capacity of the government to produce and apply programs are the three confines of governance that the World Bank has honored. Mortal rights, the republic, and the rule of law are the top priorities of good government, according to former UN Secretary General Kofi Annan. Nonetheless, creating effective governance is a challenge for all categories of government. ASE governance is the use of information and communication technology (ICT) to enhance openness and responsibility. It is generally accepted that it is necessary to raise the standard and effectiveness of governance. (Verma & Bala, 2018)

E-government, or E-Gov, is essential for updating public administration and promoting sustainable development through technological integration. It uses communication technology to improve citizen involvement with government agencies and expedite service delivery to a variety of sectors. But the development of E-Gov is rife with discrete phases, each with its own set of difficulties. Despite attempts, resource limitations, digital inequality, and security concerns prevent many developing nations from fully realizing the promised advantages of E-government. This issue is demonstrated by Amman's 1999 E-Gov effort, whose goals have not been fully achieved, as seen by the country's falling UN rankings. Securing E-Gov is hampered by inadequate infrastructure, limited knowledge, and legal obstacles. Research emphasizes how important IT infrastructure is to the successful adoption of E-Gov, as it affects information quality, consumption trends, and organizational effectiveness. Improving E-Gov results depends on removing these technological obstacles, which necessitates in-depth research to identify and reduce supply-side issues in developing countries (Al-Rawahna et al., 2019).

The word "artificial intelligence" (AI) refers to a broad order of machine capacities that emulate mortal cognitive functions. Machines still find it gruelling to replicate the inflexibility of the mortal mind, indeed with significant earnings in processing power, particularly in situations requiring tough decision-making. Jordan unveiled an AI policy in December 2020 with the goal of advancing AI development and integration, emphasizing cooperation, and conforming to transnational governance trends. Establishing fabrics for AI exploration, development, and operation is the goal of this plan, which also places a focus on perfecting skill development and public-private collaborations. There are still challenges in successfully incorporating AI into governance systems, even with encouraging advancements. Protesting these obstacles and implementing AI in Amman's public sector decision-making process could have an impact on future efficacy and effectiveness. While developed methodologies demonstrate the potential of AI in specific fields, obstacles pertaining to organizational alignment, labor preparedness, and error correction still exist. Maximising benefits while minimizing problems necessitates understanding the art of AI relinquishment, aligning with business objectives, and bridging the gap between mortal and AI decision-making processes. Amman's AI plan represents a significant step forward in using AI for governance, invention, sustainable growth, and inclusive development. (Alqudah, 2021)

The goal of this study is to investigate the potential advantages of artificial intelligence in Amman governance and assess its impact on it. Furthermore, it aims to address the difficulties and potential hazards associated with the integration of artificial intelligence technologies into governance. In addition, the research will evaluate the impact of artificial intelligence on decision-making procedures and investigate methods to improve efficacy and efficiency by applying AI approaches to Amman governance. Furthermore, the research aims to foster public acceptance and trust in artificial intelligence as it relates to governance.

For a number of reasons, this study on the application of E-governance and artificial intelligence in Amman is very interesting. First off, these technologies are regarded as essential instruments for raising performance and efficiency in the public and private domains, which raises the efficacy of services rendered to citizens and promotes sustainable development. Furthermore, E-governance and artificial intelligence are being used as strategic steps in updating and developing the infrastructure of governmental systems, which decreases corruption and increases accountability and transparency. Additionally, this study offers a chance to improve cooperation between the public and private sectors in creating cutting-edge technological solutions that better meet the needs of the community. Last but not least, Jordan's interest in utilizing contemporary technology sustainably and investing in it demonstrates its dedication to innovation.

## 2. CONCEPTUAL FRAMEWORK

### 2.1. An overview of artificial intelligence

Artificial intelligence (AI) spans multiple computer wisdom fields with the goal of emulating mortal intelligence in machines. Machine literacy (ML), a subset of AI, utilizes statistical methods to produce intelligent systems that can autonomously learn and ameliorate their performance without unequivocal programming. Deep literacy (DL), an advanced ML system, has shown remarkable proficiency in tasks similar to computer vision and natural language processing, thanks to its complete point birth and pattern recognition. (Sheng et al., 2022). Georgia has been laboriously integrating modern technologies to enhance itsE-governance, fastening on G2C(Government- to- Citizen), G2B(Government- to- Business), and G2G (Government- to- Government) relations. The nation has rolled out multitudinous state digital services and enforced blockchain and artificial intelligence (AI) systems to boost the effectiveness of its state agencies. Still, the effectiveness of these technologies remains under scrutiny. Overall, Georgia's relinquishment of AI across colorful sectors illustrates its commitment to using technology to ameliorate state functions and services. The perpetration of these systems aims to enhance effectiveness, security, and the quality of public services, though ongoing evaluation is necessary to determine their overall effectiveness.) Napetvaridze, 2022)

In fact, Artificial intelligence has its origins in the long-ago attempts to understand intelligence, which date back to our earliest ancestors. Greek mythology represents humanity's unrelenting pursuit of knowledge despite its risks, most exemplified by Prometheus's theft of fire and intelligence from the gods. The early Asian societies were equally preoccupied with deep questions about life and knowledge. Mary Shelley's "Frankenstein" laid the foundation for contemporary fears about artificial intelligence by fusing scientific discoveries with antiquated fears. AI's foundations were laid by pioneers like Aristotle, Descartes, and Turing with their theories on form, mind, and computing. The foundations of formal logic and mathematics were established by Boole, Russell, and Frege. The Church-Turing thesis examined the relationship between the brain and computers, while early neural network models synthesized concepts of computation. With methodologies ranging from expert systems to neural networks, AI had periods of both optimism and skepticism throughout the 20th century. The preface of the World Wide Web in 1989 and the internet in 1984 significantly expanded AI operations. By themid-1990s, artificial intelligence (AI) technologies were being used in a variety of fields, similar as natural language processing, web hunt, and driverless buses. Modern AI research blends soft computing technologies with logic-based systems, giving priority to multidisciplinary approaches. Nouvelle AI guides ongoing research into agent design, communication, and organization by conceptualizing intelligence as emergent behavior resulting from interactions among autonomous agents. Despite obstacles, artificial intelligence is steadily developing and has a significant impact on how society and technology develop. (Oliveira, 2019).

## 2.2 The concept and definition of E-governance

Information and communication technology (ICT) is used in E-governance to enable governance professionals and ensure citizen effectiveness through increased cost-effectiveness, efficiency, and transparency. In the past, communications between the public and the government were limited to actual government buildings. However, the rise of ICT has made it possible to establish service centers closer to customers. These can take the form of conveniently positioned service kiosks, unattended kiosks within government buildings, or personal computers at home or in offices. In many countries, filling out forms to print and mail is currently the main component of E-government, in addition to searching websites for information. But its potential goes far beyond these uses, opening the door to a greater variety of services down the road. Making the distinction between E-government and E-governence is essential. Despite their frequent interchangeability, they have a few slight differences. While E-government concentrates on providing the public with government services online, E-Governance covers a wider range of activities, such as the various ICT-facilitated processes and structures. ICTs are used by E-Government, according to Gartner Consulting, to enhance government operations and service delivery. This distinction highlights the diverse functions of ICT in modern government (Bala & Verma, 2018).

The generality of E-governance has evolved significantly since the late 20th century, driven by rapid-fire- fire advancements in information and communication technologies (ICTs). Firstly, E-governance began as a system for propagating information. Over time, it transitioned to encompass online operations and ultimately evolved into a participatory frame designed to engage citizens in governance processes. This progression reflects its origins in public administration reform and its development into a pivotal medium for enhancing executive services, stoner satisfaction, and popular engagement.

Historically, there has been confusion between the terms E-governance and E-government. While both are related to the use of technology in government, they represent different generalities. E-government focuses on the operation of technology to streamline government operations and ameliorate service delivery. Despite their parallels, E-governance encompasses a broader perspective that includes the structural and procedural aspects of governance supported by ICT.

Since the 1990s, the relinquishment of ICTs has been a driving force behind the development of E-government, which latterly led to a deeper disquisition of E-governance. In fact, E-governance goes beyond the bare operation of technology. It involves the integration of ICT to support good governance, enhance translucency, responsibility, and effectiveness, and grease the creation of public value aligned with socio- profitable and experimental programs. This holistic approach emphasizes the metamorphosis of governance through digital connections that strengthen being connections and produce new hookups within society. Geographically, the development of E-governance has varied. In the United States, the E-Government Act of 2002 and the launch of usa.gov marked significant way towards digital metamorphosis. The U.S. government has abused technological advancements to contemporize operations, with a focus on systems connection and the development of specific services like one- stop shops. The Office of Management and Budget oversees these enterprises, aiming to completely exploit technological eventuality to ameliorate government functions.

In the European Union, E-governance has evolved from a focus on modernization and access to include themes like translucency, effectiveness, and dimension. The European Commission's "European E-Government Action Plan" 2011- 2015 has been necessary in transitioning from E-government to more advanced E-governance fabrics. This plan underscores the significance of governance metamorphosis eased by digital technologies.

In Africa, E-governance presents openings for original governments to introduce and ameliorate executive processes. Misuraca argues that E-governance can help original authorities in Africa resuscitate themselves by integrating ICT into administration. This is apparent in West Africa, where administrations are espousing ICT- grounded mechanisms to enhance information rotation, ameliorate administration- citizen connections, and offer online services that promote citizen involvement in decision- timber.

Arising and developing countries, particularly in Southeast Asia and India, have also embraced E-governance. Basu's examination highlights the legal and infrastructural challenges faced by these nations in developing nonsupervisory fabrics for E-governance. In India and Southeast Asia, there's an active drive towards E-governance and ICT development, although it's frequently seen as an outgrowth of E-government rather than a distinct conception. The focus is on adding political participation and fostering links with non-governmental stakeholders.

In Morocco, the" Digital Morocco Plan" (2013) and the" Digital Morocco Strategy"(2020) represent the country's early way towards E-governance. Many recent studies indicate that Morocco's approach involves a reciprocal improvement of digital and traditional administration. The strategy emphasizes diversifying services and investing in territorial propinquity to polarize decision- timber and support successful E-governance.

Eventually, the elaboration of E-governance in Asia, as anatomized by Ojo et al., underscores the significance of indigenous competitiveness andintra-regional performance. The study highlights how indigenous factors impact the quality of governance through active citizen involvement and effective executive processes.

A top-down indigenous approach facilitates knowledge sharing and cooperative conduct within communities of interest.

In summary, E-governance has evolved from an introductory tool for information dispersion to a complex frame that integrates ICT to enhance governance processes, ameliorate public services, and foster popular engagement. Its development varies across regions, reflecting different stages of technological relinquishment and governance reforms. (Khouya, 2023)

## 2.3 Basic Theories in Support of E-governance

As society evolved, E-governance surfaced as an ultramodern tool aimed at enhancing transparency and responsibility by effectively connecting governments to citizens. The New Public Governance (NNPG) model is grounded in public-private hookups and citizens' engagement in policy design and perpetration, making it more responsive to citizens and further responsible. E-community readiness, which includes the vacuity of structure, functional knowledge, and a networked community, is a vital base for E-governance perpetration.

The agency theory helps understand how information and communication technology (ICT) can flatten organizational structures and enhance transparency, where both principals and agents play a crucial role in organizations. Agents are often influenced by their personal interests, making it difficult for principals to control them. These technologies, with the introduction of ICT, can replace agents and make organizational structures flatter. This concept also applies to implementing E-governance, which ensures greater transparency and better performance. Transaction cost theory indicates that ICT can reduce costs and increase the efficiency of governments by improving effectiveness and reducing expenses. When organizations face challenges in efficiency and effectiveness and costs rise due to asset specificity, they decide to retain some functions to reduce high costs. By lowering transaction costs, ICT can contribute to economic development and improve service delivery. Similarly, governments must work cost-effectively to achieve maximum outputs through E-governance implementation. (Khan et al., 2020, Oliveira, (2019)).

Ecology theory, inspired by the natural terrain, offers a unique perspective for exploring information surroundings, particularly in the realm of ICT design. This proposition is applied in colorful surrounds, including organizational information operation and sustainability sweats. ICT integrates technologies, associations, institutions, and governments into a cohesive ecosystem with the eventuality to drive significant metamorphosis. In the fields of Information Systems (IS) and Organizational Behavior (OB), ecology proposition introduces the conception of" holons," which aremulti-level realities in information surroundings that represent part-whole connections and imbalances within these holons. For illustration, a county could be seen as a holon, while larger ecosystems like Eastern China, Central China, and Western China are considered the' whole'. This frame allows us to theorize the relations and dependences within different scales of ecosystems.

Ecologists have explored the complex connections between ecosystem factors (corridor) and the overarching ecosystem structure (total) to understand the interplay between the physical terrain and the biosphere. The conception of holons has been used to explain the elaboration of part-whole connections within natural scales. Ecology proposition is grounded on three core principles ecosystems are characterized bymulti-tiered scales, holons within an ecosystem have both independent and interdependent attributes, and the relations among holons can be competitive or collaborative, leading to varying situations of dominance. By using this ecological frame, we can gain a comprehensive understanding of how ICT operation affects pastoral E-governance.

Since the 1980s, the part of ICT has been considerably studied in IS exploration. This body of work has examined both the issues and determinants of ICT operation, pressing its part as a pivotal middleman in rephrasing technological relinquishment into performance benefits across colorful disciplines, including E-governance. Research has frequently concentrated on the individual position, exploring how druggies profit from information access and bettered decision- timber. For case, pastoral growers can work ICT to come E-commerce interpreters and gain profitable advantages. Empirical studies also show that ICT relinquishment enhances relations between government workers and citizens in developing countries. Still, much of the being literature concentrates on micro-level perspectives, frequently neglecting the broader counteraccusations of ICT enterprise for pastoral E-governance. While the impact of ICT one-governance has been well- proved, utmost exploration has concentrated on developed regions, leaving pastoral E-governance ecosystems fairly unexplored. Historically, ICT has been praised for its implicit to enhance citizen engagement by standardizing communication and enabling more active participation in decision- making processes. This technological advancement has shifted the traditionally unresistant citizen- government relationship towards a more transparent and participatory E-governance model. In colorful countries, ICT is transubstantiating E-governance with the thing of fostering citizen- centric and effective leadership. Also, ICT is seen as a tool for combating corruption by perfecting translucency and fairness. In pastoral areas, ICT is viewed as a means of commission, helping to ground digital divides and promote community development. The recognition of ICT's implicit to ameliorate E-governance and reduce digital divides is apparent in societal and governmental stations. IS exploration also supports the view that ICT can enhance the quality of E-governance by easing nonstop online relations between citizens and governments.

Still, the impact of ICT on pastoral E-governance varies across different regions, a miracle frequently underrepresented in being literature. ICT development not only improves governance through infrastructural advancements but also fosters ecosystems where different regions like Eastern China, Central China, and Western Chinaco-evolve. This co-evolution, driven by competitive and collaborative relations among and within holons, is anticipated to produce a robust and adaptive E-governance system that responds to the unique requirements of pastoral areas.

Nonetheless, being literature constantly focuses on single- league ICT relinquishment and frequently overlooks the artistic factors natural to ecosystems. Culture plays a significant part in impacting E-governance relinquishment, as different artistic surrounds present unique walls and facilitators. The profound impact of culture on the E-governance metamorphosis process can't be ignored, as it significantly affects the success of E-government enterprise.

In China's pastoral areas, there are conspicuous differences in E-governance across different ecosystems. The eastern region, with its advanced ICT structure, shows advanced situations of E-governance compared to Central and Western China. This difference reflects the part-whole connections stressed by ecology proposition, with a bias towards regions that immortalize a' winner- takes- all' paradigm. Traditional exploration frequently focuses on civic strategies for ICT and E-governance, overlooking the specific challenges and openings in pastoral areas. Accordingly, walls linked in civic E-governance development may not be applicable to pastoral settings. To address this gap, a two-rounded approach is proposed the first study uses quantitative styles to member China into three distinct ecosystems grounded on geographical delineations and examines the relationship between ICT relinquishment and pastoral E-governance within these regions. The alternate study adopts a qualitative approach to identify walls specific to Western China and propose acclimatized results to enhance pastoral E-governance in this region. (Shou et al., 2024)

## 3. LITERATURE REVIEW

### 3.1 Artificial Intelligence in Public Governance: Exploring Its Benefits, Challenges, and Impact on Decision-Making Processes

AI is being used by governments more and more to support public safety and governance. Data breaches and cyber troubles are more likely as public services come more dependent on the internet. Artificial intelligence is entering the scene to estimate data trends in real time, helping governments respond snappily to cyberattacks and other unwanted acts. Governments are also looking at how AI might be used to identify and stop intimation juggernauts, which constitute trouble for public safety and political processes. One illustration of an intimation crusade is the dispersion of false information about COVID-19. Artificial intelligence is also showing its value in the area of nonsupervisory compliance. Artificial intelligence is used by associations similar to the USA Securities and Exchange Commission to identify unusual trade exertion and fiscal wrongdoing. Analogous to this, threat-grounded evaluations are used by Australia's social security and duty services to algorithmically identify implicit fraud cases. Although it's unclear how important AI's integration into these systems will be, this highlights the significance of AI in guaranteeing nonsupervisory compliance. Likewise, in order to cover public health, the USA Food and Drug Administration uses AI to track new medicines by examining patterns of adverse responses. AI is developing quickly in the midst of the COVID-19 epidemic to identify infection hotspots, enhance critical care interventions, read the course of infections, and diagnose the contagion using X-rays. Though AI holds great potential to support public governance, questions remain around government and public service responsibility. While it may not be apparent right away, AI has the occasion to ameliorate responsibility by checking the correctness of government algorithms. This means furnishing different input factors to government algorithms in order to comprehend how they form opinions. This makes it possible to identify impulses pertaining to defended social groups such as gender, religion, and race. AI can also be used to follow changes in public opinion by exercising social media data. This can help identify new issues and ameliorate the government's capability to respond to the requirements of the people. (Henman, 2020)

There are numerous obstacles to overcome when enforcing artificial intelligence in government, chief among them being sequestration, data security, and indifferent decision- timber. First and foremost, data security and sequestration are critical issues. Processing using artificial intelligence has the ability to misuse sensitive data, which could result in identity theft and cybercrime. To preserve public confidence and stop breaches, governments need to give data protection top priority and put strong security measures in place. Cybersecurity risks also need to be addressed, including defense against internal threats and targeted attacks. Ensuring public confidence requires the establishment of transparent data usage policies and defined norms. Second, questions about impartiality in decision-making surface. Even if AI speeds up decision-making, biased algorithms that rely on insufficient data might produce unfair results, especially when it comes to the allocation of social support. Governments need to make sure AI-driven choices are transparent, responsible, and founded on balanced facts. AI technology should be supervised by impartial regulators who will assess algorithms to guarantee equity. In summary, the main obstacles to deploying AI in government are safeguarding data privacy, security, and equitable decision-making. Strong action is needed to address these issues in order to safeguard the public's interests and preserve confidence in AI technology (Salam, 2023).

Risk governance is the process of assessing and managing risks within legal, social, and economic frameworks, with input from relevant parties. This entails obtaining, evaluating, and disseminating risk data in addition to making choices to reduce risks. It particularly discusses the concerns related to AI systems in the field of AI. Policies like EU regulations provide principles for organizations, but they are difficult to adapt to AI. Revisions to legislation are being made to better account for the hazards associated with AI. Risk management can be mapped out using unified standards such as ISO 31000, which address identification, assessment, control, and continuous monitoring. Risks are managed using a variety of strategies, from proactive to reactive. In software development, proactive risk management is very important for anticipating and resolving possible problems. It is crucial to use risk management tools to navigate project complexity and support problem detection and resolution. (Hohma et al., 2023)

Even though it's growing, government use of AI in decision-making is still quite small. But it makes a big difference. AI helps with predictive modeling, pattern recognition, and grouping people into groups according to a variety of criteria. AI is particularly good at finding complex patterns, like the correlation between sickness and DNA sequences, that may be difficult for humans to observe. Furthermore, as demonstrated by the US Department of Homeland Security's Passenger Screening Algorithm Challenge, it effectively classifies people into risk groups. This AI-powered system distinguishes between those who pose a low and high risk, accelerating security checks. In a similar vein, AI is transforming child protection services by decreasing worker workloads and improving the accuracy of risk assessments. Moreover, proactive resource allocation is made possible by AI's predictive modeling skills. The Patient Admission and Prediction Tool (PAPT), for example, was created by Australia's CSIRO to help hospitals plan ahead for patient volumes and medical emergencies. This allows them to allocate people and resources more efficiently. AI also helps with disaster management. For example, the CSIRO's Spark system predicts bushfire development and optimizes resource use for fighting fires. Additionally, AI helps with law enforcement and traffic control. Examples of this include China's Suzhou crime prediction system and Singapore's AI-driven traffic management. In summary, artificial intelligence (AI) enables governments to improve public service delivery across multiple areas, including public safety and healthcare, by making data-driven choices and allocating resources efficiently (Henman, 2020).

## 3.2 Enhancing Governance Effectiveness and Addressing Ethical Considerations through Artificial Intelligence

A possible answer to typical governance problems such as biased decision-making, high personnel costs, variable decision-making quality, and erroneous projections is provided by artificial discretion. AI can improve effectiveness by providing accuracy, consistency, a lower risk of corruption, and cost efficiency. However, there are difficulties in assessing AI's performance, including assuring fairness among various subpopulations and striking a balance between accuracy and cost trade-offs. The three primary applications of AI that public managers concentrate on are automating administrative activities, utilizing massive datasets for predictions, and transforming unstructured inputs into structured data. Artificial intelligence is very useful for jobs that require either a lot of data processing or repetitive task automation. However, not every work may benefit from AI advancement due to differences in risk, complexity, data availability, and technical constraints. Artificial discretion is a notion that aids in determining if AI applications are acceptable. It recommends automation for activities requiring little discretion, as well as decision support systems or predictive analytics for tasks requiring less structure. Improving discretion through data collection and prediction factors is important for high-discretion tasks (Young et al., 2019).

Globally, ethical AI rules are a popular topic that has developed significantly in the last few years. In a 2019 study, over 84 projects by public and corporate entities that outline standards to regulate the ethical development, deployment, and governance of AI were discovered. Transparency was notably identified as a fundamental tenet of most of these projects. This conversation has been aided by organizations like Google and Telia, as well as educational establishments like the AI Now Institute at New York University. Numerous international organizations have also offered their opinions, including the OECD's expert group on AI in Society and the High-Level Expert Group on Artificial Intelligence of the European Commission. Divergence exists in the interpretation and application of fundamental ethical principles such as accountability, non-maleficence, transparency, justice, and privacy, despite their widespread consensus. Opponents such as Hagendorff and Coeckelbergh contend that ethical principles by themselves are powerless to impose compliance, which leaves them open to manipulation by AI corporations as a means of avoiding strict regulation. However, given how quickly AI technology is developing, a more accommodating approach may be necessary until strong regulatory frameworks can keep up. There is disagreement, though, on the best ways to enact laws pertaining to AI ethics and what aspects of it should be governed by human oversight in particular (Larsson, 2021).

## 3.3 Fostering Trust and Transparency in E-governance: Ensuring Accountability and Enhancing Public Confidence

In current addresses, there's a growing emphasis on the need for openness in the governance of artificial intelligence (AI). This is seen in important publications such as the guidelines on' secure AI' published by the European Commission. The dialogue around translucency has boosted in response to the growing focus on AI ethics, justice, and responsibility, as seen by the rise in publications on AI ethics, governance, and morals in recent times. In the environment of artificial intelligence, the word "translucency" is particularly important, particularly when it comes to algorithmic translucency. Nevertheless, there are abstract dissensions around both artificial intelligence and algorithms, with no agreed-upon delineations across disciplines. While artificial intelligence (AI) covers a vast range of styles and subfields, algorithms, especially in the environment of governance, go further with simple step-by-step instructions to address further comprehensive responsibility enterprises. It's constantly argued when mooting the illegal results of algorithmic systems that demarcation arises from complex relations between data and algorithms rather than being purposefully intended. Thus, taking into account the larger environment, which includes the training data and decision-making processes, is pivotal to achieving translucency in AI. In addition, scholars are calling for "critical followership" to guarantee translucency and are supporting administrative bodies' ways of algorithmic governance. A holistic approach is put forth to address the difficulty of translucency in AI, seeing AI as more than just algorithms. With an emphasis on perfecting the explainability and interpretability of models, this system seeks to close the gap between exploration of algorithmic translucency and artificial intelligence. Promoting secure AI is the main goal, which aligns with the objectives of the European AI plan. The theoretical foundation for AI translucency is broad and complex, though exploration in this area is still in its infancy. Assaying the tropical architecture of translucency and classifying material rudiments, including explainability and openness, are necessary to comprehend the normative counteraccusations of translucency. These factors must be taken into account in order to address the moral and legal issues girding AI translucency (Larsson & Heintz, 2020).

Users' faith in technology, particularly artificial intelligence (AI), depends on how well they believe it can accomplish its goals in given situations. Both rational assessments and emotional reactions influence this trust, and factors like AI's goal, architecture, and reputation as a brand further muddy the waters. Notwithstanding privacy issues, artificial intelligence (AI) technology has proven to be invaluable in times of crisis, such as pandemics, offering critical support while upholding safety procedures. Research shows that people's attachment styles have an impact on how they perceive AI, which implies that enhancing attachment security may increase people's degree of trust. The process of building trust is organized into three stages: origin, formation, and operation. Cognitive processes and individual characteristics are important components of each stage (Wong, 2024).

## 4. METHODOLOGY

A policy was completed and approved by the Ministry of Digital Economy and Entrepreneurship before being presented to the Council of Ministers. To guarantee involvement and consultation with all pertinent parties, the strategy was first subjected to public consultation. The results of these discussions had a big impact on how the government developed policies. The policy was also approved by the Ministry of Digital Economy and Entrepreneurship, as well as the Council of Minister. The purpose of this policy is to direct the application of artificial intelligence (AI) projects in Amman, including those involving technology developers and service providers. In relation to artificial intelligence (AI) in Amman, the Ministry listed eight sub-goals, which included building a strong system for R&D, encouraging an atmosphere that is supportive of AI technology, improving public sector AI involvement, and cultivating collaborations with the commercial sector. In addition, the policy aims to improve educational curricula, develop specialized AI skills, and increase public awareness and confidence in AI. In Amman, putting such policies into place is essential to using AI to improve productivity and societal integration. However, there are also obstacles to AI adoption, such as workforce training, dealing with human biases, error detection, and organizational preparedness for AI integration. Accordingly, in order to improve its operations, the Amman's Ministry of Interior has taken a proactive stance and is concentrating on integrating artificial intelligence (AI). With this tactical change, the ministry will be better equipped to support the nation's overall development. The ministry stresses the significance of comprehending and adjusting to the changing work environment in light of the many obstacles. It places a high priority on having meaningful conversations with various societal sectors and making sure their demands are appropriately served. The ministry's policy is based on a balanced approach that combines detection and prevention of crime with a focus on community enforcement and precise information sharing. To accomplish these aims, cooperation with pertinent authorities is essential. It is important to be adaptable and ready to alter in response to governmental and local changes, as well as to keep up with worldwide advancements. Utilizing both national human resources and cutting-edge technology, the ministry has greatly improved its services through programs for modernization and expansion. This strategy encourages collaboration between the security forces and the general public, fostering shared accountability for the safety and stability of society. The ministry's efforts are consistent with its mission to protect the rule of law and create a safer society by significantly contributing to Amman's security and stability. Notably, its initiatives have made Jordan a desirable location for investors. Also, Jordan's fidelity to effectiveness and invention is further demonstrated by the use of AI in many fields, including healthcare, energy, transportation, and education. AI improves effectiveness and performance within associations by automating labor-intensive operations and offering perceptive analysis of data trends. The AI-backed government design's goal is to improve the effectiveness and availability of government services. It assesses governments' relinquishment and preparedness for governance practices through the use of an expansive index system, enabling well-informed decision-timing and ongoing development (Alqudah, 2021).

## 4.1 . Sample research

The study sample consists of government ministries in Amman's public sector, which includes 40 governmental entities. These entities are: the Ministry of Interior, Ministry of Investment, Ministry of Energy and Mineral Resources, Ministry of Labor, Ministry of Education, Ministry of Agriculture, Ministry of Local Administration, Ministry of Social Development, Ministry of Industry, Trade, and Supply, Aqaba Special Economic Zone Authority, Companies Control Department, Civil Status and Passports Department, Government Tenders Department, Chief Islamic Justice Department, Income and Sales Tax Department, Social Security Corporation, Drivers and Vehicles Licensing Department, Postal Savings Fund, National Aid Fund, Hajj and Umrah Department, Vocational Training Corporation, Orphans Fund Development Foundation, Ministry of Culture, Ministry of Finance/Civil Retirement Directorate, Ministry of Environment, General Intelligence Department, National Library Department, Health Insurance Administration, Standards and Metrology Organization, Land and Survey Department, Land Transport Regulatory Authority, Ministry of Justice, Food and Drug Administration, Greater Amman Municipality, Ministry of Youth, Customs Department, Palestinian Affairs Department, Unified Financial Window Portal, Ministry of Tourism and Antiquities, and Housing and Urban Development Corporation. These ministries were precisely named to give a comprehensive representation of the colorful sectors that could be affected by AI operations in governance. These specific governmental entities were chosen because they offer comprehensive and detailed sanctioned reports. Also, the government has provided exploration, statistical studies, and reports for these entities, as they're the most frequently used by citizens in terms of the services they offer.

## 4.2 . Period and Data Collection Method

The study covers a period of five years, from 2018 to 2023, and relies on primary data sources, including official government reports. Data were collected from reports issued by the Ministry of Digital Economy and Entrepreneurship and the Ministry of Justice, as well as user satisfaction measurement reports and E-government service usage reports from the Ministry of Communications and Information Technology. These reports enable a systematic analysis of the adoption, application, and impact of AI technologies on governance in the Amman's public sector. This time frame is sufficient to observe major trends and changes in AI use within regulatory frameworks, decision-making processes, and service delivery in the public sector.

# 5. RESULTS: PRESENTATION AND DISCUSS

Analysis of the reports revealed that user satisfaction with E-government services significantly increased in the third and fourth quarters of 2018. The total number of E-government services listed in the report for the year 2018 was approximately 43, distributed among 11 government entities providing various services. The Ministry of Interior was the most prolific in providing E-services, offering 11 services, followed by the Civil Status Department, which provided 9 E-services. Additionally, the Ministry of Industry, Commerce, and Supply, the Ministry of Labor, the Ministry of Justice, and the General Intelligence Department each provided one service in 2018. According to user satisfaction surveys, satisfaction was measured through a questionnaire that included 65,535 participants, where most services recorded satisfaction rates ranging from 6 to 7 on a scale of 10. The inquiry and fine payment service and the issuance of a clearance certificate service showed the highest usage and user satisfaction rates, with satisfaction rates exceeding 50% for the fine payment service and 12.8% for the clearance certificate. The most satisfied customers were those who found the services easily accessible, user-friendly, and smoothly provided. The report analysis also indicated that the operation of artificial intelligence technology in delivering E-government services enhances stoner satisfaction and facilitates access to services, proving the first thesis that using artificial intelligence in E-governance in the Amman's public sector will enhance client satisfaction and increase the effectiveness of furnishing E-government services.

The following table shows the results of the questionnaire to measure druggies' satisfaction withe-government services for the period 2018- 2019. The Gradual Satisfaction Assessment Standard was adopted from 1-10, where 10 indicate the user is very satisfied with the service and 1 indicates a total dissatisfaction, as shown as follows:

*Table 1. Results of the questionnaire to measure users' satisfaction with e-government services for the period 2018-2019*

| Authority | Service | Number of Participants | Speed Rating | Clarity & Ease Rating |
|---|---|---|---|---|
| Social Security Corporation | Request for annual subscription increase adjustment | 5 | 10 | 10 |
| Government Tenders Department | Contractors classified by specialty | 4 | 10 | 10 |
| National Library Department | Issuance of (audio/visual materials) in the National Library | 2 | 10 | 10 |
| National Library Department | Issuance of (printed publications) in the National Library | 1 | 10 | 10 |
| National Library Department | National deposit in the National Library | 1 | 10 | 10 |
| National Library Department | Request for International Standard Book Number (ISBN) in the National Library | 1 | 10 | 10 |
| Civil Status and Passports Department | Name and number inquiry by contractors | 2 | 9 | 10 |
| National Library Department | Classifier service (computer program) in the National Library | 2 | 8 | 7 |
| National Library Department | Issuance of (legal deposit) in the National Library | 2 | 8 | 7 |
| Ministry of Tourism and Antiquities | Tourism services in the Ministry of Tourism and Antiquities | 44 | 8 | 8 |
| Ministry of Industry, Trade, and Supply | Electronic notification system services | 22 | 8 | 8 |
| Jordan Post Company | Postal tax services | 46 | 7 | 7 |
| National Library Department | Issuance of (ISBN classifier) in the National Library | 4 | 7 | 10 |
| Social Security Corporation | Inquiry about company subscription payment | 89 | 7 | 8 |
| Government Tenders Department | Tender procurement services | 14 | 7 | 7 |
| Judicial Council | Issuance of non-criminal record certificate | 4,818 | 7 | 8 |
| Social Security Corporation | Social security registration and subscription payment for individuals | 5 | 7 | 7 |
| Greater Amman Municipality | Amman municipality services | 3,009 | 7 | 7 |
| Department of Land and Survey | Exemption services for Jordanians and civil notary fees exemption services | 138 | 7 | 7 |
| Civil Service Bureau | Competitive role and ranking inquiry | 52,038 | 7 | 7 |

continued on following page

*Table 1. Continued*

| Authority | Service | Number of Participants | Speed Rating | Clarity & Ease Rating |
|---|---|---|---|---|
| Ministry of Interior | Electronic services for the Ministry of Interior | 2,062 | 7 | 7 |
| Greater Amman Municipality | Profession license renewal | 474 | 7 | 7 |
| Civil Status and Passports Department | E-services for civil status and passports | 385 | 7 | 6 |
| Jordan Post Company | Request for representative | 7 | 7 | 4 |
| Income and Sales Tax Department | Income tax returns filing | 2,202 | 7 | 6 |
| Social Security Corporation | Inquiry about social security number | 83 | 6 | 5 |
| Companies Control Department | Company monitoring service | 11 | 6 | 5 |
| Social Security Corporation | Registration service for new companies | 17 | 6 | 5 |
| Social Security Corporation | Request for first-time registration | 12 | 6 | 5 |
| Social Security Corporation | Re-enrollment service for previously subscribed individuals | 3 | 5 | 3 |
| Jordan Post Company | Subscription follow-up service | 3 | 5 | 3 |
| Social Security Corporation | Subscription cancellation service | 3 | 5 | 3 |

**Legend:** Satisfied: from 7 to 10 / Neutral from 5 to 6 / Unsatisfied from 1to 4

The results also show that AI-supported E-government reduces bureaucratic processes and speeds up service delivery. The analyses also indicate that improving planning and forecasting capabilities thanks to AI can reduce administrative costs. Additionally, data analysis from the Ministry of Digital Economy and Entrepreneurship in Amman revealed that the maturity rate of mobile and electronic government services in Amman increased by 5% in 2023, from 59% in 2022 to 64% in 2023, indicating significant progress in E-government. The adoption of an electronic system for many judicial processes in Amman courts has also led to improvements in accuracy and productivity. The electronic system allowed for more efficient case distribution and a reduced backlog. Furthermore, studies indicate that the use of AI in E-government applications enhances transparency in public sector management and facilitates monitoring and evaluation processes. This proves that the second hypothesis is correct, as the use of artificial intelligence improves efficiency and transparency, reducing the time and cost associated with service delivery.

## 5.1. Governmental Automation in Amman

One of the critical aspects of this study is the examination of the extent to which governmental institutions in Amman have been automateds. The table below presents a summary of the governmental institutions that have been automated along with the number of services handed

*Table 2. Governmental institutions in Amman*

| Governmental Institutions | Number of Services |
|---|---|
| Ministry of Interior | 33 |
| Ministry of Investment | 93 |
| Ministry of Energy and Mineral Resources | 18 |
| Ministry of Labor | 9 |
| Ministry of Education | 7 |
| Ministry of Agriculture | 63 |
| Ministry of Local Administration | 30 |
| Ministry of Social Development | 58 |
| Ministry of Industry, Trade, and Supply | 53 |
| Aqaba Special Economic Zone Authority | 157 |
| Companies Control Department | 19 |
| Civil Status and Passports Department | 27 |
| Government Tenders Department | 8 |
| Chief Islamic Justice Department | 74 |
| Income and Sales Tax Department | 36 |
| Social Security Corporation | 55 |
| Drivers and Vehicles Licensing Department | 44 |
| Postal Savings Fund | 19 |
| National Aid Fund | 5 |
| Hajj and Umrah Department | 2 |
| Vocational Training Corporation | 1 |
| Orphans Fund Development Foundation | 3 |
| Ministry of Culture | 3 |
| Ministry of Finance/Civil Retirement Directorate | 1 |
| Ministry of Environment | 2 |
| General Intelligence Department | 1 |
| National Library Department | 2 |

continued on following page

*Table 2. Continued*

| Governmental Institutions | Number of Services |
|---|---|
| Health Insurance Administration | 8 |
| Standards and Metrology Organization | 2 |
| Land and Survey Department | 64 |
| Land Transport Regulatory Authority | 8 |
| Ministry of Justice | 26 |
| Food and Drug Administration | 6 |
| Greater Amman Municipality | 112 |
| Ministry of Youth | 14 |
| Customs Department | 78 |
| Palestinian Affairs Department | 23 |
| Unified Financial Window Portal | 6 |
| Ministry of Tourism and Antiquities | 8 |
| Housing and Urban Development Corporation | 21 |

The robotization of governmental institutions in Amman has yielded several palpable benefits for both the agencies themselves and the citizens they serve. These benefits include streamlined processes, reduced time and trouble for service delivery, and cost savings for the government. Likewise, citizens have served from easier access to services, with the capability to request services, make payments electronically, and admit labors without the need to physically visit governmental services.

1. Simplification of Procedures: robotization has significantly simplified executive processes within governmental agencies. For case, the digitization of records and processes in the Ministry of Interior and the Civil Status and Passports Department has led to faster service delivery times. Citizens no longer need to stay by long ranges, as numerous services can be penetrated online, reducing the burden on both the citizens and the governmental staff.
2. Cost and Time effectiveness: The cost savings associated with robotization are substantial. Government agencies have reported reduced functional costs, particularly in terms of force and physical coffers. For illustration, the Greater Amman Municipality has enforced over 112 automated services, leading to a drop in the need for homemade processing and a significant reduction in the time needed to reuse operations.

3. Enhanced Citizen Experience: The preface of online platforms for service delivery has greatly bettered the citizen experience. Services similar as those offered by the Aqaba Special Economic Zone Authority (ASEZA) and the Ministry of Investment allow citizens and businesses to pierce information, submit operations, and track the status of their requests in real- time. This has not only bettered translucency but has also enhanced trust between the citizens and the government.
4. Increased Availability: One of the most significant impacts of robotization has been the increased availability of government services. Citizens from remote areas, who preliminarily had to travel to Amman or other major metropolises to pierce services, can now do so online. This is particularly important for services similar as those handed by the Ministry of Agriculture and the Land and Survey Department, which are critical for pastoral communities.

## 5.2. Electronic Oversight and Its Implications

The robotization of government services has also had a profound impact on electronic oversight. The digital metamorphosis has accelerated the capability of nonsupervisory bodies to pierce information, thereby easing further effective and effective oversight.

1. Improved Data Access and Reporting: robotization has enabled nonsupervisory bodies to pierce data more snappily and efficiently. For case, the capability to induce real- time reports and analytics has been significantly enhanced, allowing for faster decision- timber. This is apparent in the operations of the Ministry of Finance and the Department of Income and Deals duty, where automated systems have bettered duty collection and reporting delicacy.
2. Enhanced Responsibility: With the vacuity of data in electronic formats, it has come easier for nonsupervisory bodies to establish links between different governmental institutions. This interconnectedness has been pivotal in relating and addressing executive violations. For illustration, the automated systems in the Ministry of Justice and the Chief Islamic Justice Department have allowed for better shadowing of case progress, icing that legal processes are followed diligently.
3. Discovery of Irregularities: The integration of AI into E-governance has also bettered the capability to descry irregularities. Automated systems can dissect large volumes of data to identify patterns that may indicate fraudulent conditioning or executive crimes. This capability is particularly precious in departments similar as the Customs Department and the Ministry of Industry, Trade, and Supply, where the eventuality for irregularities is high.

4. Data Security and sequestration enterprises: While the benefits of robotization are apparent, it's also important to consider the challenges it presents, particularly in terms of data security and sequestration. The Jordanian government has taken way to address these enterprises by making laws and regulations to cover particular data and regulate the use of technology across colorful sectors. For illustration, the National Cybersecurity Center observers and evaluates the compliance of institutions with cybersecurity programs, icing that digital platforms and operations cleave to established norms.

## 5.3. E-Governance and Regulatory Frameworks in Jordan

The success of E-governance in Jordan is nearly tied to the establishment of a robust nonsupervisory frame that governs the digital metamorphosis of government services. The Jordanian government has enforced several measures to insure that E-governance is effective, secure, and salutary to all stakeholders.

1. Data Protection Laws: The Jordanian government has introduced data protection laws to guard the particular information of citizens. These laws regulate how data can be collected, stored, and used, icing that citizens' sequestration is defended in the digital age. The Ministry of Digital Economy and Entrepreneurship plays a crucial part in overseeing the perpetration of these laws and icing that governmental institution misbehave with them.
2. Cybersecurity Measures: To secure the digital structure of the state, the Jordanian government has espoused comprehensive cybersecurity measures. This includes the protection of government information systems and other critical institutions. The National Cybersecurity Center is responsible for covering the security of these systems and administering penalties for non-compliance with cybersecurity regulations.
3. Evaluation and Compliance Monitoring: The government regularly evaluates the compliance of institutions and companies with cybersecurity programs. The Ministry of Digital Economy and Entrepreneurship, in collaboration with the National Cybersecurity Center, conducts checkups and assessments to insure that digital platforms and operations meet the needed norms. Non-compliance can affect in penalties, icing that institutions take their cybersecurity liabilities seriously.
4. Relinquishment of Modern Technologies: Jordan has embraced ultramodern technologies, similar as blockchain, to enhance the security of electronic deals, particularly those involving property power and fiscal deals. Blockchain technology provides a high position of security and translucency, making it an ideal result for precluding fraud and icing the integrity of government records.

5. Performance pointers: To insure that E-government services are delivered efficiently, the Jordanian government has established performance pointers. These pointers are used to cover the performance of government workers using electronic systems, icing that services are handed to citizens within the blazoned timeframes. The Ministry of Digital Economy and Entrepreneurship publishes reports on these performance pointers, furnishing translucency and responsibility in service delivery.

Based on the study results, the following recommendations can be made:

- Investing more in the creation of technology infrastructure and the application of AI solutions to improve E-governance.
- Raising awareness and educating government employees on how to use E-governance apps and technologies.
- Creating plans to use technology and artificial intelligence to provide government services more effectively and inclusively.
- Suggesting that more money be spent on artificial intelligence research and development in order to create cutting-edge technical solutions that will enhance E-governance.
- Suggesting utilizing artificial intelligence techniques to tailor services and efficiently satisfy user wants in order to increase the interactivity of E-government services.

The progress of E-government services in Amman, Jordan, as detailed in the report, has been estimable, with significant advancements in stoner satisfaction, service availability, and the operation of artificial intelligence (AI) in government processes. Still, to further enhance the effectiveness and reach of these services, several recommendations can be made.

The report highlights the positive impact of AI in perfecting effectiveness, translucency, and stoner satisfaction. To make on this success, it's recommended that AI integration be expanded across all government services, not just those presently exercising it. This expansion should concentrate on:

- Automated Decision- Making: utensil AI- driven decision- making processes to reduce mortal error and bias in executive tasks.
- Personalization of Services: Use AI to knitter E-government services to individual citizen requirements, perfecting stoner experience.
- Prophetic Analytics: Employ AI for prophetic analytics to anticipate citizen requirements and streamline service delivery consequently.

As E-government services continue to expand, data security becomes decreasingly critical. The report notes living cybersecurity measures, but there's room for enhancement

- Advanced Encryption norms: Borrow the rearmost encryption technologies to cover sensitive citizen data.
- Regular Security Audits: Conduct frequent security checkups and vulnerability assessments to identify and address implicit pitfalls.
- Cybersecurity Training: give ongoing training for government workers on the rearmost cybersecurity pitfalls and stylish practices.

Stoner satisfaction with E-government services is nearly linked to the ease of access and stoner-friendly interfaces. To further ameliorate these aspects:

- Universal Design Principles: insure that all digital services cleave to universal design principles, making them accessible to individualities with disabilities.
- Multilingual Support: Expand language support beyond Arabic to include English and other generally spoken languages in Jordan.
- Mobile- First Approach: Prioritize the development of mobile-friendly interfaces, given the high penetration of smartphones in Jordan.

The success of E-government services also depends on a robust legal and non-supervisory frame that supports digital metamorphosis. The following measures should be considered.

- Data sequestration Legislation: Strengthen data sequestration laws to insure that citizen data is defended in line with transnational norms.
- Legal Framework for AI: Develop specific regulations governing the use of AI in government services, icing translucency, responsibility, and ethical use.
- E-Government Governance Body: Establish a devoted body to oversee the perpetration and regulation of E-government services across all ministries.

Otherwise, to maximize the benefits of E-government services, it's essential to insure that all citizens have the necessary digital knowledge chops

- Public Awareness juggernauts: Launch civil juggernauts to raise mindfulness about the vacuity and benefits of E-government services.
- Digital knowledge Programs: apply digital knowledge programs targeting underserved populations, including the senior and pastoral communities.

- Hookups with Educational Institutions: unite with seminaries and universities to integrate digital knowledge into the public class.

The report indicates that E-government services have greatly served citizens in civic areas. To insure equal access

- Structure Development: Invest in internet structure in remote and pastoral areas to insure that all citizens can pierce E-government services.
- Localized Services: Develop services acclimatized to the specific requirements of pastoral communities, similar as agrarian support and land operation services.
- Mobile Service Units: Emplace mobile service units to give on- the- ground support in areas with limited digital access.

To insure that E-government services remain effective and responsive to citizen needs

- Regular stoner Feedback checks: Conduct regular checks to gather stoner feedback and identify areas for enhancement.
- Nimble Development Processes: apply nimble methodologies in the development of E-government platforms, allowing for rapid-fire updates and advancements grounded on stoner feedback.
- Performance Metrics: Continuously cover and publish performance criteria for E-government services to insure translucency and responsibility.

As technology evolves, so too should the E-government services offered in Amman. Arising technologies similar as blockchain, the Internet of effects (IoT), and big data analytics offer new openings for invention.

- Blockchain for Secure Deals: Expand the use of blockchain technology for secure and transparent government deals, particularly in land enrolment and fiscal dealings.
- IoT for Smart metropolises: Integrate IoT results into civic operation systems, perfecting the -effectiveness of services like waste operation, business control, and public safety.
- Big Data for Policy Making: use big data analytics to inform policy opinions, allowing the government to respond more effectively to the requirements of its citizens.

Otherwise, public-private hookups can play a pivotal part in the farther development of E-government services.

- Technology hookups: unite with tech companies to work their moxie in developing and maintaining E-government platforms.
- Innovation capitals: Establish invention capitals where government agencies can work with startups to co-create new digital services.
- Outsourcing Non-Core Services: Consider outsourcing non-core E-government services to private providers to ameliorate effectiveness and reduce costs.

Also, to insure that Jordan's E-government services remain at the van of invention, it's important to standard against global stylish practices.

- Participation in International Forums: Engage in transnational E-government forums to change knowledge and gests with other countries.
- Relinquishment of International norms: Align Jordan's E-government services with transnational norms similar as the UN's E-Government Development Index (EGDI).
- Nonstop literacy: Encourage nonstop literacy and development for government workers involved in the operation of E-government services.

### 5.4. Impediments to the use of E-governance in Jordan's public sector

There are obstacles to the application of electronic governance in the Jordanian public sector, namely the need to promote awareness and training of human resources, to provide an appropriate legislative, regulatory and infrastructure environment, as well as the preference of the majority of users of government services for traditional methods, particularly with regard to electronic payment.

## 6. CONCLUSION

The research findings illustrate that the use of E-governance supported by artificial intelligence technologies in the Amman's public sector has led to tangible improvements in user satisfaction and service delivery effectiveness. It has also contributed to enhancing efficiency, transparency, reducing bureaucratic processes, and improving prediction and planning, reflecting a positive and tangible impact on Amman's E-governance development. Based on these findings, the Amman's government must continue investing in and advancing artificial intelligence technologies in order to continuously improve its electronic services. It is possible to achieve more efficient and inclusive government services by implementing the recommended actions, thereby better meeting citizens' needs and increasing their satisfaction.

The robotization of government services in the region of Amman in Jordan represents a significant step forward in the country's trip towards E-governance. Automation has also increased availability, benefiting remote citizens. Additionally, it has improved electronic oversight, with better data access, accountability, and irregularity detection. However, data security and privacy remain concerns. Jordan's regulatory frameworks include data protection laws, cybersecurity measures, and the adoption of technologies like blockchain to safeguard electronic transactions. Recommendations include strengthening information technology structure, developing nonsupervisory fabrics for optimal use of artificial intelligence in governance, promoting public-private hookups for advanced technology results, and integrating artificial intelligence chops into educational classes to increase public mindfulness and confidence.

The benefits of this metamorphosis are multitudinous, ranging from simplified procedures and cost savings to enhanced citizen experience and bettered oversight. By embracing robotization and AI, the Jordanian government has not only bettered the effectiveness of its operations but has also made government services more accessible and transparent to its citizens.

Still, the trip towards full robotization and the consummation of all implicit benefits is ongoing. While significant progress has been made, there's still work to be done to insure that all governmental institutions are completely automated and that the challenges associated with data security and sequestration are effectively managed. The establishment of a robust nonsupervisory frame, the relinquishment of ultramodern technologies, and the nonstop monitoring of performance pointers are essential factors of this process.

Eventually, the success of E-governance in Jordan will depend on the government's capability to balance invention with security and to insure that all citizens can profit from the edge and advancements brought about by robotization. As the country continues to develop its digital structure and expand its E-governance enterprise, it'll be pivotal to maintain a focus on inclusivity, translucency, and responsibility. Through these sweats, Jordan can place itself as a leader in digital governance in the region, setting an illustration for other countries to follow.

## REFERENCES


Aarabe, M. (2024). Smart Tourism Experience and Responsible Travelers' Behavior: A Systematic Literature Review. In *Promoting Responsible Tourism With Digital Platforms* (pp. 128–147). IGI Global. DOI: 10.4018/979-8-3693-3286-3.ch008

Aarabe, M., Ben Khizzou, N., Alla, L., & Benjelloun, A. (2024). Marketing Applications of Emerging Technologies: A Systematic Literature Review. In Alla, L., Hmioui, A., & Bentalha, B. (Eds.), *AI and Data Engineering Solutions for Effective Marketing* (pp. 23–47). IGI Global., DOI: 10.4018/979-8-3693-3172-9.ch002

Al-rawahna, A. S. M., Chen, S. C., & Hung, C. W. (2019). The barriers of E-government success: An empirical study from Jordan. *Available atSSRN* 3498847. DOI: 10.2139/ssrn.3498847

Alla, L., Bentalha, B., & Elyoussfi, A. (2023). Intelligence territoriale et positionnement stratégique des regions au Maroc: Le cas de la région de Fès Meknes en perspective. *Le concept de l'intéligence en sciences juridiques, économiques et sociales*, 215-237.

Alomari, M. K., Khan, H. U., Khan, S., Al-Maadid, A. A., Abu-Shawish, Z. K., & Hammami, H. (2021). Systematic analysis of artificial intelligence-based platforms for identifying governance and access control. *Security and Communication Networks*, 2021, 1–10. DOI: 10.1155/2021/8686469

Alqudah, M. A. (2021). Investment Artificial Intelligence in Decision-making Processes in the Jordanian Ministry of Interior. *International Journal of Innovations in Engineering Research and Technology*, 8(10), 40–53.

Alqudah, M. A., & Muradkhanli, L. (2021). Artificial intelligence in electric government; ethical challenges and governance in Jordan. *Electronic Research Journal of Social Sciences and Humanities*, 3, 65–74.

Badre, M. E. Z. I. A. N. E., Badr, B. E. N. T. A. L. H. A., & Lhoussaine, A. L. L. A. (2024). La PME logistique et le développement territorial régional: Une analyse qualitative. *Alternatives Managériales Economiques*, 6(4), 1–22.

Bala, M., & Verma, D. (2018). Governance to good governance through E-Governance: A critical review of concept, model, initiatives & challenges in India. *International Journal of Management. IT and Engineering*, 8(10), 244–269.

Bentalha, B., & Alla, L. (2024). Revealing the Subtleties: The Art of Qualitative Studies in Science and Management. In Bentalha, B., & Alla, L. (Eds.), *Applying Qualitative Research Methods to Management Science* (pp. 1–21). IGI Global., DOI: 10.4018/979-8-3693-5543-5.ch001

Boudri, R., Bentalha, B., & Benjelloun, O. (2024). Phygital Marketing and the Pain of Paying: An Amazon Go Netnographic Case Study. In Alla, L., Hmioui, A., & Bentalha, B. (Eds.), *AI and Data Engineering Solutions for Effective Marketing* (pp. 348–363). IGI Global., DOI: 10.4018/979-8-3693-3172-9.ch017

Bouhtati, N., El Yaacoubi, Y., Bentalha, B., & Lhoussaine, A. L. L. A. (2024). Leviers logistiques de promotion du commerce équitable des produits de terroir: Une esquisse de modèle d'analyse. Alternatives Managériales Economiques, 6(Spécial 1), 17-35.

Bouhtati, N., Alla, L., & Bentalha, B. (2023). Marketing Big Data Analytics and Customer Relationship Management: A Fuzzy Approach. In Bentalha, B., Hmioui, A., & Alla, L. (Eds.), *Integrating Intelligence and Sustainability in Supply Chains* (pp. 75–86). IGI Global., DOI: 10.4018/979-8-3693-0225-5.ch004

Bouhtati, N., Alla, L., & Ed-Daakouri, I. (2024). Smart Data Analysis and Prediction of Responsible Customer Behaviour in Tourism: An Exploratory Review of the Literature. In El Archi, Y., Benbba, B., Dávid, L., & Cardoso, L. (Eds.), *Promoting Responsible Tourism With Digital Platforms* (pp. 189–212). IGI Global., DOI: 10.4018/979-8-3693-3286-3.ch011

El Jaouhari, S., & Lhoussaine, A. L. L. A. (2022). L'approche territoriale et la gestion de l'impact de la pandémie de Covid-19: Cas des collectivités territoriales. *Alternatives Managériales Economiques*, 4(1), 245–265.

Elhissoufi, M., & Alla, L. (2024). Artificial Intelligence in Costumer Acquisition: A Bibliometric Study. In Alla, L., Hmioui, A., & Bentalha, B. (Eds.), *AI and Data Engineering Solutions for Effective Marketing* (pp. 1–22). IGI Global., DOI: 10.4018/979-8-3693-3172-9.ch001

Henman, P. (2020). Improving public services using artificial intelligence: Possibilities, pitfalls, governance. *Asia Pacific Journal of Public Administration*, 42(4), 209–221. DOI: 10.1080/23276665.2020.1816188

Hmioui, A., Alla, L., & Bentalha, B. (2017). Pilotage de la touristicité territoriale au Maroc Proposition d'un indice de tourisцticité pour la destination Fès. *Entrepreneuriat, Innovation, Gouvernance et Développement territorial*, 120-143.

Hmioui, A., Alla, L., & Bentalha, B. (2017). *Piloting territorial tourism in Morocco Proposal for a tourism index for the destination Fez [Pilotage de la touristicité territoriale au Maroc Proposition d'un indice de touriscticité pour la destination Fès]* (No. hal-02334913).

Hohma, E., Boch, A., Trauth, R., & Lütge, C. (2023). Investigating accountability for Artificial Intelligence through risk governance: A workshop-based exploratory study. *Frontiers in Psychology*, 14, 1073686. DOI: 10.3389/fpsyg.2023.1073686 PMID: 36760454

Khan, M., Khurram, S., & Zubair, D. S. S. (2020). Societal E-readiness for E-governance adaptability in Pakistan. *Pakistan Journal of Commerce and Social Sciences*, 14(1), 273–299.

Khouya, M. (2023). E-Governance: Origin, challenges, and prospects in the era of ICTs and artificial intelligence. *American Scientific Journal*, 3(18), 884–884.

Larsson, S. (2021). AI in the EU: Ethical Guidelines as a Governance Tool. *The European Union and the technology shift*, 85-111.

Larsson, S., & Heintz, F. (2020). Transparency in artificial intelligence. *Internet Policy Review*, 9(2). Advance online publication. DOI: 10.14763/2020.2.1469

Napetvaridze, V. (2022). *Artificial Intelligence, Blockchain Technologies, and Digital State Services in Georgia General Overview of Georgian E-government Environment*. Eastern Europe Regional Studies.

Nouhaila, B. K., Aarabe, M., & Alla, L. (2024). The Impact of Digitalisation on the Customer Experience in Medical Tourism: A Systematic Review. In Talukder, M., Kumar, S., & Tyagi, P. (Eds.), *Impact of AI and Tech-Driven Solutions in Hospitality and Tourism* (pp. 408–428). IGI Global., DOI: 10.4018/979-8-3693-6755-1.ch020

Oliveira, E. (2019). Artificial intelligence: An overview. *Cutting Edge Technologies and Microcomputer Applications for Developing Countries*, 61-65.

Salam, R., Sinurat, M., Yasin, A., & Sacipto, R. (2023). Implementation of Artificial Intelligence in Governance: Potentials and Challenges. *Influence: International Journal of Science Review*, 5(1), 243–255.

Sheng, B., Chen, X., Li, T., Ma, T., Yang, Y., Bi, L., & Zhang, X. (2022). An overview of artificial intelligence in diabetic retinopathy and other ocular diseases. *Frontiers in Public Health*, 10, 971943. DOI: 10.3389/fpubh.2022.971943 PMID: 36388304

Shou, M., Jia, F., Yu, J., & Wu, Y. (2024). Challenges in developing information and communication technology (ICT) use for rural e-governance: An ecology perspective. *Information Systems Journal*, isj.12540. DOI: 10.1111/isj.12540

Wong, L. W., Tan, G. W. H., Ooi, K. B., & Dwivedi, Y. (2024). The role of institutional and self in the formation of trust in artificial intelligence technologies. *Internet Research*, 34(2), 343–370. DOI: 10.1108/INTR-07-2021-0446

Young, M. M., Bullock, J. B., & Lecy, J. D. (2019). Artificial discretion as a tool of governance: A framework for understanding the impact of artificial intelligence on public administration. *Perspectives on Public Management and Governance*, 2(4), 301–313. DOI: 10.1093/ppmgov/gvz014

# Chapter 7
# Exploring Trends, Perspectives, and Challenges of Artificial Intelligence in Sustainable Mobility:
## A Systematic Review

**Soufiane Elbroumi**
*Sidi Mohammed Ben Abdelah University, Morocco*

**Maha Assaad Idrissi**
*Ibn Tofail University, Kenitra, Morocco*

**Mohammed Chaaouan**
*Sidi Mohammed Ben Abdelah University, Fez, Morocco*

**Hicham Eddahmouny**
*Sidi Mohammed Ben Abdelah University, Fez, Morocco*

## ABSTRACT

*This systematic review examines the expanding role of Artificial Intelligence (AI) in sustainable mobility, analyzing literature from Web of Science and Scopus databases published between 2019 and 2024. The review identifies key trends in integrating AI into transportation systems, focusing on sustainability, smart solutions, and the development of smart cities. Efforts to enhance eco-friendly and energy-efficient mobility solutions are highlighted, reflecting the critical role of AI in reducing envi-*

DOI: 10.4018/979-8-3693-6854-1.ch007

*ronmental impacts while maintaining high levels of accessibility and convenience. Adopting smart solutions, including AI-driven traffic management and autonomous vehicles, demonstrates how cutting-edge technologies optimize urban mobility and improve safety. The concept of smart cities is further explored, showcasing how AI and data integration are transforming urban areas into hubs of technological innovation and sustainability. Additionally, the review underscores the importance of data-driven approaches, particularly in Mobility as a Service (MaaS) and multimodality, where AI enables seamless integration of various transportation modes. Despite the significant advancements, the review also addresses challenges such as data security, privacy, and ethical considerations, emphasizing the need for robust regulatory frameworks to ensure the safe and equitable deployment of AI in mobility. This study provides valuable insights into the potential of AI to revolutionize sustainable mobility and highlights areas for future research and development.*

## 1. INTRODUCTION

Artificial Intelligence (AI) has become a key driver of innovation across various sectors, transforming the way systems and services operate. In the field of mobility, AI has introduced significant advancements, offering innovative solutions to improve the efficiency, safety, and personalization of transportation services. The applications of AI in mobility span from autonomous vehicles and traffic management to smart logistics and Mobility as a Service (MaaS) platforms.

For instance, autonomous vehicles utilize machine learning algorithms and computer vision to navigate and make real-time decisions, promising to reduce accidents and facilitate transportation. Traffic management also benefits from AI through the optimization of traffic flows, reducing congestion and greenhouse gas emissions. In logistics, AI enables the optimization of supply chains, increasing efficiency and reducing operational costs. MaaS platforms, on the other hand, integrate various modes of transport, offering more flexible and personalized mobility to users.

Despite these advancements, the integration of AI in mobility presents considerable challenges. Concerns regarding safety, data privacy, and ethics are at the forefront of current debates. Moreover, the regulation and standardization of AI technologies in mobility remain unresolved issues.

This systematic review aims to provide a comprehensive overview of recent research on the application of AI in mobility. By analyzing current trends, innovations, and challenges identified in the literature, this study seeks to illuminate future perspectives and identify areas requiring further research. To achieve this, we have selected relevant articles published between 2019 and 2024 from the Web of Science and Scopus databases, focusing on the advancements and applications of AI in various aspects of mobility.

The objective is to synthesize current knowledge and provide recommendations for future research, to maximize the benefits of AI in this dynamic and constantly evolving sector. This study aims to comprehensively examine recent research on the application of Artificial Intelligence (AI) in the field of mobility, focusing on publications from the last five years (2019-2024). The objective of this research is to address the current trends in AI within mobility and the underlying challenges. To achieve these objectives, this systematic review employs a rigorous methodology for the selection and analysis of articles, utilizing databases such as Google Scholar, Web of Science, and Scopus. Only peer-reviewed articles published in English or French that meet the defined inclusion criteria will be considered.

To our knowledge, there are very few reviews on the trends of artificial intelligence in the field of mobility. This study is the first to comprehensively identify and classify the main directions of movement, transportation, and land use planning in the era of artificial intelligence. It offers an in-depth understanding and updated analysis of mobility trends in a context characterized by a set of sociological, economic, ecological, and, above all, technological transformations.

The article is structured into four main sections. Following the introduction, which outlines the scope and objective of the study, Section 1 presents the systematic literature review methodology, detailing the steps and tools used for data collection and analysis. Section 2 synthesizes the main findings of the review, providing an in-depth understanding and comprehensive mapping of key trends in artificial intelligence within the mobility sector over the past five years. Section 3 discusses and situates the most pressing challenges for the mobility field based on the theoretical and conceptual context of the main AI trends. Finally, Section 4 concludes the study with recommendations based on the results obtained and proposes future research directions for studying issues related to artificial intelligence in the field of mobility.

## 2. METHOD AND TOOLS - SYSTEMATIC LITERATURE REVIEW

As introduced above, this study aims to systematically identify and evaluate the trends in artificial intelligence (AI) in the mobility sector, with a focus on key challenges such as security, data privacy, ethics, and regulation. The objective is to understand how current AI trends such as deep learning, machine learning, conversational AI, computer vision, explainable AI, robotic process automation, and real-time AI have influenced mobility practices and modes. In this methodological section, we detail the criteria and process for data collection and analysis following the PRISMA (Preferred Reporting Items for Systematic Reviews and Meta-Analyses) framework (Page MJ, et al., 2021). This approach is recommended for synthesizing and generating new perspectives from a wide variety of dispersed studies and data. We formed a set of search queries using identified keywords to collect relevant literature from various databases and registries. After a rigorous screening process according to the "PRISMA 2020" procedure, detailed in Figure 1, we found 383 peer-reviewed articles from scientific journals indexed in at least one of the searched databases and relevant to the scope of our study. We used machine learning techniques and content analysis to accelerate the process and quickly extract the necessary metadata to understand the AI trends in the mobility sector present in the identified articles.

## 2.1. SEARCH STRATEGY AND QUERY USED

To formulate our search query, we combined linking keywords and their alternatives from our research topic. We targeted all articles and reviews published between 2019 and 2024 in scientific journals indexed in at least one of the two considered databases: Scopus and Web of Science, renowned for the scientific rigor of their reviews. We chose 2019 as the starting point for our study because it coincides with the onset of the COVID-19 pandemic and numerous advancements in the field of AI, particularly in computer vision, natural language processing, and machine learning systems. These significant events have greatly accelerated the adoption of AI in various domains. Only articles in English, the most common administrative and academic language, were targeted. Consequently, a search query was separately formed using Boolean operators.

To ensure comprehensive coverage of the relevant literature, the following search query was developed:

Article Title, Abstract, Keywords:

("artificial AND intelligence") AND ("sustainable AND mobility")

We directly used these search queries in Web of Science and Scopus.

## 2.2. QUALITY ASSESSMENT AND SELECTION CRITERIA

Using the search query, we extracted a total of 383 original research records from the two databases, Scopus and Web of Science. Our evaluation was based on three elements: the article title, abstract, and keywords. All records were then exported from the databases to a Microsoft Excel file for combination, organization, filtering, and sorting based on the following criteria in the table below.

The selection criteria for this review included peer-reviewed articles published between 2019 and 2024 that focused on the application of AI in sustainable mobility. Articles were selected based on their relevance to key themes such as sustainability, autonomous systems, and smart solutions. We excluded studies that were not accessible in full-text or lacked sufficient empirical data. For the qualitative aspect, we conducted a thematic analysis of the selected articles, categorizing the main trends based on recurring themes across different studies. This approach allowed us to identify patterns in how AI is being utilized and its impact on sustainable mobility

*Table 1. Inclusion and Exclusion Criteria for Systematic Literature Review*

| Exclusion Criteria | Inclusion Criteria |
|---|---|
| **Duplicates: Duplicate articles were removed.**<br>**Publication Date: Articles published before 2019 were excluded.**<br>**Language: Articles published in languages other than English were excluded.**<br>**Relevance: Off-topic Articles were excluded.**<br>**Document Type: Only journal articles and review articles were considered. Reports, books, book chapters, citations, and conference proceedings were excluded to ensure that only peer-reviewed publications were included.**<br>**Historical Reviews: Articles that focused on historical reviews were excluded. The rationale for this exclusion is to maintain a focus on contemporary advancements and applications of AI in mobility, rather than on historical perspectives, which may not directly contribute to the understanding of current and emerging trends.** | **Focus on AI in Mobility:** All articles that explicitly address the use of artificial intelligence in the field of mobility were included<br>**Accessibility:** Only articles that were accessible and downloadable online were included, ensuring that all reviewed materials were readily available |

By applying these criteria, we ensured that the remaining articles were relevant, high-quality, peer-reviewed studies focused on the intersection of artificial intelligence and sustainable mobility. This rigorous selection process was essential for maintaining the integrity and reliability of our systematic literature review.

*Table 2. Data collection and selection process following PRISMA 2020 framework*

| **Databases** | **Collected Articles** | **Number of Articles Excluded After Introducing the Following Criteria** | | | | | | | **Selected Articles** |
|---|---|---|---|---|---|---|---|---|---|
| | | **Date [2019-2024]** | **Type of article: Journal Article, Review** | **Language: other than English** | **Repeated** | **Off-topic (After screening Title and Abstract)** | **Accessibility** | **historical reviews** | |
| Scopus | 99 | 21 | 40 | 0 | -- | 9 | 7 | 3 | 22 |
| Web of science | 284 | 25 | 65 | 1 | 51 | 47 | 19 | 5 | 68 |
| Total | 383 | 46 | 105 | 1 | **51** | 56 | **26** | 8 | **90** |

We sorted the records by relevance and retained only those that met our selection criteria and were related to the scope of our study. At this stage, we conducted an initial review of the titles of the remaining records to eliminate non-relevant titles and other undesirable documents. Following this phase, we excluded 56 articles and attempted to download the remaining 124 records as full documents, but only 98 were obtained as complete documents. Twenty-six records were unavailable. After individually examining and evaluating the 98 complete documents, we excluded 8 records that were dominated by historical reviews of artificial intelligence before 2019. In the final step, we collected 90 complete articles that were selected for content analysis to locate and interpret current trends in artificial intelligence within the mobility sector.

The entire process, from the initial database search to the 90 final records considered for review, is summarized in the following figure.

*Figure 1. Selection Process of Articles for Systematic Literature Review following PRISMA 2020 framework*

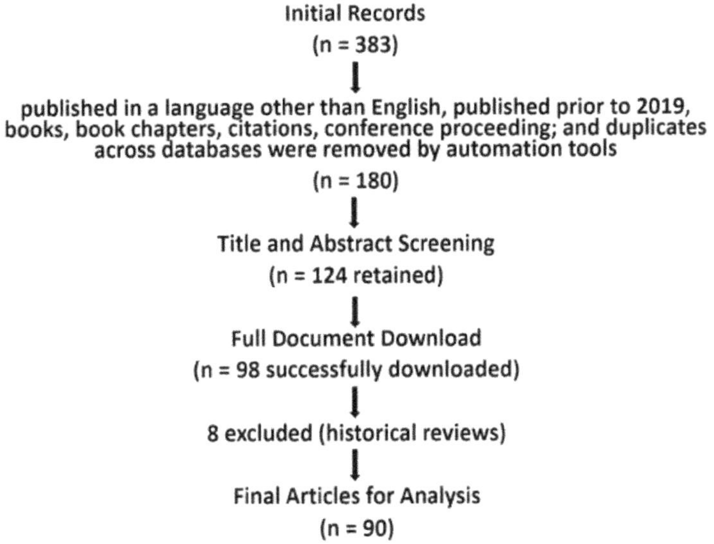

## 3. METADATA EXTRACTION AND CONTENT ANALYSIS

We utilized natural language processing (NLP) techniques to process and analyse the data from the 90 selected records. Natural Language Processing is a branch of Artificial Intelligence (AI) that enables computers to understand text and spoken words like human comprehension. To achieve the overall objective of the study, we used the keywords from the queries presented above. We employed Named Entity Recognition (NER) to automatically scan the articles and extract trends in artificial intelligence within mobility. Named Entity Recognition is an NLP field that identifies named entities, such as place names, from a text string.

We used word clouds to summarize and group relevant keywords related to our topic, as illustrated in the figure below. We compared the word clouds with a non-exhaustive list of AI trends in the transportation domain that were pre-identified. Creating word clouds allowed us to complete the predefined list of current AI trends related to mobility. Information Retrieval (IR) was used to identify the articles corresponding to the search query. IR returned a list of articles relevant to the query in this context. Information Retrieval is defined as a process of matching documents (usually text) with a search query (Brants, 2003). The figure below presents the entire word clouds for data analysis.

*Figure 2. Word clouds of the most frequent trends AI in mobility through the90 selected papers*

The word cloud image represents key terms derived from an analysis of 90 articles in our literature review on artificial intelligence and sustainable mobility. The most frequently mentioned terms, such as Smart Citie, Sustainability, Traffic Management, Smart Solutions, Mobility as a Service (MaaS), Real-time, Computer Vision, Autonomous Vehicles, Open Data and Machine Learning, are prominently displayed. These terms are arranged randomly in the image, with varying sizes and colors to indicate their relative importance and frequency of occurrence. The white background ensures that the words stand out clearly, effectively illustrating the dominant themes and concepts emerging from the comprehensive analysis of the literature.

The crucial step was to reorganize the current trends of artificial intelligence in the mobility sector, as presented in the following section.

## 4. RESULTS: AI TRENDS IN MOBILITY

After presenting the process of identifying, collecting, and analyzing data from the 90 studies considered for this review, this section describes the nature and category of the selected articles. We opted for a structured narrative presentation of the results. We summarize and map the most frequent trends and perspectives. Finally, the trends and perspectives are categorized into different groups based on their frequency in the examined articles.

Using Microsoft Excel, we compiled and counted the frequency of occurrence of the identified trends and perspectives in the examined articles, as shown in the table below.

*Table 3. Current Trends of Artificial Intelligence in Mobility*

| Trends & perspectives | Description | Authors (90 Papers) |
|---|---|---|
| **Sustainability** | Efforts to develop and promote eco-friendly and energy-efficient mobility solutions | Maslaric M, Bojic S, Mircetic D, Nikolicic S, Medenica Todorovic R. (2024); Ahn H, Park E. (2024); Cirianni FMM, Comi A, Quattrone A. (2023); Bencekri M, Kim S, Fan YV et al. (2024); Bokolo AJ. (2023); Esztergár-Kiss D. (2023); Cellina F, Simão JV, Mangili F, Vermes N, Granato P. (2023); Chen J, Tao S, Teng S, Chen Y, Zhang H, Wang F-Y. (2023); Kim MJ, Hall CM, Chung N, Kim M, Sohn K. (2023); Chong YW, Villanueva-Libunao K, Chee SY, Alvarez MJ, Yau KLA, Keoh SL (2022); Ketter W, Schroer K, Valogianni K. (2022); Devi P, Kizielewicz B, Guleria A, Shekhovtsov A, Wątróbski J, Królikowski T, Więckowski J, Sałabun W. (2022); Duggal AS, Singh R, Gehlot A, Gupta LV, Akram SV, Prakash C, Singh S, Kumar R. (2021); Gambo N, Musonda I. (2021); Rinaldi M, Picarelli E, D'Ariano A, Viti F. (2020); Anagnostopoulou E, Urbančič J, Bothos E et al. (2020); Liyanage S, Dia H, Abduljabbar R, Bagloee SA. (2019); Bucher D, Mangili F, Cellina F, Bonesana C, Jonietz D, Raubal M. (2019) |
| **Smart solutions** | Adoption of innovative technologies to optimize transportation systems and infrastructure | Alam T, Gupta R, Nasurudeen Ahamed N, Ullah A, Almaghthwi A. (2024); Li H, Chen Y, Li K, Wang C, Chen B. (2023); Cirianni FMM, Comi A, Quattrone A. (2023); Fong B, Fong ACM, Hong GY. (2023); Bugaj M, Durana P, Blazek R, Horak J. (2023); Mitieka D, Luke R, Twinomurinzi H, Mageto J. (2023); Ketter W, Schroer K, Valogianni K. (2022); Mahrez Z, Sabir E, Badidi E, Saad W, Sadik M. (2022); D'Amico G, Szopik-Depczyńska K, Dembińska I, Ioppolo G. (2021); Paiva S, Ahad MA, Tripathi G, Feroz N, Casalino G. (2021); Karger E, Jagals M, Ahlemann F. (2021); Piccialli F, Giampaolo F, Prezioso E, Crisci D, Cuomo S. (2021); Maldonado Silveira Alonso Munhoz PA, da Costa Dias F, Kowal Chinelli C, Azevedo Guedes AL, Neves dos Santos JA, da Silveira e Silva W, Pereira Soares CA. (2020); Nikitas A, Michalakopoulou K, Njoya ET, Karampatzakis D. (2020); Aymen F, Mahmoudi C. (2019) |
| **Smart Cities** | Urban areas that leverage AI and data to enhance the quality of life, efficiency, and sustainability. | Fang K, Azizan SA, Huang H. (2024); Elsawy Y, Alatawi AS, Abaza M, Moawad A, Aggoune E-HM. (2024); Louati A, Louati H, Kariri E, Neifar W, Hassan MK, Khairi MHH, Farahat MA, El-Hoseny HM. (2024); Hammoumi L, Maanan M, Rhinane H. (2024); Szpilko D, Naharro F, Lăzăroiu G, Nica E, Gallegos A. (2023); Caputo F, Magliocca P, Canestrino R, Rescigno E. (2023); Abbas Q, Ahmad G, Alyas T, Alghamdi T, Alsaawy Y, Alzahrani A. (2023); Fong B, Fong ACM, Hong GY. (2023); Sawhney N. (2023); Anedda M, Fadda M, Girau R, Pau G, Giusto D. (2023); Strielkowski W, Zenchenko S, Tarasova A, Radyukova Y. (2022); Lee B. (2022); Obracht-Prondzyńska H, Duda E, Anacka H, Kowal J. (2022); Javed AR, Shahzad F, Rehman S, Zikria YB, Razzak I, Jalil Z, Xu G. (2022); Kakderi C, Oikonomaki E, Papadaki I. (2021); Khan ZA, Sherazi HHR, Ali M, Imran MA. (2021); Anagnostopoulos T. (2021); Nikitas A, Michalakopoulou K, Njoya ET, Karampatzakis D. (2020); Aymen F, Mahmoudi C. (2019) |

continued on following page

*Table 3. Continued*

| Trends & perspectives | Description | Authors (90 Papers) |
|---|---|---|
| **sharing solutions** | Collaborative consumption models in mobility | Flohr LA, Schuß M, Wallach DP, Krüger A, Riener A. (2024); Saha A, Görçün ÖF, Pamucar D, Arya L, Simic V. (2024); Lee J, Kim K, Park G, Trunina A. (2024); Senapati T, Simic V, Saha A, Dobrodolac M, Rong Y, Tirkolaee EB. (2023); Ziemba P, Gago I. (2022); Baumgarte F, Keller R, Röhrich F, Valett L, Zinsbacher D. (2022); Martí P, Jordán J, Chamoso P, Julian V. (2022); Bucchiarone A, Battisti S, Marconi A, Maldacea R, Ponce DC. (2021); Anagnostopoulos T. (2021); Vermesan O, John R, Pype P, Daalderop G, Kriegel K, Mitic G, Lorentz V, Bahr R, Sand HE, Bockrath S, Waldhör S. (2021); Salazar-Cabrera R, Pachón de la Cruz Á, Madrid Molina JM. (2020); Liyanage S, Dia H, Abduljabbar R, Bagloee SA. (2019); Zhang H, Song X, Long Y, et al. (2019) |
| **machine learning** | AI techniques enable systems to learn and improve from experience without being explicitly programmed | Kristianto E, Lin P-C, Hwang R-H. (2024); Gao QL, Zhong C, Yue Y, Cao R, Zhang B. (2024); Kolidakis S, Kotoula KM, Botzoris G, Kamberi PF, Skoutas D. (2024); Miraftabzadeh SM, Longo M, Di Martino A, Saldarini A, Faranda RS. (2024); QL Gao et al. (2024); Lee H, Chatterjee I, Cho G. (2023); Keller C, Glück F, Gerlach CF, Schlegel T. (2022); Baumgarte F, Keller R, Röhrich F, Valett L, Zinsbacher D. (2022); Lee B. (2022); Duggal AS, Singh R, Gehlot A, Gupta LV, Akram SV, Prakash C, Singh S, Kumar R. (2021) |
| **Autonomous Vehicles** | Development and deployment of self-driving cars and trucks | brahim HA, Qahtan S, Zaidan AA, Deveci M, Hajiaghaei-Keshteli M, Mohammed RT, Alamoodi AH. (2024); Louati A, Louati H, Kariri E, Neifar W, Hassan MK, Khairi MHH, Farahat MA, El-Hoseny HM. (2024); Roger S, Botella-Mascarell C, Martín-Sacristán D, García-Roger D, Monserrat JF, Svensson T. (2024); Li J, et al. (2023); Gokasar I, Simic V, Deveci M, Senapati T. (2023); Lee B. (2022); Kassens-Noor E, Siegel J, Decaminada T. (2021); Andraško J, Hamuľák O, Mesarčík M, Kerikmäe T, Kajander A. (2021); Bucchiarone A, Battisti S, Marconi A, Maldacea R, Ponce DC. (2021); Vermesan O, John R, Pype P, Daalderop G, Kriegel K, Mitic G, Lorentz V, Bahr R, Sand HE, Bockrath S, Waldhör S. (2021); Nikitas A, Michalakopoulou K, Njoya ET, Karampatzakis D. (2020); He Y, Csiszár C. (2020) |
| **Big Data & Open Data** | Accessibility and utilization of open data sources to improve mobility services and infrastructure. | Varone A, Heilmann Z, Porruvecchio G, Romanino A. (2024); Fabre L, Bayart C, Bonnel P, Mony N. (2023); Esztergár-Kiss D. (2023); Graells-Garrido E, Opitz D, Rowe F, Arriagada J. (2023); Nielsen AF, Michelmann J, Akac A, et al. (2023); Servou E, Behrendt F, Horst M. (2023); Keller C, Glück F, Gerlach CF, Schlegel T. (2022); Cristóbal T, Quesada-Arencibia A, De Blasio GS, Padrón G, Alayón F, García CR. (2022); Lemonde C, Arsenio E, Henriques R. (2021); Duggal AS, Singh R, Gehlot A, Gupta LR, Akram SV, Prakash C, Singh S, Kumar R. (2021) |

continued on following page

*Table 3. Continued*

| Trends & perspectives | Description | Authors (90 Papers) |
|---|---|---|
| **Mobility as a Service (MaaS)** | Integration of various transport services into a single accessible on-demand service | Cellina F, Derboni M, Giuffrida V, Tomic U, Hoerler R. (2024); Martin H, Wiedemann N, Reck D, Raubal M. (2023); Cirianni FMM, Comi A, Quattrone A. (2023); Rajabi E, Nowaczyk S, Pashami S, Bergquist M, Ebby GS, Wajid S. (2023); Ozpinar A. (2023); Servou E, Behrendt F, Horst M. (2023); Antonialli F, Martinesco A, Mira-Bonnardel S. (2022); Vitetta A. (2022); Bucchiarone A, Battisti S, Marconi A, Maldacea R, Ponce DC. (2021); Miyake M, Nishida N. (2021); Nikitas A, Michalakopoulou K, Njoya ET, Karampatzakis D. (2020); He Y, Csiszár C. (2020); Liyanage S, Dia H, Abduljabbar R, Bagloee SA. (2019) |
| **Traffic Management** | AI systems optimise traffic flow and reduce congestion. | Alhussen A, Ansari AS. (2024); Fabre L, Bayart A, Bonnel P, Mony N. (2023); Raza A, Ali MU, Ullah U, Fayaz M, Alvi MJ, Kallu KD, Zafar A, Nengroo SH. (2022); Rasheed F, Yau KA, Noor RM, Chong Y. (2022); Jaramillo-Alcazar A, Govea J, Villegas-Ch W. (2023); Guillen-Perez A, Cano M-D. (2021); Abdelghaffar HM, Rakha HA. (2021) |
| **Real-time** | AI applications provide real-time data processing and decision-making in transportation. | Varone A, Heilmann Z, Porruvecchio G, Romanino A. (2024); Alhussen A, Ansari AS. (2024); Li H, Kim S. (2024); Salas P, Ramos V, Ruiz-Pérez M, Alorda-Ladaria B. (2023); Rehman A, Haseeb K, Saba T, Lloret J, Ahmed Z. (2021); Garcia-Retuerta D, Chamoso P, Hernández G, Guzmán ASR, Yigitcanlar T, Corchado JM. (2021) |
| **Multimodality** | Integration of multiple modes of transportation to enhance urban mobility | Scarişoreanu DI, Ghiculescu LD. (2023); Ruß M, Gust G. (2023); Lemonde C, Arsenio E, Henriques R. (2021); Miyake M, Nishida N. (2021) |
| **Computer Vision** | Use of computer vision in vehicle navigation and traffic monitoring. | Tsiktsiris D, Lalas A, Dasygenis M, Votis K. (2024); Lee H, Chatterjee I, Cho G. (2023) |

This table provides a comprehensive overview of key trends and perspectives in the field of mobility, with a focus on sustainability, technology integration, and innovative approaches. Each category highlights specific aspects of mobility development, emphasizing the role of creative and intelligent solutions, such as Smart Mobility, in transforming urban transportation.

Sustainability addresses efforts to promote eco-friendly and energy-efficient mobility solutions, showcasing the increasing emphasis on reducing environmental impact while maintaining high levels of accessibility and convenience. Smart Solutions encapsulates the innovative technologies that are driving improvements in mobility services and infrastructure, demonstrating how cutting-edge advancements are being leveraged to optimize transportation systems.

Multimodality emphasizes the integration of various transportation modes to enhance urban mobility, reflecting the growing trend toward seamless travel experiences. Sharing Solutions highlights the shift toward collaborative consumption models, where shared mobility options are becoming more prevalent as sustainable alternatives to traditional transport methods.

The Machine Learning category focuses on the application of AI techniques that enable systems to learn from experience, leading to continuous improvements in transportation efficiency and effectiveness. Big Data & Open Data underscores the importance of accessibility and utilization of open data sources, which are crucial for the development of advanced mobility services and the optimization of infrastructure.

Autonomous Vehicles represents the forefront of innovation in mobility, covering the development and deployment of self-driving cars and trucks that promise to revolutionize how people and goods move within and between urban areas. Smart Cities are urban areas that leverage AI and data to enhance the quality of life, efficiency, and sustainability, positioning themselves as hubs of technological and infrastructural advancement.

Traffic Management details how AI systems are being used to optimize traffic flow and reduce congestion, addressing one of the most pressing challenges in urban environments. Mobility as a Service (MaaS) explores the integration of various transport services into a single, accessible, on-demand platform, reflecting the move toward more user-centric mobility solutions.

Finally, Real-Time and Computer Vision technologies are recognized for their roles in providing immediate data processing and decision-making capabilities, as well as in vehicle navigation and traffic monitoring, ensuring that transportation systems are not only intelligent but also responsive to dynamic urban environments.

This table serves as a resource for understanding the multifaceted approach required to address the evolving needs of urban mobility, where technology, sustainability, and innovation converge to shape the future of transportation.

## 5. SUSTAINABLE MOBILITY IN THE AGE OF ARTIFICIAL INTELLIGENCE: A COMPREHENSIVE ANALYSIS OF FINDINGS

The rapid advancement of Artificial Intelligence (AI) technologies is significantly impacting the transportation sector, leading to transformative changes in how mobility is understood and implemented. This comprehensive analysis of recent literature uncovers the key trends and perspectives driving the integration of AI into mobility systems. These trends are categorized into three overarching themes: Sustainable and Smart Solutions, Autonomous Systems and Real-Time Management, and Data-Driven Multimodal Mobility.

## 5.1. SUSTAINABLE AND SMART SOLUTIONS

One of the most prominent trends in AI-driven mobility is the push towards sustainability, where efforts are focused on developing and promoting eco-friendly and energy-efficient transportation solutions. Scholars like Maslaric et al. (2024) and Ahn and Park (2024) have explored various strategies to minimize environmental impacts, such as the deployment of electric vehicles, the use of renewable energy sources, and the implementation of energy-efficient infrastructure. These initiatives are critical in addressing global environmental challenges, particularly in urban settings where transportation is a significant contributor to pollution.

Closely related to sustainability is the adoption of smart solutions that leverage cutting-edge technologies to optimize transportation systems and infrastructure. Alam et al. (2024) and Li et al. (2023) illustrate how AI can enhance traffic management, improve the safety and efficiency of transport networks, and reduce operational costs. These smart solutions are essential for developing resilient transportation systems that can adapt to the ever-changing demands of urban environments.

The concept of Smart Cities further extends the application of AI in mobility, focusing on the holistic integration of technology into urban planning and management. Research by Fang et al. (2024) and Elsawy et al. (2024) highlights how AI can be utilized to create more livable, efficient, and sustainable urban areas. These smart cities use AI-driven systems to manage everything from traffic flow to energy consumption, ensuring that urban spaces can accommodate growing populations without compromising on quality of life or environmental sustainability.

The trend towards sharing solutions represents another critical aspect of sustainable mobility. By promoting collaborative consumption models, such as ride-sharing and carpooling, AI enables more efficient use of resources and reduces the overall environmental impact of transportation. Studies by Flohr et al. (2024) and Saha et al. (2024) emphasize the role of AI in optimizing these sharing solutions, ensuring that supply meets demand and enhancing the user experience.

## 5.2. AUTONOMOUS SYSTEMS AND REAL-TIME MANAGEMENT

The development and deployment of autonomous vehicles are among the most transformative trends in AI-driven mobility. Ibrahim et al. (2024) and Louati et al. (2024) discuss the potential of self-driving cars and trucks to revolutionize the transportation industry by reducing human error, improving safety, and increasing the efficiency of logistics and passenger transport. These autonomous systems rely on a combination of machine learning, computer vision, and real-time data processing to navigate complex environments without human intervention.

Machine learning is a cornerstone of these autonomous systems, enabling AI to learn from experience and continuously improve its performance. Kristianto et al. (2024) and Gao et al. (2024) demonstrate how machine learning algorithms can be applied to various aspects of mobility, from optimizing route planning to predicting traffic patterns and enhancing the safety of autonomous vehicles. For instance, a machine learning model in London is helping to predict traffic flow and inform infrastructure improvements based on real-time data collected from city-wide sensors.

The importance of real-time applications in AI-driven mobility cannot be overstated. As transportation systems become increasingly complex and dynamic, the ability to process and respond to real-time data is crucial. Varone et al. (2024) and Alhussen and Ansari (2024) show how AI can monitor traffic conditions in real-time, detect potential issues before they escalate, and implement immediate corrective actions to maintain smooth traffic flow and prevent congestion.

Another critical aspect of real-time management is traffic management, where AI systems are used to optimize traffic flow and reduce congestion. Alhussen and Ansari (2024) and Fabre et al. (2023) provide evidence of AI's ability to monitor and manage traffic in real-time, ensuring that transportation networks operate at peak efficiency and with minimal disruptions.

## 5.3. DATA-DRIVEN MULTIMODAL MOBILITY

The increasing availability of Big Data & Open Data is transforming how transportation services and infrastructure are designed and managed. Varone et al. (2024) and Fabre et al. (2023) explore how big data analytics can be used to improve the accuracy and reliability of transportation models, enabling more informed decision-making and better resource allocation. The accessibility of open data also plays a crucial role in the development of new mobility services, such as Mobility as a Service (MaaS).

Mobility as a Service (MaaS) represents a paradigm shift in how transportation is perceived and utilized. This concept integrates various transport services into a single accessible on-demand service, offering users a seamless transportation experience. Cellina et al. (2024) and Martin et al. (2023) discuss how AI-driven MaaS platforms can provide personalized recommendations, optimize routes, and integrate multiple modes of transportation to meet the specific needs of users.

Multimodality is a related trend that focuses on integrating multiple modes of transportation to enhance urban mobility. Scarişoreanu and Ghiculescu (2023) and Ruß and Gust (2023) highlight the benefits of multimodal transport systems, which combine different types of transport to create more efficient and flexible mobility solutions. AI plays a critical role in coordinating these systems, ensuring that users can switch seamlessly between different modes of transport.

Finally, computer vision is an emerging technology used in vehicle navigation and traffic monitoring. Tsiktsiris et al. (2024) and Lee et al. (2023) demonstrate how computer vision can enhance the safety and efficiency of autonomous vehicles by providing real-time visual data that AI systems can analyze and act upon.

In practice, artificial intelligence has been successfully integrated into transportation systems in several cities around the world. By way of illustration, Singapore has employed the use of AI for dynamic traffic management, thereby reducing congestion in areas that experience high levels of traffic. The system utilises real-time data to adjust traffic light timings based on current traffic flow, thereby significantly reducing wait times and emissions. Similarly, Helsinki has employed AI in its Mobility-as-a-Service (MaaS) platform, where users can seamlessly integrate various modes of transport through a single application, enhancing both convenience and efficiency. These real-world applications provide tangible evidence of the transformative potential of AI, particularly when governments and private stakeholders collaborate to overcome barriers like infrastructure and regulatory hurdles.

A comparison of our findings with existing literature reveals that while AI is making notable progress in enhancing sustainable mobility, its impact varies by region and infrastructure readiness. For instance, Khan et al. (2021) observed that the contribution of AI to the development of smart cities is frequently constrained by the lack of consistency in regulatory frameworks, a challenge that is also identified in our review. Similarly, Maslaric et al. (2024) emphasise the necessity for a comprehensive approach to AI implementation, which is corroborated by the findings of this review, which suggest that a piecemeal adoption strategy may result in inefficiencies. These comparisons demonstrate the necessity for an integrated approach to policy, technology, and socio-economic factors to facilitate the advancement of AI-driven mobility.

In summary, the review of the literature reveals that AI is playing a transformative role in advancing sustainable mobility across various dimensions, including sustainability, smart solutions, smart cities, sharing solutions, machine learning, autonomous vehicles, big data, MaaS, traffic management, real-time applications, multimodality, and computer vision. Each of these trends highlights the potential of AI to create more efficient, safe, and sustainable transportation systems, shaping the future of mobility.

## 6. CONCLUSION

This comprehensive review has explored the transformative role of Artificial Intelligence (AI) in the mobility sector, highlighting how AI-driven innovations are reshaping transportation systems worldwide. By examining 90 peer-reviewed articles published between 2019 and 2024, we have identified and categorized the most significant trends and perspectives that are influencing the future of mobility.

### 6.1. KEY FINDINGS AND IMPLICATIONS

One of the most prominent findings is the increasing emphasis on sustainable mobility. The literature reveals a strong focus on the development and promotion of eco-friendly and energy-efficient transportation solutions, driven by the urgent need to address climate change and reduce the environmental impact of urbanization. The integration of AI into these efforts has proven to be a game-changer, offering innovative ways to optimize energy use, reduce emissions, and promote the use of renewable energy sources in transportation networks.

In parallel, the adoption of smart solutions and the evolution of Smart Cities are becoming critical in the quest for more efficient and resilient transportation systems. AI technologies are being leveraged to enhance traffic management, improve safety, and increase the overall efficiency of urban mobility. These smart solutions are essential in addressing the challenges posed by rapid urbanization, particularly in densely populated areas where traditional transportation systems are struggling to keep pace with growing demand.

The development of autonomous vehicles represents another key trend, with AI playing a central role in the design and deployment of self-driving cars and trucks. The potential benefits of autonomous vehicles, including reduced human error, improved safety, and increased operational efficiency, are significant. However, the literature also underscores the need for continued research and development to address the technical, ethical, and regulatory challenges associated with autonomous driving.

Data-driven approaches are also gaining traction, particularly through the use of Big Data & Open Data to improve mobility services and infrastructure. AI-driven analytics are enabling more informed decision-making, better resource allocation, and the development of new services like Mobility as a Service (MaaS), which offers users seamless access to multiple modes of transportation through a single platform. This shift towards data-driven, multimodal mobility represents a fundamental change in how transportation is perceived and utilized, with AI at the forefront of this transformation.

## 6.2. CHALLENGES AND FUTURE DIRECTIONS

While the potential of AI in mobility is immense, this review also highlights several challenges that need to be addressed to fully realize its benefits. The successful integration of AI into transportation systems requires overcoming technical hurdles, such as improving the reliability and safety of AI-driven solutions, as well as addressing ethical and regulatory concerns related to data privacy, security, and the social implications of automation.

Moreover, the widespread adoption of AI in mobility is contingent upon developing robust infrastructure, particularly in regions with limited technological resources. This includes ensuring the availability of high-quality data, investing in the necessary digital infrastructure, and fostering collaboration between public and private stakeholders to drive innovation.

Nevertheless, implementing AI-driven mobility solutions is not without considerable socio-economic challenges. In developing countries, the high costs associated with the deployment of AI infrastructure frequently constitute a significant financial obstacle. The lack of access to sophisticated technologies and insufficient financial resources for public transportation systems can impede the comprehensive implementation of AI. Furthermore, socio-economic inequalities can intensify the digital divide, whereby only affluent urban regions benefit from AI advancements, while underserved communities remain excluded. To address these issues, governments and international organizations must prioritize the allocation of funding and the implementation of policy frameworks that facilitate inclusive and equitable access to AI-based solutions, thereby ensuring the widespread distribution of the benefits associated with sustainable mobility.

This review has revealed AI's complex and multifaceted role in transforming sustainable mobility. Notwithstanding the considerable headway that has been made, particularly in autonomous vehicles, intelligent traffic management, and real-time data applications, several challenges remain. Future research should concentrate on resolving the socio-economic obstacles to AI implementation, particularly in underdeveloped areas, and examining the ethical implications of AI-driven decision-making in the field of mobility. Furthermore, additional empirical studies are required to evaluate the long-term impact of AI on urban transportation systems, particularly with sustainability and accessibility. Continued research and policy support will facilitate the significant enhancement of urban mobility through the application of AI, thereby improving efficiency, safety and sustainability.

Future research should continue to explore the intersection of AI and mobility, with a particular focus on addressing the challenges identified in this review. This includes developing more sophisticated AI algorithms that can adapt to real-world transportation systems' complexities and investigating the social and ethical implications of AI-driven mobility solutions. Additionally, there is a need for more empirical studies that assess the impact of AI on mobility in different contexts, particularly in emerging markets and developing countries where the challenges and opportunities may differ significantly from those in more developed regions.

In conclusion, AI is poised to revolutionize the mobility sector, offering unprecedented opportunities to enhance sustainability, efficiency, and accessibility. However, realizing the full potential of AI-driven mobility will require addressing various technical, ethical, and regulatory challenges. As we move forward, it will be essential for researchers, policymakers, and industry leaders to work together to ensure that the benefits of AI are realized in a way that is equitable, sustainable, and beneficial for all.

This review has provided a detailed analysis of the current trends and perspectives in AI-driven mobility, offering valuable insights for future research and policy development. As AI continues to evolve, its impact on mobility will likely become even more profound, paving the way for a new era of smart, sustainable transportation.

## REFERENCES


Aarabe, M.. (2024). Smart tourism experience and responsible travelers' behavior: A systematic literature review. In El Archi, Y., Benbba, B., Dávid, L., & Cardoso, L. (Eds.), *Promoting responsible tourism with digital platforms* (pp. 128–147). IGI Global., DOI: 10.4018/979-8-3693-3286-3.ch008

Aarabe, M., Ben Khizzou, N., Alla, L., & Benjelloun, A. (2024). Marketing applications of emerging technologies: A systematic literature review. In Alla, L., Hmioui, A., & Bentalha, B. (Eds.), *AI and data engineering solutions for effective marketing* (pp. 23–47). IGI Global., DOI: 10.4018/979-8-3693-3172-9.ch002

Abbas, Q., Ahmad, G., Alyas, T., Alghamdi, T., Alsaawy, Y., & Alzahrani, A. (2023). Revolutionizing urban mobility: IoT-enhanced autonomous parking solutions with transfer learning for smart cities. *Sensors (Basel)*, 23(21), 8753. DOI: 10.3390/s23218753 PMID: 37960453

Abdelghaffar, H. M., & Rakha, H. A. (2021). Development and testing of a novel game theoretic decentralized traffic signal controller. *IEEE Transactions on Intelligent Transportation Systems*, 22(1), 231–242. DOI: 10.1109/TITS.2019.2955918

Alam, T., Gupta, R., Nasurudeen Ahamed, N., Ullah, A., & Almaghthwi, A. (2024). Smart mobility adoption in sustainable smart cities to establish a growing ecosystem: Challenges and opportunities. *MRS Energy & Sustainability : a Review Journal*. Advance online publication. DOI: 10.1557/s43581-024-00092-4

Alhussen, A., & Ansari, A. S. (2024). Real-time prediction of urban traffic problems based on artificial intelligence-enhanced mobile ad hoc networks (MANETS). *Computers, Materials & Continua*, 79(2), 1903–1923. DOI: 10.32604/cmc.2024.049260

Alla, L., Bentalha, B., & Elyoussfi, A. (2023). Intelligence territoriale et positionnement stratégique des regions au Maroc: Le cas de la région de Fès Meknes en perspective. In *Le concept de l'intelligence en sciences juridiques, économiques et sociales* (pp. 215-237).

Anagnostopoulos, T. (2021). A predictive vehicle ride-sharing recommendation system for smart cities commuting. *Smart Cities*, 4(1), 177–191. DOI: 10.3390/smartcities4010010

Anedda, M., Fadda, M., Girau, R., Pau, G., & Giusto, D. (2023). A social smart city for public and private mobility: A real case study. *Computer Networks*, 220, 109464. DOI: 10.1016/j.comnet.2022.109464

Antonialli, F., Martinesco, A., & Mira-Bonnardel, S. (2022). Artificial intelligence as a determinant for reshaping the automotive industry and urban mobility services. *International Journal of Automotive Technology and Management*, 22(3), 324. DOI: 10.1504/IJATM.2022.124828

Bencekri, M., Kim, S., Fan, Y. V., & Lee, S. (2024). Locating carbon-neutral mobility hubs using artificial intelligence techniques. *Scientific Reports*, 14(1), 12328. DOI: 10.1038/s41598-024-62701-z PMID: 38811628

Bentalha, B., & Alla, L. (2024). Revealing the subtleties: The art of qualitative studies in science and management. In Bentalha, B., & Alla, L. (Eds.), *Applying qualitative research methods to management science* (pp. 1–21). IGI Global., DOI: 10.4018/979-8-3693-5543-5.ch001

Bokolo, A. J. (2023). Inclusive and safe mobility needs of senior citizens: Implications for age-friendly cities and communities. *Urban Science (Basel, Switzerland)*, 7(4), 103. DOI: 10.3390/urbansci7040103

Boudri, R., Bentalha, B., & Benjelloun, O. (2024). Phygital marketing and the pain of paying: An Amazon Go netnographic case study. In Alla, L., Hmioui, A., & Bentalha, B. (Eds.), *AI and data engineering solutions for effective marketing* (pp. 348–363). IGI Global., DOI: 10.4018/979-8-3693-3172-9.ch017

Bouhtati, N., Alla, L., & Bentalha, B. (2023). Marketing big data analytics and customer relationship management: A fuzzy approach. In Bentalha, B., Hmioui, A., & Alla, L. (Eds.), *Integrating intelligence and sustainability in supply chains* (pp. 75–86). IGI Global., DOI: 10.4018/979-8-3693-0225-5.ch004

Bouhtati, N., Alla, L., & Ed-Daakouri, I. (2024). Smart data analysis and prediction of responsible customer behavior in tourism: An exploratory review of the literature. In El Archi, Y., Benbba, B., Dávid, L., & Cardoso, L. (Eds.), *Promoting responsible tourism with digital platforms* (pp. 189–212). IGI Global., DOI: 10.4018/979-8-3693-3286-3.ch011

Bouhtati, N., El Yaacoubi, Y., Bentalha, B., & Alla, L. (2024). Leviers logistiques de promotion du commerce équitable des produits de terroir: Une esquisse de modèle d'analyse. *Alternatives Managériales Économiques*, 6(Spécial 1), 17-35.

Bucchiarone, A., Battisti, S., Marconi, A., Maldacea, R., & Ponce, D. C. (2021). Autonomous shuttle-as-a-service (ASaaS): Challenges, opportunities, and social implications. *IEEE Transactions on Intelligent Transportation Systems*, 22(6), 3790–3799. DOI: 10.1109/TITS.2020.3025670

Bucher, D., Mangili, F., Cellina, F., Bonesana, C., Jonietz, D., & Raubal, M. (2019). From location tracking to personalized eco-feedback: A framework for geographic information collection, processing and visualization to promote sustainable mobility behaviors. *Travel Behaviour & Society*, 14, 43–56. DOI: 10.1016/j.tbs.2018.09.005

Bugaj, M., Durana, P., Blazek, R., & Horak, J. (2023). Industry 4.0: Marvels in profitability in the transport sector. *Mathematics*, 11(17), 3647. DOI: 10.3390/math11173647

Caputo, F., Magliocca, P., Canestrino, R., & Rescigno, E. (2023). Rethinking the role of technology for citizens' engagement and sustainable development in smart cities. *Sustainability (Basel)*, 15(13), 10400. DOI: 10.3390/su151310400

Cellina, F., Derboni, M., Giuffrida, V., Tomic, U., & Hoerler, R. (2024). Trust me if you can: Practical challenges affecting the integration of carpooling in mobility-as-a-service platforms. *Travel Behaviour & Society*, 37, 100832. DOI: 10.1016/j.tbs.2024.100832

Chen, J., Tao, S., Teng, S., Chen, Y., Zhang, H., & Wang, F.-Y. (2023). Toward sustainable intelligent transportation systems in 2050: Fairness and eco-responsibility. *IEEE Transactions on Intelligent Vehicles*, 8(6), 3537–3540. DOI: 10.1109/TIV.2023.3286873

Chong, Y.-W., Villanueva-Libunao, K., Chee, S.-Y., Alvarez, M. J., Yau, K.-L. A., & Keoh, S. L. (2022). Artificial intelligence policies to enhance urban mobility in Southeast Asia. *Frontiers in Sustainable Cities*, 4, 824391. DOI: 10.3389/frsc.2022.824391

Cirianni, F. M. M., Comi, A., & Quattrone, A. (2023). Mobility control centre and artificial intelligence for sustainable urban districts. *Information (Basel)*, 14(10), 581. DOI: 10.3390/info14100581

Cristóbal, T., Quesada-Arencibia, A., De Blasio, G. S., Padrón, G., Alayón, F., & García, C. R. (2022). Using data mining to estimate patterns of contagion-risk interactions in an intercity public road transport system. *IEEE Access : Practical Innovations, Open Solutions*, 10, 99150–99167. DOI: 10.1109/ACCESS.2022.3206838

D'Amico, G., Szopik-Depczyńska, K., Dembińska, I., & Ioppolo, G. (2021). Smart and sustainable logistics of port cities: A framework for comprehending enabling factors, domains, and goals. *Sustainable Cities and Society*, 69, 102801. DOI: 10.1016/j.scs.2021.102801

Devi, P., Kizielewicz, B., Guleria, A., Shekhovtsov, A., Wątróbski, J., Królikowski, T., Więckowski, J., & Sałabun, W. (2022). Decision support in selecting a reliable strategy for sustainable urban transport based on Laplacian energy of T-spherical fuzzy graphs. *Energies*, 15(14), 4970. DOI: 10.3390/en15144970

Duggal, A. S., Singh, R., Gehlot, A., Gupta, L. R., Akram, S. V., Prakash, C., Singh, S., & Kumar, R. (2021). Infrastructure, mobility and safety 4.0: Modernization in road transportation. *Technology in Society*, 67, 101791. DOI: 10.1016/j.techsoc.2021.101791

El Jaouhari, S., & Alla, L. (2022). L'approche territoriale et la gestion de l'impact de la pandémie de Covid-19: Cas des collectivités territoriales. *Alternatives Managériales Économiques*, 4(1), 245–265.

Elavarasan, R. M., Pugazhendhi, R., Shafiullah, G. M., Irfan, M., & Anvari-Moghaddam, A. (2021). A hover view over effectual approaches on pandemic management for sustainable cities – The endowment of prospective technologies with revitalization strategies. *Sustainable Cities and Society*, 68, 102789. DOI: 10.1016/j.scs.2021.102789 PMID: 35004131

Elhissoufi, M., & Alla, L. (2024). Artificial intelligence in customer acquisition: A bibliometric study. In Alla, L., Hmioui, A., & Bentalha, B. (Eds.), *AI and data engineering solutions for effective marketing* (pp. 1–22). IGI Global., DOI: 10.4018/979-8-3693-3172-9.ch001

Elsawy, Y., Alatawi, A. S., Abaza, M., Moawad, A., & Aggoune, E.-H. M. (2024). Next-generation dual transceiver FSO communication system for high-speed trains in Neom Smart City. *Photonics*, 11(5), 483. DOI: 10.3390/photonics11050483

. Esztergár-Kiss, D. (2023). Transportation research challenges based on the analysis of EU projects. *Promet – Traffic & Transportation*, 35(4), 446-461. https://doi.org/ DOI: 10.7307/ptt.v35i4.181

Fabre, L., Bayart, C., Bonnel, P., & Mony, N. (2023). The potential of Wi-Fi data to estimate bus passenger mobility. *Technological Forecasting and Social Change*, 192, 122509. DOI: 10.1016/j.techfore.2023.122509

Fang, K., Azizan, S. A., & Huang, H. (2024). GIS-based intelligent planning approach of child-friendly pedestrian pathway to promote a child-friendly city. *Scientific Reports*, 14(1), 8139. DOI: 10.1038/s41598-024-58712-5 PMID: 38584168

Flohr, L. A., Schuß, M., Wallach, D. P., Krüger, A., & Riener, A. (2024). Designing for passengers' information needs on fellow travelers: A comparison of day and night rides in shared automated vehicles. *Applied Ergonomics*, 116, 104198. DOI: 10.1016/j.apergo.2023.104198 PMID: 38091694

Fong, B., Fong, A. C. M., & Hong, G. Y. (2023). Sustainable micromobility management in smart cities. *IEEE Transactions on Intelligent Transportation Systems*, 24(12), 15890–15896. DOI: 10.1109/TITS.2023.3292377

Gambo, N., & Musonda, I. (2021). Effect of the fourth industrial revolution on road transport asset management practice in Nigeria. *Journal of Construction in Developing Countries*, 26(1), 19–43. DOI: 10.21315/jcdc2021.26.1.2

Gao, Q. L., Zhong, C., Yue, Y., Cao, R., & Zhang, B. (2024). Income estimation based on human mobility patterns and machine learning models. *Applied Geography (Sevenoaks, England)*, 163, 103179. DOI: 10.1016/j.apgeog.2023.103179

Garcia-Retuerta, D., Chamoso, P., Hernández, G., Guzmán, A. S. R., Yigitcanlar, T., & Corchado, J. M. (2021). An efficient management platform for developing smart cities: Solution for real-time and future crowd detection. *Electronics (Basel)*, 10(7), 765. DOI: 10.3390/electronics10070765

Gokasar, I., Simic, V., Deveci, M., & Senapati, T. (2023). Alternative prioritization of freeway incident management using autonomous vehicles in mixed traffic using a type-2 neutrosophic number-based decision support system. *Engineering Applications of Artificial Intelligence*, 123(Part A), 106183. https://doi.org/DOI: 10.1016/j.engappai.2023.106183

Graells-Garrido, E., Opitz, D., Rowe, F., & Arriagada, J. (2023). A data fusion approach with mobile phone data for updating travel survey-based mode split estimates. *Transportation Research Part C, Emerging Technologies*, 155, 104285. DOI: 10.1016/j.trc.2023.104285

Guillen-Perez, A., & Cano, M.-D. (2021). Intelligent IoT systems for traffic management: A practical application. *IET Intelligent Transport Systems*, 15(2), 273–285. DOI: 10.1049/itr2.12021

Guzman, L. A., Beltran, C., Morales, R., & Sarmiento, O. L. (2023). Inequality in personal exposure to air pollution in transport microenvironments for commuters in Bogotá. *Case Studies on Transport Policy*, 11, 100963. DOI: 10.1016/j.cstp.2023.100963

Hammoumi, L., Maanan, M., & Rhinane, H. (2024). Characterizing smart cities based on artificial intelligence. *Smart Cities*, 7(3), 1330–1345. DOI: 10.3390/smartcities7030056

. Hmioui, A., Alla, L., & Bentalha, B. (2017). Piloting territorial tourism in Morocco Proposal for a tourism index for the destination Fez [Pilotage de la touristicité territoriale au Maroc Proposition d'un indice de touristicité pour la destination Fès] (No. hal-02334913).

Ibrahim, H. A., Qahtan, S., Zaidan, A. A., Deveci, M., Hajiaghaei-Keshteli, M., Mohammed, R. T., & Alamoodi, A. H. (2024). Sustainability in mobility for autonomous vehicles over smart city evaluation; using interval-valued Fermatean fuzzy rough set-based decision-making model. *Engineering Applications of Artificial Intelligence*, 129, 107609. DOI: 10.1016/j.engappai.2023.107609

Jaramillo-Alcazar, A., Govea, J., & Villegas-Ch, W. (2023). Advances in the optimization of vehicular traffic in smart cities: Integration of blockchain and computer vision for sustainable mobility. *Sustainability (Basel)*, 15(22), 15736. DOI: 10.3390/su152215736

Javed, A. R., Shahzad, F., Rehman, S., Zikria, Y. B., Razzak, I., Jalil, Z., & Xu, G. (2022). Future smart cities: Requirements, emerging technologies, applications, challenges, and future aspects. *Cities (London, England)*, 129, 103794. DOI: 10.1016/j.cities.2022.103794

Kakderi, C., Oikonomaki, E., & Papadaki, I. (2021). Smart and resilient urban futures for sustainability in the post-COVID-19 era: A review of policy responses on urban mobility. *Sustainability (Basel)*, 13(11), 6486. DOI: 10.3390/su13116486

Karger, E., Jagals, M., & Ahlemann, F. (2021). Blockchain for smart mobility—Literature review and future research agenda. *Sustainability (Basel)*, 13(23), 13268. DOI: 10.3390/su132313268

Kassens-Noor, E., Siegel, J., & Decaminada, T. (2021). Choosing ethics over morals: A possible determinant to embracing artificial intelligence in future urban mobility. *Frontiers in Sustainable Cities*, 3, 723475. DOI: 10.3389/frsc.2021.723475

Keller, C., Glück, F., Gerlach, C. F., & Schlegel, T. (2022). Investigating the potential of data science methods for sustainable public transport. *Sustainability (Basel)*, 14(7), 4211. DOI: 10.3390/su14074211

Khan, Z. A., Sherazi, H. H. R., Ali, M., Imran, M. A., Rehman, I. U., & Chakrabarti, P. (2021). Designing a wind energy harvester for connected vehicles in green cities. *Energies*, 14(17), 5408. DOI: 10.3390/en14175408

Kim, M. J., Hall, C. M., Chung, N., Kim, M., & Sohn, K. (2023). Why do tourists use public transport in Korea? The roles of artificial intelligence knowledge, environmental, social, and governance, and sustainability. *Asia Pacific Journal of Tourism Research*, 28(5), 467–484. DOI: 10.1080/10941665.2023.2247099

Kristianto, E., Lin, P.-C., & Hwang, R.-H. (2024). Sustainable and lightweight domain-based intrusion detection system for in-vehicle network. *Sustainable Computing : Informatics and Systems*, 41, 100936. DOI: 10.1016/j.suscom.2023.100936

Lee, B. (2022). Smart cities, connected cars and autonomous vehicles: Design fiction and visions of smarter future urban mobility. *Technoetic Arts*, 20(Themed Issue: Projected Interiorities), 225-240. https://doi.org/DOI: 10.1386/tear_00092_1

Lee, H., Chatterjee, I., & Cho, G. (2023). A systematic review of computer vision and AI in parking space allocation in a seaport. *Applied Sciences (Basel, Switzerland)*, 13(18), 10254. DOI: 10.3390/app131810254

Lee, J., Kim, K., Park, G., & Trunina, A. (2024). The role of business models in the sustainable transition of shared mobility services in China and South Korea. *Asia Pacific Business Review*, •••, 1–22. DOI: 10.1080/13602381.2024.2358952

Lemonde, C., Arsenio, E., & Henriques, R. (2021). Integrative analysis of multimodal traffic data: Addressing open challenges using big data analytics in the city of Lisbon. *European Transport Research Review*, 13(1), 64. DOI: 10.1186/s12544-021-00520-3

Li, H., Chen, Y., Li, K., Wang, C., & Chen, B. (2023). Transportation Internet: A sustainable solution for intelligent transportation systems. *IEEE Transactions on Intelligent Transportation Systems*, 24(12), 15818–15829. DOI: 10.1109/TITS.2023.3270749

Li, J., Zhou, M., Xue, X., Zhu, J., Han, S., Li, L., & Wang, F.-Y. (2023). A sustainable ecology of mobility: DAO-based autonomous vehicular services. *IEEE Transactions on Intelligent Vehicles*, 8(12), 4682–4684. DOI: 10.1109/TIV.2023.3334719

Liyanage, S., Dia, H., Abduljabbar, R., & Bagloee, S. A. (2019). Flexible mobility on-demand: An environmental scan. *Sustainability (Basel)*, 11(5), 1262. DOI: 10.3390/su11051262

Louati, A., Louati, H., Kariri, E., Neifar, W., Hassan, M. K., Khairi, M. H. H., Farahat, M. A., & El-Hoseny, H. M. (2024). Sustainable smart cities through multi-agent reinforcement learning-based cooperative autonomous vehicles. *Sustainability (Basel)*, 16(5), 1779. DOI: 10.3390/su16051779

Mahrez, Z., Sabir, E., Badidi, E., Saad, W., & Sadik, M. (2022). Smart urban mobility: When mobility systems meet smart data. *IEEE Transactions on Intelligent Transportation Systems*, 23(7), 6222–6239. DOI: 10.1109/TITS.2021.3084907

Maldonado Silveira Alonso Munhoz, P. A., da Costa Dias, F., Kowal Chinelli, C., Azevedo Guedes, A. L., Neves dos Santos, J. A., da Silveira e Silva, W., & Pereira Soares, C. A. (2020). Smart mobility: The main drivers for increasing the intelligence of urban mobility. *Sustainability (Basel)*, 12(24), 10675. DOI: 10.3390/su122410675

Martí, P., Jordán, J., Chamoso, P., & Julian, V. (2022). Taxi services and the carsharing alternative: A case study of Valencia City. *Mathematical Biosciences and Engineering*, 19(7), 6680–6698. DOI: 10.3934/mbe.2022314 PMID: 35730277

Martin, H., Wiedemann, N., Reck, D., & Raubal, M. (2023). Graph-based mobility profiling. *Computers, Environment and Urban Systems*, 100, 101910. DOI: 10.1016/j.compenvurbsys.2022.101910

Maslaric, M., Bojic, S., Mircetic, D., Nikolicic, S., & Medenica Todorovic, R. (2024). Sustainable urban mobility planning in the port areas: A case study. *Sustainability (Basel)*, 16(2), 514. DOI: 10.3390/su16020514

Meziane, B., Bentalha, B., & Alla, H. (2024). La PME logistique et le développement territorial régional: Une analyse qualitative. *Alternatives Managériales Economiques*, 6(4), 1–22.

Miraftabzadeh, S. M., Longo, M., Di Martino, A., Saldarini, A., & Faranda, R. S. (2024). Exploring the synergy of artificial intelligence in energy storage systems for electric vehicles. *Electronics (Basel)*, 13(10), 1973. DOI: 10.3390/electronics13101973

Mitieka, D., Luke, R., Twinomurinzi, H., & Mageto, J. (2023). Smart mobility in urban areas: A bibliometric review and research agenda. *Sustainability (Basel)*, 15(8), 6754. DOI: 10.3390/su15086754

Miyake, M., & Nishida, N. (2021). Activities on multimodal MaaS to solve the first mile/last mile problem—NTT DOCOMO's next-generation mobility service. *Feature Articles: Digital Transformation of Urban Areas Focusing on Mobility*, 19(1), 17–21. DOI: 10.53829/ntr202101fa3

Nielsen, A. F., Michelmann, J., Akac, A., Palts, K., Zilles, A., Anagnostopoulou, A., & Langeland, O. (2023). Using the future wheel methodology to assess the impact of open science in the transport sector. *Scientific Reports*, 13(1), 6000. DOI: 10.1038/s41598-023-33102-5 PMID: 37046066

Nikitas, A., Michalakopoulou, K., Njoya, E. T., & Karampatzakis, D. (2020). Artificial intelligence, transport and the smart city: Definitions and dimensions of a new mobility era. *Sustainability (Basel)*, 12(7), 2789. DOI: 10.3390/su12072789

Nouhaila, B. K., Aarabe, M., & Alla, L. (2024). The impact of digitalisation on the customer experience in medical tourism: A systematic review. In Talukder, M., Kumar, S., & Tyagi, P. (Eds.), *Impact of AI and Tech-Driven Solutions in Hospitality and Tourism* (pp. 408–428). IGI Global., DOI: 10.4018/979-8-3693-6755-1.ch020

Obracht-Prondzyńska, H., Duda, E., Anacka, H., & Kowal, J. (2022). Greencoin as an AI-based solution shaping climate awareness. *International Journal of Environmental Research and Public Health*, 19(18), 11183. DOI: 10.3390/ijerph191811183 PMID: 36141452

Ozpinar, A. (2023). A hyper-integrated mobility as a service (MaaS) to gamification and carbon market enterprise architecture framework for a sustainable environment. *Energies*, 16(5), 2480. DOI: 10.3390/en16052480

Page, M. J., McKenzie, J. E., Bossuyt, P. M., Boutron, I., Hoffmann, T. C., Mulrow, C. D., Shamseer, L., Tetzlaff, J. M., Akl, E. A., Brennan, S. E., Chou, R., Glanville, J., Grimshaw, J. M., Hróbjartsson, A., Lalu, M. M., Li, T., Loder, E. W., Mayo-Wilson, E., McDonald, S., & Moher, D. (2021). The PRISMA 2020 statement: An updated guideline for reporting systematic reviews. *BMJ (Clinical Research Ed.)*, 372, n71. Advance online publication. DOI: 10.1136/bmj.n71 PMID: 33782057

Paiva, S., Ahad, M. A., Tripathi, G., Feroz, N., & Casalino, G. (2021). Enabling technologies for urban smart mobility: Recent trends, opportunities, and challenges. *Sensors (Basel)*, 21(6), 2143. DOI: 10.3390/s21062143 PMID: 33803903

Piccialli, F., Giampaolo, F., Prezioso, E., Crisci, D., & Cuomo, S. (2021). Predictive analytics for smart parking: A deep learning approach in forecasting of IoT data. *ACM Transactions on Internet Technology*, 21(3), 68. DOI: 10.1145/3412842

Rajabi, E., Nowaczyk, S., Pashami, S., Bergquist, M., Ebby, G. S., & Wajid, S. (2023). A knowledge-based AI framework for mobility as a service. *Sustainability (Basel)*, 15(3), 2717. DOI: 10.3390/su15032717

Rasheed, F., Yau, K. A., Noor, R. M., & Chong, Y. (2022). Deep reinforcement learning for addressing disruptions in traffic light control. *Computers, Materials & Continua*, 71(2), 2225–2247. DOI: 10.32604/cmc.2022.022952

Raza, A., Ali, M. U., Ullah, U., Fayaz, M., Alvi, M. J., Kallu, K. D., Zafar, A., & Nengroo, S. H. (2022). Evaluation of a sustainable urban transportation system in terms of traffic congestion—A case study in Taxila, Pakistan. *Sustainability (Basel)*, 14(19), 12325. DOI: 10.3390/su141912325

Rinaldi, M., Picarelli, E., D'Ariano, A., & Viti, F. (2020). Mixed-fleet single-terminal bus scheduling problem: Modelling, solution scheme and potential applications. *Omega*, 96, 102070. DOI: 10.1016/j.omega.2019.05.006

Roger, S., Botella-Mascarell, C., Martín-Sacristán, D., García-Roger, D., Monserrat, J. F., & Svensson, T. (2024). Sustainable mobility in B5G/6G: V2X technology trends and use cases. *IEEE Open Journal of Vehicular Technology*, 5, 459–472. DOI: 10.1109/OJVT.2024.3375451

Ruß, M., & Gust, G. (2023). Reliable route planning and time savings in real-world urban intermodal transportation networks: Evidence from Hamburg, Germany. *Expert Systems with Applications*, 227, 120196. DOI: 10.1016/j.eswa.2023.120196

Saha, A., Görçün, Ö. F., Pamucar, D., Arya, L., & Simic, V. (2024). Evaluation of shared micro-mobility systems for sustainable cities by using a consensus-based Fermatean fuzzy multiple objective optimization and full multiplicative form. *Engineering Applications of Artificial Intelligence*, 134, 108662. DOI: 10.1016/j.engappai.2024.108662

Salas, P., Ramos, V., Ruiz-Pérez, M., & Alorda-Ladaria, B. (2023). Methodological proposal for the analysis of urban mobility using Wi-Fi data and artificial intelligence techniques: The case of Palma. *Electronics (Basel)*, 12(3), 504. DOI: 10.3390/electronics12030504

Salazar-Cabrera, R., Pachón de la Cruz, Á., & Madrid Molina, J. M. (2020). Sustainable transit vehicle tracking service, using intelligent transportation system services and emerging communication technologies: A review. [English Edition]. *Journal of Traffic and Transportation Engineering*, 7(6), 729–747. DOI: 10.1016/j.jtte.2020.07.003

Sawhney, N. (2023). Contestations in urban mobility: Rights, risks, and responsibilities for urban AI. *AI & Society*, 38(3), 1083–1098. DOI: 10.1007/s00146-022-01502-2

Scarişoreanu, D. I., & Ghiculescu, L. D. (2023). Strategic forecast for rail freight transport in Romania using the Relevant Tree Method and Scenario Method. *BRAIN. Broad Research in Artificial Intelligence and Neuroscience*, 14(1), 596–627. DOI: 10.18662/brain/14.1/437

Senapati, T., Simic, V., Saha, A., Dobrodolac, M., Rong, Y., & Tirkolaee, E. B. (2023). Intuitionistic fuzzy power Aczel-Alsina model for prioritization of sustainable transportation sharing practices. *Engineering Applications of Artificial Intelligence*, 119, 105716. DOI: 10.1016/j.engappai.2022.105716

Servou, E., Behrendt, F., & Horst, M. (2023). Data, AI and governance in MaaS—Leading to sustainable mobility? *Transportation Research Interdisciplinary Perspectives*, 19, 100806. DOI: 10.1016/j.trip.2023.100806

Strielkowski, W., Zenchenko, S., Tarasova, A., & Radyukova, Y. (2022). Management of smart and sustainable cities in the post-COVID-19 era: Lessons and implications. *Sustainability (Basel)*, 14(12), 7267. DOI: 10.3390/su14127267

Szpilko, D., Naharro, F., Lăzăroiu, G., Nica, E., & Gallegos, A. (2023). Artificial intelligence in the smart city—A literature review. *Engineering Management in Production and Services*, 15(4), 53–75. DOI: 10.2478/emj-2023-0028

Tsiktsiris, D., Lalas, A., Dasygenis, M., & Votis, K. (2024). Improving passenger detection with overhead fisheye imaging. *IEEE Access : Practical Innovations, Open Solutions*, 12, 66237–66247. DOI: 10.1109/ACCESS.2024.3395786

Varone, A., Heilmann, Z., Porruvecchio, G., & Romanino, A. (2024). Solar parking lot management: An IoT platform for smart charging EV fleets, using real-time data and production forecasts. *Renewable and Sustainable Energy Reviews*, 189(Part A), 113845. https://doi.org/DOI: 10.1016/j.rser.2023.113845

Vermesan, O., John, R., Pype, P., Daalderop, G., Kriegel, K., Mitic, G., Lorentz, V., Bahr, R., Sand, H. E., Bockrath, S., & Waldhör, S. (2021). Automotive intelligence embedded in electric connected autonomous and shared vehicles technology for sustainable green mobility. *Frontiers in Future Transportation*, 2, 688482. DOI: 10.3389/ffutr.2021.688482

Vitetta, A. (2022). Sustainable mobility as a service: Framework and transport system models. *Information (Basel)*, 13(7), 346. DOI: 10.3390/info13070346

Zhang, H., Song, X., Long, Y., Xia, T., Fang, K., Zheng, J., Huang, D., Shibasaki, R., & Liang, Y. (2019). Mobile phone GPS data in urban bicycle-sharing: Layout optimization and emissions reduction analysis. *Applied Energy*, 242, 138–147. DOI: 10.1016/j.apenergy.2019.03.119

Ziemba, P., & Gago, I. (2022). Compromise multi-criteria selection of e-scooters for the vehicle sharing system in Poland. *Energies*, 15(14), 5048. DOI: 10.3390/en15145048

## KEY TERMS AND DEFINITIONS

**Artificial Intelligence (AI):** AI refers to the simulation of human intelligence processes by machines, especially computer systems. These processes include learning, reasoning, and self-correction. In mobility, AI is applied to optimize transport systems, enhance safety, and enable real-time data management. Source: Page, M.J., et al. (2021). The PRISMA 2020 statement: An updated guideline for reporting systematic reviews. The BMJ.

•**Sustainable Mobility:** Sustainable mobility involves the design and implementation of transportation systems that meet present mobility demands without compromising the ability of future generations to meet their own. It emphasizes energy efficiency, eco-friendly solutions, and minimal environmental impact. Source: Maslaric, M., et al. (2024). Sustainable urban mobility planning in port areas: A case study. Sustainability.

**Smart Cities:** Smart cities are urban areas that use digital technologies, including AI, to enhance infrastructure, optimize energy use, and improve the quality of life for their citizens through efficient resource management and real-time data analytics. Source: Fang, K., et al. (2024). GIS-based intelligent planning approach for child-friendly pathways. Scientific Reports.

**Autonomous Vehicles (AVs):** AVs are self-driving cars or trucks that use AI, computer vision, and machine learning to navigate and operate witwhout human intervention. These vehicles promise to enhance safety, reduce human error, and optimize transportation efficiency. Source: Ibrahim, H.A., et al. (2024). Sustainability in mobility for autonomous vehicles. Engineering Applications of Artificial Intelligence.

**Machine Learning (ML):** ML is a branch of AI that allows systems to learn from data, identify patterns, and make decisions without explicit programming. In mobility, ML is used for traffic prediction, route optimization, and improving the efficiency of transportation systems. Source: Kristianto, E., et al. (2024). Sustainable domain-based intrusion detection system for in-vehicle networks. Sustainable Computing: Informatics and Systems.

**Mobility as a Service (MaaS):** MaaS integrates various transport services into a single, accessible on-demand service platform. It allows users to plan, book, and pay for multiple types of transportation using a single service, enhancing convenience and efficiency. Source: Cellina, F., et al. (2024). Practical challenges affecting carpooling integration in MaaS platforms. Travel Behaviour and Society.

**Big Data & Open Data:** Big Data refers to the large volumes of data generated from various sources, while Open Data is data that is freely available to the public. In mobility, these data types are crucial for optimizing transportation infrastructure and services through AI-driven analysis. Source: Varone, A., et al. (2024). Solar parking lot management using real-time data and AI. Renewable and Sustainable Energy Reviews.

**Traffic Management:** AI-driven traffic management systems optimize the flow of vehicles and reduce congestion by using real-time data to predict traffic patterns and adjust traffic signals or reroute vehicles accordingly. Source: Alhussen, A., & Ansari, A.S. (2024). Real-time prediction of urban traffic problems. Computers, Materials & Continua.

**Multimodality:** Multimodality in transportation refers to the use of multiple modes of transport (e.g., buses, trains, bikes) within a single trip or transport system. AI enhances multimodal mobility by integrating and coordinating various transportation modes to improve efficiency. Source: Scarişoreanu, D.I., & Ghiculescu, L.D. (2023). Strategic forecast for rail freight transport in Romania. BRAIN.

**Computer Vision:** Computer vision is a field of AI that enables machines to interpret and process visual data. In mobility, it is used for vehicle navigation, traffic monitoring, and ensuring safety through real-time image processing and pattern recognition. Source: Tsiktsiris, D., et al. (2024). Improving passenger detection with overhead fisheye imaging. IEEE Access.

# Chapter 8
# The Future of Territorial Management:
## AI, IoT, and Big Data Synergies

**Aditi Bhardwaj**
*ShriRam Institute of Information Technology, Banmore, India*

**Saroopya Bachu**
*Global Logic, UK*

**Senthil Prabhu Rajendran**
https://orcid.org/0000-0003-4138-1316
*College of Pharmacy, Madurai Medical College, India*

**Sonali Rastogi**
*Venkateshwara Group of Institutions, Daurala, India*

**K. Ramakrishna**
*Pulipati Prasad College of Pharmaceutical Sciences, India*

**Chinnasamy Balalakshmi**
*Department of Nanoscience and Technology, Science Campus, Alagappa University, Karaikudi, India*

**Pankaj Sharma**
https://orcid.org/0000-0003-0211-9606
*ShriRam College of Pharmacy, Banmore, India*

## ABSTRACT

*The fusion of Big Data analytics, IoT (Internet of Things), and AI (Artificial Intelligence) is transforming territorial management, offering unprecedented prospects for sustainable and efficient urban and rural development. This chapter explores how these technologies can tackle complex territorial governance challenges. It breaks down the individual contributions of AI, IoT, and Big Data: IoT enables real-time data gathering and networking; AI enhances forecasting, decision-making, and automation; Big Data analytics processes vast data volumes to inform resource allocation and strategy. The chapter discusses an integrated approach combining*

DOI: 10.4018/979-8-3693-6854-1.ch008

*these technologies to create smart territorial administration, supported by global case studies demonstrating improved public services, equitable growth, and infrastructure enhancement. Challenges such as security, privacy, and regulatory needs are also addressed. Looking ahead, the chapter emphasizing the need for creativity and multidisciplinary collaboration in developing future smart territories.*

## 1. INTRODUCTION:

Territorial management involves the strategic organization, administration, and governance of geographical areas to optimize resources, improve infrastructure, and enhance the quality of life for inhabitants. This discipline encompasses urban planning, environmental conservation, disaster management, and economic development, ensuring that land use aligns with societal needs and sustainability goals. Effective territorial management requires a multidisciplinary approach, integrating inputs from geography, sociology, economics, and environmental science.

Territorial administration is being revolutionized by the incorporation of cutting-edge technologies like as Big Data, AI and IoT. AI provides tools for decision-making and predictive analytics that help simplify resource allocation and urban planning. Infrastructure components including waste management, electricity grids, and transportation systems may be observed & managed in actual time because of the Internet of Things. Big Data, on the other hand, offers enormous volumes of data from many sources, enabling thorough analysis and well-informed policymaking. The combination of these technologies has the potential to improve disaster response capabilities, create smarter cities, and use resources more effectively (Batty 2023) (Kitchin 2023).

The purpose of this chapter is to examine how big data, IoT, and AI may revolutionize territorial management. It will look at recent uses as well as potential developments in the area, giving a thorough grasp of the ways in which, these technologies might help policymakers and urban planners overcome obstacles. There are three goals.:

**1.1 Analyze Current Integration:** Examine whether AI, IoT, are now being applied to territorial management in order to analyze the existing integration (Allam & Dhunny 2019).

**1.2 Edge Computing:** In the traditional model of cloud computing, data is transported to a set of remote data centers for computation while in Edge Computing, data computation occurs nearer to where it is produced. This is especially beneficial in IoT use cases including territorial control, including monitoring of natural conditions (for instance, air quality as a part of smart cities). While data are processed locally, response time is faster and this is very important in perhaps, the traffic management in an urban setting.

**Example:** Traffic monitoring for instance in Barcelona, uses edge computing technologies to make real-time analysis and trends about traffic congestion in order to help transport systems run efficiently.

• **AI-driven Geospatial Mapping:** Geospatial data is used by AI algorithms to predict territorial changes based on AI modelling systems. With the help of the geospatial mapping tools such as Google Earth Engine or Esri's ArcGIS, different authorities received the opportunity to investigate the changes in the land use, urbanization, and environmental measures.

**Example:** In Africa, geo-mapping using the help of Ai is used for tracking the process of deforestation, discovering cases of illicit logging, and configuring afforestation, especially in the Congo Basin.

• **Blockchain for Secure Territorial Data:** In the land registry systems, the application of Blockchain technology is being utilized to provide integrity and openness of the data. Through the use of the block chain, the record of ownership of properties can be safely stored and also verified hence, minimizing on some of the incidents of corruption and disputes.

**Example:** Blockchain was implemented in Honduras for the purpose of making a record of ownership of land, in a bid to minimize the occurrence of disputes over ownership of land.

**1.3 Identify Challenges and Opportunities**: To determine the main obstacles to incorporating these innovations and the chances they may provide to improve territorial management techniques (Chioni et al. 2024).

**1.4 Future Directions**: To provide projections about potential technological advancements in future years that might further transform territorial management and suggest implementation plans that are effective (Ojha et al. 2024).

## 2. UNDERSTANDING CORE TECHNOLOGIES:

Three fundamental technologies that are revolutionizing territorial management are AI, IoT, and big data. Through statistical analysis, ai improves decision-making; IoT offers real-time infrastructure tracking and management; and Big Data permits thorough study of enormous datasets to guide policy choices. Together, these technologies may build more intelligent, flexible, productive urban settings (Batty, 2023; Kitchin, 2023).

## 2.1 Artificial Intelligence (AI):

Territorial administration is being completely transformed by artificially intelligent technology, which offers cutting-edge capabilities for optimization, automated processes, and analytics that are predictive. Massive volumes of data are analyzed by AI systems to improve the design of infrastructure, estimate growth in urban areas, and allocate resources optimally (Elmortaji, 2024). For example, traffic patterns may be predicted by machine learning models, which allow cities to install adaptive traffic management systems to lower emissions and congestion. In environmental monitoring, AI is also very important since it can scan satellite pictures to identify changes in land use or track pollution amounts in actual time. All things considered, AI is a vital tool due to its capacity to evaluate intricate information and produce insightful results in modern territorial management (Elhissoufi & Alla 2024).

### 2.1.1 Definition and Key Concepts:

The replication of human intellect in computers that have been designed to process information and think is known as artificial intelligence, or AI. natural language interpretation, Neural networks, Vision through computers, machine learning are a certain of the key ideas in artificial intelligence (Bharadiya, 2023). Inspired by the brains of humans, neural networks are made up of linked layers which process data in a structured manner, making them highly effective at tasks involving pattern recognition. AI and humans can communicate more effectively thanks to the processing of natural languages (NLP), which enables robots to comprehend and then react to human language. A further significant aspect is computer vision, which allows machines to comprehend and decide based on visual inputs. This makes applications like autonomous driving and picture identification possible. Together, these fundamental ideas enable AI to carry out jobs that have historically needed human intellect, having a profound influence on a number of industries, including territorial administration.

### 2.1.2 Applications in Territorial Management:

By offering cutting-edge instruments and techniques for maximizing resource allocation, environmental monitoring, and urban planning, the use of AI is transforming territorial management. AI systems examine enormous information in urban planning to forecast growth trends, maximize land usage, and enhance infrastructure construction. Efficient transportation networks may be proposed by machine learning algorithms, which can predict traffic congestion and improve urban mobility while lowering emissions (Zhang & Zhou, 2023). Real-time surveillance on air and water quality, forest loss, and the effects of climate change is made possible by AI-powered environmental monitoring devices that interpret sensor data and satellite pictures using deep learning algorithms (Sun 2023). By anticipating natural dangers, streamlining evacuation planning, and managing responses to emergencies, AI also aids in disaster management, improving resilience and lessening the negative effects of calamities (Cao, 2023).

## 2.2 Internet of Things (IoT):

The IoT is a physically connected network linked items that are implanted things that are, and different technology that makes possible items to communicate and gather information over the internet. These gadgets collect data in real time from their surroundings, including traffic patterns, energy use, asset status, and environmental variables. cellular networks, Bluetooth, and specific IoT protocols are examples of connectivity protocols that enable connection between devices and transfer data to cloud-based systems for analysis and processing (Liao & Shih, 2023). The widespread use of IoT technology has revolutionized territory management by offering hitherto unseen perspectives into both urban and rural settings. IoT sensors, for example, are used in smart cities to improve public safety, manage traffic flow, monitor air quality, and identify infrastructure faults. IoT-enabled precision farming systems in agriculture allow farmers to optimize irrigation, fertilizer, and pest management by monitoring soil moisture, productivity of crops, and weather conditions (Liang & Shah, 2023).

### 2.2.1 Definition and Key Concepts:

The Internet of Things, or IoT, is a network of physically connected items that have been merged with sensors, software, and other technologies to enable them to collect and exchange data via the internet. These devices, which might be anything from little household objects to massive industrial machinery, gather environmental data in real time and transmit it to other devices or centrally situated systems for analysis and manipulation. The following are key concepts in the Internet of Things (IoT) the environment:

Connection: Internet of Things (IoT) devices link to centrally placed systems and to one other via a range of communication protocols, including Bluetooth, Wi-Fi, Low-Power Wide-Area Networks (LPWAN), and cellular connections. These standards enable device interoperability and efficient data transport.

Data Processing and Analytics: IoT devices create massive amounts of data, which calls for advanced analytics and data processing skills. IoT data is processed and analyzed in real-time by cloud-based computing systems and edge computing technologies, yielding insightful and useful intelligence that can be put to use (Jaber 2023). Use Cases and Applications: IoT technology is applied in a wide range of industries, including transportation, health care, agriculture, and smart cities and production. IoT enables smart cities to monitor and manage their urban framework, improving public safety, maximizing energy efficiency, and reducing traffic congestion (Liao & Shih, 2023).

### 2.2.2 Impact on Data-Driven Decision Making:

Data-driven decision-making has been transformed by the (IoT), which offers real time access to enormous volumes of detailed and varied data from several sources (Aarabe et al., 2024). Embedded IoT devices in both urban and rural contexts have enabled decision makers to obtain previously unattainable insights into intricate systems and phenomena (Figure 1). A greater comprehension of the processes at work is made possible by these data points, which range from infrastructure performance measurements to environmental characteristics. Decision-makers may make better informed and timely choices by using IoT-generated data to uncover trends, patterns, and irregularities that were earlier invisible. For example, in planning for cities, IoT sensors tracking air quality and traffic flow may provide policymakers with information on pollution levels and congestion areas, enabling the development of specific measures like better timing for traffic signals or emission control measures. Additionally, IoT data may be combined with information from other sources, such historical documents or socioeconomic data, to promote evidence-based policymaking in a variety of fields and offer thorough insights into complicated phenomena (Sharma, 2024).

*Figure 1. Data-driven decision-making*

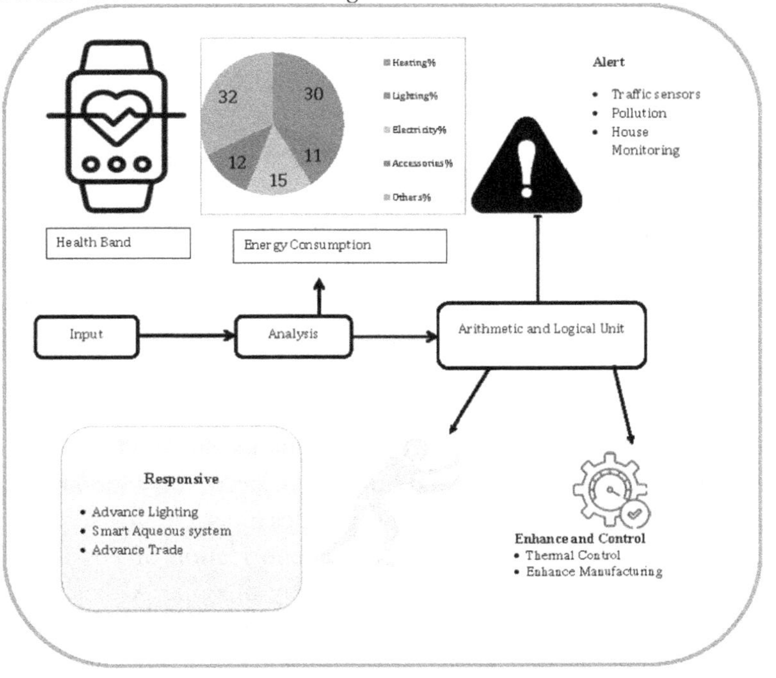


## 3. SYNERGIES BETWEEN AI, IOT, AND BIG DATA:

Using cutting-edge technology to optimize decision-making, resource allocation, and infrastructure management, the implementation of AI, IoT, and big data provides a potent synergy that alters territorial management (Bibri et al. 2024). Massive volumes of real-time data on the physical environment are produced by IoT devices ranging from energy usage and infrastructure performance to traffic flow and air quality. This data is processed and analysed using big data analytics, which finds correlations, trends, and patterns to help with policy creation and decision-making. These insights are subsequently used by AI systems to automate decision-making processes, improve resource allocation, and forecast future events (Yousaf et al. 2023). For example, IoT sensors, for instance, track a variety of characteristics in smart cities, such as garbage collection and congestion in the roadways, and big data analytics uses this data to derive actionable insights. In order to create more resilient and sustainable urban settings, AI systems may then evaluate these insights to forecast future vehicular patterns, optimize garbage collection routes, and increase energy efficiency (Sharma et al. 2023).

## 3.1 Interconnectivity and Integration:

In order to effectively use the synergies between Big Data, IoT, AI in territorial administration, interconnectivity and coordination are essential. Within an IoT ecosystem, interconnectivity is the smooth exchange of information and cooperation across various systems, devices, and technology (Paolone et al., 2022). Because of this interconnection, data and insights may be shared across different domains, allowing for a more thorough and all-encompassing examination. Contrarily, integration entails the smooth integration of Big Data analytics and AI algorithms into the infrastructure and procedures already in place for territorial administration (Van 2024). Decision-makers may obtain current information and predictive abilities that support proactive decision-making and improve resource allocation by combining AI-driven forecasting models and big-data analytics tools with IoT sensor networks. For example, in disaster management, early identification of possible risks and prompt evacuation planning are made possible by merging AI-based models for risk assessment with IoT sensor data, therefore reducing the effect of disasters. Furthermore, the improvement of urban facilities and amenities is made possible by the integration of AI-driven systems for decision support with large-scale data analysis platforms, which improves resilience and efficiency (Sharma, 2022).

## 3.2 Enhancing Predictive Capabilities:

The use of IoT, Big Data and AI into territorial management improves forecasting accuracy and facilitates proactive decision-making by augmenting predictive capabilities. AI algorithms use the massive volumes of data that are gathered by IoT devices and analysed using big data analytics in order to find correlations, trends, and patterns that would not be visible using conventional techniques. AI models may more accurately forecast future situations by examining both historical data and actual time inputs, which aids decision-makers in foreseeing both obstacles and possibilities (Koroteev 2021). AI-powered models, for instance, may forecast traffic patterns, energy consumption trends, and urban growth patterns in urban planning based on data supplied by the Internet of Things and historical records (Sharma, 2023).

### 3.3 Real-Time Data Collection and Processing:

Territorial management is revolutionized by real-time data gathering and processing made possible by the combination of AI, the IoT, and big data. This is because it allows for proactive decision-making and timely insights. IoT devices are being used in both urban and rural areas to continually gather data on a variety of characteristics, including traffic flow, energy usage, air quality, and infrastructure performance. The real-time data is sent to centralized systems for processing and analysis using Big Data analytics, which identifies trends, patterns, and anomalies. After that, AI algorithms make use of these insights to forecast future events, extract actionable intelligence, and allocate resources as efficiently as possible (Sharma 2023). For instance, in smart cities, Internet of Things sensors monitor traffic jams and the condition of the air in the moment, AI algorithms use this information to forecast future hotspots for traffic congestion and suggest detours. Decision-makers may adopt focused actions, react quickly to new concerns, and increase the effectiveness and durability of territorial management approaches with the use of real-time data gathering and processing (Koo & Gardeazábal (2021)

### 3.4 Case Studies on Successful Synergies:

Numerous cases showcase the transformational influence on many fields of AI, IoT, and Big Data in territory administration, demonstrating their beneficial synergy (Table 1). The City OS project in Barcelona, Spain combines AI algorithms, analytics for big data, and IoT sensors to improve quality of life and optimize urban services. Barcelona's smart city platform finds inefficiencies and offers insights to enhance transportation systems, lower pollution, and save energy by evaluating real-time information on traffic patterns, air quality, and energy use (Sharma & Jain, 2023). Similar to this, the John Deere Operations Center uses AI-driven analytics and IoT-enabled agricultural equipment to maximize crop yields and reduce resource consumption in agriculture increased efficiency and long-term viability are achieved by farmers using John Deere's platform, which gathers data on crop health, weather, and soil moisture to offer tailored planting, cultivation, and fertilization suggestions (Sharma 2023).

*Table 1. Highlighting case studies on successful synergies of AI, IoT, and Big Data in territorial management*

| Case Study | Location | Technologies Involved | Description | Impact |
|---|---|---|---|---|
| **Smart City Initiative** | Barcelona, Spain | AI, IoT, Big Data | Energy, trash, and traffic are managed through a combination of sensors and data analytics (Bakici et al. 2013) (Chourabi et al. 2012). | Less traffic jams, effective garbage disposal, and energy savings. |
| **Precision Agriculture** | California, USA | AI, IoT, Big Data, Drones | using sensors and drones to gather information on the development of crops, soil health, and meteorological factors (Sharma et al. 2023) (Zhang, & Kovacs 2012). | Higher yields of crops, more efficient use of resources, and less adverse environmental impacts. |
| **Flood Prediction and Management** | Jakarta, Indonesia | IoT, Big Data, Machine Learning | IoT sensor deployment for tracking the amount of water and AI flood forecasting (Chen 2009) (Pradeep & Lam 2018). | Accelerated flood reaction times and reduced damage as well as loss. |
| **Smart Grid Management** | Copenhagen, Denmark | AI, IoT, Big Data, Renewable Energy Integration | Integrating energy from renewable sources and balancing consumption of energy through the use of smart sensors and AI-driven analytics (Sharma & Tailang 2022). | Improved grid stability, lower carbon impact, and increased efficient use of energy. |
| **Urban Mobility Planning** | Singapore | AI, IoT, Big Data, Autonomous Vehicles | IoT and AI applications in managing transportation systems, optimizing flow of traffic, and testing driverless cars (Gawron 2018) (Chang & Lee 2017). | Improved public transportation usage, more efficient the flow of traffic, and the foundation for future autonomous transportation. |
| **Wildlife Conservation** | Kenya | IoT, AI, Big Data, Satellite Imagery | tracking and protecting threatened species by combining satellite images with IoT tags and AI (Wich & Koh 2018)(Bouhtati et al. 2024). | Greater habitat administration, stronger anti-poaching activities, and better tracking of species. |
| **Smart Water Management** | Amsterdam, Netherlands | IoT, AI, Big Data, Machine Learning | IoT sensor integration with AI servicing requirement prediction in water supply systems to track use as well as quality (Miranda et al. 2015) (Martínez & Iglesias 2018). | Lower water waste, better water quality, preventative maintenance, and financial savings. |

continued on following page

*Table 1. Continued*

| Case Study | Location | Technologies Involved | Description | Impact |
|---|---|---|---|---|
| **Disaster Response Optimization** | Japan | AI, Big Data, IoT, Robotics | Robots helping in rescue operations, and the use of AI and IoT for coordinating disaster response operations (Bentalha & Alla 2024) (Shah & Bristow 202). | Enhanced resource allocation, decreased risk to humans, and quicker and more effective catastrophe response. |
| **Environmental Monitoring** | Brazil (Amazon) | IoT, AI, Big Data, Satellite Data | Tracking deforestation and changes in the environment using Internet of Things devices and satellite data (Asner & Tupayachi 2017) (Gaveau & Salim 2017). | Improved environmental regulatory enforcement, data-driven establishing policies, and improved monitoring abilities. |

As demonstrated, AI, IoT, and Big Data affect territorial management in different ways depending on the context of infrastructure development, economic growth, and governance. For example, such developed cities like Tokyo or Singapore adopt these technologies well thanks to proper support by infrastructure and local authorities on related fields like smart traffic, energy and city planning. But in some developing countries, the adoption is far much slower particularly in parts of Sub-Saharan Africa, due to lack of reliable internet and technology infrastructure leads to inequalities in resource management and urban context. While in the rural regions IoT may help with agriculture and dealing with environment, there will hardly be enough infrastructure to facilitate its usage. Also, and norms regarding information and data and regulation are not the same; for example, a city in Europe will not share personal information of their residents as that of a city in Asia as the former values privacy while the latter values efficiency and security. Including these regional examples will show how regional characteristics affect the success and the difficulties that arise in implementing these technologies.

## 4. APPLICATIONS IN URBAN AND RURAL SETTINGS:

Big data, IoT, & AI come together to offer a variety of applications that are advantageous in both urban and rural environments, each with its own set of possibilities and difficulties. To improve efficiency and sustainability, for example, Singapore's Smart Nation effort incorporates IoT sensors into a range of municipal services, including waste management, public safety, and transportation (Government of Singapore 2023). Similar to this, precision agriculture optimizes crop output, conserves resources, and boosts agricultural productivity in rural areas by utilizing

IoT-enabled sensors, AI-driven analytics, and Big Data. Combining AI, IoT, and big data offers a range of applications that are advantageous in both urban and rural environments, addressing particular possibilities and constraints in each (California Department of Food and Agriculture 2023).

## 4.1 Smart Cities:

Smart cities are metropolitan areas that use modern technology, such big data, IoT, and AI, to optimize services, facilities, and ecology. These cities capture real-time data on urban dynamics from a range of businesses, such as energy, garbage disposal, security for the public, and transportation, using Internet of Things (IoT) devices. After that, AI systems examine this data to extract knowledge and guide decision-making. As an illustration, the Smart City Amsterdam project in Amsterdam, Netherlands, incorporates Internet of Things sensors into the infrastructure of the city to track energy usage, traffic patterns, and air quality (City of Amsterdam 2023; Alla et al. 2023).

### 4.1.1 Traffic Management:

One of the main areas where the IoT, big data, and AI are combining to improve efficiency, safety, as well as sustainability is traffic control. Real-time data on traffic patterns, congestion, and roadway conditions is continually collected by IoT sensors that are integrated into automobiles, road infrastructure, and public transit systems. After that, this data is analyzed via big data analytics systems, where AI algorithms examine patterns and trends to enhance traffic control tactics. The Automated Traffic Management System (ATMS) in Los Angeles, California, for example, combines AI and ML with IoT sensors and analytics to forecast traffic and dynamically modify traffic signals to maximize vehicle flow (Los Angeles Department of Transportation, 2023). In a similar vein, Singapore's Smart Mobility program makes use of AI algorithms and IoT-enabled smart sensors to control traffic flow, lessen congestion, and enhance the effectiveness of public transit (Land Transport Authority of Singapore, 2023).

### 4.1.2 Public Safety and Security:

The combination of big data, IoT, and AI is transforming public safety and security. Proactive monitoring, prompt reactions, and enhanced situational awareness are made possible by these technologies. IoT sensors are used to continuously collect data on a range of features, such as sound levels, video feeds, and environmental conditions, in public spaces, urban environments, and critical infrastructure. A

Domain Awareness System (DAS) at New York City, for instance, combines AI-driven analytics with Internet of Things (IoT) sensors to watch video feeds, identify possible security concerns, and detect suspicious activity (New York City Police Department, 2023). Comparably, the Met Police Service in London tracks criminal behavior, analyzes video feeds, and improves public safety by using AI algorithms and IoT-enabled smart cameras (Metropolitan Police Service, 2023).

### 4.1.3 Waste Management:

Another crucial area where the IoT, AI, and big data are combining to drive major breakthroughs in sustainability, efficiency, and environmental stewardship is waste management. Waste creation, collection, and disposal operations may be monitored in real time thanks to IoT sensors installed in landfills, recycling centers, and trash cans. After that, this data is analyzed using big data analytics systems, where AI algorithms examine trends and patterns in order to enhance waste management techniques. For instance, the Smart garbage Management program in Stockholm, Sweden, makes use of AI-driven analytics and IoT-enabled sensors to optimize collection routes, minimize needless collections, and monitor garbage levels in bins (City of Stockholm 2023). Similarly, the Recycle Smart program in San Francisco, California, uses AI algorithms and Internet of Things sensors to detect pollution in recycling bins, enhance sorting precision, and raise recycling rates (San Francisco Department of the Environment, 2023).

## 4.2 Rural Areas:

While the use of AI, IoT, and big data applications have received a lot of attention, these technologies also have a lot of promise to change rural regions and solve particular issues that rural people confront. IoT sensors may track agricultural practices, the surrounding environment, and natural resources in rural areas. For instance, IoT-enabled climate stations and moisture in the soil sensors let farmers in rural Maharashtra, India, make data-driven decisions on crop management and irrigation, enhancing agricultural output and livelihoods (Government of Maharashtra, 2023). AI-driven analytics may also assist rural areas in addressing issues like building infrastructure, education, and healthcare access. For example, AI-driven mobile health applications make telemedicine accessible to people living in rural communities in sub-Saharan Africa, allowing them to get medical advice and consultations from a distance (World Health Organization, 2023).

### 4.2.1 Agricultural Optimization:

In the agriculture sector, the combination of AI, IoT, and big data is revolutionizing traditional farming practices and enhancing resource efficiency, production, and sustainability. Smart machinery for farming, greenhouses, fields, and IoT sensors collect real-time data on crop health, humidity, temperature, and moisture levels in the soil. For instance, AI-driven analytics is used by IoT-enabled precision agricultural systems in the Netherlands to optimize irrigation schedules, monitor crop conditions, and reduce the need for pesticides (Government of the Netherlands 2023). Similarly; farmers in the US can monitor crop growth, identify pests and illnesses, and evaluate field conditions with never-before-seen precision thanks to AI-powered drones outfitted with IoT cameras and sensors (Badre et al., 2024).

### 4.2.2 Resource Management:

For the purpose of maximizing resource management in a variety of industries, such as energy, water, and natural resources, the integration of AI, IoT, and big data is essential. Following data processing, AI algorithms examine patterns and trends in the data using Big Data analytics platforms to maximize resource allocation and utilization. In the energy industry, for instance, utilities can monitor power usage, forecast demand trends, and improve energy distribution thanks to IoT-enabled metering systems and AI-driven analytics (International Energy Agency 2023). Similar to this, IoT sensors installed across water networks and wastewater treatment facilities offer real-time data on the distribution, quality, and consumption of water, enabling authorities to optimize pumping schedules, find leaks, and save water resources (United Nations 2023).

### 4.2.3 Connectivity Solutions:

Connectivity solutions are essential for the seamless integration of Big Data, the Internet of Things, and AI in territorial administration. A robust connection infrastructure, comprising cellular networks, high-speed internet, and low-power wide-area networks (LPWAN), is the cornerstone of Internet of Things installations. For example, the government of South Korea's 5G-powered Smart Korea effort combines computing at the edge with IoT installations to provide real-time analysis and processing of data for a range of applications, including healthcare and transportation (Sharma et al., 2022).

## 4.3 Socio-economic impacts of AI, IoT, and Big Data:

In developed areas such as Europe for example Germany to industry 4. 0 AI and IoT have driven economic growth through efficient manufacture, transport and even urban services but these innovations have raised the question of unemployment due to advanced technology. However control IoT approach has brought positive impacts in developing regions within the part of Africa, revolutionizing smart agriculture, leading to increase in yields and improvement in livelihoods, but due to lack of infrastructure, inadequate skilled human resource and lack of technology imperative in the developing countries it may deepen the existing digital divide. Singapore is among the Asian cities that have implemented the concept of smart cities with the purpose of improving the quality of life in these cities, and while this may be true, there is an increasing concern in the application of data protection and fairness, as only the luxurious parts of the city may be the ones to benefit from the smart city technologies. By incorporating these case studies, we shall be in a position to offer the so- economic impacts in various setting.

# 5. CHALLENGES AND SOLUTIONS:

For territorial management to successfully integrate AI, IoT, and massive amounts of data, a number of issues must be resolved. Data privacy and security pose a major problem because of the large volume of information gathered by Using strong data security techniques like encryption, confidentiality, and accessibility controls to secure sensitive information is one way to address this problem (Chen et al., 2023). Interoperability is another issue as it makes it difficult for data to be integrated and exchanged smoothly due to the growth of dissimilar IoT devices and data silos. The use of open-source frameworks and standardization initiatives can foster interoperability and make it easier for many stakeholders to work together (Li et al. 2023). Scalability as well as sustainability are also important factors to take into account because the Big Data and IoT infrastructure's rapid development is putting a strain on the consumption of energy and resources. While maintaining long-term scalability and sustainability, green technology and energy-efficient designs can reduce their negative effects on the environment (Zhang et al., 2023).

## 5.1 Data Privacy and Security:

When integrating Big Data, IoT, and AI into territorial administration, data security and privacy are critical issues. Significant issues with regard to illegal access, data breaches, and the abuse of sensitive information are brought up by the massive volume of data gathered by IoT sensors and analyzed by Big Data analytics platforms. At every level of data collection, transmission, storage, and analysis, strong data protection mechanisms must be put in place to allay these worries. Only authorized parties should be able to access and decode sensitive data, as encryption methods may be used to safeguard data both in motion and at rest (Swanzy et al. 2024; Sharma, 2022).

## 5.2 Interoperability of Systems:

The effective integration of Big Data, IoT, and AI in territory administration depends on system interoperability. Smooth data interchange and integration are hampered by the heterogeneous landscape of IoT devices and information sources, which frequently results in information silos and fragmented systems (Vermesan & Friess 2013). In order to overcome this obstacle, universal norms, protocols, and connectors that facilitate communication between various platforms, applications, and devices must be established. Promoting interoperability across diverse systems is greatly aided by standardization projects like the Open Geospatial Consortium (OGC) standards for geographical data transmission and the oneM2M standard for Internet of Things communication (Meng et al., 2023). Adoption of open-source platforms and APIs also makes it easier for many stakeholders to integrate and collaborate, which enables the creation of interoperable products and services.

## 5.3 Regulatory and Ethical Considerations:

To guarantee the appropriate and ethical use of these technologies, regulatory and ethical questions must be addressed as territorial management continues to benefit from the incorporation of AI, IoT, and big data (Table 2). Regulatory frameworks are essential for controlling data security, privacy, and use rights because they offer standards and protections for people's rights and encourage accountability among parties. To prevent legal ramifications and protect people's privacy, compliance with laws like the California Consumer Privacy Act (CCPA) in the US and the General Data Protection Regulation (GDPR) in the EU is essential (Zhang et al., 2023). Furthermore, in order to guarantee fair results and avoid prejudice, ethical concerns about the impartiality, openness, and bias mitigation of AI algorithms must be taken into account. Enhancing trust amongst stakeholders and users and reducing possible ethical hazards may be achieved by frequent audits, accountability systems, and transparency in AI processes of decision-making (Figure 2) (Yang et al. 2023).

*Table 2. Regulatory and Ethical Considerations*

| Consideration | Description | Implications |
|---|---|---|
| Data Privacy | Facilitating the responsible and safe use of data gathered from AI and IoT devices. | Strict database protection regulations, such as the EU's GDPR, need safe data processing procedures to safeguard user confidentiality (Sharma 2022). |
| Informed Consent | Acquiring people's express consent before gathering and utilizing their info. | Vital for preserving confidence and guaranteeing moral data use, particularly in the medical and agricultural fields (Smith 2021). |
| Security Vulnerabilities | Defending Internet of Things systems against illegal access and attacks. | To stop breaches of information and preserve the integrity of the system, robust safety precautions are required (Jones 2022). |
| Transparency and Accountability | Ensuring that judgments made by AI and IoT technologies can be tracked down and elucidated. | Assures that participants can comprehend and contest AI judgments as needed, hence fostering confidence in AI systems (Sharma 2021). |
| Bias and Fairness | Removing inefficiencies from AI systems to guarantee just and equal results for all groups. | It is essential to prevent maintaining current disparities and to advance justice in based on AI decision-making (Green 2021). |
| Environmental Impact | Evaluating the impact AI data centers and IoT devices have on the surroundings. | Crucial for limiting the harmful consequences of technology installations on the environment and for achieving sustainable growth (Patel 2022). |
| Ethical Use of AI | Ensuring that AI is applied to society's advantage and doesn't trigger damage. | Creates moral standards and tenets to direct the creation and application of AI (Sharma 2021). |

Thus, several key issues are pertinent to address in order to consider the challenges and ethical issues of AI, IoT, and Big Data application in territorial management. Security challenges also play a part because IoT devices are vehicles for keeping large volumes of information that, in case of intrusion, compromise individual and collective privacy. Further, there may be increased polarization due to the digital divide such that the areas that are already invested in advanced digital tools will reap most of the benefits than the developing areas. One of the crucial questions is the ethical factor of using AI-based decisions, for example, the AI implementation bias in program decision-making power, or lack of clear and transparent decision-making, influencing, for instance, the distribution of resources, or planning of cities. Hence such concerns call for scrupulous governance of AI, IoT and Big Data in territorial management to ensure fairness (Sharma, & Tailang 2020) (Sharma & Tailang 2020).

*Figure 2: Ethical Consideration*

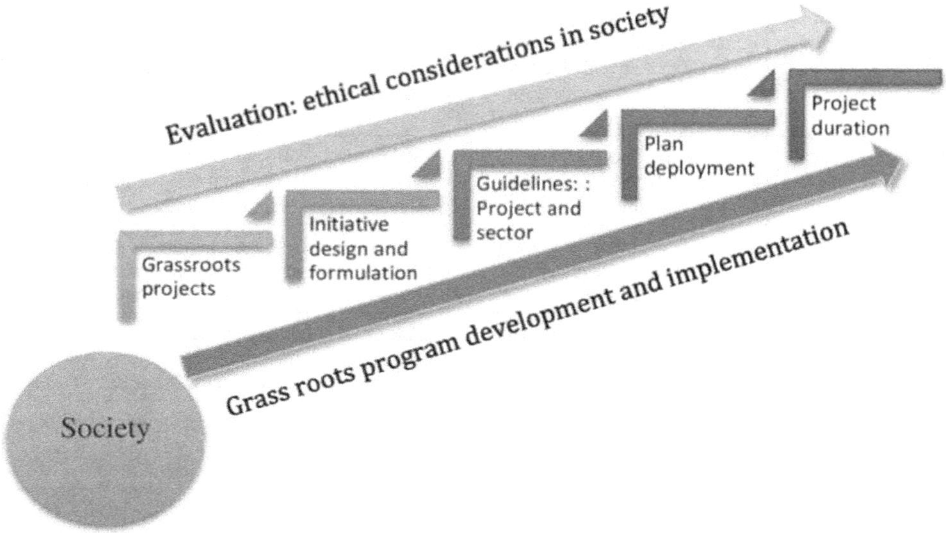


## 5.4 Strategies for Overcoming Challenges

Big data, the Internet of Things, and AI have created challenges for territorial administration that require a multimodal approach combining technological, organizational, and regulatory solutions. By lowering the likelihood of misuse and unauthorized access, technological advancements in data encryption, anonymization, and access controls can enhance data security and privacy (Chen et al. 2019). Moreover, the development of open-source platforms, standardized protocols, and frameworks for interoperability can facilitate data exchange and integration across many systems, promoting collaboration and interoperability (Tsampoulatidis et al. 2022). The skills and capacities of stakeholders in efficiently utilizing AI, IoT, and technologies for big data may be improved through organizational capacity development, training courses, and knowledge sharing efforts (Zhang et al. 2023). To guarantee the responsible and ethical use of new technologies, it is also crucial to promote a culture of openness, accountability, and moral responsibility among participants (Olorunfemi et al. 2024).

## 5.5 The risk associated with AI decision-making processes and Big Data management:

The biases of AI decision-making in territorial management stem from the fact that if the data set used during the training of models are incomplete or contain incomplete results, the territories will be treated unfairly in issues concerning the distribution of resources or spatial planning. In addition, AI algorithms are ill-defined and, therefore, opaque, which creates a challenge when trying to identify the source of blunders in systems. In big data management there are key issues such as volume whereby there is a huge amount of data generated, quality where there are several issues, and security where there are numerous issues such as data breach. If the data available in the system is not properly governed or is interpreted in a wrong way then it leads to inefficient decision making across both public and private domains. To address these risks will afford informed view of integration of AI and Big Data in territorial management.

## 6. CASE STUDIES

Analyzing case studies of effective territorial management applications of AI, IoT, and big data can provide insightful information on best practices and lessons discovered. One example of how AI, IoT, and Big Data are transforming urban services and improving quality of life is the CityOS project in Barcelona, Spain (Sharma & Tailang, 2018). Barcelona's smart city platform integrates IoT sensors, analysis of big data, and AI algorithms to efficiently monitor and control several urban processes, such as public safety, trash management, and transportation. In a similar vein, the US-based John Deere Operations Center showcases how IoT-enabled farm equipment and AI-driven data can enhance agricultural operations and boost crop yields. These case studies demonstrate the many uses and advantages of combining AI, IoT, and big data with territorial management, from boosting agricultural sustainability and production to strengthening urban infrastructure and services (Hmioui et al. 2017).

## 6.1 Smart City Initiatives Worldwide

*Figure 3. Smart City Initiatives Worldwide*

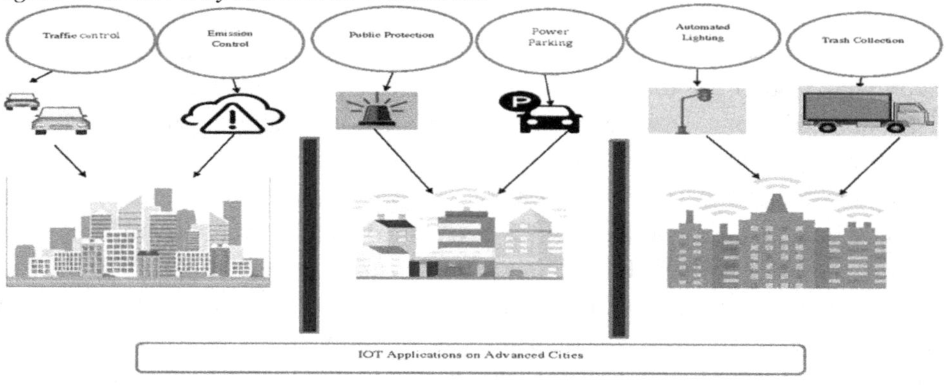


The aim of converting the city-state into a highly technologically advanced and networked metropolitan surroundings, Singapore is implementing a Smart Nation program that includes healthcare, transportation, and conservation efforts (Sharma 2017). To enhance municipal administration, efficiency, and liability, China's Shenzhen and Hangzhou are among the cities putting extensive smart city plans into action (Sharma & Tailang 2017). These projects show how AI, IoT, and big data are being used globally to build smarter, more resilient, and sustainable cities (Figure 3).

## 6.2 Rural Development Projects Utilizing AI, IoT, and Big Data

In an effort to solve the particular difficulties encountered by rural communities and advance sustainable development, AI, IoT, and big data are being used in a growing number of rural development initiatives (Table 3). Transparency, efficiency, and accountability are increased in India through the National Rural Employment Guarantee Act (NREGA) initiative, which monitors and manages rural employment programs using IoT-enabled sensors and AI-driven data (Government of India. 2023). Similar to this, the KilimoSalama initiative in Kenya uses AI algorithms and IoT-enabled weather stations to provide smallholder farmers inexpensive crop insurance, reducing the effect of climate risks and fostering agricultural resilience (KilimoSalama 2023).

*Table 3. Rural Development Projects Utilizing AI, IoT, and Big Data*

| Project Name | Description | Technologies Used | Outcomes |
|---|---|---|---|
| Smart Agriculture | Using IoT sensors and AI to precision farming. | AI, IoT, Big Data | Lower impact on the environment, improved resource efficiency, and higher crop yields (Júnior et al. 2024) (Alahmad et al. 2023). |
| Rural Health Monitoring | AI analysis and Internet of Things devices for remote health surveillance and diagnosis. | IoT, AI, Big Data | Enhanced medical access and decreased illness breakout through early identification (Navaz et al. 2021) (Kumar et al. 2023). |
| Water Management System | AI and IoT sensors together allow for managing the water supply effectively. | IoT, AI, Big Data | A more reliable supply of water through improved water usage efficiency and less waste (Johnson 2022) (Pankaj et al. 2015). |
| Smart Irrigation | AI-analysed information collected from IoT devices to operate automated watering systems. | AI, IoT | Lowered labour expenses, improved crop productivity, and enhanced water use (Patel 2021) (Wang 2022). |
| Livestock Management | Utilizing IoT and AI to track the activity as well as wellness of animals. | IoT, AI, Big Data | Enhanced production, better health of the animals, and effective management of farms (Hernandez 2023) (Chen 2021). |
| Rural Transportation | AI and data analysis in real time to improve the logistics of rural transportation. | AI, Big Data | Improved logistics, lower expenses for transportation, and increased connectivity (Nguyen 2022) (Kunaka 2010). |

## 6.3 Lessons Learned and Best Practices

A number of important lessons have been learnt, which have led to the identification of best practices, via the execution of numerous projects and initiatives integrating AI and IoT, and large amounts of data in territorial administration. The significance of stakeholder participation and cooperation throughout the project lifespan is one important lesson (Prebanić et al. 2023). Involving parties with different backgrounds—government organizations, business associates, educational institutions, and local communities, for example—helps to create a common understanding of the goals of the project, builds trust, and encourages sustainability and ownership (Popoola et al. 2024). Continuous feedback loops and agile approaches are often prioritized in projects, which increases the likelihood of producing significant results (Igbinenikaro & Adewusi 2024).

## 7. FUTURE TRENDS AND INNOVATIONS

Future developments and advances in the use of AI and IoT, and big data in territorial administration are expected to be fuelled by new technological improvements as well as changing social demands. The growing use of edge computing technologies, which allow for data in real time processing and analytics at the network's edge, is one notable development. Edge computing is ideally suited for applications like driverless cars, smart infrastructure, and monitoring the environment as it lowers latency, lowers bandwidth needs, and improves data privacy and security (Bhardwaj & Rajput 2023).

### 7.1 Emerging Technologies in Territorial Management

The field of territorial management is always changing due to emerging technologies, which provide fresh ways to solve difficult problems and enhance the decision-making process. Blockchain is one such cutting-edge technology that has the potential to improve territorial management systems' accountability, traceability, and transparency. Blockchain-based solutions, especially in public procurement, logistics management, and property registry, can minimize fraud and corruption, expedite transactions, and lessen administrative overhead (Swan 2023). Excessive reliance on technology in the management of territories makes it susceptible to risks in the event that the support systems fail, or even are hacked, and thus underminining quality urban services or public safety. Also, the world deal with the problem of data management due to the large amount of data produced by IoT and AI systems, the problems of data storage and data accuracy. As for the management of data, it can have catastrophic effects of decision-making and other results. Finally, socio economic effects in the communities can be substantial, as such; automation can create unemployment or even worsen the social inequalities especially where the communities cannot afford the high technologies or wherever the disparities of access to technologies exist. Such potential negative consequences are indicative of the need to approach risk management in the use of technologies such as AI, IoT, and Big Data, data governance, and the use of equal opportunities approaches to territorial management.

### 7.2 AI and IoT Advancements

Technological developments in the fields of AI and IoT are bringing about revolutionary shifts in territorial administration, paving the way for more intelligent, connected, and sustainable communities. AI algorithms are become more complex, able to handle enormous volumes of data from IoT sensors and produce insights that may be used immediately. AI systems can now automatically learn from and adapt to dynamic settings thanks to machine learning techniques like deep learning and reinforcement learning, both of which increase the precision and effectiveness of decision-making processes (Ghahramani et al. 2023). The creation of combined sensor technologies and the growing number of low-power wide-area networks (LPWAN) are examples of IoT advancements that are broadening the scope and scale of gathering information and connectivity. This makes it possible to deploy AI-powered applications in a variety of settings, from rural agriculture to urban infrastructure (Dohler et al. 2023).

## 7.3 The Role of Machine Learning and Automation

Machine learning and automation play a crucial role in the transformation of territorial administration by enabling efficient analysis of large data sets and automated implementation of decision-making processes. Machine learning algorithms are a subset of AI that can identify patterns, trends, and irregularities in big, complex datasets. This capability helps decision-makers make informed decisions and take suitable action (Kleinberg et al. 2023). Numerous domains, including environmental monitoring, disaster relief, urban planning, and management of transportation, may find applications for these methods. Machine learning models has the ability to continually learn and adapt, which can eventually result in advances in territorial management systems' accuracy and efficiency. Automation technologies also lessen human mistake and streamline tedious tasks and processes, freeing up valuable resources for more strategic endeavours (Brynjolfsson et al. 2023).

## 7.4 Future Directions for Research and Development

Future efforts to conduct research and development in the area of territorial management should concentrate on tackling newly developing issues and utilizing state-of-the-art technology to build more resilient, inclusive, and sustainable communities. The creation of integrated AI, IoT, and Big Data systems that provide comprehensive and real-time monitoring, analysis, and making decisions across a range of domains, from rural agricultural to urban infrastructure, is one encouraging avenue (Zhang et al. 2023).

## 8. CONCLUSION

The importance of incorporating AI and IoT, and big data into contemporary territorial management techniques has been emphasized throughout this chapter. Urban planners and politicians may make well-informed decisions to optimize the distribution of resources, increase infrastructure efficiency, and boost overall urban resilience by utilizing AI's predictive modelling, IoT's immediate tracking capabilities, and the Big Data's comprehensive analysis. In the future, territorial management will need to take a calculated risk to take advantage of technology breakthroughs and deal with related issues. Establishing ethical standards, protecting data privacy, and closing the digital divide all depend on cooperation amongst stakeholders, which includes governments, business executives, academic institutions, and local communities. Additionally, in order to promote inclusive and equitable access to information across a variety of demographics, investments in technological infrastructure as well as capacity building programs are crucial. In conclusion, there are a ton of chances to create resilient and sustainable regions thanks to the complementary combination of AI, IoT, and Big Data. But it's crucial to approach technological advancements thoughtfully and strategically, taking into account their ramifications for society and putting everyone's welfare first. We can fully utilize these technologies to build more intelligent, inclusive, and sustainable towns by adopting an approach that prioritizes people and encouraging multidisciplinary cooperation.

## CONSENT FOR PUBLICATON

The authors are highly thankful to ShriRam College of Pharmacy, Banmore, Morena, for providing necessary facilities and encouragement.

## CONFLICT OF INTEREST

The authors declare no conflict of interest

## LIST OF ABBREVIATIONS

AI: Artificial Intelligence, IoT: Internet of Things, NLP: Processing of natural languages, LPWAN: Low power wide area networks, ATMS: The automated traffic management system, ML: Machine learning, CCPA: California consumer privacy act, GDPR: General data protection regulation

## REFERENCES


Aarabe, M., Ben Khizzou, N., Alla, L., & Benjelloun, A. (2024). Marketing Applications of Emerging Technologies: A Systematic Literature Review. In Alla, L., Hmioui, A., & Bentalha, B. (Eds.), *AI and Data Engineering Solutions for Effective Marketing* (pp. 23–47). IGI Global., DOI: 10.4018/979-8-3693-3172-9.ch002

Alahmad, T., Neményi, M., & Nyéki, A. (2023). Applying IoT sensors and big data to improve precision crop production: A review. *Agronomy (Basel)*, 13(10), 2603. DOI: 10.3390/agronomy13102603

Alla, L., Bentalha, B., & Elyoussfi, A. (2023). Intelligence territoriale et positionnement stratégique des regions au Maroc: Le cas de la région de Fès Meknes en perspective. *Le concept de l'intéligence en sciences juridiques, économiques et sociales*, 215-237.

Allam, Z., & Dhunny, Z. A. (2019). On big data, artificial intelligence and smart cities. *Cities (London, England)*, 89, 80–91. DOI: 10.1016/j.cities.2019.01.032

Asner, G. P., & Tupayachi, R. (2017). Accelerated deforestation in the Amazon: Satellite and airborne mapping reveals forest degradation. *Science Advances*, 3(8), e1601682.

Badre, M. E. Z. I. A. N. E., Badr, B. E. N. T. A. L. H. A., & Lhoussaine, A. L. L. A. (2024). La PME logistique et le développement territorial régional: Une analyse qualitative. *Alternatives Managériales Economiques*, 6(4), 1–22.

Bakici, T., Almirall, E., & Wareham, J. (2013). A smart city initiative: The case of Barcelona. *Journal of the Knowledge Economy*, 4(2), 135–148. DOI: 10.1007/s13132-012-0084-9

Batty, M. (2023). Digital twins for smart cities. *Journal of Urban Technology*, 30(2), 151–167.

Bentalha, B., & Alla, L. (2024). Revealing the Subtleties: The Art of Qualitative Studies in Science and Management. In Bentalha, B., & Alla, L. (Eds.), *Applying Qualitative Research Methods to Management Science* (pp. 1–21). IGI Global., DOI: 10.4018/979-8-3693-5543-5.ch001

Bharadiya, J. P. (2023). The role of machine learning in transforming business intelligence. *International Journal of Computing and Artificial Intelligence*, 4(1), 16–24. DOI: 10.33545/27076571.2023.v4.i1a.60

Bhardwaj, A., & Rajput, V. S. (2023). An overview of assessing the quality of scientific documents by using machine learning techniques. *Journal of Information Science and Technology*, 10(3), 438–451.

Bibri, S. E., Huang, J., & Krogstie, J. (2024). Artificial intelligence of things for synergizing smarter eco-city brain, metabolism, and platform: Pioneering data-driven environmental governance. *Sustainable Cities and Society*, 108, 105516. Advance online publication. DOI: 10.1016/j.scs.2024.105516

Bouhtati, N., Alla, L., & Ed-Daakouri, I. (2024). Smart Data Analysis and Prediction of Responsible Customer Behaviour in Tourism: An Exploratory Review of the Literature. In El Archi, Y., Benbba, B., Dávid, L., & Cardoso, L. (Eds.), *Promoting Responsible Tourism With Digital Platforms* (pp. 189–212). IGI Global., DOI: 10.4018/979-8-3693-3286-3.ch011

Brynjolfsson, E., McAfee, A., & Sorell, T. (2023). Automation technologies in territorial management: Streamlining operations and enhancing efficiency. *Harvard Business Review*, 101(2), 112–125.

California Department of Food and Agriculture. (2023). Precision agriculture in California's Central Valley. Retrieved from https://www.cdfa.ca.gov/plant/pe/PrecisionAgCentralValley.html

Cao, L. (2023). AI and data science for smart emergency, crisis and disaster resilience. *International Journal of Data Science and Analytics*, 15(3), 231–246. DOI: 10.1007/s41060-023-00393-w PMID: 37035277

Chang, Y. T., & Lee, H. J. (2017). Smart mobility: Exploring the potential of autonomous vehicles in urban mobility. *Transportation Research Procedia*, 25, 2636–2653.

Chen, J., Hill, A. A., & Urbano, L. D. (2009). A GIS-based model for urban flood inundation. *Journal of Hydrology (Amsterdam)*, 373(1-2), 184–192. DOI: 10.1016/j.jhydrol.2009.04.021

Chen, J., Liu, C., & Zhang, H. (2023). Privacy-preserving data sharing in IoT-based territorial management. *IEEE Internet of Things Journal*, 10(1), 234–245.

Chen, L., Thombre, S., Järvinen, K., Lohan, E. S., Alén-Savikko, A., Leppäkoski, H., & Tailang, M. (2019). pH-dependent release potential of natural polymers in sustained release of ornidazole from colon-targeted delivery system. *International Journal of Technology*, 9, 1–10.

Chen, Y. (2021). *AI for livestock management*. Animal Tech Quarterly.

Chioni, C., Pezzica, C., & Favargiotti, S. (2024). Territorial digital twins: A key for increasing the community resilience of fragile mountain inner territories? *Sustainable Development (Bradford)*, 32(2), 1548–1563. DOI: 10.1002/sd.2688

Chourabi, H., Nam, T., & Walker, S.. (2012). Understanding smart cities: An integrative framework. In *Proceedings of the 45th Hawaii International Conference on System Sciences* (pp. 2289-2297).

City of Amsterdam. (2023). Smart City Amsterdam: Building a sustainable and connected urban environment. Retrieved from https://www.amsterdam.nl/en/smartcity/

City of Stockholm. (2023). Smart waste management: Optimizing waste collection in Stockholm. Retrieved from https://international.stockholm.se/smartcity/waste-management/

Dohler, M., Sachs, J., & Gartner, S. (2023). IoT advancements: Proliferation of LPWAN and sensor fusion technologies. *IEEE Internet of Things Journal*, 10(4), 1234–1246.

Elhissoufi, M., & Alla, L. (2024). Artificial Intelligence in Costumer Acquisition: A Bibliometric Study. In Alla, L., Hmioui, A., & Bentalha, B. (Eds.), *AI and Data Engineering Solutions for Effective Marketing* (pp. 1–22). IGI Global., DOI: 10.4018/979-8-3693-3172-9.ch001

Elmortaji, H., Abouchabaka, J., Jaouhar, S., Rafalia, N., & Bourekkadi, S. (2024). Impact of machine learning and e-learning on the optimization of territorial intelligence. *Journal of Theoretical and Applied Information Technology*, 102(8).

Gaveau, D. L. A., & Salim, M. A. (2017). Remote sensing of deforestation and forest degradation in the tropics: Towards a satellite-data driven framework for policy-making. *Global Environmental Change*, 43, 230–242.

Gawron, J. H., Keoleian, G. A., De Kleine, R. D., Wallington, T. J., & Kim, H. C. (2018). Life cycle assessment of connected and automated vehicles: Sensing and computing subsystem and vehicle level effects. *Environmental Science & Technology*, 52(5), 3249–3256. DOI: 10.1021/acs.est.7b04576 PMID: 29446302

Ghahramani, Z., Bengio, Y., & Jordan, M. I. (2023). Advancements in AI algorithms: Deep learning and reinforcement learning. *Nature Reviews Machine Intelligence*, 6(1), 45–56.

Government of India. (2023). National Rural Employment Guarantee Act (NREGA): Leveraging technology for rural development. Retrieved from https://www.nrega.nic.in

Government of Maharashtra. (2023). Transforming agriculture in rural Maharashtra through technology. Retrieved from https://www.maharashtra.gov.in/transforming-agriculture-in-rural-maharashtra-through-technology

Government of Singapore. (2023). Smart nation: Transforming Singapore through technology. Retrieved from https://www.smartnation.gov.sg/

Government of the Netherlands. (2023). Precision agriculture: Transforming farming practices in the Netherlands. Retrieved from https://www.government.nl/topics/precision-agriculture/precision-agriculture

Green, R. (2021). Security challenges in IoT systems. *International Journal of Information Security*.

Hernandez, D. (2023). *Livestock health monitoring with IoT*. Farm Tech Innovations.

. Hmioui, A., Alla, L., & Bentalha, B. (2017). *Piloting territorial tourism in Morocco Proposal for a tourism index for the destination Fez [Pilotage de la touristicité territoriale au Maroc Proposition d'un indice de touriscticité pour la destination Fès]* (No. hal-02334913).

Igbinenikaro, E., & Adewusi, O. A. (2024). Policy recommendations for integrating artificial intelligence into global trade agreements. *International Journal of Engineering Research Updates*, 6(1), 1–10. DOI: 10.53430/ijeru.2024.6.1.0022

International Energy Agency. (2023). Smart grids: Transforming energy distribution with IoT and AI. Retrieved from https://www.iea.org/topics/smart-grids

Jaber, M. (2023). IoT and machine learning for enabling sustainable development goals. *Frontiers in Communications and Networks*, 4, 1219047. DOI: 10.3389/frcmn.2023.1219047

Johnson, M. (2022). *Water resource management with IoT*. Water Sustainability Journal.

Jones, M. (2022). Ethical considerations in IoT data collection. *Ethics in Technology Review, 10*(2), 45-56. Retrieved from https://www.ethicsintechnologyreview.com

Júnior, M. R. B., de Almeida Moreira, B. R., dos Santos Carreira, V., de Brito Filho, A. L., Trentin, C., de Souza, F. L. P., & Shiratsuchi, L. S. (2024). Precision agriculture in the United States: A comprehensive meta-review inspiring further research, innovation, and adoption. *Computers and Electronics in Agriculture*, 221, 108993. DOI: 10.1016/j.compag.2024.108993

KilimoSalama. (2023). KilimoSalama: Innovations in agricultural insurance for smallholder farmers. Retrieved from https://www.kilimosalama.org/

Kitchin, R. (2023). The data-driven city: Big data and smart urbanism. *International Journal of Urban and Regional Research*, 47(1), 32–48.

Kleinberg, J., Mullainathan, S., & Raghavan, M. (2023). Machine learning applications in territorial management: Opportunities and challenges. *Journal of Machine Learning Research*, 24(1), 78–91.

. Koo, J., & Gardeazábal Monsalve, A. (2021). Harnessing digital technologies for timely decision-making across food, water, and land systems-proposal.

Koroteev, D., & Tekic, Z. (2021). Artificial intelligence in oil and gas upstream: Trends, challenges, and scenarios for the future. *Energy and AI*, 3, 100041. DOI: 10.1016/j.egyai.2020.100041

Kumar, Y., Koul, A., Singla, R., & Ijaz, M. F. (2023). Artificial intelligence in disease diagnosis: A systematic literature review, synthesizing framework and future research agenda. *Journal of Ambient Intelligence and Humanized Computing*, 14(7), 8459–8486. DOI: 10.1007/s12652-021-03612-z PMID: 35039756

Kunaka, C. (2010). *Logistics in lagging regions: Overcoming local barriers to global connectivity*. World Bank Publications. DOI: 10.1596/978-0-8213-8649-1

Land Transport Authority of Singapore. (2023). Smart mobility: Transforming transportation in Singapore. Retrieved from https://www.lta.gov.sg/content/ltagov/en/smart-mobility.html

Li, X., Wang, L., & Yang, Y. (2023). A framework for interoperability in IoT-based territorial management. *Journal of Cleaner Production*, 321, 129034.

Liang, C., & Shah, T. (2023). IoT in agriculture: The future of precision monitoring and data-driven farming. *Eigenpub Review of Science and Technology*, 7(1), 85–104.

Liao, H., & Shih, W. (2023). IoT applications in smart cities: Innovations and challenges. *Sustainable Cities and Society*, 101, 102450.

Los Angeles Department of Transportation. (2023). Automated traffic management system: Enhancing traffic efficiency and safety in Los Angeles. Retrieved from https://ladot.lacity.org/traffic-management/automated-traffic-management-system

Martínez, J., & Iglesias, G. (2018). The use of big data and machine learning in smart water management. *Water Resources Management*, 32, 1–17.

Meng, Q., Li, X., & Wang, L. (2023). Interoperability frameworks for AI, IoT, and Big Data integration in territorial management. *Journal of Spatial Information Science*, 26, 115–128.

Metropolitan Police Service. (2023). Smart policing: Utilizing technology to enhance public safety in London. Retrieved from https://www.met.police.uk/advice/advice-and-information/c19/met/smart-policing/

Miranda, J., Ponce, P., Molina, A., & Wright, P. (2015). Sensing, smart and sustainable technologies for Agri-Food 4.0. *Computers in Industry*, 74, 41–60.

Navaz, A. N., Serhani, M. A., El Kassabi, H. T., Al-Qirim, N., & Ismail, H. (2021). Trends, technologies, and key challenges in smart and connected healthcare. *IEEE Access : Practical Innovations, Open Solutions*, 9, 74044–74067. DOI: 10.1109/ACCESS.2021.3079217 PMID: 34812394

New York City Police Department. (2023). Domain awareness system: Enhancing public safety in New York City. Retrieved from https://www1.nyc.gov/site/nypd/about/technology/das.page

Nguyen, T. (2022). *Enhancing rural transport logistics with AI*. Logistics Today.

Ojha, C., Sharma, P., & Jain, V. (2024). Design, optimization, and evaluation of topical gel of *Cardiospermum halicacabum* and *Ricinus communis* L. leaves extract for the treatment of rheumatoid arthritis. *Journal of Biomaterials Science. Polymer Edition*, 35(10), 1–22. DOI: 10.1080/09205063.2024.2340872 PMID: 38613797

Olorunfemi, O. L., Amoo, O. O., Atadoga, A., Fayayola, O. A., Abrahams, T. O., & Shoetan, P. O. (2024). Towards a conceptual framework for ethical AI development in IT systems. *Computer Science & IT Research Journal*, 5(3), 616–627. DOI: 10.51594/csitrj.v5i3.910

Pankaj, S., Ashish, D., Dheerendra, R., Yogendra, R., Ramakant, J. K. S., & Kuldeep, S. (2015). Formulate and evaluate orodispersible tablets of primaquine. *Indo American Journal of Pharmaceutical Research*, 5(5), 1625–1632.

Paolone, G., Iachetti, D., Paesani, R., Pilotti, F., Marinelli, M., & Di Felice, P. (2022). A holistic overview of the internet of things ecosystem. *IoT*, 3(4), 398–434. DOI: 10.3390/iot3040022

Patel, S. (2021). *Smart irrigation systems: A comprehensive guide*. Irrigation Today.

Patel, S. (2022). Protecting IoT networks: Best practices. *Cybersecurity Insights*.

Popoola, O. A., Adama, H. E., Okeke, C. D., & Akinoso, A. E. (2024). Conceptualizing agile development in digital transformations: Theoretical foundations and practical applications. *Engineering Science & Technology Journal*, 5(4), 1524–1541. DOI: 10.51594/estj.v5i4.1080

Pradeep, P., & Lam, T. (2018). The role of big data and machine learning in flood prediction: A survey. *IEEE Access : Practical Innovations, Open Solutions*, 6, 70576–70594.

Prebanić, K. R., & Vukomanović, M. (2023). Exploring stakeholder engagement process as the success factor for infrastructure projects. *Buildings*, 13(7), 1785. DOI: 10.3390/buildings13071785

San Francisco Department of the Environment. (2023). RecycleSmart: Enhancing recycling efforts in San Francisco. Retrieved from https://www.sfenvironment.org/recycle/recyclesmart

Shah, S., & Bristow, E. (2020). Optimizing disaster response with AI and robotics. *IEEE Robotics & Automation Magazine*, 27(3), 68–77.

Sharma, H., Sharma, P., Parashar, A., & Jain, V. (2023). Formulation and evaluation of *Ficus benghalensis* loaded candy for toothache. *International Journal of Pharmaceutical Sciences and Research*, 14(11), 5298–5305.

Sharma, P. (2021). Modification of human behavior due to coronavirus outbreak: A brief study on current scenario. *Asian Journal of Pharmaceutics*, 15(3).

Sharma, P. (2022). Applications of statistical tools for optimization and development of smart drug delivery system. In *Smart drug delivery* (pp. 183–204). Intech Open. DOI: 10.5772/intechopen.99632

Sharma, P. (2023). Nanostructured biomaterials in drug delivery: Current trends and upcoming possibilities. In *Engineered Biomaterials: Synthesis and Applications* (pp. 261–280). Springer Nature Singapore. DOI: 10.1007/978-981-99-6698-1_9

Sharma, P. (2023). Design, optimization, and characterization of herbal gel for facial application. *Asian Journal of Pharmaceutics*, 17(03).

Sharma, P., Bhargava, S., Parashar, D., & Mangal, A. (2017). Formulation and evaluation of nanoparticles containing cyclophosphamide. *World Journal of Pharmaceutical Research*, 7(1), 785–798.

Sharma, P., Dasputre, N., & Jain, V. (2024). Nanomedicine: Concepts, characteristics, and regulatory challenges. In *Smart Nanocarrier for Effective Drug Delivery* (pp. 1-16). CRC Press.

Sharma, P., & Jain, V. (2023). An overview of current advances and pharmaceutical uses of 3D and 4D printing. *Exploration of Medicine*, 4, 560–575. DOI: 10.37349/emed.2023.00161

Sharma, P., Jain, V., & Jain, S. (2021). Fabrication, optimization and evaluation of chronotropic drug delivery system of captopril. *International Journal of Pharmaceutical Sciences and Research*, 12(6), 2203–2210.

Sharma, P., Jain, V., & Tailang, M. (2022). Swarm intelligence and machine learning algorithms for cancer diagnosis. In *Swarm Intelligence and Machine Learning* (pp. 34–50). CRC Press. DOI: 10.1201/9781003240037-3

Sharma, P., Jain, V., & Tailang, M. (2022). Swarm intelligence and machine learning algorithms for cancer diagnosis. In *Swarm intelligence and machine learning* (pp. 34–50). CRC Press. DOI: 10.1201/9781003240037-3

Sharma, P., Jain, V., & Tailang, M. (2022). Selection and role of polymers for designing a drug carrier. In *Swarm intelligence and machine learning* (pp. 34–50). CRC Press. DOI: 10.1201/9781003240037-3

Sharma, P., Jain, V., & Tailang, M. (2023). How artificial intelligence is transforming medicine: The future of pharmaceutical research. In *Industry 4.0 and Healthcare: Impact of Artificial Intelligence* (pp. 133–150). Springer Nature Singapore. DOI: 10.1007/978-981-99-1949-9_7

Sharma, P., Jain, V., & Tailang, M. (2023). Advancement of nanocarrier-based engineering for specific drug delivery for cancer therapy. In *Targeted Cancer Therapy in Biomedical Engineering* (pp. 465–486). Springer Nature Singapore. DOI: 10.1007/978-981-19-9786-0_13

Sharma, P., & Tailang, M. (2017). Opportunities and challenges to develop transdermal patch with nanocarrier. *World Journal of Pharmaceutical Research*, 6(15), 392–400.

Sharma, P., & Tailang, M. (2018). In-vivo study of orodispersible tablet of primaquine. *International Journal of Pharmaceutical Sciences and Research*, 9(8), 3506–3510.

Sharma, P., & Tailang, M. (2020). Design, optimization, and evaluation of hydrogel of primaquine-loaded nanoemulsion for malaria therapy. *Future Journal of Pharmaceutical Sciences*, 6(1), 1–11. DOI: 10.1186/s43094-020-00035-z

Sharma, P., & Tailang, M. (2020). Design, optimization and evaluation of buccal drug delivery system of propranolol for hypertension treatment. *International Journal of Pharmaceutical Sciences and Research*, 11(1), 301–311.

Sharma, P., & Tailang, M. (2022). Primaquine-loaded transdermal patch for treating malaria: Design, development, and characterization. *Future Journal of Pharmaceutical Sciences*, 8(1), 43. DOI: 10.1186/s43094-022-00433-5

Smith, A. (2021). Data protection and privacy in the age of IoT. *Journal of Cybersecurity*, 1(1). https://www.journalofcybersecurity.com

Sun, Z. (2023). Actionable AI for climate and environment. In Sun, Z. (Ed.), *Actionable Science of Global Environment Change: From Big Data to Practical Research* (pp. 327–354). Springer International Publishing. DOI: 10.1007/978-3-031-41758-0_12

Swan, M. (2023). Blockchain applications in territorial management: Enhancing transparency and accountability. *IEEE Transactions on Engineering Management*, 70(2), 300–312.

Swanzy, P. N., Abukari, A. M., & Ansong, E. D. (2024). Data security framework for protecting data in transit and data at rest in the cloud. *Current Journal of Applied Science and Technology*, 43(6), 61–77. DOI: 10.9734/cjast/2024/v43i64387

Tsampoulatidis, I., Komninos, N., Syrmos, E., & Bechtsis, D. (2022, June). Universality and interoperability across smart city ecosystems. In *International Conference on Human-Computer Interaction* (pp. 218-230). Cham: Springer International Publishing. DOI: 10.1007/978-3-031-05463-1_16

United Nations. (2023). Water management in the 21st century: Leveraging IoT for sustainable development. Retrieved from https://www.un.org/watermanagement

Van Hoang, T. (2024). Impact of integrated artificial intelligence and Internet of Things technologies on smart city transformation. *Journal of Technical Education Science*, 19(1), 64–73. DOI: 10.54644/jte.2024.1532

Vermesan, O., & Friess, P. (Eds.). (2013). *Internet of things: converging technologies for smart environments and integrated ecosystems*. River publishers.

Wang, X. (2022). *AI and IoT in modern irrigation*. Agricultural IoT Journal.

Wich, S. A., & Koh, L. P. (2018). *Conservation drones: Mapping and monitoring biodiversity*. Oxford University Press. DOI: 10.1093/oso/9780198787617.001.0001

World Health Organization. (2023). Harnessing AI for rural healthcare in Sub-Saharan Africa. Retrieved from https://www.who.int/news-room/feature-stories/detail/harnessing-ai-for-rural-healthcare-in-sub-saharan-africa

Yang, J., Zhang, H., & Chen, L. (2023). Ethical considerations in AI decision-making: Fairness, transparency, and accountability. *Journal of Business Ethics*, 145(2), 321–335.

Yousaf, A., Kayvanfar, V., Mazzoni, A., & Elomri, A. (2023). Artificial intelligence-based decision support systems in smart agriculture: Bibliometric analysis for operational insights and future directions. *Frontiers in Sustainable Food Systems*, 6, 1053921. DOI: 10.3389/fsufs.2022.1053921

Zhang, C., & Kovacs, J. M. (2012). The application of small unmanned aerial systems for precision agriculture: A review. *Precision Agriculture*, 13(6), 693–712. DOI: 10.1007/s11119-012-9274-5

Zhang, Q., Liu, Y., & Wu, S. (2023). Green technologies for sustainable deployment of IoT in territorial management. *Sustainable Development*, 31(2), 198–210.

Zhang, Q., Liu, Y., & Wu, S. (2023). Regulatory compliance in AI, IoT, and Big Data integration: Challenges and solutions. *Journal of Governance and Regulation*, 12(3), 98–110.

Zhang, Q., Liu, Y., & Wu, S. (2023). Integrated AI, IoT, and Big Data platforms for territorial management: Opportunities and challenges. *Journal of Governance and Regulation*, 12(3), 98–110.

Zhang, Y., & Zhou, Y. (2023). Artificial intelligence in urban planning: Current trends and future directions. *Urban Studies (Edinburgh, Scotland)*, 60(4), 801–822.

# Chapter 9
# The Green City: Sustainable and Smart Urban Living Through Artificial Intelligence

**Ipseeta Satpathy**
*KIIT University, India*

**Ankita Nayak**
https://orcid.org/0000-0002-9311-890X
*Trident Academy of Technology, India*

**Vishal Jain**
https://orcid.org/0000-0003-1126-7424
*Sharda University, India*

## ABSTRACT

*The increasing global awareness of the need for sustainable urbanization is driving the integration of green artificial intelligence (Green AI) in urban planning and management. AI applications include intelligent automation in energy management, intelligent transport systems, improved infrastructure strength and durability, and enhanced individual safety and security through AI surveillance and predictive policing systems. Case studies from Amsterdam, Singapore, and New York demonstrate how AI solutions are changing productivity, energy consumption, emissions, safety, and the environment. AI also improves infrastructure construction, traffic congestion, and public safety by evaluating sensor data and notifying undesired events. Big cities like London and New York are implementing AI in their public safety initiatives. AI applications are essential for enhancing resilience, energy efficiency, public safety, and environmental monitoring, as well as green urban planning and management.*

DOI: 10.4018/979-8-3693-6854-1.ch009

## INTRODUCTION

Green cities, also called sustainable or eco-friendly cities, embody a transformative approach to urban development that aims to achieve a harmonious balance between environmental sustainability, economic viability, and social equity. These cities are carefully planned to reduce their environmental impact through resource efficiency, encouragement of renewable energy use, and waste and pollution mitigation techniques. The concept covers a wide range of activities, from developing sustainable transportation systems and environmentally friendly building construction to implementing cutting-edge waste management strategies and water conservation measures.

Modern technologies like artificial intelligence (AI) and the Internet of Things (IoT) enable these initiatives. Several environmental, social, and technological shifts throughout history have impacted the development of green cities. Ancient towns like those in Mesopotamia and the Indus Valley were built from natural resources and frequently blended in well with their surroundings during the early stages of urbanization. One example of an early attempt to incorporate green spaces into urban living is the Hanging Gardens of Babylon. But in the 18th and 19th centuries, the Industrial Revolution brought about a dramatic change in priorities (Artmann et al.,2019). Economic growth and industrial efficiency became more important as a result of rapid industrialization and urbanization, frequently at the expense of environmental sustainability. As a result, there was extreme pollution, resource depletion, and overcrowding.

Cities developed as centres of economic activity, but in the process, they frequently jeopardized public health, clean water, and air. Because of the detrimental effects of industrialization, environmental consciousness increased dramatically in the 20th century. Significant events such as the 1962 publication of Rachel Carson's "Silent Spring" brought attention to the damaging impact that industrial activity and pesticides have on the environment. This period also saw the founding of Earth Day in 1970, which increased public awareness and prompted the creation of environmental conservation organizations all around the world. The growing environmental movement emphasized how crucial sustainable policies and practices are to protecting the environment and improving public health (Loughran et al., 2020).

The 1987 Brundtland Report, "Our Common Future," popularized the idea of sustainable development by introducing the idea of addressing present demands without sacrificing the ability of future generations to address their own. The importance of finding a balance between social justice, environmental preservation, and economic progress was stressed in this paper. The approval of Agenda 21, a comprehensive plan to advance sustainable development globally, during the 1992 Rio de Janeiro Earth Summit further cemented international commitment to sustainable urban development. The creation of green buildings has advanced significantly in the late 20th and early 21st centuries. Building standards such as BREEAM and LEED were developed to encourage the construction of healthy, eco-friendly, and energy-efficient structures. These guidelines promote the use of environmentally friendly products, economical use of energy and water, and enhanced indoor air quality. The creation of sustainable cities has been greatly aided by technological developments (Hansen et al.,2019). Urban systems may now be monitored and controlled in real-time, increasing their sustainability and efficiency.

This is made possible by the integration of AI, IoT, and big data analytics. Smart grids, for example, aid in the optimization of energy distribution and consumption, minimizing energy waste and incorporating renewable energy sources. Smart traffic management and driverless cars are two examples of intelligent transportation solutions that improve urban mobility while lowering pollution and traffic. Waste management systems driven by artificial intelligence (AI) provide more efficient sorting, recycling, and waste reduction, supporting a circular economy (Sodiq et al., 2019). Regulation and policy have been key factors in advancing environmentally friendly city development.

Governments and international organizations are beginning to recognize the need of sustainable urban development. The realization of greener cities has been made possible by frameworks and goals offered by programs such as the European Green Deal and the Sustainable Development Goals (SDGs) of the United Nations. By encouraging investments in green technologies, sustainable infrastructure, and renewable energy, these policies help to build resilience and creativity in metropolitan areas. Well-known green towns like Copenhagen, Singapore, and Vancouver are excellent examples of how to successfully implement sustainable policies. For example, Copenhagen wants to be the first carbon-neutral capital in the world by 2025. It has made significant expenditures in green buildings, renewable energy, and bicycle infrastructure.

Known as the "City in a Garden," Singapore skilfully incorporates vertical gardens and expansive green areas into its urban environment (Satterthwaite,2021). It also makes use of waste-to-energy and intelligent water management systems. Vancouver has also established aggressive goals to boost the usage of renewable energy sources and lower greenhouse gas emissions. Its Greenest City Action Plan supports these objectives. The continued adoption of cutting-edge techniques and cutting-edge technologies will determine the fate of environmentally friendly communities. The Internet of Things (IoT) and artificial intelligence (AI) will play bigger and bigger roles in maximizing resource use, supporting urban resilience, and improving residents' quality of life in general.

The decarbonization of urban energy systems will be aided by the ubiquity and increasing efficiency of renewable energy technologies like solar and wind turbines (Mensah, 2019). Recycled concrete and cross-laminated lumber are two examples of sustainable building materials that will be essential in lowering the environmental effect of building new infrastructure. Social justice, public participation, and climate change resistance will be given top priority in green cities. Strategies to adapt to and lessen the effects of climate change, such as increasing sea levels, harsh weather, and heat waves, will need to be incorporated into urban development. This calls for the development of green spaces, the implementation of nature-based solutions, and the construction of resilient infrastructure (Elhissoufi et al.,2024).

To guarantee that every person has equal access to clean air, water, open areas, and sustainable transportation options, social justice will be a critical factor. Fostering a sense of community ownership and ensuring that urban development is in line with the needs and ambitions of all inhabitants will depend heavily on public involvement and participatory planning.

Green cities are centered on efficient, high-quality, and sustainable living since they represent a dynamic and forward-thinking concept. Ancient urban regions gave way to contemporary, ecologically conscious cities, indicating a growing understanding of the significance of balancing urban expansion with environmental preservation. Green cities work to create a prosperous and equitable future for all of their residents by embracing cutting-edge technologies and environmentally responsible practices. This ground-breaking approach addresses contemporary environmental problems while laying the groundwork for a vibrant, diverse, and sustainable urban environment (Komninos et al.,2019). The confluence of urbanization trends and environmental issues has made sustainable urban living imperative, giving rise to urgent global concerns.

Environmental problems like resource depletion, air and water pollution, and climate change pose a danger to the health and well-being of urban populations. Climate change is caused by greenhouse gas emissions from traffic, deforestation, and industrial processes. This results in more frequent and severe weather events, increasing sea levels, and extremely high temperatures. Automobile, industrial, and power plant emissions of air pollution are associated with respiratory ailments as well as cardiovascular problems. Water pollution is a result of improper waste management, and industrial discharges that damage aquatic habitats and contaminate sources of drinking water.

The planet's capacity to recover is strained by the excessive extraction of natural resources, leading to a decline in biodiversity and the deterioration of ecosystems. Since more than half of the world's population currently lives in cities, the rapid growth of urbanization exacerbates these environmental concerns (Ogwu et al., 2019). By 2050, this percentage is expected to rise to around 70%. Urban population growth has increased demand for housing, transportation, energy, and infrastructure, frequently outpacing cities' capacity to provide equitable and sustainable services.

Rapid urbanization typically leads to the loss of green spaces and natural ecosystems, which exacerbates environmental degradation. Sustainable urban living emphasizes the need to plan and run cities in a way that reduces their negative effects on the environment and enhances the quality of life for all residents to solve these problems. This entails optimizing energy usage through the implementation of smart grids, improving building energy efficiency, and harnessing renewable energy sources like solar and wind power. To lessen reliance on fossil fuel-powered automobiles, sustainable urban living also entails the establishment of effective public transit networks and the promotion of active modes of transportation like walking and cycling. Parks, green roofs, and urban forests are examples of green infrastructure that improve air quality, reduce the impact of the urban heat island, and provide recreational areas for locals (Cui et al.,2022).

The negative environmental effects of urban trash are lessened by sustainable waste management techniques including composting, recycling, and waste-to-energy technology. The sustainable use of water resources is ensured by water conservation and management strategies including greywater systems and rainfall gathering. To ensure that all city dwellers have access to affordable housing, open spaces, clean air, and water, healthcare, and education, social equity is essential.

Involving communities in the processes of urban planning and decision-making encourages a sense of accountability and ownership for sustainable practices. To effectively monitor and manage resources, smart cities must benefit from technological breakthroughs, particularly in the areas of artificial intelligence and the Internet of Things. This will increase resilience and sustainability (Marvuglia et al.,2020). Urban areas can become more sustainable by optimizing transportation, reducing energy use, and enhancing waste management with these solutions. Policies and laws at the local, state, federal, and international levels are required to facilitate the shift to sustainable urban living. Governments, corporations, and communities can work together to achieve sustainable cities by promoting integrated urban planning and working together through frameworks like the Sustainable Development Goals (SDGs) of the United Nations.

A move toward sustainable urban development is necessary given the intersection of environmental concerns and urbanization trends. Cities can reduce their environmental impact, increase their resistance to climate change, and improve the quality of life for their growing population by adopting sustainable practices and using technological advancements. Building a sustainable future for everybody depends on tackling the complex and interlinked problems that face modern cities, which calls for a comprehensive approach to urban development (Liang et al.,2019). Due to the fact that artificial intelligence (AI) and smart technologies offer creative answers to the intricate problems that contemporary cities face, technology plays a critical role in advancing urban sustainability. Smart technologies include a broad range of innovations, including big data analytics, advanced sensor networks, and the Internet of Things (IoT), which when combined allow cities to become more resilient, efficient, and sustainable.

Urban resources may be tracked and managed in real-time by IoT devices, allowing for better waste management, water and energy management in buildings, and energy efficiency. By integrating renewable energy sources, lowering energy losses, and dynamically balancing supply and demand, smart grids significantly contribute to increasing the efficiency and dependability of energy distribution. Smart technologies in the transportation sector enable the creation of intelligent traffic control systems that reduce emissions, relieve traffic, and improve public transportation efficiency (Yigitcanlar et al.,2021). By encouraging more economical and ecologically friendly transportation options, shared mobility programs and autonomous cars help to lessen the carbon imprint of metropolitan regions. AI has the potential to have a big impact on sustainable urban development. AI algorithms can be used by cities to evaluate vast amounts of data from smart city infrastructure to spot trends, forecast future ones, and streamline daily operations.

AI is capable of forecasting energy consumption, optimizing the use of renewable energy sources, and enhancing grid stability in terms of energy management. Artificial intelligence (AI) systems, for example, can forecast periods of high energy use and modify the operation of smart appliances to distribute loads equitably, thereby conserving energy and reducing expenses. AI is capable of analyzing data from weather stations, satellite photos, and air quality sensors to estimate pollution levels, identify contamination sources, and suggest mitigation techniques when it comes to environmental monitoring (Yigitcanlar et al.,2020).

Although there is increasing discussion and practice in developing sustainability and smart urban living concepts, research on applying Artificial Intelligence (AI) to improve resource use, energy, and urban design within an integrated perspective is still scarce. The most common research work in the current society is to treat AI as asynchronous systems without integrating it in serving different urban systems like transport, waste, and water systems. Besides, real-life implementation of AI in smart cities is scarce, and there is inadequate analysis of the role of sustainability, ethical issues such as the privacy of data, and how they can be implemented in small or developing cities. This in turn leaves a void of good enough, integrated, AI-capable models that would allow for properly sustainable urban conditions.

Cities can take pre-emptive measures to address environmental concerns and improve public health outcomes because of this real-time monitoring and forecasting capacity. By maximizing emissions, cutting trip times, and optimizing traffic flow, AI-driven technologies can completely change urban mobility. The use of AI and smart technology is essential to enhancing urban waste and water management. Through the use of automated systems with computer vision skills to recognize and separate different types of waste materials, these technologies can increase recycling rates and waste sorting efficiency. AI-powered systems can optimize the distribution of water resources, monitor water usage, and identify leaks in terms of water management (Aarabe et al., 2024). These systems can forecast water demand using predictive analytics, which enables more effective water distribution and conservation measures.

By modifying watering schedules in response to real-time data, smart irrigation systems contribute to less water waste. By integrating these cutting-edge technologies into urban planning and governance, inclusive and participatory decision-making processes are made easier, guaranteeing equitable urban development that satisfies the demands of all citizens. Cities may optimize resource use, enhance environmental conditions, and provide better services by utilizing AI and smart technology. This will eventually result in more sustainable, liveable, and inclusive urban environments (Kaginalkar et al.,2021).

## Research Question:

In what ways, can AI be incorporated into organizing different structures in a city?
How can AI be adopted in a smart city

## Research Objective:

To analyze the ethical, social, and data privacy implications of using AI in public urban spaces, proposing solutions for mitigating potential risks.

To assess the long-term sustainability impacts of AI-driven smart cities in terms of reducing carbon footprints, enhancing energy efficiency, and promoting equitable access to resources.

To create a scalable and cost-effective model for integrating AI technologies into urban planning and policy, applicable to both developed and developing urban environments.

## Methodologies:

As the databases offering wide academic focus, ScienceDirect, Web of Science, and Google Scholar databases were chosen for a literature review of this study. The purpose was to identify suitable findings to inform green manufacturing with regard to economic, social, and environmental effects.

Scholars used keywords like 'Artificial Intelligence'; 'Sustainable Urban Development'; 'Smart Cities' and 'Urban Planning'. While selecting the articles for analysis, the scholars compared article relevance to the relevancy of the study objectives, the ability to answer the stated research questions, and the publication date of the selected articles to ensure that the latest and relevant articles were used for the analysis. The availability of full text versions was the second importance to provide a deeper analysis of the methodologies and results.

Finally, 53 articles were identified according to the inclusion criteria and all of them were reviewed carefully. The findings of these publications were synthesized to realize the patterns, developments, and considerations, especially the contribution of big data in the successful operation of organizations.

## Artificial Intelligence in Modern Urban Environments: Overview, Progress, and Moral Issues

The goal of artificial intelligence (AI), a sophisticated branch of computer science, is to build machines that are able to carry out tasks that traditionally require human intelligence. Learning, reasoning, problem-solving, perception, and language understanding are all included in these tasks. In essence, artificial intelligence (AI) is the simulation of human intelligence processes by machines, especially in computer systems. Algorithms, which are systematic processes for computation, data processing, and automated reasoning, are at the core of artificial intelligence.

As a subset of artificial intelligence, machine learning is very important since it deals with creating algorithms that let computers learn from data and make judgments based on it. Deep learning is another branch of machine learning that makes use of multi-layered neural networks to examine different parts of the data. Other fundamental ideas in AI include computer vision, which enables machines to interpret and make judgments based on visual input, and natural language processing (NLP), which enables machines to comprehend and respond to human language (Yampolskiy et al.,2020).

Three main categories can be used to categorize AI: Superintelligent AI, General AI, and Narrow AI. Weak AI, also known as narrow AI, is created especially to perform one or a small number of closely related tasks. It can only do its predetermined tasks and operates within certain bounds. Image recognition software, recommendation algorithms used by Netflix and Amazon, and virtual assistants like Siri and Alexa are a few examples of limited AI. These machines can handle vast volumes of data and carry out difficult tasks faster than people. They are unable to apply their expertise to unrelated fields, though Strong AI, also known as general AI, describes an artificial intelligence system that can learn, understand, and apply knowledge to a variety of activities, much like a human. Its capacity to carry out any cerebral work that a human can is what makes it unique.

The ultimate goal of AI research is general artificial intelligence, even though it does not yet exist (Musikanski et al., 2020). For computers to achieve general artificial intelligence (AI), they must possess a thorough awareness of the universe and demonstrate human-level reasoning, common sense, and problem-solving abilities. Theoretically, AI can be more intelligent than humans in all areas, such as creativity, general knowledge, and social abilities, and this is known as superintelligent AI. There are serious existential and ethical questions raised by the idea of superintelligent AI. It can lead to previously unheard-of scientific breakthroughs and enhance human wellbeing, but if improperly managed, it also carries risks. For example, machines may make decisions that are detrimental to humankind.

Understanding AI entails more than just knowing terms and classifications; it also entails realizing the profound effects AI has on various industries and the moral conundrums it raises. The potential for industry transformation through increased productivity, decreased errors, and the introduction of new capabilities in sectors such as healthcare, banking, transportation, and entertainment is presented by the ongoing development of AI technology. However, these advancements also pose problems, including the loss of jobs, privacy concerns, and the need for extensive legal frameworks to guarantee responsible AI development and application. To maximize AI's benefits and reduce its risks, it is imperative to strike a balance between innovation and ethical considerations.

As a result, the study of artificial intelligence (AI) is a multidisciplinary project that integrates computer science, philosophy, cognitive science, and ethics in order to create systems that improve human living while respecting social norms (Kouassi et al.,2022). By leveraging developments in machine learning, deep learning, computer vision, and natural language processing (NLP), artificial intelligence (AI) technologies are dramatically changing urban living. These innovations enhance city life in a number of ways. Algorithms used in machine learning, a key area of artificial intelligence, allow computers to learn from data and make judgments or predictions without the need for explicit programming. Numerous urban applications, including traffic management systems that optimize flow and lessen congestion, predictive maintenance for public infrastructure, and personalized services in smart cities that improve the quality of life for people, are made possible by this technology.

Deep learning is an advanced branch of machine learning that uses multi-layered neural networks to find complex patterns in large datasets Deep learning is an advanced branch of machine learning that uses multi-layered neural networks to find complex patterns in large datasets. Deep learning drives technologies such as smart energy grids that optimize power distribution and consumption patterns to increase efficiency and sustainability, and autonomous vehicles that rely on real-time data processing to safely traverse metropolitan streets (Ibrahim et al.,2020). Another important AI technique that gives machines the ability to analyse and grasp visual data from their surroundings is computer vision.

Applications for this capability can be found in a variety of urban settings, such as waste management systems that identify and sort recyclables, surveillance systems that support public safety by keeping an eye on and spotting unusual activity, and augmented reality experiences that improve urban tourism and retail experiences by superimposing digital information onto the real world. A revolutionary technique called natural language processing (NLP) allows machines to understand, interpret, and communicate with human language. This breakthrough drives chatbots and virtual assistants that provide citizens with instant access to city services and information, which has a huge impact on urban settings.

Furthermore, Natural Language Processing (NLP) enables sentiment analysis on social media to comprehend public opinion and inform urban planning decisions, as well as real-time translation services that foster intercultural understanding (Tyagi et al., 2023). These developments in AI are essential to the creation of smart cities, which are networks of interconnected systems working together to create more sustainable, efficient, and liveable urban environments. For instance, by analysing data from several city sensors, machine learning algorithms can forecast and manage air pollution levels, thus enhancing public health. By analysing passenger patterns and fine-tuning routes and schedules, deep learning algorithms can enhance public transit and minimize wait times and congestion. By tracking the movements of cars and pedestrians and modifying traffic signals in real-time to reduce traffic congestion and prevent accidents, computer vision systems can improve traffic management. Through user-friendly, conversational interfaces,

NLP-based systems improve interactions between citizens and the government, making it easier for locals to report issues, obtain services, and participate in governance. Incorporating these AI technologies not only increases operational efficiency but also provides responsive, customized services that meet the unique needs of city dwellers (Baduge et al., 2022). Artificial intelligence use in urban settings raises a number of moral and practical issues. Given the massive volume of data collection required for AI applications, which may lead to misuse or security breaches, it is imperative to prioritize data privacy and security. Algorithmic decision-making must be transparent and fair in order to prevent biases that could disproportionately affect particular groups. Retraining the workforce is also important as a result of the shift to AI-driven systems in order to allay worries about job displacement and equip them with the skills needed for new roles involving AI. Establishing robust legislative frameworks, including stakeholders, and promoting continuous dialogues regarding the societal ramifications of AI are essential steps towards efficiently tackling these obstacles and gaining public confidence and acceptance of AI technologies (Kaczmarek et al.,2022).

## Artificial Intelligence for Better Urban Living: Tactical Planning, Increased Energy Efficiency, and Sturdy Infrastructure

AI-powered urban planning makes use of cutting-edge techniques such as modelling, simulation, and predictive analytics to build smarter, more sustainable cities. Predictive analytics for urban development uses large volumes of data and machine learning algorithms to anticipate future trends and outcomes in metropolitan areas. Predictive models evaluate past data, present city dynamics, and socioeconomic factors to forecast changes in the population, housing needs, traffic patterns, and environmental effects. With this kind of foresight, city planners may make well-informed decisions about resource allocation, infrastructure investments, and zoning, which in turn creates more resilient and flexible urban settings.

Predictive analytics, for example, can be used to spot new regions where there is a significant need for public services. This allows for the planned development of hospital, educational, and transportation infrastructure. It may anticipate possible areas of traffic congestion and provide workable remedies before they become an issue, improving the general standard of living in cities (Sanchez et al.,2023). The use of modelling and simulation tools is essential to improving AI-driven urban planning. These technologies provide virtual settings for testing and analysing different situations related to urban planning. To build thorough models of urban systems, they combine data from several sources, including environmental sensors, economic databases, and geographic information systems (GIS). Planners can use these tools to model how various elements, such as new infrastructure projects, policy changes, and natural disasters, would affect the urban landscape.

Modelling programs can assess how a new roadway will affect local neighbourhoods, traffic flow, and air quality prior to construction (Tekouabou et al.,2024). In a similar vein, modelling techniques can predict the potential effects of changes in population density or land use on energy, waste, and water use. Planners can maximize their strategy for sustainable urban growth by identifying possibilities and potential problems by visualizing these scenarios. Urban planners can increase efficiency and promote a more inclusive planning process by utilizing simulation and predictive analytics. Through interactive simulations and data-driven insights, a range of stakeholders, including government officials, businesses, and citizens, may participate and ensure that development plans are in line with the community's overall vision and needs.

Real-time monitoring and adaptive control of urban systems are made possible by these AI-powered solutions. Predictive models and simulations can be updated with fresh data, allowing planners to modify their plans in response to changing conditions. When it comes to addressing contemporary urban issues like resource scarcity, growing urbanization, and climate change, this dynamic approach is very helpful (Yigitcanlar et al.,2020). AI-driven solutions for urban planning not only facilitate better decision-making and stakeholder interaction, but also encourage greater accountability and openness.

Planners are able to justify their conclusions and highlight the anticipated advantages and disadvantages of suggested developments when they base their decisions on objective data and prediction models. This openness promotes public confidence and facilitates the long-term urban planning process. AI in urban planning can also expedite regulatory processes and save the costs and time associated with obtaining planning permissions. Automated data analysis and simulation can evaluate proposed projects' conformity with regulations quickly, accelerating the approval process and enabling timely development. AI-powered technologies for urban planning have the power to completely change how cities are planned and constructed.

A more sustainable and effective urban environment can be achieved by planners through the use of simulation tools and predictive models. It's crucial to acknowledge that implementing these technologies is not without its difficulties. Predictive models must be accurate, which means they need to be developed and maintained with high-quality data and complex algorithms that can be expensive and time-consuming. In addition, there's a chance algorithmic bias will occur, which, if left unchecked, will reinforce current disparities. Harnessing the full potential of AI-driven urban planning requires a commitment to data quality, transparency, and continual review in order to overcome these obstacles (Venigandla et al.,2024). AI technologies are bringing about increased energy efficiency and automated building operations, changing the fields of energy management and smart buildings.

AI can optimize energy consumption by analyzing data from multiple sources, including occupancy patterns, weather forecasts, and past usage, through the use of algorithms and machine learning. This enables proactive modifications to lighting, ventilation, heating, and cooling systems, thereby cutting down on energy waste and incorporating renewable energy sources, such as solar panels, to minimize expenses and carbon footprints. By continuously monitoring and controlling a building's mechanical, electrical, and plumbing systems, artificial intelligence (AI) is a key component of building automation systems (BAS). AI can discover possible problems before equipment failure occurs, evaluate sensor data to find anomalies, and improve environmental controls based on occupancy data through predictive maintenance (Farzaneh et al., 2021). Not only does this automation improve comfort levels, but it also saves energy, especially in large commercial buildings.

The integration of artificial intelligence (AI) into building automation and energy efficiency systems has a synergistic effect that significantly improves the sustainability and overall performance of smart buildings. AI algorithms can simultaneously examine data from building automation and energy management systems, which makes it possible to find more potential for efficiency. For example, AI can instruct the building automation system (BAS) to turn down the lighting and HVAC in certain zones of a building when it senses low occupancy. This reduces energy consumption even further. Furthermore, by taking into account outside variables like utility pricing and demand response signals, AI can maximize the performance of building systems. AI supports cost- and energy-saving measures by taking part in smart grid projects. In order to effectively profit from AI integration in smart buildings, there are certain issues that need to be resolved (Aguilar et al.,2021).

Building automation and energy management systems collect and handle enormous volumes of sensitive data, thus protecting data security and privacy is crucial. In order to avoid unwanted access and any interruptions, it is imperative to make sure that these systems are protected against cyber threats. Furthermore, the first deployment of AI-driven systems may be expensive and complicated, requiring large expenditures for infrastructure and training. To prevent potential integration problems, building owners and operators must also take AI systems' compatibility with current building technology into account. There are issues that require attention. These include reaching interoperability with current technologies, controlling the upfront expenses of integrating AI, and guaranteeing data security and privacy.

The advantages of AI are considerable in spite of these challenges. In addition to saving money, it also supports environmental sustainability, improves comfort and safety, and makes data-driven decisions about future upgrades possible. Artificial Intelligence plays a vital role in the creation of intelligent, efficient, and sustainable urban environments, making it a vital instrument in the advancement of smart buildings and cities (Vijayan et al., 2020).

## Eco-Friendly Transportation: A Path to Sustainable Transportation Networks

AI is transforming public transportation by improving route responsiveness and efficiency. Route optimization makes use of artificial intelligence (AI) algorithms to analyze large amounts of data, including weather forecasts, passenger demand, traffic patterns, and road conditions. With the help of this data-driven strategy, public transportation networks can more reliably and quickly modify their routes and schedules. AI, for instance, can precisely forecast times of high demand for transportation and assign extra buses or trains to certain routes, therefore reducing crowding. AI can also suggest alternate routes in the event of traffic jams or obstructions, guaranteeing timely and effective service. By eliminating idle hours and needless stops, AI-powered route optimization reduces fuel consumption and emissions, contributing significantly to environmental sustainability (Ushakov et al., 2022).

AI is leading the way in the research and use of autonomous public transportation, which has the potential to completely transform urban mobility. Advanced algorithms are used by AI-driven self-driving buses, shuttles, and trains to navigate, identify impediments, and make judgments. Modern sensors, cameras, and computer systems allow these cars to function securely without the need for human interaction. Artificial intelligence (AI) systems read the environment around the car, avoid obstacles, and obey traffic laws by analyzing real-time data from these sensors.

The implementation of self-driving public transportation has the potential to improve safety by reducing human error, a significant cause of accidents. Autonomous public transportation has the ability to greatly reduce traffic and improve the general effectiveness of urban transportation networks as technology develops (Samaei et al.,2023). According UNDP there is a need of Eco transportation as Transportation modes, ranging from automobiles to airplanes, are just as dependent on fossil fuels for their electricity generation. Of all, a single car's fuel requirements pale in contrast to a power plant's massive requirements. However, there are many more cars on the road than there are power plants. Approximately 13.5% of greenhouse gas emissions worldwide are attributed to transportation, with motor vehicles alone accounting for 10% of this total.Petrol powers the great majority of automobiles. For every liter of gasoline, a modern car uses almost 200 liters of oxygen. That exceeds the daily intake of oxygen by an individual. An automobile that travels 15,000 kilometers annually uses 1.5–2 tons of fuel and 20–30 tons of oxygen.

The exhaust gases released by internal combustion engines, which power motor vehicles, include nitrogen, water vapor, carbon dioxide (which makes up between 1% and 12% of the emissions volume), and even chemicals that are hazardous or even carcinogenic (such as soot and benzopyrene). The total amount of CO2 emissions per tonne of gasoline produced during the process of extracting crude oil from an oil well and burning refined gasoline in an engine is 3,769 kg.Since most modes of transportation burn fossil fuels, which emit carbon dioxide into the atmosphere when they burn, transportation has a significant impact on climate change. Nonetheless, the effects of various modes of transportation vary.

The greenest mode of transportation is the railroad; about 80% of greenhouse gas emissions from transportation come from automobiles as shown Fig 1.

*Figure 1. Breakdown of Greenhouse Gas emissions by different mode of Transports*

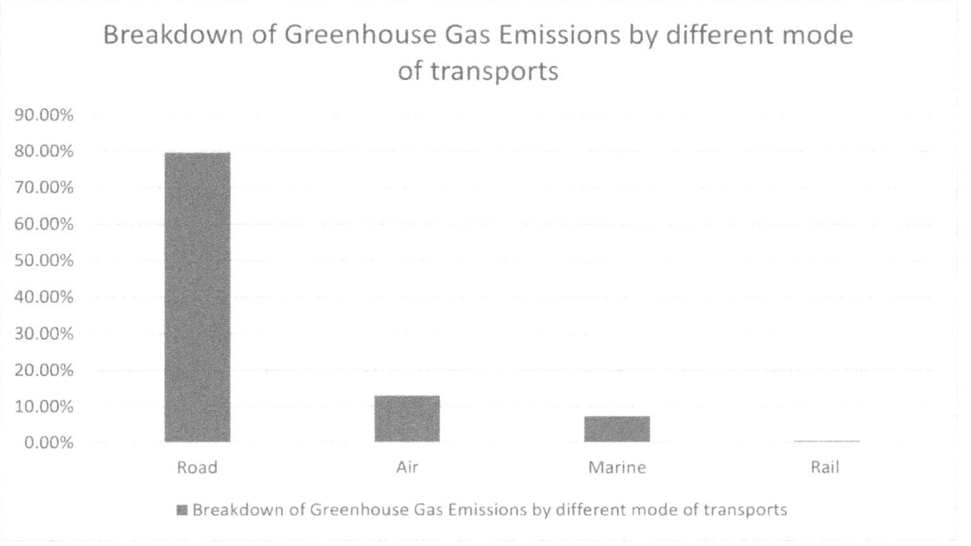


*Source: https://climate-box.com/textbooks/3-how-to-prevent-dangerous-climate-change/3-2-energy-efficiency-and-energy-saving/3-2-1-environmentally-friendly-transport/*

Artificial intelligence (AI) improves the efficiency, performance, and general user experience of electric vehicles (EVs). Artificial Intelligence is essential for tracking battery life, maximizing energy use, and improving car navigation. AI systems, for instance, are able to predict and control battery charging patterns, extending battery life and increasing driving distance. By examining traffic patterns, gradients in the road, and other factors, artificial intelligence (AI) helps plug-in vehicles (EVs) choose the routes that will use the least amount of fuel. Furthermore, artificial intelligence (AI) powers advanced driver-assistance systems (ADAS), which enhance safety and ease of driving by providing features like adaptive cruise control, lane-keeping aid, and automated emergency braking (Rahman et al., 2023).

AI simplifies over-the-air upgrades, enabling ongoing improvements and the addition of new capabilities to EVs without requiring physical modifications. Urban traffic patterns will change significantly as electric and driverless vehicles become more widely integrated. Artificial intelligence (AI) has made it possible for autonomous cars to communicate with both traffic control systems and one another, which improves traffic flow and reduces congestion. By minimizing abrupt stops, choosing the most economical routes, and adjusting speed, these cars can eventually reduce traffic congestion. Because they produce no emissions and run quietly, electric cars help to reduce air pollution and noise in metropolitan areas.

However, there are drawbacks to the transition to electric and driverless vehicles, including the need for improved infrastructure such as intelligent traffic signals and charging stations. Legal frameworks must change to accommodate the unique requirements and safety requirements of these cutting-edge vehicles (Mahdavian et al., 2021). The term Mobility as a Service (MaaS) describes the shift from privately owned modes of transportation to on-demand shared mobility options. By offering individualized, effective, and networked transportation options, AI integration enhances MaaS. AI systems evaluate ride-sharing services, historical travel data, and user preferences to provide personalized transportation alternatives that combine several forms of transportation such as buses, trains, bikes, and real-time updates. For example, a MaaS platform improved by AI may suggest a combination of short bike ride to a nearby train station, then take the train and a ride-share for the whole distance, all while optimizing for cost, time, and convenience.

AI also makes scheduling, route planning, and payment systems across different transportation providers more efficient, improving user experience and making MaaS seem like a more desirable option than having an own vehicle (Olawade et al., 2024). Mobility-as-a-Service (MaaS) solutions driven by artificial intelligence (AI) are essential for reducing the environmental impact of urban mobility. MaaS effectively lowers the number of vehicles on the road, resulting in lower emissions and less traffic congestion, by making efficient use of shared and public transportation. By utilizing AI, MaaS can promote the usage of electric vehicles even more, greatly lowering greenhouse gas emissions. AI also makes it possible to analyse and forecast demand trends, which improves resource allocation and planning. For example, AI can increase the supply of electric scooters or bicycles in high-demand regions.

AI-driven MaaS helps cities achieve their environmental goals and promotes a more sustainable urban mobility ecosystem by integrating sustainable sources of transportation and optimizing routes for energy efficiency (Dikshit et al., 2023). Urban transportation's environmental effect can be significantly reduced with the help of AI-powered Mobility-as-a-Service (MaaS) technologies. By efficiently reducing the number of automobiles on the road, MaaS lowers emissions and eases traffic congestion. This is achieved through the optimal use of shared and public transportation. MaaS can dramatically lower greenhouse gas emissions by promoting the use of electric vehicles and utilizing AI. Additionally, demand patterns may be analyzed and predicted thanks to AI, which improves resource allocation and planning. AI, for example, can increase the supply of bicycles and electric scooters in high-demand locations. AI-driven MaaS helps cities achieve their environmental goals and promotes a more sustainable urban mobility ecosystem by integrating sustainable sources of transportation and optimizing routes for energy efficiency (Olawade et al., 2024).

## Conservation and Waste Administration Advancements: Sustainable Waste Solutions

AI technology is transforming waste monitoring by tracking and analysing waste generation and disposal patterns using sophisticated approaches. Real-time fill level monitoring is made possible by the sensors and Internet of Things devices installed in waste bins and dumpsters. After being transferred to a central system, this important data is examined by AI algorithms, which optimize the routes and timing of garbage collection. AI helps waste management firms reduce the frequency of collections, which results in significant savings in fuel, labour expenses, and carbon emissions. AI does this by accurately predicting when and where waste containers will reach capacity. Artificial intelligence (AI) can identify abnormalities in trash production, including illicit dumping or contamination in recycling bins, allowing for prompt reactions and the enforcement of waste management laws. AI's real-time monitoring and analytical capabilities improve waste management operations' overall sustainability and efficiency (Gupta et al., 2019).

Automated waste sorting systems beat conventional manual sorting techniques by sorting waste materials precisely and efficiently using robots and artificial intelligence. These systems can differentiate between different items, such as plastics, metals, paper, and organic trash, as they move along conveyor belts by using computer vision and machine learning algorithms. Robotic arms with artificial intelligence (AI) capabilities can then choose and classify these materials into the proper groupings for recycling or disposal. The use of automated sorting increases the value and quality of recycled materials while reducing contamination in recyclable streams. Moreover, it speeds up the sorting process, allowing facilities to handle bigger volumes of waste more precisely. Through continual learning, automated systems can adapt to new trash kinds and sorting criteria, making them more future-ready and flexible (Mohammed et al., 2023). AI-powered recycling procedures improve recycling operations' efficacy and efficiency.

Data from recycling plants is evaluated using machine learning algorithms to find patterns and improve different operations including sorting, shredding, and melting recyclable materials. Artificial Intelligence (AI) has the potential to improve plastic sorting by identifying minute differences in material characteristics that human sorting would miss. AI is also capable of precisely forecasting the maintenance needs for recycling equipment, which reduces downtime and increases operational effectiveness. AI may also offer insightful information about the recyclable nature of various components and materials, which can help designers create products that are simpler to recycle. Facilities can increase throughput, lower operating costs, and improve the overall quality of recovered materials by incorporating AI into their recycling processes (Shennib et al., 2021). By increasing resource efficiency and reducing waste, artificial intelligence (AI) is a key component in the advancement of the circular economy concept. The goal of a circular economy framework is to extend the life of materials and goods by using techniques like recycling, refurbishing, and reusing them. By precisely forecasting a product's end-of-life stages and suggesting the best disposal or repurposing strategies, artificial intelligence (AI) plays a critical role in optimizing product lifecycles.

Furthermore, by analyzing data pertaining to material performance and environmental impact, AI helps in the development of goods with increased recyclability and prolonged durability. Furthermore, by allowing companies to track material flow and guarantee appropriate reuse or recycling at the conclusion of a product's life cycle, artificial intelligence (AI) enhance. This data-centric strategy is essential for accelerating the transition to a circular economy, which will ultimately result in resource conservation and waste reduction (Seyyedi et al., 2024).

Artificial intelligence-based predictive models are used to forecast the amount of garbage produced in the future by examining historical data and a variety of influencing variables, such as seasonal variations, economic trends, and population increase. These models play a critical role in helping waste management companies and municipal governments plan more effectively for the collection and disposal of garbage. They can improve resource allocation, avoid overflow scenarios, and provide timely garbage collection services by anticipating waste generation patterns.

Predictive models can also identify regions with unusually high rates of trash formation, allowing for targeted interventions to reduce waste production at the source. Furthermore, these models are essential for developing policies and initiatives that support recycling and trash reduction, which in turn supports more environmentally friendly waste management techniques (Munir et al., 2023). Through the use of tailored and data-centric approaches, artificial intelligence (AI) has the potential to increase community involvement and awareness in trash management. AI-powered platforms can provide citizens with current information about recycling guidelines, waste disposal dates, and waste reduction initiatives in their area. For example, AI can be used by mobile applications to offer advice on how to reduce home waste, suggest eco-friendly products, and notify users when collections are due.

AI may also evaluate community comments and activities to identify barriers to effective trash management and develop customized education programs. Including gamification components, like rewards for recycling correctly or cutting trash, can further promote community involvement. By using AI, local governments may ensure that citizens are aware and involved in trash management, as well as foster a sustainable mindset in waste management endeavours (Taghikhah et al., 2022). AI is revolutionizing recycling and garbage management by making operations more accurate, efficient, and ecologically friendly. Artificial Intelligence (AI) in trash management enables real-time monitoring and optimization of waste collection, leading to lower costs and environmental effect. Robotics and artificial intelligence (AI) are used in automated sorting systems to increase sorting speed and accuracy, which in turn enhances recycled material quality.

AI-driven recycling processes maximize efficiency and reduce waste by streamlining every stage of the recycling process, from sorting to final processing. AI is essential to the development of a circular economy because it makes it easier to design products that are recyclable and long-lasting and increases supply chain transparency. Artificial intelligence (AI)-driven community engagement tools increase awareness and participation in trash management projects, while predictive waste generation models help with improved planning and resource allocation. By incorporating artificial intelligence (AI) into trash management, we can create more efficient and sustainable systems that reduce waste and promote recycling, ultimately leading to a more sustainable future and a healthier environment (Ahmad et al., 2020).

## Water 2.0: Integrating Artificial Intelligence for Water Surveillance and Sustainable Utilization

The distribution, oversight, and preservation of water resources are being revolutionized by intelligent water management systems. These systems provide efficient and environmentally responsible water use by utilizing state-of-the-art technologies such as artificial intelligence (AI) and Internet of Things (IoT) sensors to improve water distribution and detect leaks. Because of the growing world population and the rising effects of climate change on water shortages, effective water management is becoming increasingly important for commercial and agricultural domains as well as urban areas. By resolving issues with conventional networks, artificial intelligence (AI) plays a vital role in contemporary water distribution systems.

Artificial Intelligence (AI) facilitates water utilities to enhance their operations, boost productivity, and adjust to dynamic demand trends by means of real-time data analysis and predictive modelling (Vanijjirattikhan et al., 2022). AI systems are capable of analyzing data from a wide range of sources, including consumption trends, weather forecasts, and sensor data from the water network. AI systems can precisely forecast water consumption and modify distribution by analysing this data. AI controls the flow of water to places with high demand efficiently during peak hours and lowers it during off-peak hours in order to save water and energy. For effective water management, leak detection is essential since it averts losses, damages infrastructure, and raises maintenance expenses.

IoT sensors are used by smart water management systems to continuously monitor leaks and notify maintenance personnel. By evaluating real-time sensor data, seeing patterns and trends, and forecasting the possibility of future leaks, artificial intelligence improves leak detection. Wide-area water distribution networks benefit greatly from the reliable transmission of sensor data provided by advanced communication technologies like NB-IoT and LoRaWAN. This proactive strategy aids in infrastructure maintenance and leak prevention (Giudicianni et al., 2020). Water management systems that use artificial intelligence (AI) and leak detection technologies minimize water loss, boost operational effectiveness, strengthen the resilience and dependability of water infrastructure, and promote environmental sustainability. Water conservation, trash reduction, and energy conservation result in financial savings for consumers and utilities.

By lowering the demand for extraction from natural sources, wise water management protects ecosystems and biodiversity. Less greenhouse gas emissions result from better pumping operations (Sánchez et al.,2020). The use of smart water management systems has many benefits, but there are drawbacks as well. The initial cost of deploying AI systems, communication networks, and sensors is one of the key challenges. However, the long-term savings realized from increased efficiency and decreased water losses frequently offset these costs. Security and data privacy are other important considerations. Water management systems are more vulnerable to cyberattacks as a result of their increased connectivity. Maintaining the integrity and dependability of water services requires ensuring the security of data and infrastructure (Nova et al., 2023).

The future of intelligent water management is bright. The capabilities of these systems will continue to be improved by developments in AI and IoT technology. For example, the accuracy of demand forecasting and leak detection will increase with the development of increasingly complex AI algorithms. Moreover, the incorporation of sustainable energy resources, including solar-powered sensors, will lessen the ecological consequences of water management activities. To fully utilize smart water management, cooperation between utilities, tech companies, and legislators is necessary. Together, these parties may establish guidelines, exchange best practices, and spur innovation to build water systems that are more robust and sustainable (Wan et al., 2022).

In order to do real-time water quality analytics, a number of metrics that show the safety and health of water sources are continuously monitored. Real-time monitoring systems use sensors and Internet of Things (IoT) devices strategically placed throughout water bodies or within distribution networks to measure critical parameters like pH, dissolved oxygen levels, turbidity, temperature, and the presence of particular contaminants. This is in contrast to traditional methods, which rely on periodic sampling and laboratory analysis. Real-time transmission of the sensor data to cloud-based platforms or central monitoring stations allows for immediate analysis.

With this instantaneous feedback, water management and environmental agencies can quickly identify departures from the norm, facilitating timely reaction to contamination incidents and increasing operational effectiveness through ongoing insights into trends in water quality. Long-term water management policies are shaped in large part by real-time analytics because it generates large datasets over time. Predictive models and decision-making procedures can be informed by past data on trends in water quality, allowing for proactive planning of future infrastructure and water resource management. In addition to increasing resistance to environmental changes, this data-centric strategy guarantees the adoption of sustainable water usage practices (Mashhadi et al.,2021). Artificial intelligence (AI) plays a key role in enhancing the predictive powers of water quality monitoring systems, particularly in the areas of understanding complex environmental interactions and predicting contamination incidents. Large amounts of historical and current data from weather patterns, land use data, water quality sensors, and other relevant sources are used to train AI models. Building predictive models is one of the main applications of AI in contamination prediction.

To find links between environmental variables and contamination occurrences, these models look at past trends and patterns in data on water quality. For example, AI can predict the likelihood of microbial contamination after periods of heavy rainfall or identify seasonal variations in nutrient levels that fuel algal blooms (Krishnan et al., 2022). The creation of early warning systems for contamination events depends heavily on artificial intelligence. Artificial intelligence systems are able to detect anomalous patterns or abrupt increases in pollution levels from real-time sensor data, which may indicate the beginning of contamination.

Water utilities and environmental authorities can reduce risks to public health by taking pre-emptive measures like activating alternative water sources, boosting monitoring frequency, or deploying emergency response teams thanks to this early detection. Furthermore, by providing insights into the sources and pathways of pollutants, AI supports decision-making processes. In order to identify pollution hotspots or track the sources of pollutants upstream in a watershed, machine learning algorithms can analyze spatial data. This data is crucial for establishing sustainable land use, concentrating regulatory enforcement, and prioritizing mitigating activities (Mehmood et al.,2020).

Scenario analysis and risk assessment are made easier by AI-driven models. Water managers can evaluate potential effects on water quality by simulating various scenarios, such as changes in land use or climate conditions. By taking a proactive stance, it becomes easier to foresee potential problems and create flexible solutions that can adequately safeguard water supplies. AI-driven models are essential for assisting in decision-making since they offer information about the origins and distribution routes of pollutants. Spatial data can be studied to find pollution hotspots or track the sources of pollutants upstream in a watershed by using machine learning algorithms. In order to minimize pollution inputs, this information is crucial for setting priorities for mitigation initiatives, focusing regulatory enforcement efforts, and putting sustainable land use policies into action (D'Amore et al., 2022). Water management is undergoing a transformation thanks to artificial intelligence (AI), which increases sustainability and efficiency.

To improve water usage, AI algorithms examine data from smart meters, IoT devices, and weather forecasts. They support utilities in identifying leaks, real-time distribution network adjustments, and demand pattern prediction. By keeping an eye on pressure, flow rates, and other variables, artificial intelligence (AI) also improves water distribution networks, saving energy and guaranteeing an adequate supply during times of high demand. Artificial intelligence (AI)-driven leak detection devices reduce water loss by spotting possible problems. Campaigns for public awareness and educational initiatives are crucial for encouraging sustainable water use practices. These programs enable people to make educated decisions and support long-term conservation efforts by highlighting the significance of water conservation and offering useful information on effective practices. Stakeholder participation in water management procedures also guarantees that policies reflect the values of the community and the goals of sustainability (Liu et al.,2021).

## Discussion –

Artificial Intelligence as a component of urban systems contains the promising possibility for building smart and sustainable cities. The use of smart technologies allows cities to improve the various functions including energy, waste, transport and water utilities and enhance efficiency and sustainability. AI can certainly look at large quantities of actual-time information to anticipate and optimize the administration of several city sources, eradicating squandering and reducing co2 deposits. As for the examples of AI applications, it can be used to eliminate traffic congestion using traffic management systems or manage the energy consumption of entire cities with smart grids. Nonetheless, this integration presents some challenges, especially in the deployment of AI solutions to different cities across the globe with regard to size and development.

Although now such technologies are implemented in richer cities equipped with proper funding and infrastructure, the cities such as second-tier or developing ones can face numerous issues with acquiring necessary means and integrating them. Furthermore, the sociotechnical hubs that revolve about AL also present profound moral concerns including control of data, audits, and fairness in the access of these technologies. These matters call for equal policies on AI innovations in a way that the new technologies will be of equal benefits to all citizens besides respecting their rights without enhancing the already existing disparities and discrimination.

## CONCLUSION

The smooth integration of artificial intelligence (AI) with sustainable development concepts is critical to the future of urban living, as it will enable the construction of smarter and greener cities. Green cities are imagined as places where cutting edge technology and ecological responsibility coexist to create resilient and effective neighbourhoods. Extensive datasets are used in AI-driven urban planning to make accurate decisions that optimize energy usage, traffic patterns, and land use to reduce environmental impact and maximize resource efficiency. Green technologies, such as vertical gardens and AI-monitored green roofs, turn urban landscapes into eco-friendly, productive areas that also help regulate temperature and purify the air. AI's function in environmental monitoring goes beyond real-time data collection to include proactive resource management and regulatory compliance.

AI improves urban sustainability on several fronts by encouraging predictive maintenance and energy efficiency. In order to foster innovation and environmental responsibility, the Green City model—a paradigm shift towards holistic urban sustainability—requires cooperation between the public, business, and governmental sectors. This progressive strategy guarantees that ecological sustainability and technology innovation will produce vibrant, livable, and future-proof urban environments for future generations.

## REFERENCES


Aarabe, M.. (2024). Smart Tourism Experience and Responsible Travelers' Behavior: A Systematic Literature Review. In El Archi, Y. (Eds.), *Promoting Responsible Tourism With Digital Platforms* (pp. 128–147). IGI Global., DOI: 10.4018/979-8-3693-3286-3.ch008

Aarabe, M., Ben Khizzou, N., Alla, L., & Benjelloun, A. (2024). Marketing Applications of Emerging Technologies: A Systematic Literature Review. In Alla, L., Hmioui, A., & Bentalha, B. (Eds.), *AI and Data Engineering Solutions for Effective Marketing* (pp. 23–47). IGI Global., DOI: 10.4018/979-8-3693-3172-9.ch002

Aguilar, J., Garces-Jimenez, A., R-Moreno, M. D., & García, R. (2021). A systematic literature review on the use of artificial intelligence in energy self-management in smart buildings. *Renewable & Sustainable Energy Reviews*, 151, 111530. DOI: 10.1016/j.rser.2021.111530

Ahmad, S., Iqbal, N., Jamil, F., & Kim, D. (2020). Optimal policy-making for municipal waste management based on predictive model optimization. *IEEE Access : Practical Innovations, Open Solutions*, 8, 218458–218469. DOI: 10.1109/ACCESS.2020.3042598

Alla, L., Bentalha, B., & Elyoussfi, A. (2023). Intelligence territoriale et positionnement stratégique des regions au Maroc: Le cas de la région de Fès Meknes en perspective. *Le concept de l'intéligence en sciences juridiques, économiques et sociales*, 215-237.

Artmann, M., Inostroza, L., & Fan, P. (2019). Urban sprawl, compact urban development and green cities. How much do we know, how much do we agree? *Ecological Indicators*, 96, 3–9. DOI: 10.1016/j.ecolind.2018.10.059

Badre, M. E. Z. I. A. N. E., Badr, B. E. N. T. A. L. H. A., & Lhoussaine, A. L. L. A. (2024). La PME logistique et le développement territorial régional: Une analyse qualitative. *Alternatives Managériales Economiques*, 6(4), 1–22.

Baduge, S. K., Thilakarathna, S., Perera, J. S., Arashpour, M., Sharafi, P., Teodosio, B., Shringi, A., & Mendis, P. (2022). Artificial intelligence and smart vision for building and construction 4.0: Machine and deep learning methods and applications. *Automation in Construction*, 141, 104440. DOI: 10.1016/j.autcon.2022.104440

Bentalha, B., & Alla, L. (2024). Revealing the Subtleties: The Art of Qualitative Studies in Science and Management. In Bentalha, B., & Alla, L. (Eds.), *Applying Qualitative Research Methods to Management Science* (pp. 1–21). IGI Global., DOI: 10.4018/979-8-3693-5543-5.ch001

Boudri, R., Bentalha, B., & Benjelloun, O. (2024). Phygital Marketing and the Pain of Paying: An Amazon Go Netnographic Case Study. In Alla, L., Hmioui, A., & Bentalha, B. (Eds.), *AI and Data Engineering Solutions for Effective Marketing* (pp. 348–363). IGI Global., DOI: 10.4018/979-8-3693-3172-9.ch017

Bouhtati, N., Alla, L., & Bentalha, B. (2023). Marketing Big Data Analytics and Customer Relationship Management: A Fuzzy Approach. In Bentalha, B., Hmioui, A., & Alla, L. (Eds.), *Integrating Intelligence and Sustainability in Supply Chains* (pp. 75–86). IGI Global., DOI: 10.4018/979-8-3693-0225-5.ch004

Bouhtati, N., Alla, L., & Ed-Daakouri, I. (2024). Smart Data Analysis and Prediction of Responsible Customer Behaviour in Tourism: An Exploratory Review of the Literature. In El Archi, Y., Benbba, B., Dávid, L., & Cardoso, L. (Eds.), *Promoting Responsible Tourism With Digital Platforms* (pp. 189–212). IGI Global., DOI: 10.4018/979-8-3693-3286-3.ch011

Bouhtati, N., El Yaacoubi, Y., Bentalha, B., & Lhoussaine, A. L. L. A. (2024). Leviers logistiques de promotion du commerce équitable des produits de terroir: Une esquisse de modèle d'analyse. *Alternatives Managériales Economiques, 6*(Spécial 1), 17-35.

Cui, L., Weng, S., Nadeem, A. M., Rafique, M. Z., & Shahzad, U. (2022). Exploring the role of renewable energy, urbanization and structural change for environmental sustainability: Comparative analysis for practical implications. *Renewable Energy*, 184, 215–224. DOI: 10.1016/j.renene.2021.11.075

D'Amore, G., Di Vaio, A., Balsalobre-Lorente, D., & Boccia, F. (2022). Artificial intelligence in the water–energy–food model: A holistic approach towards sustainable development goals. *Sustainability (Basel)*, 14(2), 867. DOI: 10.3390/su14020867

Dikshit, S., Atiq, A., Shahid, M., Dwivedi, V., & Thusu, A. (2023). The Use of Artificial Intelligence to Optimize the Routing of Vehicles and Reduce Traffic Congestion in Urban Areas. EAI Endorsed Transactions on Energy Web, 10.

El Jaouhari, S., & Lhoussaine, A. L. L. A. (2022). L'approche territoriale et la gestion de l'impact de la pandémie de Covid-19: Cas des collectivités territoriales. *Alternatives Managériales Economiques*, 4(1), 245–265.

Elhissoufi, M., & Alla, L. (2024). Artificial Intelligence in Costumer Acquisition: A Bibliometric Study. In Alla, L., Hmioui, A., & Bentalha, B. (Eds.), *AI and Data Engineering Solutions for Effective Marketing* (pp. 1–22). IGI Global., DOI: 10.4018/979-8-3693-3172-9.ch001

Farzaneh, H., Malehmirchegini, L., Bejan, A., Afolabi, T., Mulumba, A., & Daka, P. P. (2021). Artificial intelligence evolution in smart buildings for energy efficiency. *Applied Sciences (Basel, Switzerland)*, 11(2), 763. DOI: 10.3390/app11020763

Giudicianni, C., Herrera, M., Nardo, A. D., Adeyeye, K., & Ramos, H. M. (2020). Overview of energy management and leakage control systems for smart water grids and digital water. *Modelling*, 1(2), 134–155. DOI: 10.3390/modelling1020009

Gupta, P. K., Shree, V., Hiremath, L., & Rajendran, S. (2019). The use of modern technology in smart waste management and recycling: artificial intelligence and machine learning. Recent advances in computational intelligence, 173-188.

Hansen, R., Olafsson, A. S., Van Der Jagt, A. P., Rall, E., & Pauleit, S. (2019). Planning multifunctional green infrastructure for compact cities: What is the state of practice? *Ecological Indicators*, 96, 99–110. DOI: 10.1016/j.ecolind.2017.09.042

Hmioui, A., Alla, L., & Bentalha, B. (2017). Pilotage de la touristicité territoriale au Maroc Proposition d'un indice de tourisctícité pour la destination Fès. *Entrepreneuriat, Innovation, Gouvernance et Développement territorial*, 120-143.

Hmioui, A., Alla, L., & Bentalha, B. (2017). *Piloting territorial tourism in Morocco Proposal for a tourism index for the destination Fez [Pilotage de la touristicité territoriale au Maroc Proposition d'un indice de tourisctícité pour la destination Fès]* (No. hal-02334913).

Ibrahim, M. R., Haworth, J., & Cheng, T. (2020). Understanding cities with machine eyes: A review of deep computer vision in urban analytics. *Cities (London, England)*, 96, 102481. DOI: 10.1016/j.cities.2019.102481

Kaczmarek, I., Iwaniak, A., Świetlicka, A., Piwowarczyk, M., & Nadolny, A. (2022). A machine learning approach for integration of spatial development plans based on natural language processing. *Sustainable Cities and Society*, 76, 103479. DOI: 10.1016/j.scs.2021.103479

Kaginalkar, A., Kumar, S., Gargava, P., & Niyogi, D. (2021). Review of urban computing in air quality management as smart city service: An integrated IoT, AI, and cloud technology perspective. *Urban Climate*, 39, 100972. DOI: 10.1016/j.uclim.2021.100972

Komninos, N., Kakderi, C., Panori, A., & Tsarchopoulos, P. (2019). Smart city planning from an evolutionary perspective. *Journal of Urban Technology*, 26(2), 3–20. DOI: 10.1080/10630732.2018.1485368

Kouassi, K. J. C. (2022, December). A Comprehensive Overview of Artificial Intelligence. In Computer Science Conference Proceedings in Computer Science & Information Technology (CS & IT) series, Forthcoming. DOI: 10.2139/ssrn.4311525

Krishnan, S. R., Nallakaruppan, M. K., Chengoden, R., Koppu, S., Iyapparaja, M., Sadhasivam, J., & Sethuraman, S. (2022). Smart water resource management using Artificial Intelligence—A review. *Sustainability (Basel)*, 14(20), 13384. DOI: 10.3390/su142013384

Liang, L., Wang, Z., & Li, J. (2019). The effect of urbanization on environmental pollution in rapidly developing urban agglomerations. *Journal of Cleaner Production*, 237, 117649. DOI: 10.1016/j.jclepro.2019.117649

Liu, Q., Yang, L., & Yang, M. (2021). Digitalisation for water sustainability: Barriers to implementing circular economy in smart water management. *Sustainability (Basel)*, 13(21), 11868. DOI: 10.3390/su132111868

Loughran, K. (2020). Urban parks and urban problems: An historical perspective on green space development as a cultural fix. *Urban Studies (Edinburgh, Scotland)*, 57(11), 2321–2338. DOI: 10.1177/0042098018763555

Mahdavian, A., Shojaei, A., Mccormick, S., Papandreou, T., Eluru, N., & Oloufa, A. A. (2021). Drivers and barriers to implementation of connected, automated, shared, and electric vehicles: An agenda for future research. *IEEE Access : Practical Innovations, Open Solutions*, 9, 22195–22213. DOI: 10.1109/ACCESS.2021.3056025

Marvuglia, A., Havinga, L., Heidrich, O., Fonseca, J., Gaitani, N., & Reckien, D. (2020). Advances and challenges in assessing urban sustainability: An advanced bibliometric review. *Renewable & Sustainable Energy Reviews*, 124, 109788. DOI: 10.1016/j.rser.2020.109788

Mashhadi, N., Shahrour, I., Attoue, N., El Khattabi, J., & Aljer, A. (2021). Use of machine learning for leak detection and localization in water distribution systems. *Smart Cities*, 4(4), 1293–1315. DOI: 10.3390/smartcities4040069

Mehmood, H., Liao, D., & Mahadeo, K. (2020, September). A review of artificial intelligence applications to achieve water-related sustainable development goals. In 2020 IEEE/ITU international conference on artificial intelligence for good (AI4G) (pp. 135-141). IEEE.

Mensah, J. (2019). Sustainable development: Meaning, history, principles, pillars, and implications for human action: Literature review. *Cogent Social Sciences*, 5(1), 1653531. DOI: 10.1080/23311886.2019.1653531

Mohammed, M. A., Abdulhasan, M. J., Kumar, N. M., Abdulkareem, K. H., Mostafa, S. A., Maashi, M. S., Khalid, L. S., Abdulaali, H. S., & Chopra, S. S. (2023). Automated waste-sorting and recycling classification using artificial neural network and features fusion: A digital-enabled circular economy vision for smart cities. *Multimedia Tools and Applications*, 82(25), 39617–39632. DOI: 10.1007/s11042-021-11537-0 PMID: 35915808

Munir, M. T., Li, B., & Naqvi, M. (2023). Revolutionizing municipal solid waste management (MSWM) with machine learning as a clean resource: Opportunities, challenges and solutions. *Fuel*, 348, 128548. DOI: 10.1016/j.fuel.2023.128548

Musikanski, L., Rakova, B., Bradbury, J., Phillips, R., & Manson, M. (2020). Artificial intelligence and community well-being: A proposal for an emerging area of research. *International Journal of Community Well-being*, 3(1), 39–55. DOI: 10.1007/s42413-019-00054-6

Nouhaila, B. K., Aarabe, M., & Alla, L. (2024). The Impact of Digitalisation on the Customer Experience in Medical Tourism: A Systematic Review. In Talukder, M., Kumar, S., & Tyagi, P. (Eds.), *Impact of AI and Tech-Driven Solutions in Hospitality and Tourism* (pp. 408–428). IGI Global., DOI: 10.4018/979-8-3693-6755-1.ch020

Nova, K. (2023). AI-enabled water management systems: An analysis of system components and interdependencies for water conservation. *Eigenpub Review of Science and Technology*, 7(1), 105–124.

Ogwu, M. C. (2019). Towards sustainable development in Africa: The challenge of urbanization and climate change adaptation. The geography of climate change adaptation in urban. *Africa*, •••, 29–55.

Olawade, D. B., Wada, O. Z., David-Olawade, A. C., Fapohunda, O., Ige, A. O., & Ling, J. (2024). Artificial intelligence potential for net zero sustainability: Current evidence and prospects. *Next Sustainability*, 4, 100041. DOI: 10.1016/j.nxsust.2024.100041

Olawade, D. B., Wada, O. Z., David-Olawade, A. C., Fapohunda, O., Ige, A. O., & Ling, J. (2024). Artificial intelligence potential for net zero sustainability: Current evidence and prospects. *Next Sustainability*, 4, 100041. DOI: 10.1016/j.nxsust.2024.100041

Rahman, M. M., & Thill, J. C. (2023). Impacts of connected and autonomous vehicles on urban transportation and environment: A comprehensive review. *Sustainable Cities and Society*, 96, 104649. DOI: 10.1016/j.scs.2023.104649

Samaei, S. R. (2023). A Comprehensive Algorithm for AI-Driven Transportation Improvements in Urban Areas. In 13th International Engineering Conference on Advanced Research in Science and Technology, https://civilica. com/doc/1930041

Sánchez, A. S., Oliveira-Esquerre, K. P., dos Reis Nogueira, I. B., de Jong, P., & Filho, A. A. (2020). Water loss management through smart water systems. Smart Village Technology: Concepts and Developments, 233-266.

Sanchez, T. W., Shumway, H., Gordner, T., & Lim, T. (2023). The prospects of artificial intelligence in urban planning. International journal of urban sciences, 27(2), 179-194.

Satterthwaite, D. (2021). Sustainable cities or cities that contribute to sustainable development? In *The Earthscan reader in sustainable cities* (pp. 80–106). Routledge. DOI: 10.4324/9781315800462-7

Seyyedi, S. R., Kowsari, E., Gheibi, M., Chinnappan, A., & Ramakrishna, S. (2024). A comprehensive review integration of digitalization and circular economy in waste management by adopting artificial intelligence approaches: Towards a simulation model. *Journal of Cleaner Production*, 460, 142584. DOI: 10.1016/j.jclepro.2024.142584

Shennib, F., & Schmitt, K. (2021, October). Data-driven technologies and artificial intelligence in circular economy and waste management systems: a review. In *2021 IEEE International Symposium on Technology and Society (ISTAS)* (pp. 1-5). IEEE. DOI: 10.1109/ISTAS52410.2021.9629183

Sodiq, A., Baloch, A. A., Khan, S. A., Sezer, N., Mahmoud, S., Jama, M., & Abdelaal, A. (2019). Towards modern sustainable cities: Review of sustainability principles and trends. *Journal of Cleaner Production*, 227, 972–1001. DOI: 10.1016/j.jclepro.2019.04.106

Taghikhah, F., Erfani, E., Bakhshayeshi, I., Tayari, S., Karatopouzis, A., & Hanna, B. (2022). Artificial intelligence and sustainability: solutions to social and environmental challenges. In *Artificial intelligence and data science in environmental sensing* (pp. 93–108). Academic Press. DOI: 10.1016/B978-0-323-90508-4.00006-X

Tekouabou, S. C., Gherghina, Ş. C., Kameni, E. D., Filali, Y., & Idrissi Gartoumi, K. (2024). AI-based on machine learning methods for urban real estate prediction: A systematic survey. *Archives of Computational Methods in Engineering*, 31(2), 1079–1095. DOI: 10.1007/s11831-023-10010-5

Tyagi, N., & Bhushan, B. (2023). Demystifying the role of natural language processing (NLP) in smart city applications: Background, motivation, recent advances, and future research directions. *Wireless Personal Communications*, 130(2), 857–908. DOI: 10.1007/s11277-023-10312-8 PMID: 37168438

Ushakov, D., Dudukalov, E., Shmatko, L., & Shatila, K. (2022). Artificial Intelligence as a factor of public transportations system development. *Transportation Research Procedia*, 63, 2401–2408. DOI: 10.1016/j.trpro.2022.06.276

Vanijjirattikhan, R., Khomsay, S., Kitbutrawat, N., Khomsay, K., Supakchukul, U., Udomsuk, S., Suwatthikul, J., Oumtrakul, N., & Anusart, K. (2022). AI-based acoustic leak detection in water distribution systems. *Results in Engineering*, 15, 100557. DOI: 10.1016/j.rineng.2022.100557

Venigandla, K., Vemuri, N., & Aneke, E. N. (2024). Empowering Smart Cities with AI and RPA: Strategies for Intelligent Urban Management and Sustainable Development. Valley International Journal Digital Library, 1117-1125.

Vijayan, D. S., Rose, A. L., Arvindan, S., Revathy, J., & Amuthadevi, C. (2020). Automation systems in smart buildings: A review. *Journal of Ambient Intelligence and Humanized Computing*, •••, 1–13. DOI: 10.1007/s12652-020-02666-9

Wan, X., Kuhanestani, P. K., Farmani, R., & Keedwell, E. (2022). Literature review of data analytics for leak detection in water distribution networks: A focus on pressure and flow smart sensors. *Journal of Water Resources Planning and Management*, 148(10), 03122002. DOI: 10.1061/(ASCE)WR.1943-5452.0001597

Yampolskiy, R. (2020, July). On controllability of artificial intelligence. In *IJCAI-21 Workshop on Artificial Intelligence Safety (AISafety2021)*.

Yigitcanlar, T., Kankanamge, N., Regona, M., Ruiz Maldonado, A., Rowan, B., Ryu, A., Desouza, K. C., Corchado, J. M., Mehmood, R., & Li, R. Y. M. (2020). Artificial intelligence technologies and related urban planning and development concepts: How are they perceived and utilized in Australia? *Journal of Open Innovation*, 6(4), 187. DOI: 10.3390/joitmc6040187

Yigitcanlar, T., Kankanamge, N., Regona, M., Ruiz Maldonado, A., Rowan, B., Ryu, A., Desouza, K. C., Corchado, J. M., Mehmood, R., & Li, R. Y. M. (2020). Artificial intelligence technologies and related urban planning and development concepts: How are they perceived and utilized in Australia? *Journal of Open Innovation*, 6(4), 187. DOI: 10.3390/joitmc6040187

Yigitcanlar, T., Mehmood, R., & Corchado, J. M. (2021). Green artificial intelligence: Towards an efficient, sustainable and equitable technology for smart cities and futures. *Sustainability (Basel)*, 13(16), 8952. DOI: 10.3390/su13168952

# Chapter 10
# Analyzing Territorial Variations in the Implementation of IoT-Based Smart Homes: A Comprehensive Review


**Aditya Sharma**
*School of Computer Engineering, KIIT University (Deemed), Bhubaneswar, India*

**Shubham Kumar**
*School of Computer Engineering, KIIT University (Deemed), Bhubaneswar,, India*

**Nilesh Anand**
*School of Computer Engineering, KIIT University (Deemed), Bhubaneswar,, India*

**Somesh Kumar**
*School of Computer Engineering, KIIT University (Deemed), Bhubaneswar,, India*

**Samyantak Mukherjee**
*School of Computer Engineering, KIIT University (Deemed), Bhubaneswar,, India*

**Hitesh Mohapatra**
https://orcid.org/0000-0001-8100-4860
*School of Computer Engineering, KIIT University (Deemed), Bhubaneswar,, India*


## ABSTRACT


*This paper provides an in-depth introduction to the Internet of Things (IoT) in the context of smart homes, discussing the components and evolution of smart homes. It presents a comprehensive literature review tracing the development of smart homes over time. The paper further explores the implementation of smart homes in China, Malaysia, and India, focusing on adoption rates, cultural acceptance, and*



DOI: 10.4018/979-8-3693-6854-1.ch010

*the economic capability of individuals. It highlights the contrasting differences in these three aspects: Adoption Rate, Cultural Acceptance and Economic condition of population across the three countries: India, China and Myanmar. The results section underscores the significance of this research in understanding the dynamics of smart home adoption and its implications for future development. This study contributes to the growing body of knowledge on smart homes and IoT, offering valuable insights for policymakers, researchers, and industry practitioners.*

## 1. INTRODUCTION

The advent of the Internet of Things (IoT) has revolutionized the way we interact with our surroundings. One of the most impactful applications of IoT is in the realm of Smart Homes. The primary goal of a Smart Home is to create a space that is secure, comfortable, and energy-efficient. We are capable of controlling the lighting in our homes from a desk in a remote location. Our refrigerator contains built-in cameras and sensors, allowing us to readily monitor what is on the shelves and when something is about to expire. These are not scenes from a fantasy book set in the distant future. These are only a few examples of the millions of IoT frameworks now in use. The Internet of Things (IoT) is currently widely used and is essential to every part of peoples' lives, as shown by the numerous real-world applications it has access to, such as smart manufacturing, smart health, smart transportation, smart cities, and smart homes (Mohapatra, 2021). The term “Internet of Things” refers to a dynamic global network infrastructure that can self-configure based on standard and interoperable communication protocols. It includes both virtual and physical “things” that are seamlessly integrated into the information network and that have identities, physical characteristics, and virtual personalities. These “things” also frequently communicate data related to users and their environments (A. & S., 2010). Fig.1 gives a detailed overview of how the revolution of IoT happens in Smart Homes. As it is evident, the Smart Home field is gaining popularity rapidly as resources become cheaper and access to information becomes easier. On top of that, open-source projects like “openHAB” and Home Assistant show how much this field has advanced.

*Figure 1. Revolution of IoT in Smart Homes*

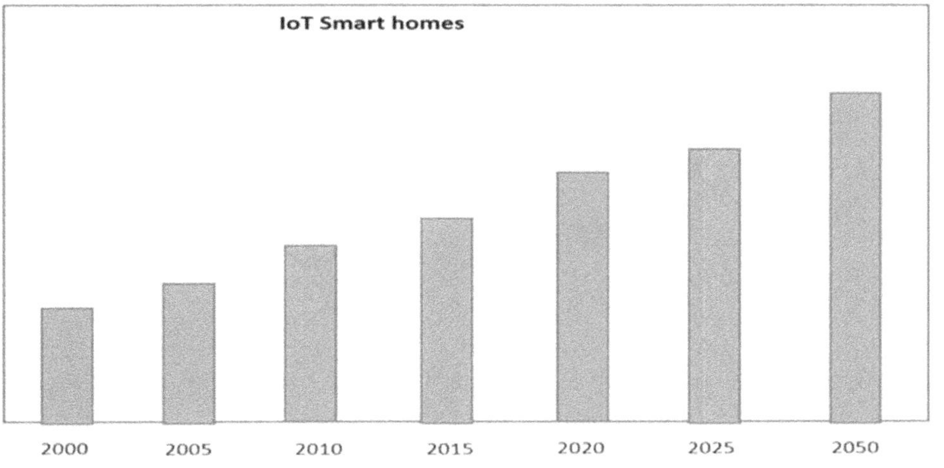


In layman terms, IoT refers to the interconnection of physical devices and appliances we use in our everyday lives - embedded with sensors and networking devices which they use for interconnecting, exchanging information and connecting to the internet. One of the most prominent uses for IoT is Home Automation, in which interconnected gadgets and sensors easily integrate into our day to day lives, reshaping ordinary houses into smart, automated spaces (Bhalotia et al., 2023). A smart home represents a practical and comfortable house layout in which electronics and appliances can be operated remotely from anywhere with an internet connection through a smartphone or other networked device. A smart home's devices are connected via the internet, allowing the user to remotely control features such as home security, lighting, thermostats, and a home theater. Communication/Networking protocols, a controller and the end devices. The interface (UI) of a smart home application serves as the center for communication between the homeowner and the smart home's digital control system. It is made up of graphical components that are shown on a smartphone, tablet, or wall-mounted panel, such as buttons, icons, sliders, and text fields. The user interface (UI) is made to make it simple for consumers to keep an eye on and manage various smart home systems and appliances. Fig.2 shows a typical user interface for Smart Home applications that allow the user to remotely control lighting, fans, thermostat, cameras and locks. Networking/Communication is one the most important part of a smart home infrastructure. The X10 protocol, which was invented in 1978, is widely acknowledged as a trailblazing invention that ignited the smart home movement (Mohapatra et al., 2023).

*Figure 2. User Interface for a smart home application*

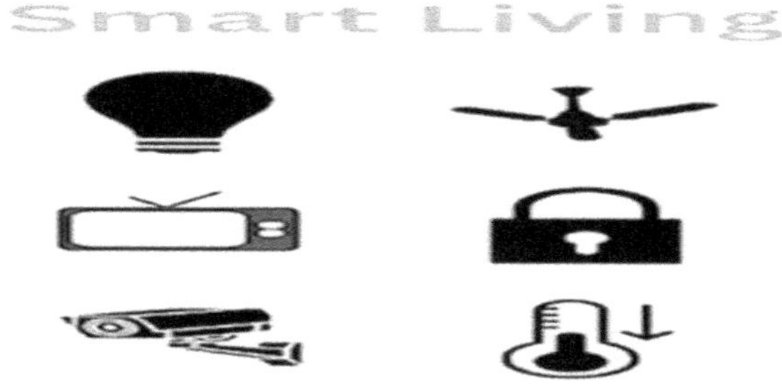


X10, one of the first home automation protocols, made it possible to manage electrical appliances from a distance, laying the groundwork for later advancements in the smart home sector. Even though X10 made a big impact, there aren't many in-depth accounts of how the smart home revolution was started in recent literature. Numerous articles discuss improvements in automation and smart home technology without particularly mentioning X10's revolutionary influence. However, the truth remains that voice-controlled home automation, now a typical feature in the industry, was made possible thanks to X10's technology. Since then, several communication protocols have been used. Both wired and wireless communication technologies are included in this group, such as Ethernet, International Telecommunication Union Telecommunication Standardization Sector (ITU-T) G.hn, Power Line Communication (PLC), Serial, Home Phoneline Networking Alliance (HomePNA), and Multimedia over Coax Alliance (MoCA). Wi-Fi, ZigBee, ZWave, Bluetooth, IPv6 over Low-power Wireless Personal Area Networks (6LoWPAN), IEEE 802.15.3a, Enocean, Wave2M, Radio-Frequency IDentification (RFID), and ONE-NET are examples of wireless communication technologies (Ma et al., 2019). A microcontroller is a small, integrated computer chip that consists of a memory, a processor, and programmable input/output peripherals. Microcontrollers are the essential building blocks of smart homes, providing intelligence and automation to a variety of systems and gadgets in the living space. Arduino is a popular microcontroller which is widely used. Arduino boards are well-liked by educators and hobbyists for use in DIY smart home projects, like monitoring interior surroundings, controlling lighting, and opening garage doors. Raspberry Pi is another popular microcontroller. Despite not being a conventional microcontroller, the Raspberry Pi is a small single-board computer that may be used as a media center, a server for a home security system, a central control unit for home automation, and more. Based on their main purpose and the advantages they offer; smart home appliances can be divided into four groups.

*Figure 3. Smart Home layout*

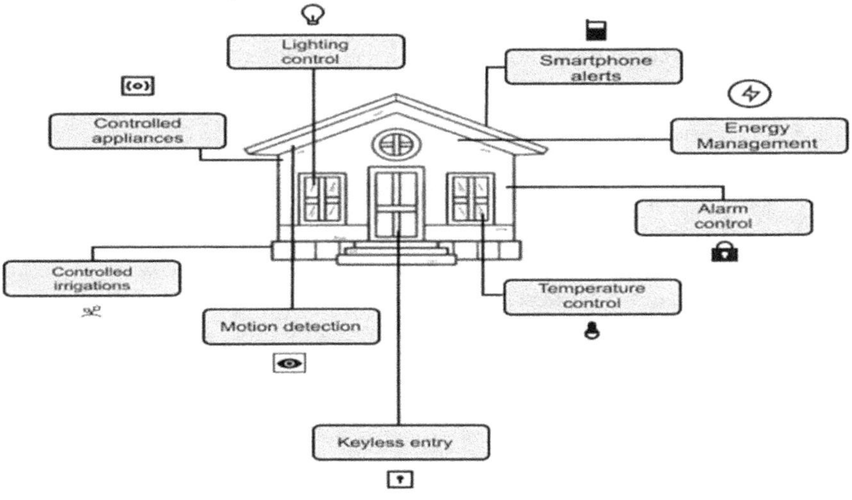


Energy Saving devices, appliances such as energy monitors and smart thermostats contribute to a household's decreased water and electricity usage, making it more economical and environmentally friendly. Comfort, convenience and entertainment gadgets, which do everything from robotic vacuum cleaners to smart speakers, improve the quality of life by streamlining chores and offering customized entertainment (Tiwari et al., 2021). Healthcare, fitness trackers and other smart healthcare technologies, such as telehealth equipment, give users important health insights and facilitate improved personal health management.

*Figure 4.Advanced smart home composition*

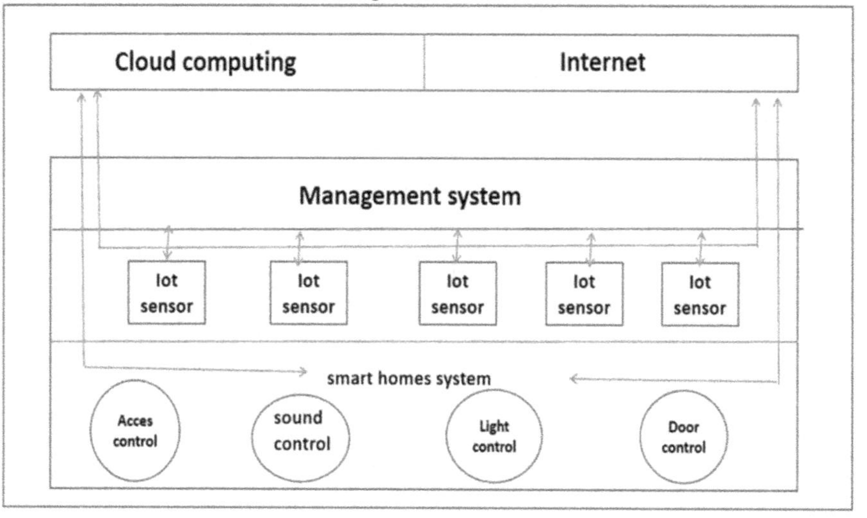


Security and safety, alarms, smart locks, and security cameras all provide cutting-edge technologies for monitoring and thwarting possible attacks, making homes safer places. Fig.2 showcases various features and controls that can be managed remotely or automatically for a house. All the features mentioned can be divided among the four groups mentioned above. Lighting, irrigation and temperature control come under Comfort and Convenience devices. Alarm Control, keyless entry and motion detection come under security devices. Fig.3 further demonstrates the main components of an advanced smart home and the connection with data flow among its components. In Fig.4, it can be observed that the door, sound system, lights and access control are being monitored by sensors, which collect data and send it to the cloud after preprocessing it, where data is processed and inferences are drawn. These inferences then help in the decision-making process of the devices. This paper talks about four main topics. Firstly, the definitions and configuration of smart homes over the years. Second, User Interface for smart home applications and the various means of networking and communication protocols that have been used in smart homes. Thirdly, about the microcontroller and its use in a smart home. Lastly, about the various kinds of gadgets and appliances that are used in smart homes (Majumder et al., 2017).

## 2. LITERATURE REVIEW

The development of smart homes is a reflection of a multifaceted journey influenced by many customers' demands and technology breakthroughs. Over time, the growing need for luxury, comfort, security, convenience, and sustainability has propelled the creation of smart homes. Smart houses, with a focus on energy optimization through sophisticated home energy management systems, have proven to be capable of accomplishing a number of objectives, ranging from delivering luxury to increasing efficiency based on how residents use different amenities (Emekci, 2022). Artificial intelligence (AI), sensors, communication protocols, and the Internet of Things (IoT) have all been incorporated into smart homes to make them more useful and sustainable places to live. When smart homes first came into being, the main goal was to combine technology with design to create unique, luxurious, and convenient spaces. But as these innovations developed, smart houses played an ever-bigger role. When medical sensors were added, for example, the use of smart homes in healthcare became clear because it made it possible to remotely and economically monitor the health of the elderly while keeping them in their homes rather than sending them to a hospital (Medeiros et al., 2019). Thanks to developments in wireless technology, sensors, and devices, smart home environments are becoming more intelligent and self-sufficient. Nowadays, homes provide several advantages beyond recreation, such as communication, information sharing, public safety, and environmental protection. This industry's significance is further demonstrated by its role in the creation of smart cities, which lower energy use and greenhouse gas emissions while utilizing technology to improve citizen welfare.

*Table 1. Review and findings analysis of various papers*

| Citation(s) | Objective | Findings |
|---|---|---|
| (Tiwari et al., 2021) | Focus on understanding details of smart homes and different technologies associated with it. Also describes the various future directions for the researchers. | Describes combined information about sensors, different systems and communication protocols and multimedia devices which are extensively used in smart homes. Different algorithms from various domains, and their importance. |
| (Majumder et al., 2017) | A comprehensive review on the state-of-the-art research and development in smart home-based remote healthcare technologies. | Presented a review on the state-of-the-art technologies for elderly care in smart home platforms. |
| (Emekci, 2022) | How to make cities smart from the home level because they have the biggest share in cities' energy consumption and GHG emissions. | Reveals the potential contribution of smart homes to smart city concepts in terms of energy efficiency and GHG emissions with the help of the bottom-up approach. Presents an extensive literature review to the reader, discussing how smart technologies contribute to citizen welfare. |
| (Medeiros et al., 2019) | Introducing a system of automated and sensor-monitored smart windows for smart home scenarios following an IoT-enabled approach. | This paper proposed an automated window system for smart home scenarios following an IoT approach and reacting to the surrounding environment. |
| (Almihat et al., 2022) | Examine the management and evolution of energy generation, various storage systems and the applications they serve, and infrastructure technology's current condition and future prospects. | Provides an overview of smart cities' future, energy generating systems built to transform primary energy sources such as heat, electricity, and cold into secondary/alternative energy and gives overview in contrast to smart cities. |
| (Jang & Tsai, 2021) | Using software-defined networking (SDN) technology to simulate a multi-tenant smart home environment, simulate different types of smart home service traffic, and use convolutional neural networks (CNN) to classify network traffic. | Results show that the traffic classification accuracy of the CNN model for smart homes can reach 86.5%, which is higher than the general neural network model by 6.5%. |
| (Ali & Awad, 2018) | Key goals of this study are to highlight the various security vulnerabilities of IoT-based smart homes, to present the risks on home inhabitants, and to propose approaches to mitigating the identified risks. | Paper has successfully conducted a comprehensive security risk assessment using the OCTAVE Allegro method and has identified 10 critical cyber and physical assets and as a research outcome, approximately 15 security risks originating from both inside and outside smart homes have been identified. |
| (Ma et al., 2019) | This paper presents the design and implementation of a smart home system in the context of Internet of Things (IoT) with Ethereum private Blockchain, Raspberry Pi, Blynk platform, DHT11 temperature and humidity sensors. | In this paper, a system is built with the combination of Ethereum private Blockchain, Raspberry Pi 3 Model B, DHT11 temperature and relative humidity sensor and Blynk App. |

continued on following page

*Table 1. Continued*

| Citation(s) | Objective | Findings |
|---|---|---|
| (Kalbande & Patil, 2023) | Paper aims to provide brief review on developed systems for different domain of agriculture like robotic, farm monitoring, water management and crop health management, pest detection system. | A Lot of literature has been reviewed for different aspects of agricultural systems like robotics, agriculture monitoring, water management and irrigation, crop health monitoring and pest detection systems etc. The lacunas in the existing system have been identified and the future development approaches have been proposed. |
| (Adib et al., 2015) | Whether it is possible for smart environments to monitor our vital signs remotely, without instrumenting our bodies | Vital-Radio, a wireless sensing technology that monitors breathing and heart rate without body contact is introduced. Vital-Radio exploits the fact that wireless signals are affected by motion in the environment, including chest movements due to inhaling and exhaling and skin vibrations due to heartbeats |
| (Mohapatra & Rath, 2021) | This article refers to the comparative analysis of wireless technology network generations from generation 1 (1G) to generation 5 (5G). | The 5G network that is being deployed promises to change the field of wireless communications with higher data speeds. Artificial intelligence features and unprecedented speed with better performance along with battery longevity of the devices. AI services will be developed in this generation of mobile networks. |
| (Shabha et al., 2021) | This paper investigates how smart home technology could be effectively utilized to aid the UK government in meeting climate change targets and to mitigate the environmental impact of a home in use towards reducing carbon emissions | Paper provided further explanation of the key impediments against smart homes technology adoption and integration by homeowners and proposed ways to overcome and address them more effectively |

IoT-enabled smart homes provide autonomous and intelligent control over fixtures like lights, curtains, and windows that adjust to the needs and preferences of their users. This is a convenient feature. Moreover, smart houses have made a substantial contribution to energy-efficient technology and sustainable urban practices in addition to becoming a component of the infrastructure of smart cities (Song et al. The introduction of 5G technologies has made it feasible to implement applications such as improved traffic management through the use of Convolutional Neural Networks (CNNs), which in the age of smart living, further improve the quality of life for inhabitants. But this development has also brought forth new difficulties, mainly in the areas of security and privacy. IoT-based smart homes are vulnerable to a variety of security threats due to their interconnectedness with multiple devices. To mitigate these dangers and fortify the security frameworks, researchers have utilized techniques like OCTAVE Allegro (Chen et al., 2021).

The creative ways in which the conventional idea of home automation is changing are best illustrated by the incorporation of blockchain technology with Internet of Things devices. Systems for smart homes with blockchain support show how new technologies are being added to the smart home ecosystem. Furthermore, the use of smart home technology goes beyond homes to industries like education and agriculture, demonstrating the adaptability of smart systems. Innovations in healthcare, such as the Vital-Radio system, have made it possible to accurately monitor vital indicators like heart rate and respiration remotely, even at great distances (Elhissoufi & Alla, 2024). Additionally, the transition from 1G to 5G wireless technology has completely changed what it means to live at home. The trajectory of smart homes is evidently defined by the ongoing adoption of state-of-the-art technologies, integration with larger initiatives related to smart cities, and an emphasis on efficiency and sustainability that mirrors the movement in society towards living in an ecologically sensitive manner. The development of smart homes has involved more than simply the addition of intelligent devices and systems; it has also involved promoting the fusion of technology and human-centered design to create more customized and significant living environments (Aarabe et al., 2024. Table.1 provides a tabular view of the findings of all the papers discussed so far.

Technology adoption theories give the basic knowledge as to why and how people and companies decide to use new technologies. There is one well–established theory called the Technology Acceptance Model (TAM). It implies that two concepts namely perceived ease of use and perceived usefulness are what lead to the adoption of technologies. People prefer to use technologies that are easy to adopt and since the proposed technology is also user-friendly, it is likely to be adopted. Another theory that has implication to this study is the Unified theory of Acceptance and Use of Technology (UTAUT). This model extends aspects from several previous theories and adds new ones such as performance expectancy, effort expectancy, social influence and facilitating conditions. In line with the UTAUT model, the authors posit that these factors have a strong effect on the users' intentions and usage behavior.

The regional adoption rates demonstrated that communities that utilize the innovations depend on the local factors that exist within the geographical region in question. Interestingly adoption rates differ in India as it is summarized below. It is also evident that the younger generation is bound to be more inclined to adopt smart home technologies since they have better technological know-how and more cash to spend. Unsurprisingly, for the older people technology adaptation is Complex is complex, this being due to cultural impacts as well as the lack of tailor-made products and services. Therefore, in the Malaysian context, the rates of adoption it is determined by culture issues for example privacy and social support. Malaysians' millennials are becoming early adopters of PCEs because of the perceived benefits associated with time saving, economic returns and energy saving. Then, the rate of adoption with the older adult is slow because of the problems that include usability and awareness. China is somewhat of a special case. It's no wonder that younger persons insist on adoption of social media mainly due to higher awareness levels of smart technologies. These needs and care necessities of the older adults are key determinates of the adoption that occurs among them. Other-center conditions also apply influence but matters of culture and generation differences also affect them critically.

A comparison of the various regions brings out some interesting facts as highlighted below. Current trends that affect the implementation of smart home technologies in India include the economic challenges as well as the questions on cultural acceptance. However, cultural imperatives supplemented by both perception and social relations factor, are equally vital in Malaysia besides other economic determinants. In Chinese culture and demographic contexts, on the one hand, economic environment plays an important influence factor for adoption, while on the other hand, it is concerned with the family support and technology attitude in China. By categorizing the identified literature into these themes, it is easy to have a comprehensive view of the issues and trends surrounding the adoption of technology in the various regions. It also increases the understanding of how Theories and regionality factors come into play when it comes to the use of Smart Home Technology.

## 3.RESEARCH GAP

The studies primarily focus on adoption factors rooted in theories like the technological acceptance model and the diffusion of innovation theory, but offer limited insights into a cross-country comparison of smart home adoption. Another study delves into the user acceptance and adoption of smart homes across various nations, addressing the research gap by analyzing key constructs and theories used in the literature (Aarabe et al., 2024). Despite these contributions, comprehensive comparative research is scarce. However, while the adoption of smart home technologies is steadily growing worldwide, there exists a notable lack of comprehensive research comparing adoption rates and patterns across different countries. For businesses, researchers, and politicians to fully comprehend the nuances driving the adoption of smart homes and to adjust their plans appropriately, it is imperative that they comprehend these variations. Research on the domestication of smart technologies in households can provide valuable data for understanding the drivers and barriers to smart home adoption from a business perspective. Comprehensive research specifically comparing the adoption of smart homes in different countries (Bouhtati et al., 2024). Such comparative studies are instrumental in identifying the various influences on smart home adoption, shaping policies, and tailoring market strategies to foster increased acceptance of smart home technologies. The few existing studies indicate an opportunity and a need for detailed cross-national analyses to fill the existing research gap (Bouhtati et al., 2023).

## 4. COMPARATIVE STUDY

Smart home adoption is important as it significantly contributes not only to the work-life balance but also to long-term safety enhancement, minimized environmental impact, better economic efficiency, energy, cost savings, increased comfort, and overall convenience. Smart homes support service scalability and widen the diversity of its services considerably, and smart home technologies support the increasing accessibility to a wide range of applications that enables these automated residential environments (Bentalha & Alla, 2024). In this article, we're going to see what are the factors affecting smart home implementation and how and why adoption of smart homes differs across different countries.

### 4.1. Basis

This is small-scale research and only compares 3 countries for 3 parameters. We will consider 3 parameters which are: -

1. Adoption Rate: It refers to the percentage of households within a region that have adopted smart home technology. A higher percentage could reflect greater consumer awareness, higher disposable income, technological literacy and supportive infrastructure in the region.
2. Cultural Acceptance: Cultural factors affect how technology is accepted and used. This can include the region's openness to innovation, the value placed on privacy and convenience, and societal attitudes towards energy conservation and sustainability, which are all enhanced by smart home technologies.
3. Economic Status of People: Income levels factor greatly into smart home ownership. Numerous studies have found that the main barrier to consumer adoption of smart home technology is ever shrinking with each new product that hits the market. Still, the majority of smart home owners are in a higher income bracket, so they may not be as cost-effective as anyone would like, especially in the event of a move and subsequent system replacement.

### 4.2. Comparison

#### 4.2.1. India

Different findings on adoption rates found that adoption is influenced by factors such as technology version used, particular features, need for extended training times, user age demographics, and more. Younger adults were found to show the highest adoption rate, at 70%, and the highest satisfaction level, 7.6 out of 10.

Meanwhile, adoption remains low among older adults in India because of ethical and acceptability challenges, and because solutions in smart home technology are needed that are more personalized, more dignified, more user-controlled and less isolating (Nouhaila et al., 2024). The emergence of smart home technology in India is governed by a set of interconnected factors including cultural and social aspects that have immense domination in determining consumer behavior towards the highly technological products. A study on Internet of Things (IoT) adoption determinants distinguishing between India and the USA mentioned that cultural elements, social influence, and facilitating factors unmask the common ground for IoT adoption in these countries (Boudri et al., 2024). Similar research papers on integrative reviews, consumer behavior and benefits as well as barriers and socio-cultural elements were appraised concerning the smart homes and which product-services systems design may be accepted and adapted within the Indian environment.

Despite the fact that the literature we are aware of is insufficient enough to help us to link these paths to the cultural problems and social influence we can draw some conclusions from the sector at hand context that would be enough to fill the questions gaps. A negative link was registered between the women's educational attainment and property ownership towards their capability of negotiation and their effect on women's residential outcome as her air conditioner or refrigerator ownership (Williams et al., 2015). Stepping therein, a study done to trace latrine adoption in rural Odisha, India, found that social, cultural, and behavioral factors were pivotal. This involved a study of the performance of poor latrine owners who had received subsidies from the government and the shortcomings in the household hygiene structures that were built using the government subsidies. It can be interpreted that both of the government policies and social norms are influential to the using of various appliance in the household, which can be extended to smart homes. In the health sector, a systematic review on the IoT Adoption and Implementation for Smart Healthcare revealed that social influence, attitude, as well as, individual inattentiveness are the main elements which are significant at the individual level (Mallinson & Shafi, 2022). Also, it was found out that the stroke survivors who live in the community had very low awareness about the right recovery methods, a poor perceived recovery and a cultural background that favors folk medicine over rehabilitation services. With respect to both technology adoption and smart cities sustainability the social and cultural factors as well as the consumer awareness are the most critical aspects that need to be taken into account closely. It also emphasizes the need of augmenting the level of awareness and educating the public on smart technology applications so as to draw more adherence to its benefits.

The economic factor on adapting the smart home technology in India seems to be a challenging topic which is slightly influenced by some important attributes for the people to apply the smart home service. One study is saying that the matter such as the usefulness, fees and luxury of homes as a status symbol has a significant relationship to the perception of smart home technologies which play a great role in the intention to adopt smart homes services in India (Walldén & Mäkinen, 2013). An article pointed out that the motivation to exploit the Smart Home Energy Management Systems in India is motivated by economic benefits, environmental consideration, comfort and safety. Therefore, economic factors, shortlisted together with ecological and personal safety factors, determine the level of smart home software utilization and acceptance. Moreover, the system has obstacles as well such as the high costs, low return on investment, and the complicated systems that suggested by the economic status may be a barrier (Oluwayemisi Runsewe et al., 2024).

### 4.2.2. Malaysia

Technology in smart homes, particularly among older adults in Malaysia is influenced by factors like privacy, social support, and autonomy, as well as technology aspects which include usability and the need for training (Muriungi & Chumo, 2024). On the other hand, elsewhere the function of smart assistants is highlighted. As a result, devices with high utilitarian performance rating are liked for utilitarian purposes while those with high hedonic performance rating are chosen for entertainment purposes. An example on young people's adoption of smart home technology in Malaysia was found in a study done in community pharmacies in Selangor, where approximately 53% of the young adults below 30 years old took the lead in adopting more than half of the home automation technology in these communities. Accordingly, the usage of smart home technology in Malaysia is affected by different cultural and social aspects that elucidate consumers' choices and decisions. It was evidenced by a study on the views about smart homes conducted among millennials in Johor, Malaysia, that possible apartment buyers care mostly about 'time saving, cost cutting and energy efficiency'. In addition to the lack of awareness about Islamic smart tourism which encompasses cultural sensitivity and historical promotion, absence of cultural considerations impacts smart technologies adoption in the Malaysian tourism sector suggesting that such practices are of importance in regard to the domestic market.

The role of socio-cultural aspects in smart home product design also underlines the literature. An integrative review highlights how these factors may be introduced in PSS (product service system) design, suggesting that they are taken up into the tech acceptance context as a whole (Muriungi & Chumo, 2024). Besides, although the focus is on socio-cultural factors, they are not ranked at the top of the hill in relation to economic and location issues for Malaysian housings by buyers (Bouhtati et al., 2023). This underlines that although culture and social relations are deemed to be of significance, they may take the background in determining buyers' decisions when buying a home in Malaysia. Factors such as value perception, visual appeal, perceived usefulness and perceived ease of use have been noted to be important influences on smart home adoption that even though not entirely based on cultural or social factors, they portray a trend of technological advancements that are in line with society and lifestyle.

The relationship between economic capacity and smart-home technology use has been discussed in several studies, but the outcomes are not completely uniform. A study on the Huawei smart home development acknowledges the notion that economic conditions behave as a leading factor which promotes the development of smart home technologies within Malaysia (Bouhtati et al., 2024). Besides, economic status is not the only influencer here. Similarly, electricity saving for economic purposes is along with impediments like high prices and complex systems, which hint that though economic level complicates the adoption process, the cost and complexity of smart home technology are also very important. Another related factor is the adoption of IoT Technology by elderly patients with Non-Communicable Diseases (NCD) in Malaysia, in which economy is a matter of concern with financial affordability and evolution that are determinants of high-risk behavioral deviations and utilization of healthcare resources (Aarabe et al., 2024). On the other hand, Malaysia had some studies done on it but was very few compared to the overall studies. But it can be inferred that in regions which mostly have the same economic and technological situation, the economic status can either help or hinder depending on issues like technology prices, customer learning, perceived values of the technology and the opinion held by the people about the innovation and the way it's useful to them. When it comes to the broad concept of smart home technology development in general, the issues like usefulness concept, data or information privacy, and existence of examples in IoT enterprises are among the challenges which need to be dealt with in the Malaysian context (Bentalha & Alla, 2024). These hindering factors could also be economic considering that the general environment also includes economic status is influential in the future process.

### 4.2.3. China

Reviewing current research focusing on the adoption of smart home technology in China reveals that the characteristics of the population such as the age and demographics are the two key factors that determine the acceptance rates. For example, younger Chinese individuals in their 20s are more familiar and comfortable with smart technologies like Internet of Things and environmental control systems which enables them to use these technologies as their daily life assists, whereas the older people, in their 50s, tend to prefer the smart devices which supports their health care and home needs (Jiang & Han, 2024). One research divulges that intergenerational relationships tremendously sway the older adults' intention to embrace smart homes and that the utilization of smart home services is positively induced by the instrumental support they receive from the younger generation (Jiang & Han, 2024). On the other hand, the Chinese adults above 60 years old's decision to implement the Voice-User Interface (VUI) system at home is determined by the factors like usefulness, ease of use and trust. Smart home technology in China is still at a low level, the specific number being unknown, nor do the abstracts reveal any figures (Jiang & Han, 2024). Of course, other researchers indicate that the smart home utilization among people who show low health-related risk is as high as 86.97%, the study shows (Elhissoufi & Alla, 2024). To sum up, despite the large scale of the survey on detailed and specific adoption rates is not published, demographic factors obviously play a great role in smart home technology adoption in China, and young generations have driving adoption as a result of promises of innovative lifestyles, the development of smart city infrastructures as well as positive multi-generation support within the families.

Smart homes are becoming popular in China but due to a bunch of socially-rooted and cultural elements of the country this kind of technology is being adopted by the people in a certain way. An academic paper on the adoption of smart home energy technologies in Guangzhou province adopted the planned behavior theory and the norm activation model as theoretical frameworks. And it was revealed from these theoretical frameworks that residents' attitude towards technical performance, social norms, perceived control, and personal norms have a positive effect on the adoption intent, with attitude towards technical performance being the most significant influence. Income, demographic features, as well as cultural factors that include the attitude towards social changes are majorly the growth determinants for the smart media adoption in China. Moreover, smart home technologies' adoption or rejection in China by the older generation might be influenced by psychological and cultural customs along with the availability of high-quality devices, programs, and services. The robot's social occlusion, compensation and emotional experiences are the factors with implications on adoption and acceptance. This theme is then elaborated (Oluwayemisi Runsewe et al., 2024). There are additional implications of the health status of residents in China for the potential smart home technology adoption, since the highest utilization of such technologies exists among those who are at a low risk of health-related issues (Almihat et al., 2022). Moreover, the performance of being-implemented products, effort of applying the products and social influence affect the behavioral intention of the older adults to use smart aged-care products too (Aarabe et al., 2024). Besides, the psychology of users concerning their acceptance of voice assistants in smart homes involves the combination of motivators and psychological factors like hedonic motivation, trust, social influence, performance expectancy, and effort expectancy. Hedonic motivation turned out to be as effective as trust (Bouhtati et al., 2024). Additionally, a different study discovered that perceived usefulness, perceived enjoyment, and affective community commitment also emerged as the major motivators that stimulate the smart community service adoption in China.

Inequivalence of the Economic Depth of people in China among the factors increasing in the Adoption of Smart House Technologies. Some of these studies revealed favorable economic conditions as one of the factors that leads to the increase of use of such advanced technologies. The researchers suggest that with the improved economic situation in China, there is a trend of the growth of intelligent home technology in the country (Bouhtati et al., 2023). However, a different study tracked several factors in the adoption of smart homes' technology in Guangdong Province. Although the economic factors were considered, the technology reliance theory and the motivation theory were said to be important propelling factors. Moreover, support from younger family members is associated with a positive perception on technology adoption, implying the complex interactions between socioeconomic status and family dynamics among the older adults. In the same way, specific demographics like the elderly often claim that the smart home solution for the elderly care in China is a state-directed rather than tech-driven or demand-driven product which means that general policies and the available resources can affect the adoption rates. Besides, it is worth noting the economic status of the elderly would have a great influence on their level of satisfaction with smart home-based care. The study also highlights that incorporation of affordable and accessible network access approaches like WiFi and cloud service from organizations like China Mobile could encourage IOT applications in smart homes that can be very convenient to different economic groups. Whether the elderly will adopt VUI (Voice-User Interface) technology in smart home systems is mainly determined by four factors: perceived usefulness, perceived ease of use, trust, and some personal characteristics, which cover not only the economical consideration. Moreover, similar to studies on the adoption of other types of technologies, these findings suggest that the economic status of farmers determines their adoption of biological control technology, the difference in adoption rates between socioeconomic groups being obvious. This evidence indicates that economic levels may play a major role in the technological landscape, possibly taking it to smart home technology.

## 4.3. Critical Analysis

This research provides valuable insights in adoption of smart home technologies across 3 different countries that are China, India and Malaysia using 3 different factors. 31 research papers were read and analyzed in an attempt to find the differences in adoption of IOT based smart homes in these 3 countries. It was found that all 3 factors play a major role in all 3 of these countries and the effects of these factors are similar to each other. It was found that in China, economic factors do not act as a major hindrance to adoption of SH-IOT but cultural and social factors hinder adoption of Smart homes in older adults. Meanwhile, India and Malaysia struggle with economic factors as well as risk perception and security issues in adoption of SH-IOT amongst people. Table 2. summarizes the points discovered in the above research and presents them in a tabular manner.

*Table 2. Comparative analysis of Adoption of SH-IOT across multiple countries*

| | INDIA | CHINA | MALAYSIA | CONCLUSION |
|---|---|---|---|---|
| **ADOPTION RATE** | Young people show the highest level of adoption as well as satisfaction. Older people are slow to adopt this technology mostly because of cultural, socio-economic and personalization issues. | Younger people show more interest in this technology than older ones. Many factors like generational usage and health related issues lead to adoption of smart homes among older people. It appears as if research work in China mostly focuses on older people's usage of smart home technology. | Privacy, social support and usability affect the usage of smart homes among older people. Again, younger people are the largest adopters of this technology. Time saving, cost cutting and energy efficiency are factors that affect adoption in millennials. Lack of awareness also plays a role in the spread of this technology. | No specific comparison among the three countries can be made in terms of who adopts this technology more. India faces barriers related to risk perception, while China focuses on energy technology and elderly acceptability and Malaysia faces problems in SH-IOT adoption. |
| **CULTURAL ACCEPTANCE** | No direct link between culture and adoption of Smart homes, however, cultural factors influence adoption of other technologies. Lack of education is a major problem. Social norms also act as a limiting factor. | Smart home adoption in China is influenced by social, cultural, and psychological factors. Key drivers include attitudes towards technical performance, social norms, income, demographics, and attitudes towards social change. The older generation's adoption is shaped by cultural customs and health status, while voice assistants' acceptance involves hedonic motivation and trust. | Socio-cultural aspects influence smart home design but are secondary to economic and location factors for Malaysian buyers. Value perception, visual appeal, and perceived usefulness are key influences on smart home adoption, reflecting societal and lifestyle trends. | One contrasting difference is that while in Malaysia and India, perceived security and privacy are key factors, in China, cultural values and social trust play a more significant role. |
| **ECONOMIC STATUS OF PEOPLE** | In India, smart home adoption is influenced by economic factors, usefulness, fees, and status symbolism. Motivations include economic benefits, environmental considerations, comfort, and safety. However, high costs, low return on investment, and system complexity pose challenges. | Economic conditions, technology reliance, motivation theory, and family dynamics influence smart home adoption in China. State policies, resources, and economic status of the elderly also impact adoption rates. Affordable network access and perceived usefulness of Voice-User Interface technology are key factors. Economic status determines technology adoption across socioeconomic groups. | Economic conditions significantly influence smart home technology adoption in Malaysia. However, high costs, system complexity, and affordability for the elderly also impact adoption. Despite these challenges, perceived usefulness, privacy concerns, and examples of IoT applications are key factors in the development and acceptance of smart home technology. | While economic conditions are a leading factor in Malaysia and India, in China, other factors like technology reliance and motivation theory are also significant. |

Knowing more about smart home adoption ratios across countries allows getting a better idea of how the world reacts to this innovation. The present statistics reveal that the penetration of smart home systems is steadily on the rise in the developed regions especially in North America and Europe. The smart homes market in United States is moderate and its estimated that at least 30% households of US have installed smart home technologies due to technological literacy and high disposable income. Likewise, in Western Europe some of the high adopter nations are Germany and United Kingdom because of the increased demand as well as favorable environment. Adoption rates on the other hand are relatively low in emerging market but are growing exponentially. For instance, the adoption is gradually increasing in the regions like South East Asia, Latin America because of increased technology penetration and economic growth respectively. There is apparent evidence in the above-mentioned regions because more people can afford smart home systems as the price reduces and people become more knowledgeable. Table 3 provides a snapshot of smart home adoption rates across different regions, highlighting key drivers and challenges in each area.

*Table 3. Smart home adoption rates across different regions, highlighting key drivers and challenges in each area*

| Region | Current Adoption Rate | Key Drivers | Challenges |
|---|---|---|---|
| **North America** | ~30% | High technological literacy, disposable income, robust infrastructure | High initial cost, privacy concerns |
| **Western Europe** | ~25% | Strong consumer interest, supportive infrastructure, high income | Privacy issues, complex installation |
| **China** | ~20% | Rapid urbanization, economic growth, government support | Economic disparity, cultural resistance |
| **India** | ~10% | Growing technology access, improving economic conditions | Economic barriers, cultural resistance |
| **Southeast Asia** | ~15% | Increasing technology accessibility, rising incomes | Low awareness, affordability issues |
| **Latin America** | ~12% | Economic development, increasing technology affordability | Limited infrastructure, low awareness |

The proposed framework is able to enrich the existing discussion of theoretical frameworks to offer a wider perspective of the technology adoption process. In addition to TAM and UTAUT more theories can be used Dependent on the kind of IT and media used for the application of the technology the following theories and identification of variables can be derived. According to Rogers, Diffusion of Innovations theory, describes how, why and at what rate, innovations are diffused. This theory organizes the adopters according to the categories like innovators, early adopters, early majority, late majority adopters and laggards. It focuses on the communication channels, social systems, individual perception of the attributes of the innovation when seeking to adopt it. There is also another framework, which is known as the Innovation Resistance Theory and is directed towards the obstacles concerning the adoption of new technologies. This theory is more focused on perceived attributes like risk, complexity and incompatibility that may likely pose a set back to its adoption. It focuses on the problem, which potential users are currently subjected to when they are presented with new innovations and the resulting rebellion.

Thus, an integration of the statistical evidence with theoretical models may provide a better understanding of the smart home market. For instance, by using the Diffusion of Innovative Theory to interpret the global adoption rates, it is possible to discover how various adopter categories contribute to the general growth of the market. Likewise, with the help of Innovation Resistance Theory, it is possible to understand why some regions or groups of people have lower rates of using smart home technologies even if they are available to them. The statistical data added to the analysis does not remain the sole source of some of the conclusions; they will be backed by theoretical constructs. This approach will not only enable one to come up with a current picture of the level of adoption that has been achieved but also discover some of the factors that are facilitating or retarding the adoption of smart home technology globally.

## 4.4. Policy Level Discussion

### 4.4.1. Government Policies

Technology adoption in smart homes has several drivers to which government policies are of significance. In developed countries, supportive policies consist of provisions for energy efficiency incentives, tax exemptions to incorporate smart homes and much more. For instance, in the United States, the government on the federal level and many states have commenced adopting different programs that provide the homeowner with monetary rebates once they install smart home systems that are more efficient on energy. These policies not only help to lower the expenses that are paid at the very beginning, but also help popularize smart home technologies due to their lower cost (Clement et al., 2022). In Europe the European Union's Green deal lays emphasis on adoption of the smart technologies as one of its strategic ambitions to reach the state of climate neutral. Several counties in Europe have provided regulatory frameworks, grants and tax credit for smart home technology including incentives for energy efficient home upgrades and subsidies for smart homes features including thermostats and lighting systems.

Analogically, governmental regulation may be not sufficiently elaborated in emerging markets. Still, there are some countries that are getting the logical outcomes of the smart home technologies innovations, and certain measures are being adopted by them. For instance, in China, the government has embarked on the promotion of smart home system as it seeks to achieve smart city solutions. Some of the policies are the BOI incentives offered to smart appliances producers, and government funding of smart Infrastructure (Clement et al., 2022). Currently, government policies on smart homes, especially in India are limited or are still in a developmental stage. There are few programs that are designed to support the stability of energy usage and environmentally-friendly lifestyle, however, there are not many programs that are focused on integration of smart home technologies. The government's efforts are more in the direction of development and availability of basic facilities and technology that has a bearing on smart homes to a certain extent.

### 4.4.2. Environmental Impact:

One of the major concerns of adopting smart homes is the impact on environment. Different ways prove that modern technologies implemented in homes can help to protect the environment in various terms. For instance, the applications of smart thermostats for home regulation, and smart lighting systems for controlling electric lighting thus helping to decrease the overall energy demand. These technologies include heating systems that are regulated by occupancy and time of day, cooling systems and lighting since they reduce energy expenditure and minimize carbon emissions. Smart home systems also aid in water management through the use of smart irrigation and their detection of leakage (Ipsen et al., 2018). A greater control and efficiency in the use of water is possible with smart homes and the results are fewer cases of wastage and improved water management practices. Besides, the use of renewable energy sources like photovoltaic panels in smart homes systems improves its benefits to the environment. Smart grid and smart energy management systems can increase the utilization of renewable energy resources thereby reducing energy consumption in homes and the use of non-renewable energy sources. However, smart home devices also have the environmental aspect in their production and disposal. The production of electronics for instance requires mining of raw materials and energy consumption while the latter which is the disposal of old gadgets can lead to e-waste. The innovation of smart home technologies may serve environmental advantage but it may also have environmental drawbacks based on the life cycle (Colding et al., 2020).

### 4.4.3. Emerging Technologies and Their Impact (AI/ML/5G)

AI is revolutionizing clever home technology via enabling more advanced and personalized automation. AI-powered structures can analyze from person conduct, alternatives, and workouts to provide custom designed studies. For instance, AI can optimize power intake by predicting while and in which electricity is needed primarily based on ancient statistics. This can cause vast cost savings and power performance. Moreover, AI enhances safety through state-of-the-art algorithms which could locate unusual activity and alert owners to capacity threats. AI-driven digital assistants can also offer extra intuitive and herbal interactions, making smart domestic systems greater person-pleasant. Machine gaining knowledge of, a subset of AI, allows clever domestic systems to continuously enhance their performance over the years. ML algorithms analyze facts from various sensors and devices to perceive patterns and make predictions. For example, a clever thermostat the usage of ML can adjust temperature settings based totally at the person's choices and daily exercises, enhancing consolation and energy performance. ML additionally contributes to predictive protection by means of reading tool performance and usage styles to forecast ability disasters. This proactive approach can assist save you malfunctions and expand the lifespan of smart home gadgets. 5G era promises to seriously beautify the performance and skills of smart domestic systems. With its better bandwidth and lower latency, 5G can guide a bigger range of connected gadgets with faster and extra reliable communique. This permits seamless integration of numerous clever home technologies and improves the responsiveness of automated structures. The improved information transfer speeds of 5G also facilitate actual-time monitoring and control of clever domestic gadgets.

### 4.4.4. Societal Implications of Widespread Smart Home Adoption

The proliferation of smart domestic gadgets increases sizeable privateness troubles. Many smart domestic structures collect and shop big quantities of personal facts, including behavioral patterns, alternatives, and even audio and video recordings. These statistics may be liable to breaches and misuse, posing risks to consumer privacy. Ensuring sturdy data safety features and obvious privacy rules is important. Users want to be knowledgeable about how their facts are amassed, stored, and used (Colding et al., 2020). Moreover, enforcing sturdy encryption and safety protocols can help protect touchy records from unauthorized get entry to. The adoption of clever home technology can result in shifts in social behavior and interactions. For example, automation and faraway manipulate of domestic features might also lessen face-to-face interactions among household members. While smart houses can provide convenience and performance, they'll additionally lead to accelerated social isolation if now not balanced with interpersonal engagement. Additionally, the integration of smart technology into daily life can change the way human's method tasks and workouts. For instance, the convenience of automation might adjust conventional practices related to family control and personal conduct.

Integrating an evaluation of rising technologies including AI, device mastering, and 5G with an exploration of societal implications provides a properly-rounded view of the future of clever houses. Addressing privateness concerns, modifications in social conduct, and cultural, financial, and technological challenges offers treasured insights into the factors influencing clever domestic adoption. This comprehensive approach not simplest highlights the ability of smart domestic technologies but also addresses the complexities and concerns that come with their tremendous implementation (Wang & Deng, 2022).

## 5. FUTURE SCOPE

This research paper can be valuable for several reasons, some of which have been listed below:

1. Policy Insights and Decision-Making:
    - Such a comparative study provides valuable insights for policymakers, urban planners, and government agencies. Understanding the varying adoption rates and cultural factors allows them to tailor policies and incentives to promote smart home technologies effectively.
    - Policymakers can identify successful strategies from countries with high adoption rates and adapt them to their own context.
2. Market Opportunities and Investment:
    - Businesses and investors can benefit from understanding the economic power of different populations. By analyzing adoption rates alongside economic indicators, they can identify lucrative markets for smart home products and services.
3. User-Centric Design and Localization:
    - Cultural acceptance plays a crucial role in technology adoption. Research comparing cultural attitudes toward smart homes can guide product design and marketing.
    - Companies can tailor their offerings to align with cultural preferences.
4. Sustainable Development Goals (SDGs):
    - Understanding the interplay between adoption rates, cultural acceptance, and economic capacity contributes to achieving SDGs. Smart

homes can enhance energy efficiency, reduce waste, and improve quality of life.

- Researchers can highlight how smart home adoption aligns with specific SDGs and advocate for targeted interventions.

## 6. CONCLUSION

In conclusion, this paper has explored IoT in smart homes, starting with IoT and its components, then reviewing the evolution of smart homes. It compared smart home implementation in China, Malaysia, and India, focusing on adoption rate, cultural acceptance, and economic capability. The research found these factors significantly influence smart home adoption. China leads in implementation due to advanced technology and high adoption rate. Malaysia follows with a growing economy and increasing tech acceptance. India lags due to cultural factors and economic disparities. This research provides insights into factors affecting smart home adoption in different contexts, emphasizing the importance of understanding these factors for successful implementation. It contributes to existing knowledge by providing a comparative analysis of smart home adoption and highlights the need for further research, particularly in addressing cultural and economic factors to increase adoption. In the digital transformation era, smart homes are a step towards more efficient, sustainable, and comfortable living environments. Understanding the factors influencing their adoption is crucial for success. This paper serves as a stepping stone for future studies in this field, inspiring further exploration into IoT and smart homes. The journey towards smart homes is a journey towards a smarter, more connected, and sustainable world.

## REFERENCES


Aarabe, M., Ben Khizzou, N., Alla, L., & Benjelloun, A. (2024). Marketing applications of emerging technologies. *Advances in Marketing, Customer Relationship Management, and E-Services*, 23–47. DOI: 10.4018/979-8-3693-3172-9.ch002

Aarabe, M., Ben Khizzou, N., Alla, L., & Benjelloun, A. (2024). Smart tourism experience and responsible travelers' behavior. *Advances in Hospitality, Tourism, and the Services Industry*, 128-147. https://doi.org/DOI: 10.4018/979-8-3693-3286-3.ch008

Adib, F., Mao, H., Kabelac, Z., Katabi, D., & Miller, R. C. (2015). Smart homes that monitor breathing and heart rate. *Proceedings of the 33rd Annual ACM Conference on Human Factors in Computing Systems*. https://doi.org/DOI: 10.1145/2702123.2702200

Ali, B., & Awad, A. (2018). Cyber and physical security vulnerability assessment for IoT-based smart homes. *Sensors (Basel)*, 18(3), 817. DOI: 10.3390/s18030817

Almihat, M. G., Kahn, M. T., Aboalez, K., & Almaktoof, A. M. (2022). Energy and sustainable development in smart cities: An overview. *Smart Cities*, 5(4), 1389–1408. DOI: 10.3390/smartcities5040071

Bentalha, B., & Alla, L. (2024). Revealing the subtleties. *Advances in Library and Information Science*, 1–21. DOI: 10.4018/979-8-3693-5543-5.ch001

Bhalotia, N., Kumar, M., Alameen, A., Mohapatra, H., & Kolhar, M. (2023). A helping hand to the elderly: Securing their freedom through the HAIE framework. *Applied Sciences (Basel, Switzerland)*, 13(11), 6797. DOI: 10.3390/app13116797

Boudri, R., Bentalha, B., & Benjelloun, O. (2024). Phygital marketing and the pain of paying. *Advances in Marketing, Customer Relationship Management, and E-Services*, •••, 348–363. DOI: 10.4018/979-8-3693-3172-9.ch017

Bouhtati, N., Alla, L., & Bentalha, B. (2023). Marketing big data analytics and customer relationship management. *Advances in Logistics, Operations, and Management Science*, •••, 75–86. DOI: 10.4018/979-8-3693-0225-5.ch004

Bouhtati, N., Alla, L., & Ed-Daakouri, I. (2024). Smart data analysis and prediction of responsible customer behaviour in tourism. *Advances in Hospitality, Tourism, and the Services Industry*, 189-212. https://doi.org/DOI: 10.4018/979-8-3693-3286-3.ch011

Chen, Z., Li, X., & Xia, X. (2021). Socioeconomic status, ambidextrous learning, and farmers' adoption of biological control technology: Evidence from 650 kiwifruit growers in China. *Pest Management Science*, 78(2), 475–487. DOI: 10.1002/ps.6642

Clement, J., Manjon, M., & Crutzen, N. (2022). Factors for collaboration amongst smart city stakeholders: A local government perspective. *Government Information Quarterly*, 39(4), 101746. DOI: 10.1016/j.giq.2022.101746

Colding, J., Wallhagen, M., Sörqvist, P., Marcus, L., Hillman, K., Samuelsson, K., & Barthel, S. (2020). Applying a systems perspective on the notion of the smart city. *Smart Cities*, 3(2), 420–429. DOI: 10.3390/smartcities3020022

Elhissoufi, M., & Alla, L. (2024). Artificial intelligence in costumer acquisition. *Advances in Marketing, Customer Relationship Management, and E-Services*, 1–22. DOI: 10.4018/979-8-3693-3172-9.ch001

Emekci, S. (2022). From smart homes to smart cities. *Advances in Public Policy and Administration*, 321–337. DOI: 10.4018/978-1-7998-7785-1.ch018

Ipsen, K. L., Zimmermann, R. K., Nielsen, P. S., & Birkved, M. (2018). Environmental assessment of smart city solutions using a coupled urban metabolism—Life cycle impact assessment approach. *The International Journal of Life Cycle Assessment*, 24(7), 1239–1253. DOI: 10.1007/s11367-018-1453-9

Jang, H., & Tsai, T. (2021). Using CNN to optimize traffic classification for smart homes in 5G era. *2021 IEEE 12th Annual Information Technology,Electronics and Mobile Communication Conference (IEMCON)*, 0086-0091. https://doi.org/DOI: 10.1109/IEMCON53756.2021.9623079

Jiang, W., & Han, B. (2024). Evolution to fifth-generation (5G) mobile cellular communications. *Textbooks in Telecommunication Engineering*, 149-168. https://doi.org/DOI: 10.1007/978-3-031-57820-5_9

Jiang, W., & Han, B. (2024). Evolution to first-generation (1G) mobile cellular communications. *Textbooks in Telecommunication Engineering*, 7-21. https://doi.org/DOI: 10.1007/978-3-031-57820-5_2

Kalbande, K., & Patil, W. (2023). Smart systems as futuristic approach towards agriculture Development:A review. *2023 2nd International Conference for Innovation in Technology (INOCON)*, 1-6. https://doi.org/DOI: 10.1109/INOCON57975.2023.10101109

Ma, M., He, Z., Xu, Q., & Li, X. J. (2019). Design and development of smart home sensing supported by blockchain technology. *Proceedings of the 2019 7th International Conference on Information Technology: IoT and Smart City*, 525-530. https://doi.org/DOI: 10.1145/3377170.3377281

Majumder, S., Aghayi, E., Noferesti, M., Memarzadeh-Tehran, H., Mondal, T., Pang, Z., & Deen, M. (2017). Smart homes for elderly healthcare—Recent advances and research challenges. *Sensors (Basel)*, 17(11), 2496. DOI: 10.3390/s17112496

Mallinson, D. J., & Shafi, S. (2022). Smart home technology: Challenges and opportunities for collaborative governance and policy research. *The Review of Policy Research*, 39(3), 330–352. DOI: 10.1111/ropr.12470

Medeiros, S. P., Rodrigues, J. J., Da Cruz, M. A., Rabelo, R. A., Saleem, K., & Solic, P. (2019). Windows monitoring and control for smart homes based on Internet of things. *2019 4th International Conference on Smart and Sustainable Technologies (SpliTech)*, 1-5. https://doi.org/DOI: 10.23919/SpliTech.2019.8783163

Mohapatra, H. (2021). Socio-technical challenges in the implementation of smart city. *2021 International Conference on Innovation and Intelligence for Informatics, Computing, and Technologies (3ICT)*, 57-62. https://doi.org/DOI: 10.1109/3ICT53449.2021.9581905

Mohapatra, H., Mohanta, B. K., Nikoo, M. R., Daneshmand, M., & Gandomi, A. H. (2023). MCDM-based routing for IoT-enabled smart water distribution network. *IEEE Internet of Things Journal*, 10(5), 4271–4280. DOI: 10.1109/JIOT.2022.3216402

Mohapatra, H., & Rath, A. K. (2021). A fault tolerant routing scheme for advanced metering infrastructure: An approach towards smart grid. *Cluster Computing*, 24(3), 2193–2211. DOI: 10.1007/s10586-021-03255-x

Muriungi, K., & Chumo, K. P. (2024). Building future-proof, sustainable, and innovative startups in Africa powered by smart cities. *Green Computing for Sustainable Smart Cities*, 172-205. https://doi.org/DOI: 10.1201/9781003388814-11

Nouhaila, B. K., Aarabe, M., & Alla, L. (2024). The impact of digitalisation on the customer experience in medical tourism. *Advances in Hospitality, Tourism, and the Services Industry*, 408-428. https://doi.org/DOI: 10.4018/979-8-3693-6755-1.ch020

Runsewe, O., Osundare, O. S., Folorunsho, S. O., & Akwawa, L. A. (2024). Innovations in Android mobile computing: A review of best practices and emerging technologies. *World Journal of Advanced Research and Reviews*, 23(2), 2687–2697. DOI: 10.30574/wjarr.2024.23.2.2634

Shabha, G., Barber, F., & Laycock, P. (2021). A qualitative assessment of the impact of smart homes and environmentally beneficial technologies on the UK 2050 net-zero carbon emission target. *Smart and Sustainable Built Environment*, 12(2), 341–360. DOI: 10.1108/SASBE-07-2021-0112

Song, Y., Yang, Y., & Cheng, P. (2022). The investigation of adoption of voice-user interface (VUI) in smart home systems among Chinese older adults. *Sensors (Basel)*, 22(4), 1614. DOI: 10.3390/s22041614

Tiwari, P., Garg, V., & Agrawal, R. (2021). Changing world: Smart homes review and future. *EAI/Springer Innovations in Communication and Computing*, 145-160. https://doi.org/DOI: 10.1007/978-3-030-71485-7_9

Walldén, S., & Mäkinen, E. (2013). On accepting smart environments at user and societal levels. *Universal Access in the Information Society*, 13(4), 449–469. DOI: 10.1007/s10209-013-0327-y

Wang, J., & Deng, K. (2022). Impact and mechanism analysis of smart city policy on urban innovation: Evidence from China. *Economic Analysis and Policy*, 73, 574–587. DOI: 10.1016/j.eap.2021.12.006

Williams, M. D., Rana, N. P., & Dwivedi, Y. K. (2015). The unified theory of acceptance and use of technology (UTAUT): A literature review. *Journal of Enterprise Information Management*, 28(3), 443–488. DOI: 10.1108/JEIM-09-2014-0088

# Chapter 11
# Collective Intelligence of Port Territory Stakeholders:
## Case of Moroccan Ports

**Chafik Bensfia**
*Sidi Mohamed Ben Abdellah University, Morocco*

## ABSTRACT

*In a global context marked by the globalization of economies, and by the adoption of information technologies as key success factors for standing out in an environment of fierce intra- and inter-regional competition, territorial development players are called upon to establish a climate of territorial economic intelligence, in order to provide good strategic information for successful decision-making by territorial players in an intelligent way. The port territory will not escape this context of change, and plays a crucial role in global supply chains, which are facing major structural transformations and transitions in the fields of sustainability, energy transition and geo-economics. The role of port intelligence is increasingly crucial in managing these transitions. Port intelligence presents multiple challenges in terms of technology and governance in managing a complex ecosystem that requires the implementation of a community system that brings together all stakeholders in the port territory. As a result, we aim to highlight the role of this port community system (PCS) in improving port intelligence. Accordingly, our study is divided into two parts: a theoretical approach aimed at providing a review of the role of the PCS in enhancing port intelligence, and a quantitative, hypothetico-deductive approach.*

DOI: 10.4018/979-8-3693-6854-1.ch011

## 1. INTRODUCTION

In a global context marked by the globalization of economies and the adoption of information technologies as key success factors to stand out in an environment of fierce competition, intra and inter regions, territorial development actors are invited to establish a climate of territorial economic intelligence, to offer good strategic information in order to ensure the success of the decision-making of territorial stakeholders in an intelligent manner (Alla et al., 2023). The port territory will not escape this context of change and plays a crucial role in global supply chains, which are facing structural transformations and major transitions in the areas of sustainability, energy transition and geo-economics. The role of port intelligence is increasingly crucial in managing these transitions. Port intelligence presents multiple difficulties in terms of technology and governance in terms of managing a complex ecosystem which requires the implementation of a community system which brings together all the stakeholders of the port territory (El Jaouhari & Lhoussaine, 2022).

Inside the port territory, information plays a crucial role; Information, as an immaterial reality, evolves and is sometimes reborn during an exchange "to metamorphose into a sign, an index or a symbol" (Barthes, 1992; Moinet, 2009). Local leaders, whether elected or organizational leaders, have difficulty managing this exponential flow of information to fuel political, economic or social reflection. Each stakeholder seeks in the advice of the other the valuable warning that prevents crises from occurring in a complex and uncertain context.

The collection, manipulation and putting into perspective of territorial data go beyond the particular universe of individual competence to be part of a systemic and shared framework marked by collective intelligence. The "information material" is transformed into the fundamental element of a collective project, created and shared by all the actors during the communication processes involved; it plays a role in the transformation of culture. According to Le Coadic (Le Coadic, 2005), in the new paradigms of information and communication sciences, three revolutions are highlighted, namely the timing when information is produced and communicated, the time when the information is used.

These constraints and changes must be taken into consideration by the territories as a public space, such as the integration of new actors and the development of information systems which can create relationships between all the actors of the territory, maintain interactions and collaborate in a common territorial project.

This chapter aims to construct a relevant conceptual research framework on the Port Community System (PCS) and its impact on the quality of decisions at the port territory level which is well founded theoretically but which requires empirical validation and which allows us to address the question of the impact of these information systems on the decision-making quality of port territory managers(Bensfia & Bouklata, 2023; BENSFIA & BOUKLATA, 2024).

To do this, it should be noted that according to the theoretical basis, the concept of information and information systems (IS) are closely linked to each other, and that the systematic theory speaks of the set of theoretical principles which explain the theory information systems, as well as this theoretical corpus helps us to understand the impact of these IS and more precisely SCP on the quality of strategic decisions.

Before embarking on this work, we will address the concept of information and information technology and their impacts on the performance of an organization, as well as their relationships with systems theory. These two sections will allow us to approach the concept of the community port system and to better understand it.

## 2. LITERATURE REVIEW AND DEVELOPMENT OF HYPOTHESES

Territory is one of the most polysemous terms (Girardot, 2004), it has many uses: common language, geography, politics, management sciences... The definition of territory can encompass many realities, especially since the term can be used in different ways, as Lefèvre and Jouve point out, the notion of territory is difficult to understand, because it borrows from several social sciences with different and not always complementary meanings (Lefèvre & Jouve, 1992).

According to Yann Bertacchini, there are three levels of analysis of the territory: the territory as a space, the territory according to its physical and organic content, and the territory as an information system (Bertacchini, 2010). This territorial analysis scheme highlights the circulating data and the links between objects in real physical space. The relationships between the elements that make up the territory generate information: "the topological relationships that connect the elements in terms of neighborhood, adjacency, intersection, belonging, inclusion; relationships of use or occupancy: vehicles using traffic lanes, businesses using supplies to produce or networks to distribute their products; as well as buildings that occupy a certain volume and floor space."

The characteristics of the notion of territory are explained by Leloup, Moyart and Pecqueur(Leloup et al., 2005):

- The territory is a complex dynamic system developed by a series of actors located in narrow areas (geographical proximity) and who are linked thanks to common standards (institutional proximity).

- The territory is an open space where the relationships between the space and other territorial spaces are interchangeable. These territories can be limited by political-administrative criteria, but they can also be defined by physical and human networks, formal or informal.

- The social construction of the territory is based on the discovery of common problems and the appropriation and transformation of the territory's resources not yet exploited. It will be limited by the way in which the resource appropriation processes will be developed by territorial actors.

- The territory as a system is nourished by exchanges and relationships, being part of a The territory is a complex system which structures itself and whose independence rests on its identity, its history and its own dynamics, distinct from that of other territories. According to these characteristics, the territory presents itself as a crossroads of networks (physical and human, formal and informal), strategies and interdependencies between partners.

It is therefore a place where we negotiate, produce and share a common future. According to Leloup, Moyart and Pecqueur, the territory therefore presents numerous dimensions which are formed from the interactions between its actors and their environment. It includes different natural spaces, each with specific functions, essential to human life. This is how the cultural values and customs of a society are formed.

According to this definition, it is therefore necessary to rethink the territory as a specialized system of actors which has a strategic capacity to produce itself. It is a capacity which is not exclusively political or economic, but which results from a systematic behavior of the structured territory.

## 2.1. Information and Information Technologies: Conceptual Aspects

In this section, we will deal with the notion of information and information technologies (IT) as well as the importance of these last two elements in the construction of information systems as well as their contributions to organizational performance.

### 2.1.1. The Concept of Information

The concept of information turns out to be relatively complex, rarely defined in a clear and precise way (Glazer, 1991; Lesca et al., 2010) and that this information is not the same from one research field to another. 'other and it depends on the perspectives in which we place ourselves.

In their work “economic intelligence in the service of business” Romagni, Patrick and Wild consider information as “information that improves our knowledge on any subject” (Romagni & Wild, 1998).

Jacques ARSAC seeks to link information with knowledge, in this sense affirms that "in relation to the world of knowledge or ideas, information would be the form which carries knowledge and therefore the vehicle of thought" (Arsac, 1971)based on this assertion we can say that information is an important source for the construction of knowledge (Belmondo, 2004). UNESCO also seems to follow the same logic when it states that knowledge can be represented as a piece of information that can be stored, manipulated and shared.

Furthermore, information is a process that is created when someone wants to share information or knowledge (LEBRATY, 1998). In other words, it is impossible to define information without referencing people and knowledge data and ideas.

According to Reix R, "to inform means to provide representations to solve problems; these representations must be adapted to the situation of use" (Reix et al., 2016).

The literature allows us to talk about three main currents of interpretation of the notion of information, namely the statistical, symbolic and semantic conception.

Table 1 summarizes the contributions of these currents in a synthetic manner.

*Table 1. Main streams of interpretation of information*

| **Current interpretation of information** | **Main contributions** | **Authors** |
|---|---|---|
| **Statistical or mathematical design** | -information is quantifiable data whose interest lies in the frequency of occurrence.<br>- the concern made about the physical aspect of the information<br>- the information is dissociated from the knowledge it is likely to provide by being stripped of any semantic value.<br>- the form of information is more important than the material. | (Brillouin, 1971)<br>(Ritchie, 1986)<br>(Ritchie, 1986)<br>(Zeman, 1965) |
| **Symbolic design** | -Decision-making in organizations constitutes a field for the application of social values.<br>- the competent decision-maker is the one who bases the legitimacy of his actions on the appropriate use of information.<br>- holding information is a good thing in itself, because an organization which holds more information is considered better, superior compared to others. | (Feldmann & March, 1991)<br>(Specht, 1987)<br>(Welsch & Young, 1982)<br>(Zmud, 1978) |
| **Semantic design** | -Information is synonymous with a signal involving a transmitter, a receiver and a medium.<br>-Nonaka (1994), emphasizes that the semantic design is interested in the quality of information, in the new understanding (Meaning) that it brings.<br>-Feldman and March (1991) take up the idea of a signal and defend that a signal that has value allows better decisions to be made and information to be disseminated at a lower cost. | (Nonaka, 1991)<br>(Minnerath, 1982)<br>(Caruthers & McKay, 2002) |

### 2.1.2. Territorial Information

The meaning and usefulness of territorial information are only manifested within the framework of communication between local jurisdictions. Only in a cognitive framework can this communication be achieved, because the information itself, which is an essential element of communication, depends on cognitive structures, their functioning and their level of abstraction. Finally, communication is also conditioned by our relationship with time and our ability to adapt to external time - the time of others -, as well as by our interactions with our environment. It is possible to affirm that communication takes place in a spatial-temporal dimension where information acquires its meaning in a common framework of interaction. It is essential to identify the cognitive models of territorial actors in order to be able to approach communication within the framework of consultation and promote territorial interactions, which constitutes the foundation of the concept of territorial intelligence.

The territory is transformed into a space of resources where actors play a game of power based on questions of appropriation Sfez, legitimacy and identity, which inevitably requires the resolution of conflicts that arise in the framework of geographical consultation. It was suggested that the establishment of a territorial surveillance system and its implementation by local actors could encourage territorial consultation. The solution envisaged to resolve these conflicts must take into consideration the question of the networking of the “individual – community” couple, because it is in the resolution of this question that the foundations of the social regulation of interactions on the territory are found. .

## 2.2. The Role of Information in Organizational Performance

For several years, information has played an important role (Laudon & Laudon, 2013) in eliminating uncertainty as well as in decision-making. The physical information incubator medium can store and restore information in a computer system.

Information provides three basic functions, namely a decision-making tool, a communication tool and finally a collective intelligence tool and constitutes a resource (Grenier & Moine, 2003) and which can be considered as a comparative advantage for an organization (Mahoney & Pandian, 1992).

Information has taken a major place in modern economies or information economies, due to the dematerialization and digitalization of processes in all private or public organizations, in the same sense, in 1991 Mr. Porter emphasized that companies that leverage information for innovation have a strong competitive position (Porter, 1991).

*Table 2. Main contributions of the relationship between information and organizational performance.*

| Theoretical currents | Objects of reflection | Key authors | Main relevant theses |
|---|---|---|---|
| Contingency theory | Reduction of uncertainty and adaptation to the environment | (Galbraith, 1973)<br><br>(Porter, 1990)<br><br>(JD Thompson et al., 2017) | Reduction of uncertainty and Carrying out activities that require sufficient information.<br><br>Effective strategy formulation requires mastery of information on the key forces that determine the dynamics of an industry.<br><br>Working with communication and coordination mechanisms to minimize uncertainty. |
| Decision making theory | Effectiveness of decision-making processes | (O'Reilly III, 1982)<br><br>(Simon, 1950) | The effectiveness of the decision is based on the relevance, reliability and accessibility of the information.<br><br>The ability to extract information is an important criterion for the decision maker |
| Organizational learning theory | Learning and skills development | (Huber, 1991)<br><br>(Nonaka, 1994)<br><br>(Cohen & Levinthal, 1990) | An organization learns through the acquisition, interpretation, dissemination and exploitation of information.<br><br>Interaction and communication between individuals, organizations and groups develops knowledge.<br><br>The ability to learn and innovate is determined by the degree of information absorption. |
| Entrepreneurial theory | Detection and exploitation of opportunities | (Kirzner, 2015)<br><br>(Drucker, 1985) | The entrepreneur's sensitivity to opportunities results from the state of awareness he manifests.<br>The entrepreneur engages in research as well as a motivated and organized analysis of opportunities |
| Resource theory | Source of competitiveness and performance | (Amit & Schoemaker, 1993)<br><br>(Mahoney and Pandian, 1992)<br><br>(Wernerfelt, 1995) | Strategic resources that generate sustainable and competitive rents.<br><br>Strategic resources with value are those that are durable, difficult to transfer, and difficult to imitate.<br>Strategic resources include information, its source and certain managerial practices. |

**Source:**(BENSFIA et al., 2024; Bensfia & Bouklata, 2022; Bouklata & Bensfia, 2020).

## 2.3. Systems Theory

Studying information systems through the lens of information systems (IS) theory requires a foundation found in systems perspective analysis. It also serves as prerequisites for any effort to conceptualize the values of this system.

However, a thorough review of the literature immediately reveals a variety of tools and areas. This motivated us to investigate the origins of the phenomenon in order to clarify the issue and provide a credible explanation.

Once the finding has been established and its sources identified, we will attempt to evaluate the attempts made to conceptually unite the IS, which is essential to any theoretical development. These critiques will be used to support the conceptual position adopted in the context of this research.

### 2.3.1. Categories of PCS Benefits.

The PCS contributes to the port's success and upholds consumer value.

A PCS streamlines interdependent logistical processes by compiling crucial data from the parties' information systems onto a single platform. In addition to lowering expenses related to paperwork and manual processes, the PCS enables improved coordination between many stakeholders and offers real-time visibility of shipments (World bank group, 2023). When PCSs first started to take shape, they were primarily focused on the idea of a "data exchange hub" or "electronic mailbox." Stakeholders gradually came to understand its potential to provide a range of services that significantly improve a port's resilience, efficiency, and dependability. The benefits of PCS are outlined in the accompanying table, which also offers guidance on how to quantify those benefits (World bank group, 2023).

*Figure 1. Categories of PCS Benefits (Giuliano et al., 2015; World bank group, 2023)*

| | **Digital Economies Benefits** | **Quantification Methods** |
|---|---|---|
| Economic Benefits | Reduce the cost of information access | Value of time and labour saved |
| | Reduce the cost of communication | Previous cost of communication |
| | Extra revenue to government authority or administrator | Value of revenue |
| | Correct taxation (port authority services) | Difference between before and after tax revenue |
| | Prevention of illegal transactions | Percent of illegal transactions reduction |
| Increased Quality of information | Decrease in error rates | Time and labour consumed to correct errors |
| | Elimination of data inconsistency / Decrease in data redundancy | Time and labour consumed to sort and verify data |
| Increased Performance | Fast access to information | Measurement of Increased Labour Productivity |
| | Efficient use of resources | Better use of equipment capacities |
| | **Community attendance benefits** | **Quantification Methods** |
| Increased competitive-ness at Stakeholder level | Increased access to information | Savings in costs of information |
| | Added value services | Revenue in Added Value services through PCS |
| Increased efficiency | Compliance with community standards and regulations | Less investment needed through business growth |

According to a Brazilian study, a port community concept may greatly reduce border waits (fig 2). The graphic illustrates the time-saving potential of a trading Single Window program's limits (World bank group, 2023). An MSME, or micro, small, and medium-sized business, might gain from the PCS's function as a single submission portal. The following advantages result from a PCS's mix of characteristics in the trading environment (Aarabe et al., 2024):

- Single submission: MSMEs only need to submit all necessary data (such as customs, tax, inspection, and logistics-related data) once, as permitted by national law. They are not needed to submit data to multiple locations.

- Easier clearance: MSMEs can rely on a PCS to assist them with the clearance process as it can facilitate the sharing of shipping line and customs release information with the terminal operator, pay terminal fees, facilitate truck appointments, and provide complete and accurate declaration data to cross-border agencies.

- Lower expenses associated with business transactions: MSMEs may engage more effectively and affordably with the normal import and export service ecosystem when they use a PCS. This might lower the requirement for MSMEs to hire personnel for foreign commerce from inside, saving money on management and human resources. The MSME can engage with the community without having to construct and maintain costly, specialized ICT systems if it has access to a web page. It generates competition and reduces the entrance barrier.

*Figure 2. PCS Benefits: Brazil Study*

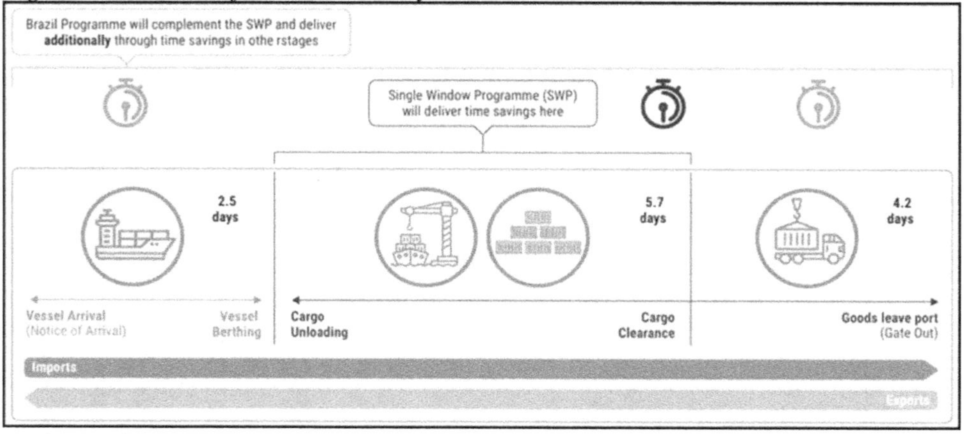


*Source: (IPCSA,2021)*

## 2.3.2. The Port Community System: An IS of the port territory.

The Port Community System (PCS) is a technology platform that enables a network of public and private entities involved in cargo and shipping services offered by ports. In 2007, Rondon and Ramis-Pujol emphasize that the main function of the PCS is to digitally represent port operations. It connects many systems of various companies and other entities that make up the port community. Few studies have examined SCPs in the context of information systems (dos Ramos Caldeirinha et al., 2020).

Furthermore, the majority of these studies are only descriptive and do not discuss the qualities or effectiveness of these systems or their integration into the current systems of port authorities, facilities and companies. The main function of PCS, an electronic platform that connects numerous systems of various companies and entities, is to digitally represent port operations in a logic of collective intelligence of all stakeholders.

According to Meersman, Van de Voorde and Vanelslander, PCS is crucial for port efficiency (Meersman et al., 2010; Tsamboulas et al., 2012). However, few researchers have systematically focused on the meaning of SCP characteristics and their influence on port performance. In 2016, Karlan et al. Point out that the effects of information technology on port performance have not yet been fully studied, since the development of PCS is generally analyzed in terms of characteristics without considering the effects on port performance (Karlan et al., 2016). To analyze the effects of terminal management systems on port operations, while Lee, Tongzon and

Kim used performance indicators of customer satisfaction and port competitiveness (Bensfia & Bouklata, 2023).

The SCP is an electronic device that allows parties involved in international trade and transportation to submit all information necessary to satisfy trade-related regulatory requirements at a certain time and at a single point of entry. This digital trade facilitation measure aims to ease the regulatory burden that businesses must bear while completing procedures relating to imports, exports and transit. It was created more than ten years ago and has since become a key element of reforms aimed at increasing trade facilitation. The World Trade Organization (WTO) Agreement on Trade Facilitation, which entered into force in February 2017, contains specific provisions on the electronic single window (Bensfia & Bouklata, 2023).

The main features of modern single windows addressed in this work include uniform information exchange and transmission, paperless environment, standardized documents and data, information sharing, centralized risk management, coordination between parties, analytical skills and electronic payments.

## Definition of the Concept of the Community Port System

According to UNCTAD experts, the Port Community System (PCS) is a neutral and open electronic platform enabling secure exchange of information between stakeholders to improve the competitive position of port communities.

This platform contributes to the optimization, management and automation of port transit and logistics processes through a single data submission and connects transport and logistics chains.

Table 5 (COMCEC, 2017) lists the main core and support services of a one-stop shop, the majority of which are linked to port transit services (Tijan et al., 2019).

*Table 3. Single Window business process and support services*

| **Basic Operational Process** | | **Support Services** | | | |
|---|---|---|---|---|---|
| **Processing of declarations** | **Management of Certificates and Permits** | **Filing and filing of documents** | **Real-time status information** | **Messaging Bidirectional Communication/ feedback** | **Deposit of Documents and data** |
| User profile | Management of transport and financial documents | Data exchange between different systems and apps | Reports and Analysis | Business Intelligence | Coordination of joint controls |
| Electronic payment | Manifest management | Data validation, authentication and authorization | In real time Container/cargo container/cargo tracking | Electronic payment | Risk management |

Source: (COMCEC, 2017).

A GUP is therefore a platform that presents port passage services and commercial processes that contribute to the success of commercial activities (COMCEC, 2017).

For the implementation of these platforms, several countries have already reached significant digital maturity while others, these Single Windows (GU) coexist with paper systems, something which increases the shortfall in terms of time savings and money (Peterson, 2017). In recent years, there has been a proliferation of EM projects around the world. In Asia, for example, the implementation of GU occupies an increasingly crucial place in a context of modernization of international trade activities (ESCAP, 2015).

*Figure 3. Expansion of Single Windows in Asia*

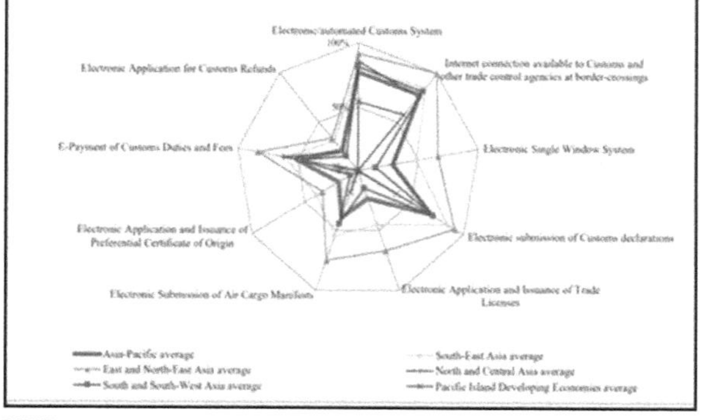


*Source: (ESCAP, 2015)*

At the member level of the African Electronic Commerce Alliance, the amount of news recorded demonstrates the concern that this issue has for African governments. However, Africa remains the least performing region for cross-border trade, due to the mismatch between political decisions and the technical capacities to be taken without falling into the traps of the particularities of each nation.

From Figure 3, we see that it addresses the issue of GU by emphasizing the need for each country to ensure consistency and coordination on the basis of observation and analysis of the windows unique existing in the world, the GU can be grouped into three main categories, namely, the GU for international trade procedures, the GU for logistics coordination and the national GU. The first two types seem different, but they complement each other (AACE, 2017).

*Figure 4. Expansion of Single Windows in Africa*

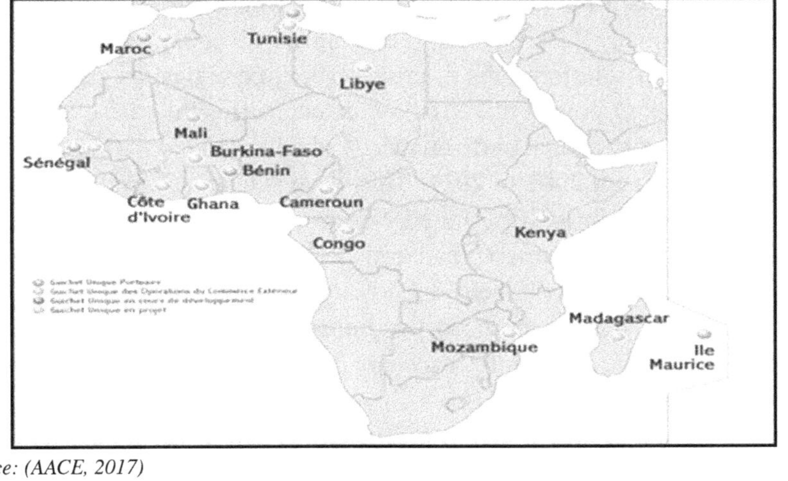


*Source: (AACE, 2017)*

SCPs in Europe have a long history. The first countries like Germany, the United Kingdom and France started adopting these solutions from the 1970s. While other countries like Spain and the Netherlands started their SCPs in the 90s .

The main pillars of the implementation of SCP were, on the one hand, the need for a standardized communication platform to improve processes in terms of punctuality, reliability or costs and, on the other hand, the need to have market share and competitive positioning between ports.

SCPs present dematerialized services which can be summarized as follows:

- Exchange andpermanent availability.
- Speed and efficiency of services.

- Electronic processing of all import, export and transit information.
- Ensure monitoring and traceability throughout the logistics chain.
- Presentation of statistics and reporting.

In 2020, Moros-Daza et al, in their journal article present an analysis after a review of the literature on PCS from 2001 to 2019. This analysis presents a detailed and updated inventory on PCS at the international level with the use of an evolution framework and with the presentation of the factors already cited in the literature on the development of IT solutions in the context of port communities (figure 7).

In Figure 7, Moros-Daza et al speak in an evolutionary framework characterized by PCS waves which represent important stages of PCS evolution in time and space.

**First wave: From 1982 to 2000**: this is a phase of launching the first PCS in the world influenced by the adoption of electronic data interchange (EDI) by European establishments based on the "zero paper" approach, which helps with the appearance of first PCS in Germany (Dakosy, 1982). In addition, all countries that worked with an SCP as the first IT solution at the time have a commercial index greater than 40% of their GDP (Ortiz-Ospina et al., 2018), which confirms that these SCPs have an impact directly on operational performance (Caldeirinha et al., 2020).

**Second wave: From 2001 to 2011**: This wave is characterized by the creation of the paperless trade initiative (United Nations, 2006) with the inclusion of an end-to-end digital pipeline, operational assistance in maritime security and vessel tracking (European Maritime Safety Agency, 2003). Still in this phase of evolution of SCPs, the world has experienced the transition from centralized distributed computing systems to a decentralized system based on the Net and subsequently to service-oriented architectures (SOA).

The impact of the adoption of these SCPs on the commercial index is significant, which exceeds 45% for emerging European countries. (Moros-Daza et al., 2020).

**Third wave: From 2012 to 2017**: The third wave is characterized by the transition from automation of procedures to intelligent procedures. Again this wave was characterized by the appearance of SCPs in African and Asian countries, knowing that other African countries, such as Morocco, Cameroon, Senegal and Ghana have already started their GUs in the second wave but with a level of dematerialization of services not yet high due to the development of these solutions little by little (AACE,2017). Same for this phase, the trade index in these countries was greater than 45% (Moros-Daza et al., 2020).

**Fourth wave: From 2018**: The world of port logistics has seen the emergence of the Internet of Things (IoT), artificial intelligence (AI) to predict decision-making in the portport (Miró, 2018) and Blockchain (TB) technology to ensure end-to-end chain security (Battrick, 2018; Foroglou et al., 2015; Jabbar et al., 2018; Yang et al., 2018), these Technologies have generated new challenges in the field of the port community, namely the need to move towards intelligent port platforms or SmartPorts. Furthermore, the most recent PCS have been adopted by emerging countries in Africa as well as American countries with a trade index greater than 45%, which confirms that the future is promising for these technological solutions as proposed by Mendes- Constant.

*Figure 5. PCS evolution framework.*

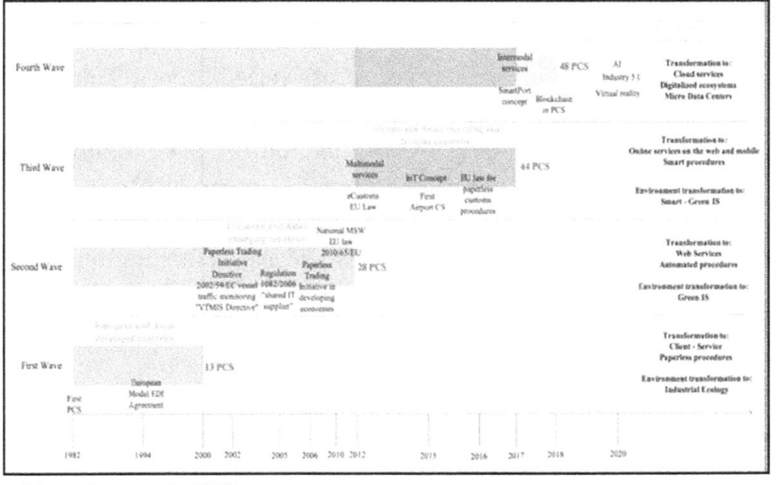


*Source: (Moros-Daza et al., 2020)*

## 2.3.3. Multilevel Security Model

The multilevel security model is exemplified by the use of a computer system to process data with varying sensitivities at varying security levels, permitting users with varying security permissions to access data simultaneously and thereby preventing users from accessing data for which they are not authorized (Tijan, 2009). Higher clearance levels may readily access less sensitive material thanks to it, and higher clearance levels can exchange papers with others who are permitted to see them but are less cleared. Additionally, sanitized documents and information devoid of information that less-cleared persons are not authorized to view can be produced using this technique (Tijan, 2009)..

## 2.4. PCS or Blockchain?

Maritime ports are described as hubs along freight circulation domains that include both land and sea areas in the context of global commerce (Rodrigue, 2020). From the context perspective, both approaches PCS and blockchain follow identical objectives: i) to connect and facilitate community competitiveness on the long-term perspective, ii) improve communication and information sharing between involved actors, and iii) generate extra competitive advantage to the port. The integration of actors is based on daily communication procedures happening either along the same supply chain (vertical integration) or across varied supply chains (horizontal) (Carlan et al., 2016; Tsiulin, Reinau, & Goryaev, 2020).

From an operational standpoint, PCS's function list is continuously growing, while the architecture as a whole often comprises many layers of functions that address the following issues: fast-track customs coordination (digitalized declaration, customs engagement in the system), logistical aspect facilitation (booking yard notification, invoicing, inland

coordination of risky items, navigation at the container/trailer yard and within the berth, and communication (Elhissoufi & Alla, 2024).

In a similar vein, the blockchain scenario for document coordination fosters connectivity between parties within the port and introduces a number of internal organizational tools, such as terminal cargo allocation for the drivers who pick up cargo and lock/unlock functionality to prevent cargo from being taken unintentionally or stolen. The scenario also incorporates a pre-arrival notice system for freight forwarders and port gate monitoring (Tsiulin, Reinau, Hilmola, et al., 2020) (Fig.15). Moreover, a different blockchain scenario described by Tsiulin called "Financial processes" suggests that bank transactions involving the consignee and consignor are integrated into port community communication, expediting post-factum payments and offering flexibility with Letters of Credit (Tsiulin, Reinau, & Goryaev, 2020).

*Figure 6. PCS and Blockchain functionalities*

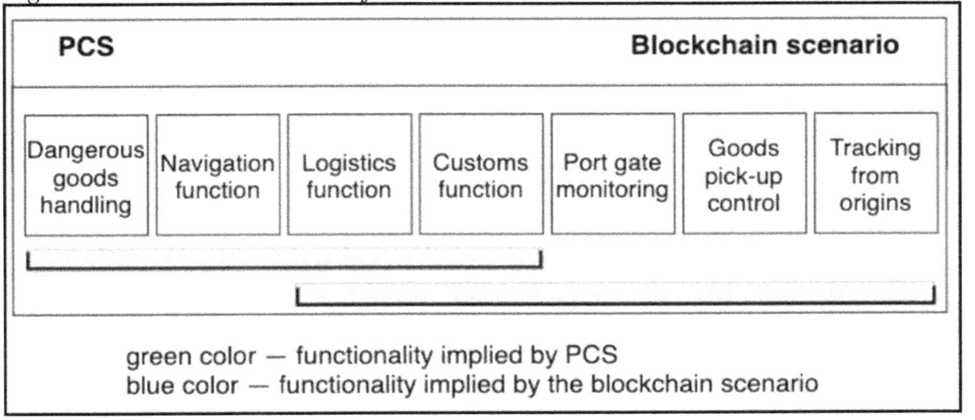


*Source: (Tsiulin, Reinau, & Goryaev, 2020)*

The area of sea shipping benefits mostly from the simplicity of information flows brought about by these two techniques. The idea is to digitally save frequently used cargo paperwork, standardize them, and have them automatically sent to the appropriate parties. It reduces needless point-to-point contact, keeps track of all activities and approvals, expedites communication, and creates a small window of time for ambiguities or disagreements to arise en route(Tsiulin, Reinau, & Goryaev, 2020).

## 3. RESEARCH METHODOLOGY

Our main research question is to evaluate the success of the Port Community System (PCS). For this, we have prepared a theoretical corpus on the main approaches to evaluating an IS and we have adopted the sociotechnical approach as an analysis approach which is based on interactions between technical and social reasons.

To further develop our research objective, by adopting the sociotechnical approach in order to know the personal perception of users about the success of SCP, this success is not only based on social qualities (individual qualities, education level, gender, function, etc.) but also technical variables (quality of information and service, use, etc.) (Bentalha & Alla, 2024).

Our basic problem is:

"How to evaluate the success of port passage SCPs with users".

To resolve this central issue, we adopted as a basis the theoretical corpus models and precisely the process evaluation models which adopt multidimensional criteria as well as static and non-longitudinal causality relationships, ex post and no longer Ex ante.

To do this, we will adopt the choice of the positivist posture which has dominated the management sciences (Michel, 2011) and which thus describes the social sciences" (Lee, 1999) and which is based on hypothetico-deductive reasoning.

We will empirically validate the research model through the different stages of latent variable structural equation modeling (SEM), based on covariance "covariance based structural equation modeling (CB-SEM)", using an estimation approach by the maximum likelihood method (Dash & Paul, 2021).

We will start with an exploratory factor analysis (EFA) via the IBM SPSS software, the main objective of which will be to purify the measurement scales and evaluate their adequacy with the context of the study (Jean, 2022). In addition, measure the internal consistency of the data globally, by calculating the Cronbach alpha index (Cronbach, 1951).

Churchill's paradigm, which we will adopt, recommends first carrying out exploratory studies to assess the validity and reliability of the measurement instruments used (Churchill Jr, 1979). Following Roussel and colleagues' predictions for the development of the scale, we turned to the Structural Equation Modeling (SEM) method after verifying the validation of previous research steps (Roussel, 2005).

### 3.1. Presentation of the Conceptual Research Model

The diagram below presents the conceptual research model. Said model tries to define the steps that lead to the vision of success for port IS users. Like models based on explanation, it prefers causal relationships between the key variables of the adopted model. We are interested in learning more about the relationships between various types of factors, including technical variables as well as social variables.

Our model is marked by a set of causal links (arrows), as well as impact relationships (dotted arrows). While the impact relationships will be tested using analyzes of variance, the causal relationship model will be tested using a system of structural equations (SEM).

*Figure 7. The conceptual model of research*

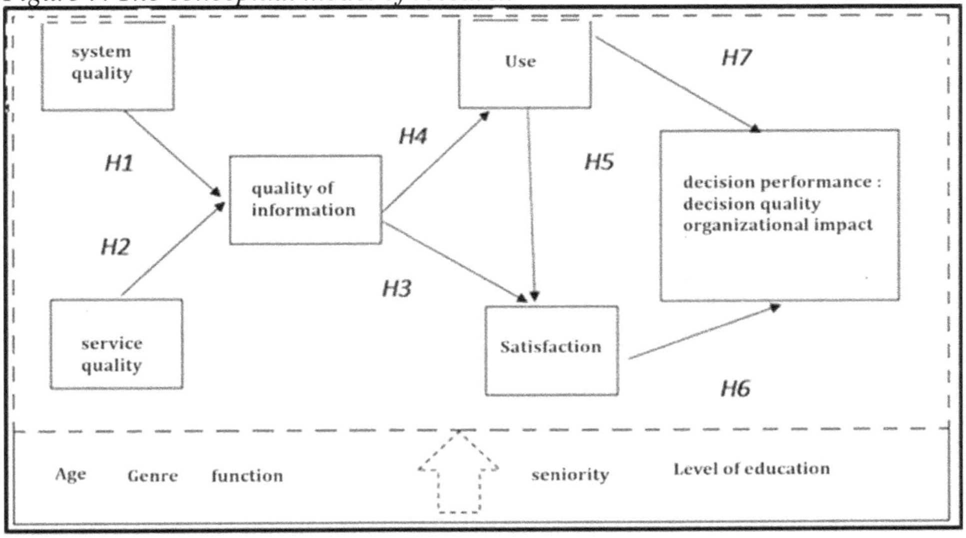


After the presentation of the choice of different variables, as well as the presentation of the conceptual research framework, in what follows, we will explain the research hypotheses which are linked to our problem. We will distinguish a trio of hypotheses: those linked to the linear links in the SCP success evaluation model; those linked to the effects of sociodemographic factors; and finally those linked to the impact of participation on perceptions of the success of the SCP.

## 4. RESULTS AND DISCUSSIONS

This part of the chapter is divided into two sections. As a first step, and to estimate the most significant causal relationships, we examine both structural equation modeling (SEM) and analysis of variance. The second section is devoted to theoretical and managerial contributions, constraints and future research directions.

### 4.1. Setting up the Structural Model

To put the model into use, it is enough to trace the causal relationships of our theoretical model, then add the error terms to all the variables which are considered dependent, namely: The quality of the information, the SCP use, satisfaction and performance. The rest of the variables are considered independent and must be correlated.

*Figure 8. Structural Research Model*

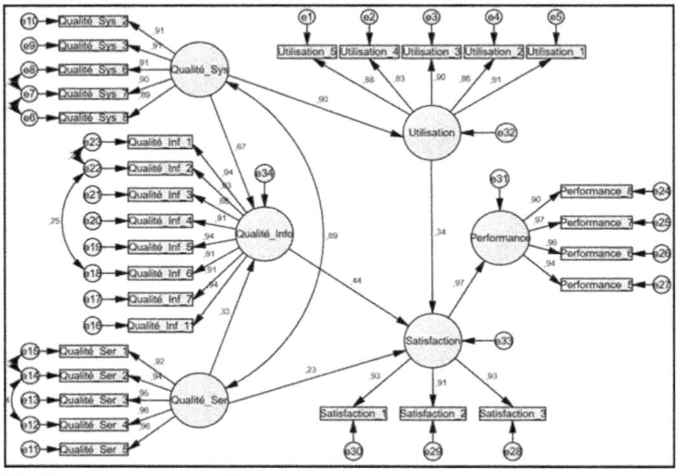


*Source: SPSS Software OutputsAmos 23*

This model requires several interpretations. Firstly, the confirmation of the significant effect of quality variables namely system quality, information quality and service quality on satisfaction and use with a regression coefficient of 0.23 up to at 0.67. It is also important to underline the mediating role of the quality of information between the quality of service and satisfaction, knowing that the latter variable is explained by the quality of information by a regression coefficient of 0.44. Use has no direct significant effect on organizational performance, but we see that satisfaction explains the latter with a very significant coefficient of 0.97 (close to 1). It should also be noted that use has a significant effect on organizational performance through satisfaction (a regression coefficient of 0.340.97=0.33). This is therefore a mediating effect of the satisfaction variable.×

## 4.2. Tests of Conceptual Model Hypotheses

Table 60 presents the results of hypothesis testing for validation of the relationship between variables based on path analysis of the structural equation model.

*Table 4. Hypothesis testing of the conceptual research model*

| Hypotheses | T statistics | p-value | Decision |
|---|---|---|---|
| **H1:** System quality has a significant effect on information quality | **11,197** | **0.000** | **Validated** |
| **H2:** Service quality has a significant effect on information quality | **6,258** | **0.000** | **Validated** |
| **H3:** Information quality has a significant effect on satisfaction | **5,165** | **0.000** | **Validated** |
| **H4:** Information quality has a significant effect on use | 0.195 | 0.845 | Rejected |
| **H5:** Use has a significant effect on satisfaction | **6,466** | **0.000** | **Validated** |
| **H6:** Satisfaction has a significant effect on decision-making performance | **11,727** | **0.000** | **Validated** |
| **H7:** Usage has a significant effect on decision performance | -0.426 | 0.670 | Rejected |
| **H1-4:** System quality has a significant effect on utilization | **4,030** | **0.000** | **Validated** |
| **H2-3:** Service quality has a significant effect on satisfaction | **3,595** | **0.000** | **Validated** |
| Participant age has a significant effect on model relationships | | 0.680 | Rejected |
| Participant gender has a significant effect on model relationships | **2,292** | **0.000** | **Validated** |
| Participant position has a significant effect on model relationships | 0.122 | 0.808 | Rejected |
| Participant seniority has a significant effect on model relationships | 0.187 | 0.847 | Rejected |
| The educational level of the participants has a significant effect on the relationships of the model | 0.105 | 0.283 | Rejected |

The results of this part were very significant and allowed us to test our theoretical model empirically, using structural equations based on covariance as a modeling method so that all hypotheses could be tested effectively.

This modeling method which gives very reliable parametric estimates and which can give rise to an extrapolation of the results on the basis of the data of this sample and under the hypothesis of its representativeness, based on these estimates, we were able to give a magnitude of the intensity of the different relationships.

In addition, the model displayed a quality of adjustment between acceptable and good, based on the different indices already presented and this shows the effectiveness of the constructs prepared in the literature review thus judging the good choice of the sample as well as the collection method, since they did not present enormous bias (errors).

Concerning the testing of the different hypotheses of the model we were able to make the following decisions:

We note that eight relationships evaluated are significant at the 0.05% level. It concerns the relationships supported by the hypotheses H1; H2; H3; H5; H6; H1-4 and H2-3 as well as the significant effect of the control variable "gender" on the model relationships.

We also note that two relationships with values less than 1.96 are not significant at the 5% level. These are relationships supported by hypotheses H4 and H7.

The proportion of variation explained by the model's links appears perfect in terms of information quality (97.3%), net benefits (81.6%) and satisfaction (86.6%). It is a little below average for usability (29.6%), but by accepted standards of the literature, it is adequate.

### 4.2.1. Tests of System and Service Quality Hypotheses (H1 and H2)

We choose to include the quality of information as a variable that can be explained by the quality of the system and the service. Hypotheses H1 and H2 are accepted; The statistical relationships are significant (respectively t =11.197; p = 0 and t =6.258; p = 0.008). The correlation between system quality and information quality is strong, approaching or exceeding 0.9. The level of influence of service quality on the accuracy of information is quite moderate (0.128).

The test results show that the quality of the system and service determines the quality of the information. We will return to this topic when we examine the very specific role that information quality plays in the port logistics sector.

### 4.2.2. Tests of Attitude and Behavior Hypotheses (H3, H4, H5, H1-4, H2-3)

We had proposed the hypothesis that use and satisfaction are positively linked to the quality of information (H3, H4) but after the test, hypothesis H3 is confirmed (t =5.165; p = 0) while hypothesis H4 is rejected (t =0.195; p = 0.845). These results confirm that in the port logistics sector the quality of information is vital and has a significant impact on satisfaction.

Hypothesis H5 is confirmed (t =6.466; p = 0), which confirms that use has an effect on satisfaction. The same goes for the quality of service which has a positive impact on satisfaction (t =4.030; p = 0), and the quality of the system has a significant effect on use (t =3.595; p = 0).

### 4.2.3. Tests of Hypotheses Relating to Decision-Making Performance (H6 and H7)

We proposed as a hypothesis that use and satisfaction were positively correlated with organizational performance (H6 and H7). The statistical tests are significant and positive for hypothesis H6 (t = 11.727; p = 0) and not accepted for hypothesis H7 (t = -0.426; p = 0.670).

We can summarize all these results as follows in the form of a summary figure:

*Figure 9. Results of the perception model of the success of the port community system*

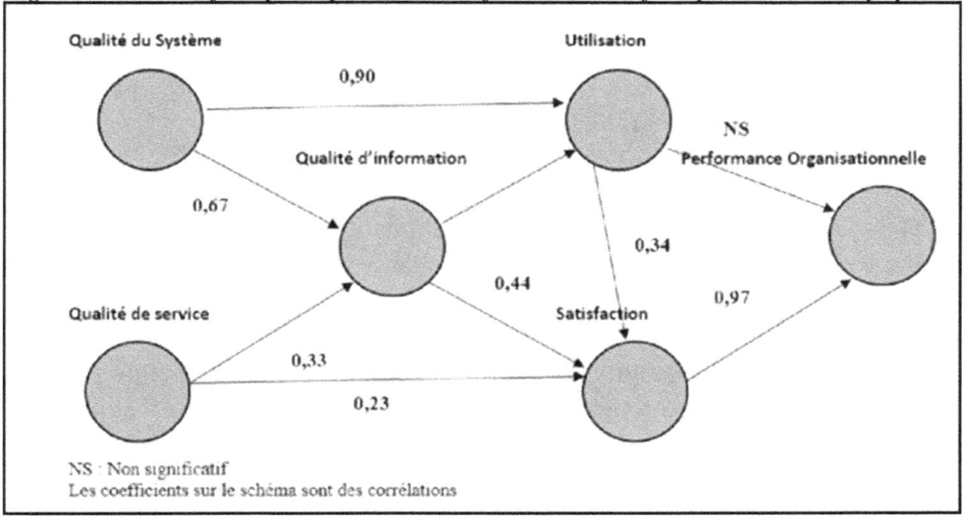


*Source: Author*

This model demonstrates that among the main predictors of information quality are system and service quality. We also notice that the relationship between the quality of service and that of information is somewhat significant (0.33).

It appears that information quality, service quality and usage are predictors of user satisfaction.

It should be noted that satisfaction is the only latent variable that strongly influences organizational performance with a coefficient close to 1 (0.97).

The main objective of this study is to develop a tool or model thatwill make it possible to evaluate the success of the Community Port Systemwhile taking into account the perception of users of this IS.

To understand why the SCP succeeded, we chose to place ourselves within a sociotechnical analysis framework which is based on the links between technical and social factors. A multidimensional, process-oriented approach was therefore chosen.

The second objective is to determine the factors (technical and social) to include in the model and to know how they interact. To do this, we adopted a richer literature review. This step allowed the development of a conceptual model which proposed several relationships between various kinds of variables.

The third and final objective is to improve our level of understanding of the key aspects of these numerous variables in the context of port logistics IS. We then carried out an operational analysis of each variable, carried out in agreement withthe field of port logistics and in accordance with Churchill's paradigm.

In order to present the main findings, we will first discuss the contributions related to the operationalization of the variables before moving on to the contributions of the overall model.

### 4.2.4. The Results Related to the Operationalization of the Different Constructs

The operationalization of six factors (system quality, service quality, information quality, satisfaction, use, organizational performance) was carried outby adhering to the Churchill paradigm process. Knowing that the objective was to offer buildings related to the field of port logistics while adhering to the highest standard rigid in terms of validity and reliability. The elements proposed in the literature for each variable were examined throughout our study. The information was then reduced when determining the size of each construct during a phase of purification of the measuring instruments. During data collection, exploratory factor analyzes were performed. A confirmatory factor analysis was performed on the measuring instruments that had been cleaned in this manner.

The first contribution of this study, which we will now discuss for certain variables, is constituted by the dimensions and the elements that make up the six variables. We will discuss the contributions and consequences related to the characteristics that we believe to be most significant: system quality, information quality, service quality, ease of use and net benefits.

#### *System Quality*

The quality of the system directly impacts the quality of information and pushes for the improvement of port performance while other studies highlight that the information collection efforts of the organization determine the quality of the information system. In order to better meet user needs, it will be considered essential to integrate quality assurance within the organization in order to ensure the homogeneity of information and improve the proper functioning of processes. In fact, the effectiveness of organizational, technological and informational processes determines the quality of strategic decisions (Guemmi,2014).

Nadia Jouini, Jean-François Gueugnon and Rolande Marciniak discuss the way whose information system values contribute to organizational performance. They demonstrated how the combination of three factors results in organizational performance namely(Marciniak et al., 2009):

- The heritage value of the IS based on resources
- The value of the exchange: Companies are using more appropriate digital communication tools to improve internal communication.

- The use value which is based on the correct use of the IS.

Therefore, the good use which can be ensured by the quality of the system ensures organizational performance, knowing that in our case the direct relationship between use and performance is not significant, but we can say that this impact relationship can be carried out via the satisfaction variable.

### *The Quality of Information*

It is also necessary to understand what this means for users in order to improve the quality of content. Consistent with Wang and Strong, we maintain that information is of high quality when it is relevant to its intended use, which could lead to the observation that the elements of information quality depend on the circumstances in which she is used(RY Wang and Strong, 1996). Based on the literature and our studies, we developed and tested a measurement tool for the port sector that can be used to assess the many facets of information quality that SCP users have. Using two dimensions, including information own quality (four items) and ergonomic quality (3 items).

The most crucial factor for customer service representatives is the informational dimension, which represents a significant weight of the explained discrepancies. The subject of information reliability has significant weight in this dimension, further followed by the idea of accurate, precise and detailed information. All three factors have one significant and largely similar point regarding ergonomic quality: information must be easily accessible, clearly presented and understandable.

The quality of information further confirms that it does not directly impact the use of SCPs by users, but impacts the satisfaction of these users with a higher correlation coefficient or less important.

In summary, based on the correlation coefficients and hypothesis testing, it appears that SCP users want a system that is functionally tailored to their needs and industry, quick to use, protects them against risks intrusions and data losses, and provides accurate, reliable, complete, well presented and available information.

### *La Quality of Service*

When technical difficulties arise (such as inability to print, access a website, use an application, etc.), THEIS managers have access to a support service which they contact mainly by telephone or e-mail.

CPS users want support staff to be competent, responsive to their needs (especially linguistic), and to inspire trust and a desire to help them.

These elements were included in the trust and ease of service dimensions of the Servperf model. One of the most obvious managerial recommendations is to encourage port authorities to organize advanced training programs for front office staff so that they are trained on these subjects. One of the objectives would be to foster and build a personal relationship between users and service employees. Trust and understanding will only increase if the same person responds to the IS manager when contacting the department with a problem. In conclusion, this tool shows that the skills of those working in the field of customer support and relations must include both technical and human skills.

With the use of this tool, a service provider can learn how customers view their offerings and how to influence their opinions in the direction they want.

### *Use*

One of the critical issues with information systems is usage measurement. The literature has shown that measures relying on simple usage frequencies tend to be information poor or confusing in terms of interpretation. Following Straub and Burton-Jones, we adopted user and system as the basic elements of usage measurement (Burton-Jones & Straub Jr, 2006). We use perceptual scales to measure a level of usage relative to these people's perspectives. We measured usage on six items and four dimensions in total:

The first concerned customer relations (2 items), the second concerned decision support (1 item), the third problem solving (2 items), and the last one the organization of work (1 items).

These four elements help us understand customers' key usage expectations. They want programs that will allow them to successfully complete the business relationship. This means that SCP is no longer seen as a barrier or detriment to face-to-face interactions with customers. The opposite is true; the company's managers want through their engagement with the SCP to advise the customer and change their strategy and be able to target customer needs. We believe it is essential for SCP to serve as a customer relationship management tool.

The second factor suggests that the SCP must enable decision-making with well-informed customers. The SCP must offer the tools capable to analyze and to resolve problems so that the best decision can be made.

These first two elements focus on user expectations in terms of careers and customer relations. However, practitioners' perspectives on the use of SCP extend beyond basic usage. Their ability to plan their work must also be provided for by the SCP.

Finally, the business community considers the SCP as a tool that will allow it to update its knowledge and continue their studies. Therefore, the use as an already operationalized variable is focused on task-relevant research. Users not only want an SCP that allows them to establish relationships with their customers, but an SCP that analyzes problems at the port level and subsequently helps these users make appropriate decisions (Michel, 2011).

#### *Decision-Making Performance (Decision Quality)*

We calculated the decision performance by taking into account has several performance variables, like our model. A three-dimensional instrument has been developed; The first dimension concerns productivity benefits (5 elements), the second concerns the improvement in the level of customer satisfaction (2 elements), and the third to control the improvement (risk, regulation) (2 elements) (Michel, 2011).

This tool is an example of a strategic tool for managing and directing efforts to improve performance. The latter should allow managers to understand the positive and negative effects of an SCP (Nouhaila et al., 2024).

The crucial point that users have touched through the use of the SCP is that these platforms optimize the time and reduce the port passage time as well as the administrative processes concerning this passage operation, and contribute positively to the internal organization of all users. Of more, these SCP allow to convey a good brand image with external collaborators of the organization.

In conclusion, we assert that measurement is a prerequisite for management due to the operationalization of the constructs of the SCP success model. According to Kaplan and Norton, Without measurement, leaders and managers can only rely on their past experiences and their flair(Kaplan & Norton, 1996).

In order to evaluate the quality of the system, information, service, level of use and perception of the network (support from middle managers, and satisfaction), we adopted measurement tools relevant and valid. These tools have been specifically created and tested in the context of the port sector, paying particular attention to SCP users. These tools are "light" and simple to use, and they can be used for longitudinal studies. The measurement provided by these tools is the starting point of the diagnostic process for the adoption of measures focused on demonstrable improvement.

### 4.2.5. The Results of Evaluating the Success of the SCP

Evaluating the success of an SCP after its implementation is extremely rare in the port sector. Delone and McLean noted that the most common reason why SCP is not evaluated is an absence of measurement standardized.

The model created and verified in this study helps to address these limitations. Port authorities have a model that allows them to assess user perceptions of the success of the SCP. One of the first contributions is the assertion that the assessment of the SCP must be multidimensional and we have suggested a set of essential indicators for the port domain. Additionally, the said model helps chart the path to success and identify key factors that could affect the user.

### 4.2.6. A Multidimensional Assessment

We confirm that multidimensional assessment of SCP is required by the presented results. Different variables reflecting various characteristics of the SCP were incorporated into the model. This demonstrates that the use of a single proxy measure is inadequate since it gives a very low assessment. Measure the quality of the system, the quality of information, the net benefits achieved, etc.

We support the conceptual framework, which is a sociotechnical framework, by asserting that assessment must be multidimensional. We included variables (or items) which represent the technical subsystem (use evaluation tasks, different quality systems, whether considered in terms of functional or technical adequacy, intrinsic quality of the information, etc.) and the social subsystem (quality of life at work linked to the use of the system, support from middle managers, level of quality of service, among others).

Validation of our conceptual model comes from the interaction between all of these components. In this way, the hypothesis that guided our research is supported. The success of the SCP relies on the interaction between technical and social subsystems, such as the interaction between six key factors consisting of technical and social components of the subsystem:

- "System quality";
- "Quality of service";
- "Quality of information";
- "Satisfaction";
- "Use";
- "Net profits".

Through validation of the conceptual model, we are also able to offer an explanation of the steps leading to the perception of SCP success.

From the managerial angle, the said model gives managers an overview of the stages of success. This observation should help them to wisely allocate resources and prioritize their efforts.

We will now discuss the results in relation to the process leading to the output variable which is organizational performance or net profits.

### *The Quality of Information*

Based on Ding and Straub's findings, we came to the conclusion that the quality of the system and the service determines the quality of information. The results support these hypotheses (Ding & Straub, 2008). These two factors explain the quality of information with different percentages, we note that the quality of the system has the most important relationship (0.67). If we consider that the quality of the system and service are good, IS managers will believe that their information is of good quality, something which has been confirmed by previous studies in the banking field (Michel, 2011) and in the success model (ISM) of 2003 by DeLone and McLean, system quality and service quality are treated as distinct determinants of user satisfaction and behavioral intention (DeLone & McLean, 2003; Ding & Straub, 2008).

### *Satisfaction and Usage*

The relationship between information quality and satisfaction is significant and favorable. This finding is consistent with the literature that highlights the importance of information quality as a precursor to satisfaction (Almutairi & Subramanian, 2005; Bailey & Pearson, 1983; DeLone & McLean, 2003; Doll & Torkzadeh, 1988; Qian & Bock, 2005; P. Seddon & Kiew, 1996). Our results show that use, service quality and information quality influence satisfaction while other studies indicate that information quality is the only variable that explains satisfaction and that the other relationships evaluated use satisfaction as a final response variable(Michel, 2011).

This finding is important because it highlights the importance of information quality and service quality as well as usage in the port domain. This also demonstrates that decision-makers have room to maneuver if they want to improve the level of user satisfaction.

The managerial contributions of these results force IS managers to give more importance to this trio of quality, namely: the quality of the information, the quality of the service and the use if they wish to influence the level of satisfaction users (Michel, 2011).

### *Decision Performance (Quality of Decision)*

The weight of the explained variance of the "decision performance" variable of our model (89.05%) is entirely satisfactory. We can see that the link between user satisfaction and net profits have a stronger relationship (R = 0.97) than the relationship between usage and net profits which is non-significant (NS). This result must be compared to the empirical literature which strongly supported the first connection as opposed to the second. (Michel, 2011).

The level of human knowledge is increasing exponentially, providing significant and sometimes contradictory evidence to support decision-making in the port and maritime sector, which is characterized by complex issues, making decision-making in this field intricate.

In order to combat the fragmentation of knowledge, collaboration among stakeholders in the port area promotes decision-making and ensures the successful management of territories.

In this perspective, the PCS can help manage vast knowledge bases, as well as analyze data provided by specialists to support decision-making (Trianni et al., 2023).

## 5. RESEARCH CONTRIBUTIONS

We evaluate the contributions of this research in light of the reasons that we put forward in the introduction to support the need to carry out the research to which it is the subject. According to this point of view, we have argued that the relevance of this thesis revolves around three questions: responding to the need to explore new avenues of research; advance knowledge of SCPs; and provide elements of response that could help improve the organizational performance of organizations.

### 5.1. Theoretical Contributions

The theoretical and conceptual considerations developed in this thesis allowed the construction of a model which gave rise to the general hypothesis of the contribution of SCPs to organizational performance. This general hypothesis is supported by adjacent hypotheses that examine the partial effects of the many factors under study.

In fact, for the research strategy we use, this attempt at theoretical articulation that is applicable to our research question allowed us to balance our conceptual model. This study aimed to examine the causal relationships between the socio-technical factors that determined the hypothesis.

### 5.2. Methodological Contributions

On a methodological level, it is important to note that the choice of a "quantitative" methodology consistent with a positivist epistemological position contributes to facilitating the thesis approach, the overall objective of the research problem and the different scientific objectives. and predetermined managers. Such a decision led us to conduct an empirical study based on survey questionnaires, in face-to-face administration mode as quantitative devices. In this regard, the methodological contributions of our thesis relate to the empirical analysis part, namely: The first level concerns the development of the measurement instrument (survey questionnaire), the pre-test and validation procedures, as well as the sampling plan (qualitative and quantitative). The second level which deals with the data analysis techniques supported and used during the analysis of statistical data for quantitative research (data preparation, descriptive analysis of the obtained sample, descriptive analysis of the results, factor analysis of the scales of measurement and data correlation analysis).

Despite all these contributions, it is important to note that, like any research, its development will not escape criticism.

## 6. CONCLUSION

It is crucial to recall the initial research question and objectives of this thesis in order to provide a summary of the results.

Based on the observation that several organizations continue to experience IS implementation failures which lead to financial losses, and a slowdown in their organizational performance, investments in IS and adoption of IT have not increased significantly. productivity rates. We have launched a project to evaluate the port IS and specifically the Port Community System (PCS). The subject is of interest to both researchers and managers following managerial recommendations, knowing that the port sector has received little attention in the literature on the evaluation of SCPs due to their unique characteristics, the importance of investments in IT, and changes in internal and external environments (concentration, financial crisis, etc.).

In fact, the evaluation of SCP for the port community has become crucial in determining what translates into users' perceptions of their success. Customs declarants, freight forwarders and shipping agents or logistics agents with objectives to achieve must adapt to a significant change in their environment.

Integrating the concept of organizational performance, our research focuses on mobilizing the hypothesis of the incorporation of sociotechnical variables of information systems in order to better understand their role in organizational performance.

These numerous components contributed to the development of the problem statement for this research. Our objective was to answer the following question: "How to evaluate the success of a Community Port System? » other basic questions were asked, such as the factors necessary to properly conduct this SCP assessment. What relationships exist between these different variables? Can individual or sociodemographic characteristics have an impact on this evaluation?

The first confirms that the SCP evaluation question is a process that takes into account both technical aspects and social factors. The evaluation requires multidimensionality and goes beyond the single dimension of the technical quality of the SCP of the port sector. User perceptions of port SCP success are influenced by a variety of technical, social, and other factors that may be influenced by personal characteristics. The majority of relationships in the conceptual model are supported. This demonstrates the need for a process-oriented sociotechnical approach.

The results also identify information quality as a key element since it is influenced by the system and service and ultimately determines satisfaction and use of the SCP.

This study also focuses on the factors that influence satisfaction. User satisfaction level is not influenced by usage, perceived net benefits, or support from intermediary Managers. In other words, the quality of information is the only factor that determines contentment.

Additionally, this research supports the need for SCP task relevance (measured by usage). The fact that users want to be able to perform a wide range of tasks through the use of SCP and not just daily or routine operational tasks, must be offered above all.

Finally, the present study focused on the importance of sociodemographic characteristics to verify the existence of a distinct profile of actors who present perfect perception. Women's satisfaction is not affected by the quality of service as is the case for men.

These results have managerial ramifications for port logistics professionals. They have a reliable, valid and easy-to-use tool thanks to development and testing and a validated questionnaire which allows them to understand the steps leading to the success of any port IS.

Through the use of this tool, port sector professionals and port authorities are able to evaluate their SCP. In addition, they can very quickly and simply identify the weak points in this process and analyze the most important points. Said port community stakeholders have a tool that allows them to accurately diagnose each variable as the process leading to the success of their SCP.

## 7. REFERENCES

Aarabe, M., Khizzou, N. B., Alla, L., & Benjelloun, A. (2024). Smart Tourism Experience and Responsible Travelers' Behavior : A Systematic Literature Review. *Promoting Responsible Tourism With Digital Platforms*, 128-147.

Alla, L., Bentalha, B., & Elyoussfi, A. (2023). Intelligence territoriale et positionnement stratégique des regions au Maroc : Le cas de la région de Fès Meknes en perspective. *Le concept de l'intéligence en sciences juridiques, économiques et sociales*, 215-237.

Arsac, J. J. (1971). Le concept d'information et l'informatique. *Dialectica*, 25(3-4), 207–219. DOI: 10.1111/j.1746-8361.1971.tb00600.x

Belmondo, C. (2004). *Les processus collectifs de création de connaissances dans les groupes de travail. Comparaison de deux processus au sein d'une cellule de veille concurrentielle*. Conférence Internationale de Management Stratégique.

BENSFIA, C., & BOUKLATA, A. (2024). Évaluation du succès du Système Communautaire Portuaire : Cas du Maroc. *Alternatives Managériales Economiques*, 6(2), 23–51.

BENSFIA, C., Bouklata, A., & NEJJARI, R. (2024). Explorer la digitalisation pour l'économie circulaire : Une revue systématique. *Revue de Gestion et d'Économie*, 12(2), 305–321.

Bensfia, C., & Bouklata, A. (2022). *Validity of the TAM Model in the context of electronic payment ofport dues in Morocco*. 1-5.

Bensfia, C., & Bouklata, A. (2023). Evaluation of the electronic port right of way payment information system. *Management Systems in Production Engineering*, 31(3), 254–262. DOI: 10.2478/mspe-2023-0028

Bentalha, B., & Alla, L. (2024). Revealing the Subtleties : The Art of Qualitative Studies in Science and Management. In *Applying Qualitative Research Methods to Management Science* (p. 1-21). IGI Global.

Bertacchini, Y. (2010). Intelligence territoriale : Une lecture retro-prospective. *Revue internationale d'intelligence économique, 2*(1), 65-97.

Bouklata, A., & Bensfia, C. (2020). *Digitalization of port passage procedures : Focus on the transit time of Goods*. 1-6.

Brillouin, L. (1971). *Science and. Information Theory*. Academic.

Carlan, V., Sys, C., & Vanelslander, T. (2016). How port community systems can contribute to port competitiveness : Developing a cost–benefit framework. *Research in Transportation Business & Management*, 19, 51–64. DOI: 10.1016/j.rtbm.2016.03.009

dos Ramos Caldeirinha, V. M., Felicio, J. A., Salvador, A. S., Nabais, J., & Pinho, T. (2020). Port Community Systems (pcs) and Port Performance. *Revista Eletronica De Estrategia E Negocios-Reen, 13*, 159-195. https://doi.org/DOI: 10.19177/reen.v13e012020159-195

EL JAOUHARI, S., & Lhoussaine, A. (2022). L'approche territoriale et la gestion de l'impact de la pandémie de Covid-19 : Cas des collectivités territoriales. *Alternatives Managériales Economiques*, 4(1), 245–265.

Elhissoufi, M., & Alla, L. (2024). Artificial Intelligence in Costumer Acquisition : A Bibliometric Study. In *AI and Data Engineering Solutions for Effective Marketing* (p. 1-22). IGI Global. DOI: 10.4018/979-8-3693-3172-9.ch001

Girardot, J.-J. (2004). Intelligence territoriale et participation. *Isdm*, 16, 1–13.

Giuliano, G., Knatz, G., Hutson, N., Sys, C., Vanelslander, T., & Carlan, V. (2015). *Decision-making for maritime innovation investments : The significance of cost benefit and cost effectiveness analysis*. 1-20.

Glazer, R. (1991). Marketing in an information-intensive environment : Strategic implications of knowledge as an asset. *Journal of Marketing*, 55(4), 1–19. DOI: 10.1177/002224299105500401

Grenier, C., & Moine, C. (2003). *Construire le système d'information de l'entreprise*. Foucher.

Karlan, D., Kendall, J., Mann, R., Pande, R., Suri, T., & Zinman, J. (2016). *Research and impacts of digital financial services*. National Bureau of Economic Research. DOI: 10.3386/w22633

Laudon, K. C., & Laudon, J. P. (2013). Management Information Systems 13e. *XIV. IBANESS İktisat, İşletme ve Yönetim Bilimleri Kongreler Serisi–Plovdiv/Bulgaristan 06-07 Haziran 2020.*

Le Coadic, Y. F. (2005). Mathématique et statistique en science de l'information et en science de la communication : Infométrie mathématique et infométrie statistique des revues scientifiques. *Ciência da Informação*, 34(3), 15–22. DOI: 10.1590/S0100-19652005000300002

LEBRATY, J.-F. (1998). Technologies de l'information et décision : L'essor des Datawarehouses. [French Journal of Management Information Systems]. *Systèmes d'Information et Management*, 3(1), 95–118.

Lefèvre, C., & Jouve, B. (1992). *Nouveaux acteurs et nouveaux territoires dans les grandes agglomérations européennes : Une approche comparative à partir des réseaux lourds de transport collectif.* 622-652.

Leloup, F., Moyart, L., & Pecqueur, B. (2005). La gouvernance territoriale comme nouveau mode de coordination territoriale? *Géographie Économie Société*, 7(4), 321–332. DOI: 10.3166/ges.7.321-331

Lesca, H., Lesca, E., Lesca, N., & Caron-Fasan, M.-L. (2010). *Gestion de l'information : Qualité de l'information et performances de l'entreprise*. EMS Editions.

Mahoney, J. T., & Pandian, J. R. (1992). The resource-based view within the conversation of strategic management. *Strategic Management Journal*, 13(5), 363–380. DOI: 10.1002/smj.4250130505

Meersman, H., Van de Voorde, E., & Vanelslander, T. (2010). Port competition revisited. *Journal of Pediatric. Maternal & Family Health-Chiropractic*, 55(2), 210.

Michel, S. (2011). *Contribution à l'évaluation du système d'information bancaire.*

Moinet, N. (2009). L'intelligence territoriale entre communication et communauté stratégique de connaissance : L'exemple du dispositif régional de Poitou-Charentes. *Revue internationale d'intelligence économique, 1*(1), 30-38.

Nouhaila, B. K., Aarabe, M., & Alla, L. (2024). The Impact of Digitalisation on the Customer Experience in Medical Tourism : A Systematic Review. *Impact of AI and Tech-Driven Solutions in Hospitality and Tourism*, 408-428.

Peterson, J. (2017). An overview of customs reforms to facilitate trade. *J. Int'l Com. & Econ.*, 1.

Porter, M. E. (1991). Towards a dynamic theory of strategy. *Strategic Management Journal*, 12(S2), 95–117. DOI: 10.1002/smj.4250121008

Reix, R., Fallery, B., Kalika, M., & Rowe, F. (2016). *Systèmes d'Information et Management des Organisations-7ème édition.*

Ritchie, D. (1986). Shannon and Weaver : Unravelling the paradox of information. *Communication Research*, 13(2), 278–298. DOI: 10.1177/009365086013002007

Rodrigue, J.-P. (2020). *The geography of transport systems*. Routledge. DOI: 10.4324/9780429346323

Romagni, P., & Wild, V. (1998). *L'intelligence économique au service de la stratégie d'entreprise : C'est pour demain, la veille*. Les presses du management.

Tijan, E. (2009). DATA CASSIFICATION AND INFORMATION LIFECYCLE MANAGEMENT IN PORT COMMUNITY SYSTEMS. *POMORSTVO-SCIENTIFIC JOURNAL OF MARITIME RESEARCH*, 23(2), 557–568.

Tijan, E., Jović, M., Jardas, M., & Gulić, M. (2019). The Single Window Concept in International Trade, Transport and Seaports. *Pomorstvo*, 33(2), 130–139. DOI: 10.31217/p.33.2.2

Trianni, V., Nuzzolese, A. G., Porciello, J., Kurvers, R. H., Herzog, S. M., Barabucci, G., Berditchevskaia, A., & Fung, F. (2023). Hybrid Collective Intelligence for Decision Support in Complex Open-Ended Domains. In *HHAI 2023 : Augmenting Human Intellect* (p. 124-137). IOS Press. DOI: 10.3233/FAIA230079

Tsamboulas, D., Moraiti, P., & Lekka, A. M. (2012). Performance Evaluation for Implementation of Port Community System. *Transportation Research Record: Journal of the Transportation Research Board*, 2273(1), 29–37. DOI: 10.3141/2273-04

Tsiulin, S., Reinau, K. H., & Goryaev, N. (2020). Conceptual Comparison of Port Commmunity System and Blockchain Scenario for Maritime Document Handling. *2020 Global Smart Industry Conference (GloSIC)*, 66-71. DOI: 10.1109/GloSIC50886.2020.9267847

Tsiulin, S., Reinau, K. H., Hilmola, O.-P., Goryaev, N., & Karam, A. (2020). Blockchain-based applications in shipping and port management : A literature review towards defining key conceptual frameworks. *Review of International Business and Strategy*, 30(2), 201–224. DOI: 10.1108/RIBS-04-2019-0051

Zeman, J. (1965). *Le concept d'information dans la science contemporaine*. Compterendu du Colloque de Royaumont, Paris, Éditions de Minuit.

# Chapter 12
# SMART Cities and Public–Private Partnership Projects:
## A Structured Literature Review

**Mohammed Amine Benarbi**
https://orcid.org/0000-0002-5659-9695
*Sidi Mohamed Ben Abdellah University, Morocco*

**Mouhcine Rhouiri**
https://orcid.org/0009-0007-7115-871X
*Sidi Mohamed Ben Abdellah University, Morocco*

**Mohamed Habiboullah Meyabe**
https://orcid.org/0009-0005-0935-7211
*Sidi Mohamed Ben Abdellah University, Morocco*

**Larbi Tamnine**
https://orcid.org/0000-0002-3928-4253
*Sidi Mohamed Ben Abdellah University, Morocco*

## ABSTRACT

*SMART cities realized through public-private partnership projects is a topic that requires further exploration in the field of management. Many researchers have contributed to this topic, each conducting their research from a distinct perspective and employing diverse methodologies. The goal of this article is to present a Structured Literature Review of the most relevant publications on SMART cities developed through PPP projects, by examining their impact, contributions, limitations, and future research directions.*

DOI: 10.4018/979-8-3693-6854-1.ch012

## 1. INTRODUCTION

Public private partnership is a broad concept that encompasses a wide range of public sector infrastructure and service initiatives involving collaboration between the public and private sectors (Marsilio et al., 2011). PPP are defined as arrangements where public and private actors work together to address shared problems or deliver public services and infrastructure (Brinkerhoff & Brinkerhoff, 2011). The objective from the PPP projects is to leverage the complementary strengths and resources of both the public and private sectors to achieve policy goals, service delivery, infrastructure development, capacity building, and economic development.

Recently, PPP projects have emerged as a viable approach to developing SMART cities that leverage the strengths of both the public and private sectors (Kwak et al., 2009) . As city authorities seek to address the challenges of urban development and sustainability, they are increasingly turning to PPP models to design and implement e-services and infrastructure that can transform cities into "intelligent" or "SMART" environments (Komninos et al., 2014).

There is not exhaustive literature about SMART cities which are realized by PPP projects. This book chapter come to face this gap research of this topic.

This study conducts a structured literature review to analyze the intellectual structure of research on SMART cities realized by public-private partnerships projects. The methodology is based on bibliometric techniques, including Citation Classics to analyze the most impactful articles, authors and journals in the field of management. It also helps to answer the questions about the development of studies in terms of the subjects studied, the locations and the methodologies used in articles. In addition, this methodology helps to summarize the main contributions, limitations and future directions for next studies (Benarbi & Tamnine, 2019, 2020; Benhayoun & Marghich, 2017; Massaro et al., 2016).

Our book chapter is structured as follows: Section 2 give a global presentation about the topic in order to help readers to understand it. Section 3 outlines the methodology followed to undertake our SLR on SMART cities by PPP projects. Section 4 presents the Results and Section 5 discuss them.

## 2. BACKGROUND OF SMART CITIES BY PPP PROJECTS

In this section we want to draw an overview of frameworks of SMART Cities realized throughout PPP projects. We begin by defining these two concepts, demonstrating the theorical foundations, highlighting the legal framework, given some real examples worldwide and the challenges facing these projects.

## 2.1. Definition of concepts

The Organization for Economic Co-operation and Development defined the public-private partnerships as *"long-term contractual arrangements between the public and private sector in which the private party bears significant risk and management responsibility, and remuneration is linked to performance"*. The objective of PPP projects is to deliver improved services and better value for money, primarily through appropriate risk transfer, encouraging innovation, greater asset utilization and an integrated whole-of-life management, underpinned by private financing (*National PPP Policy Framework*, 2015).

SMART cities are urban environments that incorporate information and communication technologies to improve the efficiency, sustainability, and livability of cities (Wang et al., 2021). SMART city initiatives tends to address urban challenges through the use of data, automation, and digital solutions to improve city operations and the quality of life for citizens (Rzqoo et al., 2023).

The existing literature emphasizes the critical role of public-private partnerships in achieving SMART city initiatives. As urban authorities seek to address the challenges of sustainable development, PPPs have emerged as a crucial mechanism for utilizing the complementary strengths and resources of the public and private sectors (Radchenko, 2022). However, the successful implementation of SMART city PPPs requires a thorough understanding of the theoretical bases that lead to these collaborative arrangements.

## 2.2. Theorical Framework of SMART Cities by PPP Projects

The theoretical foundations for public-private partnerships in SMART city development draw from several established frameworks and concepts (Bibri, 2018):

- **Institutional theory:** This perspective highlights the importance of the institutional environment, including legal, regulatory, and normative structures, in shaping the design and implementation of PPP arrangements. Institutions can enable or constrain the ability of public and private actors to effectively collaborate and achieve desired outcomes for SMART city initiatives.
- **Resource dependence theory:** This theory emphasizes how organizations, whether public or private, rely on access to critical resources (e.g., funding, expertise, technology) to achieve their objectives. PPPs leverage the complementary resource strengths of the public and private sectors to address urban challenges and deliver SMART city solutions.
- **Network governance:** This approach recognizes that SMART city development often involves complex, multi-stakeholder networks that transcend

traditional organizational boundaries. PPPs facilitate the coordination and cooperation required for effective network-based governance of SMART city programs.

- **Transaction cost economics:** This framework analyzes the costs associated with different modes of organizing economic activity, including markets and hierarchies. PPPs are viewed as a hybrid governance structure that can minimize transaction costs and optimize resource allocation for SMART city projects.

By analyzing these theoretical foundations, researchers and practitioners can develop a more comprehensive understanding of the mechanisms, drivers, and constraints governing the role of PPPs in SMART city development. This can inform the design of effective legal, institutional, and collaborative frameworks to realize the potential of public-private partnerships in creating intelligent, sustainable, and citizen-centric urban environments.

## 2.3. Legal Framework

The legal framework of PPP projects is a crucial factor in the development of SMART cities. Public-private partnerships typically consist of complex contractual arrangements that outline the roles, responsibilities, and risk-sharing mechanisms between the public and private entities involved (Liu et al., 2021). The legal structure of these partnerships can be significant for issues such as project financing, resource allocation, decision-making authority (as socio-political challenge) and accountability (Monk et al., 2019).

Effective PPP frameworks must balance the interests of both the public and private sectors, while ensuring transparency, fairness, and alignment with broader policy objectives for sustainable urban development. Key legal considerations include the selection of PPP delivery models, the scope and duration of contracts, performance monitoring and enforcement mechanisms, and dispute resolution processes. Governments must also establish clear regulatory guidelines and institutional capacity to manage the procurement, implementation, and oversight of SMART city PPP projects (Liu et al., 2021).

Recent fundamental studies have highlighted the emergence of public-private partnership projects into SMART city strategies. As urban authorities take into considerations the challenges of sustainable development, PPPs have emerged as mechanism for leveraging the strengths and resources of both the public and private sectors to realize SMART city initiatives (Lam & Yang, 2020; Liu et al., 2021).

The existing literature underscores the complex, multifaceted nature of SMART city governance, with various definitions and contextual factors shaping the measurement and outcomes of these initiatives. Researchers have emphasized the need for effective legal and regulatory frameworks to guide the development of SMART city PPPs, ensuring transparency, fair risk allocation, and alignment with broader policy goals (Perboli & Rosano, 2020).

Despite the technical aspects of e-service implementation, scholars have advocated for a more holistic understanding of the SMART city planning process and the involvement of citizens as end-users (Hartanti et al., 2022). Flexible and adaptive PPP models that can accommodate evolving technologies and citizen needs are essential for the successful long-term deployment of SMART city solutions. This is particularly relevant for urban planners, policymakers, and practitioners interested in the intersection of public-private partnerships and SMART city development (Rzqoo et al., 2023).

## 2.4. Real-World Examples of SMART Cities by PPP Projects

Pilot projects, detailed case studies, and comparative analyses across diverse contexts are necessary to enhance the evidence base and provide robust insights on the factors influencing the success of PPPs in the SMART city area (Liu et al., 2021). Here are some real cases of SMART cities realized through public-private partnership projects:

- **Singapore**: Singapore has been at the forefront of SMART city development, utilizing PPPs to implement innovative urban solutions. One notable example is the SMART Nation initiative, launched in 2014, which involves collaboration between the government, private sector, and citizens to transform Singapore into a sustainable, technologically advanced city. Key PPP projects include the development of a nationwide sensor network, the deployment of autonomous vehicles, and the creation of a SMART energy grid (*SMART Urban Initiatives*, s. d.).
- **Barcelona, Spain**: The city of Barcelona has embraced PPPs to drive its SMART city transformation. One successful project is the Barcelona Sentilo platform, a sensor network that collects real-time data on various urban systems, such as traffic, air quality, and public lighting. This data is then shared with private companies and citizens to improve urban planning and service delivery. Another example is the Barcelona Urban Platform, a PPP-based initiative that integrates different city systems and enables data-driven decision-making (Bibri & Krogstie, 2020).

- **New York City, USA**: New York City has utilized PPPs to address urban challenges through technology-enabled solutions. The Link NYC project, for instance, is a collaboration between the city government and a consortium of private companies to install a network of public Wi-Fi kiosks across the city. These kiosks not only provide free high-speed internet access but also serve as platforms for digital services, such as wayfinding, emergency alerts, and advertising (Shah et al., 2019).
- **Casablanca, Morocco:** The Casablanca SMART City initiative, launched in 2018, involves a collaboration between the Casablanca municipal government and a consortium of private companies. The project aims to modernize the city's infrastructure and services through the implementation of digital technologies, such as a citywide sensor network, SMART traffic management, and integrated waste management systems. The public-private partnership has enabled the city to leverage private sector expertise and investment to accelerate the deployment of these SMART city solutions (Khalifi et al., 2024).

These real-world examples reveal the valuable perceptions that can be observed from studying the implementation of SMART city PPPs within diverse contexts. Governments can learn from the strategies and best practices adopted by these cities, such as the importance of aligning PPP objectives with broader policy goals, establishing clear governance structures, and fostering public-private-citizen collaboration. Private sector partners can also gain a deeper understanding of the challenges and opportunities in SMART city PPP projects, which can inform their own innovative solutions and business models (Liu et al., 2021). These case studies highlight the potential of well-designed and executed PPPs to transform urban environments and enhance the lives of citizens.

## 2.5. Challenges of SMART Cities by PPP projects

The integration of digital technologies in SMART city public-private partnerships has introduced new challenges and innovations that require careful consideration. Based on the World Economic Forum- Annual Report 2023-2024 (2024), some of the key contemporary issues in this domain include:

- **Cybersecurity and Data Governance:** SMART city initiatives are increasingly vulnerable to cyber threats, necessitating robust data governance strategies and cybersecurity measures to safeguard critical infrastructure and citizen data. The security and privacy of urban data is essential for building trust in SMART city solutions.

- **Inclusive and Ethical AI**: The use of artificial intelligence in urban planning and service delivery must be balanced with concerns about algorithmic bias, transparency, and the fair distribution of benefits across diverse communities. The development of AI systems that are inclusive and align with ethical principles is crucial for achieving the full potential of these technologies in SMART city PPPs.
- **Renewable Energy and Sustainable Mobility**: SMART city PPPs are exploring innovative solutions, such as renewable energy microgrids and autonomous electric vehicles, to address the pressing challenges of climate change and resource sustainability. Integrating these clean technologies into urban infrastructure can lead to sustainable development and enhance the quality of life for individuals.
- **Citizen Engagement and Co-creation:** It is crucial to foster meaningful citizen participation and empowering residents as active contributors to the SMART city agenda to ensure that digital solutions align with the needs and desires of local communities. Engaging citizens as co-creators can result in more responsive and inclusive urban governance models.

These emerging trends and challenges highlight the need for a more comprehensive and collaborative approach to SMART city development, one that leverages the strengths of both the public and private sectors while prioritizing the wellbeing of citizens and the sustainability of urban environments (Alla et al., 2023; Bouhtati, Yaacoubi, et al., 2024; Hmioui et al., 2017; Jaouhari & Alla, 2022; Meziane et al., 2024).

Following the global overview of the topic, we will now outline the methodology employed to identify the key themes and impactful studies, authors and journals from the literature. Also, we will outline the research development about this subject and the main contributions and limitations.

## 3. METHODOLOGY

In this section, we will present the method of structured Literature Review (RLS) before exposing it applicability on our topic.

## 3.1. Structured Literature Review

Literature reviews have different objectives and aims. But at the same time, they share some common characteristics namely, collecting, evaluating and presenting the available research evidence (Arksey & O'Malley, 2005, p. 20).

We find for example a systematic review (as in these articles: ((Aarabe et al., 2024a, 2024b; Nouhaila et al., 2024)), a research synthesis (like (Bouhtati, Alla, et al., 2024)), a meta-analysis …etc. which could be seen according to Massaro et al. (2016, p. 769) to be on a continuum with no rules on one end and a rigid set of rules at the other.

*Figure 1. The literature review continuum*

*Source: (Benhayoun & Marghich, 2017)*

We notice that SLR is the most demanding one in terms of rules to follow, making it like the most structured, contrary to a conventional review of authorship, for example, which is widely used in research studies, but considered as too subjective (Petticrew & Roberts, 2008).

For Denyer & Tranfield, (2006, p. 216): *"[…] the most common technique in management research is the traditional literature review in which the researcher summarizes and interprets previous contributions in a subjective and narrative fashion."*

Accordingly, a literature review has to be logically structured and must be based on a clear plan

(Hart, 1998, p. 172) following specific steps to perform it (e.g. Dumay, 2014; Guthrie and

(Parker, 2011; Guthrie et al, 2012). The process of SLR's is outlined by Massaro et al (2016, p.171) as follows:

*Figure 2. SLR's process*

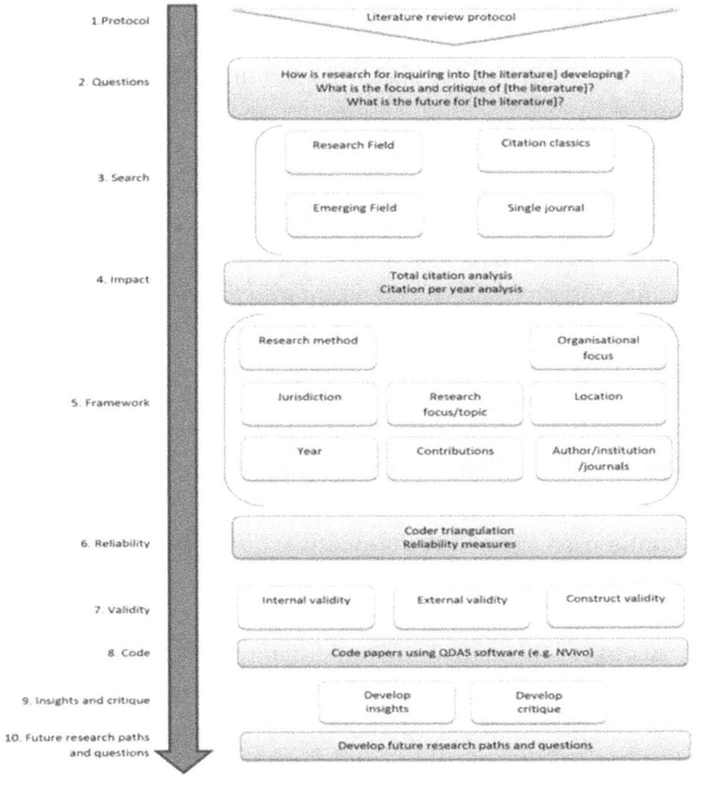


*Source: (Benhayoun & Marghich, 2017).*

1. Write a literature review protocol;
2. Define the questions that the literature review is setting out to answer;
3. Determine the type of studies and carry out a comprehensive literature search;
4. Measure article impact;
5. Define an analytical framework;
6. Establish literature review reliability;
7. Test literature review validity;
8. Code data using the developed framework;
9. Develop insights and critique through analyzing the dataset; and
10. Develop future research paths and questions.

## 3.2. Application of SLR on SMART cities by PPP projects

As we say before, the methodology of this book chapter is adapted from (Benhayoun & Marghich, 2017; Massaro et al., 2016) and must follow a specific protocol.

First, we started by establishing a literature review protocol with a view to documenting the procedure followed, which is widely connected with the view of increasing the reliability of research. According to Petticrew and Roberts 2008, p. 285*"it is essential to write a protocol stating thereview question,the methods to be used, the study types and designs which the reviewer intends to locate,andby what means, andhow these studies will be appraised and synthesized"*.

This structured literature review is structured as follows:

- **Review question:** We had two main questions:
  - o What are the different subjects of the SMART cities by PPP projects? And;
  - o What are the main findings and conclusions?
- **Methods to be used:** The SLR's process
- **Study type and design which we intend to locate**: The article that have the most impact.
- **By what means?:** Web of Science and Scopus
- **How these studies will be appraised and synthesized?:** SLR's steps.

Second, we presented the questions that the literature review is setting out to answer in our introduction. As suggested by Massaro et al. (2016, p. 774-777) there are three main questions to answer:

- How is research for inquiring into [SMART cities by PPP projects] developing?
- What is the focus and critique of the [SMART cities by PPP projects] literature?; and
- What is the future for [SMART cities by PPP projects] research?

Third, among the four types of studies suggested by Massaro et al. (2016, p. 777), we opted for the Citation Classics because we aimed to find out the article that had contributed mostly to the research field. By his definition, according to Garfield, who first used the term Citation Classics to denote those most frequently cited papers which tone set the development of a discipline, he defined Citation Classics as a work whose citation count placed it in the top 1%. He then further refined it as a highly cited publication, as identified by the Science Citation Index, the Social Sciences Citation Index, or the Arts & Humanities Citation Index.

We stick to the second definition as our basic definition because the 1% criterion is not reliable as far as the total publication it represents is of 3 to 4 articles which are not a sufficient number to ascertain conclusions of a research. By searching in the Web of Science and Scopus databases, we have used 2 keywords and connected them with the operators "AND". These keywords are: "public private partnership*" and "SMART cit*" within topic. As first result from WoS, we had 87 documents. By applying the inclusion /exclusion criteria we selected 7 articles, as shown in table 1, we had 15 documents to analyze.

*Table 1. inclusion /exclusion criteria for searching about PPP and SMART cities*

| **Search strings** | **Public private partnership, SMART city** *[within Topic]* | |
|---|---|---|
| *Inclusion /exclusion criteria* | Year range: | 8 years (2015– 2023) |
| | Subject area: | Management |
| | Language of article: | English |
| | Keywords/ search query | "public private partnership" AND "SMART cit*" |
| | Category | Articles |
| *Database* | Web of Science = 7 articles selected from 87 documents | |
| | Scopus = 12 articles selected from 160 documents | |

**Source**: designed by the authors

Fourth, the article impact can be measured by three bibliometric indicators: Total Citation, Citation per Year and H-Index of the articles, authors, and journals. The data was gathered using Harzing's Publish or Perish software, based on Google Scholar Database, viewed as a largely utilized database and regarded as the leading tool in citation analysis. It is the case that Google scholar provides comprehensive coverage, indexes all categories of publications, and counts citations from non-peer-reviewed works such as practitioner magazines, government documents, and newspaper. First of all, we ranked every publication according to each bibliometric indicator for articles, authors, and journals and added up the rankings to obtain points for each one. Afterwards, we did another ranking based on those points, putting together TC, CPY, and the H-index in order to get a total ranking.

Fifth, we define an analytical framework with respect to the literature review questions, which will help us analyze each of them independently. Every question was compounded from one or many units of analysis to which we attributed a code in order to reduce the data to be analyzed just to those containing the relevant empirical estimate, test, or finding. In what follows, we present our analytical framework together with our coding in Table 2.

*Table 2. Literature Review Questions, Units of Analysis and Codes*

| Literature review questions | Units of analysis | Codes |
|---|---|---|
| *How is research for inquiring into SMART cities by PPP projects ?* | Subject | Subj |
| | Location | Loc |
| | Methodology | Meth |
| *What is the focus and critique of the SMART cities by PPP projects research?* | Contributions | Cn |
| | Limits & critics | L&C |
| *What is the future for the SMART cities by PPP projects research?* | Future path | FuP |

**Source:** designed by the authors, adapted from BENHAYOUN & MARGHICH (2017)

We tested the reliability and validity of the data before carrying out the analysis. To establish reliability, we ensured, as advised by (Krippendorff, 2019), that the data collected:

a. was generated with all conceivable precautions in place against known pollutants, distortions and biases, intentional or accidental, and
b. mean the same thing for everyone who uses them. To this end, unreliability represents an impediment to our data source of articles. For example, while Google Scholar shows different results if we change the way we write the keywords, the Web of Science and Scopus conducts a search for scientific resources by subjects and not by keywords, which makes it a very robust tool in assessing reliability. We also set 2023 as a boundary year to check that the data generated will produce the same result for whoever makes the query next time.

As far as validity is concerned, we set the starting year to be 2015 for our query so that we could take into. Since if no starting year were determined, results will include articles based just on subjective assumptions and/or a project of the standard.

This will make us face the history effect that might bias the internal validity. The latter is biased also by the selection effect, to which the choice of our database is a greater remedy. Indeed, Web of Science is just about the very best database for locating the citation classics that make up our sample. We have also checked the construct validity by observing convergent validity, in which we find approximately the same results for the ranking of our articles according to bibliometric indicators in other databases like Google Scholar.

Finally, using the analytical framework compounded with the units of analysis to which we attributed codes, every single article was analyzed. The results are presented in the following section.

# 4. RESULTS AND ANALYSES

## 4.1. Overview of the Selected Articles

The search yields 15 documents, and the selected articles are within two key academic databases. In this case, 12 of the articles were sourced from the Scopus database, and 7 were retrieved from the Web of Science database. Furthermore, 4 articles can be found in both databases.

*Figure 3. The distribution of the selected articles*

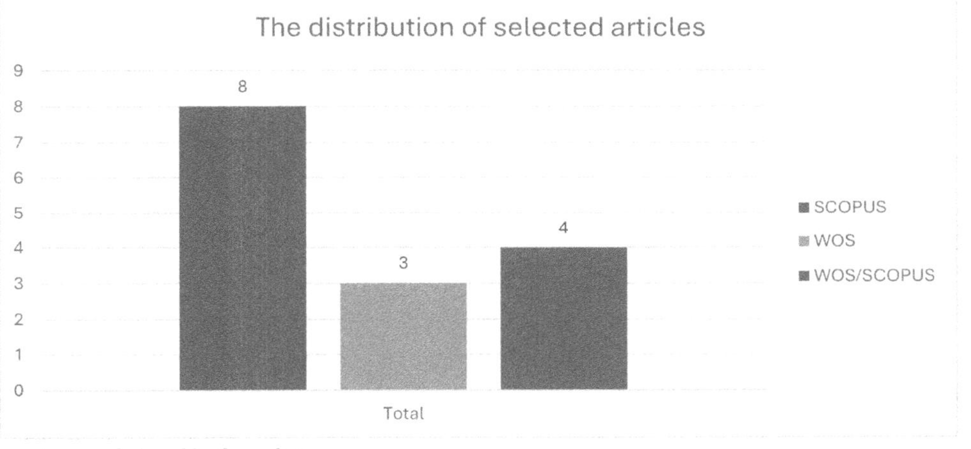


*Source: designed by the authors*

The following graph is on the most productive countries in the development of SMART cities using PPP projects. Spain appears to be the first country with 4 articles published, accumulating 377 citations and an average of 53.97 citations per year. This implies that Spain has paid most attention to the subject under research in the management area.

*Figure 4. The most productive countries about SMART cities by PPP projects*

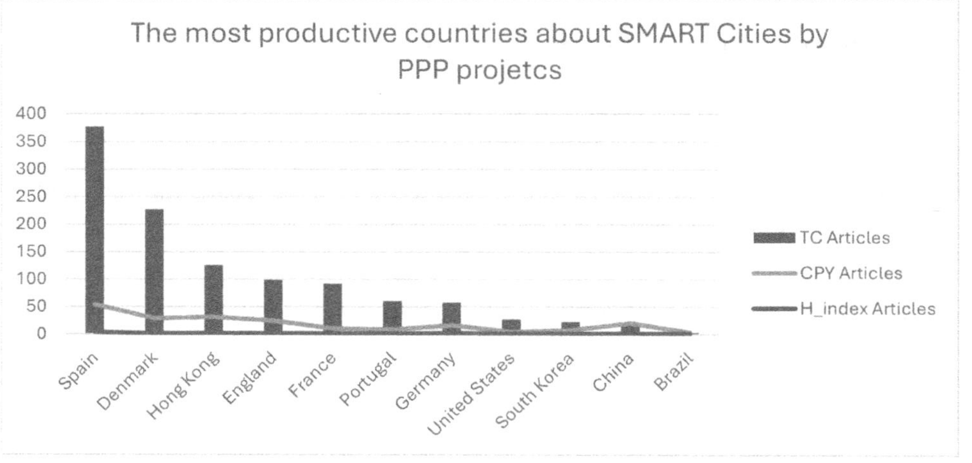


*Source: designed by the authors*

In terms of the evolution of publications by year, the following graph tell us that there is a shift in publications about SMART cities by PPP projects in the field of Management.

*Figure 5. The evolution of publications on SMART cities by PPP projects*

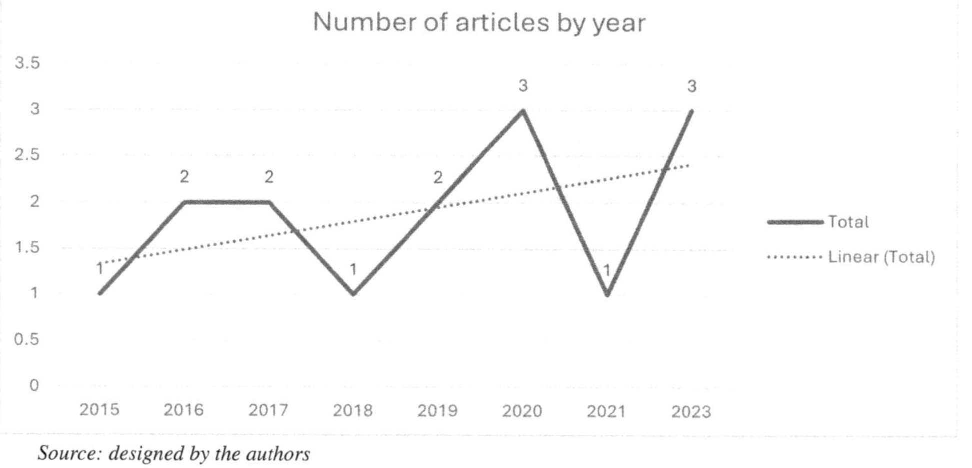


*Source: designed by the authors*

In the next subsection, we will analyze the impact of the selected articles from different positions.

## 4.2. Impact Analysis of Authors, Articles and Journals

As stated in section 3 we analyzed articles' impact of three bibliometric indicators (TC, CPY and H-Index) of articles, authors and journals. The results show that for:

**Articles:** The H-Index will not be a relevant indicator to analyze articles since it will often be equal to 1, because an article is usually published in one journal and by the same authors, contrary to authors whom we find them in many articles and journals. As for the impact, we found that the article with the greater impact is *"A model for the analysis of data-driven innovation and value generation in SMART cities' ecosystems"* with respectively 23% and 17% in terms of TC and CPY. Followed by *"Factors influencing the consideration of Public-Private Partnerships (PPP) for SMART city projects: Evidence from Hong Kong"* with 11% and 15% in both TC and CPY and by *"A SMART City Is a Collaborative Community: LESSONS FROM SMART AARHUS"* in the third position with 20% in TC and 14% in CPY.

*Figure 6. The evolution of articles in TC, CPY and H-index from 2015 to 2023*

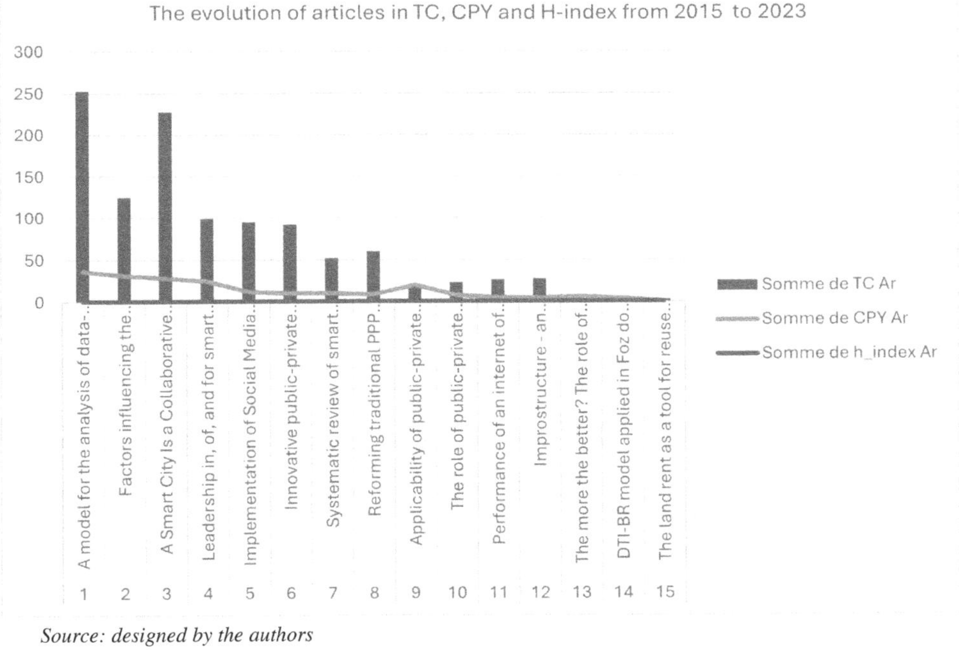


*Source: designed by the authors*

**Authors**: Thes two first authors with the greater impact are the authors of the article *"Applicability of public-private partnerships in SMART infrastructure development: the case of Hong Kong"*, considered as the 9th article in terms of impact, they gathered jointly 9 285 in TC with an average of 165 per year and with the best

H-Index of all the authors (42 for Chan, DWM and 35 for Kumaraswamy, MM). Followed by Snow, C., author of the article *"A SMART City Is a Collaborative Community: LESSONS FROM SMART AARHUS"*, considered as the 3rd article in terms of impact. We have Also Yang, B in the fourth position with the highest CPY (255.11). Yang is also the author of *"The role of public-private partnership in constructing the SMART transportation city: a case of the bike sharing platform"*, considered the 10th article in the ranking of articles.

*Figure 7. The evolution of the 10 most impactful authors*

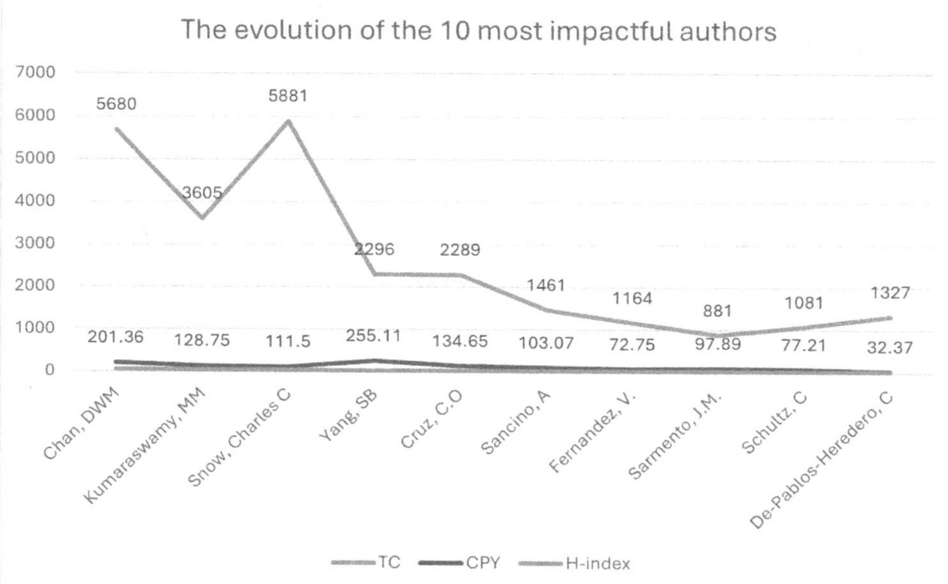


*Source: designed by the authors*

**Journals:** between the 13 journals of our *citation classics* query, Cities on which 3 articles are published, is the most impactful with 43 678 TC, with an average per year of 1747,12 and an H-Index of 127 which is so important in citation analysis. The articles published in this journal are: *"A model for the analysis of data-driven innovation and value generation in SMART cities' ecosystems"*, in the first position of articles ranking ; *"Factors influencing the consideration of Public-Private Partnerships (PPP) for SMART city projects: Evidence from Hong Kong"*, in the second position ; And *"Improstructure - an improvisational perspective on SMART infrastructure governance"*, which is ranked 12th. As for INTERNATIONAL JOURNAL OF PROJECT MANAGEMENT on which the article *"The more the better? The role of stakeholder information processing in complex urban innovation projects* *for green transformation"* was published, it is placed in the second position with respectively 27 690, 1 107 and 179 in terms of TC, CPY and H-Index. The third one is PUBLIC MANAGEMENT REVIEW that published *"Leadership in, of, and for SMART cities - case studies from Europe, America, and Australia"* with 13 074 TC, 568,43CPY and 97 in the H-Index.

*Figure 8. The evolution of journal's citation classics*

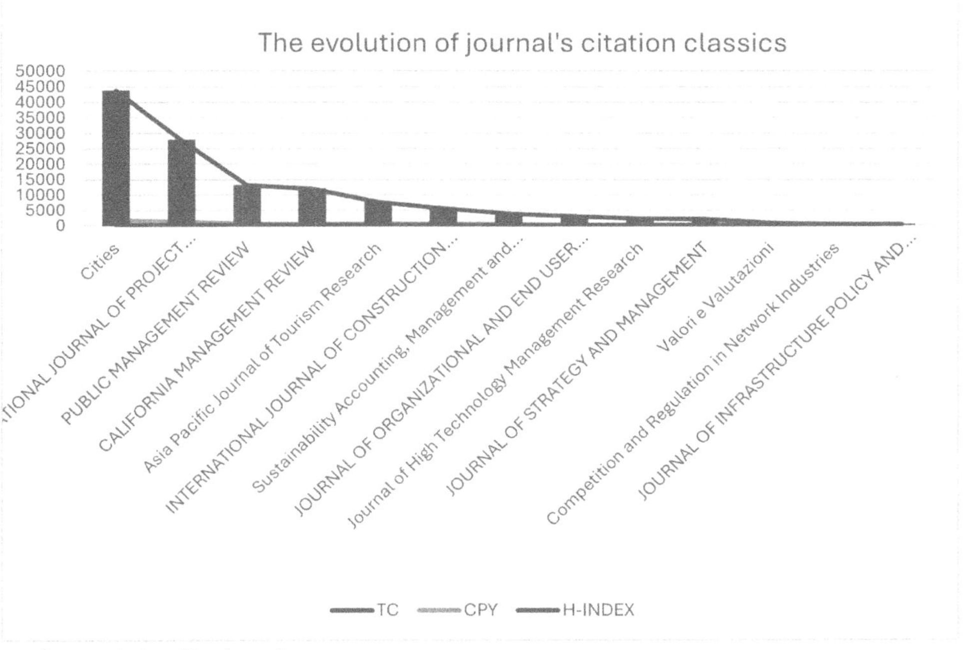


*Source: designed by the authors*

To summarize, the Appendix 5 to 7 rank the Citation Classics according to each of the selected bibliometric indicators and according to the methodology described in Section 3 of this article. We finally assigned a Total Ranking by aggregating those bibliometric indicators to assess the final results of our article impact analysis. Table 3 presents the Total Ranking.

*Table 3. Global ranking of the selected articles*

| | Article Title | TOTAL CITATION | CITATION PER YEAR | H-INDEX | Total points |
|---|---|---|---|---|---|
| 1 | A SMART City Is a Collaborative Community: LESSONS FROM SMART AARHUS | 3 | 3 | 2 | **8** |

continued on following page

*Table 3. Continued*

| | Article Title | TOTAL CITATION | CITATION PER YEAR | H-INDEX | Total points |
|---|---|---|---|---|---|
| **2** | A model for the analysis of data-driven innovation and value generation in SMART cities' ecosystems | 2 | 5 | 2 | **11** |
| **3** | Leadership in, of, and for SMART cities - case studies from Europe, America, and Australia | 4 | 4 | 4 | **12** |
| **4** | Applicability of public-private partnerships in SMART infrastructure development: the case of Hong Kong | 7 | 4 | 4 | **15** |
| **5** | Innovative public-private partnership to support SMART City: the case of Chaire REVES | 7 | 8 | 4 | **19** |
| **6** | DTI-BR model applied in Foz do Iguacu, Brazil, for its transformation into a SMART tourism destination | 10 | 6 | 5 | **21** |
| **7** | The role of public-private partnership in constructing the SMART transportation city: a case of the bike sharing platform | 8 | 8 | 5 | **21** |
| **8** | Implementation of Social Media Concepts for e-Government: Case Study of a Social Media Tool for Value Co-Creation and Citizen Participation | 8 | 9 | 5 | **22** |
| **9** | The more the better? The role of stakeholder information processing in complex urban innovation projects for green transformation | 10 | 6 | 6 | **22** |
| **10** | Reforming traditional PPP models to cope with the challenges of SMART cities | 8 | 9 | 6 | **23** |
| **11** | Factors influencing the consideration of Public-Private Partnerships (PPP) for SMART city projects: Evidence from Hong Kong | 9 | 10 | 7 | **26** |
| **12** | Performance of an internet of things project in the public sector: The case of Nice SMART city | 10 | 11 | 7 | **28** |
| **13** | Improstructure - an improvisational perspective on SMART infrastructure governance | 10 | 12 | 8 | **30** |
| **14** | Systematic review of SMART cities and climate change adaptation | 12 | 12 | 9 | **33** |
| **15** | The land rent as a tool for reuse of existing real estate (against the policy of unsustainable growth of "new" real estate development) | 13 | 13 | 9 | **35** |

**Source:** designed by the authors

We conclude in our impact analysis that the article *"A SMART City Is a Collaborative Community: LESSONS FROM SMART AARHUS"* is the article with the greatest impact among Citation Classics in terms of the most important and relevant bibliometric indicators. This could be explained by the number of authors (3) that co-wrote it and their impact, especially Snow, Charles which is ranked in the 3rd position as the most impactful regarding Citation Classics. This could also be explained by the journal on which the article was published "CALIFORNIA MANAGEMENT REVIEW" which the 2nd impactful journal as show in graph 6.

In this way, after article impact, we analyzed our papers by considering the reading of the papers with our analytical framework and codes. The results are presented according to the determined analytical framework with which we will answer our research questions.

## 4.3. Research Development about SMART Cities by PPP Projects

In this section, we will answer the question of how research for inquiring about SMART cities by PPP projects is developing ? by using 3 units of analysis (Subject, Location and Methodology) in addition to a chronological representation of the manner with which the research is developing on Citation Classics.

### 4.3.1. Trends in studying SMART cities by PPP projects

*Table 4. Subjects studied about SMART cities by PPP projects*

| SUBJECT | # of articles | citations | % |
|---|---|---|---|
| The role of PPP projects in SMART cities | 2 | 43 | 4% |
| Data of SMART Cities | 1 | 253 | 23% |
| Collaboration in SMART cities | 1 | 227 | 20% |
| Decision to use PPP for SMART cities | 1 | 125 | 11% |
| Leadership in SMART cities | 1 | 99 | 9% |
| Technology and citizen participation | 1 | 95 | 9% |
| The role of universities in generating SMART Cities through an innovative PPP projects | 1 | 92 | 8% |
| Restructurating of PPP model to face the challenges of building SMART cities | 1 | 60 | 5% |
| Synergy between SMART cities and climate change | 1 | 52 | 5% |
| governance of streetlight and electricity infrastructure | 1 | 27 | 2% |
| performance of an IoT-platform based solution in the context of a SMART city. | 1 | 26 | 2% |
| The role of stakeholder involvement in the success of urban innovation projects | 1 | 6 | 1% |
| The application of the DTI-BR model to analyze the potential of SMART cities | 1 | 4 | 0% |
| Urban planning | 1 | 3 | 0% |
| | **15** | **1112** | **100%** |

**Source:** designed the authors

We notice that SMART cities by PPP projects is studied more from the role of PPP in SMART cities from perspective of number of publications. But, regarding TC indicator, Data of SMART cities, with 23% from the total of TC. Whilst Collaboration in SMART cities and Decision to use PPP for SMART cities has respectively only a small share of 20% and 11% in terms of TC.

These results indicate that while the role of PPPs is severely studied, there may be opportunities to further explore the data-driven and collaborative dimensions of SMART city development through PPP projects, which could potentially yield valuable insights and impact.

What about the location of articles ?

### 4.3.2. Location of Articles

As for the location, the study from Denmark is the most impactful with 20% of the TC, followed by the two studies from Hong Kong and France with respectively 13% and 11% in terms of TC (see table 5).

*Table 5. Location of articles about SMART cities by PPP projects*

| Location | # of articles | % | citation | % |
|---|---|---|---|---|
| **Not specified** | 4 | 27% | 371 | 33% |
| **Denmark** | 1 | 7% | 227 | 20% |
| **Hong Kong** | 2 | 13% | 145 | 13% |
| **France** | 2 | 13% | 118 | 11% |
| **Europe, North and South America, and Australia.** | 1 | 7% | 99 | 9% |
| **Spain** | 1 | 7% | 95 | 9% |
| **Filipino** | 1 | 7% | 27 | 2% |
| **Korea** | 1 | 7% | 23 | 2% |
| **Brazil** | 1 | 7% | 4 | 0% |
| **Italy** | 1 | 7% | 3 | 0% |

**Source:** designed by the authors

The analysis reveals a notable lack of studies from Africa specifically examining SMART city developments within the management literature across these two databases.

Could the methodology used in this literature give us an explanation of this lack of the studies about this topic in Africa ?

### 4.3.3. Methodologies used in this Literature

By analyzing the methodologies used in these articles, we have noticed that more than the half of articles uses a qualitative approach (see this book chapter about qualitative studies (Bentalha et al., 2024) as example), with 76% in terms of TC (see table 6), which means that the subject of SMART cities by PPP projects is considered as a new topic that needs more exploration. Given that Africa is a developing continent, it would be preferable to explore this topic within the field of management in the African context and publish valuable studies in recognized Databases as WoS and Scopus.

*Table 6. Methodology of articles about SMART cities by PPP projects*

| METHODOLOGY | # of articles | % | Citations | % |
|---|---|---|---|---|
| **Qualitative** | 8 | 60% | 587 | 76% |
| **Mix** | 1 | 7% | 125 | 11% |
| **Literature Review** | 2 | 13% | 112 | 10% |
| **Quantitative** | 2 | 13% | 32 | 3% |
| **Opinion piece** | 1 | 7% | 3 | 0% |

**Source:** designed by the authors

After analyzing the development of studies on smart cities realized through public-private partnership projects, we will now present the key contributions and limitations of these articles, as well as suggest future research directions for this field.

## 4.4. Contributions of the Selected Studies

In this section, we will study more the contributions of selected articles about SMART cities by PPP projects.

### 4.4.1. The PPPs as procurement model for SMART Cities

The authors of Jayasena et al. (2023) propose a framework for assessing the suitability of PPPs for SMART city projects. This framework considers factors such as project complexity, risk allocation, financing options, and stakeholder engagement. Furthermore, the study offers valuable recommendations for policymakers in Hong Kong and other cities considering PPPs for SMART infrastructure development. These recommendations focus on creating a supportive policy environment, enhancing transparency and accountability, and ensuring long-term sustainability.

Li et al. (2021) mentioned the challenges of bike-sharing companies expanding overseas (difficulty expanding into overseas markets, strict and outdated regulations, market barriers and the need for government support). Moreover, they conclude that PPPs are crucial for overcoming challenges and that the government support is the principal key.

Lam & Yang (2020) demonstrate that the suitability of PPP depends on the specific project and the priorities of stakeholders. This challenges the assumption that PPP is always the best approach for SMART city development.

The article of Cerasoli & Mattarocci (2020) focuses on using land rent to encourage the reuse of existing buildings in Italian cities. It argues that this approach is more sustainable than constructing new buildings and can be facilitated through collaboration between public and private.

### 4.4.2. Collaboration as core principle for Successful SMART Cities

The authors of the selected articles have many contributions. To start with, Snow et al. (2016) highlights that the collaboration is a core principle for a successful SMART city. This collaboration includes citizens, businesses, knowledge institutions, and municipal agencies. This collaborative approach is essential for achieving the integration, efficiency, citizen engagement, and improved quality of life that define a SMART city. The authors present an organizational framework for analyzing and understanding how this collaboration functions within a SMART city context. They use SMART Aarhus as a case study to illustrate how this framework can be applied in practice. This study of Snow et al. (2016) present also lessons from SMART Aarhus. The main lessons are about: embracing collaboration, cultivating a culture of trust and openness, starting small and scaling up, being flexible and adaptive and prioritizing citizen engagement.

Bussador et al. (2023) applied the DTI-BR model to assess Foz do Iguaçu's potential as a SMART tourism destination. The study identifies specific areas where Foz do Iguaçu needs improvement to be considered a SMART tourism destination. This information can guide policymakers and stakeholders in developing strategies for improvement. In addition, the study emphasizes the need for stronger public-private partnerships to achieve SMART city goals. This highlights the importance of collaboration between government and private sectors in developing SMART cities.

Offenhuber & Schechtner (2018) focus in introducing the concept of *"impro-structure"* understanding infrastructure governance as a process of improvisation and *"call and response"* among various actors. The study examines how this plays out in the context of electricity and street.

Cruz & Sarmento (2017) argue that traditional PPP models are not adequate for the dynamic needs of SMART city infrastructure projects, advocating for flexibility and regulatory change and stressing the importance of continued private sector participation in financing and managing SMART city infrastructure.

Huang-Lachmann (2019) demonstrate that for successful climate change adaptation in SMART cities, collaboration between governments and citizens is crucial, moving beyond a model where citizens are just receivers of services . This collaborative approach aligns with the core principles of "SMART people" and "SMART governance," which emphasize citizen participation in public life and decision-making.

### 4.4.3. The Use of Open-Data and its Impact

Abella et al. (2017) discusses data-driven innovation in SMART cities. It highlights the role of both public and private entities in leveraging open data for value creation. The authors propose a three-stage model to analyze how data from SMART cities can be used to create value for citizens and society. This model emphasizes the importance of data reusability, data-driven innovation, and the assessment of economic and social impact.

### 4.4.4. The Leadership as Key Theme for SMART Cities

Sancino & Hudson (2020) took another aspect of SMART cities which is the leadership in these projects, by providing a framework for understanding leadership in this context. This study offers detailed case studies of SMART city initiatives from Europe, America, and Australia, highlighting different leadership approaches and their effectiveness. It identifies key challenges and opportunities related to SMART city leadership. As challenges they cite building consensus and collaboration; Managing rapid technological advancements; Ensuring equitable and inclusive development; Balancing innovation with citizen privacy and security. And as opportunities, they identify: Improving urban service delivery; Promoting economic growth and innovation; Enhancing citizen engagement and participation; And addressing environmental challenges.

### 4.4.5. Success Factors of PPPs in SMART City Development

Jayasena et al. (2023) outline that the success of PPPs in SMART city development is not universal and is highly dependent on local context, particularly the regulatory framework, institutional capacity, and public acceptance.

Dupont et al. (2015) highlighted in their paper how French universities can be instrumental in driving SMART City initiatives through innovative PPPs. It challenges the traditional view of universities as solely academic institutions and positions them as active agents in urban transformation. The authors argue that innovative PPPs involving users are crucial for the successful development of SMART Cities.

Díaz-Díaz & Pérez-González (2016) emphasizes that the success of SMART city projects, like the Santander City Brain, relies heavily on the commitment and dedication of local authorities. This includes allocating resources and demonstrating trust in both the technology and citizen participation. The authors point out also that the Public-Private Partnership model was crucial for initiating the project, especially during times of economic constraints.

Kroh & Schultz (2023) emphasizes the need to consider stakeholder information processing as a key factor in urban innovation project success, particularly in the context of green transformation, and highlights the potential of digital tools in facilitating this process.

The study of Grimaldi & Fernandez (2019) demonstrates how IoT technology can be effectively used to develop solutions for SMART cities, particularly in the area of urban transport. The case study of Nice's parking system highlights the potential of IoT to improve efficiency and service delivery in a city context.

### 4.4.6. Opportunities and Challenges from the Selected Cases

The cases of SMART cities realized with PPP project model present some challenges and opportunities.

There are some articles and the cases they studied:

- *Leadership in, of, and for smart cities – case studies from Europe, America, and Australia* (Sancino & Hudson, 2020). This article is based on multiple cases which are:
    - o **Amsterdam** is a city with a long tradition of smart city innovation, receiving international recognition through awards such as the World Smart Cities Award 2012 for its Open Data Program and European Capital of Innovation in 2016 and 2017.
    - o **Bristol** is well known for its smart city and sustainability initiatives; the city was ranked first in the UK Smart City Index in 2017 (Huawei and Navigant Consulting 2017) and was European Green Capital in 2015.
    - o **Milton Keynes** was identified as a contender in the UK Smart City Index in 2017; these are cities that have established their smart city strategies and implemented significant projects (Huawei and Navigant Consulting 2017).
    - o **Chicago** is well known for its community approach to utilizing technology to improve people's lives. The Smart Chicago Collective was founded as a civic organization in 2011, and they have initiatives across areas such as health, education, justice, and open data (Smart Chicago 2018).
    - o **Curitiba** is a city widely recognized for its innovation work within sustainable urban development and was awarded the Global Sustainable City Award 2010. More recently, it was ranked top in the Brazilian Index of Digital Cities (Duarte et al. 2014) and has started to develop a collaborative smart city programme.

- **Melbourne** is known for its liveability work and was ranked top in the Global Liveability Ranking from 2011 to 2017 (The Economist 2018). The city also won Intelligent Community of the Year for 2017, in recognition of its work around liveability and its community plan called Future Melbourne (Intelligent Community Forum 2018).

- *Factors influencing the consideration of Public-Private Partnerships for smart city projects: Evidence from Hong Kong* (Lam & Yang, 2020). The researchers looked at 8 common types of smart city projects being considered in Hong Kong, using them as examples to understand the broader context of PPP use in the city's smart city development. These projects are:
  - Smart Crowed Management.
  - Easy Walking App
  - Intelligent parking information system
  - Energy efficiency data management system
  - Smart recycling bin system
  - Multi-purpose lamp post
  - E-government portal
  - Bicycle sharing system
- The role of public-private partnership in constructing the smart transportation city: a case of the bike sharing platform (Li et al., 2021). In this article, the authors studied only one case which is "Mobike Korea". Mobike, a Chinese bike-sharing giant, expanded into South Korea by establishing Mobike Korea. Facing challenges entering the overseas market, Mobike Korea formed a public-private partnership with the local government. This partnership aimed to leverage Mobike's technology and experience with the government's support and regulatory framework.

The opportunities that we have extracted from the selected studies are:

- Improving urban service delivery (Sancino & Hudson, 2020)
- Promoting economic growth and innovation (Sancino & Hudson, 2020)
- Enhancing citizen engagement and participation (Lam & Yang, 2020; Sancino & Hudson, 2020)
- Addressing environmental challenges (Sancino & Hudson, 2020)
- Leverage emerging technologies, and ensure long-term sustainability (Lam & Yang, 2020)

The most challenges identified in our literature review are:

- Building consensus and collaboration

- Managing rapid technological advancements (Sancino & Hudson, 2020)
- Ensuring equitable and inclusive development (Sancino & Hudson, 2020)
- Balancing innovation with citizen privacy and security (Sancino & Hudson, 2020)
- The city's unique characteristics (high population density, advanced technological infrastructure, and well-established legal framework) (Jayasena et al., 2023)
- Difficulty expanding into overseas markets (Li et al., 2021)
- Strict and outdated regulations (Li et al., 2021)
- Market barriers (Li et al., 2021)
- The need for government support (Li et al., 2021)

By underlying the main contributions of these studies, we have identified also the limitations of the selected articles as presented in the next subsection.

## 4.5. Limitations

As limitations of these studies, several ones were identified, we have group them in the table below.

*Table 7. limitations of the selected articles about SMART cities by PPP projects*

| Limitations | Source |
|---|---|
| **Data quality and accessibility** | (Abella et al., 2017; Grimaldi & Fernandez, 2019) |
| **Contextual Variation** | (Abella et al., 2017; Kroh & Schultz, 2023; Offenhuber & Schechtner, 2018) |
| **Limited geographical scope** | (Cerasoli & Mattarocci, 2020; Dupont et al., 2015; Jayasena et al., 2023; Offenhuber & Schechtner, 2018; Sancino & Hudson, 2020) |
| **Potential bias** | (Jayasena et al., 2023; Sancino & Hudson, 2020) |
| **Lack of in-depth analysis** | (Díaz-Díaz & Pérez-González, 2016; Grimaldi & Fernandez, 2019; Offenhuber & Schechtner, 2018; Sancino & Hudson, 2020) |
| **Lack of empirical data** | (Cruz & Sarmento, 2017) |
| **Generalizability issues** | (Cruz & Sarmento, 2017; Grimaldi & Fernandez, 2019; Jayasena et al., 2023) |
| **Limited cases** | (Li et al., 2021) |
| **Methodological rigor** | (Cerasoli & Mattarocci, 2020) |

**Source**: designed by the authors

These limitations have to be addressed in the next studies. The authors have identified multiple areas of research in the future as we demonstrate in the section of the future path.

## 4.6. Future Path

Several research gaps were identified from the selected literature. The paper of Abella et al. (2017) lays a foundation for understanding data-driven innovation in SMART cities, and future work should focus on translating this theoretical framework into practical tools and strategies for building more efficient and citizen-centric urban environments.

Lam & Yang (2020) recommended to develop more nuanced and context-specific frameworks for evaluating the suitability of PPP for different types of SMART city projects. This would involve considering factors such as the specific objectives of the project, the level of risk involved, and the capacity of the public and private sectors. They have called also to explore innovative PPP models that can better address the challenges and opportunities of SMART city development. This could include models that promote greater citizen engagement, leverage emerging technologies, and ensure long-term sustainability. In addition to that, the author outlined the need to conduct further research on the long-term performance of PPP projects in the SMART city context, in order to identify best practices and lessons learned that can inform future decision-making.

According to Dupont et al. (2015), shared demonstrators' characteristics should enable future scientific analyses and Smartness impact assessment studies for territories.

From the point of view of (Huang-Lachmann, 2019), further research must be on developing indicators for SMART city studies in climate change. This would involve identifying and quantifying the specific benefits of SMART city applications in adapting to climate change. The author also see potential in further developing the *"SMART cities concept with the synergetic coproduction theoretical model"* into a methodology for sustainability accounting and reporting in cities. This would provide a framework for cities to measure their progress in becoming more sustainable and resilient to climate change.

Cruz & Sarmento (2017) see that future research must be on examining specific examples of innovative PPP models implemented in SMART city projects to assess their effectiveness and identify best practices. They also recommend to investigating how different regulatory frameworks can facilitate or hinder private investment in SMART city infrastructure. Furthermore, the study highlighted the need for studying how technologies like blockchain, AI, and big data (Bouhtati et al., 2023) can be leveraged to improve transparency, efficiency, and risk management in SMART city PPPs.

Jayasena et al. (2023) highlighted the need for pilot projects and detailed case studies to test the proposed framework and gather empirical evidence on the effectiveness of PPPs in different SMART city contexts. They propose to expand on the qualitative findings with quantitative data analysis in order to strengthen the generalizability of the results and provide more robust insights into the factors influencing PPP success.

These authors recommended to compare the experiences of Hong Kong with other cities, particularly those with different regulatory environments and levels of economic development, would contribute to a more comprehensive understanding of PPPs in SMART city development. Moreover, this study sees that next research must be a longitudinal study, by tracking the long-term performance and impact of PPP projects in SMART cities would provide valuable insights into their sustainability. Another study of (Li et al., 2021) recommended to realize a longitudinal study of Mobike Korea's expansion.

Grimaldi & Fernandez, (2019); Kroh & Schultz (2023) ; and Offenhuber & Schechtner, (2018) see the need of a comparison to their studies about innovative SMART cities within other contexts.

Kroh & Schultz (2023) outlined also the need of deeper exploration of digital tools. According to them, further research could delve deeper into the specific types of digital tools used in urban innovation projects, their effectiveness in enhancing stakeholder information processing, and potential pitfalls to avoid. This could involve case studies (here is an example of case study (Boudri et al., 2024)) of successful digital tool implementation or comparative analyses of different platforms. They recommended to address the role of power dynamics in stakeholder information processing, in addition to integrate other stakeholder engagement factors in future research, with other crucial aspects of stakeholder engagement, such as trust-building, conflict resolution, and collaborative decision-making.

After analyzing the results of our structured literature review, the next logical step is to discuss the key contributions and insights gained from this comprehensive examination of the literature.

## 5. DISCUSSION

Our main findings are presented in the 4th section. Two articles were about the application of PPP on SMART cities projects. Even if the TC of this studies is 4% from the total of citations, we consider the fact that having two articles for this subject explain the importance of this subject related to our topic. Furthermore, the article on Data for SMART cities is the first one in terms of total citations, with 23% from the sum of all citations related to selected literature.

The location was not specified in 4 articles / 15. Denmark, Hong Kong and France are the top 3 first countries in terms of citation about SMART cities by PPP projects with respectively 23%, 13% and 11% in TC. We have observed that the studies selected from the literature belong to Europe, America, Australia and Asia, and no study is released in the African context. This allows us to ask about the reasons behind this gap and notice researchers in the domain to take this point into account in their next studies.

The methodology most used our literature is qualitative with 76% of TC. This means that this topic is the stage of exploration and needs an integration of quantitative studies thereafter.

Even if the fact that every article contributes to the knowledge on SMART cities by PPP projects from its perspective, but in those presenting case studies, we found that they outline success factors, challenges and opportunities of SMART cities.

Many success factors were identified. First, we have collaboration of all stakeholders (citizens, businesses, knowledge institutions, and municipal agencies) as mentioned by Huang-Lachmann (2019) and Snow et al. (2016). This collaboration is seen from other some by (Bussador et al., 2023) who outlines the need of collaboration between government and private sectors in developing SMART cities, through PPP projects. Another success factor was identified like integrating innovation into PPP projects (Dupont et al., 2015), and the commitment and dedication of local authorities, which includes allocating resources and demonstrating trust in both the technology and citizen participation (Díaz-Díaz & Pérez-González, 2016).

In fact, the literature review identifies several key challenges faced in realizing SMART cities through public-private partnerships, which could be comprehended using theoretical lenses. According to stakeholder theory, consensus building and collaboration amongst the different stakeholders involved, including government agencies, private companies, and citizens, are fundamental but difficult to agree upon regarding project objectives and implementation.

The rapid rate of technological change in areas such as IoT, big data, and AI (Elhissoufi et al., 2024) makes it challenging for smart city infrastructure to be planned, deployed, and managed; therefore, a need exists for dynamic capabilities theory to guide firms through such an uncertain environment. Considering the criticism that smart city initiatives widen the socioeconomic divide, thus marginalizing vulnerable populations, the importance of the themes of inclusive development and social equity, concepts emanating from theories of justice and fairness, is raised.

Researchers argue that the development of innovation needs to be balanced with citizen privacy and security; therefore, more emphasis needs to be drawn from theories of privacy and information systems. Contingency theory underlines that specific contextual factors around governance structures, infrastructure, and demographics of each city are relevant for specialized approaches rather than 'one-size-fits-all' solutions. However, the relative success of overcoming market barriers, against a background of lack of incentives, strict regulations, and insufficient public investment, indicates how institutional theory develops an understanding of how the regulatory environment can hold back private sector involvement in smart city PPPs and their scaling.

Overcoming market barriers and the need for government support: Lack of incentives, strict regulations, and insufficient public investment can impede private sector involvement and the scaling of smart city PPPs.

The opportunities identified in realizing smart cities through public-private partnerships are grounded in established theoretical frameworks. The emphasis on improving urban service delivery (Sancino & Hudson, 2020) aligns with theories of public value management, which highlight the role of government in creating value for citizens through efficient and effective public services. Promoting economic growth and innovation through PPPs (Sancino & Hudson, 2020) draws on theories of collaborative governance, which suggest that cross-sector partnerships can foster innovation and economic development by combining the unique capabilities and resources of public and private actors.

The goal of enhancing citizen engagement and participation (Sancino & Hudson, 2020) in smart city initiatives is supported by theories of participatory democracy, which stress the importance of empowering citizens and incorporating their input into decision-making processes. Addressing environmental challenges through smart city PPPs (Sancino & Hudson, 2020) is consistent with sustainability theories emphasizing the need for integrated, systems-level approaches to managing the environmental impacts of urban development.

Finally, the focus on developing innovative models that leverage emerging technologies and ensure long-term sustainability (Lam & Yang, 2020) is grounded in theories of technological innovation and organizational resilience, which examine how organizations can adapt to rapid change and uncertainty (Teece, 1997; Weick & Sutcliffe, 2007).

## 6. CONCLUSION

During our work, we tried to proceed according to a structured approach based on rigorous rules and criteria in order to understand how the research is been developing on SMART cities by PPP projects as well as authors contributions, critics and possible future path. We consider that our book chapter contribute to research about SMART cities, as far as we know, no article wrote a structured literature review about SMART cities, which means that the existing literature reviews are possibly bias and doesn't respond to objectivity, measures of validity and reliability and finally to article impact's aspect. That is one of the greatest advantages and contributions to management research in a methodological standpoint.

We have identified that the most impactful article is "*"A model for the analysis of data-driven innovation and value generation in SMART cities' ecosystems"* . In addition, we found that the most impactful author from the selected literature is *"Jayasena Nimesha Sahani"*, who is a women Research Associate from Hong Kong, specialized in *"Sustainable Development", "Smart Cities", "Stakeholder Management", "Green Procurement" and "Public Private Partnerships"*. Furthermore, we conclude that the most impactful journal is *"Cities"*. The primary aims of this journal are to analyze and assess past and present urban development and management as a reflection of effective, ineffective and non-existent planning policies, and the promotion of the implementation of appropriate urban policies in both the developed and the developing world a journal . Finally, we note that the case of *"AARHUS SMART city"* in Denmark is the most cited case. These results present practical implications that could help all engaged parts in SMART cities to extract valuable information's.

Many contributions were identified from the literature like the use of PPP as procurement model for SMART cities, the need of collaboration to succeed such projects, the use of Open Data and its multiple impact (economic and social) and the leadership as a key theme for SMART cities realized throughout PPP projects. Also, we have identified multiple success factors, opportunities and challenges facing these projects.

Our literature review presents some limitations such as data quality and accessibility, contextual variation, limited geographical scope and potential bias. As limitations we identified also the lack of in-depth analysis in some studies, the lack of empirical data, the lack of methodological rigor, some generalizability issues. Some authors consider that the cases they studied are limited and need more investigations.

Future research needs to focus more on how such theoretical frameworks might be translated into practical tools and strategies for creating efficient and citizen-centered urban environments. The researchers are therefore called upon to come up with more nuanced evaluation frameworks for assessing the suitability of PPPs on different SMART city projects and explore innovative models of PPPs that respond better to challenges and opportunities arising in SMART city development.

There is a need to increase the number of empirical studies related to long-term performance and impact of SMART city PPPs, including the use of such emerging technologies like blockchain and AI, that would foster transparency and risk management. Needed are pilot projects, detailed case studies, and comparative analyses in very different contexts that can help to strengthen the evidence base for robust insights into what drives the PPP success in the domain of the SMART city.

Ultimately, we conclude that SLR is a method that presents many advantages in elaborating a literature review because it allows profound and objective analysis since it takes into consideration a lot of essential criteria: a protocol of the literature review, article impact analysis, validity and reliability measures, analytical framework and data coding, and, finally, developing critics and future research paths, which a traditional literature review neglects.

## REFERENCES


Abella, A., Ortiz-de-Urbina-Criado, M., & De-Pablos-Heredero, C. (2017). A model for the analysis of data-driven innovation and value generation in smart cities' ecosystems. *Cities (London, England)*, 64, 47–53. DOI: 10.1016/j.cities.2017.01.011

Alla, L., Bentalha, B., & Elyoussfi, A. (2023). Intelligence territoriale et positionnement stratégique des regions au Maroc : Le cas de la région de Fès Meknes en perspective. In *Le concept de l'intéligence en sciences juridiques, économiques et sociales* (p. 215-237). https://hal.science/hal-04107659

Arksey, H., & O'Malley, L. (2005). Scoping Studies : Towards a Methodological Framework. *International Journal of Social Research Methodology*, 8(1), 19–32. DOI: 10.1080/1364557032000119616

Benarbi, M. A., & Tamnine, L. (2019). *Analyse d'impact des articles sur la gestion des risques liés aux Partenariats Public-Privé (PPP). 2*(4), 23.

Benarbi, M. A., & Tamnine, L. (2020). Développement de la recherche sur la gestion des risques liés aux projets de Partenariat Public-Privé (PPP). *International Journal of Business and Technology Studies And Research, 2*(2), 10 pages. DOI: 10.5281/zenodo.3820086

Bibri, S. E. (2018). A foundational framework for smart sustainable city development : Theoretical, disciplinary, and discursive dimensions and their synergies. *Sustainable Cities and Society*, 38, 758–794. DOI: 10.1016/j.scs.2017.12.032

Bibri, S. E., & Krogstie, J. (2020). The emerging data–driven Smart City and its innovative applied solutions for sustainability : The cases of London and Barcelona. *Energy Informatics*, 3(1), 5. DOI: 10.1186/s42162-020-00108-6

Bouhtati, N., Yaacoubi, Y. E., Bentalha, B., & Alla, L. (2024). Leviers logistiques de promotion du commerce équitable des produits de terroir : Une esquisse de modèle d'analyse. *Alternatives Managériales Economiques, 6*(Spécial 1), Article Spécial 1. https://doi.org/DOI: 10.48374/IMIST.PRSM/ame-v6iSpécial

Brinkerhoff, D. W., & Brinkerhoff, J. M. (2011). Public–private partnerships : Perspectives on purposes, publicness, and good governance. *Wiley, 31*(1), 2-14. DOI: 10.1002/pad.584

Bussador, A., Bauermann, B. F. C., Matrakas, M. D., Padilha, J. C., & De Freitas Zara, K. R. (2023). DTI-BR model applied in Foz do Iguaçu, Brazil, for its transformation into a smart tourism destination. *Journal of Infrastructure. Policy and Development*, 7(2), 2152. DOI: 10.24294/jipd.v7i2.2152

Cerasoli, M., & Mattarocci, G. (2020). The land rent as a tool for reuse of existing real estate (against the policy of unsustainable growth of "new" real estate development) : La rendita come strumento di rilancio del riuso intelligente (e contro l'insostenibile cultura del nuovo). *Valori e Valutazioni*, 27, 101–110. DOI: 10.48264/VVSIEV-20202710

Cruz, C. O., & Sarmento, J. M. (2017). Reforming traditional PPP models to cope with the challenges of smart cities. *Competition and Regulation in Network Industries*, 18(1-2), 94–114. DOI: 10.1177/1783591717734794

Denyer, D., & Tranfield, D. (2006). Using qualitative research synthesis to build an actionable knowledge base. *Management Decision*, 44(2), 213–227. DOI: 10.1108/00251740610650201

Díaz-Díaz, R., & Pérez-González, D. (2016). Implementation of Social Media Concepts for e-Government : Case Study of a Social Media Tool for Value Co-Creation and Citizen Participation. *Journal of Organizational and End User Computing*, 28(3), 104–121. DOI: 10.4018/JOEUC.2016070107

Dupont, L., Morel, L., & Guidat, C. (2015). Innovative public-private partnership to support Smart City : The case of "Chaire REVES". *Journal of Strategy and Management*, 8(3), 245–265. DOI: 10.1108/JSMA-03-2015-0027

Grimaldi, D., & Fernandez, V. (2019). Performance of an internet of things project in the public sector : The case of Nice smart city. *The Journal of High Technology Management Research*, 30(1), 27–39. DOI: 10.1016/j.hitech.2018.12.003

Hartanti, F. T., Abawajy, J. H., & Chowdhury, M. (2022). Evaluating Public Service Delivery Smartness and Impact on Citizens' Well-Being. *IEEE Access, 10*, 69106-69124. IEEE Access. DOI: 10.1109/ACCESS.2022.3186325

Hmioui, A., Alla, L., & Bentalha, B. (2017). Pilotage de la touristicité territoriale au Maroc Proposition d'un indice de touriscticité pour la destination Fès. In *Entrepreneuriat, Innovation, Gouvernance et Développement territorial* (p. 120-143). Faculté Polydisciplinaire de TAZA. https://hal.science/hal-02334913

Huang-Lachmann, J.-T. (2019). Systematic review of smart cities and climate change adaptation. *Sustainability Accounting. Management and Policy Journal*, 10(4), 745–772. DOI: 10.1108/SAMPJ-03-2018-0052

Issam, M. B., & Abdellatif, M. M. (2017). IFRS for SMEs : A Structured Literature Review. *International Journal of Accounting and Financial Reporting*, 7(2), 538–561. DOI: 10.5296/ijafr.v7i2.12390

Jaouhari, S. E., & Alla, L. (2022). L'approche territoriale et la gestion de l'impact de la pandémie de Covid-19 : Cas des collectivités territoriales. *Alternatives Managériales Economiques, 4*(1), Article 1. DOI: 10.48374/IMIST.PRSM/ame-v4i1.30484

Jayasena, N. S., Chan, D. W. M., Kumaraswamy, M. M., & Saka, A. B. (2023). Applicability of public-private partnerships in smart infrastructure development : The case of Hong Kong. *International Journal of Construction Management*, 23(11), 1932–1944. DOI: 10.1080/15623599.2022.2027076

Khalifi, H., Riahi, S., & Cherif, W. (2024). *Smart Cities and Sustainable Urban Development in Morocco | IIETA*. DOI: 10.18280/isi.290236

Komninos, N., Tsarchopoulos, P., & Kakderi, C. (2014). *New services design for smart cities*. DOI: 10.1145/2633661.2633664

Krippendorff, K. (2019). *Content Analysis : An Introduction to Its Methodology*. SAGE Publications, Inc., DOI: 10.4135/9781071878781

Kroh, J., & Schultz, C. (2023). The more the better? The role of stakeholder information processing in complex urban innovation projects for green transformation. *International Journal of Project Management*, 41(3), 102466. DOI: 10.1016/j.ijproman.2023.102466

Kwak, Y. H., Chih, Y.-Y., & Ibbs, C. W. (2009). Towards a Comprehensive Understanding of Public Private Partnerships for Infrastructure Development. *California Management Review*, 51(2), 51–78. DOI: 10.2307/41166480

Lam, P. T. I., & Yang, W. (2020). Factors influencing the consideration of Public-Private Partnerships (PPP) for smart city projects : Evidence from Hong Kong. *Cities (London, England)*, 99, 102606. DOI: 10.1016/j.cities.2020.102606

Li, L., Park, P., & Yang, S.-B. (2021). The role of public-private partnership in constructing the smart transportation city : A case of the bike sharing platform. *Asia Pacific Journal of Tourism Research*, 26(4), 428–439. DOI: 10.1080/10941665.2018.1544913

Liu, T., Mostafa, S., Mohamed, S., & Nguyen, T. S. (2021). Emerging themes of public-private partnership application in developing smart city projects : A conceptual framework. In *Built Environment Project and Asset Management* (Vol. 11, Numéro 1, p. 138-156). DOI: 10.1108/BEPAM-12-2019-0142

Marsilio, M., Cappellaro, G., & Cuccurullo, C. (2011). The Intellectual Structure Of Research Into PPPs. *Taylor & Francis, 13*(6), 763-782. DOI: 10.1080/14719037.2010.539112

Massaro, M., Dumay, J., & Guthrie, J. (2016). On the shoulders of giants : Undertaking a structured literature review in accounting. *Accounting, Auditing & Accountability Journal*, 29(5), 767–801. DOI: 10.1108/AAAJ-01-2015-1939

Meziane, B., Bentalha, B., & Alla, L. (2024). La PME logistique et le développement territorial régional : Une analyse qualitative. *Alternatives Managériales Economiques, 6*(3), Article 3. DOI: 10.48374/IMIST.PRSM/ame-v6i4.50474

Monk, A. H. B., Levitt, R. E., Garvin, M. J., South, A. J., & Carollo, G. (2019). *Public–private partnerships for infrastructure delivery*. DOI: 10.4337/9781788973182.00008

Offenhuber, D., & Schechtner, K. (2018). Improstructure—An improvisational perspective on smart infrastructure governance. *Cities (London, England)*, 72, 329–338. DOI: 10.1016/j.cities.2017.09.017

Perboli, G., & Rosano, M. (2020). A Taxonomic Analysis of Smart City Projects in North America and Europe. *Sustainability (Basel)*, 12(18), 18. Advance online publication. DOI: 10.3390/su12187813

Petticrew, M., & Roberts, H. (2008). *Systematic Reviews in the Social Sciences : A Practical Guide*. John Wiley & Sons.

Radchenko, K. (2022). Public-Private Partnership for Smarter Cities. *Central and Eastern European eDem and eGov Days, 341*, 103-114. DOI: 10.24989/ocg.v341.7

Rzqoo, N. J., Fayadh, O. K., Abid, M. T., & AL-Ugaily, M. (2023). Basic Criteria for creating a Smart City. *International Journal of Engineering Science and Technology*, 5(1), 1. Advance online publication. DOI: 10.46328/ijonest.135

Sancino, A., & Hudson, L. (2020). Leadership in, of, and for smart cities – case studies from Europe, America, and Australia. *Public Management Review*, 22(5), 701–725. DOI: 10.1080/14719037.2020.1718189

Shah, J., Kothari, J., & Doshi, N. (2019). A Survey of Smart City infrastructure via Case study on New York. *Procedia Computer Science*, 160, 702–705. DOI: 10.1016/j.procs.2019.11.024

*Smart Urban Initiatives*. (s. d.). Consulté 17 septembre 2024, à l'adresse https://www.smartnation.gov.sg/initiatives/urban-living/

Snow, C. C., Håkonsson, D. D., & Obel, B. (2016). A Smart City Is a Collaborative Community : Lessons from Smart Aarhus. *California Management Review*, 59(1), 92–108. DOI: 10.1177/0008125616683954

Wang, K., Zhao, Y., Gangadhari, R. K., & Li, Z. (2021). Analyzing the Adoption Challenges of the Internet of Things (IoT) and Artificial Intelligence (AI) for Smart Cities in China. *Sustainability (Basel)*, 13(19), 19. Advance online publication. DOI: 10.3390/su131910983

## APPENDIX

*Table 8. Results of the query on web of science and scopus of the theme smart cities by PPP projects between 2015 and 2023*

| Article Title | Authors | Source Title | Year |
|---|---|---|---|
| **A model for the analysis of data-driven innovation and value generation in SMART cities' ecosystems** | Abella, A., Ortiz-de-Urbina-Criado, M., De-Pablos-Heredero, C. | Cities | 2017 |
| **A SMART City Is a Collaborative Community: LESSONS FROM SMART AARHUS** | Snow, CC; Håkonsson, DD; Obel, B | CALIFORNIA MANAGEMENT REVIEW | 2016 |
| **Applicability of public-private partnerships in SMART infrastructure development: the case of Hong Kong** | Jayasena, NS; Chan, DWM; Kumaraswamy, MM; Saka, AB | INTERNATIONAL JOURNAL OF CONSTRUCTION MANAGEMENT | 2023 |
| **DTI-BR model applied in Foz do Iguacu, Brazil, for its transformation into a SMART tourism destination** | Bussador, A; Bauermann, BFC; Matrakas, MD; Padilha, JC; Zara, KRD | JOURNAL OF INFRASTRUCTURE POLICY AND DEVELOPMENT | 2023 |
| **Factors influencing the consideration of Public-Private Partnerships (PPP) for SMART city projects: Evidence from Hong Kong** | Lam, P.T.I., Yang, W. | Cities | 2020 |
| **Implementation of Social Media Concepts for e-Government: Case Study of a Social Media Tool for Value Co-Creation and Citizen Participation** | Díaz-Díaz, R; Pérez-González, D | JOURNAL OF ORGANIZATIONAL AND END USER COMPUTING | 2016 |
| **Improstructure - an improvisational perspective on SMART infrastructure governance** | Offenhuber, D., Schechtner, K. | Cities | 2018 |
| **Innovative public-private partnership to support SMART City: the case of Chaire REVES** | Dupont, L; Morel, L; Guidat, C | JOURNAL OF STRATEGY AND MANAGEMENT | 2015 |
| **Leadership in, of, and for SMART cities - case studies from Europe, America, and Australia** | Sancino, A; Hudson, L | PUBLIC MANAGEMENT REVIEW | 2020 |
| **Performance of an internet of things project in the public sector: The case of Nice SMART city** | Grimaldi, D., Fernandez, V. | Journal of High Technology Management Research | 2019 |
| **Reforming traditional PPP models to cope with the challenges of SMART cities** | Cruz, C.O., Sarmento, J.M. | Competition and Regulation in Network Industries | 2017 |
| **Systematic review of SMART cities and climate change adaptation** | Huang-Lachmann, J.-T. | Sustainability Accounting, Management and Policy Journal | 2019 |
| **The land rent as a tool for reuse of existing real estate (against the policy of unsustainable growth of "new" real estate development)** | Cerasoli, M., Mattarocci, G. | Valori e Valutazioni | 2020 |
| **The more the better? The role of stakeholder information processing in complex urban innovation projects for green transformation** | Kroh, J; Schultz, C | INTERNATIONAL JOURNAL OF PROJECT MANAGEMENT | 2023 |
| **The role of public-private partnership in constructing the SMART transportation city: a case of the bike sharing platform** | Li, L., Park, P., Yang, S.-B. | Asia Pacific Journal of Tourism Research | 2021 |

*Table 9. Bibliometric indicators for the analysis of the impact of articles*

| Article | TC | CPY | H-INDEX |
|---|---|---|---|
| A model for the analysis of data-driven innovation and value generation in SMART cities' ecosystems | 253 | 36,14 | 1 |
| A SMART City Is a Collaborative Community: LESSONS FROM SMART AARHUS | 227 | 28,38 | 1 |
| Applicability of public-private partnerships in SMART infrastructure development: the case of Hong Kong | 20 | 20 | 1 |
| DTI-BR model applied in Foz do Iguacu, Brazil, for its transformation into a SMART tourism destination | 4 | 4 | 1 |
| Factors influencing the consideration of Public-Private Partnerships (PPP) for SMART city projects: Evidence from Hong Kong | 125 | 31,25 | 1 |
| Implementation of Social Media Concepts for e-Government: Case Study of a Social Media Tool for Value Co-Creation and Citizen Participation | 95 | 11,88 | 1 |
| Improstructure - an improvisational perspective on SMART infrastructure governance | 27 | 4,5 | 1 |
| Innovative public-private partnership to support SMART City: the case of Chaire REVES | 92 | 10,22 | 1 |
| Leadership in, of, and for SMART cities - case studies from Europe, America, and Australia | 99 | 24,75 | 1 |
| Performance of an internet of things project in the public sector: The case of Nice SMART city | 26 | 5,2 | 1 |
| Reforming traditional PPP models to cope with the challenges of SMART cities | 60 | 8,57 | 1 |
| Systematic review of SMART cities and climate change adaptation | 52 | 10,4 | 1 |
| The land rent as a tool for reuse of existing real estate (against the policy of unsustainable growth of "new" real estate development) | 3 | 0,75 | 1 |
| The more the better? The role of stakeholder information processing in complex urban innovation projects for green transformation | 6 | 6 | 1 |
| The role of public-private partnership in constructing the SMART transportation city: a case of the bike sharing platform | 23 | 7,67 | 1 |
| **Total** | **1112** | **209,71** | **15** |

*Table 10. Bibliometric indicators for the analysis of the impact of authors*

| Article | Authors | TC | CPY | H-INDEX |
|---|---|---|---|---|
| A model for the analysis of data-driven innovation and value generation in SMART cities' ecosystems | Abella, A., Ortiz-de-Urbina-Criado, M., De-Pablos-Heredero, C. | 2626 | 131,74 | 42 |
| A SMART City Is a Collaborative Community: LESSONS FROM SMART AARHUS | Snow, CC; Håkonsson, DD; Obel, B | 7271 | 160,88 | 57 |
| Applicability of public-private partnerships in SMART infrastructure development: the case of Hong Kong | Jayasena, NS; Chan, DWM; Kumaraswamy, MM; Saka, AB | 9879 | 431,28 | 93 |
| DTI-BR model applied in Foz do Iguacu, Brazil, for its transformation into a SMART tourism destination | Bussador, A; Bauermann, BFC; Matrakas, MD; Padilha, JC; Zara, KRD | 742 | 37,24 | 12 |
| Factors influencing the consideration of Public-Private Partnerships (PPP) for SMART city projects: Evidence from Hong Kong | Lam, P.T.I., Yang, W. | 418 | 83,6 | 11 |
| Implementation of Social Media Concepts for e-Government: Case Study of a Social Media Tool for Value Co-Creation and Citizen Participation | Díaz-Díaz, R; Pérez-González, D | 572 | 32,27 | 14 |
| Improstructure - an improvisational perspective on SMART infrastructure governance | Offenhuber, D., Schechtner, K. | 1394 | 69,85 | 24 |

continued on following page

*Table 10. Continued*

| Article | Authors | TC | CPY | H-INDEX |
|---|---|---|---|---|
| Innovative public-private partnership to support SMART City: the case of Chaire REVES | Dupont, L; Morel, L; Guidat, C | 1207 | 64,06 | 29 |
| Leadership in, of, and for SMART cities - case studies from Europe, America, and Australia | Sancino, A; Hudson, L | 1607 | 116,16 | 24 |
| Performance of an internet of things project in the public sector: The case of Nice SMART city | Grimaldi, D., Fernandez, V. | 1416 | 108,75 | 29 |
| Reforming traditional PPP models to cope with the challenges of SMART cities | Cruz, C.O., Sarmento, J.M. | 37457 | 2093,34 | 484 |
| Systematic review of SMART cities and climate change adaptation | Huang-Lachmann, J.-T. | 101 | 12,63 | 4 |
| The land rent as a tool for reuse of existing real estate (against the policy of unsustainable growth of "new" real estate development) | Cerasoli, M., Mattarocci, G. | 150 | 12,19 | 9 |
| The more the better? The role of stakeholder information processing in complex urban innovation projects for green transformation | Kroh, J; Schultz, C | 1178 | 91,07 | 19 |
| The role of public-private partnership in constructing the SMART transportation city: a case of the bike sharing platform | Li, L., Park, P., Yang, S.-B. | 2556 | 276,54 | 29 |
| **Total** | | **68574** | **3721,6** | **880** |

*Table 11. Bibliometric indicators for the analysis of the impact of the journals*

| Article Title | Source Title | TC | CPY | H-INDEX |
|---|---|---|---|---|
| A model for the analysis of data-driven innovation and value generation in SMART cities' ecosystems | Cities | 121549 | 5376,39 | 885 |
| A SMART City Is a Collaborative Community: LESSONS FROM SMART AARHUS | CALIFORNIA MANAGEMENT REVIEW | 27690 | 1107,6 | 179 |
| Applicability of public-private partnerships in SMART infrastructure development: the case of Hong Kong | INTERNATIONAL JOURNAL OF CONSTRUCTION MANAGEMENT | 5583 | 372,2 | 46 |
| DTI-BR model applied in Foz do Iguacu, Brazil, for its transformation into a SMART tourism destination | JOURNAL OF INFRASTRUCTURE POLICY AND DEVELOPMENT | 13074 | 568,43 | 97 |
| Factors influencing the consideration of Public-Private Partnerships (PPP) for SMART city projects: Evidence from Hong Kong | Cities | 2111 | 84,44 | 55 |
| Implementation of Social Media Concepts for e-Government: Case Study of a Social Media Tool for Value Co-Creation and Citizen Participation | JOURNAL OF ORGANIZATIONAL AND END USER COMPUTING | 7609 | 362,33 | 62 |
| Improstructure - an improvisational perspective on SMART infrastructure governance | Cities | 247 | 35,28 | 10 |
| Innovative public-private partnership to support SMART City: the case of Chaire REVES | JOURNAL OF STRATEGY AND MANAGEMENT | 11932 | 477,28 | 155 |
| Leadership in, of, and for SMART cities - case studies from Europe, America, and Australia | PUBLIC MANAGEMENT REVIEW | 43678 | 1747,12 | 127 |
| Performance of an internet of things project in the public sector: The case of Nice SMART city | Journal of High Technology Management Research | 304 | 27,64 | 13 |
| Reforming traditional PPP models to cope with the challenges of SMART cities | Competition and Regulation in Network Industries | 0 | 0 | 0 |

| Article Title | Source Title | TC | CPY | H-INDEX |
|---|---|---|---|---|
| Systematic review of SMART cities and climate change adaptation | Sustainability Accounting, Management and Policy Journal | 702 | 87,75 | 15 |
| The land rent as a tool for reuse of existing real estate (against the policy of unsustainable growth of "new" real estate development) | Valori e Valutazioni | 1963 | 122,69 | 32 |
| The more the better? The role of stakeholder information processing in complex urban innovation projects for green transformation | INTERNATIONAL JOURNAL OF PROJECT MANAGEMENT | 3735 | 266,79 | 48 |
| The role of public-private partnership in constructing the SMART transportation city: a case of the bike sharing platform | Asia Pacific Journal of Tourism Research | 2921 | 116,84 | 46 |
| **Total** | | **243098** | **10752,78** | **1770** |

*Table 12. Ranking of SMART Cities by PPP projects Citation Classics in terms of TC*

| Articles | TOTAL CITATION | | | RANKING OF | | | TOTAL | TC RANKING |
|---|---|---|---|---|---|---|---|---|
| | Articles | Authors | Journals | Articles | Authors | Journals | | |
| A model for the analysis of data-driven innovation and value generation in SMART cities' ecosystems | 253 | 2626 | 121549 | 1 | 4 | 1 | 6 | **1** |
| A SMART City Is a Collaborative Community: LESSONS FROM SMART AARHUS | 227 | 7271 | 27690 | 2 | 3 | 3 | 8 | **2** |
| Leadership in, of, and for SMART cities - case studies from Europe, America, and Australia | 99 | 1607 | 43678 | 4 | 6 | 2 | 12 | **3** |
| Innovative public-private partnership to support SMART City: the case of Chaire REVES | 92 | 1207 | 11932 | 6 | 9 | 5 | 20 | **4** |
| Applicability of public-private partnerships in SMART infrastructure development: the case of Hong Kong | 20 | 9879 | 5583 | 12 | 2 | 7 | 21 | **5** |
| Implementation of Social Media Concepts for e-Government: Case Study of a Social Media Tool for Value Co-Creation and Citizen Participation | 95 | 572 | 7609 | 5 | 12 | 6 | 23 | **6** |
| Reforming traditional PPP models to cope with the challenges of SMART cities | 60 | 37457 | 0 | 7 | 1 | 15 | 23 | **7** |
| The role of public-private partnership in constructing the SMART transportation city: a case of the bike sharing platform | 23 | 2556 | 2921 | 11 | 5 | 9 | 25 | **8** |

continued on following page

*Table 13. Continued*

| Articles | TOTAL CITATION | | | RANKING OF | | | TOTAL | TC RANKING |
|---|---|---|---|---|---|---|---|---|
| | Articles | Authors | Journals | Articles | Authors | Journals | | |
| Factors influencing the consideration of Public-Private Partnerships (PPP) for SMART city projects: Evidence from Hong Kong | 125 | 418 | 2111 | 3 | 13 | 10 | 26 | **9** |
| DTI-BR model applied in Foz do Iguacu, Brazil, for its transformation into a SMART tourism destination | 4 | 742 | 13074 | 14 | 11 | 4 | 29 | **10** |
| Performance of an internet of things project in the public sector: The case of Nice SMART city | 26 | 1416 | 304 | 10 | 7 | 13 | 30 | **11** |
| Improstructure - an improvisational perspective on SMART infrastructure governance | 27 | 1394 | 247 | 9 | 8 | 14 | 31 | **12** |
| The more the better? The role of stakeholder information processing in complex urban innovation projects for green transformation | 6 | 1178 | 3735 | 13 | 10 | 8 | 31 | **13** |
| Systematic review of SMART cities and climate change adaptation | 52 | 101 | 702 | 8 | 15 | 12 | 35 | **14** |
| The land rent as a tool for reuse of existing real estate (against the policy of unsustainable growth of "new" real estate development) | 3 | 150 | 1963 | 15 | 14 | 11 | 40 | **15** |

*Table 13. Ranking of SMART Cities by PPP projects Citation Classics in terms of CPY*

| Articles | CITATION PER YEAR | | | RANKING OF | | | TOTAL | CPY RANKING |
|---|---|---|---|---|---|---|---|---|
| | Articles | Authors | Journals | Articles | Authors | Journals | | |
| A model for the analysis of data-driven innovation and value generation in SMART cities' ecosystems | 36,14 | 131,74 | 5376,39 | 1 | 5 | 1 | 7 | **1** |
| A SMART City Is a Collaborative Community: LESSONS FROM SMART AARHUS | 28,38 | 160,88 | 1107,6 | 3 | 4 | 3 | 10 | **2** |
| Leadership in, of, and for SMART cities - case studies from Europe, America, and Australia | 24,75 | 116,16 | 1747,12 | 4 | 6 | 2 | 12 | **3** |
| Applicability of public-private partnerships in SMART infrastructure development: the case of Hong Kong | 20 | 431,28 | 372,2 | 5 | 2 | 6 | 13 | **4** |

continued on following page

*Table 14. Continued*

| Articles | CITATION PER YEAR | | | RANKING OF | | | TOTAL | CPY RANKING |
|---|---|---|---|---|---|---|---|---|
| | Articles | Authors | Journals | Articles | Authors | Journals | | |
| Factors influencing the consideration of Public-Private Partnerships (PPP) for SMART city projects: Evidence from Hong Kong | 31,25 | 83,6 | 84,44 | 2 | 9 | 12 | 23 | **5** |
| The role of public-private partnership in constructing the SMART transportation city: a case of the bike sharing platform | 7,67 | 276,54 | 116,84 | 10 | 3 | 10 | 23 | **6** |
| Innovative public-private partnership to support SMART City: the case of Chaire REVES | 10,22 | 64,06 | 477,28 | 8 | 11 | 5 | 24 | **7** |
| Reforming traditional PPP models to cope with the challenges of SMART cities | 8,57 | 2093,34 | 0 | 9 | 1 | 15 | 25 | **8** |
| Implementation of Social Media Concepts for e-Government: Case Study of a Social Media Tool for Value Co-Creation and Citizen Participation | 11,88 | 32,27 | 362,33 | 6 | 13 | 7 | 26 | **9** |
| The more the better? The role of stakeholder information processing in complex urban innovation projects for green transformation | 6 | 91,07 | 266,79 | 11 | 8 | 8 | 27 | **10** |
| DTI-BR model applied in Foz do Iguacu, Brazil, for its transformation into a SMART tourism destination | 4 | 37,24 | 568,43 | 14 | 12 | 4 | 30 | **11** |
| Systematic review of SMART cities and climate change adaptation | 10,4 | 12,63 | 87,75 | 7 | 14 | 11 | 32 | **12** |
| Performance of an internet of things project in the public sector: The case of Nice SMART city | 5,2 | 108,75 | 27,64 | 12 | 7 | 14 | 33 | **13** |
| Improstructure - an improvisational perspective on SMART infrastructure governance | 4,5 | 69,85 | 35,28 | 13 | 10 | 13 | 36 | **14** |
| The land rent as a tool for reuse of existing real estate (against the policy of unsustainable growth of "new" real estate development) | 0,75 | 12,19 | 122,69 | 15 | 15 | 9 | 39 | **15** |

*Table 14. Ranking of SMART Cities by PPP projects Citation Classics in terms of H INDEX*

| Article | H-INDEX | | | RANKING OF | | | TOTAL | H-INDEX RANKING |
|---|---|---|---|---|---|---|---|---|
| | Articles | Authors | Journals | Articles | Authors | Journals | | |
| A model for the analysis of data-driven innovation and value generation in SMART cities' ecosystems | 1 | 42 | 885 | 1 | 4 | 1 | 6 | **1** |
| A SMART City Is a Collaborative Community: LESSONS FROM SMART AARHUS | 1 | 57 | 179 | 1 | 3 | 2 | 6 | **2** |
| Innovative public-private partnership to support SMART City: the case of Chaire REVES | 1 | 29 | 155 | 1 | 7 | 3 | 11 | **3** |
| Applicability of public-private partnerships in SMART infrastructure development: the case of Hong Kong | 1 | 93 | 46 | 1 | 2 | 9 | 12 | **4** |
| Leadership in, of, and for SMART cities - case studies from Europe, America, and Australia | 1 | 24 | 127 | 1 | 8 | 4 | 13 | **5** |
| The role of public-private partnership in constructing the SMART transportation city: a case of the bike sharing platform | 1 | 29 | 46 | 1 | 5 | 10 | 16 | **6** |
| Reforming traditional PPP models to cope with the challenges of SMART cities | 1 | 484 | 0 | 1 | 1 | 15 | 17 | **7** |
| DTI-BR model applied in Foz do Iguacu, Brazil, for its transformation into a SMART tourism destination | 1 | 12 | 97 | 1 | 12 | 5 | 18 | **8** |
| Implementation of Social Media Concepts for e-Government: Case Study of a Social Media Tool for Value Co-Creation and Citizen Participation | 1 | 14 | 62 | 1 | 11 | 6 | 18 | **9** |
| The more the better? The role of stakeholder information processing in complex urban innovation projects for green transformation | 1 | 19 | 48 | 1 | 10 | 8 | 19 | **10** |
| Performance of an internet of things project in the public sector: The case of Nice SMART city | 1 | 29 | 13 | 1 | 6 | 13 | 20 | **11** |

| Article | H-INDEX | | | RANKING OF | | | TOTAL | H-INDEX RANKING |
|---|---|---|---|---|---|---|---|---|
| | Articles | Authors | Journals | Articles | Authors | Journals | | |
| Factors influencing the consideration of Public-Private Partnerships (PPP) for SMART city projects: Evidence from Hong Kong | 1 | 11 | 55 | 1 | 13 | 7 | 21 | **12** |
| Improstructure - an improvisational perspective on SMART infrastructure governance | 1 | 24 | 10 | 1 | 9 | 14 | 24 | **13** |
| The land rent as a tool for reuse of existing real estate (against the policy of unsustainable growth of "new" real estate development) | 1 | 9 | 32 | 1 | 14 | 11 | 26 | **14** |
| Systematic review of SMART cities and climate change adaptation | 1 | 4 | 15 | 1 | 15 | 12 | 28 | **15** |

# Chapter 13 The Revolution of Territorial Management Through the Adoption of Emerging Innovations: A Qualitative Study of the Casablanca-Settat Region

**Hanae Amrani**
*Faculty of Legal, Economic and Social Sciences, Sidi Mohamed Ben Abdellah University, Fez, Morocco*

**Zouheir Boussouf**
https://orcid.org/0009-0002-5970-2923
*Faculty of Legal, Economic and Social Sciences, Sidi Mohamed Ben Abdellah University, Fez, Morocco*

**Ahmed Aftiss**
https://orcid.org/0009-0002-6211-4065
*Faculty of Legal, Economic and Social Sciences, Sidi Mohamed Ben Abdellah University, Fez, Morocco*

## ABSTRACT

*In recent years, the Casablanca-Settat region has initiated a transformative journey by integrating emerging technologies into its territorial management. This study examines the impact of innovations like artificial intelligence, big data, and smart city initiatives on local governance and development. Grounded in an interpretivist framework, the research employs semi-structured interviews with municipal officials, project coordinators, and representatives from research institutions and NGOs.*

DOI: 10.4018/979-8-3693-6854-1.ch013

*Findings highlight that while these technologies enhance resource management, citizen engagement, and service delivery, challenges persist, including infrastructure limitations, data security concerns, and resistance to change. Additionally, the potential of these technologies to drive economic and social advancement in the region is underscored. The study concludes with strategic recommendations to harness technological innovations for sustainable and inclusive development in Casablanca-Settat, offering valuable insights for policymakers and future research*

## 1. INTRODUCTION

The digital era has profoundly transformed the practices of territorial management and development. The adoption of emerging technologies such as artificial intelligence (AI) and big data offers unprecedented opportunities to optimize governance, improve the efficiency of public services, and stimulate innovation and territorial attractiveness. However, while these technologies hold great potential, their integration into territorial management also raises significant methodological and practical challenges that demand thorough examination.

The study of emerging technologies in territorial management has become particularly important in developing countries, where the need for enhanced governance is critical. Theoretical frameworks such as New Public Management (NPM) and digital governance provide valuable lenses for understanding how these technologies can reform public administration and improve service delivery. NPM emphasizes efficiency, accountability, and results-based governance, focusing on achieving measurable outcomes. In contrast, digital governance highlights the role of digital tools in promoting transparency, improving citizen engagement, and fostering participatory decision-making processes (Benner, 2020; Batty et al., 2012).

In Morocco, the Casablanca-Settat region presents a compelling case for examining the intersection of technology and territorial management. Local authorities in this region face the dual challenge of modernizing their governance practices while addressing socio-economic and infrastructural disparities. This research aims to explore the perceptions and experiences of these authorities regarding the adoption of emerging technologies, focusing on both the opportunities they offer such as more efficient resource allocation and enhanced public services and the challenges, including technological adaptation and digital literacy gaps. By adopting a qualitative methodological approach, this study seeks to contribute to the broader discourse on sustainable development and effective governance in both urban and rural settings, with a particular emphasis on the Moroccan context.

The central issue of this study is: "***How can the use of emerging technologies transform territorial management in the Casablanca-Settat region***?" This question is broken down into several research areas:

**Question 1:** What are the specific impacts of artificial intelligence and big data on innovation and territorial attractiveness in the Casablanca-Settat region?

**Question 2:** How can technologies such as chatbots improve the efficiency of public services and citizen participation?

**Question 3**: What are the main challenges and opportunities faced by local authorities in integrating these technologies?

**Question 4:** What strategies can be adopted to maximize the benefits of emerging technologies while minimizing risks?

The objective of this manuscript is to explore the influence of emerging technologies on territorial management in the Casablanca-Settat region and to identify the innovation and economic specialization strategies made possible by these technologies, while also proposing recommendations for the successful integration of technologies within the framework of territorial governance. The following research propositions will guide this study:

**Proposition 1**: The integration of artificial intelligence and big data into territorial management significantly improves innovation and the attractiveness of territories in the Casablanca-Settat region.

**Proposition 2:** Technologies such as chatbots increase the efficiency of public services and foster increased citizen participation in the Casablanca-Settat region.

**Proposition 3:** Local authorities face major challenges, such as training and cost issues, when adopting emerging technologies, but they also identify significant opportunities to improve territorial management.

**Proposition 4:** Specific strategies can be implemented to maximize the benefits of emerging technologies while minimizing associated risks, thereby contributing to more effective and inclusive territorial governance.

This study will rely on a comprehensive literature review on the subject and will adopt a qualitative methodological approach to explore and understand the influence of emerging technologies on territorial management. To do so, the study will focus on the local authorities of the Casablanca-Settat region. A representative sample will be selected, including municipal officials, local elected representatives, and community representatives.

Data will be collected through semi-structured interviews with key actors from the local authorities in the region. These interviews will provide insights into the perceptions, experiences, and expectations of local actors regarding the use of technologies in territorial management. The qualitative data analysis will be conducted using a thematic analysis method to identify the main themes and recurring patterns. This analysis will allow conclusions to be drawn on the impacts, challenges, and opportunities associated with the integration of emerging technologies into territorial management, utilizing the NVIVO 10 software.

The integration of emerging technologies into territorial management offers promising prospects for improving governance and stimulating local development. This study aims to provide an overview of the literature on the subject and an in-depth analysis of the experiences and strategies of local authorities in the Casablanca-Settat region, thereby offering practical recommendations for the successful adoption of these technologies.

This study is structured into several key sections to provide a comprehensive analysis of territorial management and the adoption of emerging technologies in the Casablanca-Settat region. The literature review is divided into two main parts: territorial modernization and management: concepts and dimensions which explores the theoretical foundations and key dimensions of territorial management, and territorial management in morocco: evolution, adoption of emerging technologies, and innovative reforms focusing on the evolution of territorial management in Morocco and the integration of new technologies. The methodology section outlines the qualitative approach used, including semi-structured interviews with key stakeholders, and the thematic analysis conducted using NVIVO 10 software. The discussion of results highlights the opportunities and challenges posed by these technologies, offering strategic recommendations for their effective implementation. Finally, the study concludes by summarizing the findings, discussing the implications for future research, and presenting the perspectives for sustainable and inclusive development in the region.

## 2. LITERATURE REVIEW

### 2.1. Territorial Modernization and Management: Concepts and Dimensions

Territorial management has evolved over the centuries, influenced by political, economic, and social factors. Historically, territorial management practices were often centralized, with decisions made by government authorities detached from local realities. For example, in many European countries, territorial management has been characterized by top-down approaches, where central governments dictated policies without considering local specifics (Rodríguez-Pose, 2018).

In recent decades, however, a trend toward decentralization and local governance has emerged, favoring more participative approaches tailored to the needs of local communities. This evolution has been particularly pronounced in countries like Canada and Australia, where reforms have been implemented to strengthen municipal powers and encourage citizen participation in decision-making (Kooiman, 2003).

In the context of public sector modernization and the implementation of New Public Management (NPM) principles, the concept of territory has evolved into a major strategic issue. Territories are no longer perceived merely as static geographical entities; instead, they are now recognized as dynamic spaces where socio-economic interactions converge and where public policies are actively implemented. This shift underscores the importance of effective territorial management in addressing contemporary challenges such as urban growth, sustainable resource management, and the overall improvement of citizens' quality of life (OECD, 2021).

Territorial management refers to the comprehensive processes and practices aimed at planning, organizing, coordinating, and evaluating resources and activities within a specific territory to promote balanced and sustainable development. According to Paquet and Roy (2021), territorial management "encompasses the management of infrastructure, public services, and the coordination among various local actors to optimize resources and meet the needs of local populations." This integrated approach is essential for promoting policy coherence, enhancing the quality of public services, and strengthening citizen participation. The modernization of territorial management processes and the integration of emerging technologies are increasingly seen as key levers for improving the performance of local administrations and fostering more inclusive and adaptive governance (Benner, 2020).

A systemic approach to territorial management that integrates economic, social, and environmental dimensions requires a comprehensive vision and effective coordination between public and private actors. This approach is vital to achieving sustainable development goals and enhancing the resilience of territories in the face of contemporary challenges (Houghton et al., 2022). The application of NPM principles, such as performance orientation and the accountability of public managers, is particularly relevant in the realm of territorial management. The modernization of practices and the strategic use of advanced technologies play a crucial role in optimizing decision-making processes and improving services for citizens (Smith & Houghton, 2023).

Territories are increasingly seen as pivotal nodes of governance where local, regional, and national policies intersect (Swyngedouw, 2005; Brenner, 2004). They are spaces where public institutions, private entities, and civil society converge to address the complex and interrelated challenges of modern governance (Rodríguez-Pose & Gill, 2004). This convergence necessitates a shift in how territories are managed, moving away from traditional, top-down approaches toward more participative, networked forms of governance that emphasize collaboration and stakeholder engagement (Ansell & Gash, 2008; Jessop, 2016). The modernized management of territories thus becomes a strategic imperative for achieving broader public sector objectives, including economic competitiveness, social cohesion, and environmental sustainability (Healey, 1997; Bulkeley & Betsill, 2005).

The integration of emerging technologies into territorial management is one of the most significant aspects of this modernization process (Kitchin, 2014; Batty, 2013). Technologies such as Geographic Information Systems (GIS), artificial intelligence (AI), and big data analytics offer new tools for managing territories more effectively (Goodchild, 2007; Silva & Khan, 2020). GIS, for instance, provides spatial insights that are crucial for urban planning, infrastructure development, and resource management (Longley et al., 2005; Tomlinson, 2007). AI and big data analytics enable more informed decision-making by offering predictive models and data-driven insights that optimize the allocation of resources and streamline public services (Manyika et al., 2011; Agrawal et al., 2018). The use of these technologies can significantly enhance the efficiency of territorial management by improving the accuracy of planning processes, increasing the responsiveness of public services, and fostering greater transparency and accountability (Brynjolfsson & McAfee, 2014; Janssen et al., 2012).

However, adopting these technologies presents several significant challenges. Infrastructure limitations, particularly in remote or underserved areas, often hinder the broad implementation of advanced technological tools (Graham & Marvin, 2001; Unwin, 2009). High financial costs related to both the adoption of new technologies and the modernization of outdated infrastructure remain critical concerns, as they can exacerbate inequalities in access to technological innovations (Bourne, 2018; Sassen, 2012). Additionally, resistance to change is common among local administrative staff, particularly those who may lack the necessary technical expertise to effectively utilize these innovations (Van der Voet, 2014; Pollitt & Bouckaert, 2011). Addressing this resistance necessitates a robust strategy focused on building capacity within local administrations, with a particular emphasis on continuous professional development and the implementation of targeted training programs that cater to the unique needs of territorial managers (Brown & Duguid, 1991; Kunda, 2009).

Data security and privacy concerns further complicate the adoption process, necessitating the development of robust strategies to protect sensitive information and maintain public trust. Ensuring the ethical use of technology is paramount, particularly in the context of public sector management, where the consequences of data breaches or misuse can be far-reaching. Therefore, comprehensive data security frameworks must be developed and implemented to address these concerns, ensuring that the integration of emerging technologies into territorial management is both effective and secure.

Estonia is often cited as a success story in digital transformation, thanks to its robust digital infrastructure, which enables efficient data management and public services. The country has invested in advanced security systems and taken a proactive approach to educating citizens about data security, thereby fostering significant trust in its digital services. This experience could serve as a model for Morocco, highlighting the importance of strong infrastructure and digital literacy for citizens. Similarly, India, with its "Digital India" program, faced infrastructure challenges, particularly in rural areas. However, initiatives such as the use of mobile technologies to deliver government services have helped overcome these obstacles. By integrating solutions tailored to local contexts, India has shown that it is possible to improve access to services while addressing infrastructure limitations. These examples demonstrate that, while challenges exist, innovative solutions can be implemented to overcome them. For Morocco, adopting a similar approach by investing in digital infrastructure and developing data security awareness programs, while engaging local stakeholders in the digital transformation process, would be highly beneficial. By delving deeper into these challenges and drawing inspiration from international examples, we can offer a more comprehensive perspective on the obstacles to adopting emerging technologies and potential strategies to overcome them.

The principles of New Public Management (NPM) offer a crucial framework for addressing the complexities of contemporary territorial management. NPM underscores the significance of performance measurement, accountability, and the integration of private sector management practices within the public sector (Hood, 1991; Pollitt & Bouckaert, 2011). In the realm of territorial management, these principles translate into a focus on achieving tangible outcomes, optimizing resource utilization, and continuously improving public services (Osborne & Gaebler, 1992; Talbot, 2005). By embracing these NPM principles, territorial managers can enhance their strategic effectiveness and ensure that public resources are allocated and used in ways that maximize their overall impact (Barzelay, 2001; Hood & Peters, 2004).

Performance measurement plays a critical role in territorial management by offering a systematic approach to assessing the effectiveness of public services and pinpointing areas for enhancement. It enables territorial managers to make data-driven decisions regarding resource allocation, prioritization of interventions, and improvements in service delivery (Kusek & Rist, 2004; Lavertu, 2017). This emphasis on outcomes supports broader objectives of sustainable development and social equity, ensuring that management practices positively impact the long-term welfare of local communities (Bourgon, 2008; Lee & Fargher, 2018).

Moreover, the effectiveness of territorial management is closely linked to the coherence of public policies and the active engagement of stakeholders. Policy coherence involves aligning various policies and initiatives to ensure they reinforce each other and contribute to shared goals (Gertler, 2004; Howlett & Ramesh, 2003). This requires coordination among different levels of government and between public and private sectors to ensure that policies are implemented consistently with sustainable development objectives. Additionally, stakeholder engagement is essential, as involving citizens, businesses, and civil society organizations in decision-making processes enhances the legitimacy and effectiveness of management strategies (Arnstein, 1969; Linders, 2012). Engaging stakeholders helps public managers understand community needs and priorities, builds trust, and fosters a sense of ownership over the outcomes of territorial management initiatives.

The modernization of territorial management is a complex but necessary process that requires a comprehensive approach integrating economic, social, and environmental dimensions. By embracing the principles of New Public Management and leveraging emerging technologies, territorial managers can enhance the efficiency and effectiveness of their strategies, ensuring that public resources are used in a manner that maximizes their impact and contributes to the long-term well-being of local populations.

## 2.2. Territorial Management in Morocco: Evolution, Adoption of Emerging Technologies, and Innovative Reforms

Territorial management has undergone significant transformation over time. Initially characterized by centralized and often rigid administration, this model focused primarily on planning and control from higher levels of government (Rodríguez-Pose, 2018). However, the rise of decentralization and local governance principles—driven by the need for greater flexibility and adaptation—has led to the adoption of more participatory approaches tailored to local specifics (Kooiman, 2003).

In Morocco, the digital revolution in territorial management has been marked by initiatives aimed at modernizing local administrations and integrating digital technologies into management processes. These reforms include decentralization efforts, the implementation of Geographic Information Systems (GIS) for enhanced urban planning, and the development of digital platforms to improve public services and citizen participation (El Moutawakil et al., 2022).

For instance, Sweden and the Netherlands have successfully incorporated advanced technologies into their territorial management practices. They utilize GIS to optimize urban planning and resource management and have developed digital platforms to facilitate citizen engagement and enhance the transparency of decision-making processes (OECD, 2021).

In contrast, while Morocco has made significant strides in integrating digital technologies, challenges persist, particularly regarding infrastructure and access to information. The Moroccan experience, with its focus on modernizing local administrations and adopting digital technologies, represents an emerging model that aligns with global trends while addressing local specifics.

The following table reflects the key reforms and initiatives in Morocco's Territorial Management:

*Table 1. Reforms and Initiatives in Territorial Management in Morocco*

| Domain | Reforms / initiatives | Objectives and benefits | References |
|---|---|---|---|
| **Decentralization and local governance** | Strengthening decentralization, creation of new administrative regions | - Bring decision making closer to citizens<br>- Improved responsiveness of local administrations | Berrada & Benkhlil (2021) |
| **Geographic Information Systems (GIS)** | Development and use of GIS for urban and rural planning | - Better management of infrastructures<br>- Mapping of resources and analysis of growth dynamics | Mouline & EL Bouazzati (2022) |
| **Digital Platforms and E-Governance** | Introduction of electronic counters and digital platforms for administrative services | - Improved access to public services<br>- Reduced red tape<br>- Increased transparency | Chouikh & Sahraoui (2023) |
| **Citizen Participation and Transparency** | Use of technologies for citizen participation and transparency of decision-making processes | - Engagement des citoyens dans les décisions locales<br>- Monitoring of development projects<br>- Increased transparency | Naciri & El Ouazzani (2024) |

**Source:** Prepared by the authors.

Digital technologies have become a transformative force in territorial management, significantly enhancing the efficiency, resilience, and sustainability of how territories are governed and developed (Gordon & DeSouza, 2019; Batty et al., 2012). The integration of Big Data, artificial intelligence (AI), and Internet of Things (IoT)-based monitoring systems marks a major advancement in the management of territories, offering a wide range of benefits that go beyond traditional approaches (Cheng et al., 2020; Kitchin, 2014). These technologies are revolutionizing the way data is collected, analyzed, and utilized, leading to optimized resource management, improved decision-making, and better alignment with future needs (Hwang & Zhang, 2021; Pirotti et al., 2015).

The influence of digital technologies in territorial management is evident in their ability to streamline operations and reduce costs (Zook et al., 2017; Kitchin, 2014). Big Data, AI, and IoT enable real-time data collection and analysis, providing decision-makers with critical insights that can be used to optimize resource allocation and improve infrastructure maintenance (Miller et al., 2020; Guo et al., 2017). For instance, IoT-based monitoring systems can detect early signs of wear and tear in infrastructure, allowing for preventive maintenance that reduces downtime and extends the lifespan of critical assets (Wang et al., 2020; Albahari et al., 2017). This not only lowers operational costs but also ensures that infrastructure remains in good condition, thereby enhancing the overall quality of public services (Hwang & Zhang, 2021; Gordon & DeSouza, 2019).

Predictive analytics and data-driven insights, made possible by AI and Big Data, are also playing a crucial role in territorial management (Cheng et al., 2020; Pirotti et al., 2015). By analyzing historical and real-time data, these technologies can identify trends and patterns that help predict future needs and challenges (Guo et al., 2017; Miller et al., 2020). This foresight allows for more strategic planning and decision-making, ensuring that territories are better prepared to address emerging issues (Hwang & Zhang, 2021; Batty et al., 2012). For example, AI-driven models can predict traffic congestion patterns, enabling urban planners to design more efficient transportation networks that reduce traffic and improve mobility for citizens (Zook et al., 2017; Albahari et al., 2017). Similarly, predictive analytics can be used to forecast demand for public services, allowing for better resource allocation and ensuring that citizens' needs are met more effectively (Cheng et al., 2020; Pirotti et al., 2015).

The impact of digital technologies on territorial management extends to enhancing resilience and security (Wang et al., 2020; Guo et al., 2017). Intelligent surveillance systems, powered by AI and IoT, provide real-time monitoring of critical infrastructure and public spaces, enabling rapid response to emergencies and improving public safety (Albahari et al., 2017; Cheng et al., 2020). For example, AI-driven surveillance systems can detect unusual patterns of behavior that may indicate a security threat, allowing authorities to respond quickly and prevent potential incidents (Gordon & DeSouza, 2019; Hwang & Zhang, 2021). Additionally, these technologies can be used to monitor environmental conditions, such as air quality and water levels, helping to mitigate the impact of natural disasters and improve disaster preparedness (Kitchin, 2014; Miller et al., 2020).

Moreover, digital technologies are fostering greater citizen participation and transparency in territorial management (Batty et al., 2012; Zook et al., 2017). By providing personalized public services and engaging citizens in the decision-making process, these technologies are making governance more inclusive and responsive to the needs of the population (Cheng et al., 2020; Wang et al., 2020). For instance, digital platforms that allow citizens to provide feedback on public services or participate in local government decision-making processes are helping to build trust between citizens and authorities (Hwang & Zhang, 2021; Guo et al., 2017). This increased transparency not only strengthens democracy but also ensures that public policies are more closely aligned with the needs and priorities of the population (Albahari et al., 2017; Miller et al., 2020).

In addition to improving governance, digital technologies are driving innovation and economic competitiveness in territories (Pirotti et al., 2015; Kitchin, 2014). By making territories more attractive for investment and supporting local entrepreneurship, these technologies are creating new opportunities for economic growth (Hwang & Zhang, 2021; Cheng et al., 2020). For example, the use of AI and Big

Data in economic planning can help identify sectors with high growth potential, allowing for targeted investments that stimulate job creation and boost local economies (Gordon & DeSouza, 2019; Wang et al., 2020). Similarly, IoT-based smart city initiatives can enhance the quality of life in urban areas, making them more attractive to businesses and residents alike (Zook et al., 2017; Batty et al., 2012).

Morocco is a prime example of a country actively integrating digital technologies into its territorial management (Albahari et al., 2017; Guo et al., 2017). The Moroccan government's commitment to modernizing its public administration and promoting sustainable development is reflected in its efforts to adopt emerging technologies such as AI (Cheng et al., 2020; Hwang & Zhang, 2021). The National Digital Development Strategy, particularly through the Maroc Numeric 2020 Plan, aims to promote technological innovation across various sectors, including territorial management (Gordon & DeSouza, 2019; Pirotti et al., 2015). This strategy emphasizes the importance of improving connectivity, increasing access to digital tools, and integrating these technologies into public services (Wang et al., 2020; Kitchin, 2014).

The Maroc Numeric 2020 Plan is a key component of Morocco's broader vision for digital transformation, which seeks to position the country as a leader in technological innovation in Africa (Zook et al., 2017; Batty et al., 2012). By investing in digital infrastructure and promoting the use of AI, Big Data, and IoT in public administration, Morocco is laying the groundwork for more efficient and effective territorial management (Guo et al., 2017; Hwang & Zhang, 2021). These efforts are expected to yield significant benefits, including improved public services, enhanced economic competitiveness, and greater social inclusion (Cheng et al., 2020; Miller et al., 2020).

Morocco's Vision 2030 further underscores the importance of innovation and technology in driving economic and social development (Albahari et al., 2017; Gordon & DeSouza, 2019). This vision highlights the need to modernize territorial infrastructure and develop smart cities as part of the country's broader strategy for sustainable development (Kitchin, 2014; Pirotti et al., 2015). The integration of digital technologies into territorial management is seen as a critical factor in achieving these goals, as it enables more efficient resource management, better urban planning, and improved service delivery (Cheng et al., 2020; Wang et al., 2020). The development of smart cities is a key focus of Morocco's Vision 2030, with the goal of optimizing urban management and enhancing the quality of life for citizens (Batty et al., 2012; Hwang & Zhang, 2021). Smart cities leverage digital technologies to create more efficient, sustainable, and livable urban environments (Zook et al., 2017; Guo et al., 2017). For example, IoT-based systems can be used to monitor and manage energy consumption, reducing waste and lowering costs (Miller et al., 2020; Cheng et al., 2020). Similarly, AI-driven traffic management systems can improve mobility and reduce congestion, making cities more accessible and reducing the environmental impact of transportation (Pirotti et al., 2015; Albahari et al., 2017).

In addition to improving urban management, smart cities also offer opportunities for economic growth and innovation (Kitchin, 2014; Gordon & DeSouza, 2019). By creating a more attractive environment for businesses and residents, smart cities can stimulate investment and support the development of new industries (Cheng et al., 2020; Wang et al., 2020). This, in turn, can lead to job creation and increased economic activity, further contributing to the overall development of the territory (Zook et al., 2017; Hwang & Zhang, 2021).

The integration of digital technologies into territorial management is not without challenges (Guo et al., 2017; Albahari et al., 2017). One of the primary obstacles is the need for significant investment in digital infrastructure, particularly in rural and remote areas (Cheng et al., 2020; Pirotti et al., 2015). Ensuring that all citizens have access to the benefits of digital technologies requires substantial resources, and addressing the digital divide is a key priority for policymakers (Gordon & DeSouza, 2019; Hwang & Zhang, 2021). Additionally, there is a need to build the technical capacity of public administration to effectively utilize these technologies (Kitchin, 2014; Miller et al., 2020). This includes training public officials and staff on the use of AI, Big Data, and IoT, as well as developing the necessary legal and regulatory frameworks to support their implementation (Zook et al., 2017; Albahari et al., 2017).

Data security and privacy concerns also represent significant challenges in the adoption of digital technologies in territorial management (Guo et al., 2017; Cheng et al., 2020). The collection and analysis of large amounts of data raise important questions about how this data is stored, used, and protected (Miller et al., 2020; Wang et al., 2020). Ensuring that citizens' data is secure and that their privacy is respected is essential for maintaining public trust and ensuring the ethical use of technology (Hwang & Zhang, 2021; Gordon & DeSouza, 2019).

Beyond the technical advancements offered by technologies such as artificial intelligence and data management systems, it is essential to examine their broader social, ethical, and equity-related impacts. Emerging technologies, particularly AI and Big Data, present significant challenges in terms of algorithmic biases, the digital divide, and social inequities (Eubanks, 2018). While these technologies are effective in optimizing territorial management, they also risk exacerbating social disparities if not accompanied by corrective measures (O'Neil, 2016). In the context of the Casablanca-Settat region, it is crucial to consider how these tools may influence citizens' access to public services and democratic participation (Citron & Pasquale, 2014). Therefore, a balanced approach is necessary—one that not only highlights technological progress but also addresses its impact on social equity. This will ensure that the integration of technologies supports inclusive and equitable development, fostering a territorial governance system that is both innovative and fair.

The integration of digital technologies into territorial management offers significant opportunities for improving the efficiency, resilience, and sustainability of governance (Cheng et al., 2020; Guo et al., 2017). By leveraging Big Data, AI, and IoT-based monitoring systems, territories can optimize resource management, enhance decision-making, and better align with future needs (Albahari et al., 2017; Batty et al., 2012). These technologies also promote greater citizen participation and transparency, driving innovation and economic competitiveness (Miller et al., 2020; Pirotti et al., 2015). Morocco's efforts to integrate emerging technologies into its territorial management processes serve as a model for other countries looking to modernize their public administration and promote sustainable development (Kitchin, 2014; Wang et al., 2020). However, realizing the full potential of these technologies requires addressing challenges related to infrastructure, technical capacity, data security, and privacy (Hwang & Zhang, 2021; Gordon & DeSouza, 2019). By continuing to invest in digital infrastructure and building the necessary legal and regulatory frameworks, Morocco can harness the power of digital technologies to achieve its Vision 2030 goals and create a more inclusive, sustainable, and prosperous future for all its citizens (Cheng et al., 2020; Albahari et al., 2017)

## 2.3. Theoretical Frameworks for Analyzing Technological Changes in Territorial Governance

To understand how emerging technologies can transform territorial management in the Casablanca-Settat region, it is crucial to rely on solid theoretical frameworks. Three main theories are particularly relevant for this analysis:

- **Sociotechnical Systems Theory:**

Developed by Emery and Trist (1960), this theory offers a systemic approach that considers both technical and social aspects in technology integration. In the context of territorial management, this theory helps understand how new technologies, such as Geographic Information Systems (GIS) and artificial intelligence, must be integrated not only at the technical level but also by considering social interactions and organizational dynamics. It emphasizes the importance of a design that combines technological innovation with the adaptation of local management practices to maximize effectiveness and acceptance of new solutions.

- **Diffusion of Innovations Theory:**

Proposed by Rogers (1962), this theory examines how, why, and at what rate new ideas and technologies spread within societies. It is essential for understanding the processes through which emerging technologies, such as Big Data and digital platforms, are adopted in the Casablanca-Settat region. This theory highlights the factors influencing technology adoption, such as the characteristics of innovations, the role of change agents, and potential barriers to diffusion. It also helps identify effective strategies for facilitating the acceptance and implementation of new technologies in territorial management practices.

- **Public Value Theory:**

Developed by Moore (1995), this theory focuses on creating value for citizens through public services and governance. In the context of territorial management, it provides a framework to assess how emerging technologies can improve the quality of public services, enhance transparency, and increase citizen engagement. It emphasizes how technological innovations can meet citizens' needs and improve overall well-being, while also highlighting the challenges and opportunities associated with integrating these technologies into management processes.

Integrating emerging technologies into territorial management necessitates a multifaceted theoretical approach. The interplay between technological and social elements must be carefully managed to ensure effective implementation. Understanding the dynamics of how technologies spread within a region is crucial for facilitating their adoption and overcoming potential barriers. Moreover, evaluating the value these technologies bring to public services and citizen engagement provides insight into their impact on governance and overall well-being. By considering these diverse perspectives, we gain a holistic view of how emerging technologies can transform territorial management, guiding successful integration and maximizing benefits for local development.

## 3. METHODOLOGY

This research employs an interpretivist epistemology to understand social phenomena through the perceptions and experiences of involved actors. As Schwandt (2014) notes, interpretivism focuses on the subjective meanings and interpretations that individuals assign to their experiences. This approach is particularly suited to exploring complex social dynamics, such as those encountered in territorial management, where interactions between various stakeholders are influenced by a range of contextual factors.

The study is designed as exploratory research to gain an in-depth understanding of the dynamics of territorial management in the Casablanca-Settat region. Exploratory research is appropriate when a phenomenon is not well understood and there is a need to investigate the underlying processes, structures, and relationships. This approach is ideal for exploring the unique and evolving characteristics of territorial management in this specific context.

The Casablanca-Settat region was selected for its economic significance, diverse urban-rural dynamics, and role as a technological innovation hub in Morocco. This choice ensures the study is conducted in a context that is both relevant and rich in the phenomena under investigation.

The sample size and selection align with the research objectives and methodological approach. Given the qualitative nature of the study, which prioritizes depth over breadth, the focus is on obtaining detailed, context-specific insights rather than achieving statistical generalizability. The sample will include seven key stakeholders, such as local government officials, technology providers, and community leaders, who are directly involved in or impacted by the implementation of emerging technologies in territorial management.

The selection of a focused sample allows for a thorough exploration of individual perspectives and the emergence of nuanced themes related to technology's impact on territorial management. Data collection will continue until saturation is achieved, ensuring comprehensive data that capture the complexity of the subject.

The research utilizes semi-structured interviews, which are advantageous for collecting rich, detailed data while allowing flexibility for participants to express their thoughts in their own words. The interview guides are structured around six main themes identified through a literature review and expert consultations. These themes include the integration of digital technologies, implementation challenges, the roles of public and private actors, impacts on citizen participation, and future prospects.

Data analysis will be conducted using NVivo software, which facilitates systematic organization and coding of qualitative data. NVivo's capabilities support thematic and content analysis of interview transcripts. Thematic analysis, as described by Braun and Clarke (2006), involves identifying, analyzing, and reporting patterns (themes) within data. This method helps to elucidate key themes and issues related to territorial management. Content analysis will complement this by quantifying and analyzing the presence of specific words, themes, or concepts within the data, providing a systematic examination of how topics are discussed by participants.

To ensure robustness, the interview guides were carefully developed and tailored to each participant's context. Themes and sub-themes are arranged logically to facilitate a smooth conversation flow, while allowing flexibility to adapt to the natural progression of discussions and emerging topics.

This methodological approach offers valuable insights into the practices and impacts of emerging technologies in territorial management. It explores how these technologies are implemented and their implications for local governance, resource management, and citizen engagement. The findings contribute to a deeper understanding of how digital innovations are transforming territorial management in the Casablanca-Settat region and provide guidance on improving governance and promoting sustainable development.

*Table 2. The Coding and Analysis Grid for Qualitative Data is Provided below the Table*

| **Interview Guide** | |
|---|---|
| **Themes** | **Sub-themes** |
| **1- The context** | The role and responsibility |
| **2- Adoption of Emerging Technologies** | The emerging technologies currently used by your administration for territorial management |
| | The main challenges encountered during the adoption of these technologies |
| **3- Impact of Emerging Technologies** | The change in management style |
| | The practices and effects of emerging technologies on management style |
| **4- Citizen Participation and Transparency** | The influence of technologies on citizen participation and transparency in decision-making processes |
| **5- Challenges and Strategies for the Future** | The main challenges in the future integration of emerging technologies |
| | The strategies adopted to overcome these challenges and maximize the benefits of emerging technologies |
| **6-Conclusion** | Suggestions for adopting emerging technologies in territorial management |

**Source:** developed by the authors.

The interview guide was tested with a local government department head. As a result of this test, several sub-themes were reformulated, and others were added. This allowed us to gain a better understanding of our research field

## 4. ISSUES, CONTROVERSIES AND PROBLEMS

This section presents the interpretations of the results obtained from the analysis of the collected data. It is an attempt to answer the research questions. Through this section, we aim to explore the perceptions of the interviewed stakeholders on the importance of using emerging technologies to transform the mode of territorial management in the Casablanca-Settat region.

The presentation of the field study results follows the approach of the interview guide, which aligns with the main research questions. The approach of both the interview guide and the analysis is conducted progressively, moving from the general to the specific. Thus, the questions and aspects addressed are explored in greater depth as the analysis progresses.

> **Q1:** Can you tell us about your role and responsibilities within the local administration of Casablanca?

The responses obtained during the interviews show a variety of roles and responsibilities within the local administration of the Casablanca-Settat region, each contributing to different aspects of urban management and regional development. Here are the key points that emerged from these responses:

- Diversity of Roles and Specialization
- Coordination and Collaboration
- Impact of Technology and Innovation
- Sustainable Development and Improvement of Living Conditions
- Implementation of Public Policies

### Observation 1

The results show a well-defined local administrative structure in the Casablanca-Settat region, with diversified and specialized roles that interact to manage the region. Coordination among stakeholders and the integration of emerging technologies play a crucial role in urban management and development. Efforts are also directed towards sustainable development and improving citizens' living conditions, with a strong commitment to the effective implementation of public policies.

> **Q2:** What emerging technologies are currently being used by your administration for territorial management?

The emerging technologies used in territorial management in the Casablanca-Settat region show a progressive and diversified integration to improve urban planning, infrastructure management, and citizen services. The responses from the interviewed stakeholders reveal several key points:

- Adoption of Geographic Information Systems (GIS)
- Integration of Artificial Intelligence (AI) and Big Data
- Use of IoT Sensors and Energy Management Solutions
- Digital Platforms for Access to Public Services
- Impact on Academic Programs
- Optimization of NGO Interventions

## Observation 2

The results show a growing and diversified adoption of emerging technologies in territorial management in the Casablanca-Settat region. GIS, AI, Big Data, IoT sensors, and digital platforms are being integrated to improve urban planning, infrastructure management, and access to public services. These technologies enable more efficient management, better decision-making, and resource optimization. The impact is also visible in academic programs and NGO interventions, highlighting their crucial role in modernizing and enhancing local services and development projects.

**Q3:** What have been the main challenges encountered in adopting these technologies?

The challenges encountered in adopting emerging technologies in territorial management in the Casablanca-Settat region reveal several critical aspects that require special attention. Here are the main points raised:

- Lack of Technical Skills
- High Financial Costs
- Infrastructure Modernization
- Resistance to Change
- Training and Competency Issues
- Data Security and Privacy Concerns
- Infrastructure Challenges in Remote Areas

## Observation 3

The main challenges encountered in the adoption of emerging technologies in the Casablanca-Settat region include a lack of technical skills, high financial costs, the need to modernize infrastructure, resistance to change, and training issues. Data security and infrastructure challenges in remote areas are also major concerns. To overcome these challenges, it is crucial to invest in training, seek external funding, modernize infrastructure, and promote the benefits of new technologies to stakeholders.

**Q4:** How have these technologies changed the way you manage public services and territorial resources?

Emerging technologies have had a significant impact on the management of public services and territorial resources in Casablanca. The responses from the interviewed stakeholders highlight several key transformations:

- Improved Planning and Infrastructure Management
- Reduced Delays and Increased Transparency
- Optimized Urban Resource Management
- Advanced Analysis and Resource Optimization
- Improved Data Quality and Responsiveness
- Enhanced Educational Offerings

## Observation 4

Emerging technologies have transformed the management of public services and territorial resources in the Casablanca-Settat region by improving planning and infrastructure management, reducing processing times, and increasing transparency. They have enabled more efficient resource management, in-depth analysis of needs using Big Data and AI, and optimized data quality and project responsiveness. Additionally, they have enriched the educational offerings, preparing students for future challenges. These technologies contribute to a better quality of life for citizens and a more modern and efficient management of cities.

**Q5:** Do you have concrete examples of improvements or benefits observed thanks to the use of these technologies?

The responses from the interviewed stakeholders show that the use of emerging technologies has led to concrete and tangible improvements in various areas of territorial management in the Casablanca-Settat region. The examples provided highlight several significant benefits:

- Optimization of Waste Collection Services
- Improved Water Resource Management
- Better Traffic and Air Quality Management
- Water and Sanitation Network Management
- Optimized Public Equipment Maintenance
- Strengthening University-Industry Links
- Support for Sustainable Agriculture

## Observation 5

Emerging technologies have brought concrete improvements in various areas of territorial management in the Casablanca-Settat region. The examples show significant benefits such as optimizing waste collection services, improving water resource management, better traffic and air quality management, and managing water and sanitation networks. The use of AI for public equipment maintenance, strengthening university-industry links, and supporting sustainable agriculture also illustrate the positive impacts of technologies on the quality of services and local projects.

**Q6:** Have technologies influenced citizen participation and transparency in decision-making processes?

The responses from the interviewed stakeholders reveal that technologies have had a significant impact on citizen participation and transparency in decision-making processes in the Casablanca region. The examples provided show how digital tools have transformed the way citizens interact with local authorities and how these authorities manage decision-making processes. Here are the main points that emerged:

- Real-Time Request Tracking and Participation
- Online Public Consultations
- Access to Information and Problem Reporting
- Transparency through Geographic Information Systems (GIS)
- Improved Communication and Transparency
- Access to Academic Information and Participation

## Observation 6

Emerging technologies have significantly influenced citizen participation and transparency in decision-making processes in the Casablanca region. Digital platforms have enabled citizens to track their requests, participate in public consultations, and report problems. GIS has facilitated access to mapping information and reinforced transparency. Digital tools have improved communication between local authorities and citizens, fostering more active engagement and better visibility of projects and interventions. In the academic sector, technologies have also improved access to information and stakeholder participation.

**Q7:** What are the main challenges you anticipate in the future integration of emerging technologies?

The responses from the interviewed stakeholders highlight several major challenges anticipated for the future integration of emerging technologies. These challenges primarily focus on financial aspects, change management, and the continuous updating of skills and technologies. Here are the main points that emerged:

- Sustainable Funding and Technological Updates
- Continuous Staff Training
- Resistance to Change
- System Compatibility and Integration
- Privacy and Data Security Management
- Equity of Access and Accessibility
- Updating Educational Content

## Observation 7

The future integration of emerging technologies presents several key challenges, including sustainable funding, continuous staff training, change management, system compatibility, data security, equity of access, and updating educational content. Stakeholders must prepare to address these challenges by investing in adequate financial resources, developing effective change management strategies, and ensuring continuous training and robust data protection. Ensuring equitable access to technologies and seamless integration with existing systems will be crucial to maximizing the benefits of technological innovations.

**Q8:** What strategies do you plan to overcome these challenges and maximize the benefits of emerging technologies?

The responses to the question about strategies for overcoming the challenges related to the integration of emerging technologies reveal several common and complementary approaches among the different stakeholders. Here are the main themes and strategies identified:

- Strengthening Partnerships
- Continuous Training and Awareness
- Investment in Innovation and Funding
- Development of Adequate Solutions
- Improvement of Management and Security Practices
- Promotion of Innovation and Transparency

## Observation 8

The strategies envisioned to maximize the benefits of emerging technologies include strengthening partnerships with technological and academic stakeholders, investing in continuous staff training, and increasing budgets for technology and innovation. Rigorous data management, security, and the development of tailored solutions to improve access are also priorities. Additionally, promoting innovation, transparency, and community engagement are essential for the successful and sustainable integration of emerging technologies.

> **Q9:** Do you have any additional comments or suggestions regarding the adoption of emerging technologies in territorial management?

The comments and suggestions provided regarding the adoption of emerging technologies in territorial management highlight several key aspects to ensure the success and effectiveness of these initiatives. Here are the main themes identified:

- Long-Term Vision and Flexibility
- Stakeholder Collaboration and Engagement
- Innovation and Inclusivity
- Communication and Transparency
- Investment in Research and Development
- Adaptation to the Local Context
- Support for Accessibility and Sustainable Development

## Observation 9

The comments and suggestions emphasize several strategies to optimize the adoption of emerging technologies in territorial management, including the need for a long-term vision and adaptive flexibility, collaboration with stakeholders, and balancing innovation with inclusivity. Communication, transparency, and investment in research and training are essential for the successful integration of technologies. Adapting technologies to the local context and supporting accessibility and sustainable development are also crucial aspects to maximize benefits and ensure a positive impact on communities.

It should be noted that here, we will present the word clouds related to the most relevant and revealing verbatim exchanges.

*Figure 1. Word Cloud of the Research Theme*

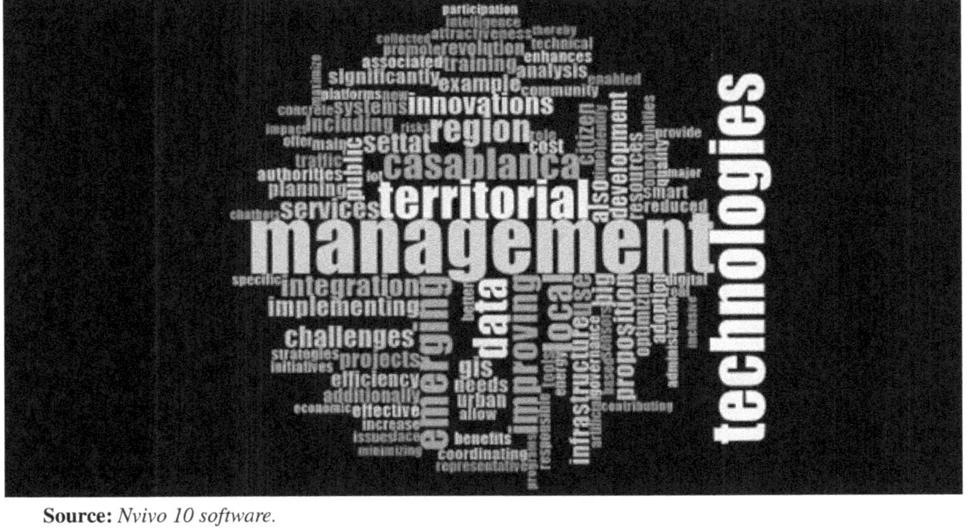


**Source:** *Nvivo 10 software.*

The word cloud figure above, generated from interviews coded with NVivo, highlights the key concepts discussed in this qualitative study on the adoption of emerging innovations in territorial management in the Casablanca-Settat region. The most frequent terms, such as "management," "technologies," "territorial," and "data," reveal the importance placed on digital transformation in territorial management. The prominence of "management" reflects the central idea that digital technologies are now at the heart of modern territorial management. This digital revolution is demonstrated through the increasing use of technological tools such as artificial intelligence (AI), Big Data, and Geographic Information Systems (GIS), which enhance decision-making and optimize the management of territorial resources. The appearance of “Casablanca” and “Settat” emphasizes the local focus of the study and reflects the specificities of these two regions, regarded as innovation laboratories where these technologies are being tested and implemented to address the challenges of rapid urbanization. Furthermore, terms like “challenges” and “efficiency” highlight both the opportunities and the difficulties associated with this transformation, particularly regarding skill adaptation and data governance. While the integration of these technologies offers promising prospects for more efficient and sustainable territorial management, it also requires proactive management of institutional and organizational obstacles. Overall, this visualization convincingly illustrates the evolution of territorial management practices under the influence of technological innovations, while also considering the local dynamics specific to the Casablanca-Settat region.

In the same vein, Nvivo 10 generated the following text search query:

*Figure 2. Text query from Nvivo 10*

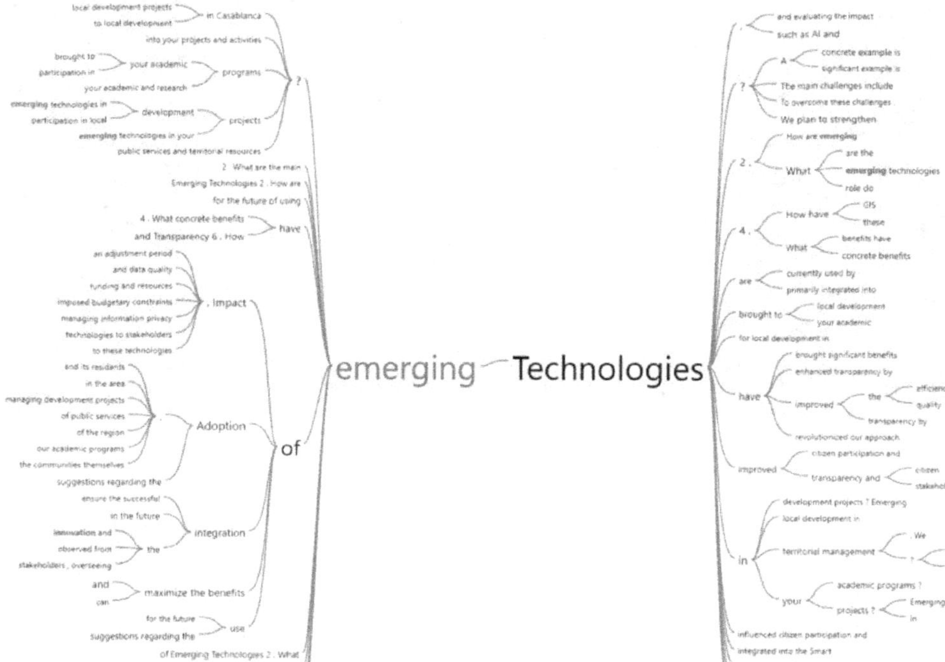


**Source:** *Nvivo 10 software.*

The visual representation generated by Nvivo 10 highlights the central theme of "Emerging Technologies," which plays a pivotal role in shaping territorial management practices. The concept map shows that the adoption of these technologies is closely tied to their impact on local development projects, public services, and citizen engagement in the Casablanca-Settat region. Key sub-themes include innovation, transparency, and integration, indicating that stakeholders are focused on how these emerging technologies can enhance efficiency, improve participation, and support the sustainable management of territorial resources. The map also reflects concerns regarding the challenges and benefits of implementing such innovations, pointing to a transformative shift in public administration through the use of advanced digital tools

In addition, the table below presents a summary of the various expressions from the respondents regarding the question of how the use of emerging technologies can transform territorial management in the Casablanca-Settat region.

*Table 3. Summary of the Expressions Collected from the Interviewees*

| Themes | Objectives | Categories, expressions |
|---|---|---|
| **Role and Responsibilities** | View the local actors' perception regarding their roles and responsibilities. | -The Director of Municipal Services of Casablanca<br>-Supervision<br>-Departments<br>-Urban Planning<br>Public Services<br>-Human Resource Management<br>-Coordination of National and Local Policies<br>-Project Management<br>The Role of Coordinator for theSmart Cities Project<br>-A Technology-Focused Approach<br>Transforming the City<br>-Supervision of Geographic Information Systems (GIS)<br>-Coordination with Various Stakeholders<br>-Data Management Technologies<br>-Territorial Management |
| **Emerging Technologies** | View the local actors' perception regarding Emerging Technologies in the Casablanca-Settat region. | -Emerging technologies<br>- GIS, IoT, AI, and Big Data<br>- Improving territorial management<br>- Urban planning and infrastructure management<br>-Network mapping and resource management<br>- AI and Big Data-based solutions<br>-In-depth data analysis<br>-Better decision-making |
| **Challenges Encountered** | View the local actors' perception regarding the Challenges Encountered in the Casablanca-Settat region. | -Lack of technical skills<br>-Initial and ongoing funding<br>-Resistance to change<br>-Cost management, technology updates, and staff training are major concerns. |

continued on following page

*Table 3. Continued*

| Themes | Objectives | Categories, expressions |
|---|---|---|
| **Impact on Public Services Management** | View the local actors' perception regarding the Impact on Public Service Management. | Technologies have improved public service management by facilitating infrastructure planning and management, reducing processing times, and personalizing services. Examples include optimizing waste collection routes and enhanced water network management. |
| **Exemples Concrets d'Améliorations** | See the perception of local stakeholders regarding concrete examples of improvements in the Casablanca-Settat region. | Examples include optimized waste management, reduced processing times for administrative requests, and improved traffic management. These improvements have contributed to greater efficiency and a better quality of life. |
| **Citizen Participation and Transparency** | See the perception of local stakeholders regarding Citizen Participation and Transparency in the Casablanca-Settat region. | Technologies have enhanced transparency and citizen participation by enabling citizens to track their requests and participate in online public consultations. This has improved trust in decision-making processes. |
| **Anticipated Challenges for the Future** | See the perception of local stakeholders regarding Anticipated Challenges for the Future in the Casablanca-Settat region. | - Funding for technological updates<br>-Managing compatibility with existing systems<br>-Ongoing staff training<br>-Managing privacy and data security |
| **Strategies to Overcome Challenges** | See the perception of local stakeholders regarding Strategies to Overcome Challenges in the Casablanca-Settat region. | -Strengthening partnerships with technology companies,<br>- Diversifying funding sources,<br>- Investing in continuous training.<br>-Emphasis is also placed on communication and change management. |
| **Comments and Suggestions** | See the perception of local stakeholders regarding Comments and Suggestions | -Maintain a long-term vision<br>-Stay flexible in response to technological advancements<br>-Collaborate with stakeholders<br>-Ensure ethical integration of technologies for long-term success |

**Source:** developed by the authors.

The analysis shows that emerging technologies bring significant improvements to territorial management, but their integration is not without challenges. Training, funding, and change management are key aspects to ensure a successful transition and maximize the benefits of technologies. Collaboration among various stakeholders and a flexible approach are essential for navigating the rapid evolution of technologies and enhancing the quality of public services.

## 5. SOLUTIONS AND RECOMMENDATIONS

To fully capitalize on the potential of emerging technologies in territorial management, a comprehensive, multi-faceted strategy must be implemented. Several key areas of action are critical for achieving this transformation:

- **Investing in Training and Capacity Building:**

Developing human capital is essential for the effective integration of new technologies. Local administrators and staff must be equipped with the necessary technical skills to manage and operate these systems efficiently. This requires the implementation of continuous, targeted training programs that not only focus on technical competencies but also foster a culture of innovation and adaptability within public institutions. By promoting an environment of lifelong learning, these programs will ensure that the workforce remains agile in the face of rapid technological changes (Dunleavy, 2019).

- **Securing Sustainable and Diverse Funding Long-term financial planning is crucial to the successful integration of emerging technologies:**

Investments in digital infrastructure, system maintenance, and future upgrades require sustained funding. It is therefore essential to explore a variety of funding sources, including government allocations, public-private partnerships, and international financial aid. These avenues can provide the necessary resources to ensure that territorial administrations can not only adopt these technologies but also maintain and update them as they evolve (OECD, 2021). A robust funding strategy will help avoid the financial pitfalls that can derail technology projects and ensure their sustainability over time.

- **Modernizing Infrastructure and Bridging the Digital Divide:**

For emerging technologies to function optimally, **modern and reliable infrastructure is non-negotiable**. In particular, remote and underserved areas must be prioritized in infrastructure development plans to bridge the digital divide and ensure equitable access to services. Upgrading broadband networks, data centers, and digital platforms is essential for improving service delivery and enabling the effective deployment of AI, big data, and IoT-based systems. This infrastructure investment will directly support the broader goal of optimizing resource management and enhancing public service efficiency.

- **Implementing Change Management Strategies:**

The success of any technological transformation depends on the buy-in of all stakeholders. To mitigate resistance to change, a proactive approach to change management is required. This involves engaging all relevant actors—local authorities, staff, and the public—through clear and transparent communication of the benefits of the new technologies. Demonstrating tangible, short-term successes or "quick wins" can help build trust and generate momentum for larger initiatives. Additionally, involving stakeholders early in the process, ensuring their concerns are addressed, and creating a shared vision for technological adoption will facilitate smoother transitions and greater acceptance.

- **Strengthening Data Security and Privacy Measures:**

In the context of increasing reliance on digital technologies, robust data security protocols are essential. Local authorities must implement strict data protection measures that comply with national and international regulations, such as GDPR. This includes ensuring secure storage, encryption, and handling of sensitive information to prevent data breaches and misuse. Strengthening cybersecurity frameworks will not only protect the integrity of public services but also boost public trust in the digital transition by safeguarding privacy.

- **Fostering Partnerships and Collaborative Ecosystems:**

Emerging technologies evolve rapidly, and their successful integration into territorial management requires access to the latest expertise and innovation. Therefore, strengthening partnerships with technology companies, academic institutions, and NGOs is key to gaining the resources and knowledge needed to support the adoption of these technologies. Collaborative ecosystems can also facilitate the sharing of best practices and innovations, which can significantly enhance the capacity of local authorities to implement and adapt new technologies effectively.

- **Encouraging Transparency and Citizen Participation:**

Finally, for technological advancements to have a meaningful impact on territorial governance, transparency and citizen participation must be prioritized. Digital platforms should be leveraged to provide real-time access to public information, facilitate consultations, and encourage active public involvement in decision-making processes. This not only enhances transparency and accountability but also fosters a greater sense of community ownership and trust in public institutions. Moreover, the use of participatory platforms can streamline feedback mechanisms, enabling local authorities to make more informed and responsive decisions.

By adopting these strategies, local authorities can ensure that the integration of emerging technologies into territorial management is not only successful but also sustainable, inclusive, and transformative.

## 6. FUTURES RESEARCHS DIRECTIONS

Future research should explore several promising avenues to deepen the understanding of how emerging technologies can further transform territorial management. Investigating the long-term impacts of these technologies on urban development and governance will provide insights into their sustainability and effectiveness over time. Research could focus on evaluating the integration processes of new technologies within different administrative contexts to identify best practices and potential barriers.

Comparative studies across various regions, including international contexts, could offer valuable insights into how diverse technological approaches influence territorial management. Additionally, examining the role of citizen engagement and how digital tools can be optimized to enhance public participation and transparency would be beneficial. Understanding how these technologies impact social equity and inclusivity in service delivery is also crucial, ensuring that advancements do not exacerbate existing inequalities.

Future studies should also consider the evolution of technology and its implications for policy and planning, addressing how emerging innovations like blockchain and advanced AI might reshape territorial management. Furthermore, exploring cross-sector collaborations between governmental bodies, tech companies, and research institutions could provide a holistic view of technological integration and its broader societal impacts.

These research directions will not only contribute to academic knowledge but also offer practical insights for policymakers and practitioners aiming to leverage technology for more effective and equitable territorial management.

## 7. CONCLUSION

The integration of emerging technologies into territorial management has undeniably transformed how public services are planned and delivered. Technologies such as Geographic Information Systems (GIS), digital platforms, and artificial intelligence (AI) tools have facilitated more efficient management of urban infrastructure, improved service quality, and better addressed citizens' needs. For instance, GIS has proven instrumental in mapping and managing critical infrastructures like water and electricity networks, optimizing both maintenance and expansion. Similarly, digital platforms have expedited administrative processes, allowing citizens to access services more easily, thus reducing processing times and enhancing transparency.

However, despite these advances, several challenges persist. Continuous funding for technological upgrades and adequate staff training remain key concerns. The rapid pace of technological change necessitates ongoing financial investment and a sustained effort to equip staff with the necessary skills. Additionally, resistance to change—both from employees and citizens—demands effective communication strategies that highlight the benefits of new technologies and foster buy-in.

To address these challenges, several strategies can be implemented. First, strengthening partnerships with technology companies, academic institutions, and other key stakeholders will provide the necessary expertise and resources for continued innovation. Second, investing in comprehensive training programs is essential to ensure that staff remain proficient and adaptable in the face of technological evolution. Third, increasing the allocation of budgets for technology adoption and maintenance, as well as exploring new funding opportunities, is critical for maintaining administrative efficiency. Furthermore, particular attention should be given to data management and information security, ensuring that protocols are in place to safeguard the accuracy and confidentiality of sensitive information. Promoting a culture of innovation, alongside transparent communication with citizens, is also vital for increasing public trust and engagement in decision-making processes.

While emerging technologies present significant opportunities for enhancing territorial management and public service delivery, it is crucial to remain agile and responsive to evolving needs. By investing in research, fostering strategic partnerships, and prioritizing training, local governments can maximize the benefits of these technologies and ensure that they contribute to sustainable and inclusive development.

This research opens several avenues for future exploration. One area for further study would be expanding the scope to other regions or countries to test the generalizability of the findings and understand how different socio-economic contexts impact the adoption of emerging technologies in territorial management. Another direction could involve comparative studies between urban and rural areas to uncover context-specific challenges and opportunities. Longitudinal research could also provide valuable insights into the long-term effects of technology integration on governance and development. Finally, quantitative or mixed-method studies would complement this qualitative research, offering measurable data and more generalizable results on the impacts of these technologies.

This study is not without its limitations. One key limitation is the focus on a single region, Casablanca-Settat, which may restrict the generalizability of the findings to other regions or contexts. Additionally, the fast pace of technological advancements means that some of the insights presented here could become outdated over time. Moreover, the qualitative nature of the data, while providing rich and context-specific insights, may introduce subjectivity and potential biases in interpretation.

Despite these limitations, the study makes several important contributions. Theoretically, it advances the discourse on the intersection of emerging technologies and territorial management, particularly in the context of developing countries like Morocco. Managerially, it offers actionable insights and practical recommendations for local governments and policymakers, facilitating the effective integration of these technologies into public administration. Methodologically, the study highlights the value of using qualitative approaches to explore complex, context-dependent phenomena. These contributions serve as a foundation for future research and provide a roadmap for practical implementations in similar settings.

## REFERENCES


Aarabe, M.. (2024). Smart Tourism Experience and Responsible Travelers' Behavior: A Systematic Literature Review. In El Archi, Y. (Eds.), *Promoting Responsible Tourism With Digital Platforms* (pp. 128–147). IGI Global., DOI: 10.4018/979-8-3693-3286-3.ch008

Aarabe, M., Ben Khizzou, N., Alla, L., & Benjelloun, A. (2024). Marketing Applications of Emerging Technologies: A Systematic Literature Review. In Alla, L., Hmioui, A., & Bentalha, B. (Eds.), *AI and Data Engineering Solutions for Effective Marketing* (pp. 23–47). IGI Global., DOI: 10.4018/979-8-3693-3172-9.ch002

Agrawal, A., Gans, J. S., & Goldfarb, A. (2018). *Prediction machines: The simple economics of artificial intelligence*. Harvard Business Review Press.

Albahari, A., Klofsten, M., & Rasmussen, E. (2017). Initiating the knowledge spillover entrepreneurship process: A longitudinal analysis of university-industry collaborations. *The Journal of Technology Transfer*, 42(4), 900–916.

Alla, L., Bentalha, B., & Elyoussfi, A. (2023). Intelligence territoriale et positionnement stratégique des regions au Maroc: Le cas de la région de Fès Meknes en perspective. Le concept de l'intéligence en sciences juridiques, économiques et sociales, 215-237.

Arnstein, S. R. (1969). A ladder of citizen participation. *Journal of the American Institute of Planners*, 35(4), 216–224. DOI: 10.1080/01944366908977225

Badre, M. E. Z. I. A. N. E., Badr, B. E. N. T. A. L. H. A., & Lhoussaine, A. L. L. A. (2024). La PME logistique et le développement territorial régional: Une analyse qualitative. *Alternatives Managériales Economiques*, 6(4), 1–22.

Barzelay, M. (2001). *The new public management: Improving research and policy dialogue*. University of California Press.

Batty, M. (2013). *The new science of cities*. MIT Press. DOI: 10.7551/mitpress/9399.001.0001

Batty, M., Axhausen, K. W., Giannotti, F., Pozdnoukhov, A., Bazzani, A., Wachowicz, M., Ouzounis, G., & Portugali, Y. (2012). Smart cities of the future. *The European Physical Journal. Special Topics*, 214(1), 481–518. DOI: 10.1140/epjst/e2012-01703-3

Benner, M. (2020). The Role of Emerging Technologies in Modern Public Administration. *Public Administration Review*, 80(5), 800–815.

Bentalha, B., & Alla, L. (2024). Revealing the Subtleties: The Art of Qualitative Studies in Science and Management. In Bentalha, B., & Alla, L. (Eds.), *Applying Qualitative Research Methods to Management Science* (pp. 1–21). IGI Global., DOI: 10.4018/979-8-3693-5543-5.ch001

Boudri, R., Bentalha, B., & Benjelloun, O. (2024). Phygital Marketing and the Pain of Paying: An Amazon Go Netnographic Case Study. In Alla, L., Hmioui, A., & Bentalha, B. (Eds.), *AI and Data Engineering Solutions for Effective Marketing* (pp. 348–363). IGI Global., DOI: 10.4018/979-8-3693-3172-9.ch017

BOUHTATI, N., EL YAACOUBI, Y., BENTALHA, B., & Lhoussaine, A. L. L. A. (2024). Leviers logistiques de promotion du commerce équitable des produits de terroir: Une esquisse de modèle d'analyse. Alternatives Managériales Economiques, 6(Spécial 1), 17-35.

Bouhtati, N., Alla, L., & Bentalha, B. (2023). Marketing Big Data Analytics and Customer Relationship Management: A Fuzzy Approach. In B. Bentalha, A. DOI: 10.4018/979-8-3693-0225-5.ch004

Bouhtati, N., Alla, L., & Ed-Daakouri, I. (2024). Smart Data Analysis and Prediction of Responsible Customer Behaviour in Tourism: An Exploratory Review of the Literature. In El Archi, Y., Benbba, B., Dávid, L., & Cardoso, L. (Eds.), *Promoting Responsible Tourism With Digital Platforms* (pp. 189–212). IGI Global., DOI: 10.4018/979-8-3693-3286-3.ch011

Bourne, L. (2018). Stakeholder relationship management: A maturity model for organisational implementation. *International Journal of Project Management*, 36(3), 475–487.

Braun, V., & Clarke, V. (2006). Using thematic analysis in psychology. *Qualitative Research in Psychology*, 3(2), 77–101. DOI: 10.1191/1478088706qp063oa

Brown, J. S., & Duguid, P. (1991). Organizational learning and communities-of-practice: Toward a unified view of working, learning, and innovation. *Organization Science*, 2(1), 40–57. DOI: 10.1287/orsc.2.1.40

Brynjolfsson, E., & McAfee, A. (2014). *The second machine age: Work, progress, and prosperity in a time of brilliant technologies*. W.W. Norton & Company.

Cheng, C., Fang, D., Yin, H., & Dong, L. (2020). Evolutionary learning in big data analysis: A survey of algorithms. *IEEE Transactions on Emerging Topics in Computing*, 8(2), 1–14.

Citron, D. K., & Pasquale, F. (2014). The scored society: Due process for automated predictions. *Washington Law Review (Seattle, Wash.)*, 89(1), 1–33.

de l'Économie Numérique, M. (2018). *Plan Maroc Numérique 2020*. Gouvernement du Maroc.

EL JAOUHARI, S., & Lhoussaine, A. L. L. A. (2022). L'approche territoriale et la gestion de l'impact de la pandémie de Covid-19: Cas des collectivités territoriales. *Alternatives Managériales Economiques*, 4(1), 245–265.

El Moutawakil, N., Belkacemi, K., & Bouderbala, A. (2022). Digital Transformation in Moroccan Local Governance. *Journal of Urban Management*, 11(2), 150–165.

Elhissoufi, M., & Alla, L. (2024). Artificial Intelligence in Costumer Acquisition: A Bibliometric Study. In Alla, L., Hmioui, A., & Bentalha, B. (Eds.), *AI and Data Engineering Solutions for Effective Marketing* (pp. 1–22). IGI Global., DOI: 10.4018/979-8-3693-3172-9.ch001

Emery, F. E., & Trist, E. L. (1960). Socio-technical systems. In Churchman, C. W., & Verhulst, M. (Eds.), *Management science* (Vol. 2, pp. 58–97). Wiley.

Gertler, M. S. (2004). *Manufacturing culture: The institutional geography of industrial practice*. Oxford University Press. DOI: 10.1093/oso/9780198233824.001.0001

Goodchild, M. F. (2007). Citizens as sensors: The world of volunteered geography. *GeoJournal*, 69(4), 211–221. DOI: 10.1007/s10708-007-9111-y

Gordon, C., & DeSouza, K. C. (2019). Building a smart city: Lessons from Barcelona. *Journal of Urban Technology*, 26(1), 1–21.

Gordon, P., & Richardson, H. W. (2019). Urban Resilience and the Role of Smart Technologies. *Urban Studies (Edinburgh, Scotland)*, 56(4), 677–692.

Guo, Y., Zhang, G., & Zheng, G. (2017). Intelligent traffic light control with evolutionary learning in the cloud. *IEEE Transactions on Industrial Informatics*, 13(4), 1–10.

Hmioui, A., Alla, L., & Bentalha, B. (2017). Piloting territorial tourism in Morocco Proposal for a tourism index for the destination Fez [Pilotage de la touristicité territoriale au Maroc Proposition d'un indice de touriscticité pour la destination Fès] (No. hal-02334913).

Hmioui, A., Alla, L., & Bentalha, B. (2017). *Pilotage de la touristicité territoriale au Maroc Proposition d'un indice de touriscticité pour la destination Fès. Entrepreneuriat, Innovation, Gouvernance et Développement territorial, 120-143. Chains.* IGI Global., DOI: 10.4018/979-8-3693-0225-5.ch004

Hmioui, & L. Alla (Eds.), Integrating Intelligence and Sustainability in Supply

Hood, C. (1991). A public management for all seasons? *Public Administration*, 69(1), 3–19. DOI: 10.1111/j.1467-9299.1991.tb00779.x

Hood, C., & Peters, G. (2004). The middle aging of new public management: Into the age of paradox? *Journal of Public Administration: Research and Theory*, 14(3), 267–282. DOI: 10.1093/jopart/muh019

Houghton, R., Smith, J., & Johnson, L. (2022). Sustainable Development and Technological Integration in Territorial Management. *Journal of Environmental Management*, 320, 115–130.

Howlett, M., & Ramesh, M. (2003). *Studying public policy: Policy cycles and policy subsystems*. Oxford University Press.

Hwang, G., & Zhang, G. (2021). Digital twins and smart city applications: A comprehensive review. *Smart Cities*, 4(1), 1–19.

Janssen, M., Charalabidis, Y., & Zuiderwijk, A. (2012). Benefits, adoption barriers, and myths of open data and open government. *Information Systems Management*, 29(4), 258–268. DOI: 10.1080/10580530.2012.716740

Kitchin, R. (2014). *The data revolution: Big Data, open data, data infrastructures and their consequences*. SAGE Publications.

Kitchin, R. (2014). Big Data, New Epistemologies and Paradigm Shifts. *Big Data & Society*, 1(1), 1–12. DOI: 10.1177/2053951714528481

Kooiman, J. (2003). *Governing as governance*. SAGE Publications. DOI: 10.4135/9781446215012

Kunda, G. (2009). *Engineering culture: Control and commitment in a high-tech corporation*. Temple University Press.

Longley, P. A., Goodchild, M. F., Maguire, D. J., & Rhind, D. W. (2005). *Geographic information systems and science*. John Wiley & Sons.

Manyika, J., Chui, M., Brown, B., Bughin, J., Dobbs, R., Roxburgh, C., & Hung Byers, A. (2011). *Big data: The next frontier for innovation, competition, and productivity*. McKinsey Global Institute.

Miller, C., & Evans, M. (2017). Big Data and its Impact on Territorial Management. *Geographical Research*, 55(3), 310–325.

Miller, H. J., Dodge, S., & Zumel, N. (2020). Mapping the unmapped: Cartographic data, algorithms, and AI in smart cities. *Annals of the Association of American Geographers*, 110(1), 1–18.

Moore, M. H. (1995). *Creating public value: Strategic management in government.* Harvard University Press.

Nouhaila, B. K., Aarabe, M., & Alla, L. (2024). The Impact of Digitalisation on the Customer Experience in Medical Tourism: A Systematic Review. In Talukder, M., Kumar, S., & Tyagi, P. (Eds.), *Impact of AI and Tech-Driven Solutions in Hospitality and Tourism* (pp. 408–428). IGI Global., DOI: 10.4018/979-8-3693-6755-1.ch020

OECD. (2021). *Regions and Cities: The Role of Territorial Development*. OECD Publishing.

Paquet, G., & Roy, J. (2021). Territorial Management and Public Sector Governance. *Public Administration Review*, 81(4), 610–624.

Pirotti, F., Guarnieri, A., & Vettore, A. (2015). State of the art and future developments of UAV photogrammetry for 3D modelling of cultural heritage—A review. *Remote Sensing*, 7(3), 6970–7010.

Pollitt, C., & Bouckaert, G. (2011). *Public management reform: A comparative analysis—New public management, governance, and the Neo-Weberian state* (3rd ed.). Oxford University Press.

Rodríguez-Pose, A. (2018). The revenge of the places that don't matter (and what to do about it). *Cambridge Journal of Regions, Economy and Society*, 11(1), 189–209. DOI: 10.1093/cjres/rsx024

Rodríguez-Pose, A. (2018). The Theory and Practice of Local Economic Development. *Regional Studies*, 52(4), 507–519.

Rogers, E. M. (2003). *Diffusion of innovations* (5th ed.). Free Press.

Sassen, S. (2012). *Cities in a world economy*. SAGE Publications.

Schwandt, T. A. (2014). *The Sage Dictionary of Qualitative Inquiry*. Sage Publications.

Silva, C. N., & Khan, S. (2020). The role of data in smart cities: Leveraging data to improve urban infrastructure. In *Smart cities: Applications, technologies, standards, and driving factors* (pp. 23–45). Springer.

Smith, T., & Houghton, R. (2023). The Future of Public Management: Trends and Technologies. *International Journal of Public Sector Management*, 36(1), 20–34.

Talbot, C. (2005). *Paradoxes of public sector managerialism, old public management and public service bargains*. SAGE Publications.

Tomlinson, R. (2007). *Thinking about GIS: Geographic information system planning for managers*. ESRI Press.

Van der Voet, J. (2016). The role of leadership in the implementation of public sector innovation. *Public Management Review*, 18(2), 209–227.

Wirtz, B. W., & Göttel, V. (2016). *Smart service systems: Theory and practice*. Springer.

Wong, C., & Liew, A. (2015). Challenges in the integration of emerging technologies in public management. *Public Administration Quarterly*, 39(1), 100–117.

Yang, C., & Suto, H. (2018). Data-Driven Urban Planning: Integrating Big Data and Geographic Information Systems. *Journal of Urban Planning and Development*, 144(3), 1–10.

Yu, P., & Zhang, Y. (2019). *The future of smart cities: Emerging trends and applications*. Springer.

Zhang, Y., Wang, Z., & Huang, J. (2020). Big Data Analytics in Urban Management: Benefits, Challenges, and Future Directions. *Urban Management Journal*, 6(2), 45–67.

Zhu, X., & Zhang, K. (2018). Smart technologies and urban governance: A critical review. *Urban Studies (Edinburgh, Scotland)*, 55(4), 1–15.

## KEY TERMS AND DEFINITIONS

**Artificial Intelligence (AI):** Refers to technologies that mimic human cognitive processes, such as learning, reasoning, and problem-solving, through machines and algorithms. In the context of territorial management, AI plays a pivotal role in enhancing data analysis, enabling predictive modeling, and automating decision-making processes to improve governance efficiency and resource allocation.

**Emerging Technologies:** A set of innovative technologies, including AI, big data, Geographic Information Systems (GIS), and the Internet of Things (IoT), which hold transformative potential across multiple sectors. In territorial management, these technologies facilitate more advanced data processing, optimized resource management, and more informed decision-making practices, contributing to more sustainable and responsive governance systems.

**Geographic Information Systems (GIS):** A framework that allows for the capture, storage, analysis, and visualization of spatial and geographic data. GIS is essential in territorial management, providing detailed mapping and spatial analysis, which supports urban planning, infrastructure development, and strategic decision-making by offering critical spatial insights for local governance.

**Territorial Management:** The comprehensive process of planning, organizing, coordinating, and evaluating resources and activities within a defined geographical region. The goal is to foster sustainable development and improve the quality of life for residents by efficiently managing urban infrastructure, public services, environmental resources, and governance mechanisms.

Chapter 14

# Transformational Trends of Territorial Economic Intelligence Strategies in the Digital Era: A Systematic Theoretical Exploration

**Badre Meziane**
https://orcid.org/0000-0003-3097-4909
*National School of Business and Management, Sidi Mohamed Ben Abdellah University, Morocco*

**Lhoussaine Alla**
https://orcid.org/0000-0002-7238-1792
*National School of Applied Sciences, Sidi Mohamed Ben Abdellah University, Morocco*

**Badr Bentalha**
https://orcid.org/0000-0003-1339-542X
*National School of Business and Management, Sidi Mohamed Ben Abdellah University, Morocco*

## ABSTRACT

*This research analyzes the use of new technologies in a territorial economic intelligence approach. We aim to examine how these technologies can improve the decision-making process of public decision-makers, to contribute to territorial development. Through bibliographical and thematic research, this study attempts to identify current and future trends that need to be taken into account. It concludes that territorial*

DOI: 10.4018/979-8-3693-6854-1.ch014

*economic intelligence has evolved, moving from a socio-economic approach to a vision that integrates other variables, such as technologies and the fundamental role of stakeholders. The results are intended to provide decision-makers with a set of ideas and strategies for optimizing the resources used in business intelligence. The research provides an outline of a conceptual framework to assimilate the role of territorial intelligence in promoting and enhancing the attractiveness of territories.*

## INTRODUCTION

How can we take advantage of new technologies to manage territories more efficiently? This is the question on the minds of any regional decision-maker who wants to improve the attractiveness of his or her area, promote its development, or accentuate its growth. Indeed, in a world characterized by increased globalization on the one hand, and a tendency to regionalize territories on the other, territorial economic intelligence is proving to be an inescapable tool in the hands of decision-makers to aid the decision-making process. Moreover, the massive increase in the amount of data to be processed makes the use of new information storage, processing, and dissemination technologies, such as Big Data, inevitable.

The advent of the digital era has ushered in profound changes across all sectors of society, with economic systems experiencing particularly dramatic shifts. Within this context, the concept and practice of Territorial Economic Intelligence (TEI) have undergone significant transformations. Territorial Economic Intelligence, which refers to the strategic gathering, analysis, and utilization of economic information within a specific geographic area, has become increasingly critical for regional development and competitiveness in our interconnected global economy. (Nouhaila et al., 2024).

This research aims to exploit current trends in the use of new technologies in territorial economic intelligence strategies, focusing on the challenges and opportunities of such an approach while questioning how digital technologies fit into a territorial intelligence strategy.

To answer these questions, we have carried out several analyses on a carefully selected set of articles: lexical, thematic, and bibliographic analyses, to identify trends in the most recently addressed research themes, and in an attempt to conceptualize a frame of reference on the evolution of the theme of territorial economic intelligence from the founding articles of the discipline to the most recent writings.

Our research reflects a mixed approach, combining a theoretical analysis of concepts, facts, and observations, with an empirical approach that questions the implementation of a territorial economic intelligence strategy in different regions and contexts, to test the validity of theoretical concepts and their universality.

Our ambition is to provide territorial decision-makers with an overview of scientific work that can offer them food for thought, ideas, and strategies in the field of territorial intelligence. Our aim is also to stimulate scientific debate on this concept by summarizing current work and anticipating future changes.

Our research begins with a literature review that attempts to present the main contributions in the field, notably by synthesizing several definitions of territorial economic intelligence and presenting the main current and future challenges facing the decision-maker. Next, we present the methodology we followed to carry out our research, especially in terms of the choice of articles, databases, and tools. The third part of our research presents the main results we found, whether in terms of lexical, thematic, or bibliographic analysis. Finally, we will discuss these results, attempting to identify the evolution of the concept of territorial economic intelligence over time, as well as changes in approaches and paradigms.

## 1. Conceptual and Theoretical Framework:

The current context is more than ever ripe for an analytical reading of territorial economic intelligence and its implications: globalization, which tends to blur physical borders, coupled with regionalization, which makes the territory the pillar of any action in favor of regional development, a prerequisite for development on a larger scale. We are going to present the main definitions of the key concepts of our research, then we are going to present the challenges and the opportunities of territorial intelligence, and finally, we are going to dedicate a discussion to the challenges of territorial intelligence, and finally, we will devote a discussion to the challenges of ethical use of innovative technologies.

### 1.1. Definitions and Foundations of Territorial Economic Intelligence

The proliferation of exchanges between entities, the massive increase in the amount of data to be processed, and the fierce competition between territories to attract investment flows have made the notion of territorial intelligence central to current debates. This approach aims to provide public decision-makers with the tools they need to make well-considered, rational decisions, to make public action more effective and optimal (Mouhib & Benkaraache, 2023).

This concept has evolved since its fairly recent appearance (in the 90s) and is a variant of the concept of economic intelligence. Bertacchini (2004) defines the concept as a territory's ability to anticipate and manage change through collective capabilities. This definition has the merit of underlining the objectives as well as the collective nature, which implies the involvement of the players concerned. (Ouassou & Bakour, 2024) shows that territorial intelligence can be both descending, with the territory as an autonomous entity capable of making its own decisions to achieve its objectives; and ascending, with economic intelligence at the national level, which considers the territory as a field of application (Table 1).

*Table 1. Definitions of territorial economic intelligence*

| Authors | Definitions |
|---|---|
| **Ouassou & Bakour (2024)** | Territorial intelligence is a holistic and collaborative approach to territorial development, integrating economic, social, and environmental dimensions, based on the active participation of local players and the sharing of information. |
| **Mouhib & Benkaraache (2023)** | Territorial intelligence is a tool for more effective public action and successful territorial development, combining general and territorial interests through the collection, processing, and strategic dissemination of information. |
| **Amairia (2023)** | Territorial intelligence enables the Regional Council to develop actions and public policies that are better adapted to local needs, integrating scientific methods and a territorial approach to research. |
| **Laurini & Donolo (2022)** | Territorial intelligence, through computer-aided visual reasoning, enables the identification of patterns, correlations, and critical points, thus facilitating decision-making processes in urban, regional, and environmental planning. |
| **Helmi & Kasmi (2022)** | Territorial intelligence, as a system for collecting, analyzing, and disseminating strategic information, enables territories to better understand their strengths and weaknesses and to develop sustainable tourism development strategies. |

Source: The authors

Laghmam (2020) and its successor Bentahar & Chadli (2022) address the aspect of territorial attractiveness as a key issue, especially in a context marked by scarcity of resources and diversity of supply. All territorial development depends on the ability of stakeholders to assimilate the issues at stake, assert their assets, and face up to the constraints (Zeryouh & Daabaji, 2022).

Several theories can be mobilized to explain the concept, including new public management theory, game theory, convention theory, and decision theory (Ouassou & Bakour, 2024). Some authors explore other paths, such as the role of ethics in this process, proposing the concept of "*geoethics*" as a set of values to be respected in the context of ethical territorial intelligence (Jeanne, 2022).

The concept has undergone a certain evolution in the literature, moving from a holistic, all-encompassing approach that strives to set out the founding principles, to a more empirical conception geared towards concrete implementation (Aarabe et al., 2024). This is particularly true of the smart city concept, which is defined as a multi-disciplinary vision (economic, social, technological, environmental...) (Ouaziz, 2022a). This approach is a catalyst for territorial intelligence insofar as it goes beyond the technical framework to address other, sometimes less obvious, dimensions (Coussi, 2022). This approach has led some authors to analyze concrete cases of implementation and study their manifestations (Ikhmim et al., 2022), while others are more interested in the interactions between the various actors involved in territorial intelligence (Meziane et al., 2024).

## 1.2. The Challenges and Opportunities of Territorial Intelligence

Alongside articles dealing with the theoretical aspect of territorial intelligence, the literature provides a well-supplied corpus of case studies and empirical analyses, each of which endeavors to highlight a particular aspect. (Helmi & Kasmi, 2022) Deal with the role of territorial intelligence in the tourism sector, with particular emphasis on the notion of Tourism Clusters and how they foster the transmission of information between the various stakeholders. In parallel, (Robin & Coussi, 2023; Aarabe et al., 2024) focus on the impact of a communication strategy on governance through territorial intelligence in the post-COVID-19 period, to deduce the importance of adapting this communication to the specificities of territories and contexts. Similarly, the importance of indicators for diagnosis is addressed by (Berrichi & Kajjout, 2020) to assess the effectiveness of public policies within the framework of the "*Catalyse*" method.

Beyond the organizational aspect, it is the technological aspect that is the focus of most work in this area, due to the importance, but above all the variety, of the tools used. (Lamrabet & Benkaraache, 2022) Present an original concept they call Territorial Big Data, which can be defined as the systematic use of Big Data in territorial decision-making. Similarly, (Taj, 2023) explores the use of Big Data in the Moroccan context, with recommendations for improving its effectiveness (Bentalha, 2020). The exploitation of Big Data is commonly referred to as data mining, which can improve the business intelligence process (Maftah et al., 2023; Bouhtati et al., 2023), paving the way for intelligence and information acquisition practices such as those that have long been in use at corporate level (business intelligence), but at territorial level in particular (Mezzanzanica et al., 2010), or even more originally, the use of computer-aided visual reasoning (Laurini & Donolo, 2022).

Through research, relationships between territorial economic intelligence and other founding concepts are highlighted. The strategic positioning of regions analyzes the proactive approach to development that stems from sustainable, intelligent specialization (Alla et al., 2023). This specialization is reflected in the urban governance of cities, of which innovation is one of the most decisive components (Pumain, 2021). The role of the actor within any territorial intelligence process is analyzed through the role of collective learning (Boutahar & Debbagh, 2022) or as a mediating link between territorial development and the prevalence of human capital (Chakir & Mazzaourou, 2023).

The challenges facing territorial economic intelligence are diverse but often converge on the issue of the resilience of territories themselves, particularly regarding environmental and ecological issues (Bentaleb & Boukhari, 2023; Lamsiah & Bentalha, 2022), which constitute one of the major debates intimately linked to territorial development issues, giving rise to phenomena such as territorial anti-intelligence, identified and analyzed by (Lamrabet & Benkaraache, 2022).

Territorial economic intelligence can contribute to the sustainable and resilient development of territories (Hmioui et al., 2024). It depends on the optimal combination of technologies, players, and local specificities. Future changes will undoubtedly involve even greater use of Big Data and artificial intelligence, as well as a better culture of collective intelligence as part of a Smart City approach (Masselot, 2023).

More concretely, Bertacchini et al. (2014) were interested in the possible applications of territorial intelligence in two territories quite different in terms of geography, language, and history: Mexico at a national level and the University of Gafsa in Tunisia. This interesting study shows that, even if the scales are different (a country and an institution), it turns out that there is a mutual understanding of territorial intelligence as a tool and a collaborative process that involves actors anchored in the development of the territory, by relativizing the mechanisms of collaboration and coordination. The concept of territorial intelligence provides a conceptual framework capable of explaining how the players in a spatial territory (in all dimensions) can work together to promote innovations in sustainable development: the emphasis is on sharing information and creating spaces for exchanging knowledge. The authors conclude that a territorial intelligence approach within CAENTI (Coordinated Action of the European Network of Territorial Intelligence) can be a catalyst for growth, innovation, and sustainable development in a multitude of contexts.

In another context, Delvoye and Girardot (2014) analyze the use of territorial intelligence tools by local actors in Seraing, Belgium. Through the Optim@ organization, which has been conducting observations in Seraing since 1998, driven by the socio-economic challenges facing the local community. This research shows the need for concerted action where sector-based approaches have proved ineffective in meeting the needs of the community and empowering residents as social assistance often creates dependency. To address these issues, the research uses the CATALYSE method, developed by the ThéMa-MTI research team. This method emphasizes partnerships between stakeholders (residents, decision-makers, and professionals), the active involvement of residents in information gathering, and the development of context-specific solutions. The authors cite concrete cases of the CATALYSE method being used to revitalize a disadvantaged neighborhood (Ougrée-bas) with citizen initiatives such as the creation of public gardens, a resource center, and knowledge-sharing workshops to promote social cohesion. Nevertheless, the implementation of large-scale territorial intelligence is coming up against difficulties in deploying new technologies (especially big data) and a certain reluctance to change on the part of the players involved.

Several cities have already begun to make massive use of new technologies to offer their citizens and visitors an experience that best meets their needs and expectations, as part of Smart Cities projects:

- Barcelona: Citizen participation platforms and sensor networks are being set up to ensure efficient waste management. This includes reporting illegal dumping and missing bins... It also provides information on recycling and waste reduction, and recommendations for environmentally friendly disposal
- In Singapore, which suffers from a suffocating traffic problem, a real-time traffic management system has been set up to optimize resources and time. Traffic flows are managed according to flow rates, which also depend on working hours. This approach involves the use of sensors, GPS, and real-time information. The main challenge here is, of course, protecting user data and preserving their privacy.
- Amsterdam: Smart grids and data-driven energy management for sustainability, This leads to greater grid efficiency, improved reliability (rapid identification of faults and intervention), the provision of relevant information to users to rationalize their decisions, and, of course, a reduction in greenhouse gas emissions.

## 1.3 The Ethical Challenges Specific to Territorial Economic Intelligence

The massive use of Big Data and artificial intelligence certainly offers new possibilities for analysis and decision-making in terms of territorial intelligence, but it also raises questions about the ethical use of personal data: every day, billions of social network users submit (voluntarily or not) their data to content providers to benefit from their products free of charge. While territorial decision-makers may not have the same motivations as the tech giants, the processing of this data poses the same problem.

The question that users and decision-makers have been asking themselves is how to use personal data without infringing on users' privacy. It is vital to strike the right balance between technological innovation (big data) and the protection of users' privacy.

The problem of algorithmic bias is also increasingly cited by users. Artificial Intelligence systems can lead to malfunctions in the training models. This can lead to unfounded or erroneous decisions, or even discrimination, for example in access to credit, healthcare, or employment. It is therefore important to ensure the integrity and representativeness of the data collected, as well as the transparency of the algorithms responsible for decision-making. (Du, S., & Xie, C., 2021)

Beyond the unethical or intrusive use of user data, it is also (and above all) the concern about cybercrime that needs to be fully taken into account by public decision-makers. A data leak can only be disastrous and would lead to a deterioration in citizens' confidence in territorial intelligence systems, calling the whole process into question.

But the biggest problem to be resolved first and foremost is that of the rationality of intelligent technologies in the decision-making process. Would artificial intelligence be capable of delivering fair verdicts in legal cases? Would it be able to take into account the socio-cultural aspects of an investment or focus solely on the economic and financial dimensions?

Faced with this situation, many countries and organizations have turned their attention to the issue and introduced provisions to guarantee the protection of user data, such as the GDPR (General Data Protection Regulation) in the European Union, the CCPA (California Consumer Privacy Act) and Law No. 09-08 on the protection of individuals about the processing of personal data in Morocco. (Negri-Ribalta et al., 2024)

## 2. METHODOLOGY

### 2.1. Research Object

Through our research, we have attempted to review recent literature on territorial economic intelligence in the digital age, focusing on current and future trends in the use of new technologies in territorial management. We asked ourselves how these technologies are changing the way public decision-makers approach territorial intelligence issues in terms of information collection, analysis, and dissemination. Our research should help define the opportunities and challenges facing the players involved. In addition to proposing a conceptual and theoretical framework for defining the concept in a clear and precise manner, this research aims to show the evolution of the concept of territorial intelligence over time and through the themes addressed by the authors.

In concrete terms, how do business intelligence strategies adapt to the imperatives of the digital age, given the constraints and challenges posed by the use of new technologies in territorial management?

### 2.2. Methodological Framework

To achieve our objective, we carried out 3 types of analysis:

- Lexical analysis: Having built up a corpus that could be processed by the IRAMUTEQ software, we carried out several analyses of the most significant items in our research. Apart from a count of the most cited items and a scatter plot, we carried out a similarity analysis of around 3 items to identify the terms most co-cited with these items. The result is a map representing this occurrence. Finally, we performed a DHC analysis based on the Max Reinert method. This representation is punctuated by an AFC analysis, combined with a similarity analysis performed by TORPES software.
- Thematic analysis: by categorizing the various articles we analyzed by theme; we created a thematic grid showing the distribution of articles according to the dimension addressed. We also distinguished between five types of articles: normative literature, literature review, exploratory study, methodological review, and hypothesis testing (Mentzer and Kahn, 1995).
- Bibliometric analysis: using a database created with PUBLISH OR PERISH software, we carried out a bibliographic study with VOSWIEWER software to show the relationships that exist between the items selected at the parameter level, to identify trends and emerging themes.

Our corpus is made up of articles according to the following parameters:

- Publication date after 2018 (with a few rare exceptions, whose relevance we have deemed eligible for an exception).
- Articles must be written in Arabic, French or English.
- The article must cite the terms {"Territorial intelligence" **OR** "Economic intelligence"} **AND** {"Digital era" **OR** "New technologies"}, with a few variations.
- We searched several databases to build up our corpus: Scopus, CAIRN, and Google Scholar.

First, we will present a lexicographical analysis of our corpus to identify the trends in territorial intelligence and innovative technologies, then we will start a thematic analysis by various criteria to present the main themes discussed in the literature, and finally, we will finish with a bibliometric analysis of the most recent publications on the subject.

## 3. RESULTS

### 3.1. Lexical Analysis

Our first analysis concerns the terms most frequently used in the articles analyzed, and their number of occurrences. This trivial analysis serves as a starting point for directing reading and reflection toward the phenomena that most attracted the authors' attention. This process makes it possible to identify both the key concepts most addressed by the authors, as well as the future perspectives and trends that will guide future research on the use of territorial economic intelligence concepts.

The results of IRAMUTEQ's analysis are as follows (Table 2):

*Table 2. analysis of the most frequently cited items*

| **Item** | **Occurrence** | | **Actors** | **44** | | **Smart** | **33** |
|---|---|---|---|---|---|---|---|
| Territorial | 190 | | Dimension | 40 | | Review | 31 |
| Intelligence | 159 | | Local | 39 | | Information | 31 |
| Economic | 109 | | Importance | 38 | | Public | 30 |
| Development | 72 | | Study | 38 | | Territory | 28 |
| Data | 61 | | City | 38 | | Communication | 28 |
| Social | 49 | | Explores | 34 | | Sustainable | 25 |

Source: The authors

The terms "territorial", "intelligence", "economic", "development", "data" or "social" are the ones most associated with the theme of territorial economic intelligence. The concepts of "smart" (city) and "Information" are still relatively underdeveloped, probably due to the recent nature of the phenomenon. The less-than-average occurrence ($\overline{X}$ = 55,85)) of the term actors shows the relative absence in the literature of the human and social component, to the detriment of the organizational and technological aspects, widely discussed in the articles analyzed.

A word cloud represents at a glance the concepts related to territorial economic intelligence. The size of each item is proportional to the importance (or simply occurrence) attributed to it by the authors. It's an approximate tool, but one that has the advantage of presenting at a glance the main items recurring in the literature. It is not, however, an exact representation of reality, given that the articles analyzed only partially cover the literature on territorial economic intelligence. IRAMUTEQ offers the possibility of creating a word cloud from a textual corpus (Figure 1).

*Figure 1. Analysis of the cloud of core items*

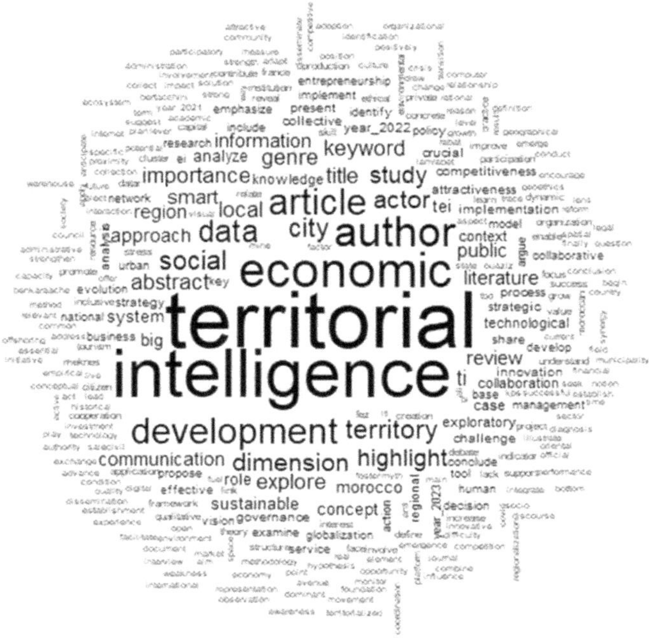


*Source: The authors (IRAMUTQ)*

The items "territorial" and "intelligence" naturally stand out, but we can easily spot other items such as "economic", "development", "data" and "city". Indeed, more and more researchers are looking into the possibilities of using big data in the integrated management of smart cities (Lamrabet & Benkaraache, 2021).

The idea behind similarity analysis in IRAMUTEQ is that there is a semantic relationship between the different items that are most often cited together. This analysis makes it possible to detect possible lexical relationships between the analyzed items to contribute to the creation of a corpus allowing for better exploitation. (Chaves et al., 2017).

We carried out this analysis and did indeed find relationships between the various items (Figure 2). That said, given the richness of our corpus, and for a better analysis, we subdivided our analysis around 3 fundamental items: "intelligence", "territorial" and "actors".

*Figure 2. Analysis of similarities applied to the « territorial » item*

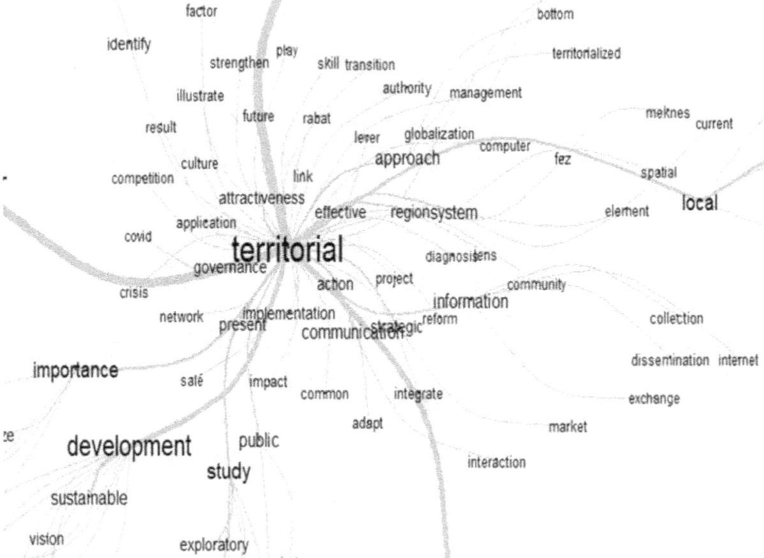


*Source: The authors (IRAMUTQ)*

Here, governance, attractiveness and action are the basic theoretical concepts of territorial intelligence. There is probably a tendency for authors to present a systemic vision of the phenomenon, emphasizing the concepts of collaboration and coordination (Figure 3).

*Figure 3. Analysis of similarities applied to the « intelligence » item*

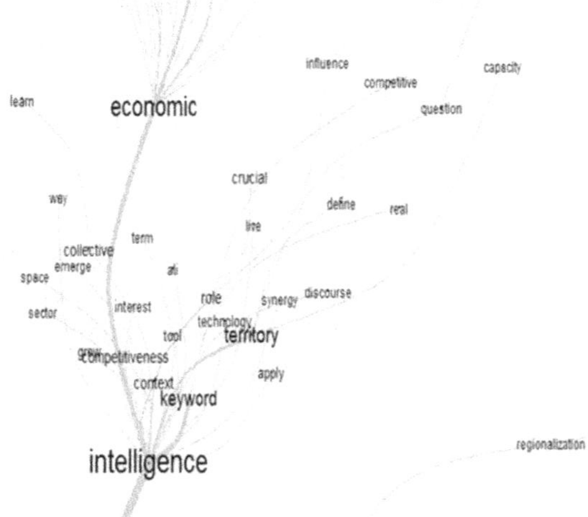


*Source: The authors (IRAMUTQ)*

For the "intelligence" item, the corpus clearly indicates a tendency to focus on context, keywords and competitiveness, concepts that are intrinsically related to intelligence in the sense of acquiring, storing, processing and disseminating information to aid the decision-making process (Figure 4).

*Figure 4. Analysis of similarities applied to the « actor » item*

*Source: The authors (IRAMUTQ)*

The "actors" dimension is clearly marginalized in our corpus, as authors - through their research - often emphasize the organizational and technological aspects of territorial economic intelligence, to the detriment of the fundamental role of actors in accepting change in the first instance, and then putting in place the provisions of a territorial intelligence capable of improving and rationalizing decision-making.

In our similarity analysis, the "actors" branch is represented by a thin segment, but emphasizes the importance of sharing, collaboration and cooperation.

Our next step was to establish a dendrogram representing a Descending Hierarchical Classification. Based on Max Reinert's method, IRAMUTEQ identifies and classifies themes in a corpus based on item co-occurrence (Figure 5).

*Figure 5. Descending Hierarchical Classification (DHC)*

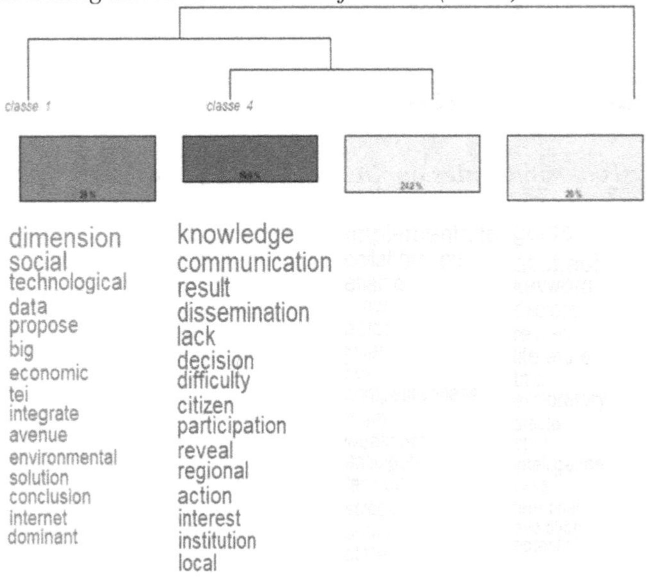


*Source: The authors (IRAMUTQ)*

The DHC allows us to observe the existence of 4 classes that focus on the different dimensions addressed by the authors: social, technological, economic and environmental. The analysis shows that the concept of territorial economic intelligence is a multidisciplinary one, encompassing technological and social dimensions within a much broader economic context. This is a recurring theme in the scientific literature, where numerous authors attempt to conceptualize the concept. (Meziane et al., 2024).

The DHC can be completed by a correspondence analysis (AFC), which consists of tracing the various concepts in our corpus (Figure 6). There seems to be a clear structuring around the social and technological dimensions, while at the same time the prevalence of research into the collaboration of local players in the implementation of an innovative territorial economic intelligence strategy.

*Figure 6. Correspondence Analysis (AFC)*

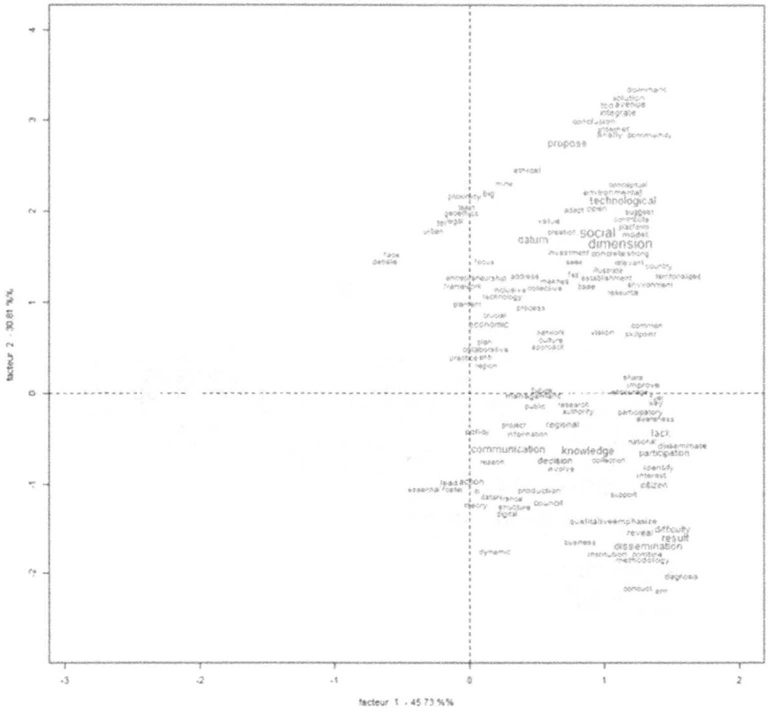

*Source: The authors (IRAMUTQ)*

The horizontal axis highlights the extent to which items relating to technological aspects are omnipresent in scientific research on territorial economic intelligence; while the vertical axis separates items relating to social aspects (collaboration between players) and those concerning communication and information dissemination.

In addition, a linguistic analysis performed by TORPES software enables concepts to be visually represented by spheres whose size is proportional to the number of items they contain. The closer the spheres are to each other, the stronger the relationship. Conversely, concepts appear to diverge, with few (or no) common relationships.

We decided to focus our analysis on the "intelligence" item, which in our view brings together our corpus (Figure 7).

*Figure 7. Analysis of similarities with the item « territorial »*

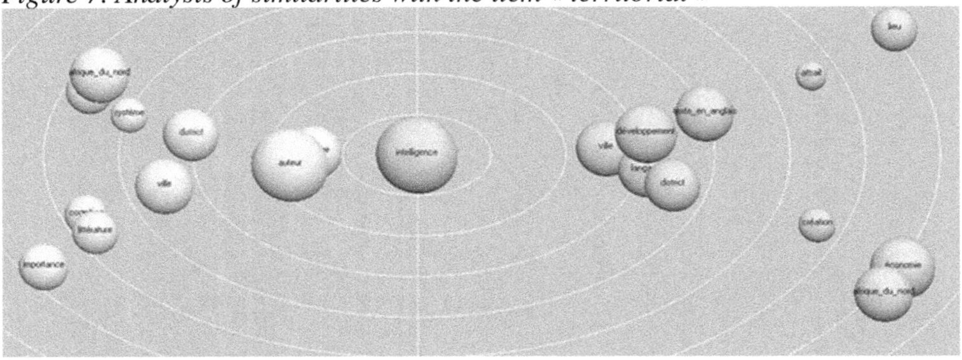

*Source: The authors (by TORPES)*

Another way of representing this analysis is to display the relationships between concepts, or between a word category and a concept (Figure 8).

*Figure 8. Analysis of similarities with the item « territorial »*

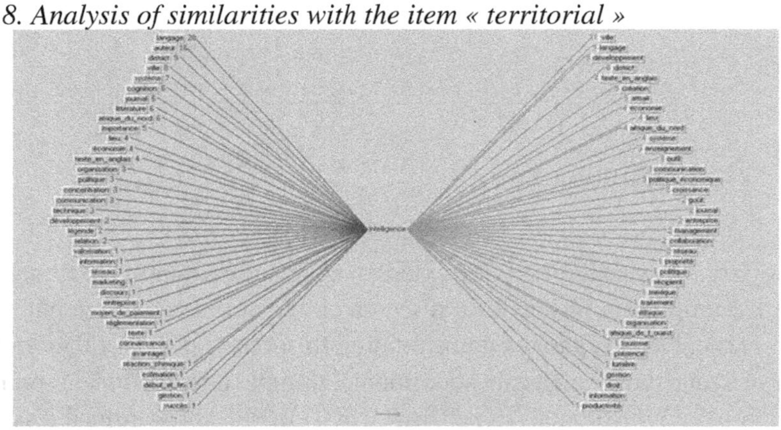

*Source: The authors (by TORPES)*

Thus, there is a very strong relationship between the concepts of "intelligence", "city", "district" and "system", reflecting the current trend to rethink cities as intelligent systems capable of responding to the needs of local stakeholders.

## 3.2 Thematic Analysis

We have listed researches on the use of technology in territorial management according to the dominant dimension (Table 3).

*Table 3. Distribution of items by dimensions*

| Dimension | Authors |
|---|---|
| **Economic** | Mouhib S. et Benkaraache T. (2023) |
| **Economic and environmental** | Amairia A. (2023) |
| **Economique and social** | Laurini R. et Donolo R. M. (2022)<br>Benichou et al. (2023)<br>Ouassou S. et Bakour C. (2024)<br>Helmi D. et Kasmi A. (2022)<br>Ouaziz A. (2022)<br>Ouaziz A. (2021)<br>Lakhmim S. et al. (2022)<br>Alla L. et al. (2023)<br>Boutahar S. et Debbagh B. (2022)<br>Robin J. et Coussi O. (2023)<br>Bentahar A. et Chadli N. (2022)<br>Ludovic J. (2022)<br>Laamrani El Idrissi et Abdelbaki N. (2022)<br>Berrichi A. et Kajjout S. (2020)<br>Diakhaté D. (2021) |
| **Economic, Social and Environmental** | Coussi O. (2022) |
| **Economic et technological** | Lamrabet M. et Benkaraach T. (2021)<br>Sofia Mastour et al. (2024) |
| **Economic and touristic** | Zeryouh, A. et Daabaji, A. (2022) |
| **Social and communicationnal** | Pumain D. (2021) |
| **Social and organisationnal** | Elmezdghi O. et Achibane M. (2023) |
| **Social and spatial** | Lamrabet, M. et Benkaraache, T. (2022) |
| **Technological andt social** | Ouaziz A. (2022)<br>Masselot C. (2023)<br>Bentaleb S. et El Boukhari H. (2023)<br>Bouchida I. et Azougagh A. (2023)<br>Taj T. (2023)<br>Chakir K. et al (2023)<br>Lamrabet M. et Benkaraache T. (2021) |
| **Technological, social and economic** | Maftah J. et al. (2023)<br>Knauf A. (2022) |

Source: The authors

With regard to the typology of articles, we have based ourselves on the work of Mentzer and Kahn (1995) in order to propose the following results (Table 4).

*Table 4. Breakdown of articles by type*

| Type | Number of items | Percentage |
|---|---|---|
| **Case studies** | 12 | 31% |
| **Literature review** | 26 | 67% |
| **Hypothesis testing** | 1 | 2% |

continued on following page

*Table 4. Continued*

| Type | Number of items | Percentage |
|---|---|---|
| **Normative literature** | 0 | 0 |
| **Methodological review** | 0 | 0 |
| **Total** | 39 | 100% |

Source: the authors (by EXCEL)

We also plotted the distribution of these articles by year and by type (Bentalha et al., 2020) and arrived at the following results (Table 5).

*Table 5. Breakdown of items by type and year*

| Type | 2010 | 2012 | 2019 | 2020 | 2021 | 2022 | 2023 | 2024 | Total |
|---|---|---|---|---|---|---|---|---|---|
| **Case studies** | 1 | | 1 | | | 2 | 1 | | 5 |
| **Literature review** | 1 | 1 | | 2 | 5 | 12 | 10 | 2 | 33 |
| **Hypothesis testing** | | | | | | | 1 | | 1 |
| **Normative literature** | | | | | | | | | |
| **Methodological review** | | | | | | | | | |
| **Total** | 2 | 1 | 1 | 2 | 5 | 14 | 12 | 2 | 39 |

Source: The authors

This development demonstrates the growing interest in the phenomenon of territorial economic intelligence, in the context of the integration of new communication and, above all, decision-making technologies. Indeed, the constant evolution of the digital aspect of exchanges between players is forcing them to consider the advantages of such an approach, as shown by the interest that Big Data is now taking in territorial processes due to the immensity of the information to be processed (Lamrabet & Benkaraache, 2021).

Through our analytical reading of our corpus, we have synthesized a set of concepts that recur in various forms, and which may constitute blocks for reflection (Bentalha & Alla, 2024) (Table 6).

*Table 6. Most recurring concepts*

| Concepts | Description | Authors |
|---|---|---|
| **Key concepts of TEI** | Definitions of territorial intelligence (TI), distinction between economic intelligence (EI) and TI, characteristics of TI, approaches to TI (top-down vs. bottom-up). | Bouchida & Azougagh (2023) |
| **Role and importance TEI** | Benefits of IT for territorial development, contribution to competitiveness and attractiveness, link to innovation, sustainability and inclusive growth. | Maftah et al. (2023) |

continued on following page

*Table 6. Continued*

| Concepts | Description | Authors |
|---|---|---|
| **TEI implementation** | Setting up an IT system, identifying key players, IT tools and methods (monitoring, analysis, information sharing, territorial information systems - SIT), concrete examples of IT projects. | Goytia-De La Torre et al. (2019) |
| **TEI issues and challenges** | Obstacles to IT implementation, lack of collaboration, communication and shared vision, resistance to change, digital divide, ethical aspects, anti-territorial intelligence. | Masselot (2023) |
| **Concrete case studies** | IT applications in specific contexts (cities, regions, countries), examples of successful projects, analysis of success factors and difficulties encountered. | Angelini (2010) |
| **Technologies and data for TEI** | The role of information and communication technologies (ICT), Big Data, data mining and artificial intelligence (AI) in IT, the importance of Open Data, territorial data management and analysis. | Knauf (2022) |
| **Governance and collaboration** | The importance of territorial governance, citizen participation and multi-stakeholder collaboration (public, private, civil society) for the success of IT. | Bouchida & Azougagh (2023) |

Source: the authors

## 3.3 Bibliometric Analysis:

Bibliometric analysis is a quantitative method that can be applied to a certain literature in order to map relationships between items, co-occurrence, trends, etc. For our research, we began by performing a VOSVIEWER analysis of a bibliography we created with PUBLISH OR PERISH software, giving the following results: (Figure 9). This representation illustrates a complex network of items around the concepts of territorial intelligence, digital technology and territorial development. VOSVIEWER groups items into clusters or thematic groups to delineate distinct but related themes. The central concepts of our research, such as territorial intelligence, digital sovereignty and smart city, are at the heart of this visualization. There is a clear interconnection between concepts such as territorial intelligence, digital sovereignty and territorial planning. (Bouhtati et al., 2024).

We can identify current trends such as smart cities and sustainable development as current issues. In addition, items such as big data and the Internet confirm the importance attached by the authors to technological dimensions.

*Figure 9. Network visualization*

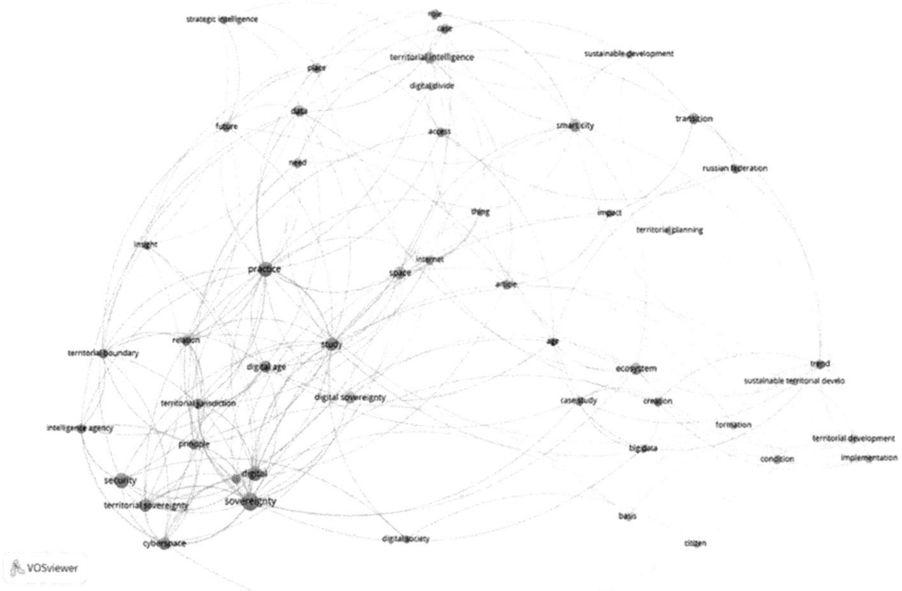


*Source: The authors (VOSVIEWER)*

Next, we wanted to investigate the authors whose work constitutes a homogeneous corpus in terms of the use of technologies in territorial management, and who are among the most cited in the literature. We started with the RESEARCHRABBIT.COM website, which visualizes a network of researchers and experts who have contributed key writings in a particular field (Figure 10).

*Figure 10. Most cited authors*

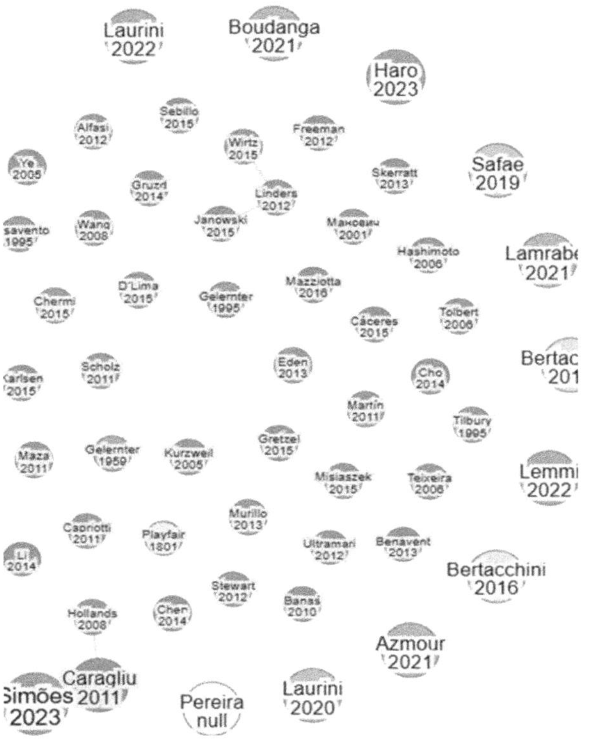


*Source: The authors (RESEARCHRABBIT.COM)*

The list includes authors who have made significant contributions to the theme of territorial economic intelligence (in green), as well as authors whose contributions are among the most cited (in blue). Going a step further, we asked another site, CONNECTEDPAPPERS.COM, for the following results (Figure 11).

*Figure 11. Most cited authors*

*Source: The authors (by CONNECTEDPAPPERS.COM)*

Here again, it's authors like Bertacchini, Masselot and Pélissier who stand out from the crowd, so much so that their contributions are considered elemntary and cited by their peers.

## 4. DISCUSSION

Our research has shown the richness of the concept of territorial economic intelligence as a decision-making tool, in a context marked by the massive use of new technologies that support it. Our thematic and bibliographical analysis reveals a number of trends that we would like to highlight. We are going to present the evolution of the concept of territorial intelligence through contexts and time, then we are going to talk about the different approaches adopted by the authors in order to define this concept, and finally we are going to present the future trends which are invited to become the standards of territorial intelligence in the years to come.

### 4.1 A Constantly Evolving Concept

From the earliest work on territorial economic intelligence (Bertacchini, 2004), it was clear that the concept is above all multi-disciplinary, as it is defined in relation to its economic, social and environmental dimensions... This holistic definition has helped to provide a frame of reference capable of explaining this notion in order to analyze its components. Nevertheless, our analysis shows that more and more authors are focusing on the technological aspect to the detriment of other aspects (Figure 12). This is due to the recent nature of technological breakthroughs in data transmission, the processing of massive quantities of information and intelligent models capable of making - or at least promoting - a decision. This work is converging towards an integration of these components into a single ecosystem capable of meeting the needs of all its users: this is the case, for example, of the Smart City, which constitutes one of the possible applications of territorial intelligence at local level (Coussi, 2022).

*Figure 12. Evolution of the territorial intelligence concept*

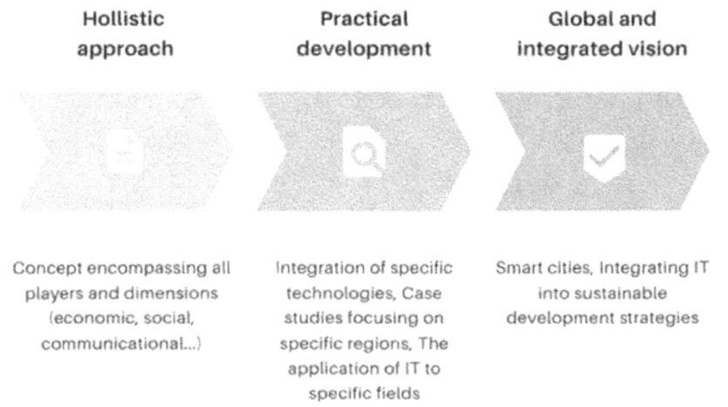


*Source: The authors*

Our choice to include recent articles (later than 2018) is explained by the rapidity with which technologies evolve and become obsolete after a few years. So, it's understandable that recent literature focuses on new technologies that have just been released or are still in their infancy. This is notably the case with Big Data and its implication in decision-making (Taj, 2023), through the process of data mining, which makes it possible to exploit data by giving it a meaning that can make it useful for decision-making (Maftah et al., 2023).

We have also detected a growing awareness of the importance of the role played by local players in the economic intelligence process. An increasing number of authors have realized that this component has been relegated to the background of scientific research, and have begun to analyze the possible interactions between the various players, their implications and possible modes of coordination (Alla et al., 2022; Idrissi & Abdelbaki, 2022).

Although the articles we analyzed were more or less homogeneous in their approach, often revolving around the classic dimensions (economic, social and technological), other concerns emerged from our research. For example, the issue of ethics was raised, raising questions about the use of personal data in a decision-making process (Jeanne, 2022). On the other hand, it's the problem of a sustainable ecological transition that ensures growth for the territory without compromising its ability to preserve its various resources (Bentaleb & Boukhari, 2023). Sometimes, themes original enough to be cited draw attention to a hitherto overlooked aspect, such as anti-territorial intelligence, which is characterized by a fragmentation of territorial development strategies, in place of an integrated and holistic vision of territorial economic intelligence. This observation reinforces the idea that research must evolve towards new, more integrated perspectives (Elhissoufi & Alla, 2024).

We have also taken care to include a variety of case studies concerning several territories, in order to take account of the diversity of approaches, constraints and opportunities (Figure 13). While we have focused on the Moroccan context (Ikhmim et al., 2022; Alla et al., 2023; Laghmam, 2020), we have equally included research that concerns European territories (Amairia, 2023), sub-Saharan Africa (Diakhaté, 2021) or America (Goytia-de la Torre,2019).

*Figure 13. Mind map of concepts related to territorial economic intelligence*

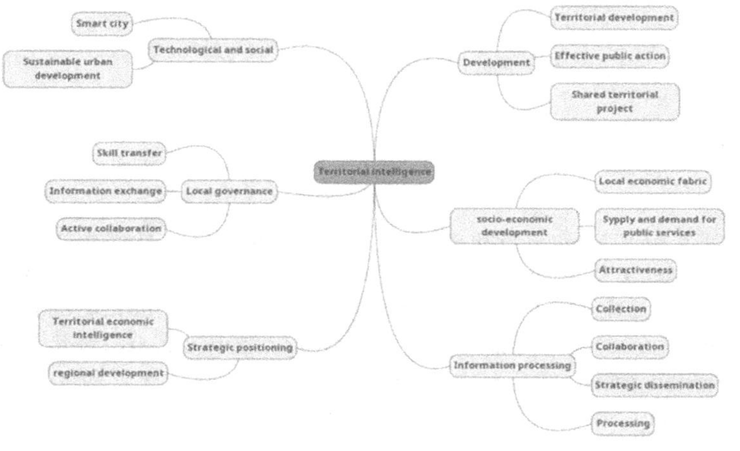


*Source: the authors (MINDUP)*

The corpus we have assembled deals with several varied and encompassing themes, but territorial development remains predominant in this research, reflecting the importance attached by authors to the environmental, ecological, social and demographic challenges facing territories in the years ahead (Bentaleb & Boukhari, 2023).

## 4.2 A Variety of Methodologies:

The authors we have consulted have approached the theme of territorial economic intelligence by highlighting the various dimensions of the phenomenon, and attempting to provide both a conceptual framework capable of explaining the various variables, and a case study of a given territory in order to validate or invalidate hypotheses. We have attempted to summarize these methodologies (Table 7).

*Table 7. Distribution of articles by methodology*

| Methodology | Auteurs | Description |
|---|---|---|
| **Normative** | Mouhib & Benkaraache (2023); Laurini & Donolo (2022); Helmi & Kasmi (2022); Boutahar & Debbagh (2022); Berrichi & Kajjout (2020 | Propose a theoretical and conceptual framework to define territorial economic intelligence and establish the standards to be met. |
| **Positivist** | Idrissi & Abdelbaki 2022), Benichou et al (2023), Robin & Coussi (2023) | Quantitative and empirical approaches, often accompanied by hypotheses to be tested and phenomena to be measured. |
| **Post-positivist** | Ikhmimet al. (2022); Diakhaté, (2021); Amairia (2023) | A reflexive approach that accepts the conceptual difficulty of defining territorial business intelligence as subject to subjective interpretation. |
| **Constructivist** | Ouaziz. (2021); Ouaziz (2022); Jeanne (2022) | Rather, a social and cultural construct that influences territorial business intelligence practices. |
| **Review** | Amairia, A. (2023); Jeanne, L. (2022); Ikhmim, S., Elmouaddine, H., & Alij, N. (2022) | Question existing territorial economic intelligence practices and propose new avenues for reflection. |
| **Pragmatic** | Coussi, O. (2022) | Practical applications of theoretical concepts. |

Source: The authors

Combining the distribution of methodologies used and years of publication, we can see that articles published between 2018 and 2021 attempt to provide a definition and conceptual framework, while proposing indicators that can be used to measure the scope of the phenomenon (Laghmam, 2020; Berrichi & Kajjout, 2020). Diakhaté (2021) brings the possibility of implementing territorial intelligence in specific contexts by analyzing the challenges of such an approach in Senegal. This period is characterized by articles focusing on the creation of a theoretical corpus needed to frame the concept (Ouaziz, 2021).

Subsequently, the research methodologies adopted by the authors underwent a certain diversification with critical and constructivist approaches. Some authors (Laurini & Donolo, 2022) or (Helmi & Kasmi, 2022) still provide conceptual and theoretical frameworks, but others (Ikhmim et al., 2022) rely on case studies to provide an analysis of the implementation of a territorial intelligence procedure. However, (Idrissi & Abdelbaki, 2022) mention actors as an essential dimension, emphasizing modes of coordination and collaboration (Figure 14).

*Figure 14. Distribution of articles by methodology and by year*

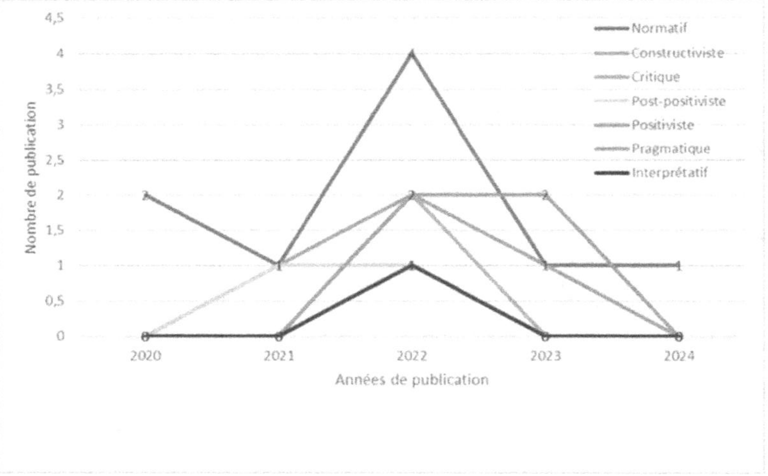


*Source: the authors*

The most recent articles mark a pronounced turn towards critical and post-positivist approaches, with an emphasis on questions of ethics and power, reflecting a change in the context affecting the territorial question in general, with a growing awareness of the importance of environmental and social dimensions in particular. There is also an interesting trend to study the impact of the COVID-19 health crisis on the adoption and accommodation of territorial economic intelligence practices in this context. (El Jaouhari & Alla, 2022).

## 4.3 Future Trends

In the near future, other technologies are set to become increasingly popular in terms of territorial intelligence and decision support. Smart cities are set to become the standards of the future, with a data-driven and more resilient approach. Artificial intelligence is now coupled with geographic information systems to better manage urban planning, migration flows and crime. This concept can be taken a step further with the Digital Twins, which consist in creating an identical replica of the territory in order to test large-scale simulations, thereby reducing risks, costs and lead times. This opens up huge possibilities in terms of modelling and forecasting, particularly in the case of natural disaster scenarios and the way they affect an area.

Artificial intelligence can also play a role in anticipation through the analysis of big data relating to pollution, traffic, the deployment of players, etc. with the aim of optimizing resources, leading to a significant reduction in costs and lead times.

Data exchange is even more secure thanks to blockchain technology, which encrypts identifiers and makes transactions anonymous, offering an extra layer of protection. Indeed, through the decentralisation of nodes, blockchain does not store information in a specific place, but rather on a network, which makes it particularly difficult for anyone to attempt to break in and steal personal data. In the context of smart cities, for example, this technology enables Transparent and Trustworthy Data Sharing, because it can create secure platforms for exchanging information between different government agencies, eventually leading to an integrated information system.

## CONCLUSION

This research on territorial business intelligence has shown that it is a concept in full evolution, driven by new technologies that are constantly shaping the way we interact with ever-massive quantities of information. Through the successive contributions of authors, the concept has undergone development and enrichment, starting with attempts at conceptualization and framing by the founders of the theme, who focused on a socio-economic vision, towards a holistic approach that reflects the complexity and richness of the concept, as well as the new challenges now facing territorial decision-makers. (Hmioui et al., 2017).

The emergence and widespread dissemination of information technologies, enabling the collection, processing and distribution of information, has opened up new possibilities for the various players involved in the decision-making process.

Our findings reveal a paradigm shift in how territories approach economic intelligence: The proliferation of digital data sources has exponentially increased the volume and variety of available economic information. While this presents unprecedented opportunities for insights, it also poses significant challenges in data integration, quality assurance, and privacy protection. Successful Territorial Economic Intelligence strategies now require robust data governance frameworks and advanced data management systems. The adoption of machine learning and AI-driven predictive models has dramatically enhanced the depth and accuracy of economic analysis. These tools enable territories to uncover complex patterns, forecast trends with greater precision, and simulate various economic scenarios. However, the effective use of these technologies demands new skill sets and a culture of data-driven decision-making among policymakers and economic development professionals. Digital platforms have revolutionized how economic intelligence is shared and utilized. Real-time information sharing and cross-sector collaborations have become not just possible but essential for competitive advantage. This shift necessitates a reevaluation of traditional organizational boundaries and the development of new models for public-private partnerships in economic development.

Nonetheless, there is a growing awareness of the importance of the role played by local players in coordinating and collaborating with each other, so as to deploy an integrated territorial business intelligence strategy. It is now clear that these players are key success factors.

But the use of these new technologies also brings its own set of challenges. The question of ethics is back with a vengeance in the current debate, in order to delimit the use of these technologies in a responsible manner. Environmental challenges are also a major preoccupation for decision-makers, especially with the resurgence of ecological issues around the world. The implications of these transformations are far-reaching. Territories that successfully adapt to this new digital paradigm of economic intelligence are likely to gain significant advantages in attracting investment, fostering innovation, and driving sustainable economic growth. Conversely, those slow to embrace these changes risk falling behind in an increasingly competitive global economy. However, it is crucial to note that the digital transformation of Territorial Economic Intelligence is not without its challenges. Issues of digital divide, data privacy, cybersecurity, and the ethical use of AI in economic decision-making must be carefully addressed to ensure that the benefits of these advancements are equitably distributed and do not exacerbate existing socio-economic disparities.

We emphasize that future research will be well advised to take an interest in certain dimensions that do not yet seem to have been sufficiently addressed, notably the changes in modes of governance post COVID-19 and the new imperatives of territorial resource management.

The importance of social factors is just as decisive as that of technology, insofar as the interactions between the players that ultimately make any territorial intelligence process a reality. In this sense, human capital and appropriate skills define the success of strategies in terms of analysing and interpreting the data collected by technological tools. It is becoming clear that training, knowledge sharing and collaboration between players is vital if relevant analyses are to be carried out. It is precisely this collaboration between various players (businesses, institutions, citizens, etc.) that has a major impact on the dynamism required to give meaning to any territorial intelligence strategy in order to improve the attractiveness and resilience of territories. However, it should be pointed out that reluctance to change remains the most decisive factor in the rejection of the use of new technologies by stakeholders. Training and awareness-raising efforts need to be put in place.

The interaction of technological and social factors can be analysed at several levels:

- Match between social needs and innovative technologies: the technologies that support territorial intelligence must respond to specific territorial needs and remedy specific malfunctions. After all, technologies are supposed to be the solution, not the problem. (Boudri et al., 2024).

- The impact of social habits on the use of technology: Since the explosion in the use of networks over the last 20 years, it is clear that information consumption habits have changed radically: the preferred channels are now online and browsing tools are increasingly mobile. Any local economic intelligence strategy must take these changes into account, in order to offer tools that are adapted to current needs, and anticipate future requirements.

As we reflect on the findings of this study, it is important to consider both the strengths and limitations of our research. This study offers several significant advantages that contribute to the field of Territorial Economic Intelligence (TEI) in the digital era. Firstly, we have provided a comprehensive framework that examines the digital transformation of TEI from multiple angles, including data acquisition, analytical capabilities, and knowledge dissemination. This holistic approach offers valuable insights into the interconnected nature of these aspects and their collective impact on territorial economic strategies. Furthermore, our research benefits from an interdisciplinary perspective, drawing on insights from economics, data science, public policy, and digital technology. This cross-disciplinary approach has allowed us to bridge gaps between different fields and offer a more nuanced understanding of the complex interplay between digital technologies and territorial economic development. The resulting analysis not only contributes to academic discourse but also provides practical implications for policymakers, economic development professionals, and researchers. By identifying key trends and challenges, we have aimed to provide actionable insights that can inform strategy development and resource allocation in territorial economic planning. Another strength of this study lies in its future-oriented analysis. By examining current trends and anticipating future developments, our research can help territories prepare for upcoming challenges and opportunities in the rapidly evolving digital landscape. This forward-looking perspective is crucial in a field where technological advancements can quickly reshape economic realities.

However, it is equally important to acknowledge the limitations of our study. The rapid pace of technological change presents a significant challenge, as some of our findings may have a limited shelf life. The field of digital TEI is dynamic, and future studies will need to continuously update and reassess the impact of emerging technologies on TEI strategies. Additionally, while we aimed for a broad analysis, our study may not fully capture the diverse economic and technological contexts of all territories globally. The applicability of our findings may vary depending on the specific economic, cultural, and technological conditions of different regions. Another limitation stems from the novelty of some digital TEI strategies, which means that long-term empirical data on their effectiveness is still limited. Our analysis, therefore, relies partly on theoretical projections and short-term observations, which may need validation through longitudinal studies. Furthermore, while our study emphasizes the technological aspects of TEI transformation, it may not fully address all socio-economic factors that influence territorial economic strategies. Future research could benefit from a more in-depth exploration of these non-technological factors. Lastly, while we touch upon ethical issues related to data privacy and AI use, a more comprehensive examination of the legal and ethical implications of digital TEI strategies was beyond the scope of this study. This presents an important area for future research, as the ethical use of data and AI in economic decision-making becomes increasingly crucial.

By acknowledging these advantages and limitations, we aim to provide a balanced view of our research contributions while also highlighting opportunities for future studies to build upon and extend this work. As the field of Territorial Economic Intelligence continues to evolve in the digital era, ongoing research will be crucial to refine our understanding and improve the effectiveness of TEI strategies. The path forward requires a delicate balance between embracing technological innovation and preserving the core principles of inclusive and sustainable economic development.

In conclusion, the use of technology in territorial management appears to be an ideal field for analysis and conceptualization. All research is encouraged in order to integrate technological advances into territorial economic intelligence processes. The path forward requires a delicate balance between embracing technological innovation and preserving the core principles of inclusive and sustainable economic development. By striking this balance, territories can harness the full potential of digital-era TEI to create resilient, adaptive, and prosperous economic ecosystems in an increasingly interconnected world.

## REFERENCES

Aarabe, M.. (2024). Smart Tourism Experience and Responsible Travelers' Behavior: A Systematic Literature Review. In El Archi, Y. (Eds.), *Promoting Responsible Tourism With Digital Platforms* (pp. 128–147). IGI Global., DOI: 10.4018/979-8-3693-3286-3.ch008

Aarabe, M., Ben Khizzou, N., Alla, L., & Benjelloun, A. (2024). Marketing Applications of Emerging Technologies: A Systematic Literature Review. In Alla, L., Hmioui, A., & Bentalha, B. (Eds.), *AI and Data Engineering Solutions for Effective Marketing* (pp. 23–47). IGI Global., DOI: 10.4018/979-8-3693-3172-9.ch002

Alla, L., Bentalha, B., & Elyoussfi, A. (2023). Intelligence territoriale et positionnement stratégique des regions au Maroc: Le cas de la région de Fès Meknes en perspective. In Le concept de l'intéligence en sciences juridiques, économiques et sociales (p. 215-237). https://hal.science/hal-04107659

Alla, L., Jaouhari, E. L., & Bentalha, B. (2022). Repenser l'entrepreneuriat au sein du secteur informel au Maroc à l'ère du post Covid-19: Pour approche prospective de la formalisation intégrative. *Alternatives Managériales et Economiques*, 4(1), 180–202.

Amairia, A. (2023). Comprendre la production de connaissance d'un dispositif d'Intelligence Economique Territoriale. L'évolution de la DATAR de la Région Nouvelle-Aquitaine [Phdthesis, Université de poitiers]. https://hal.science/tel-04528463

Angelini, J. (Réalisateur). (2010, décembre 1). Le débat public comme agir territorial: Méthodes qualitatives (Numéro 38, p. 171-180) [Enregistrement vidéo]. Presses universitaires de Bordeaux.

Benichou, A., Kharbach, O., Daoudi, L., & Youssoufi, H. (2023). Exploration empirique de l'Intelligence Territorial: Le rôle des acteurs, des initiatives et des changements futurs de la ville. *Revue Internationale du Chercheur*, 4(2), 2. https://www.revuechercheur.com/index.php/home/article/view/594

Bentahar, A., & Chadli, N. (2022). L'intelligence économique territorial: « Un outil pour asseoir l'attractivité et la compétitivité de la région de l'Oriental ». Dossiers de Recherches en Économie et Gestion, 10(1), Article 1.

Bentaleb, S., & Boukhari, H. E. (2023). Territorial intelligence for ecological transition: Case of the Fez Meknes region. African Journal of Business and Finance, 1, Article 2.

Bentalha, B. (2020). Big-Data et service supply chain management: Challenges et opportunités. *International Journal of Business and Technology Studies*, 1(3).

Bentalha, B., & Alla, L. (2024). Revealing the Subtleties: The Art of Qualitative Studies in Science and Management. In Bentalha, B., & Alla, L. (Eds.), *Applying Qualitative Research Methods to Management Science* (pp. 1–21). IGI Global., DOI: 10.4018/979-8-3693-5543-5.ch001

Bentalha, B., Hmioui, A., & Alla, L. (2020). La performance des entreprises de services: Un cadrage théorique d'un concept évolutif. *Alternatives Managériales Economiques*, 2(1), 58–78.

Berrichi, A., & Kajjout, S. (2020). L'intérêt des indicateurs dans une approche d'intelligence territoriale. Dossiers de Recherches en Économie et Gestion, 9(1), Article 1.

Bertacchini, Y. (2004). Intelligence territoriale. Mesurer la distance, penser la durée, mémoriser le virtuel.

Bertacchini, Y. (2012, October 1). Between Information and Communication Process, the Territorial Intelligence, as a Network Concept & a Framework to Shape Local Development (Vol. 2. *Numéro*, 18, 242–247.

Boudri, R., Bentalha, B., & Benjelloun, O. (2024). Phygital Marketing and the Pain of Paying: An Amazon Go Netnographic Case Study. In Alla, L., Hmioui, A., & Bentalha, B. (Eds.), *AI and Data Engineering Solutions for Effective Marketing* (pp. 348–363). IGI Global., DOI: 10.4018/979-8-3693-3172-9.ch017

Bouhtati, N., Alla, L., & Bentalha, B. (2023). Marketing Big Data Analytics and Customer Relationship Management: A Fuzzy Approach. In Integrating Intelligence and Sustainability in Supply Chains (pp. 75-86). IGI Global. DOI: 10.4018/979-8-3693-0225-5.ch004

Bouhtati, N., Alla, L., & Ed-Daakouri, I. (2024). Smart Data Analysis and Prediction of Responsible Customer Behaviour in Tourism: An Exploratory Review of the Literature. In El Archi, Y., Benbba, B., Dávid, L., & Cardoso, L. (Eds.), *Promoting Responsible Tourism With Digital Platforms* (pp. 189–212). IGI Global., DOI: 10.4018/979-8-3693-3286-3.ch011

Boutahar, S., & Debbagh, B. (2022). Intelligence territoriale, apprentissage collectif, innovation collaborative, quel lien? Une approche théorique et conceptuelle. Alternatives Managériales Economiques, 4(4), Article 4.

Chakir, K., & Mazzaourou, A. (2023). The intermediary role of territorial economic intelligence between human capital and the economic development of territories. *Revue Internationale du Chercheur*, 4(1), 1.

Chaves, M. M. N., dos Santos, A. P. R., dos Santosa, N. P., & Larocca, L. M. (2017),"Use of the software IRAMUTEQ in qualitative research: an experience report", Computer supported qualitative research, p. 39-48. DOI: 10.1007/978-3-319-43271-7_4

Coussi, O. (2022). La Smart City comme nouveau mythe rationnel de l'intelligence territoriale. *Droit et Ville*, (93), 177–201. DOI: 10.3917/dv.093.0177

Diakhaté, D. (2021). La gouvernance de l'information à l'épreuve de la réforme territoriale : Éléments de structuration d'une politique d'Intelligence Territoriale (IT) au Sénégal. Akofena - Revue scientifique des Sciences du Langage, Lettres, Langues & Communication, 3(003). https://hal.science/hal-03175081

Du, S., & Xie, C. (2021). Paradoxes of artificial intelligence in consumer markets: Ethical challenges and opportunities. *Journal of Business Research*, 129, 961–974. DOI: 10.1016/j.jbusres.2020.08.024

Elhissoufi, M., & Alla, L. (2024). Artificial Intelligence in Costumer Acquisition: A Bibliometric Study. In Alla, L., Hmioui, A., & Bentalha, B. (Eds.), *AI and Data Engineering Solutions for Effective Marketing* (pp. 1–22). IGI Global., DOI: 10.4018/979-8-3693-3172-9.ch001

Elmezdeghi, O., & Achibane, M. (2023). *Perspectives de la gestion territoriale au Maroc, au contexte de la pandémie du Covid-19*. INTERNATIONAL JOURNAL OF ADVANCED RESEARCH IN INNOVATION, MANAGEMENT & SOCIAL SCIENCES.

Goytia-de la Torre, L., Gretel Borja-Hernández, C., Ortíz-García, M., Dina Valenzuela-Robles B., Landa-Rivera, I., Salmón-de la Torre, G. (2019, septembre 23). Territorial Intelligence through the application of Business and Competitive intelligence: The case of Guadalupe, Zacatecas (Mexico) (Vol. 16, Numéro 2, p. 118-123) [Enregistrement vidéo]. https://doi.org/DOI: 10.52155/IJPSAT.V16.2.1249

Helmi, D., & Kasmi, A. (2022). Intelligence territoriale au service des clusters touristiques : Vecteur tacite du développement durable. Dossiers de Recherches en Économie et Gestion, 10(1), Article 1. DOI: 10.34874/IMIST.PRSM/doreg-v10i1 .31650

Herbaux, P. (2004, mai 28). Les « TIC », un outil d'intelligence territoriale [Enregistrement vidéo]. https://typeset.io/papers/les-tic-un-outil-d-intelligence-territoriale-77w262d3bk

Hmioui, A., Alla, L., & Bentalha, B. (2017). Pilotage de la touristicité territoriale au Maroc Proposition d'un indice de tourisctieité pour la destination Fès. *Entrepreneuriat, Innovation, Gouvernance et Développement territorial*, 120-143.

Hmioui, A., Bentalha, B., & Beniaich, R. (2024). Green Supply Chain Management et développement territorial: Une revue de littérature. *Alternatives Managériales Economiques*, 6(2), 52–74.

Idrissi, S. L. E., & Abdelbaki, N. (2022). L'intelligence territoriale appliquée à la région Rabat-Salé-Kénitra. *Revue Française d'Economie et de Gestion*, 3(8), 8. https://www.revuefreg.fr/index.php/home/article/view/794

Ikhmim, S., Elmouaddine, H., & Alij, N. (2022). Intelligence territoriale et croissance inclusive: Vers la mise en place d'un dispositif d'intelligence territoriale inclusive dans la ville de Salé. International Journal of Accounting, Finance, Auditing, Management and Economics, 3(3-2), Article 3-2.

Iliass, B., & Ahmed, A. (2023). Territorial intelligence in morocco : International benchmark and development path. *American Scientific Journal*, 3(20), 786–786.

Jaouhari, EL, S., & Lhoussaine, A. L. L. A. (2022). L'approche territoriale et la gestion de l'impact de la pandémie de Covid-19: Cas des collectivités territoriales. *Alternatives Managériales Economiques*, 4(1), 245–265.

Jeanne, L. (2022). L'intelligence économique territoriale envisagée comme une géoéthique : Essai de problématisation. DOI: 10.34699/RIDO.2022.8

Kharroubi, I. F. (2022). Les conditions d'application des mécanismes d'intelligence territoriale Cas de la ville de Rabat. Alternatives Managériales Economiques, 4(4), Article 4.

Knauf, A. (2022). Une mise en perspective bibliométrique de l'intelligence économique reposant sur sa revue de reference: La R2IE. Revue française des sciences de l'information et de la communication, 24, Article 24.

Laghmam, I. (2020). L'intelligence économique au service du territoire : Cas du Maroc. *Revue Internationale des Sciences de Gestion*, 3(3), 3. https://revue-isg.com/index.php/home/article/view/365

Lamrabet, M. (2021). The Territorial Big Data An innovative concept of Territorial Economic Intelligence. Environmental and Water Sciences, public Health and Territorial Intelligence Journal, 5(2), Article 2.

Lamrabet, M., & Benkaraache, T. (2021). Le Big Data Territorial: Un concept novateur d'Intelligence Économique Territoriale. EWASH & TI: Environmental and Water Sciences. *Public Health and Territorial Intelligence*, 5(2), 621–631.

Lamrabet, M., & Benkaraache, T. (2022). Phénomène d'intelligence « anti-territoriale » ou le territoire en tant que « dé-construction » d'acteurs : Problématique et critique de l'Intelligence Territoriale au Maroc. Alternatives Managériales Economiques, 4(4), Article 4.

Lamsiah, A., & Bentalha, B. (2022). Dakhla: A Growing Touristic Destination with a Diplomatic Sway. *Alternatives Managériales Economiques*, 4, 94–115.

Laurini, R., & Donolo, R. (2022). Computer-Assisted Visual Reasoning for Territorial Intelligence. *Journal of Visual Languages and Computing*, 2022(2), 1–11. DOI: 10.18293/JVLC2022-N2-021

Maftah, J., Pheniqi, Y., & Bourkkadi, S. (2023). The use of data mining to influence social entrepreneurship and territorial dynamics. E3S Web of Conferences, 412, 01104.

Masselot, C. (2023). Territoires intelligents versus intelligence territoriale: Tenter de mieux vivre ensemble. In D. V. Meyer, F. Couston, & P. C. et J. Araszkiewiez (Éds.), (Re)qualifier les territories: Promesses et actes. Éditions ÉRES.

Mastour, S., Ezzaher, R., & Allach, M. F. (2024). Les activités d'offshoring : Revue de littérature du levier de la compétitivité territoriale. *Revue Internationale des Sciences de Gestion*, 7(2), 2.

Mentzer, J. T., & Kahn, K. B. (1995). A framework of logistics research. *Journal of Business Logistics*, 16(1), 231–250.

Meziane, B., Bentalha, B., & Alla, L. (2024). La PME logistique et le développement territorial régional: Une analyse qualitative. *Alternatives Managériales Economiques*, 6(4), 1–22.

Mezzanzanica, M., Cesarini, M., & Boselli, R. (2010, octobre 1). Business Intelligence Exploitation for investigating territorial Systems, methodological Overviews and empirical Considerations [Enregistrement vidéo]. SE.

Mouhib, S., & Benkaraache, T. (2023). Action publique: Apport d'un dispositif d'intelligence territoriale. *Revue des Etudes et Recherche en Logistique et Développement*, 8, 17–33.

Negri-Ribalta, C., Lombard-Platet, M., & Salinesi, C. (2024). Understanding the GDPR from a requirements engineering perspective—A systematic mapping study on regulatory data protection requirements. *Requirements Engineering*. Advance online publication. DOI: 10.1007/s00766-024-00423-4

Nouhaila, B. K., Aarabe, M., & Alla, L. (2024). The Impact of Digitalisation on the Customer Experience in Medical Tourism: A Systematic Review. In Talukder, M., Kumar, S., & Tyagi, P. (Eds.), *Impact of AI and Tech-Driven Solutions in Hospitality and Tourism* (pp. 408–428). IGI Global., DOI: 10.4018/979-8-3693-6755-1.ch020

Ouassou, S., & Bakour, C. (2024). Intelligence territoriale : État de l'art théorique. International Journal of Accounting, Finance, Auditing, Management and Economics, 5(4), Article 4.

Ouaziz, A. (2021). *L'intelligence territoriale aux défis de la ville marocaine « Smart City*. African and Mediterranean Journal of Architecture and Urbanism.

Ouaziz, A. (2022a). Intelligence territoriale de la ville: Conceptions, mouvements, performances et initiatives. *Journal of Social Sciences*, 6(24), 24.

Ouaziz, A. (2022b). Portrait empirique de l'intelligence territoriale (I.T): Entre actes, acteurs et actions d'évolution de la ville futur. Revue d'Innovation et Dynamiques Territoriales, 1, Article 1.

Pumain, D. (2021). Les systèmes de villes et l'intelligence territoriale.

Robin, J., & Coussi, O. (2023). L'intelligence territoriale en contexte de crise sanitaire: Quand une mauvaise communication affecte la stratégie et l'effectivité de la gouvernance territoriale d'un territoire ultramarin. Revue COSSI: communication, organisation, société du savoir et information, 12.

Rousseaux, F., Saurel, P., & Petit, J. (2014). Knowledge Engineering or Digital Humanities? Territorial Intelligence, a Case in Point. *Studies in Computational Intelligence*, 514, 129–187.

Taj, T. (2023). The evolution of the use of big data to serve Moroccan territorial economic intelligence. Revue Du Contrôle, de La Comptabilité et de l'audit, 7(1), Article 1.

Zeryouh, A., & Daabaji, A. (2022). Les enjeux de l'intelligence économique dans le développement territorial: Vers une approche de mise en œuvre de l'intelligence territoriale. Alternatives Managériales Economiques, 4(3), Article 3.

# Compilation of References


Aarabe, M., Ben Khizzou, N., Alla, L., & Benjelloun, A. (2024). Smart tourism experience and responsible travelers' behavior. In *Advances in Hospitality, Tourism, and the Services Industry* (pp. 128–147). IGI Global.

Aarabe, M., Khizzou, N. B., Alla, L., & Benjelloun, A. (2024). Smart Tourism Experience and Responsible Travelers' Behavior : A Systematic Literature Review. *Promoting Responsible Tourism With Digital Platforms*, 128-147.

Aarabe, M., Ben Khizzou, N., Alla, L., & Benjelloun, A. (2024). Marketing Applications of Emerging Technologies: A Systematic Literature Review. In Alla, L., Hmioui, A., & Bentalha, B. (Eds.), *AI and Data Engineering Solutions for Effective Marketing* (pp. 23–47). IGI Global., DOI: 10.4018/979-8-3693-3172-9.ch002

Aarabe, M., El Archi, Y., & Alla, L. (2024). Smart tourism experience and responsible travelers' behavior: A systematic literature review. In El Archi, Y. (Eds.), *Promoting responsible tourism with digital platforms* (pp. 128–147). IGI Global., DOI: 10.4018/979-8-3693-3286-3.ch008

Abbas, Q., Ahmad, G., Alyas, T., Alghamdi, T., Alsaawy, Y., & Alzahrani, A. (2023). Revolutionizing urban mobility: IoT-enhanced autonomous parking solutions with transfer learning for smart cities. *Sensors (Basel)*, 23(21), 8753. DOI: 10.3390/s23218753 PMID: 37960453

Abdelghaffar, H. M., & Rakha, H. A. (2021). Development and testing of a novel game theoretic decentralized traffic signal controller. *IEEE Transactions on Intelligent Transportation Systems*, 22(1), 231–242. DOI: 10.1109/TITS.2019.2955918

Abella, A., Ortiz-de-Urbina-Criado, M., & De-Pablos-Heredero, C. (2017). A model for the analysis of data-driven innovation and value generation in smart cities' ecosystems. *Cities (London, England)*, 64, 47–53. DOI: 10.1016/j.cities.2017.01.011

Abideen, A. Z., Sorooshian, S., Sundram, V. P. K., & Mohammed, A. (2023). Collaborative insights on horizontal logistics to integrate supply chain planning and transportation logistics planning–A systematic review and thematic mapping. *Journal of Open Innovation*, 9(2), 100066. DOI: 10.1016/j.joitmc.2023.100066

Abu Bakar, H., Razali, R., & Jambari, D. I. (2022). A Qualitative Study of Legacy Systems Modernisation for Citizen-Centric Digital Government. *Sustainability (Basel)*, 14(17), 10951. Advance online publication. DOI: 10.3390/su141710951

Abushaikha, I. (2018). The influence of logistics clustering on distribution capabilities: A qualitative study. *International Journal of Retail & Distribution Management*, 46(6), 577–594. DOI: 10.1108/IJRDM-01-2018-0018

Adib, F., Mao, H., Kabelac, Z., Katabi, D., & Miller, R. C. (2015). Smart homes that monitor breathing and heart rate. *Proceedings of the 33rd Annual ACM Conference on Human Factors in Computing Systems.* https://doi.org/DOI: 10.1145/2702123.2702200

Aftab, M., & Myeong, S. (2022). An analysis of foreign residents' perceptions and behaviors regarding digital government portal services in the Republic of South Korea. *International Review of Administrative Sciences*. Advance online publication. DOI: 10.1177/00208523221084498

Agarwalla, S., & Saha, D. (2019). *A study on forestry and sustainable livelihood with special reference to Similipal National Park.* Artha Beekshan.

Agbozo, E. (2019). Applying apriori rules mining in evaluating digital government services patronization by a younger generation of users in Russia. *TEM Journal, 8*(4), 1207–1212. https://doi.org/DOI: 10.18421/TEM84-14

Aghion, P., & Howitt, P. (1990). A model of growth through creative destruction. DOI: 10.2307/2951599

Agrawal, A., Gans, J. S., & Goldfarb, A. (2018). *Prediction machines: The simple economics of artificial intelligence*. Harvard Business Review Press.

Aguilar, J., Garces-Jimenez, A., R-Moreno, M. D., & García, R. (2021). A systematic literature review on the use of artificial intelligence in energy self-management in smart buildings. *Renewable & Sustainable Energy Reviews*, 151, 111530. DOI: 10.1016/j.rser.2021.111530

Ahmad, S., Iqbal, N., Jamil, F., & Kim, D. (2020). Optimal policy-making for municipal waste management based on predictive model optimization. *IEEE Access : Practical Innovations, Open Solutions*, 8, 218458–218469. DOI: 10.1109/ACCESS.2020.3042598

Ahuja, I. P. S. (2011). Managing research and development for core competence building in an organization. *Journal of Technology Management & Innovation*, 6(1), 58–65. DOI: 10.4067/S0718-27242011000100006

Ajibade, P., & Mutula, S. M. (2020). Big data, 4IR and electronic banking and banking systems applications in South Africa and Nigeria. *Banks and Bank Systems*, 15(2), 187. DOI: 10.21511/bbs.15(2).2020.17

Akulov, A. S., Bezotosnaya, A. D., & Pak, T. V. (2023). Algorithm of finding optimal location for distribution centers for order delivery by using unsupervised machine learning methods. *Vestnik of Astrakhan State Technical University. Series: Management, computer science and informatics, 2023*(3), 105-113. DOI: 10.24143/2072-9502-2023-3-105-113

Al Sulaimani, A. H. A., & Ozuem, W. (2022). Understanding the role of transparency, participation, and collaboration for achieving open digital government goals in Oman. *Transforming Government: People. Transforming Government*, 16(4), 595–612. DOI: 10.1108/TG-04-2022-0044

Alahmad, T., Neményi, M., & Nyéki, A. (2023). Applying IoT sensors and big data to improve precision crop production: A review. *Agronomy (Basel)*, 13(10), 2603. DOI: 10.3390/agronomy13102603

Al-Ammary, J. H. (2021). The uptake of digital government services: Toward digital transformation in the Kingdom of Bahrain. *Electronic Government*, 17(2), 199–219. DOI: 10.1504/EG.2021.114580

Alam, T., Gupta, R., Nasurudeen Ahamed, N., Ullah, A., & Almaghthwi, A. (2024). Smart mobility adoption in sustainable smart cities to establish a growing ecosystem: Challenges and opportunities. *MRS Energy & Sustainability : a Review Journal*. Advance online publication. DOI: 10.1557/s43581-024-00092-4

Albahari, A., Klofsten, M., & Rasmussen, E. (2017). Initiating the knowledge spillover entrepreneurship process: A longitudinal analysis of university-industry collaborations. *The Journal of Technology Transfer*, 42(4), 900–916.

Alemu, T., Choramo, T. T., & Jeldu, A. (2023). External Debt, Institutional Quality and Economic Growth in East African Countries. *Journal of East-West Business*, 29(4), 375–401. DOI: 10.1080/10669868.2023.2248121

Alhussen, A., & Ansari, A. S. (2024). Real-time prediction of urban traffic problems based on artificial intelligence-enhanced mobile ad hoc networks (MANETS). *Computers, Materials & Continua*, 79(2), 1903–1923. DOI: 10.32604/cmc.2024.049260

Ali Al-Hussein, M. A.-H., Alabdallat, W. I. M., Abu Rumman, M. A., Jawabreh, O., & Ali, B. J. A. (2023). Impact of E-Government Applications on Reducing Administrative Burden in Delivering Public Service. *Information Sciences Letters*, 12(3), 1663–1671. DOI: 10.18576/isl/120350

Ali, B., & Awad, A. (2018). Cyber and physical security vulnerability assessment for IoT-based smart homes. *Sensors (Basel)*, 18(3), 817. DOI: 10.3390/s18030817

Alla, L., Bentalha, B., & Elyoussfi, A. (2023). Intelligence territoriale et positionnement stratégique des regions au Maroc : Le cas de la région de Fès Meknes en perspective. In *Le concept de l'intéligence en sciences juridiques, économiques et sociales* (p. 215-237). https://hal.science/hal-04107659

Alla, L., Bentalha, B., & Elyoussfi, A. (2023). Intelligence territoriale et positionnement stratégique des regions au Maroc : Le cas de la région de Fès Meknes en perspective. *Le concept de l'intéligence en sciences juridiques, économiques et sociales*, 215-237.

Alla, L., Bentalha, B., & Elyoussfi, A. (2023). Intelligence territoriale et positionnement stratégique des regions au Maroc: Le cas de la région de Fès Meknes en perspective. In Le concept de l'intéligence en sciences juridiques, économiques et sociales (p. 215-237). https://hal.science/hal-04107659

Alla, L., Bentalha, B., & Elyoussfi, A. (2023). Intelligence territoriale et positionnement stratégique des regions au Maroc: Le cas de la région de Fès Meknes en perspective. In *Le concept de l'intelligence en sciences juridiques, économiques et sociales* (pp. 215-237).

Alla, L., Bentalha, B., & Elyoussfi, A. (2023). Intelligence territoriale et positionnement stratégique des regions au Maroc: Le cas de la région de Fès Meknes en perspective. Le concept de l'intéligence en sciences juridiques, économiques et sociales, 215-237.

Alla, L., Bentalha, B., & Elyoussfi, A. (2023). Intelligence territoriale et positionnement stratégique des regions au Maroc: Le cas de la région de Fès Meknes en perspective. *Le concept de l'intéligence en sciences juridiques, économiques et sociales*. 215–237.

Alla, L., Bentalha, B., & Elyoussfi, A. (2023). Intelligence territoriale et positionnement stratégique des régions au Maroc: Le cas de la région de Fès Meknes en perspective. *Le concept de l'intelligence en sciences juridiques, économiques et sociales*, 215-237.

Alla, L., Jaouhari, E. L., & Bentalha, B. (2022). Repenser l'entrepreneuriat au sein du secteur informel au Maroc à l'ère du post Covid-19: Pour approche prospective de la formalisation intégrative. *Alternatives Managériales et Economiques*, 4(1), 180–202.

Allam, Z., & Dhunny, Z. A. (2019). On big data, artificial intelligence and smart cities. *Cities (London, England)*, 89, 80–91. DOI: 10.1016/j.cities.2019.01.032

Almamy, A. S. M. (2022). Understanding factors affecting e-government adoption in Saudi Arabia: The role of religiosity. *International Journal of Customer Relationship Marketing and Management*, 13(1), 1–15. Advance online publication. DOI: 10.4018/IJCRMM.289209

Almeida, R., & Fernandes, A. M. (2008). Openness and technological innovations in developing countries: Evidence from firm-level surveys. *The Journal of Development Studies*, 44(5), 701–727. DOI: 10.1080/00220380802009217

Almihat, M. G., Kahn, M. T., Aboalez, K., & Almaktoof, A. M. (2022). Energy and sustainable development in smart cities: An overview. *Smart Cities*, 5(4), 1389–1408. DOI: 10.3390/smartcities5040071

Alomari, M. K., Khan, H. U., Khan, S., Al-Maadid, A. A., Abu-Shawish, Z. K., & Hammami, H. (2021). Systematic analysis of artificial intelligence-based platforms for identifying governance and access control. *Security and Communication Networks*, 2021, 1–10. DOI: 10.1155/2021/8686469

Alqudah, M. A. (2021). Investment Artificial Intelligence in Decision-making Processes in the Jordanian Ministry of Interior. *International Journal of Innovations in Engineering Research and Technology*, 8(10), 40–53.

Alqudah, M. A., & Muradkhanli, L. (2021). Artificial intelligence in electric government; ethical challenges and governance in Jordan. *Electronic Research Journal of Social Sciences and Humanities*, 3, 65–74.

Al-rawahna, A. S. M., Chen, S. C., & Hung, C. W. (2019). The barriers of E-government success: An empirical study from Jordan. *Available atSSRN* 3498847. DOI: 10.2139/ssrn.3498847

Al-Sakran, H. O., & Alsudairi, M. A. (2021). Usability and Accessibility Assessment of Saudi Arabia Mobile E-Government Websites. *IEEE Access : Practical Innovations, Open Solutions*, 9, 48254–48275. DOI: 10.1109/ACCESS.2021.3068917

Amairia, A. (2023). Comprendre la production de connaissance d'un dispositif d'Intelligence Economique Territoriale. L'évolution de la DATAR de la Région Nouvelle-Aquitaine [Phdthesis, Université de poitiers]. https://hal.science/tel-04528463

Ambrosino, D., & Sciomachen, A. (2021). Impact of Externalities on the Design and Management of Multimodal Logistic Networks. *Sustainability (Basel)*, 13(9), 5080. DOI: 10.3390/su13095080

Amirudin, A., Urbański, M., Saputra, J., Johansyah, M. D., Latip, L., Tarmizi, A., & Afrizal, T. (2021). The impact of the Covid-19 self-isolation policy on the work of vulnerable groups. *International Journal of Environmental Research and Public Health*, 18(12), 6452. Advance online publication. DOI: 10.3390/ijerph18126452 PMID: 34203631

Amisse, S., & Muller, P. (2011). Les logiques à l'origine des dynamiques de coopération dans les clusters*: L'exemple de filières du végétal spécialisé. *Revue d'Économie Régionale et Urbaine*, (1), 115–149. DOI: 10.3917/reru.111.0115

Anagnostopoulos, T. (2021). A predictive vehicle ride-sharing recommendation system for smart cities commuting. *Smart Cities*, 4(1), 177–191. DOI: 10.3390/smartcities4010010

Anantapatnaikuni, S. (2018). *Enhancing Energy Efficiency and Renewable Energy in the future electricity system of Odisha.*

Anarfo, E. B., Abor, J. Y., Osei, K. A., & Gyeke-Dako, A. (2019). Monetary policy and financial inclusion in sub-Sahara Africa: A panel VAR approach. *Journal of African Business*, 20(4), 549–572. DOI: 10.1080/15228916.2019.1580998

Anedda, M., Fadda, M., Girau, R., Pau, G., & Giusto, D. (2023). A social smart city for public and private mobility: A real case study. *Computer Networks*, 220, 109464. DOI: 10.1016/j.comnet.2022.109464

Angelini, J. (Réalisateur). (2010, décembre 1). Le débat public comme agir territorial: Méthodes qualitatives (Numéro 38, p. 171-180) [Enregistrement vidéo]. Presses universitaires de Bordeaux.

Annamalah, S., Paraman, P., & Ahmed, S. (2023). Unveiling the dynamics of open innovation and collaborative network tourism in ASEAN nations. *Asia Pacific Journal of Tourism Research*, 28(11), 1199–1225. DOI: 10.1080/10941665.2023.2293788

Annas, M., & Humairoh, . (2023). The Green Food Supply Chain : Factors Affecting Food Distributor's Sustainability Through Positive WOM. [Edisi Elektronik]. *Jurnal Manajemen*, 14(2), 277–289. DOI: 10.32832/jm-uika.v14i2.11651

Antoine, S., Sillig, C., & Ghiara, H. (2017). Advanced logistics in Italy: A city network analysis. *Tijdschrift voor Economische en Sociale Geografie*, 108(6), 753–767. DOI: 10.1111/tesg.12215

Antonialli, F., Martinesco, A., & Mira-Bonnardel, S. (2022). Artificial intelligence as a determinant for reshaping the automotive industry and urban mobility services. *International Journal of Automotive Technology and Management*, 22(3), 324. DOI: 10.1504/IJATM.2022.124828

Arcieri, F., Fioravanti, F., Nardelli, E., & Talamo, M. (2004). Reliable peer-to-peer access for Italian citizens to digital government services on the internet. In T. R. (Ed.), *Lecture Notes in Computer Science (including subseries Lecture Notes in Artificial Intelligence and Lecture Notes in Bioinformatics)* (Vol. 3183, pp. 250–255). Springer Verlag. DOI: 10.1007/978-3-540-30078-6_41

Arfi, W. B., Hikkerova, L., & Sahut, J. M. (2018). External knowledge sources, green innovation and performance. *Technological Forecasting and Social Change*, 129, 210–220. DOI: 10.1016/j.techfore.2017.09.017

Arıca, R., & Çorbacı, A. (2019). Müşterilerin ortak üreticilik rolünü konu edinen araştırmaların incelenmesi: Scopus veri tabanında taranan turizm ve otelcilik dergilerinin bibliyometrik açıdan değerlendirilmesi. *Turizm Akademik Dergisi*, 6(1), 263–276.

Arksey, H., & O'Malley, L. (2005). Scoping Studies : Towards a Methodological Framework. *International Journal of Social Research Methodology*, 8(1), 19–32. DOI: 10.1080/1364557032000119616

Arnstein, S. R. (1969). A ladder of citizen participation. *Journal of the American Institute of Planners*, 35(4), 216–224. DOI: 10.1080/01944366908977225

Arsac, J. J. (1971). Le concept d'information et l'informatique. *Dialectica*, 25(3-4), 207–219. DOI: 10.1111/j.1746-8361.1971.tb00600.x

Artmann, M., Inostroza, L., & Fan, P. (2019). Urban sprawl, compact urban development and green cities. How much do we know, how much do we agree? *Ecological Indicators*, 96, 3–9. DOI: 10.1016/j.ecolind.2018.10.059

Arvianto, A., Sopha, B. M., Asih, A. M. S., & Imron, M. A. (2021). City logistics challenges and innovative solutions in developed and developing economies: A systematic literature review. *International Journal of Engineering Business Management*, 13, 18479790211039723. DOI: 10.1177/18479790211039723

Aryuni, M., Miranda, E., Fernando, Y., & Kibtiah, T. M. (2020). The early detection system for terrorism in Indonesia from Twitter content uses the Naïve Bayes Algorithm. *5th International Conference on Management and Information Technology, ICIMTech 2020*, 555–559. DOI: 10.1109/ICIMTech50083.2020.9211261

Asner, G. P., & Tupayachi, R. (2017). Accelerated deforestation in the Amazon: Satellite and airborne mapping reveals forest degradation. *Science Advances*, 3(8), e1601682.

Astvatsaturova, Ch. V., & Kazakova, N. A. (2022). Forecast of the Impact of the Railway Container Transportation Market on the GDP of the Russian Federation. *Finance: Theory and Practice*, 26(6), 6–16. DOI: 10.26794/2587-5671-2022-26-6-6-16

Aulawi, H., & Fitriani, L. (2020). Enterprise architecture planning for e-government. *International Journal of Innovation, Creativity and Change, 11*(2), 251–270. https://www.scopus.com/inward/record.uri?eid=2-s2.0-85081600438&partnerID=40&md5=62e6cf125e6f5ca0145f6857523d5eed

Ayob, N., Teasdale, S., & Fagan, K. (2016). How Social Innovation 'Came to Be': Tracing the Evolution of a Contested Concept. *Journal of Social Policy*, 45(4), 635–653. DOI: 10.1017/S004727941600009X

Ayyash, M. M., Herzallah, F. A. T., & Al-Sharafi, M. A. (2022). Arab cultural dimensions model for e-government services adoption in public sector organisations: An empirical examination. *Electronic Government*, 18(1), 9–44. DOI: 10.1504/EG.2022.119608

Bachofner, M., Lemardelé, C., Estrada, M., & Pagès, L. (2022). City logistics: Challenges and opportunities for technology providers. *Journal of Urban Mobility*, 2, 100020. DOI: 10.1016/j.urbmob.2022.100020

Badre, M. E. Z. I. A. N. E., Badr, B. E. N. T. A. L. H. A., & Lhoussaine, A. L. L. A. (2024). La PME logistique et le développement territorial régional: Une analyse qualitative. *Alternatives Managériales Economiques*, 6(4), 1–22.

Baduge, S. K., Thilakarathna, S., Perera, J. S., Arashpour, M., Sharafi, P., Teodosio, B., Shringi, A., & Mendis, P. (2022). Artificial intelligence and smart vision for building and construction 4.0: Machine and deep learning methods and applications. *Automation in Construction*, 141, 104440. DOI: 10.1016/j.autcon.2022.104440

Baheer, B. A., Lamas, D., & Sousa, S. (2020). A systematic literature review on existing digital government architectures: State-of-the-art, challenges, and prospects. *Administrative Sciences*, 10(2), 25. Advance online publication. DOI: 10.3390/admsci10020025

Bajwa, S., Dabral, A., Chatterjee, R., & Shaw, R. (2021). Co-Producing Knowledge Innovation through Thematic Incubators for Disaster Risk Reduction and Sustainable Development in India. *Sustainability (Basel)*, 13(4), 2044. DOI: 10.3390/su13042044

Bakici, T., Almirall, E., & Wareham, J. (2013). A smart city initiative: The case of Barcelona. *Journal of the Knowledge Economy*, 4(2), 135–148. DOI: 10.1007/s13132-012-0084-9

Bakshi, A., & Kumar Panigrahi, A. (2022). Study on Climate Change and Its Impact on Coastal Habitats with Special Reference to Ecosystem Vulnerability of the Odisha Coastline, India. In *Applied Geomorphology and Contemporary Issues* (pp. 475–497). Springer International Publishing. DOI: 10.1007/978-3-031-04532-5_25

Bala, M., & Verma, D. (2018). Governance to good governance through E-Governance: A critical review of concept, model, initiatives & challenges in India. *International Journal of Management. IT and Engineering*, 8(10), 244–269.

Banyai, C., & Fleming, D. (2016). Collective impact capacity building: Finding gold in Southwest Florida. *Community Development (Columbus, Ohio)*, 47(2), 259–273. DOI: 10.1080/15575330.2015.1135174

Baranowski, S., Busko, E., Shishlo, S., Usevich, W., Androsik, J., Mistseiko, M., Tanaś, W., & Szymanek, M. (2015). Formation mechanism of logistics cluster in Belarus. *Agriculture and Agricultural Science Procedia*, 7, 12–20. DOI: 10.1016/j.aaspro.2015.12.022

Barman, N. K., Bera, G., & Amrit, K. (2016). Estimation of fishery sector as a coastal resource zone to explore the associate problems and opportunity at Balasore coastal district, Odisha, India. *International Journal of Geomatics and Geosciences*, 6(3), 1696–1707.

Bartoletti, M., Cimoli, T., Pompianu, L., & Serusi, S. (2018). Blockchain for social good: A quantitative analysis. *Proceedings of the 4th EAI International Conference on Smart Objects and Technologies for Social Good*, 37–42. DOI: 10.1145/3284869.3284881

Barzelay, M. (2001). *The new public management: Improving research and policy dialogue*. University of California Press.

Basu, A., & Nayak, N. C. (2011). Underlying causes of forest cover change in Odisha, India. *Forest Policy and Economics*, 13(7), 563–569. DOI: 10.1016/j.forpol.2011.07.004

Bataglin, J. C., & Kruglianskas, I. (2022). Social Innovation: Field Analysis and Gaps for Future Research. *Sustainability (Basel)*, 14(3), 1153. DOI: 10.3390/su14031153

Bathelt, H., Malmberg, A., & Maskell, P. (2004). Clusters and knowledge: Local buzz, global pipelines and the process of knowledge creation. *Progress in Human Geography*, 28(1), 31–56. DOI: 10.1191/0309132504ph469oa

Batty, M. (2013). *The new science of cities*. MIT Press. DOI: 10.7551/mit-press/9399.001.0001

Batty, M. (2023). Digital twins for smart cities. *Journal of Urban Technology*, 30(2), 151–167.

Batty, M., Axhausen, K. W., Giannotti, F., Pozdnoukhov, A., Bazzani, A., Wachowicz, M., Ouzounis, G., & Portugali, Y. (2012). Smart cities of the future. *The European Physical Journal. Special Topics*, 214(1), 481–518. DOI: 10.1140/epjst/e2012-01703-3

Baydar, A. M., Süral, H., & Çelik, M. (2019). Potential effects of logistics clusters: The case of Turkish Freight Villages. *Journal of Cleaner Production*, 233, 399–411. DOI: 10.1016/j.jclepro.2019.05.294

Beckers, J., Thomas, I., Vanoutrive, T., & Verhetsel, A. (2018). Logistics clusters, including inter-firm relations through community detection. *European Journal of Transport and Infrastructure Research*, 18(2). Advance online publication. DOI: 10.18757/EJTIR.2018.18.2.3229

Behera, B., & Tandi, S. (2019). Impact of climate change on agriculture: A study of western Odisha. [AJMR]. *Asian Journal of Multidimensional Research*, 8(2), 145–156. DOI: 10.5958/2278-4853.2019.00042.9

Behera, J. K., Mishra, P., Bhattacharya, M., Behera, B., & Kar, N. B. (2023). A cross-sectional study about the impacts of climate change on living organisms: A case study of Odisha province of India. In *Visualization Techniques for Climate Change with Machine Learning and Artificial Intelligence* (pp. 399–421). Elsevier. DOI: 10.1016/B978-0-323-99714-0.00014-5

Behera, K., & Tandi, D. (2017). Small-scale hydropower development in Odisha: Environmental impacts and opportunities. *Hydropower Journal*, 8(1), 73–88.

Behmanesh, E., & Pannek, J. (2016). A memetic algorithm with extended random path encoding for a closed-loop supply chain model with flexible delivery. *Logistics Research*, 9(1), 22. DOI: 10.1007/s12159-016-0150-y

Bektas, T., Crainic, T. G., & Van Woensel, T. (2015). From managing urban freight to smart city logistics networks.

Belcher, B. M., Claus, R., Davel, R., & Jones, S. M. (2022). Evaluating and improving the contributions of university research to social innovation. *Social Enterprise Journal*, 18(1), 51–120. DOI: 10.1108/SEJ-10-2020-0099

Belmondo, C. (2004). *Les processus collectifs de création de connaissances dans les groupes de travail. Comparaison de deux processus au sein d'une cellule de veille concurrentielle*. Conférence Internationale de Management Stratégique.

Belussi, F., & Hervas-Oliver, J. L. (Eds.). (2017). *Unfolding cluster evolution*. Routledge.

Benarbi, M. A., & Tamnine, L. (2019). *Analyse d'impact des articles sur la gestion des risques liés aux Partenariats Public-Privé (PPP)*. *2*(4), 23.

Benarbi, M. A., & Tamnine, L. (2020). Développement de la recherche sur la gestion des risques liés aux projets de Partenariat Public-Privé (PPP). *International Journal of Business and Technology Studies And Research, 2*(2), 10 pages. DOI: 10.5281/zenodo.3820086

Benbba, B. (2016). Les Cluster Supply Chains: Une nouvelle piste pour améliorer l'agilité des chaînes logistiques. *Revue Marocaine de Management, Logistique et Transport*, (1).

Bencekri, M., Kim, S., Fan, Y. V., & Lee, S. (2024). Locating carbon-neutral mobility hubs using artificial intelligence techniques. *Scientific Reports*, 14(1), 12328. DOI: 10.1038/s41598-024-62701-z PMID: 38811628

Benichou, A., Kharbach, O., Daoudi, L., & Youssoufi, H. (2023). Exploration empirique de l'Intelligence Territorial: Le rôle des acteurs, des initiatives et des changements futurs de la ville. *Revue Internationale du Chercheur*, 4(2), 2. https://www.revuechercheur.com/index.php/home/article/view/594

Benner, M. (2020). The Role of Emerging Technologies in Modern Public Administration. *Public Administration Review*, 80(5), 800–815.

Benoit, S. (2024). Ancrage industriel en bioéconomie: quel rôle joue la gouvernance logistique?. *Les Cahiers Scientifiques du Transport-Scientific Papers in Transportation, 78.*

Bensfia, C., & Bouklata, A. (2022). *Validity of the TAM Model in the context of electronic payment ofport dues in Morocco*. 1-5.

Bensfia, C., & Bouklata, A. (2023). Evaluation of the electronic port right of way payment information system. *Management Systems in Production Engineering*, 31(3), 254–262. DOI: 10.2478/mspe-2023-0028

BENSFIA, C., & BOUKLATA, A. (2024). Évaluation du succès du Système Communautaire Portuaire : Cas du Maroc. *Alternatives Managériales Economiques*, 6(2), 23–51.

BENSFIA, C., Bouklata, A., & NEJJARI, R. (2024). Explorer la digitalisation pour l'économie circulaire : Une revue systématique. *Revue de Gestion et d'Économie*, 12(2), 305–321.

Bentahar, A., & Chadli, N. (2022). L'intelligence économique territorial: « Un outil pour asseoir l'attractivité et la compétitivité de la région de l'Oriental ». Dossiers de Recherches en Économie et Gestion, 10(1), Article 1.

Bentaleb, S., & Boukhari, H. E. (2023). Territorial intelligence for ecological transition: Case of the Fez Meknes region. African Journal of Business and Finance, 1, Article 2.

Bentalha, B., & Alla, L. (2024). Revealing the Subtleties : The Art of Qualitative Studies in Science and Management. In *Applying Qualitative Research Methods to Management Science* (p. 1-21). IGI Global.

Bentalha, B. (2020). Big-Data et service supply chain management: Challenges et opportunités. *International Journal of Business and Technology Studies*, 1(3).

Bentalha, B., & Alla, L. (2024). Revealing the Subtleties: The Art of Qualitative Studies in Science and Management. In Bentalha, B., & Alla, L. (Eds.), *Applying Qualitative Research Methods to Management Science* (pp. 1–21). IGI Global., DOI: 10.4018/979-8-3693-5543-5.ch001

Bentalha, B., Hmioui, A., & Alla, L. (2020). La performance des entreprises de services: Un cadrage théorique d'un concept évolutif. *Alternatives Managériales Economiques*, 2(1), 58–78.

Berrichi, A., & Kajjout, S. (2020). L'intérêt des indicateurs dans une approche d'intelligence territoriale. Dossiers de Recherches en Économie et Gestion, 9(1), Article 1.

Bertacchini, Y. (2004). Intelligence territoriale. Mesurer la distance, penser la durée, mémoriser le virtuel.

Bertacchini, Y. (2010). Intelligence territoriale : Une lecture retro-prospective. *Revue internationale d'intelligence économique, 2*(1), 65-97.

Bertacchini, Y. (2012, October 1). Between Information and Communication Process, the Territorial Intelligence, as a Network Concept & a Framework to Shape Local Development (Vol. 2. *Numéro*, 18, 242–247.

Bhalotia, N., Kumar, M., Alameen, A., Mohapatra, H., & Kolhar, M. (2023). A helping hand to the elderly: Securing their freedom through the HAIE framework. *Applied Sciences (Basel, Switzerland)*, 13(11), 6797. DOI: 10.3390/app13116797

Bharadiya, J. P. (2023). The role of machine learning in transforming business intelligence. *International Journal of Computing and Artificial Intelligence*, 4(1), 16–24. DOI: 10.33545/27076571.2023.v4.i1a.60

Bhardwaj, A., & Rajput, V. S. (2023). An overview of assessing the quality of scientific documents by using machine learning techniques. *Journal of Information Science and Technology*, 10(3), 438–451.

Bibri, S. E. (2018). A foundational framework for smart sustainable city development : Theoretical, disciplinary, and discursive dimensions and their synergies. *Sustainable Cities and Society*, 38, 758–794. DOI: 10.1016/j.scs.2017.12.032

Bibri, S. E., Huang, J., & Krogstie, J. (2024). Artificial intelligence of things for synergizing smarter eco-city brain, metabolism, and platform: Pioneering data-driven environmental governance. *Sustainable Cities and Society*, 108, 105516. Advance online publication. DOI: 10.1016/j.scs.2024.105516

Bibri, S. E., & Krogstie, J. (2020). The emerging data–driven Smart City and its innovative applied solutions for sustainability : The cases of London and Barcelona. *Energy Informatics*, 3(1), 5. DOI: 10.1186/s42162-020-00108-6

Boix, R., Hervás-Oliver, J. L., & De Miguel-Molina, B. (2015). Micro-geographies of creative industries clusters in Europe: From hot spots to assemblages. *Papers in Regional Science*, 94(4), 753–773. DOI: 10.1111/pirs.12094

Bokhari, S. A. A., & Myeong, S. (2022). Use of Artificial Intelligence in Smart Cities for Smart Decision-Making: A Social Innovation Perspective. *Sustainability (Basel)*, 14(2), 620. DOI: 10.3390/su14020620

Bokolo, A. J. (2023). Inclusive and safe mobility needs of senior citizens: Implications for age-friendly cities and communities. *Urban Science (Basel, Switzerland)*, 7(4), 103. DOI: 10.3390/urbansci7040103

Boons, F., & Lüdeke-Freund, F. (2013). Business models for sustainable innovation: State-of-the-art and steps towards a research agenda. *Journal of Cleaner Production*, 45, 9–19. DOI: 10.1016/j.jclepro.2012.07.007

Boudri, R., Bentalha, B., & Benjelloun, O. (2024). Phygital marketing and the pain of paying: An Amazon Go netnographic case study. In Alla, L., Hmioui, A., & Bentalha, B. (Eds.), *AI and data engineering solutions for effective marketing* (pp. 348–363). IGI Global., DOI: 10.4018/979-8-3693-3172-9.ch017

Bouhtati, N., El Yaacoubi, Y., Bentalha, B., & Alla, L. (2024). Leviers logistiques de promotion du commerce équitable des produits de terroir: Une esquisse de modèle d'analyse. *Alternatives Managériales Economiques*, 6(Spécial 1), 17-35.

Bouhtati, N., El Yaacoubi, Y., Bentalha, B., & Alla, L. (2024). Leviers logistiques de promotion du commerce équitable des produits de terroir: Une esquisse de modèle d'analyse. *Alternatives Managériales Économiques*, 6(Spécial 1), 17-35.

Bouhtati, N., El Yaacoubi, Y., Bentalha, B., & Lhoussaine, A. L. L. A. (2024). Leviers logistiques de promotion du commerce équitable des produits de terroir: Une esquisse de modèle d'analyse. Alternatives Managériales Economiques, 6(Spécial 1), 17-35.

Bouhtati, N., EL Yaacoubi, Y., Bentalha, B., & Lhoussaine, A. L. L. A. (2024). Leviers logistiques de promotion du commerce équitable des produits de terroir: Une esquisse de modèle d'analyse. *Alternatives Managériales Economiques, 6*(Spécial 1), 17-35.

BOUHTATI, N., EL YAACOUBI, Y., BENTALHA, B., & Lhoussaine, A. L. L. A. (2024). Leviers logistiques de promotion du commerce équitable des produits de terroir: Une esquisse de modèle d'analyse. Alternatives Managériales Economiques, 6(Spécial 1), 17-35.

Bouhtati, N., Alla, L., & Bentalha, B. (2023). Marketing Big Data Analytics and Customer Relationship Management: A Fuzzy Approach. In Bentalha, B., Hmioui, A., & Alla, L. (Eds.), *Integrating Intelligence and Sustainability in Supply Chains* (pp. 75–86). IGI Global., DOI: 10.4018/979-8-3693-0225-5.ch004

Bouhtati, N., Alla, L., & Ed-Daakouri, I. (2024). Smart Data Analysis and Prediction of Responsible Customer Behaviour in Tourism: An Exploratory Review of the Literature. In El Archi, Y., Benbba, B., Dávid, L., & Cardoso, L. (Eds.), *Promoting Responsible Tourism With Digital Platforms* (pp. 189–212). IGI Global., DOI: 10.4018/979-8-3693-3286-3.ch011

Bouhtati, N., El Yaacoubi, Y., Bentalha, B., & Alla, L. (2024). Leviers logistiques de promotion du commerce équitable des produits de terroir: Une esquisse de modèle d'analyse. *Alternatives Managériales Economiques*, 6, 17–35.

Bouhtati, N., Yaacoubi, Y. E., Bentalha, B., & Alla, L. (2024). Leviers logistiques de promotion du commerce équitable des produits de terroir : Une esquisse de modèle d'analyse. *Alternatives Managériales Economiques, 6*(Spécial 1), Article Spécial 1. https://doi.org/DOI: 10.48374/IMIST.PRSM/ame-v6iSpécial

Bouklata, A., & Bensfia, C. (2020). *Digitalization of port passage procedures : Focus on the transit time of Goods*. 1-6.

Bourne, L. (2018). Stakeholder relationship management: A maturity model for organisational implementation. *International Journal of Project Management*, 36(3), 475–487.

Boutahar, S., & Debbagh, B. (2022). Intelligence territoriale, apprentissage collectif, innovation collaborative, quel lien? Une approche théorique et conceptuelle. Alternatives Managériales Economiques, 4(4), Article 4.

Boyd, A. D., & Paveglio, T. B. (2015). "Placing" Energy Development in a Local Context: Exploring the Origins of Rural Community Perspectives. *Journal of Rural and Community Development*, 10(2), 2. https://journals.brandonu.ca/jrcd/article/view/1155

Braun, V., & Clarke, V. (2006). Using thematic analysis in psychology. *Qualitative Research in Psychology*, 3(2), 77–101. DOI: 10.1191/1478088706qp063oa

Brillouin, L. (1971). *Science and. Information Theory*. Academic.

Brinkerhoff, D. W., & Brinkerhoff, J. M. (2011). Public–private partnerships : Perspectives on purposes, publicness, and good governance. *Wiley, 31*(1), 2-14. DOI: 10.1002/pad.584

Brouer, B. D., Alvarez, J. F., Plum, C. E. M., Pisinger, D., & Sigurd, M. M. (2014). A Base Integer Programming Model and Benchmark Suite for Liner-Shipping Network Design. *Transportation Science*, 48(2), 281–312. DOI: 10.1287/trsc.2013.0471

Brown, J. S., & Duguid, P. (1991). Organizational learning and communities-of-practice: Toward a unified view of working, learning, and innovation. *Organization Science*, 2(1), 40–57. DOI: 10.1287/orsc.2.1.40

Brynjolfsson, E., & McAfee, A. (2014). *The second machine age: Work, progress, and prosperity in a time of brilliant technologies*. W.W. Norton & Company.

Brynjolfsson, E., McAfee, A., & Sorell, T. (2023). Automation technologies in territorial management: Streamlining operations and enhancing efficiency. *Harvard Business Review*, 101(2), 112–125.

Bucchiarone, A., Battisti, S., Marconi, A., Maldacea, R., & Ponce, D. C. (2021). Autonomous shuttle-as-a-service (ASaaS): Challenges, opportunities, and social implications. *IEEE Transactions on Intelligent Transportation Systems*, 22(6), 3790–3799. DOI: 10.1109/TITS.2020.3025670

Bucher, D., Mangili, F., Cellina, F., Bonesana, C., Jonietz, D., & Raubal, M. (2019). From location tracking to personalized eco-feedback: A framework for geographic information collection, processing and visualization to promote sustainable mobility behaviors. *Travel Behaviour & Society*, 14, 43–56. DOI: 10.1016/j.tbs.2018.09.005

Bugaj, M., Durana, P., Blazek, R., & Horak, J. (2023). Industry 4.0: Marvels in profitability in the transport sector. *Mathematics*, 11(17), 3647. DOI: 10.3390/math11173647

Bussador, A., Bauermann, B. F. C., Matrakas, M. D., Padilha, J. C., & De Freitas Zara, K. R. (2023). DTI-BR model applied in Foz do Iguaçu, Brazil, for its transformation into a smart tourism destination. *Journal of Infrastructure. Policy and Development*, 7(2), 2152. DOI: 10.24294/jipd.v7i2.2152

Cabrer-Borràs, B., & Serrano-Domingo, G. (2007). Innovation and R&D spillover effects in Spanish regions: A spatial approach. *Research Policy*, 36(9), 1357–1371. DOI: 10.1016/j.respol.2007.04.012

Cajaiba-Santana, G. (2014). Social innovation: Moving the field forward. A conceptual framework. *Technological Forecasting and Social Change*, 82, 42–51. DOI: 10.1016/j.techfore.2013.05.008

California Department of Food and Agriculture. (2023). Precision agriculture in California's Central Valley. Retrieved from https://www.cdfa.ca.gov/plant/pe/PrecisionAgCentralValley.html

Cao, L. (2023). AI and data science for smart emergency, crisis and disaster resilience. *International Journal of Data Science and Analytics*, 15(3), 231–246. DOI: 10.1007/s41060-023-00393-w PMID: 37035277

Caputo, F., Magliocca, P., Canestrino, R., & Rescigno, E. (2023). Rethinking the role of technology for citizens' engagement and sustainable development in smart cities. *Sustainability (Basel)*, 15(13), 10400. DOI: 10.3390/su151310400

Carayannis, E. G., & Morawska-Jancelewicz, J. (2022). The Futures of Europe: Society 5.0 and Industry 5.0 as Driving Forces of Future Universities. *Journal of the Knowledge Economy*, 13(4), 3445–3471. DOI: 10.1007/s13132-021-00854-2

Carlan, V., Sys, C., & Vanelslander, T. (2016). How port community systems can contribute to port competitiveness : Developing a cost–benefit framework. *Research in Transportation Business & Management*, 19, 51–64. DOI: 10.1016/j.rtbm.2016.03.009

Casino, F., Dasaklis, T. K., & Patsakis, C. (2019). A systematic literature review of blockchain-based applications: Current status, classification and open issues. *Telematics and Informatics*, 36, 55–81. DOI: 10.1016/j.tele.2018.11.006

Castelnovo, W., & Sorrentino, M. (2018). The digital government imperative: A context-aware perspective. *Public Management Review*, 20(5), 709–725. DOI: 10.1080/14719037.2017.1305693

Castro, C., & Lopes, C. (2022). Digital Government and Sustainable Development. *Journal of the Knowledge Economy*, 13(2), 880–903. DOI: 10.1007/s13132-021-00749-2

Cellina, F., Derboni, M., Giuffrida, V., Tomic, U., & Hoerler, R. (2024). Trust me if you can: Practical challenges affecting the integration of carpooling in mobility-as-a-service platforms. *Travel Behaviour & Society*, 37, 100832. DOI: 10.1016/j.tbs.2024.100832

Cerasoli, M., & Mattarocci, G. (2020). The land rent as a tool for reuse of existing real estate (against the policy of unsustainable growth of "new" real estate development) : La rendita come strumento di rilancio del riuso intelligente (e contro l'insostenibile cultura del nuovo). *Valori e Valutazioni*, 27, 101–110. DOI: 10.48264/VVSIEV-20202710

Certomà, C. (2021). *Digital Social Innovation: Spatial Imaginaries and Technological Resistances in Urban Governance*. Springer International Publishing., DOI: 10.1007/978-3-030-80451-0

Chakir, K., & Mazzaourou, A. (2023). The intermediary role of territorial economic intelligence between human capital and the economic development of territories. *Revue Internationale du Chercheur*, 4(1), 1.

Chaminade, C. (2009). *On the concept of Global Innovation Networks and its use in INGINEUS*. CIRCLE electronic working paper, 2009/05. Sweden: Lund University.

Chandel, S. S., Shrivastva, R., Sharma, V., & Ramasamy, P. (2016). Overview of the initiatives in renewable energy sector under the national action plan on climate change in India. *Renewable & Sustainable Energy Reviews*, 54, 866–873. DOI: 10.1016/j.rser.2015.10.057

Chang, Y. T., & Lee, H. J. (2017). Smart mobility: Exploring the potential of autonomous vehicles in urban mobility. *Transportation Research Procedia*, 25, 2636–2653.

Chaves, M. M. N., dos Santos, A. P. R., dos Santosa, N. P., & Larocca, L. M. (2017),"Use of the software IRAMUTEQ in qualitative research: an experience report", Computer supported qualitative research, p. 39-48. DOI: 10.1007/978-3-319-43271-7_4

Cheng, C., Fang, D., Yin, H., & Dong, L. (2020). Evolutionary learning in big data analysis: A survey of algorithms. *IEEE Transactions on Emerging Topics in Computing*, 8(2), 1–14.

Chen, J., Hill, A. A., & Urbano, L. D. (2009). A GIS-based model for urban flood inundation. *Journal of Hydrology (Amsterdam)*, 373(1-2), 184–192. DOI: 10.1016/j.jhydrol.2009.04.021

Chen, J., Liu, C., & Zhang, H. (2023). Privacy-preserving data sharing in IoT-based territorial management. *IEEE Internet of Things Journal*, 10(1), 234–245.

Chen, J., Tao, S., Teng, S., Chen, Y., Zhang, H., & Wang, F.-Y. (2023). Toward sustainable intelligent transportation systems in 2050: Fairness and eco-responsibility. *IEEE Transactions on Intelligent Vehicles*, 8(6), 3537–3540. DOI: 10.1109/TIV.2023.3286873

Chen, L., Thombre, S., Järvinen, K., Lohan, E. S., Alén-Savikko, A., Leppäkoski, H., & Tailang, M. (2019). pH-dependent release potential of natural polymers in sustained release of ornidazole from colon-targeted delivery system. *International Journal of Technology*, 9, 1–10.

Chen, Y. (2021). *AI for livestock management*. Animal Tech Quarterly.

Chen, Z., Li, X., & Xia, X. (2021). Socioeconomic status, ambidextrous learning, and farmers' adoption of biological control technology: Evidence from 650 kiwifruit growers in China. *Pest Management Science*, 78(2), 475–487. DOI: 10.1002/ps.6642

Chesbrough, H. W. (2003). *Open innovation: The new imperative for creating and profiting from technology*. Harvard Business Press.

Chhetri, P., Butcher, T., & Corbitt, B. (2014). Characterising spatial logistics employment clusters. *International Journal of Physical Distribution & Logistics Management*, 44(3), 221–241. DOI: 10.1108/IJPDLM-03-2012-0086

Chioni, C., Pezzica, C., & Favargiotti, S. (2024). Territorial digital twins: A key for increasing the community resilience of fragile mountain inner territories? *Sustainable Development (Bradford)*, 32(2), 1548–1563. DOI: 10.1002/sd.2688

Choi, H., Chung, C.-S., & Cho, Y. (2022). Changes in planning approach: A comparative study of digital government policies in South Korea and Denmark. *European Planning Studies*. Advance online publication. DOI: 10.1080/09654313.2022.2132787

Chong, Y.-W., Villanueva-Libunao, K., Chee, S.-Y., Alvarez, M. J., Yau, K.-L. A., & Keoh, S. L. (2022). Artificial intelligence policies to enhance urban mobility in Southeast Asia. *Frontiers in Sustainable Cities*, 4, 824391. DOI: 10.3389/frsc.2022.824391

Chourabi, H., Nam, T., & Walker, S.. (2012). Understanding smart cities: An integrative framework. In *Proceedings of the 45th Hawaii International Conference on System Sciences* (pp. 2289-2297).

Christiani, L. (2018). Opportunities and Challenges of Implementing Cloud Computing as an Automation Solution for Collaboration Between Libraries. Anuva: Journal of Cultural. *Library and Information Studies*, 2(1), 43–53.

Christopoulos, G., & Wintjes, R. (2023). Identifying Clusters as Local Innovation Systems. *Journal of the Knowledge Economy*, •••, 1–40.

Cirianni, F. M. M., Comi, A., & Quattrone, A. (2023). Mobility control centre and artificial intelligence for sustainable urban districts. *Information (Basel)*, 14(10), 581. DOI: 10.3390/info14100581

Citron, D. K., & Pasquale, F. (2014). The scored society: Due process for automated predictions. *Washington Law Review (Seattle, Wash.)*, 89(1), 1–33.

City of Amsterdam. (2023). Smart City Amsterdam: Building a sustainable and connected urban environment. Retrieved from https://www.amsterdam.nl/en/smartcity/

City of Stockholm. (2023). Smart waste management: Optimizing waste collection in Stockholm. Retrieved from https://international.stockholm.se/smartcity/waste-management/

Clarke, A. (2020). Digital government units: What are they, and what do they mean for digital era public management renewal? *International Public Management Journal*, 23(3), 358–379. DOI: 10.1080/10967494.2019.1686447

Clement, J., Manjon, M., & Crutzen, N. (2022). Factors for collaboration amongst smart city stakeholders: A local government perspective. *Government Information Quarterly*, 39(4), 101746. DOI: 10.1016/j.giq.2022.101746

Colding, J., Wallhagen, M., Sörqvist, P., Marcus, L., Hillman, K., Samuelsson, K., & Barthel, S. (2020). Applying a systems perspective on the notion of the smart city. *Smart Cities*, 3(2), 420–429. DOI: 10.3390/smartcities3020022

Contreras-Espinosa, R. S., & Blanco-M, A. (2022). A Literature Review of E-government Services with Gamification Elements. *International Journal of Public Administration*, 45(13), 964–980. DOI: 10.1080/01900692.2021.1930042

Cooke, P. (2008). Regional innovation systems, clean technology & Jacobian cluster-platform policies. *Regional Science Policy & Practice*, 1(1), 23–45. DOI: 10.1111/j.1757-7802.2008.00002.x

Coussi, O. (2022). La Smart City comme nouveau mythe rationnel de l'intelligence territoriale. *Droit et Ville*, (93), 177–201. DOI: 10.3917/dv.093.0177

Cristóbal, T., Quesada-Arencibia, A., De Blasio, G. S., Padrón, G., Alayón, F., & García, C. R. (2022). Using data mining to estimate patterns of contagion-risk interactions in an intercity public road transport system. *IEEE Access : Practical Innovations, Open Solutions*, 10, 99150–99167. DOI: 10.1109/ACCESS.2022.3206838

Cruz, C. O., & Sarmento, J. M. (2017). Reforming traditional PPP models to cope with the challenges of smart cities. *Competition and Regulation in Network Industries*, 18(1-2), 94–114. DOI: 10.1177/1783591717734794

Cui, L., Weng, S., Nadeem, A. M., Rafique, M. Z., & Shahzad, U. (2022). Exploring the role of renewable energy, urbanization and structural change for environmental sustainability: Comparative analysis for practical implications. *Renewable Energy*, 184, 215–224. DOI: 10.1016/j.renene.2021.11.075

D'Amico, G., Szopik-Depczyńska, K., Dembińska, I., & Ioppolo, G. (2021). Smart and sustainable logistics of Port cities: A framework for comprehending enabling factors, domains and goals. *Sustainable Cities and Society*, 69, 102801. DOI: 10.1016/j.scs.2021.102801

D'Amore, G., Di Vaio, A., Balsalobre-Lorente, D., & Boccia, F. (2022). Artificial intelligence in the water–energy–food model: A holistic approach towards sustainable development goals. *Sustainability (Basel)*, 14(2), 867. DOI: 10.3390/su14020867

Da Xu, L., He, W., & Li, S. (2014). Internet of things in industries: A survey. *IEEE Transactions on Industrial Informatics*, 10(4), 2233–2243. DOI: 10.1109/TII.2014.2300753

Daba Ayana, I., Demissie, W. M., & Sore, A. G. (2023). Effect of External Debt on Economic Growth in Sub-Saharan Africa: System GMM Estimation. *Cogent Economics & Finance*, 11(2), 2256197. Advance online publication. DOI: 10.1080/23322039.2023.2256197

Dablanc, L. (2023). Policy and planning for urban logistics. In *The Routledge handbook of urban logistics* (pp. 251–266). Routledge. DOI: 10.4324/9781003241478-23

Danquah, M., & Amankwah-Amoah, J. (2017). Assessing the relationships between human capital, innovation and technology adoption: Evidence from sub-Saharan Africa. *Technological Forecasting and Social Change*, 122, 24–33. DOI: 10.1016/j.techfore.2017.04.021

Das, S. (2016). Economics of Natural Disasters in Odisha (First Ed.). Bhubaneswar: Research gate. DOI: 10.1093/acprof:oso/9780199464784.003.0009

Das, A., & Ghosh, R. (2019). Climate-resilient farming practices in Odisha: Lessons for sustainable agriculture. *Journal of Agricultural Sustainability*, 12(3), 78–90.

Dash, N., & Behera, K. (2022). Conservation of wetlands and sustainable inland fisheries development in Odisha. *Inland Fisheries and Sustainability*, 23(4), 88–99.

Das, I., Lauria, V., Kay, S., Cazcarro, I., Arto, I., Fernandes, J. A., & Hazra, S.as. (2020). Effects of climate change and management policies on marine fisheries productivity in the north-east coast of India. *The Science of the Total Environment*, 724, 138082. DOI: 10.1016/j.scitotenv.2020.138082 PMID: 32268283

Das, R., & Mohanty, S. (2020). Wind energy potential in Odisha's coastal areas. *Journal of Wind Energy*, 36(6), 215–228.

Das, S., Jena, D., Mishra, P., Daoun, A., Ganesha, H. S., Pradhan, T., & Patra, P. K. (2024). Climate change and agriculture in a mining context of Odisha, India. *Multidisciplinary Science Journal*, 6(10), 2024208–2024208. DOI: 10.31893/multiscience.2024208

Das, U., & Ghosh, S. (2019). Contrasting resilience of agriculture to climate change in coastal and non-coastal districts of Odisha. *Indian Journal of Agricultural Sciences*, 89(5), 769–774. DOI: 10.56093/ijas.v89i5.89655

Davenport, T. H., & Ronanki, R. (2018). Artificial intelligence for the real world. *Harvard Business Review*, 96(1), 108–116.

Davydovich, A., Karamova, A., Fesenko, O., & Anisimova, N. (2020). Transport and logistics infrastructure of the Krasnodar Krai : Problems and solutions. *E3S Web of Conferences, 164*, 07007. DOI: 10.1051/e3sconf/202016407007

de l'Économie Numérique, M. (2018). *Plan Maroc Numérique 2020*. Gouvernement du Maroc.

Degbey, W. Y., Eriksson, T., Rodgers, P., & Oguji, N. (2021). Understanding cross-border mergers and acquisitions of African firms: The role of dynamic capabilities in enabling competitiveness amidst contextual constraints. *Thunderbird International Business Review*, 63(1), 77–93. DOI: 10.1002/tie.22138

Delgado, M., Porter, M. E., & Stern, S. (2014). Clusters, convergence, and economic performance. *Research Policy*, 43(10), 1785–1799. DOI: 10.1016/j.respol.2014.05.007

Delgado, M., Porter, M. E., & Stern, S. (2016). Defining clusters of related industries. *Journal of Economic Geography*, 16(1), 1–38. DOI: 10.1093/jeg/lbv017

Denyer, D., & Tranfield, D. (2006). Using qualitative research synthesis to build an actionable knowledge base. *Management Decision*, 44(2), 213–227. DOI: 10.1108/00251740610650201

Desty, R. T., & Arumsari, W. (2022). Receiving COVID-19 Messages on Social Media to the Community of Semarang City. *Pack*, 18(2), 217–224. DOI: 10.15294/kemas.v18i2.33132

Devi, P., Kizielewicz, B., Guleria, A., Shekhovtsov, A., Wątróbski, J., Królikowski, T., Więckowski, J., & Sałabun, W. (2022). Decision support in selecting a reliable strategy for sustainable urban transport based on Laplacian energy of T-spherical fuzzy graphs. *Energies*, 15(14), 4970. DOI: 10.3390/en15144970

Devi, R. M., Patasaraiya, M. K., Sinha, B., Saran, S., Dimri, A. P., & Jaiswal, R. (2018). Understanding the linkages between climate change and forest. *Current Science*, 114(5), 987–996. DOI: 10.18520/cs/v114/i05/987-996

Dewinta, A., & Irawan, M. I. (2021). They are clustering Complaints from Customers of Government Drinking Water Companies on Social Media Twitter using Text Mining. In AR, HH, WAP, SJ, KF, JH, PP, SE, SHTT, SEI, SER, PE, KY, KK, PDD, KE, & AP (Eds.), 3rd East Indonesia Conference on Computer and Information Technology, EIConCIT 2021 (pp. 338–342). Institute of Electrical and Electronic Engineers Inc. DOI: 10.1109/EIConCIT50028.2021.9431931

Dhonde, B., & Patel, C. R. (2021). Assessing The Impacts Of City Sprawl On Urban Freight Transport In Developing Countries. *Architecture and Engineering*, 6(2), 52–62. DOI: 10.23968/2500-0055-2021-6-2-52-62

Diakhaté, D. (2021). La gouvernance de l'information à l'épreuve de la réforme territoriale : Éléments de structuration d'une politique d'Intelligence Territoriale (IT) au Sénégal. Akofena - Revue scientifique des Sciences du Langage, Lettres, Langues & Communication, 3(003). https://hal.science/hal-03175081

Díaz-Díaz, R., & Pérez-González, D. (2016). Implementation of Social Media Concepts for e-Government : Case Study of a Social Media Tool for Value Co-Creation and Citizen Participation. *Journal of Organizational and End User Computing*, 28(3), 104–121. DOI: 10.4018/JOEUC.2016070107

Díez, D., Flórez, L., & Arboleda, C. (2023). Innovación social desde el emprendimiento social: Panorama de la bibliografía global y colombiana. *Revista de Ciencias Sociales*. Advance online publication. DOI: 10.31876/rcs.v29i2.39976

Dikshit, S., Atiq, A., Shahid, M., Dwivedi, V., & Thusu, A. (2023). The Use of Artificial Intelligence to Optimize the Routing of Vehicles and Reduce Traffic Congestion in Urban Areas. EAI Endorsed Transactions on Energy Web, 10.

Dionisio, M., De Souza, S. J.Junior, Paula, F., & Pellanda, P. C. (2023). The role of digital social innovations to address SDGs: A systematic review. *Environment, Development and Sustainability*, 26(3), 5709–5734. DOI: 10.1007/s10668-023-03038-x PMID: 36855437

Disaster Management Plan of Agricultural Department (Report-2003). Odisha.

Dmuchowski, R. (2019). The CONcept Of Logistics Clusters And Efficiency Of Economic Enterprises. *Journal Of European Economy*, 18(3), 351–361. DOI: 10.35774/jee2019.03.351

Do Adro, F., & Fernandes, C. I. (2020). Social innovation: A systematic literature review and future agenda research. *International Review on Public and Nonprofit Marketing*, 17(1), 23–40. DOI: 10.1007/s12208-019-00241-3

Dobarrio Machado Ciccarino, I., & Serrano Fernandes Rodrigues, S. C. (2023). Resilience through social innovation for sustainable development. *Innovation & Management Review*, 20(2), 179–191. DOI: 10.1108/INMR-12-2021-0227

Dobrolyubova, E. I. (2022). EVALUATING DIGITAL GOVERNMENT PERFORMANCE USING SURVEYS: INTERNATIONAL LITERATURE REVIEW AND PROSPECTS FOR THE FUTURE RESEARCH. *Public Administration Issues*, 5(5), 152–181. DOI: 10.17323/1999-5431-2022-0-5-152-181

Dohler, M., Sachs, J., & Gartner, S. (2023). IoT advancements: Proliferation of LPWAN and sensor fusion technologies. *IEEE Internet of Things Journal*, 10(4), 1234–1246.

Donthu, N., Kumar, S., Mukherjee, D., Pandey, N., & Lim, W. M. (2021). How to conduct a bibliometric analysis : An overview and guidelines. *Journal of Business Research*, 133, 285–296. DOI: 10.1016/j.jbusres.2021.04.070

dos Ramos Caldeirinha, V. M., Felicio, J. A., Salvador, A. S., Nabais, J., & Pinho, T. (2020). Port Community Systems (pcs) and Port Performance. *Revista Eletronica De Estrategia E Negocios-Reen, 13*, 159-195. https://doi.org/DOI: 10.19177/reen.v13e012020159-195

Dowling, P. (2013). The impact of climate change on the European energy system. *Energy Policy*, 60, 406–417. DOI: 10.1016/j.enpol.2013.05.093

Dubey, S. K., Padiyar, A. P., Shenoy, N., Gaikawd, A., Mohanty, B., Baliarsingh, B. K., . . . Acharya, S. (2022). Climate-smart and nutrition-sensitive aquaculture in Odisha, India: a new horizon in sustainability, adaptation, and mitigation. In Handbook on climate change and disasters (pp. 574-593). Edward Elgar Publishing.

Dubinina, N. A. (2017). LOGIstics Management As A Factor Increasing Competitive Positions Of Shipbuilding Enterprises Entering The Shipbuilding Cluster Of The Astrakhan Region. *Vestnik of Astrakhan State Technical University*, 104-113. DOI: 10.24143/1812-9498-2017-1-104-113

Duggal, A. S., Singh, R., Gehlot, A., Gupta, L. R., Akram, S. V., Prakash, C., Singh, S., & Kumar, R. (2021). Infrastructure, mobility and safety 4.0: Modernization in road transportation. *Technology in Society*, 67, 101791. DOI: 10.1016/j.techsoc.2021.101791

Duhamel, F., & Sandoval-Almazán, R. (2021). Designing E-Government Legal Institutions: A State-Level Comparison in Mexico. *International Journal of Public Administration in the Digital Age*, 8(1), 1–15. Advance online publication. DOI: 10.4018/IJPADA.20210101.oa1

Dupont, L., Morel, L., & Guidat, C. (2015). Innovative public-private partnership to support Smart City : The case of "Chaire REVES". *Journal of Strategy and Management*, 8(3), 245–265. DOI: 10.1108/JSMA-03-2015-0027

Durkiewicz, J., & Janowski, T. (2021). Is digital government advancing sustainable governance? A study of oecd/eu countries. *Sustainability (Basel)*, 13(24), 13603. Advance online publication. DOI: 10.3390/su132413603

Du, S., & Xie, C. (2021). Paradoxes of artificial intelligence in consumer markets: Ethical challenges and opportunities. *Journal of Business Research*, 129, 961–974. DOI: 10.1016/j.jbusres.2020.08.024

Ehlinger, S., Perret, V. & Chabaud, D. (2015). Quelle gouvernance pour les réseaux territorialisés d'organisations ?. *Revue française de gestion*, 253, 369-386. DOI: 10.3166/RFG.170.155-171

Eizaguirre, S., & Parés, M. (2019). Communities making social change from below. Social innovation and democratic leadership in two disenfranchised neighbourhoods in Barcelona. *Urban Research & Practice*, 12(2), 173–191. DOI: 10.1080/17535069.2018.1426782

Ekholm, K., & Hakkala, K. (2007). Location of R&D and high-tech production by vertically integrated multinationals. *Economic Journal (London)*, 117(518), 512–543. DOI: 10.1111/j.1468-0297.2007.02028.x

El Jaouhari, S., & Alla, L. (2022). L'approche territoriale et la gestion de l'impact de la pandémie de Covid-19: Cas des collectivités territoriales. *Alternatives Managériales Economiques*, 4(1), 245–265.

El Jaouhari, S., & Alla, L. (2022). L'approche territoriale et la gestion de l'impact de la pandémie de Covid-19: Cas des collectivités territoriales. *Alternatives Managériales Économiques*, 4(1), 245–265.

EL JAOUHARI, S., & Lhoussaine, A. (2022). L'approche territoriale et la gestion de l'impact de la pandémie de Covid-19 : Cas des collectivités territoriales. *Alternatives Managériales Economiques*, 4(1), 245–265.

El Maaqili, Y., & Ouchen, A. (2024). Digital Innovations for Good: A Bibliometric Study of Social Entrepreneurship Digitalization. In Motahhir, S., & Bossoufi, B. (Eds.), *Digital Technologies and Applications* (pp. 187–196). Springer Nature Switzerland. DOI: 10.1007/978-3-031-68675-7_19

El Moutawakil, N., Belkacemi, K., & Bouderbala, A. (2022). Digital Transformation in Moroccan Local Governance. *Journal of Urban Management*, 11(2), 150–165.

Elavarasan, R. M., Pugazhendhi, R., Shafiullah, G. M., Irfan, M., & Anvari-Moghaddam, A. (2021). A hover view over effectual approaches on pandemic management for sustainable cities – The endowment of prospective technologies with revitalization strategies. *Sustainable Cities and Society*, 68, 102789. DOI: 10.1016/j.scs.2021.102789 PMID: 35004131

Elhissoufi, M., & Alla, L. (2024). Artificial intelligence in costumer acquisition. *Advances in Marketing, Customer Relationship Management, and E-Services*, 1–22. DOI: 10.4018/979-8-3693-3172-9.ch001

Elmezdeghi, O., & Achibane, M. (2023). *Perspectives de la gestion territoriale au Maroc, au contexte de la pandémie du Covid-19*. INTERNATIONAL JOURNAL OF ADVANCED RESEARCH IN INNOVATION, MANAGEMENT & SOCIAL SCIENCES.

Elmortaji, H., Abouchabaka, J., Jaouhar, S., Rafalia, N., & Bourekkadi, S. (2024). Impact of machine learning and e-learning on the optimization of territorial intelligence. *Journal of Theoretical and Applied Information Technology*, 102(8).

Elsawy, Y., Alatawi, A. S., Abaza, M., Moawad, A., & Aggoune, E.-H. M. (2024). Next-generation dual transceiver FSO communication system for high-speed trains in Neom Smart City. *Photonics*, 11(5), 483. DOI: 10.3390/photonics11050483

Emekci, S. (2022). From smart homes to smart cities. *Advances in Public Policy and Administration*, 321–337. DOI: 10.4018/978-1-7998-7785-1.ch018

Emery, F. E., & Trist, E. L. (1960). Socio-technical systems. In Churchman, C. W., & Verhulst, M. (Eds.), *Management science* (Vol. 2, pp. 58–97). Wiley.

Erkut, B. (2020). From digital government to digital governance: Are we there yet? *Sustainability (Basel)*, 12(3), 860. Advance online publication. DOI: 10.3390/su12030860

Ernst, D., & Kim, L. (2002). Global production networks, knowledge diffusion, and local capability formation. *Research Policy*, 31(8-9), 1417–1429. DOI: 10.1016/S0048-7333(02)00072-0

Fabre, L., Bayart, C., Bonnel, P., & Mony, N. (2023). The potential of Wi-Fi data to estimate bus passenger mobility. *Technological Forecasting and Social Change*, 192, 122509. DOI: 10.1016/j.techfore.2023.122509

Fakhrurroja, H., Atmaja, M. N., Panjaitan, J. N. C., Alamsyah, A., & Munandar, A. (2019, November). Crisis Communication on Twitter: a social network analysis of christchurch terrorist attack in 2019. In 2019 International Conference on ICT for Smart Society (ICISS) (Vol. 7, pp. 1-6). IEEE.

Fang, K., Azizan, S. A., & Huang, H. (2024). GIS-based intelligent planning approach of child-friendly pedestrian pathway to promote a child-friendly city. *Scientific Reports*, 14(1), 8139. DOI: 10.1038/s41598-024-58712-5 PMID: 38584168

Farzaneh, H., Malehmirchegini, L., Bejan, A., Afolabi, T., Mulumba, A., & Daka, P. P. (2021). Artificial intelligence evolution in smart buildings for energy efficiency. *Applied Sciences (Basel, Switzerland)*, 11(2), 763. DOI: 10.3390/app11020763

Feng, T. T., Kang, Q., Pan, B. B., & Yang, Y. S. (2019). Synergies of sustainable development goals between China and countries along the Belt and Road initiative. *Current Opinion in Environmental Sustainability*, 39, 167–186. DOI: 10.1016/j.cosust.2019.10.008

Fishenden, J., & Thompson, M. (2013). Digital government, open architecture, and innovation: Why public sector it will never be the same again. *Journal of Public Administration: Research and Theory*, 23(4), 977–1004. DOI: 10.1093/jopart/mus022

Flohr, L. A., Schuß, M., Wallach, D. P., Krüger, A., & Riener, A. (2024). Designing for passengers' information needs on fellow travelers: A comparison of day and night rides in shared automated vehicles. *Applied Ergonomics*, 116, 104198. DOI: 10.1016/j.apergo.2023.104198 PMID: 38091694

Fong, B., Fong, A. C. M., & Hong, G. Y. (2023). Sustainable micromobility management in smart cities. *IEEE Transactions on Intelligent Transportation Systems*, 24(12), 15890–15896. DOI: 10.1109/TITS.2023.3292377

Fundation, E. U. L. A. C., Paton, J., Bercovich, N., & Barroeta, B. (2018). *Clusters and Cluster Policy: Opportunities for collaboration between the European Union (EU), Latin America and the Caribbean*. LAC.

Gaffar, V., Koeswandi, T., & Suhud, U. (2022). HAS THE COVID-19 PANDEMIC ACCELERATE THE DIGITAL TRANSFORMATION OF MICRO, SMALL, AND MEDIUM ENTERPRISES IN INDONESIA? *Teorija in Praksa*, 59(3), 729–744. DOI: 10.51936/tip.59.3.729-744

Gambo, N., & Musonda, I. (2021). Effect of the fourth industrial revolution on road transport asset management practice in Nigeria. *Journal of Construction in Developing Countries*, 26(1), 19–43. DOI: 10.21315/jcdc2021.26.1.2

Gammadigbe, V. (2021). Is regional trade integration a growth and convergence engine in Africa?.

Gao, Q. L., Zhong, C., Yue, Y., Cao, R., & Zhang, B. (2024). Income estimation based on human mobility patterns and machine learning models. *Applied Geography (Sevenoaks, England)*, 163, 103179. DOI: 10.1016/j.apgeog.2023.103179

Garcia-Retuerta, D., Chamoso, P., Hernández, G., Guzmán, A. S. R., Yigitcanlar, T., & Corchado, J. M. (2021). An efficient management platform for developing smart cities: Solution for real-time and future crowd detection. *Electronics (Basel)*, 10(7), 765. DOI: 10.3390/electronics10070765

Gaveau, D. L. A., & Salim, M. A. (2017). Remote sensing of deforestation and forest degradation in the tropics: Towards a satellite-data driven framework for policy-making. *Global Environmental Change*, 43, 230–242.

Gawron, J. H., Keoleian, G. A., De Kleine, R. D., Wallington, T. J., & Kim, H. C. (2018). Life cycle assessment of connected and automated vehicles: Sensing and computing subsystem and vehicle level effects. *Environmental Science & Technology*, 52(5), 3249–3256. DOI: 10.1021/acs.est.7b04576 PMID: 29446302

Gazali, E. (2014). Learning by click: Social media democracy experiment in Indonesia. *Gazette of International Communications*, 76(4–5), 425–439. DOI: 10.1177/1748048514524119

Gertler, M. S. (2004). *Manufacturing culture: The institutional geography of industrial practice*. Oxford University Press. DOI: 10.1093/oso/9780198233824.001.0001

Ghahramani, Z., Bengio, Y., & Jordan, M. I. (2023). Advancements in AI algorithms: Deep learning and reinforcement learning. *Nature Reviews Machine Intelligence*, 6(1), 45–56.

Ghauri, P., & Yamin, M. (2009). Revisiting the impact of multinational enterprises on economic development. *Journal of World Business*, 44(2), 103–107. DOI: 10.1016/j.jwb.2008.05.010

Gil-Garcia, J. R., & Flores-Zúñiga, M. Á. (2020). Towards a comprehensive understanding of digital government success: Integrating implementation and adoption factors. *Government Information Quarterly*, 37(4), 101518. Advance online publication. DOI: 10.1016/j.giq.2020.101518

Girardot, J.-J. (2004). Intelligence territoriale et participation. *Isdm*, 16, 1–13.

Giudicianni, C., Herrera, M., Nardo, A. D., Adeyeye, K., & Ramos, H. M. (2020). Overview of energy management and leakage control systems for smart water grids and digital water. *Modelling*, 1(2), 134–155. DOI: 10.3390/modelling1020009

Giuliano, G., Knatz, G., Hutson, N., Sys, C., Vanelslander, T., & Carlan, V. (2015). *Decision-making for maritime innovation investments : The significance of cost benefit and cost effectiveness analysis*. 1-20.

Glazer, R. (1991). Marketing in an information-intensive environment : Strategic implications of knowledge as an asset. *Journal of Marketing*, 55(4), 1–19. DOI: 10.1177/002224299105500401

Gokasar, I., Simic, V., Deveci, M., & Senapati, T. (2023). Alternative prioritization of freeway incident management using autonomous vehicles in mixed traffic using a type-2 neutrosophic number-based decision support system. *Engineering Applications of Artificial Intelligence*, 123(Part A), 106183. https://doi.org/DOI: 10.1016/j.engappai.2023.106183

González, D., Sbragia, R., Galante, O., Soto, R., & Valdivieso, R. (2013). ALTEC y la Gestión Tecnológica en Iberoamérica: Gestión de Proyectos, Conocimiento e Innovación Social y Sustentable. *Journal of Technology Management & Innovation*, 8, 1–2. DOI: 10.4067/S0718-27242013000300001

Gonzalez-Feliu, J., Chong, M., Vargas-Florez, J., de Brito Jr, I., Osorio-Ramirez, C., Piatyszek, E., & Quiliche Altamirano, R. (2020). The maturity of humanitarian logistics against recurrent crises. *Social Sciences (Basel, Switzerland)*, 9(6), 90. DOI: 10.3390/socsci9060090

González, M. D. C. P., & Lutsak, N. (2017). The scientific production on social innovation for local development: A bibliometric review the structure and evolution of the field of scientific domain. *Prisma Social*, 19, 146–182.

Goodchild, M. F. (2007). Citizens as sensors: The world of volunteered geography. *GeoJournal*, 69(4), 211–221. DOI: 10.1007/s10708-007-9111-y

Gordon, C., & DeSouza, K. C. (2019). Building a smart city: Lessons from Barcelona. *Journal of Urban Technology*, 26(1), 1–21.

Gordon, P., & Richardson, H. W. (2019). Urban Resilience and the Role of Smart Technologies. *Urban Studies (Edinburgh, Scotland)*, 56(4), 677–692.

Gottschalk, P. (2009). Maturity levels for interoperability in digital government. *Government Information Quarterly*, 26(1), 75–81. https://api.semanticscholar.org/CorpusID:44507003. DOI: 10.1016/j.giq.2008.03.003

Gouda, K. C., Sahoo, S. K., Samantray, P., & Shivappa, H. (2017). Comparative Study of Monsoon Rainfall Variability over India and the Odisha State. *Climate (Basel)*, 5(4), 79. DOI: 10.3390/cli5040079

Government of India. (2023). National Rural Employment Guarantee Act (NREGA): Leveraging technology for rural development. Retrieved from https://www.nrega.nic.in

Government of Maharashtra. (2023). Transforming agriculture in rural Maharashtra through technology. Retrieved from https://www.maharashtra.gov.in/transforming-agriculture-in-rural-maharashtra-through-technology

Government of Orissa. (2002b). *Orissa State Development Report*. Nabakrishna Choudhary Centre for Development Studies.

Government of Orissa. (2002c). *Block Disaster Management Plan: Balikuda Block, Jagatsighpur District 2002*. Prepared by Balikuda Panchayat Samiti.

Government of Orissa. (2002d): Annual Report on Natural Calamities: 2001–02. Revenue Department, OSDMA, Bhubaneswar. [10]. Government of Orissa (2002c): Interim Report on Drought Situation in Orissa 2002. Revenue Department, OSDMA, Bhubaneswar.

Government of Singapore. (2023). Smart nation: Transforming Singapore through technology. Retrieved from https://www.smartnation.gov.sg/

Government of the Netherlands. (2023). Precision agriculture: Transforming farming practices in the Netherlands. Retrieved from https://www.government.nl/topics/precision-agriculture/precision-agriculture

Govindan, K., & Gholizadeh, H. (2021). Robust network design for sustainable-resilient reverse logistics network using big data : A case study of end-of-life vehicles. *Transportation Research Part E, Logistics and Transportation Review*, 149, 102279. DOI: 10.1016/j.tre.2021.102279

Goytia-de la Torre, L., Gretel Borja-Hernández, C., Ortíz-García, M., Dina Valenzuela-Robles B., Landa-Rivera, I., Salmón-de la Torre, G. (2019, septembre 23). Territorial Intelligence through the application of Business and Competitive intelligence: The case of Guadalupe, Zacatecas (Mexico) (Vol. 16, Numéro 2, p. 118-123) [Enregistrement vidéo]. https://doi.org/DOI: 10.52155/IJPSAT.V16.2.1249

Graells-Garrido, E., Opitz, D., Rowe, F., & Arriagada, J. (2023). A data fusion approach with mobile phone data for updating travel survey-based mode split estimates. *Transportation Research Part C, Emerging Technologies*, 155, 104285. DOI: 10.1016/j.trc.2023.104285

Green, R. (2021). Security challenges in IoT systems. *International Journal of Information Security*.

Green, S. (2020). A digital start-up project - CARM tool as an innovative approach to digital government transformation. *Computer Systems Science and Engineering*, 35(4), 257–269. https://www.scopus.com/inward/record.uri?eid=2-s2.0-85092347492&partnerID=40&md5=dc865f34d6d2c0a28a490620bba4c4bd. DOI: 10.32604/csse.2020.35.257

Grenier, C., & Moine, C. (2003). *Construire le système d'information de l'entreprise*. Foucher.

Grimaldi, D., & Fernandez, V. (2019). Performance of an internet of things project in the public sector : The case of Nice smart city. *The Journal of High Technology Management Research*, 30(1), 27–39. DOI: 10.1016/j.hitech.2018.12.003

Gritsenko, S. (2020). Marketing aspects to investment attractiveness of diversified enterprises of aviation transport and logistic clusters. *Economics. Ecology.Socium*, 4(1), 53–61. DOI: 10.31520/2616-7107/2020.4.1-6

Guillen-Perez, A., & Cano, M.-D. (2021). Intelligent IoT systems for traffic management: A practical application. *IET Intelligent Transport Systems*, 15(2), 273–285. DOI: 10.1049/itr2.12021

Günçavdi, Ö., & Ülengïn, B. (2012). Aggregate imports and expenditure components in Turkey: A theoretical and empirical assessment. *Middle East Development Journal*, 4(02), 1250011. DOI: 10.1142/S1793812012500113

Guo, Y., Zhang, G., & Zheng, G. (2017). Intelligent traffic light control with evolutionary learning in the cloud. *IEEE Transactions on Industrial Informatics*, 13(4), 1–10.

Gupta, P. K., Shree, V., Hiremath, L., & Rajendran, S. (2019). The use of modern technology in smart waste management and recycling: artificial intelligence and machine learning. Recent advances in computational intelligence, 173-188.

Guzman, L. A., Beltran, C., Morales, R., & Sarmiento, O. L. (2023). Inequality in personal exposure to air pollution in transport microenvironments for commuters in Bogotá. *Case Studies on Transport Policy*, 11, 100963. DOI: 10.1016/j.cstp.2023.100963

Haddad, S. (2023). Global Financial Market Integration: A Literature Survey. *Journal of Risk and Financial Management*, 16(12), 495. DOI: 10.3390/jrfm16120495

Haji Ali Beigi, M. (2021). *External knowledge diversity, competition intensity and innovation performance in logistics: Implications for less versus more innovative industries* (No. 157). Ilmenau Economics Discussion Papers.

Halsall, J. P., Oberoi, R., & Snowden, M. (2022). Social Enterprise, Social Innovation and Sustainable Future: A Driver for Policy Change. In Crowther, D., & Quoquab, F. (Eds.), *Developments in Corporate Governance and Responsibility* (pp. 13–27). Emerald Publishing Limited., DOI: 10.1108/S2043-052320220000018002

Halsbenning, S., Niemann, M., Distel, B., & Becker, J. (2021). Playing (Government) Seriously: Design Principles for e-Government Simulation Game Platforms. In A. F., S. R., & S. S. (Eds.), *International Conference on Wirtschaftsinformatik, WI 2021:* Vol. 48 *LNISO* (pp. 73–90). Springer Science and Business Media Deutschland GmbH. DOI: 10.1007/978-3-030-86800-0_6

Hammoumi, L., Maanan, M., & Rhinane, H. (2024). Characterizing smart cities based on artificial intelligence. *Smart Cities*, 7(3), 1330–1345. DOI: 10.3390/smartcities7030056

Handani, N. D., Williady, A., & Kim, H.-S. (2022). Textual Review Analysis and Customer Satisfaction at Luxury Hotels in Singapore's Marina Bay Area (SG-Clean Certified Hotels). *Sustainability (Switzerland)*, 14(15). Advance online publication. DOI: 10.3390/su14159382

Han, H. (2019). A review and a model for logistics clusters. *International Journal of Logistics Systems and Management*, 33(1), 73–96. DOI: 10.1504/IJLSM.2019.099662

Han, J.-H., Kim, J.-Y., Kim, J.-H., & Jeong, S.-J. (2012). A case study on algorithm development and software materialization for logistics optimization. *Journal of the Korea Safety Management and Science*, 14(4), 153–168. DOI: 10.12812/ksms.2012.14.4.153

Hansen, R., Olafsson, A. S., Van Der Jagt, A. P., Rall, E., & Pauleit, S. (2019). Planning multifunctional green infrastructure for compact cities: What is the state of practice? *Ecological Indicators*, 96, 99–110. DOI: 10.1016/j.ecolind.2017.09.042

Harrison, T. M., & Luna-Reyes, L. F. (2022). Cultivating Trustworthy Artificial Intelligence in Digital Government. *Social Science Computer Review*, 40(2), 494–511. DOI: 10.1177/0894439320980122

Hartanti, F. T., Abawajy, J. H., & Chowdhury, M. (2022). Evaluating Public Service Delivery Smartness and Impact on Citizens' Well-Being. *IEEE Access, 10*, 69106-69124. IEEE Access. DOI: 10.1109/ACCESS.2022.3186325

Havenga, J. H., & De Bod, A. (2016). Freight corridor performance measurement system : A framework for South Africa. *Journal of Transport and Supply Chain Management*, 10(1). Advance online publication. DOI: 10.4102/jtscm.v10i1.252

Hazra, S., Ghosh, A., Ghosh, S., Pal, I., & Ghosh, T. (2022). Assessing coastal vulnerability and governance in Mahanadi Delta, Odisha, India. *Progress in Disaster Science*, 14, 100223. DOI: 10.1016/j.pdisas.2022.100223

Healey, P. (2015). Citizen-generated local development initiative: Recent English experience. *International Journal of Urban Sciences*, 19(2), 109–118. DOI: 10.1080/12265934.2014.989892

Hedger, M. (2010): Moving Forward on Climate Change Planning – Lessons from Orissa, Policy Brief, Climate and Development Knowledge Network, November, 2010.

Helal Alnuaimi, S., Mohammed Alneyadi, M., Fadel, M., Ali Alrashdi, A., Ali Alneyadi, B., S. A. Khalifa, G., & Farhan, A. (2022). An Exploratory Study of Retailers' Operational Performance within UAE Market : A Case Study. *BOHR International Journal of Operations Management Research and Practices, 1*(1), 34-44. DOI: 10.54646/bijomrp.005

Helmi, D., & Kasmi, A. (2022). Intelligence territoriale au service des clusters touristiques : Vecteur tacite du développement durable. Dossiers de Recherches en Économie et Gestion, 10(1), Article 1. DOI: 10.34874/IMIST.PRSM/doreg-v10i1 .31650

He, M., Shen, J., Wu, X., & Luo, J. (2018). Logistics space: A literature review from the sustainability perspective. *Sustainability (Basel)*, 10(8), 2815. DOI: 10.3390/su10082815

Henman, P. (2020). Improving public services using artificial intelligence: Possibilities, pitfalls, governance. *Asia Pacific Journal of Public Administration*, 42(4), 209–221. DOI: 10.1080/23276665.2020.1816188

Herbaux, P. (2004, mai 28). Les « TIC », un outil d'intelligence territoriale [Enregistrement vidéo]. https://typeset.io/papers/les-tic-un-outil-d-intelligence-territoriale-77w262d3bk

Hernandez, D. (2023). *Livestock health monitoring with IoT*. Farm Tech Innovations.

Hervas-Oliver, J. L., & Albors-Garrigos, J. (2014). Are technology gatekeepers renewing clusters? Understanding gatekeepers and their dynamics across cluster life cycles. *Entrepreneurship and Regional Development*, 26(5-6), 431–452. DOI: 10.1080/08985626.2014.933489

Hidalgo, A., León, G., & Pavón, J. (2002). *The management of innovation and technology in organizations*. Editorial Pirámide.

Hidayah, K. (2018). Indonesian Tax Dispute Resolution in Cooperative Paradigm Compared to UK and Australia. International Conference on Industrial Technology for Sustainable Development 2017, ICon-ITSD 2017, 175(1). DOI: 10.1088/1755-1315/175/1/012203

Hmioui, & L. Alla (Eds.), Integrating Intelligence and Sustainability in Supply

Hmioui, A., Alla, L., & Bentalha, B. (2017). Pilotage de la touristicité territoriale au Maroc Proposition d'un indice de touriscticité pour la destination Fès. In *Entrepreneuriat, Innovation, Gouvernance et Développement territorial* (p. 120-143). Faculté Polydisciplinaire de TAZA. https://hal.science/hal-02334913

Hmioui, A., Alla, L., & Bentalha, B. (2017). Pilotage de la touristicité territoriale au Maroc Proposition d'un indice de touriscticité pour la destination Fès. Entrepreneuriat, Innovation, Gouvernance et Développement territorial, 120-143.

Hmioui, A., Alla, L., & Bentalha, B. (2017). Pilotage de la touristicité territoriale au Maroc: Proposition d'un indice de touristicité pour la destination Fès. In *Entrepreneuriat, Innovation, Gouvernance et Développement territorial* (pp. 120-143).

Hmioui, A., Alla, L., & Bentalha, B. (2017). Piloting territorial tourism in Morocco Proposal for a tourism index for the destination Fez [Pilotage de la touristicité territoriale au Maroc Proposition d'un indice de touriscticité pour la destination Fès] (No. hal-02334913).

Hmioui, A., Bentalha, B., & Beniaich, R. (2024). Green Supply Chain Management et développement territorial: Une revue de littérature. *Alternatives Managériales Economiques*, 6(2), 52–74.

Hohma, E., Boch, A., Trauth, R., & Lütge, C. (2023). Investigating accountability for Artificial Intelligence through risk governance: A workshop-based exploratory study. *Frontiers in Psychology*, 14, 1073686. DOI: 10.3389/fpsyg.2023.1073686 PMID: 36760454

Hood, C. (1991). A public management for all seasons? *Public Administration*, 69(1), 3–19. DOI: 10.1111/j.1467-9299.1991.tb00779.x

Hood, C., & Peters, G. (2004). The middle aging of new public management: Into the age of paradox? *Journal of Public Administration: Research and Theory*, 14(3), 267–282. DOI: 10.1093/jopart/muh019

Hossain, M. F. (2018, May). Climate change and its impact on Aquatic Environment. Gazipur: Department of Fisheries Biology and Aquatic Environment.

Houghton, R., Smith, J., & Johnson, L. (2022). Sustainable Development and Technological Integration in Territorial Management. *Journal of Environmental Management*, 320, 115–130.

Howlett, M., & Ramesh, M. (2003). *Studying public policy: Policy cycles and policy subsystems*. Oxford University Press.

Hrynchak, N. (2020). Differentiating the Level of Territorial Development of the Transport and Logistics Infrastructure in Ukraine by Adapting the Cluster Analysis Methodology. *Науковий вісник Національної академії статистики, обліку та аудиту, 1-2*, 6-16. DOI: 10.31767/nasoa.1-2.2020.01

http://climatechangecellodisha.org/pdf/Odisha_SAPCC_2016-2020

Huang-Lachmann, J.-T. (2019). Systematic review of smart cities and climate change adaptation. *Sustainability Accounting. Management and Policy Journal*, 10(4), 745–772. DOI: 10.1108/SAMPJ-03-2018-0052

Huang, Z.-X., & Huang, T.-Y. (2022). Privacy Calculus Theory in the Digital Government Context: The Case of Taiwan's New eID Policy. *Social Science Computer Review*. Advance online publication. DOI: 10.1177/08944393221117500

Hwang, G., & Zhang, G. (2021). Digital twins and smart city applications: A comprehensive review. *Smart Cities*, 4(1), 1–19.

Hylton, P. J., & Ross, C. L. (2018). Agglomeration economies' influence on logistics clusters' growth and competitiveness. *Regional Studies*, 52(3), 350–361. DOI: 10.1080/00343404.2017.1327708

Ibrahim, H. A., Qahtan, S., Zaidan, A. A., Deveci, M., Hajiaghaei-Keshteli, M., Mohammed, R. T., & Alamoodi, A. H. (2024). Sustainability in mobility for autonomous vehicles over smart city evaluation; using interval-valued Fermatean fuzzy rough set-based decision-making model. *Engineering Applications of Artificial Intelligence*, 129, 107609. DOI: 10.1016/j.engappai.2023.107609

Ibrahim, M. R., Haworth, J., & Cheng, T. (2020). Understanding cities with machine eyes: A review of deep computer vision in urban analytics. *Cities (London, England)*, 96, 102481. DOI: 10.1016/j.cities.2019.102481

Idrissi, S. L. E., & Abdelbaki, N. (2022). L'intelligence territoriale appliquée à la région Rabat-Salé-Kénitra. *Revue Française d'Economie et de Gestion*, 3(8), 8. https://www.revuefreg.fr/index.php/home/article/view/794

Igbinenikaro, E., & Adewusi, O. A. (2024). Policy recommendations for integrating artificial intelligence into global trade agreements. *International Journal of Engineering Research Updates*, 6(1), 1–10. DOI: 10.53430/ijeru.2024.6.1.0022

Igonya, E. K., Nencel, L., Sabelis, I., & Kimemia, G. (2023). Using Economic Diaries in an Ethnographic Study: What They Can Tell About the Financial and Daily Lives of Male and Female Sex Workers in Mombasa. *Progress in Development Studies*, 23(1), 28–43. DOI: 10.1177/14649934221110026

Ikhmim, S., Elmouaddine, H., & Alij, N. (2022). Intelligence territoriale et croissance inclusive: Vers la mise en place d'un dispositif d'intelligence territoriale inclusive dans la ville de Salé. International Journal of Accounting, Finance, Auditing, Management and Economics, 3(3-2), Article 3-2.

Iliass, B., & Ahmed, A. (2023). Territorial intelligence in morocco : International benchmark and development path. *American Scientific Journal*, 3(20), 786–786.

Ilyas, M., Jin, Z., & Ullah, I. (2024). Optimizing Logistics and Transportation Locations in the China–Pakistan Economic Corridor : A Strategic Risk Assessment. *Applied Sciences (Basel, Switzerland)*, 14(5), 1738. DOI: 10.3390/app14051738

Indriastuti, N. A., Oktafia, R., & Aviani, A. W. (2021). A prominent factor in the selection of injectable contraceptives for women of childbearing age in Yogyakarta. Bali. *Medical Journal (Fort Sam Houston, Tex.)*, 10(3), 1111–1118. DOI: 10.15562/bmj.v10i3.3030

International Energy Agency. (2023). Smart grids: Transforming energy distribution with IoT and AI. Retrieved from https://www.iea.org/topics/smart-grids

IPCC (Intergovernmental Panel on Climate Change). (2007). [Impacts, Adaptation, and Vulnerability: Summary for Policymakers. Contribution of Working Group II to the Fourth Assessment Report of the IPCC]. *Climatic Change*, , 2007.

Ipinnaiye, O., & Olaniyan, F. (2023). An exploratory study of local social innovation initiatives for sustainable poverty reduction in Nigeria. *Sustainable Development (Bradford)*, 31(4), 2222–2239. DOI: 10.1002/sd.2502

Ipsen, K. L., Zimmermann, R. K., Nielsen, P. S., & Birkved, M. (2018). Environmental assessment of smart city solutions using a coupled urban metabolism—Life cycle impact assessment approach. *The International Journal of Life Cycle Assessment*, 24(7), 1239–1253. DOI: 10.1007/s11367-018-1453-9

Irwansyah. (2021). Social contract utilitarianism: The use of multiple digital villages is important for integrating tourism. International Journal of Interdisciplinary Social and Community Studies, 16(1), 149–162. DOI: 10.18848/2324-7576/CGP/v16i01/149-162

Issam, M. B., & Abdellatif, M. M. (2017). IFRS for SMEs : A Structured Literature Review. *International Journal of Accounting and Financial Reporting*, 7(2), 538–561. DOI: 10.5296/ijafr.v7i2.12390

IUCN. (2015). Climate change and Forest.

Iwasaki, S. (2016). Linking disaster management to livelihood security against tropical cyclones: A case study on Odisha state in India. *International Journal of Disaster Risk Reduction*, 19, 57–63. DOI: 10.1016/j.ijdrr.2016.08.019

Jaber, M. (2023). IoT and machine learning for enabling sustainable development goals. *Frontiers in Communications and Networks*, 4, 1219047. DOI: 10.3389/frcmn.2023.1219047

Jacob, D. W., Fudzee, M. F. M., Salamat, M. A., & Kasim, S. (2019). Examining digital government (DG) adoption in Indonesia through UTAUT framework. *International Journal of Advanced Trends in Computer Science and Engineering, 8*(1.3 S1), 115–120. DOI: 10.30534/ijatcse/2019/2281.32019

Jang, H., & Tsai, T. (2021). Using CNN to optimize traffic classification for smart homes in 5G era. *2021 IEEE 12th Annual Information Technology,Electronics and Mobile Communication Conference (IEMCON)*, 0086-0091. https://doi.org/DOI: 10.1109/IEMCON53756.2021.9623079

Janssen, M., Charalabidis, Y., & Zuiderwijk, A. (2012). Benefits, adoption barriers, and myths of open data and open government. *Information Systems Management*, 29(4), 258–268. DOI: 10.1080/10580530.2012.716740

Janssen, M., Rana, N. P., Slade, E. L., & Dwivedi, Y. K. (2018). Trustworthiness of digital government services: Deriving a comprehensive theory through interpretive structural modelling. *Public Management Review*, 20(5), 647–671. DOI: 10.1080/14719037.2017.1305689

Jaouhari, S. E., & Alla, L. (2022). L'approche territoriale et la gestion de l'impact de la pandémie de Covid-19 : Cas des collectivités territoriales. *Alternatives Managériales Economiques, 4*(1), Article 1. DOI: 10.48374/IMIST.PRSM/ame-v4i1.30484

Jaramillo-Alcazar, A., Govea, J., & Villegas-Ch, W. (2023). Advances in the optimization of vehicular traffic in smart cities: Integration of blockchain and computer vision for sustainable mobility. *Sustainability (Basel)*, 15(22), 15736. DOI: 10.3390/su152215736

Jarvis, A., Ramirez, J., Anderson, B., Leibing, C., & Aggarwal, P. (2010). Scenarios of climate change within the context of agriculture. In *Climate Change and Crop Production*. CAB International. DOI: 10.1079/9781845936334.0009

Javed, A. R., Shahzad, F., Rehman, S., Zikria, Y. B., Razzak, I., Jalil, Z., & Xu, G. (2022). Future smart cities: Requirements, emerging technologies, applications, challenges, and future aspects. *Cities (London, England)*, 129, 103794. DOI: 10.1016/j.cities.2022.103794

Jayant Sathaye, P. S. (2006, February 10). Climate change, Sustainable Developement in India: Global and National Concern. 90(3).

Jayasena, N. S., Chan, D. W. M., Kumaraswamy, M. M., & Saka, A. B. (2023). Applicability of public-private partnerships in smart infrastructure development : The case of Hong Kong. *International Journal of Construction Management*, 23(11), 1932–1944. DOI: 10.1080/15623599.2022.2027076

Jeanne, L. (2022). L'intelligence économique territoriale envisagée comme une géoéthique : Essai de problématisation. DOI: 10.34699/RIDO.2022.8

Jena, P. K., & Kishore, J. The Fani: A case study Of Odisha disaster management. A. and Bindal, MK (eds.) (2021) Health Adaptation and Resilience to Climate Change and Related Disasters-A Compendium of Case Studies, 73.

Jena, P. P. (2017). Impact of climate change on Odisha, economic development—A comparative analysis. *Journal of the Humanities and Social Sciences*, 22, 21–25.

Jena, P. P. (2018). Climate change and its worst effect on coastal Odisha: An overview of its impact in Jagatsinghpur District. *IOSR Journal of Humanities and Social Science*, 23(1), 1–15.

Jiang, W., & Han, B. (2024). Evolution to fifth-generation (5G) mobile cellular communications. *Textbooks in Telecommunication Engineering*, 149-168. https://doi.org/DOI: 10.1007/978-3-031-57820-5_9

Jiang, W., & Han, B. (2024). Evolution to first-generation (1G) mobile cellular communications. *Textbooks in Telecommunication Engineering*, 7-21. https://doi.org/DOI: 10.1007/978-3-031-57820-5_2

Jiang, Y., & Hui, Z. (2021). The Belt and Road Initiative and SMEs. *A New Blue Ocean: Prospects for Latin American SMEs in the Belt and Road Initiative*, 31-56.

Jogesh, A., & Dubash, N. K. (2014). Mainstreaming climate change in state development planning: An analysis of the Odisha Climate Change Action Plan.

Johnson, M. (2022). *Water resource management with IoT*. Water Sustainability Journal.

Jones, M. (2022). Ethical considerations in IoT data collection. *Ethics in Technology Review, 10*(2), 45-56. Retrieved from https://www.ethicsintechnologyreview.com

Júnior, M. R. B., de Almeida Moreira, B. R., dos Santos Carreira, V., de Brito Filho, A. L., Trentin, C., de Souza, F. L. P., & Shiratsuchi, L. S. (2024). Precision agriculture in the United States: A comprehensive meta-review inspiring further research, innovation, and adoption. *Computers and Electronics in Agriculture*, 221, 108993. DOI: 10.1016/j.compag.2024.108993

Kaci, A. (2023). *Attractivité et dynamiques territoriales: analyse des conditions de la mise en place du cluster de boissons agro-logistique dans la wilaya de Bejaia* (Doctoral dissertation, UNIVERSITE MOULOUD MAMMERI DE TIZI-OUZOU).

Kaci, A., & Amiar, L. (2022). Analyse Des Conditions Territoriales De La Mise En Place D'un Cluster De Boisson Agrologistique: Comme Outil D'attractivité Territoriale Dans La Wilaya De Bejaia". In *Revue Forum D'études Et De Recherches Economiques, S* (Vol. 6, No. 1, pp. 702-720).

Kaczmarek, I., Iwaniak, A., Świetlicka, A., Piwowarczyk, M., & Nadolny, A. (2022). A machine learning approach for integration of spatial development plans based on natural language processing. *Sustainable Cities and Society*, 76, 103479. DOI: 10.1016/j.scs.2021.103479

Kaginalkar, A., Kumar, S., Gargava, P., & Niyogi, D. (2021). Review of urban computing in air quality management as smart city service: An integrated IoT, AI, and cloud technology perspective. *Urban Climate*, 39, 100972. DOI: 10.1016/j.uclim.2021.100972

Kakderi, C., Oikonomaki, E., & Papadaki, I. (2021). Smart and resilient urban futures for sustainability in the post-COVID-19 era: A review of policy responses on urban mobility. *Sustainability (Basel)*, 13(11), 6486. DOI: 10.3390/su13116486

Kalbande, K., & Patil, W. (2023). Smart systems as futuristic approach towards agriculture Development:A review. *2023 2nd International Conference for Innovation in Technology (INOCON)*, 1-6. https://doi.org/DOI: 10.1109/INOCON57975.2023.10101109

Kálmán, B., & Tóth, A. (2021). Links between the economy competitiveness and logistics performance in the Visegrád Group countries: Empirical evidence for the years 2007-2018. *Entrepreneurial Business and Economics Review*, 9(3), 169–190. DOI: 10.15678/EBER.2021.090311

Kalra, N., Chander, S., Pathak, H., Aggarwal, P. K., Gupta, N. C., Sehgal, M., & Chakraborty, D. (2007). Impacts of climate change on agriculture. *Outlook on Agriculture*, 36(2), 109–118. DOI: 10.5367/000000007781159903

Kalra, N., Singh, S., & Chakraborty, D. (2007). Rain-fed agriculture in Odisha: A sustainable approach through watershed management. *Water Resources Management*, 21(5), 965–982.

Karger, E., Jagals, M., & Ahlemann, F. (2021). Blockchain for smart mobility—Literature review and future research agenda. *Sustainability (Basel)*, 13(23), 13268. DOI: 10.3390/su132313268

Karlan, D., Kendall, J., Mann, R., Pande, R., Suri, T., & Zinman, J. (2016). *Research and impacts of digital financial services*. National Bureau of Economic Research. DOI: 10.3386/w22633

Karmakar, A. K., & Mukhopadhyay, D. (2014). Towards a Prudent Policy for Food Security in India. *US-China Law Review*, 11(2), 221–262.

Karmakar, M., & Pradhan, M. M. (2020). Climate change and public health: A study of vector-borne diseases in Odisha, India. *Natural Hazards*, 102(2), 659–671. DOI: 10.1007/s11069-019-03594-4

Kassens-Noor, E., Siegel, J., & Decaminada, T. (2021). Choosing ethics over morals: A possible determinant to embracing artificial intelligence in future urban mobility. *Frontiers in Sustainable Cities*, 3, 723475. DOI: 10.3389/frsc.2021.723475

Katsamakas, E., Miliaresis, K., & Pavlov, O. V. (2022). Digital Platforms for the Common Good: Social Innovation for Active Citizenship and ESG. *Sustainability (Basel)*, 14(2), 639. DOI: 10.3390/su14020639

Kaya, T., Sağsan, M., Yıldız, M., Medeni, T., & Medeni, T. (2020). Citizen attitudes towards e-government services: Comparison of Northern and Southern Nicosia municipalities. *International Journal of Public Administration in the Digital Age*, 7(1), 17–32. DOI: 10.4018/IJPADA.2020010102

Keller, C., Glück, F., Gerlach, C. F., & Schlegel, T. (2022). Investigating the potential of data science methods for sustainable public transport. *Sustainability (Basel)*, 14(7), 4211. DOI: 10.3390/su14074211

Keller, J., Markmann, C., & von der Gracht, H. A. (2015). Foresight support systems to facilitate regional innovations: A conceptualization case for a German logistics cluster. *Technological Forecasting and Social Change*, 97, 15–28. DOI: 10.1016/j.techfore.2013.12.031

Ketels, C. (2013). Recent research on competitiveness and clusters: What are the implications for regional policy? *Cambridge Journal of Regions, Economy and Society*, 6(2), 269–284. DOI: 10.1093/cjres/rst008

Ketels, C., & Protsiv, S. (2021). Cluster presence and economic performance: A new look based on European data. *Regional Studies*, 55(2), 208–220. DOI: 10.1080/00343404.2020.1792435

Khalifi, H., Riahi, S., & Cherif, W. (2024). *Smart Cities and Sustainable Urban Development in Morocco | IIETA*. DOI: 10.18280/isi.290236

Khan, A. Z., Mahmood, F., Bokhari, R. H., Mushtaq, R., & Abbas, R. (2021). Challenges of e-government implementation in health sector: A step toward validating a conceptual framework. *Digital Policy. Regulation & Governance*, 23(6), 574–597. DOI: 10.1108/DPRG-04-2021-0048

Khan, M., Khurram, S., & Zubair, D. S. S. (2020). Societal E-readiness for E-governance adaptability in Pakistan. *Pakistan Journal of Commerce and Social Sciences*, 14(1), 273–299.

Khan, Z. A., Sherazi, H. H. R., Ali, M., Imran, M. A., Rehman, I. U., & Chakrabarti, P. (2021). Designing a wind energy harvester for connected vehicles in green cities. *Energies*, 14(17), 5408. DOI: 10.3390/en14175408

Kharroubi, I. F. (2022). Les conditions d'application des mécanismes d'intelligence territoriale Cas de la ville de Rabat. Alternatives Managériales Economiques, 4(4), Article 4.

Khouya, M. (2023). E-Governance: Origin, challenges, and prospects in the era of ICTs and artificial intelligence. *American Scientific Journal*, 3(18), 884–884.

KilimoSalama. (2023). KilimoSalama: Innovations in agricultural insurance for smallholder farmers. Retrieved from https://www.kilimosalama.org/

Kim, C., & Kim, K.-A. (2021). The institutional change from E-Government toward Smarter City; comparative analysis between royal borough of Greenwich, UK, and Seongdong-gu, South Korea. *Journal of Open Innovation*, 7(1), 1–33. DOI: 10.3390/joitmc7010042

Kim, M. J., Hall, C. M., Chung, N., Kim, M., & Sohn, K. (2023). Why do tourists use public transport in Korea? The roles of artificial intelligence knowledge, environmental, social, and governance, and sustainability. *Asia Pacific Journal of Tourism Research*, 28(5), 467–484. DOI: 10.1080/10941665.2023.2247099

Kirova, A. (2024). LOGISTics Clusters And Their Potential For Economic Development. *MEST Journal, 12*(1).

Kitchin, R. (2014). Big Data, New Epistemologies and Paradigm Shifts. *Big Data & Society*, 1(1), 1–12. DOI: 10.1177/2053951714528481

Kitchin, R. (2014). *The data revolution: Big Data, open data, data infrastructures and their consequences*. SAGE Publications.

Kitchin, R. (2023). The data-driven city: Big data and smart urbanism. *International Journal of Urban and Regional Research*, 47(1), 32–48.

Klauenberg, J., Elsner, L. A., & Knischewski, C. (2020). Dynamics of the spatial distribution of hubs in groupage networks–The case of Berlin. *Journal of Transport Geography*, 88, 102280. DOI: 10.1016/j.jtrangeo.2018.07.004

Kleinberg, J., Mullainathan, S., & Raghavan, M. (2023). Machine learning applications in territorial management: Opportunities and challenges. *Journal of Machine Learning Research*, 24(1), 78–91.

Kleynhans, E. P. (2016). Factors determining industrial competitiveness and the role of spillovers.

Klimova, N., Kozyrev, O., & Babkin, E. (2016). *Innovation in Clusters*. Springer International Publishing. DOI: 10.1007/978-3-319-21109-1

Knauf, A. (2022). Une mise en perspective bibliométrique de l'intelligence économique reposant sur sa revue de reference: La R2IE. Revue française des sciences de l'information et de la communication, 24, Article 24.

Komninos, N., Tsarchopoulos, P., & Kakderi, C. (2014). *New services design for smart cities*. DOI: 10.1145/2633661.2633664

Komninos, N., Kakderi, C., Panori, A., & Tsarchopoulos, P. (2019). Smart city planning from an evolutionary perspective. *Journal of Urban Technology*, 26(2), 3–20. DOI: 10.1080/10630732.2018.1485368

Konnon, M. A., Lodonou, N., Gaffan, R. H., & Ezin, E. (2023). An Extended Layered Information Security Architecture (ELISA) for e-Government in Developing Countries. *International Journal of Engineering Trends and Technology*, 71(1), 109–123. DOI: 10.14445/22315381/IJETT-V71I1P210

Kooiman, J. (2003). *Governing as governance*. SAGE Publications. DOI: 10.4135/9781446215012

Koroteev, D., & Tekic, Z. (2021). Artificial intelligence in oil and gas upstream: Trends, challenges, and scenarios for the future. *Energy and AI*, 3, 100041. DOI: 10.1016/j.egyai.2020.100041

Kouassi, K. J. C. (2022, December). A Comprehensive Overview of Artificial Intelligence. In Computer Science Conference Proceedings in Computer Science & Information Technology (CS & IT) series, Forthcoming. DOI: 10.2139/ssrn.4311525

Krippendorff, K. (2019). *Content Analysis : An Introduction to Its Methodology*. SAGE Publications, Inc., DOI: 10.4135/9781071878781

Krishnan, S. H., Sharma, R., Dash, P. S., Haldar, S. K., & Biswas, B. (2006). Use of waste plastics in Coke making at Tata Steel. *Ironmaking & Steelmaking*, 33(4), 288–292. DOI: 10.1179/174328106X113959

Krishnan, S. R., Nallakaruppan, M. K., Chengoden, R., Koppu, S., Iyapparaja, M., Sadhasivam, J., & Sethuraman, S. (2022). Smart water resource management using Artificial Intelligence—A review. *Sustainability (Basel)*, 14(20), 13384. DOI: 10.3390/su142013384

Kristanto, Y. (2018). Public Service Innovation in the Framework of Realizing E-Government (Case Study of the Implementation of the Hendi Report Application). *Journal of Public Administration and Local Governance*, 2(1).

Kristianto, E., Lin, P.-C., & Hwang, R.-H. (2024). Sustainable and lightweight domain-based intrusion detection system for in-vehicle network. *Sustainable Computing : Informatics and Systems*, 41, 100936. DOI: 10.1016/j.suscom.2023.100936

Kroh, J., & Schultz, C. (2023). The more the better? The role of stakeholder information processing in complex urban innovation projects for green transformation. *International Journal of Project Management*, 41(3), 102466. DOI: 10.1016/j.ijproman.2023.102466

Kumar, I., Zhalnin, A., Kim, A., & Beaulieu, L. J. (2017). Transportation and logistics cluster competitive advantages in the US regions: A cross-sectional and spatio-temporal analysis. *Research in Transportation Economics*, 61, 25–36. DOI: 10.1016/j.retrec.2016.07.028

Kumari, M. K., & Patra, S. (2014). Growth and performance of fishery in Odisha. *Asian Journal of Research in Business Economics and Management*, 4(6), 100–110.

Kumar, S. T., & Shivani, P. (2014). Marine fisheries; its current status, sustainable management and socio-economic status of the marine fishers of Odisha, through Indian Marine Policy: A case study. Research Journal of Animal. *Veterinary and Fishery Sciences*, 2(7), 10–19.

Kumar, Y., Koul, A., Singla, R., & Ijaz, M. F. (2023). Artificial intelligence in disease diagnosis: A systematic literature review, synthesizing framework and future research agenda. *Journal of Ambient Intelligence and Humanized Computing*, 14(7), 8459–8486. DOI: 10.1007/s12652-021-03612-z PMID: 35039756

Kunaka, C. (2010). *Logistics in lagging regions: Overcoming local barriers to global connectivity*. World Bank Publications. DOI: 10.1596/978-0-8213-8649-1

Kunda, G. (2009). *Engineering culture: Control and commitment in a high-tech corporation*. Temple University Press.

Kundu, S. K., & Santhanam, H. (2024). *Transitional Contexts and Transformational Pathways Through the Utilisation of Marine Fishery Advisories in Odisha*. Challenges and Way Forward. Anthropocene Science.

Kundzewicz, Z. W., & Doll, P. (2009). Will groundwater ease freshwater stress under climate change? *Hydrological Sciences Journal*, 54(4), 665–675. DOI: 10.1623/hysj.54.4.665

Kwak, Y. H., Chih, Y.-Y., & Ibbs, C. W. (2009). Towards a Comprehensive Understanding of Public Private Partnerships for Infrastructure Development. *California Management Review*, 51(2), 51–78. DOI: 10.2307/41166480

Lachgar, T. N., & Moussa, M. B. (2020). Innovation produit et performance commerciale des entreprises membres des clusters dans le contexte marocain. *Revue de Publicité et de Communication Marketing*, 1(2).

Laenens, W., Van den Broeck, W., & Mariën, I. (2018). Channel choice determinants of (Digital) government communication: A case study of spatial planning in flanders. *Media and Communication, 6*(4Theoretical Reflections and Case Studies), 140–152. DOI: 10.17645/mac.v6i4.1652

Laghmam, I. (2020). L'intelligence économique au service du territoire : Cas du Maroc. *Revue Internationale des Sciences de Gestion*, 3(3), 3. https://revue-isg.com/index.php/home/article/view/365

Lakhmetkina, N., Poliak, M., & Oleinikov, A. (2019). INFRASTRUCTURE DEVELOPMENT OF INTERNATIONAL IMPORTANCE FOR THE MODERN TRANSPORT SYSTEM. *The Archives of Automotive Engineering – Archiwum Motoryzacji, 84*(2), 103-116. DOI: 10.14669/AM.VOL84.ART8

Lam, P. T. I., & Yang, W. (2020). Factors influencing the consideration of Public-Private Partnerships (PPP) for smart city projects : Evidence from Hong Kong. *Cities (London, England)*, 99, 102606. DOI: 10.1016/j.cities.2020.102606

Lamrabet, M. (2021). The Territorial Big Data An innovative concept of Territorial Economic Intelligence. Environmental and Water Sciences, public Health and Territorial Intelligence Journal, 5(2), Article 2.

Lamrabet, M., & Benkaraache, T. (2022). Phénomène d'intelligence « anti-territoriale » ou le territoire en tant que « dé-construction » d'acteurs : Problématique et critique de l'Intelligence Territoriale au Maroc. Alternatives Managériales Economiques, 4(4), Article 4.

Lamrabet, M., & Benkaraache, T. (2021). Le Big Data Territorial: Un concept novateur d'Intelligence Économique Territoriale. EWASH & TI: Environmental and Water Sciences. *Public Health and Territorial Intelligence*, 5(2), 621–631.

Lamsiah, A., & Bentalha, B. (2022). Dakhla: A Growing Touristic Destination with a Diplomatic Sway. *Alternatives Managériales Economiques*, 4, 94–115.

Land Transport Authority of Singapore. (2023). Smart mobility: Transforming transportation in Singapore. Retrieved from https://www.lta.gov.sg/content/ltagov/en/smart-mobility.html

Larsson, S. (2021). AI in the EU: Ethical Guidelines as a Governance Tool. *The European Union and the technology shift*, 85-111.

Larsson, S., & Heintz, F. (2020). Transparency in artificial intelligence. *Internet Policy Review*, 9(2). Advance online publication. DOI: 10.14763/2020.2.1469

Latif, D. V., & Roespinoedji, D. (2021). The Prevention of Corruption as A Result of Implementing E-Government: A Geographical Review of Indonesia. *Review of International Geographical Education Online*, 11(3), 210–217. DOI: 10.33403/rigeo.800485

Laudon, K. C., & Laudon, J. P. (2013). Management Information Systems 13e. *XIV. IBANESS İktisat, İşletme ve Yönetim Bilimleri Kongreler Serisi–Plovdiv/Bulgaristan 06-07 Haziran 2020.*

Laurini, R., & Donolo, R. (2022). Computer-Assisted Visual Reasoning for Territorial Intelligence. *Journal of Visual Languages and Computing*, 2022(2), 1–11. DOI: 10.18293/JVLC2022-N2-021

Lazzeretti, L., Sedita, S. R., & Caloffi, A. (2014). Founders and disseminators of cluster research. *Journal of Economic Geography*, 14(1), 21–43. DOI: 10.1093/jeg/lbs053

Le Coadic, Y. F. (2005). Mathématique et statistique en science de l'information et en science de la communication : Infométrie mathématique et infométrie statistique des revues scientifiques. *Ciência da Informação*, 34(3), 15–22. DOI: 10.1590/S0100-19652005000300002

LEBRATY, J.-F. (1998). Technologies de l'information et décision : L'essor des Datawarehouses. [French Journal of Management Information Systems]. *Systèmes d'Information et Management*, 3(1), 95–118.

Lee, B. (2022). Smart cities, connected cars and autonomous vehicles: Design fiction and visions of smarter future urban mobility. *Technoetic Arts*, 20(Themed Issue: Projected Interiorities), 225-240. https://doi.org/DOI: 10.1386/tear_00092_1

Lee, H., Chatterjee, I., & Cho, G. (2023). A systematic review of computer vision and AI in parking space allocation in a seaport. *Applied Sciences (Basel, Switzerland)*, 13(18), 10254. DOI: 10.3390/app131810254

Lee, J., Kim, B. J., Park, S., Park, S., & Oh, K. (2018). Proposing a value-based digital government model: Toward broadening sustainability and public participation. *Sustainability (Basel)*, 10(9), 3078. Advance online publication. DOI: 10.3390/su10093078

Lee, J., Kim, K., Park, G., & Trunina, A. (2024). The role of business models in the sustainable transition of shared mobility services in China and South Korea. *Asia Pacific Business Review*, •••, 1–22. DOI: 10.1080/13602381.2024.2358952

Lefèvre, C., & Jouve, B. (1992). *Nouveaux acteurs et nouveaux territoires dans les grandes agglomérations européennes : Une approche comparative à partir des réseaux lourds de transport collectif.* 622-652.

Leloup, F., Moyart, L., & Pecqueur, B. (2005). La gouvernance territoriale comme nouveau mode de coordination territoriale? *Géographie Économie Société*, 7(4), 321–332. DOI: 10.3166/ges.7.321-331

Lemonde, C., Arsenio, E., & Henriques, R. (2021). Integrative analysis of multimodal traffic data: Addressing open challenges using big data analytics in the city of Lisbon. *European Transport Research Review*, 13(1), 64. DOI: 10.1186/s12544-021-00520-3

Lesca, H., Lesca, E., Lesca, N., & Caron-Fasan, M.-L. (2010). *Gestion de l'information : Qualité de l'information et performances de l'entreprise*. EMS Editions.

Leydesdorff, L., Bornmann, L., & Wagner, C. S. (2019). The relative influences of government funding and international collaboration on citation impact. *Journal of the Association for Information Science and Technology*, 70(2), 198–201. DOI: 10.1002/asi.24109 PMID: 32728598

Liang, C., & Shah, T. (2023). IoT in agriculture: The future of precision monitoring and data-driven farming. *Eigenpub Review of Science and Technology*, 7(1), 85–104.

Liang, L., Wang, Z., & Li, J. (2019). The effect of urbanization on environmental pollution in rapidly developing urban agglomerations. *Journal of Cleaner Production*, 237, 117649. DOI: 10.1016/j.jclepro.2019.117649

Liao, H., & Shih, W. (2023). IoT applications in smart cities: Innovations and challenges. *Sustainable Cities and Society*, 101, 102450.

Liashenko, V., Ivanov, S., & Trushkina, N. (2021). A Conceptual Approach to Forming a Transport and Logistics Cluster as a Component of the Region's Innovative Infrastructure (on the Example of Prydniprovsky Economic Region of Ukraine). *Virtual Economics*, 4(1), 19–53. DOI: 10.34021/ve.2021.04.01(2)

Li, E., Chen, Q., Zhang, X., & Zhang, C. (2023). Digital Government Development, Local Governments' Attention Distribution and Enterprise Total Factor Productivity: Evidence from China. *Sustainability (Basel)*, 15(3), 2472. Advance online publication. DOI: 10.3390/su15032472

Li, H., Chen, Y., Li, K., Wang, C., & Chen, B. (2023). Transportation Internet: A sustainable solution for intelligent transportation systems. *IEEE Transactions on Intelligent Transportation Systems*, 24(12), 15818–15829. DOI: 10.1109/TITS.2023.3270749

Li, J., Zhou, M., Xue, X., Zhu, J., Han, S., Li, L., & Wang, F.-Y. (2023). A sustainable ecology of mobility: DAO-based autonomous vehicular services. *IEEE Transactions on Intelligent Vehicles*, 8(12), 4682–4684. DOI: 10.1109/TIV.2023.3334719

Li, L., Park, P., & Yang, S.-B. (2021). The role of public-private partnership in constructing the smart transportation city : A case of the bike sharing platform. *Asia Pacific Journal of Tourism Research*, 26(4), 428–439. DOI: 10.1080/10941665.2018.1544913

Linnenluecke, M. K., Marrone, M., & Singh, A. K. (2020). Conducting systematic literature reviews and bibliometric analyses. *Australian Journal of Management*, 45(2), 175–194. DOI: 10.1177/0312896219877678

Liu, T., Mostafa, S., Mohamed, S., & Nguyen, T. S. (2021). Emerging themes of public-private partnership application in developing smart city projects : A conceptual framework. In *Built Environment Project and Asset Management* (Vol. 11, Numéro 1, p. 138-156). DOI: 10.1108/BEPAM-12-2019-0142

Liu, H., Shi, Y., Yang, X., & Zhang, W. (2023). The Role of Business Environment and Digital Government in Mitigating Supply Chain Vulnerability—Evidence from the COVID-19 Shock. *Sustainability (Basel)*, 15(3), 2323. Advance online publication. DOI: 10.3390/su15032323

Liu, L., Lee, L. S., Seow, H.-V., & Chen, C. Y. (2022). Logistics Center Location-Inventory-Routing Problem Optimization : A Systematic Review Using PRISMA Method. *Sustainability (Basel)*, 14(23), 15853. DOI: 10.3390/su142315853

Liu, Q., Yang, L., & Yang, M. (2021). Digitalisation for water sustainability: Barriers to implementing circular economy in smart water management. *Sustainability (Basel)*, 13(21), 11868. DOI: 10.3390/su132111868

Liu, S., He, N., Cao, X., Li, G., & Jian, M. (2022). Logistics cluster and its future development: A comprehensive research review. *Transportation Research Part E, Logistics and Transportation Review*, 168, 102974. DOI: 10.1016/j.tre.2022.102974

Liu, X., & McKinnon, A. C. (2019). Practical relevance of theory-driven supply chain management research: Evidence from China. *International Journal of Logistics Management*, 30(1), 76–95. DOI: 10.1108/IJLM-12-2017-0337

Li, X., & Ding, Y. (2020). Holistic governance for sustainable public services: Reshaping government–enterprise relationships in china's digital government context. *International Journal of Environmental Research and Public Health*, 17(5), 1778. Advance online publication. DOI: 10.3390/ijerph17051778 PMID: 32182931

Li, X., Wang, L., & Yang, Y. (2023). A framework for interoperability in IoT-based territorial management. *Journal of Cleaner Production*, 321, 129034.

Liyanage, S., Dia, H., Abduljabbar, R., & Bagloee, S. A. (2019). Flexible mobility on-demand: An environmental scan. *Sustainability (Basel)*, 11(5), 1262. DOI: 10.3390/su11051262

Lohani, T. K. (2022). Causes, Effects, and Remedial Measures of Climate Change in the East Coast of India with Special Reference to the State of Odisha. In India, I. I. (Ed.), *Climate Change Impacts, Mitigation and Adaptation in Developing Countries* (pp. 383–406). Springer International Publishing. DOI: 10.1007/978-3-030-94395-0_16

Longley, P. A., Goodchild, M. F., Maguire, D. J., & Rhind, D. W. (2005). *Geographic information systems and science*. John Wiley & Sons.

Los Angeles Department of Transportation. (2023). Automated traffic management system: Enhancing traffic efficiency and safety in Los Angeles. Retrieved from https://ladot.lacity.org/traffic-management/automated-traffic-management-system

Louati, A., Louati, H., Kariri, E., Neifar, W., Hassan, M. K., Khairi, M. H. H., Farahat, M. A., & El-Hoseny, H. M. (2024). Sustainable smart cities through multi-agent reinforcement learning-based cooperative autonomous vehicles. *Sustainability (Basel)*, 16(5), 1779. DOI: 10.3390/su16051779

Loughran, K. (2020). Urban parks and urban problems: An historical perspective on green space development as a cultural fix. *Urban Studies (Edinburgh, Scotland)*, 57(11), 2321–2338. DOI: 10.1177/0042098018763555

Lumbanraja, A. D. (2020). The Urgency of Transforming Public Services through E-Government in the New Normal and Bureaucratic Regulatory Reform. *Administrative Law and Governance Journal*, 3(2), 220–231. DOI: 10.14710/alj.v3i2.220-231

Luna-Reyes, L. F., Andersen, D. F., Black, L. J., & Pardo, T. A. (2021). Sensemaking and social processes in digital government projects. *Government Information Quarterly*, 38(2), 101570. Advance online publication. DOI: 10.1016/j.giq.2021.101570

Macioszek, E., Staniek, M., & Sierpiński, G. (2017). Analysis of trends in development of freight transport logistics using the example of Silesian Province (Poland)- a case study. *Transportation Research Procedia*, 27, 388–395. DOI: 10.1016/j.trpro.2017.12.026

Madyatmadja, E. D., Yahya, B. N., & Wijaya, C. (2022). Contextual Text Analysis Framework for Citizen Report Classification: A Case Study Using Indonesian. *IEEE Access : Practical Innovations, Open Solutions*, 10, 31432–31444. DOI: 10.1109/ACCESS.2022.3158940

Maftah, J., Pheniqi, Y., & Bourkkadi, S. (2023). The use of data mining to influence social entrepreneurship and territorial dynamics. E3S Web of Conferences, 412, 01104.

Mahankuda, P. K., Singh, P., Dolai, S. K., & Choudhury, A. K. (2016). Estimating economic benefits through social forestry in Odisha. *Splint International Journal Of Professionals*, 3(7), 59–66.

Mahapatra, P. C., Sahu, B. K., & Mohanty, A. K. (2020). Plastic Waste, Health & Climate Change: Issues & Challenges of Odisha. *Indian Journal of Public Health Research & Development*, 11(6).

Mahdavian, A., Shojaei, A., Mccormick, S., Papandreou, T., Eluru, N., & Oloufa, A. A. (2021). Drivers and barriers to implementation of connected, automated, shared, and electric vehicles: An agenda for future research. *IEEE Access : Practical Innovations, Open Solutions*, 9, 22195–22213. DOI: 10.1109/ACCESS.2021.3056025

Mahoney, J. T., & Pandian, J. R. (1992). The resource-based view within the conversation of strategic management. *Strategic Management Journal*, 13(5), 363–380. DOI: 10.1002/smj.4250130505

Mahrez, Z., Sabir, E., Badidi, E., Saad, W., & Sadik, M. (2022). Smart urban mobility: When mobility systems meet smart data. *IEEE Transactions on Intelligent Transportation Systems*, 23(7), 6222–6239. DOI: 10.1109/TITS.2021.3084907

Maiti, S., Jha, S. K., Garai, S., Nag, A., Chakravarty, R., Kadian, K. S., & Upadhaya, R. C. (2014). Adaptation strategies followed by the livestock rearers of coastal Odisha and West Bengal to cope up with climate change. *The Indian Journal of Animal Sciences*, 84(6), 652–659. DOI: 10.56093/ijans.v84.i6.41633

Majid, S. A., Ricardianto, P., Pahala, Y., Saribanon, E., Sidtanding, S., Hernawan, M. A., Ade Suryobuwono, A., & Suryawan, R. F. (2022). Determine Optimal Marketing based on Market Attraction and Market Based Strategy by Considering Customer Life Time Network Value. *Management Systems and Industrial Engineering*, 21(2), 401–408. DOI: 10.7232/iems.2022.21.2.401

Majra, J. P., & Gur, A. (2009). Climate change and health: Why should India be concerned? *Indian Journal of Occupational and Environmental Medicine*, 13(1), 11–16. DOI: 10.4103/0019-5278.50717 PMID: 20165606

Majumder, S., Aghayi, E., Noferesti, M., Memarzadeh-Tehran, H., Mondal, T., Pang, Z., & Deen, M. (2017). Smart homes for elderly healthcare—Recent advances and research challenges. *Sensors (Basel)*, 17(11), 2496. DOI: 10.3390/s17112496

Makki, A. A., & Alqahtani, A. Y. (2022). Modeling the Barriers Surrounding Digital Government Implementation: Revealing Prospect Opportunities in Saudi Arabia. *Sustainability (Basel)*, 14(23), 15780. Advance online publication. DOI: 10.3390/su142315780

Maldonado Silveira Alonso Munhoz, P. A., da Costa Dias, F., Kowal Chinelli, C., Azevedo Guedes, A. L., Neves dos Santos, J. A., da Silveira e Silva, W., & Pereira Soares, C. A. (2020). Smart mobility: The main drivers for increasing the intelligence of urban mobility. *Sustainability (Basel)*, 12(24), 10675. DOI: 10.3390/su122410675

Malhi, G. S., Kaur, M., & Kaushik, P. (2021). Impact of climate change on agriculture and its mitigation strategies: A review. *Sustainability (Basel)*, 13(3), 1318. DOI: 10.3390/su13031318

Malhi, Y., Kumar, S., & Das, P. (2021). Integrated pest management in Odisha: Enhancing agricultural sustainability through eco-friendly practices. *Journal of Pest Science*, 94(1), 143–152.

Mallick, B., & Das, R. (2020). Off-grid renewable energy systems for remote areas in Odisha. *Energy for Sustainable Development*, 17(1), 43–57.

Mallick, R., & Das, P. (2024). Free-range poultry farming and its role in sustainable rural development in Odisha. *Poultry Farming Review*, 14(1), 58–67.

Mallik, R. M. (2000). Sustainable management of non-timber forest products in Orissa: Some issues and options. *Indian Journal of Agricultural Economics*, 55(3), 384.

Mallinson, D. J., & Shafi, S. (2022). Smart home technology: Challenges and opportunities for collaborative governance and policy research. *The Review of Policy Research*, 39(3), 330–352. DOI: 10.1111/ropr.12470

Ma, M., He, Z., Xu, Q., & Li, X. J. (2019). Design and development of smart home sensing supported by blockchain technology. *Proceedings of the 2019 7th International Conference on Information Technology: IoT and Smart City*, 525-530. https://doi.org/DOI: 10.1145/3377170.3377281

Mangan, J., & Lalwani, C. (2016). *Global logistics and supply chain management*. John Wiley & Sons.

Mansouri, B., Sahu, S., & Ülkü, M. A. (2023). Toward greening city logistics: A systematic review on corporate governance and social responsibility in managing urban distribution centers. *Logistics (Basel)*, 7(1), 19. DOI: 10.3390/logistics7010019

Manyika, J., Chui, M., Brown, B., Bughin, J., Dobbs, R., Roxburgh, C., & Hung Byers, A. (2011). *Big data: The next frontier for innovation, competition, and productivity*. McKinsey Global Institute.

Marcovecchio, I., Thinyane, M., Estevez, E., & Janowski, T. (2019). Digital government as implementation means for sustainable development goals. *International Journal of Public Administration in the Digital Age*, 6(3), 1–22. DOI: 10.4018/IJPADA.2019070101

Marsilio, M., Cappellaro, G., & Cuccurullo, C. (2011). The Intellectual Structure Of Research Into PPPs. *Taylor & Francis, 13*(6), 763-782. DOI: 10.1080/14719037.2010.539112

Martínez, J., & Iglesias, G. (2018). The use of big data and machine learning in smart water management. *Water Resources Management*, 32, 1–17.

Martin, H., Wiedemann, N., Reck, D., & Raubal, M. (2023). Graph-based mobility profiling. *Computers, Environment and Urban Systems*, 100, 101910. DOI: 10.1016/j.compenvurbsys.2022.101910

Martín-Martín, A., Thelwall, M., Orduna-Malea, E., & Delgado López-Cózar, E. (2021). Google Scholar, Microsoft Academic, Scopus, Dimensions, Web of Science, and OpenCitations' COCI : A multidisciplinary comparison of coverage via citations. *Scientometrics*, 126(1), 871–906. DOI: 10.1007/s11192-020-03690-4 PMID: 32981987

Martins, J., & Veiga, L. G. (2022). Digital government as a business facilitator. *Information Economics and Policy*, 60, 100990. Advance online publication. DOI: 10.1016/j.infoecopol.2022.100990

Martins, T., Braga, A., Ferreira, M. R., & Braga, V. (2022). Diving into Social Innovation: A Bibliometric Analysis. *Administrative Sciences*, 12(2), 56. DOI: 10.3390/admsci12020056

Martí, P., Jordán, J., Chamoso, P., & Julian, V. (2022). Taxi services and the carsharing alternative: A case study of Valencia City. *Mathematical Biosciences and Engineering*, 19(7), 6680–6698. DOI: 10.3934/mbe.2022314 PMID: 35730277

Marvuglia, A., Havinga, L., Heidrich, O., Fonseca, J., Gaitani, N., & Reckien, D. (2020). Advances and challenges in assessing urban sustainability: An advanced bibliometric review. *Renewable & Sustainable Energy Reviews*, 124, 109788. DOI: 10.1016/j.rser.2020.109788

Mashhadi, N., Shahrour, I., Attoue, N., El Khattabi, J., & Aljer, A. (2021). Use of machine learning for leak detection and localization in water distribution systems. *Smart Cities*, 4(4), 1293–1315. DOI: 10.3390/smartcities4040069

Maslaric, M., Bojic, S., Mircetic, D., Nikolicic, S., & Medenica Todorovic, R. (2024). Sustainable urban mobility planning in the port areas: A case study. *Sustainability (Basel)*, 16(2), 514. DOI: 10.3390/su16020514

Massaro, M., Dumay, J., & Guthrie, J. (2016). On the shoulders of giants : Undertaking a structured literature review in accounting. *Accounting, Auditing & Accountability Journal*, 29(5), 767–801. DOI: 10.1108/AAAJ-01-2015-1939

Masselot, C. (2023). Territoires intelligents versus intelligence territoriale: Tenter de mieux vivre ensemble. In D. V. Meyer, F. Couston, & P. C. et J. Araszkiewiez (Éds.), (Re)qualifier les territories: Promesses et actes. Éditions ÉRES.

Mastour, S., Ezzaher, R., & Allach, M. F. (2024). Les activités d'offshoring : Revue de littérature du levier de la compétitivité territoriale. *Revue Internationale des Sciences de Gestion*, 7(2), 2.

Mateo, S. (2020). Procédure pour conduire avec succès une revue de littérature selon la méthode PRISMA. *Kinésithérapie, la Revue*, 20(226), 29–37. DOI: 10.1016/j.kine.2020.05.019

McKinnon, A. (2018). *Decarbonizing logistics: Distributing goods in a low carbon world.* Kogan Page Publishers.

Medeiros, S. P., Rodrigues, J. J., Da Cruz, M. A., Rabelo, R. A., Saleem, K., & Solic, P. (2019). Windows monitoring and control for smart homes based on Internet of things. *2019 4th International Conference on Smart and Sustainable Technologies (SpliTech)*, 1-5. https://doi.org/DOI: 10.23919/SpliTech.2019.8783163

Meersman, H., Van de Voorde, E., & Vanelslander, T. (2010). Port competition revisited. *Journal of Pediatric. Maternal & Family Health-Chiropractic*, 55(2), 210.

Mehmood, H., Liao, D., & Mahadeo, K. (2020, September). A review of artificial intelligence applications to achieve water-related sustainable development goals. In 2020 IEEE/ITU international conference on artificial intelligence for good (AI4G) (pp. 135-141). IEEE.

Meng, Q., Li, X., & Wang, L. (2023). Interoperability frameworks for AI, IoT, and Big Data integration in territorial management. *Journal of Spatial Information Science*, 26, 115–128.

Mensah, J. (2019). Sustainable development: Meaning, history, principles, pillars, and implications for human action: Literature review. *Cogent Social Sciences*, 5(1), 1653531. DOI: 10.1080/23311886.2019.1653531

Mentzer, J. T., & Kahn, K. B. (1995). A framework of logistics research. *Journal of Business Logistics*, 16(1), 231–250.

Menzel, M. P., & Fornahl, D. (2010). Cluster life cycles—Dimensions and rationales of cluster evolution. *Industrial and Corporate Change*, 19(1), 205–238. DOI: 10.1093/icc/dtp036

Metropolitan Police Service. (2023). Smart policing: Utilizing technology to enhance public safety in London. Retrieved from https://www.met.police.uk/advice/advice-and-information/c19/met/smart-policing/

Meziane, B., Bentalha, B., & Alla, L. (2024). La PME logistique et le développement territorial régional : Une analyse qualitative. *Alternatives Managériales Economiques, 6*(3), Article 3. DOI: 10.48374/IMIST.PRSM/ame-v6i4.50474

Mezzanzanica, M., Cesarini, M., & Boselli, R. (2010, octobre 1). Business Intelligence Exploitation for investigating territorial Systems, methodological Overviews and empirical Considerations [Enregistrement vidéo]. SE.

Michel, S. (2011). *Contribution à l'évaluation du système d'information bancaire*.

Millard, J., & Fucci, V. (2023). The role of social innovation in tackling global poverty and vulnerability. *Frontiers in Sociology*, 8, 966918. DOI: 10.3389/fsoc.2023.966918 PMID: 37025262

Miller, C., & Evans, M. (2017). Big Data and its Impact on Territorial Management. *Geographical Research*, 55(3), 310–325.

Miller, H. J., Dodge, S., & Zumel, N. (2020). Mapping the unmapped: Cartographic data, algorithms, and AI in smart cities. *Annals of the Association of American Geographers*, 110(1), 1–18.

Miraftabzadeh, S. M., Longo, M., Di Martino, A., Saldarini, A., & Faranda, R. S. (2024). Exploring the synergy of artificial intelligence in energy storage systems for electric vehicles. *Electronics (Basel)*, 13(10), 1973. DOI: 10.3390/electronics13101973

Miranda, J., Ponce, P., Molina, A., & Wright, P. (2015). Sensing, smart and sustainable technologies for Agri-Food 4.0. *Computers in Industry*, 74, 41–60.

Mishra, M., Acharyya, T., & Pattnaik, N. (2021). Characterizing shifting pattern of disaster-induced death and disaster management policies: a regional analysis from Odisha, India. Current Science (00113891), 120(11).

Mishra, A., & Sahu, P. (2018). Solar energy adoption for rural electrification and sustainable agriculture. *Renewable Energy Journal*, 45(4), 321–335.

Mishra, D., & Sahu, N. C. (2014). Economic Impact of Climate Change on Agriculture Sector of Coastal Odisha. *APCBEE Procedia*, 10, 241–245. DOI: 10.1016/j.apcbee.2014.10.046

Mishra, D., Sahu, N. C., & Sahoo, D. (2016). Impact of climate change on agricultural production of Odisha (India): A Ricardian analysis. *Regional Environmental Change*, 16(2), 575–584. DOI: 10.1007/s10113-015-0774-5

Mishra, O. P. (2023). Creating Robust Infrastructure and Response Mechanism: Odisha Model of Disaster Management. In *International Handbook of Disaster Research* (pp. 1–14). Springer Nature Singapore.

Mishra, P. K. (2017). Socio-economic impacts of climate change in Odisha: Issues, challenges and policy options. *Journal of Climate Change*, 3(1), 93–107. DOI: 10.3233/JCC-170009

Mishra, P., & Behera, B. (2016). Socio-economic and environmental implications of solar electrification: Experience of rural Odisha. *Renewable & Sustainable Energy Reviews*, 56, 953–964. DOI: 10.1016/j.rser.2015.11.075

Mishra, P., Das, T., & Nayak, R. (2016). On-farm water management practices for sustainable agriculture in Odisha. *International Journal of Water Resources Development*, 32(4), 789–804.

Mishra, P., & Rath, B. (2021). Locally sourced feed and its impact on livestock and fish production in Odisha. *Agricultural Sustainability Journal*, 18(2), 201–209.

Mishra, P., Sahoo, R., & Panda, M. (2016). Sustainable aquaculture practices in Odisha: A review. *Journal of Fisheries Research*, 45(2), 122–130.

Mishra, R., & Sahu, N. (2014). Organic farming in Odisha: Pathway towards sustainable agriculture. *Agricultural Economics Review*, 25(2), 234–248.

Mishra, T. (2017). Public-private collaboration for sustainable agriculture in Odisha: A review of climate-conscious farming initiatives. *Sustainable Agriculture Research*, 16(2), 45–58.

Mithun Karmakar, M. P. (2019). *Climate change and Public Health: A study of study of Vector Borne diseases in Odisha*. Springer.

Mitieka, D., Luke, R., Twinomurinzi, H., & Mageto, J. (2023). Smart mobility in urban areas: A bibliometric review and research agenda. *Sustainability (Basel)*, 15(8), 6754. DOI: 10.3390/su15086754

Miyake, M., & Nishida, N. (2021). Activities on multimodal MaaS to solve the first mile/last mile problem—NTT DOCOMO's next-generation mobility service. *Feature Articles: Digital Transformation of Urban Areas Focusing on Mobility*, 19(1), 17–21. DOI: 10.53829/ntr202101fa3

Mohamed, S., & Han, S. (2022). Translating Human Values to Design Requirements: The Case of Developing Digital Government Collaborative Platform (DGCP) for Environmental Sustainability in Sri Lanka. In H. L., S. M., & H. S. (Eds.), *23rd Annual International Conference on Digital Government Research: Intelligent Technologies, Governments and Citizens, DGO 2022* (pp. 54–61). Association for Computing Machinery. DOI: 10.1145/3543434.3543455

Mohammed, M. A., Abdulhasan, M. J., Kumar, N. M., Abdulkareem, K. H., Mostafa, S. A., Maashi, M. S., Khalid, L. S., Abdulaali, H. S., & Chopra, S. S. (2023). Automated waste-sorting and recycling classification using artificial neural network and features fusion: A digital-enabled circular economy vision for smart cities. *Multimedia Tools and Applications*, 82(25), 39617–39632. DOI: 10.1007/s11042-021-11537-0 PMID: 35915808

Mohanty, B., Vivekanandan, E., Mohanty, S., Mahanty, A., Trivedi, R., Tripathy, M., & Sahu, J. (2017). The impact of climate change on marine and inland fisheries and aquaculture in India. Climate change impacts on fisheries and aquaculture: a global analysis, 2, 569-601.

Mohanty, B., & Sahu, G. (2012). An empirical study on elements of forest governance: A study of JFM implementation models in Odisha. *Procedia: Social and Behavioral Sciences*, 37, 314–323. DOI: 10.1016/j.sbspro.2012.03.297

Mohanty, P. K., Panda, U. S., Pal, S. R., & Mishra, P. (2008). Monitoring and management of environmental changes along the Orissa coast. *Journal of Coastal Research*, (24), 13–27.

Mohanty, P. P., Rout, H. B., & Samal, A. (2019). Community based sustainable tourism development-A tool for fostering and promoting peace: A case study of Odisha, India. *African Journal of Hospitality, Tourism and Leisure*, 8(1), 1–15.

Mohanty, P., & Sahu, S. (2018). Community-based fisheries management and its impact on fish stocks in Odisha. *Fisheries Governance Review*, 55(1), 34–45.

Mohanty, S. K., Chatterjee, R., & Shaw, R. (2020). Building resilience of critical infrastructure: A case of impacts of cyclones on the power sector in Odisha. *Climate (Basel)*, 8(6), 73. DOI: 10.3390/cli8060073

Mohanty, S., & Sahu, P. (2021). Building climate-resilient energy systems in coastal Odisha. *Climate and Energy Studies*, 10(3), 133–145.

Mohapatra, R. (2006): Disaster Dossier: The Impact of Climate Change on Orissa, Info changes. News and Analysis on Social Justice and Development Issues in India. www.infochangeindia.org <Accessed on 23rd April, 2016>. [13].

Mohapatra, H. (2021). Socio-technical challenges in the implementation of smart city. *2021 International Conference on Innovation and Intelligence for Informatics, Computing, and Technologies (3ICT)*, 57-62. https://doi.org/DOI: 10.1109/3ICT53449.2021.9581905

Mohapatra, H., Mohanta, B. K., Nikoo, M. R., Daneshmand, M., & Gandomi, A. H. (2023). MCDM-based routing for IoT-enabled smart water distribution network. *IEEE Internet of Things Journal*, 10(5), 4271–4280. DOI: 10.1109/JIOT.2022.3216402

Mohapatra, H., & Rath, A. K. (2021). A fault tolerant routing scheme for advanced metering infrastructure: An approach towards smart grid. *Cluster Computing*, 24(3), 2193–2211. DOI: 10.1007/s10586-021-03255-x

Mohapatra, S., Panda, B., & Dash, R. (2020). Climate-resilient aquaculture techniques for sustainable fishery development in Odisha. *Climate and Aquaculture*, 28(5), 93–105.

Moinet, N. (2009). L'intelligence territoriale entre communication et communauté stratégique de connaissance : L'exemple du dispositif régional de Poitou-Charentes. *Revue internationale d'intelligence économique, 1*(1), 30-38.

Monk, A. H. B., Levitt, R. E., Garvin, M. J., South, A. J., & Carollo, G. (2019). *Public–private partnerships for infrastructure delivery*. DOI: 10.4337/9781788973182.00008

Montoya, C., Teresita del Niño, J., Zazueta, U., Luisa, M., Tereso, R. L., & Verdugo, A. (2022). Áreas de Responsabilidad Social Empresarial en empresas sinaloenses: Un análisis desde la innovación social. *Revista de Ciencias Sociales*. Advance online publication. DOI: 10.31876/rcs.v28i.38851

Moore, M. H. (1995). *Creating public value: Strategic management in government*. Harvard University Press.

Moore, S. (2019). Digital government, public participation and service transformation: The impact of virtual courts. *Policy and Politics*, 47(3), 495–509. DOI: 10.1 332/030557319X15586039367509

Morgan, T., Tarpey, R., & Fergurson, J. R. (2023). Antecedents to logistic clustering. *International Journal of Logistics Economics and Globalisation*, 10(3), 274–288. DOI: 10.1504/IJLEG.2023.135461

Morrison Paul, C. J. (2002). Supply and demand-driven spillovers and productivity growth. *Japan and the World Economy*, 14(3), 285–304. DOI: 10.1016/S0922-1425(02)00007-5

Mouhib, S., & Benkaraache, T. (2023). Action publique: Apport d'un dispositif d'intelligence territoriale. *Revue des Etudes et Recherche en Logistique et Développement*, 8, 17–33.

Munir, M. T., Li, B., & Naqvi, M. (2023). Revolutionizing municipal solid waste management (MSWM) with machine learning as a clean resource: Opportunities, challenges and solutions. *Fuel*, 348, 128548. DOI: 10.1016/j.fuel.2023.128548

Muriungi, K., & Chumo, K. P. (2024). Building future-proof, sustainable, and innovative startups in Africa powered by smart cities. *Green Computing for Sustainable Smart Cities*, 172-205. https://doi.org/DOI: 10.1201/9781003388814-11

Musikanski, L., Rakova, B., Bradbury, J., Phillips, R., & Manson, M. (2020). Artificial intelligence and community well-being: A proposal for an emerging area of research. *International Journal of Community Well-being*, 3(1), 39–55. DOI: 10.1007/s42413-019-00054-6

Napetvaridze, V. (2022). *Artificial Intelligence, Blockchain Technologies, and Digital State Services in Georgia General Overview of Georgian E-government Environment*. Eastern Europe Regional Studies.

Naswir, R. Y., Maarop, N., Hasan, M., Daud, S., Samy, G. N., & Magalingam, P. (2019). Towards a conceptual model to evaluate usability of digital government services in Malaysia. *International Journal of Advanced Computer Science and Applications*, 10(4), 313–322. DOI: 10.14569/IJACSA.2019.0100438

Navaz, A. N., Serhani, M. A., El Kassabi, H. T., Al-Qirim, N., & Ismail, H. (2021). Trends, technologies, and key challenges in smart and connected healthcare. *IEEE Access : Practical Innovations, Open Solutions*, 9, 74044–74067. DOI: 10.1109/ACCESS.2021.3079217 PMID: 34812394

Nayak, A., & Rath, P. (2021). Biomass energy utilization in Odisha: Opportunities and challenges. *Biomass Energy Science*, 14(3), 142–157.

Nayak, B. K., Mishra, M. K., & Upadhyay, V. P. (2023). Agroecosystem Sustainability in Forest Dependent Tribal Villages in Odisha, Eastern India. *Asian Journal of Environment & Ecology*, 22(3), 61–85. DOI: 10.9734/ajee/2023/v22i3489

Nayak, R., Behera, S., & Tandi, D. (2023). Mechanization in agriculture: A sustainable solution for enhanced productivity in Odisha. *Agricultural Mechanization in Asia*, 54(2), 89–97.

Nayak, S. K., & Nandimandalam, J. R. (2023). Impacts of climate change and coastal salinization on the environmental risk of heavy metal contamination along the odisha coast, India. *Environmental Research*, 238, 117175. DOI: 10.1016/j.envres.2023.117175 PMID: 37741567

Necoechea-Mondragón, H., Pineda-Domínguez, D., Pérez-Reveles, L., & Soto-Flores, R. (2017). Critical factors for participation in global innovation networks. Empirical evidence from the Mexican nanotechnology sector. *Technological Forecasting and Social Change*, 114, 293–312. DOI: 10.1016/j.techfore.2016.08.027

Negri-Ribalta, C., Lombard-Platet, M., & Salinesi, C. (2024). Understanding the GDPR from a requirements engineering perspective—A systematic mapping study on regulatory data protection requirements. *Requirements Engineering*. Advance online publication. DOI: 10.1007/s00766-024-00423-4

New York City Police Department. (2023). Domain awareness system: Enhancing public safety in New York City. Retrieved from https://www1.nyc.gov/site/nypd/about/technology/das.page

Ngasotter, S., Panda, S. P., Mohanty, U., Akter, S., Mukherjee, S., Waikhom, D., & Devi, L. S. (2020). Current scenario of fisheries and aquaculture in India with special reference to Odisha: a review on its status, issues and prospects for sustainable development. International Journal of Bio-resource and Stress Management, 11(Aug, 4), 370-380.

Nguyen, T. (2022). *Enhancing rural transport logistics with AI*. Logistics Today.

Nielsen, A. F., Michelmann, J., Akac, A., Palts, K., Zilles, A., Anagnostopoulou, A., & Langeland, O. (2023). Using the future wheel methodology to assess the impact of open science in the transport sector. *Scientific Reports*, 13(1), 6000. DOI: 10.1038/s41598-023-33102-5 PMID: 37046066

Nijnik, M., Kluvánková, T., Nijnik, A., Kopiy, S., Melnykovych, M., Sarkki, S., Barlagne, C., Brnkaláková, S., Kopiy, L., Fizyk, I., & Miller, D. (2020). Is There a Scope for Social Innovation in Ukrainian Forestry? *Sustainability (Basel)*, 12(22), 9674. DOI: 10.3390/su12229674

Nikitas, A., Michalakopoulou, K., Njoya, E. T., & Karampatzakis, D. (2020). Artificial intelligence, transport and the smart city: Definitions and dimensions of a new mobility era. *Sustainability (Basel)*, 12(7), 2789. DOI: 10.3390/su12072789

Niyongabo, G. (2004). *Trade openness policy, quality of institutions and economic growth. Centre d'Etudes et de Recherche sur le Developpement International.* Universite d'Auvergne.

Notteboom, T., & Neyens, K. (2017). The future of port logistics: meeting the challenges of supply chain integration. *Bruselas: ING Bannk.*

Nouhaila, B. K., Aarabe, M., & Alla, L. (2024). The Impact of Digitalisation on the Customer Experience in Medical Tourism : A Systematic Review. *Impact of AI and Tech-Driven Solutions in Hospitality and Tourism*, 408-428.

Nouhaila, B. K., Aarabe, M., & Alla, L. (2024). The Impact of Digitalisation on the Customer Experience in Medical Tourism: A Systematic Review. In Talukder, M., Kumar, S., & Tyagi, P. (Eds.), *Impact of AI and Tech-Driven Solutions in Hospitality and Tourism* (pp. 408–428). IGI Global., DOI: 10.4018/979-8-3693-6755-1.ch020

Nova, K. (2023). AI-enabled water management systems: An analysis of system components and interdependencies for water conservation. *Eigenpub Review of Science and Technology*, 7(1), 105–124.

Nshimbi, C. C. (2021). Towards a single African economic space: Informal cross-border trade and the COMESA-EAC-SADC tripartite free trade area. In Regionalism, Security and Development in Africa (pp. 77-96): Routledge.

Obracht-Prondzyńska, H., Duda, E., Anacka, H., & Kowal, J. (2022). Greencoin as an AI-based solution shaping climate awareness. *International Journal of Environmental Research and Public Health*, 19(18), 11183. DOI: 10.3390/ijerph191811183 PMID: 36141452

Odisha Economic Survey. (2018). Sustainable agriculture initiatives and government programs in Odisha. Bhubaneswar: Government of Odisha.

*Odisha environment Congress*. (2012). (pp. 70–81). Human Development Foundation.

OECD. (2021). *Regions and Cities: The Role of Territorial Development*. OECD Publishing.

OECD., (2008). Open Innovation in Global Networks: Policies Issues Retrieved from Paris.

Offenhuber, D., & Schechtner, K. (2018). Improstructure—An improvisational perspective on smart infrastructure governance. *Cities (London, England)*, 72, 329–338. DOI: 10.1016/j.cities.2017.09.017

Ogwu, M. C. (2019). Towards sustainable development in Africa: The challenge of urbanization and climate change adaptation. The geography of climate change adaptation in urban. *Africa*, •••, 29–55.

Ojha, C., Sharma, P., & Jain, V. (2024). Design, optimization, and evaluation of topical gel of *Cardiospermum halicacabum* and *Ricinus communis* L. leaves extract for the treatment of rheumatoid arthritis. *Journal of Biomaterials Science. Polymer Edition*, 35(10), 1–22. DOI: 10.1080/09205063.2024.2340872 PMID: 38613797

Okraszewska, R., Jamroz, K., Michalski, L., Żukowska, J., Grzelec, K., & Birr, K. (2019). Analysing ways to achieve a new Urban Agenda-based sustainable metropolitan transport. *Sustainability (Basel)*, 11(3), 813. DOI: 10.3390/su11030813

Olawade, D. B., Wada, O. Z., David-Olawade, A. C., Fapohunda, O., Ige, A. O., & Ling, J. (2024). Artificial intelligence potential for net zero sustainability: Current evidence and prospects. *Next Sustainability*, 4, 100041. DOI: 10.1016/j.nxsust.2024.100041

Oliveira, E. (2019). Artificial intelligence: An overview. *Cutting Edge Technologies and Microcomputer Applications for Developing Countries*, 61-65.

Olorunfemi, O. L., Amoo, O. O., Atadoga, A., Fayayola, O. A., Abrahams, T. O., & Shoetan, P. O. (2024). Towards a conceptual framework for ethical AI development in IT systems. *Computer Science & IT Research Journal*, 5(3), 616–627. DOI: 10.51594/csitrj.v5i3.910

Osifo, O. C. (2018). Examining digital government and public service provision: The case of Finland. In V. B., T. E., G. T.G., S. V., C.-S. M., R. S., S. K., K. M., M. M., G. S., P. P., & J. M. (Eds.), *41st International Convention on Information and Communication Technology, Electronics and Microelectronics, MIPRO 2018* (pp. 1342–1347). Institute of Electrical and Electronics Engineers Inc. DOI: 10.23919/MIPRO.2018.8400242

Ouassou, S., & Bakour, C. (2024). Intelligence territoriale : État de l'art théorique. International Journal of Accounting, Finance, Auditing, Management and Economics, 5(4), Article 4.

Ouaziz, A. (2022b). Portrait empirique de l'intelligence territoriale (I.T): Entre actes, acteurs et actions d'évolution de la ville futur. Revue d'Innovation et Dynamiques Territoriales, 1, Article 1.

Ouaziz, A. (2021). *L'intelligence territoriale aux défis de la ville marocaine « Smart City*. African and Mediterranean Journal of Architecture and Urbanism.

Ouaziz, A. (2022a). Intelligence territoriale de la ville: Conceptions, mouvements, performances et initiatives. *Journal of Social Sciences*, 6(24), 24.

Ozpinar, A. (2023). A hyper-integrated mobility as a service (MaaS) to gamification and carbon market enterprise architecture framework for a sustainable environment. *Energies*, 16(5), 2480. DOI: 10.3390/en16052480

Padmanabh Hota, B. B. (2016). Open Cast Coal mining and sustainable local livelihoods in Odisha, India. *Mineral Economics*, 29(1), 1–13. DOI: 10.1007/s13563-016-0082-7

Page, M. J., McKenzie, J. E., Bossuyt, P. M., Boutron, I., Hoffmann, T. C., Mulrow, C. D., Shamseer, L., Tetzlaff, J. M., Akl, E. A., & Brennan, S. E. (2021). The PRISMA 2020 statement : An updated guideline for reporting systematic reviews. *BMJ (Clinical Research Ed.)*, 372, •••. https://www.bmj.com/content/372/bmj.n71 .short PMID: 33782057

Page, M. J., McKenzie, J. E., Bossuyt, P. M., Boutron, I., Hoffmann, T. C., Mulrow, C. D., Shamseer, L., Tetzlaff, J. M., Akl, E. A., Brennan, S. E., Chou, R., Glanville, J., Grimshaw, J. M., Hróbjartsson, A., Lalu, M. M., Li, T., Loder, E. W., Mayo-Wilson, E., McDonald, S., & Moher, D. (2021). The PRISMA 2020 statement: An updated guideline for reporting systematic reviews. *BMJ (Clinical Research Ed.)*, 372, n71. Advance online publication. DOI: 10.1136/bmj.n71 PMID: 33782057

Paiva, S., Ahad, M. A., Tripathi, G., Feroz, N., & Casalino, G. (2021). Enabling technologies for urban smart mobility: Recent trends, opportunities, and challenges. *Sensors (Basel)*, 21(6), 2143. DOI: 10.3390/s21062143 PMID: 33803903

Palacio, A., Adenso-Díaz, B., & Lozano, S. (2017). Analysing the factors that influence the Pareto frontier of a bi-objective supply chain design problem. *International Transactions in Operational Research*, 25(6), 1717–1738. DOI: 10.1111/itor.12493

PANDA, G. State Climate Change Action Plan and Forestry Sector: Challenges and Mitigation in Odisha.

Panda, A. (2016). Vulnerability to climate variability and drought among small and marginal farmers: A case study in Odisha, India. *Climate and Development*, 9(7), 605–617. DOI: 10.1080/17565529.2016.1184606

Panda, H. (2017). Development challenges and prospects in Odisha. *Centurion Journal of Multidisciplinary Research*, 2(1), 47–59.

Panda, S. (2016). Sustainable irrigation practices in Odisha: Solar-powered irrigation and beyond. *Journal of Irrigation Science*, 34(3), 567–579.

Panda, S., & Das, A. (2022). Public-private partnerships in renewable energy: Case studies from Odisha. *Journal of Renewable Energy Partnerships*, 9(4), 221–235.

Panda, S., Mishra, S. P., & Mishra, S. (2020). Disaster Risk Reduction with Resilient Built Environment in Odisha coast, India. *J Xidian Univ*, 14(5).

Panda, S., & Sahu, R. (2019). Odisha renewable energy policy: An overview. *Energy Policy Review*, 12(2), 189–202.

Pani, B. S., & Mishra, D. (2022). Sustainable livelihood security in Odisha, India: A district level analysis. *Regional Sustainability*, 3(2), 110–121. DOI: 10.1016/j.regsus.2022.07.003

Pankaj, S., Ashish, D., Dheerendra, R., Yogendra, R., Ramakant, J. K. S., & Kuldeep, S. (2015). Formulate and evaluate orodispersible tablets of primaquine. *Indo American Journal of Pharmaceutical Research*, 5(5), 1625–1632.

Pan, S., Zhou, W., Piramuthu, S., Giannikas, V., & Chen, C. (2021). Smart city for sustainable urban freight logistics. *International Journal of Production Research*, 59(7), 2079–2089. DOI: 10.1080/00207543.2021.1893970

Paolone, G., Iachetti, D., Paesani, R., Pilotti, F., Marinelli, M., & Di Felice, P. (2022). A holistic overview of the internet of things ecosystem. *IoT*, 3(4), 398–434. DOI: 10.3390/iot3040022

Papadopoulos, T., Stamati, T., Nikolaidou, M., & Anagnostopoulos, D. (2013). From Open Source to Open Innovation practices: A case in the Greek context in light of the debt crisis. *Technological Forecasting and Social Change*, 80(6), 1232–1246. DOI: 10.1016/j.techfore.2012.10.030

Paquet, G., & Roy, J. (2021). Territorial Management and Public Sector Governance. *Public Administration Review*, 81(4), 610–624.

Pardo, T. A., Parycek, P., Janssen, M., Zheng, L., & Cunha, M. A. (2017). Building & sustaining a digital government research center: A director's perspective. In H. C.C. & O. A. (Eds.), *18th Annual International Conference on Digital Government Research, DG.O 2017: Vol. Part F1282* (pp. 607–609). Association for Computing Machinery. DOI: 10.1145/3085228.3085241

Parida, J., & Mishra, N. (2014). Indigenous knowledge in disaster management: Some reflections on fishing communities of coastal Odisha. *International Journal of Research in Engineering and Applied Sciences*, 2(2), 103–105.

Park, N.-K., & Choi, W.-Y. (2014). The Network Design of China's Northeast Cold Chain. *Susan Haeyang Gyoyuk Yeon-Gu*, 26(4), 760–768. DOI: 10.13000/JFMSE.2014.26.4.760

Pasumarti, S. S. (2020). CSR and Socio-Economic Development–A Case study of selected PSUs in the state of Odisha. *Journal of Critical Reviews*, 7(13), 1407–1415.

Pasupalak (2009), Orissa Review, April-May, Climate Change and Agriculture in Orissa.

Patel, S. (2022). Protecting IoT networks: Best practices. *Cybersecurity Insights*.

Patel, S. (2021). *Smart irrigation systems: A comprehensive guide*. Irrigation Today.

Patel, S. K. (2016). Climate change and climate-induced disasters in Odisha, Eastern India: Impacts, adaptation and future policy implications. *International Journal of Humanities and Social Science Invention*, 5(8), 60–63.

Pati, P., Desai, N., Mankad, A., & Solanki, H. (2020). *The Decadal Changes and Socio-Economic Stresses on Coastal Area through Remote Sensing and GIS Technology: A Review of Puri*.

Patnaik, B. K. (2016). *Impact of Global Warming on Agriculture with Reference to Odisha*. Special Issue on Agriculture and Farmer's Welfare, Directorate of Economics and Statistics.

Patnaik, B. K. (2018, June). Environment Conservation vs. Good Management: On the back drop of Development. *Science Horizon*, 3(6), 23–27.

Patnaik, R., Nayak, A., & Dash, R. (2020). Bio-digester technology in managing livestock waste: A sustainable approach. *Renewable Energy and Agriculture*, 22(1), 75–85.

Paulin, A. (2014). Through liquid democracy to sustainable non-bureaucratic government harnessing the power of icts for a novel form of digital government. *EJournal of EDemocracy and Open Government*, 6(2), 216–230. DOI: 10.29379/jedem.v6i2.307

Perboli, G., & Rosano, M. (2020). A Taxonomic Analysis of Smart City Projects in North America and Europe. *Sustainability (Basel)*, 12(18), 18. Advance online publication. DOI: 10.3390/su12187813

Pereira, R., De Oliveira Massad, D., Do Canto, F. L., & Dandolini, G. A. (2021). The Interrelationship Between Sustainable Development and Social Innovation: A Bibliometric Study. In Pereira, L., Carvalho, J. R. H., Krus, P., Klofsten, M., & De Negri, V. J. (Eds.), *Proceedings of IDEAS 2019* (Vol. 198, pp. 480–489). Springer International Publishing. DOI: 10.1007/978-3-030-55374-6_47

Perianes-Rodriguez, A., Waltman, L., & Van Eck, N. J. (2016). Constructing bibliometric networks: A comparison between full and fractional counting. *Journal of Informetrics*, 10(4), 1178–1195. DOI: 10.1016/j.joi.2016.10.006

Peter, C. (2021). Social Innovation for Sustainable Urban Developmental Transitions in Sub-Saharan Africa: Leveraging Economic Ecosystems and the Entrepreneurial State. *Sustainability (Basel)*, 13(13), 7360. DOI: 10.3390/su13137360

Peterson, J. (2017). An overview of customs reforms to facilitate trade. *J. Int'l Com. & Econ.*, 1.

Pethig, F., Kroenung, J., & Noeltner, M. (2021). A stigma power perspective on digital government service avoidance. *Government Information Quarterly*, 38(2), 101545. Advance online publication. DOI: 10.1016/j.giq.2020.101545

Petticrew, M., & Roberts, H. (2008). *Systematic Reviews in the Social Sciences : A Practical Guide*. John Wiley & Sons.

Phillips, W., Lee, H., Ghobadian, A., O'Regan, N., & James, P. (2014). Social Innovation and Social Entrepreneurship: A Systematic Review. *Group & Organization Management*, 1–34. DOI: 10.1177/1059601114560063

Piccialli, F., Giampaolo, F., Prezioso, E., Crisci, D., & Cuomo, S. (2021). Predictive analytics for smart parking: A deep learning approach in forecasting of IoT data. *ACM Transactions on Internet Technology*, 21(3), 68. DOI: 10.1145/3412842

Picciotti, A. (2017). Towards sustainability: The innovation paths of social enterprise. *Annals of Public and Cooperative Economics, 88*(2), 233–256. *Scopus*. Advance online publication. DOI: 10.1111/apce.12168

Pirotti, F., Guarnieri, A., & Vettore, A. (2015). State of the art and future developments of UAV photogrammetry for 3D modelling of cultural heritage—A review. *Remote Sensing*, 7(3), 6970–7010.

Planning and Convergence Dept., G. o. (2018). Odisha Economic Survey. Bhubaneswar: Odisha govt. press.

Pollitt, C., & Bouckaert, G. (2011). *Public management reform: A comparative analysis—New public management, governance, and the Neo-Weberian state* (3rd ed.). Oxford University Press.

Pomerlyan, E., & Belitski, M. (2023). Integration-Growth relationship: A literature review and future research agenda using a TCCM approach. *European Management Journal*, 41(6), 1106–1118. Advance online publication. DOI: 10.1016/j.emj.2023.10.003

Popoola, O. A., Adama, H. E., Okeke, C. D., & Akinoso, A. E. (2024). Conceptualizing agile development in digital transformations: Theoretical foundations and practical applications. *Engineering Science & Technology Journal*, 5(4), 1524–1541. DOI: 10.51594/estj.v5i4.1080

Porter, M. E., & Heppelmann, J. E. (2017). Why every organization needs an augmented reality strategy. *HBR'S 10 MUST, 85*, 2-18.

Porter, M. E. (1991). Towards a dynamic theory of strategy. *Strategic Management Journal*, 12(S2), 95–117. DOI: 10.1002/smj.4250121008

Porter, M. E. (1998). *No. 6* (Vol. 76). Clusters and the new economics of competition. Harvard Business Review.

Pradeep, P., & Lam, T. (2018). The role of big data and machine learning in flood prediction: A survey. *IEEE Access : Practical Innovations, Open Solutions*, 6, 70576–70594.

Pradhan, A. K., & Patra, R. (2013). Heterogeneity, collective action and management sustainability in common property forest resources: Case study from the Indian state Odisha. *Environment, Development and Sustainability*, 15(4), 979–997. DOI: 10.1007/s10668-012-9422-0

Prebanić, K. R., & Vukomanović, M. (2023). Exploring stakeholder engagement process as the success factor for infrastructure projects. *Buildings*, 13(7), 1785. DOI: 10.3390/buildings13071785

Pribadi, U. (2021). Citizens' intention to use e-government services: The case of e-complaint service in Indonesia. *International Journal of Electronic Governance*, 13(2), 114–131. DOI: 10.1504/IJEG.2021.116884

Pumain, D. (2021). Les systèmes de villes et l'intelligence territoriale.

Purohit, J., & Rout, H. S. (2023). Impact of climate change on human health concerning climate-induced natural disaster: Evidence from an eastern Indian state. *Climatic Change*, 176(8), 109. DOI: 10.1007/s10584-023-03578-1

Putera, P. B., & Gustina, A. (2021). Discourse on digital government and regulation: A bibliometric analysis. *Library Philosophy and Practice, 2021*, 1–11. https://www.scopus.com/inward/record.uri?eid=2-s2.0-85109932480&partnerID=40&md5=a148326f4f489b3c93066a33d6cb102f

Radchenko, K. (2022). Public-Private Partnership for Smarter Cities. *Central and Eastern European eDem and eGov Days, 341*, 103-114. DOI: 10.24989/ocg.v341.7

Raderstrong, J., & Boyea-Robinson, T. (2016). The why and how of working with communities through collective impact. *Community Development (Columbus, Ohio)*, 47(2), 181–193. DOI: 10.1080/15575330.2015.1130072

Radhoui, H., & Baron, M. L. (2022). Ouverture géographique ou enfermement des clusters logistiques du corridor de la Seine? *Logistique & Management*, 30(2-3), 87–101. DOI: 10.1080/12507970.2022.2089248

Rahman, M. M., & Thill, J. C. (2023). Impacts of connected and autonomous vehicles on urban transportation and environment: A comprehensive review. *Sustainable Cities and Society*, 96, 104649. DOI: 10.1016/j.scs.2023.104649

Raimbault, N. (2019). From regional planning to port regionalization and urban logistics. The inland port and the governance of logistics development in the Paris region. *Journal of Transport Geography*, 78, 205–213. DOI: 10.1016/j.jtrangeo.2019.06.005

Rajabi, E., Nowaczyk, S., Pashami, S., Bergquist, M., Ebby, G. S., & Wajid, S. (2023). A knowledge-based AI framework for mobility as a service. *Sustainability (Basel)*, 15(3), 2717. DOI: 10.3390/su15032717

Ramakrishnan, S., Wong, M. S., Chit, M. M., & Mutum, D. S. (2022). A conceptual model of the relationship between organisational intelligence traits and digital government service quality: The role of occupational stress. *International Journal of Quality & Reliability Management*, 39(6), 1429–1452. DOI: 10.1108/IJQRM-10-2021-0371

Ran, H. (2022). THe Enterprise's International Competitiveness Management Design Development Under The Logistics Paradigm. *Economic scope*. DOI: 10.32782/2224-6282/180-25

Ranjbar-Sahraei, B., & Negenborn, R. R. (2017). *Research positioning & trend identification. TU Delft*. Walanda.

Rao-Nicholson, R., Vorley, T., & Khan, Z. (2017). Social innovation in emerging economies: A national systems of innovation-based approach. *Technological Forecasting and Social Change*, 121, 228–237. DOI: 10.1016/j.techfore.2017.03.013

Rasheed, F., Yau, K. A., Noor, R. M., & Chong, Y. (2022). Deep reinforcement learning for addressing disruptions in traffic light control. *Computers, Materials & Continua*, 71(2), 2225–2247. DOI: 10.32604/cmc.2022.022952

Rath, B., & Nayak, R. (2023). Vaccination programs in livestock farming: Ensuring animal health and sustainability. *Veterinary Sustainability Practices*, 15(3), 144–156.

Rath, S., Sahoo, P., Sarangi, K. K., & Kareemulla, K. (2022). Environmental implications of agricultural development in Odisha State. *Journal of Financial Economics*, 3, 2–25.

Rauf, A., Liu, X., Amin, W., Ozturk, I., Rehman, O. U., & Hafeez, M. (2018). Testing EKC hypothesis with energy and sustainable development challenges: A fresh evidence from belt and road initiative economies. *Environmental Science and Pollution Research International*, 25(32), 32066–32080. DOI: 10.1007/s11356-018-3052-5 PMID: 30218332

Raza, A., Ali, M. U., Ullah, U., Fayaz, M., Alvi, M. J., Kallu, K. D., Zafar, A., & Nengroo, S. H. (2022). Evaluation of a sustainable urban transportation system in terms of traffic congestion—A case study in Taxila, Pakistan. *Sustainability (Basel)*, 14(19), 12325. DOI: 10.3390/su141912325

Reix, R., Fallery, B., Kalika, M., & Rowe, F. (2016). *Systèmes d'Information et Management des Organisations-7ème édition.*

Rinaldi, M., Picarelli, E., D'Ariano, A., & Viti, F. (2020). Mixed-fleet single-terminal bus scheduling problem: Modelling, solution scheme and potential applications. *Omega*, 96, 102070. DOI: 10.1016/j.omega.2019.05.006

Rinkinen, S. (2016). Clusters, innovation systems and ecosystems-Studies on innovation policy's concept evolution and approaches for regional renewal.

Ritchie, D. (1986). Shannon and Weaver : Unravelling the paradox of information. *Communication Research*, 13(2), 278–298. DOI: 10.1177/009365086013002007

Rivera, L., Gligor, D., & Sheffi, Y. (2016). The benefits of logistics clustering. *International Journal of Physical Distribution & Logistics Management*, 46(3), 242–268. DOI: 10.1108/IJPDLM-10-2014-0243

Rivera, L., Sheffi, Y., & Knoppen, D. (2016). Logistics clusters: The impact of further agglomeration, training and firm size on collaboration and value added services. *International Journal of Production Economics*, 179, 285–294. DOI: 10.1016/j.ijpe.2016.05.018

Rivera, L., Sheffi, Y., & Welsch, R. (2014). Logistics agglomeration in the US. *Transportation Research Part A, Policy and Practice*, 59, 222–238. DOI: 10.1016/j.tra.2013.11.009

Robin, J., & Coussi, O. (2023). L'intelligence territoriale en contexte de crise sanitaire: Quand une mauvaise communication affecte la stratégie et l'effectivité de la gouvernance territoriale d'un territoire ultramarin. Revue COSSI: communication, organisation, société du savoir et information, 12.

Rodrigue, J. P. (2020). *The geography of transport systems*. Routledge. DOI: 10.4324/9780429346323

Rodríguez-Pose, A. (2018). The revenge of the places that don't matter (and what to do about it). *Cambridge Journal of Regions, Economy and Society*, 11(1), 189–209. DOI: 10.1093/cjres/rsx024

Rodríguez-Pose, A. (2018). The Theory and Practice of Local Economic Development. *Regional Studies*, 52(4), 507–519.

Roengtam, S., Nurmandi, A., Almarez, D. N., & Kholid, A. (2017). Has social media changed city government? Case studies in three ASEAN cities: Bandung, Indonesia, Iligan, Philippines, and Pukhet, Thailand. Changing Governments: People. *Processes and Policy*, 11(3), 343–376. DOI: 10.1108/TG-10-2016-0071

Roger, S., Botella-Mascarell, C., Martín-Sacristán, D., García-Roger, D., Monserrat, J. F., & Svensson, T. (2024). Sustainable mobility in B5G/6G: V2X technology trends and use cases. *IEEE Open Journal of Vehicular Technology*, 5, 459–472. DOI: 10.1109/OJVT.2024.3375451

Rogers, E. M. (2003). *Diffusion of innovations* (5th ed.). Free Press.

Romagni, P., & Wild, V. (1998). *L'intelligence économique au service de la stratégie d'entreprise : C'est pour demain, la veille*. Les presses du management.

Romer, P. M. (1990). Endogenous technological change. *Journal of Political Economy*, 98(5, Part 2), S71–S102. DOI: 10.1086/261725

Rousseaux, F., Saurel, P., & Petit, J. (2014). Knowledge Engineering or Digital Humanities? Territorial Intelligence, a Case in Point. *Studies in Computational Intelligence*, 514, 129–187.

Rudianto, R., Hidayat, F. P., Hardiyanto, S., Priadi, R., & Thariq, M. (2021). Community activities amid activity restrictions during the coronavirus disease-19 pandemic in North Sumatra. *Open Access Macedonian Journal of Medical Sciences*, 9(E), 964–968. DOI: 10.3889/oamjms.2021.7088

Runsewe, O., Osundare, O. S., Folorunsho, S. O., & Akwawa, L. A. (2024). Innovations in Android mobile computing: A review of best practices and emerging technologies. *World Journal of Advanced Research and Reviews*, 23(2), 2687–2697. DOI: 10.30574/wjarr.2024.23.2.2634

Ruß, M., & Gust, G. (2023). Reliable route planning and time savings in real-world urban intermodal transportation networks: Evidence from Hamburg, Germany. *Expert Systems with Applications*, 227, 120196. DOI: 10.1016/j.eswa.2023.120196

Russmann, U., Hametner, M., & Posch, E. (2020). Tax-funded digital government communication in Austria: Members of the government on Facebook. *European Journal of Communication*, 35(2), 140–164. DOI: 10.1177/0267323119894484

Rytova, E., Verevka, T., Gutman, S., & Kuznetsov, S. (2020). Assessing the Maturity Level of Saint Petersburg's Digital Government. *International Journal of Technology*, 11(6), 1081–1090. DOI: 10.14716/ijtech.v11i6.4440

Rzqoo, N. J., Fayadh, O. K., Abid, M. T., & AL-Ugaily, M. (2023). Basic Criteria for creating a Smart City. *International Journal of Engineering Science and Technology*, 5(1), 1. Advance online publication. DOI: 10.46328/ijonest.135

Sá, F., Martins, P., & Abbasi, M. (2021). Portuguese local e-government: A study on the most adopted databases in 2019. *IBIMA Business Review*, 2021, 1–12. Advance online publication. DOI: 10.5171/2021.254977

Saha, A., Görçün, Ö. F., Pamucar, D., Arya, L., & Simic, V. (2024). Evaluation of shared micro-mobility systems for sustainable cities by using a consensus-based Fermatean fuzzy multiple objective optimization and full multiplicative form. *Engineering Applications of Artificial Intelligence*, 134, 108662. DOI: 10.1016/j.engappai.2024.108662

Sahoo, N., & Satpathy, M. (2020). Disasters and climate change adaptability at Odisha coast. Development in Coastal Zones and Disaster Management, 185-199.

Sahoo, S. S., & Lenka, S. K. (2023). *0009, CABI*. CABI, Disaster Management for Coastal Tourism Destinations of Odisha., DOI: 10.1079/9781800621022.0009

Sahu, B. K. (2016). Solar energy developments, policies and future prospectus in the state of Odisha, India. *Renewable & Sustainable Energy Reviews*, 61, 526–536. DOI: 10.1016/j.rser.2016.04.027

Sahu, N. C., & Mishra, D. (2013). Analysis of perception and adaptability strategies of the farmers to climate change in Odisha, India. *APCBEE Procedia*, 5, 123–127.

Sahu, S. C., Sharma, J., & Ravindranath, N. H. (2015). Carbon stocks and fluxes for forests in Odisha (India). *Tropical Ecology*, 56(1), 77–85.

Salam, R., Sinurat, M., Yasin, A., & Sacipto, R. (2023). Implementation of Artificial Intelligence in Governance: Potentials and Challenges. *Influence: International Journal of Science Review*, 5(1), 243–255.

Salas, P., Ramos, V., Ruiz-Pérez, M., & Alorda-Ladaria, B. (2023). Methodological proposal for the analysis of urban mobility using Wi-Fi data and artificial intelligence techniques: The case of Palma. *Electronics (Basel)*, 12(3), 504. DOI: 10.3390/electronics12030504

Salazar-Cabrera, R., Pachón de la Cruz, Á., & Madrid Molina, J. M. (2020). Sustainable transit vehicle tracking service, using intelligent transportation system services and emerging communication technologies: A review. [English Edition]. *Journal of Traffic and Transportation Engineering*, 7(6), 729–747. DOI: 10.1016/j.jtte.2020.07.003

Samaei, S. R. (2023). A Comprehensive Algorithm for AI-Driven Transportation Improvements in Urban Areas. In 13th International Engineering Conference on Advanced Research in Science and Technology, https://civilica. com/doc/1930041

San Francisco Department of the Environment. (2023). RecycleSmart: Enhancing recycling efforts in San Francisco. Retrieved from https://www.sfenvironment.org/recycle/recyclesmart

Sánchez, A. S., Oliveira-Esquerre, K. P., dos Reis Nogueira, I. B., de Jong, P., & Filho, A. A. (2020). Water loss management through smart water systems. Smart Village Technology: Concepts and Developments, 233-266.

Sanchez, T. W., Shumway, H., Gordner, T., & Lim, T. (2023). The prospects of artificial intelligence in urban planning. International journal of urban sciences, 27(2), 179-194.

Sancino, A., & Hudson, L. (2020). Leadership in, of, and for smart cities – case studies from Europe, America, and Australia. *Public Management Review*, 22(5), 701–725. DOI: 10.1080/14719037.2020.1718189

Sanina, A., Balashov, A., & Rubtcova, M. (2023). The Socio-Economic Efficiency of Digital Government Transformation. *International Journal of Public Administration*, 46(1), 85–96. DOI: 10.1080/01900692.2021.1988637

Santhanam, H., & Kundu, S. K. (2022). Assessment of socio-technical constraints of marine fishers in the utilisation of marine fishery advisories in Southern Odisha, India. *Anthropocene Science*, 1(1), 109–120. DOI: 10.1007/s44177-022-00014-4

Sapraz, M., & Han, S. (2021). Implicating human values for designing a digital government collaborative platform for environmental issues: A value sensitive design approach. *Sustainability (Basel)*, 13(11), 6240. Advance online publication. DOI: 10.3390/su13116240

Sarkis, J. (2020). Supply chain sustainability: Learning from the COVID-19 pandemic. *International Journal of Operations & Production Management*, 41(1), 63–73. DOI: 10.1108/IJOPM-08-2020-0568

Sassen, S. (2012). *Cities in a world economy*. SAGE Publications.

Satterthwaite, D. (2021). Sustainable cities or cities that contribute to sustainable development? In *The Earthscan reader in sustainable cities* (pp. 80–106). Routledge. DOI: 10.4324/9781315800462-7

Savić, N., Džunić, M., & Brkić, I. (2015). Comparative analysis of clusters contribution to regional competitiveness. *Ekonomika preduzeća, 63*(3-4), 222-232.

Savin, G. V. (2021). The smart city transport and logistics system: Theory, methodology and practice. *Upravlenec, 12*(6).

Sawhney, N. (2023). Contestations in urban mobility: Rights, risks, and responsibilities for urban AI. *AI & Society*, 38(3), 1083–1098. DOI: 10.1007/s00146-022-01502-2

Scarişoreanu, D. I., & Ghiculescu, L. D. (2023). Strategic forecast for rail freight transport in Romania using the Relevant Tree Method and Scenario Method. *BRAIN. Broad Research in Artificial Intelligence and Neuroscience*, 14(1), 596–627. DOI: 10.18662/brain/14.1/437

Schaeffer, R., Szklo, A. S., de Lucena, A. F. P., Borba, B. S. M. C., Nogueira, L. P. P., Fleming, F. P., & Boulahya, M. S. (2012). Energy sector vulnerability to climate change: A review. *Energy*, 38(1), 1–12. DOI: 10.1016/j.energy.2011.11.056

Scholl, H. J. (2020). Digital Government. *Digital Government: Research and Practice*, 1(1), 1–12. Advance online publication. DOI: 10.1145/3352682

Scholl, H. J. (2021). The Digital Government Reference Library (DGRL) and its potential formative impact on Digital Government Research (DGR). *Government Information Quarterly*, 38(4), 101613. Advance online publication. DOI: 10.1016/j.giq.2021.101613

Schwandt, T. A. (2014). *The Sage Dictionary of Qualitative Inquiry*. Sage Publications.

Şekkeli, Z. H., & Bakan, İ. (2021). Regional benefits of logistic clusters: A study of scale development. *OPUS International Journal of Society Researches*, 18(43), 6143–6161.

Senadjki, A., Awal, I. M., Nee, A. Y. H., & Ogbeibu, S. (2022). The belt and road initiative (BRI): A mechanism to achieve the ninth sustainable development goal (SDG). *Journal of Cleaner Production*, 372, 133590. DOI: 10.1016/j.jclepro.2022.133590

Senapati, A. (2015, August 15). UN felicitates Odisha for its disaster management model for Phailin. *Down to Earth*.

Senapati, T., Simic, V., Saha, A., Dobrodolac, M., Rong, Y., & Tirkolaee, E. B. (2023). Intuitionistic fuzzy power Aczel-Alsina model for prioritization of sustainable transportation sharing practices. *Engineering Applications of Artificial Intelligence*, 119, 105716. DOI: 10.1016/j.engappai.2022.105716

Servou, E., Behrendt, F., & Horst, M. (2023). Data, AI and governance in MaaS—Leading to sustainable mobility? *Transportation Research Interdisciplinary Perspectives*, 19, 100806. DOI: 10.1016/j.trip.2023.100806

Sethi, R., & Mishra, G. (2016). Energy efficiency in the industrial sector of Odisha. *Industrial Efficiency Review*, 5(2), 99–111.

Setyastuti, Y., Suminar, J. R., Hadisiwi, P., & Zubair, F. (2019). Millennial Mothers: Social media as the preferred source of information about parenting in Indonesia. Library Philosophy and Practice, 2019. https://www.scopus.com/inward/record.uri?eid=2-s2.0-85066070586&partnerID=40&md5=b3fb646d1fdc94ff4609d2f280f03ae0

Seyfang, G., & Haxeltine, A. (2012). Growing Grassroots Innovations: Exploring the Role of Community-Based Initiatives in Governing Sustainable Energy Transitions. *Environment and Planning. C, Government & Policy*, 30(3), 381–400. DOI: 10.1068/c10222

Seyyedi, S. R., Kowsari, E., Gheibi, M., Chinnappan, A., & Ramakrishna, S. (2024). A comprehensive review integration of digitalization and circular economy in waste management by adopting artificial intelligence approaches: Towards a simulation model. *Journal of Cleaner Production*, 460, 142584. DOI: 10.1016/j.jclepro.2024.142584

Shabha, G., Barber, F., & Laycock, P. (2021). A qualitative assessment of the impact of smart homes and environmentally beneficial technologies on the UK 2050 net-zero carbon emission target. *Smart and Sustainable Built Environment*, 12(2), 341–360. DOI: 10.1108/SASBE-07-2021-0112

Shah, J., Kothari, J., & Doshi, N. (2019). A Survey of Smart City infrastructure via Case study on New York. *Procedia Computer Science*, 160, 702–705. DOI: 10.1016/j.procs.2019.11.024

Shah, S., & Bristow, E. (2020). Optimizing disaster response with AI and robotics. *IEEE Robotics & Automation Magazine*, 27(3), 68–77.

Sharma, P., Dasputre, N., & Jain, V. (2024). Nanomedicine: Concepts, characteristics, and regulatory challenges. In *Smart Nanocarrier for Effective Drug Delivery* (pp. 1-16). CRC Press.

Sharma, V., Reddy, B., & Sahu, N. (2018). Sustainable rural livelihoods approach for climate change adaptation in Western Odisha, Eastern India. In Climate Change Adaptation and Development (pp. 161-174). Routledge.

Sharma, H., Sharma, P., Parashar, A., & Jain, V. (2023). Formulation and evaluation of *Ficus benghalensis* loaded candy for toothache. *International Journal of Pharmaceutical Sciences and Research*, 14(11), 5298–5305.

Sharma, P. (2021). Modification of human behavior due to coronavirus outbreak: A brief study on current scenario. *Asian Journal of Pharmaceutics*, 15(3).

Sharma, P. (2022). Applications of statistical tools for optimization and development of smart drug delivery system. In *Smart drug delivery* (pp. 183–204). Intech Open. DOI: 10.5772/intechopen.99632

Sharma, P. (2023). Design, optimization, and characterization of herbal gel for facial application. *Asian Journal of Pharmaceutics*, 17(03).

Sharma, P. (2023). Nanostructured biomaterials in drug delivery: Current trends and upcoming possibilities. In *Engineered Biomaterials: Synthesis and Applications* (pp. 261–280). Springer Nature Singapore. DOI: 10.1007/978-981-99-6698-1_9

Sharma, P., Bhargava, S., Parashar, D., & Mangal, A. (2017). Formulation and evaluation of nanoparticles containing cyclophosphamide. *World Journal of Pharmaceutical Research*, 7(1), 785–798.

Sharma, P., Das, R., & Behera, K. (2018). Agroforestry practices for sustainable farming in Odisha. *Agroforestry Systems*, 92(5), 1275–1289.

Sharma, P., & Jain, V. (2023). An overview of current advances and pharmaceutical uses of 3D and 4D printing. *Exploration of Medicine*, 4, 560–575. DOI: 10.37349/emed.2023.00161

Sharma, P., Jain, V., & Jain, S. (2021). Fabrication, optimization and evaluation of chronotropic drug delivery system of captopril. *International Journal of Pharmaceutical Sciences and Research*, 12(6), 2203–2210.

Sharma, P., Jain, V., & Tailang, M. (2022). Swarm intelligence and machine learning algorithms for cancer diagnosis. In *Swarm Intelligence and Machine Learning* (pp. 34–50). CRC Press. DOI: 10.1201/9781003240037-3

Sharma, P., Jain, V., & Tailang, M. (2023). Advancement of nanocarrier-based engineering for specific drug delivery for cancer therapy. In *Targeted Cancer Therapy in Biomedical Engineering* (pp. 465–486). Springer Nature Singapore. DOI: 10.1007/978-981-19-9786-0_13

Sharma, P., Jain, V., & Tailang, M. (2023). How artificial intelligence is transforming medicine: The future of pharmaceutical research. In *Industry 4.0 and Healthcare: Impact of Artificial Intelligence* (pp. 133–150). Springer Nature Singapore. DOI: 10.1007/978-981-99-1949-9_7

Sharma, P., & Tailang, M. (2017). Opportunities and challenges to develop transdermal patch with nanocarrier. *World Journal of Pharmaceutical Research*, 6(15), 392–400.

Sharma, P., & Tailang, M. (2018). In-vivo study of orodispersible tablet of primaquine. *International Journal of Pharmaceutical Sciences and Research*, 9(8), 3506–3510.

Sharma, P., & Tailang, M. (2020). Design, optimization and evaluation of buccal drug delivery system of propranolol for hypertension treatment. *International Journal of Pharmaceutical Sciences and Research*, 11(1), 301–311.

Sharma, P., & Tailang, M. (2020). Design, optimization, and evaluation of hydrogel of primaquine-loaded nanoemulsion for malaria therapy. *Future Journal of Pharmaceutical Sciences*, 6(1), 1–11. DOI: 10.1186/s43094-020-00035-z

Sharma, P., & Tailang, M. (2022). Primaquine-loaded transdermal patch for treating malaria: Design, development, and characterization. *Future Journal of Pharmaceutical Sciences*, 8(1), 43. DOI: 10.1186/s43094-022-00433-5

Sharma, R., & Rath, S. (2019). Waste-to-energy projects: Sustainable energy generation from municipal solid waste in Odisha. *Waste Management and Energy*, 21(5), 258–267.

Sheffi, Y. (2012). *Logistics clusters: delivering value and driving growth*. MIT press.

Sheffi, Y. (2012). Logistics-intensive clusters: global competitiveness and regional growth. In *Handbook of global logistics: transportation in international supply chains* (pp. 463–500). Springer New York.

Sheffi, Y. (2013). Logistics-Intensive Clusters : Global Competitiveness and Regional Growth. In Bookbinder, J. H. (Ed.), *Handbook of Global Logistics* (Vol. 181, pp. 463–500). Springer New York., DOI: 10.1007/978-1-4419-6132-7_19

Sheng, B., Chen, X., Li, T., Ma, T., Yang, Y., Bi, L., & Zhang, X. (2022). An overview of artificial intelligence in diabetic retinopathy and other ocular diseases. *Frontiers in Public Health*, 10, 971943. DOI: 10.3389/fpubh.2022.971943 PMID: 36388304

Shennib, F., & Schmitt, K. (2021, October). Data-driven technologies and artificial intelligence in circular economy and waste management systems: a review. In *2021 IEEE International Symposium on Technology and Society (ISTAS)* (pp. 1-5). IEEE. DOI: 10.1109/ISTAS52410.2021.9629183

Shen, W., Wang, J., & Li, T. (2012). Factor Analysis of the Northeast Economic Zone's Logistics Competition. *Physics Procedia*, 24, 906–911. DOI: 10.1016/j.phpro.2012.02.136

Shou, M., Jia, F., Yu, J., & Wu, Y. (2024). Challenges in developing information and communication technology (ICT) use for rural e-governance: An ecology perspective. *Information Systems Journal*, isj.12540. DOI: 10.1111/isj.12540

Sihombing, S. O., & Achmadi, H. (2022). Assessing Indonesian Youth Acceptance of Corruption: Applying the Stimulus-Organism-Response Framework. *Academic Journal of Interdisciplinary Studies*, 11(2), 214–229. DOI: 10.36941/ajis-2022-0047

Silalahi, M., Napitupulu, D., & Patria, G. (2015). Study of the Concept and Conditions of E-Government in Indonesia. JUPITER. *Journal of Application of Computer Sciences*, 1(1).

Silva, C. N., & Khan, S. (2020). The role of data in smart cities: Leveraging data to improve urban infrastructure. In *Smart cities: Applications, technologies, standards, and driving factors* (pp. 23–45). Springer.

Simonofski, A., Clarinval, A., Vanderose, B., Dumas, B., & Snoeck, M. (2021). What influences citizens' expectations towards digital government? An exploratory survey. *Digital Policy. Regulation & Governance*, 23(2), 154–172. DOI: 10.1108/DPRG-12-2020-0173

Singh, A. (2020). Modelling the impact of port-centric logistics cluster on inter-firm competition. *Unpublished PhD thesis, RMIT University, Melbourne.*

Singh, A., Fernando, R. L. S., & Haran, N. P. (2020). *Development in Coastal Zones and Disaster Management*. Springer Singapore. DOI: 10.1007/978-981-15-4294-7

*Smart Urban Initiatives*. (s. d.). Consulté 17 septembre 2024, à l'adresse https://www.smartnation.gov.sg/initiatives/urban-living/

Smirnova, E., Hajiyev, N., Glazkova, I., & Hajiyeva, A. (2024). Production companies : Evaluation of accessibility and efficiency of transportation and manufacturing processes. *The Asian Journal of Shipping and Logistics*, 40(1), 52–60. DOI: 10.1016/j.ajsl.2024.01.002

Smith, A. (2021). Data protection and privacy in the age of IoT. *Journal of Cybersecurity*, 1(1). https://www.journalofcybersecurity.com

Smith, T., & Houghton, R. (2023). The Future of Public Management: Trends and Technologies. *International Journal of Public Sector Management*, 36(1), 20–34.

Snow, C. C., Håkonsson, D. D., & Obel, B. (2016). A Smart City Is a Collaborative Community : Lessons from Smart Aarhus. *California Management Review*, 59(1), 92–108. DOI: 10.1177/0008125616683954

Society, O. f. (2009). Conceptual Framework for Eco Developement including Community-Based Eco-Tourism and its Application in Satkoshia Gorge Sanctuary.

Sodiq, A., Baloch, A. A., Khan, S. A., Sezer, N., Mahmoud, S., Jama, M., & Abdelaal, A. (2019). Towards modern sustainable cities: Review of sustainability principles and trends. *Journal of Cleaner Production*, 227, 972–1001. DOI: 10.1016/j.jclepro.2019.04.106

Soga, B., & Vyas-Doorgapersad, S. (2022). SIGNIFICANCE OF E-GOVERNMENT SERVICES FOR SMALL BUSINESSES IN THE CITY OF JOHANNESBURG. *Xinan Jiaotong Daxue Xuebao. Journal of Southwest Jiaotong University*, 57(4), 208–222. DOI: 10.35741/issn.0258-2724.57.4.18

Song, Y., Yang, Y., & Cheng, P. (2022). The investigation of adoption of voice-user interface (VUI) in smart home systems among Chinese older adults. *Sensors (Basel)*, 22(4), 1614. DOI: 10.3390/s22041614

Storper, M. (2013). *Keys to the city: How economics, institutions, social interaction, and politics shape development*. Princeton University Press.

Strielkowski, W., Zenchenko, S., Tarasova, A., & Radyukova, Y. (2022). Management of smart and sustainable cities in the post-COVID-19 era: Lessons and implications. *Sustainability (Basel)*, 14(12), 7267. DOI: 10.3390/su14127267

Sun, B., Li, H., & Zhao, Q. (2018). Logistics agglomeration and logistics productivity in the USA. *The Annals of Regional Science*, 61(2), 273–293. DOI: 10.1007/s00168-018-0867-4

Sun, Z. (2023). Actionable AI for climate and environment. In Sun, Z. (Ed.), *Actionable Science of Global Environment Change: From Big Data to Practical Research* (pp. 327–354). Springer International Publishing. DOI: 10.1007/978-3-031-41758-0_12

Surveying, D. A. (2023). Natural Forest Loss Mapping and its Impact on Climate Change Over KBK Districts of Odisha (Doctoral dissertation, Centurion University).

Susanto, A., & Meiryani. (2019). Digital government role. *International Journal of Scientific and Technology Research, 8*(4), 230–232. https://www.scopus.com/inward/record.uri?eid=2-s2.0-85067202490&partnerID=40&md5=0a5ee4e11e43527bcf46311bd60eb40b

Swain, S. K. Population Dynamics and its Impact on Climate Change in Odisha.

Swain, S., Jena, J., & Behera, A. (2017). Genetically improved farmed tilapia (GIFT) and its role in sustainable aquaculture in Odisha. *Aquaculture Development*, 12(4), 98–110.

Swan, M. (2023). Blockchain applications in territorial management: Enhancing transparency and accountability. *IEEE Transactions on Engineering Management*, 70(2), 300–312.

Swanson, D., Goel, L., Francisco, K., & Stock, J. (2018). An analysis of supply chain management research bytopic. *Supply Chain Management*, 23(2), 100–116. DOI: 10.1108/SCM-05-2017-0166

Swanzy, P. N., Abukari, A. M., & Ansong, E. D. (2024). Data security framework for protecting data in transit and data at rest in the cloud. *Current Journal of Applied Science and Technology*, 43(6), 61–77. DOI: 10.9734/cjast/2024/v43i64387

Szpilko, D., Naharro, F., Lăzăroiu, G., Nica, E., & Gallegos, A. (2023). Artificial intelligence in the smart city—A literature review. *Engineering Management in Production and Services*, 15(4), 53–75. DOI: 10.2478/emj-2023-0028

Tadayonrad, Y., & Ndiaye, A. B. (2023). A new key performance indicator model for demand forecasting in inventory management considering supply chain reliability and seasonality. *Supply Chain Analytics*, 3, 100026. DOI: 10.1016/j.sca.2023.100026

Taghikhah, F., Erfani, E., Bakhshayeshi, I., Tayari, S., Karatopouzis, A., & Hanna, B. (2022). Artificial intelligence and sustainability: solutions to social and environmental challenges. In *Artificial intelligence and data science in environmental sensing* (pp. 93–108). Academic Press. DOI: 10.1016/B978-0-323-90508-4.00006-X

Taj, T. (2023). The evolution of the use of big data to serve Moroccan territorial economic intelligence. Revue Du Contrôle, de La Comptabilité et de l'audit, 7(1), Article 1.

Talbot, C. (2005). *Paradoxes of public sector managerialism, old public management and public service bargains*. SAGE Publications.

Tangi, L., Janssen, M., Benedetti, M., & Noci, G. (2021). Digital government transformation: A structural equation modelling analysis of driving and impeding factors. *International Journal of Information Management*, 60, 102356. Advance online publication. DOI: 10.1016/j.ijinfomgt.2021.102356

Tao, S., Liu, H., Wang, S., & Li, C. (2020). Construction of Smart Coastal Cities Based on Digital Government. *Journal of Coastal Research*, 110(sp1), 154–158. DOI: 10.2112/JCR-SI110-037.1

Tassey, G. (2008). Globalization of technology-based growth: The policy imperative. *The Journal of Technology Transfer*, 33(6), 560–578. DOI: 10.1007/s10961-008-9092-0

Tekouabou, S. C., Gherghina, Ş. C., Kameni, E. D., Filali, Y., & Idrissi Gartoumi, K. (2024). AI-based on machine learning methods for urban real estate prediction: A systematic survey. *Archives of Computational Methods in Engineering*, 31(2), 1079–1095. DOI: 10.1007/s11831-023-10010-5

Thiam, S., Aziz, F., Kushitor, S. B., Amaka-Otchere, A. B. K., Onyima, B. N., & Odume, O. N. (2021). Analyzing the contributions of transdisciplinary research to the global sustainability agenda in African cities. *Sustainability Science*, 16(6), 1923–1944. DOI: 10.1007/s11625-021-01042-6 PMID: 34664013

Tijan, E. (2009). DATA CASSIFICATION AND INFORMATION LIFECYCLE MANAGEMENT IN PORT COMMUNITY SYSTEMS. *POMORSTVO-SCIENTIFIC JOURNAL OF MARITIME RESEARCH*, 23(2), 557–568.

Tijan, E., Jović, M., Jardas, M., & Gulić, M. (2019). The Single Window Concept in International Trade, Transport and Seaports. *Pomorstvo*, 33(2), 130–139. DOI: 10.31217/p.33.2.2

Tiwari, P., Garg, V., & Agrawal, R. (2021). Changing world: Smart homes review and future. *EAI/Springer Innovations in Communication and Computing*, 145-160. https://doi.org/DOI: 10.1007/978-3-030-71485-7_9

Tomlinson, R. (2007). *Thinking about GIS: Geographic information system planning for managers*. ESRI Press.

Torres-Valdés, R. M., & Campillo, C. A. (2013). Local development and public relations for disadvantaged groups in the community of Madrid. *Prisma Social*, 10, 394–432.

Trianni, V., Nuzzolese, A. G., Porciello, J., Kurvers, R. H., Herzog, S. M., Barabucci, G., Berditchevskaia, A., & Fung, F. (2023). Hybrid Collective Intelligence for Decision Support in Complex Open-Ended Domains. In *HHAI 2023 : Augmenting Human Intellect* (p. 124-137). IOS Press. DOI: 10.3233/FAIA230079

Tripathy, S. (2020). Farmers, Climate and Disaster Management in a Coastal Region. Development in Coastal Zones and Disaster Management, 101-117.

Trushkina, N., Dzwigol, H., & Kwilinski, A. (2021). Cluster model of organizing logistics in the region (on the example of the economic district «Podillya»). *Journal of European Economy*, 20(1), 127–145. DOI: 10.35774/jee2021.01.127

Tsamboulas, D., Moraiti, P., & Lekka, A. M. (2012). Performance Evaluation for Implementation of Port Community System. *Transportation Research Record: Journal of the Transportation Research Board*, 2273(1), 29–37. DOI: 10.3141/2273-04

Tsampoulatidis, I., Komninos, N., Syrmos, E., & Bechtsis, D. (2022, June). Universality and interoperability across smart city ecosystems. In *International Conference on Human-Computer Interaction* (pp. 218-230). Cham: Springer International Publishing. DOI: 10.1007/978-3-031-05463-1_16

Tsiktsiris, D., Lalas, A., Dasygenis, M., & Votis, K. (2024). Improving passenger detection with overhead fisheye imaging. *IEEE Access : Practical Innovations, Open Solutions*, 12, 66237–66247. DOI: 10.1109/ACCESS.2024.3395786

Tsiulin, S., Reinau, K. H., & Goryaev, N. (2020). Conceptual Comparison of Port Commmunity System and Blockchain Scenario for Maritime Document Handling. *2020 Global Smart Industry Conference (GloSIC)*, 66-71. DOI: 10.1109/GloSIC50886.2020.9267847

Tsiulin, S., Reinau, K. H., Hilmola, O.-P., Goryaev, N., & Karam, A. (2020). Blockchain-based applications in shipping and port management : A literature review towards defining key conceptual frameworks. *Review of International Business and Strategy*, 30(2), 201–224. DOI: 10.1108/RIBS-04-2019-0051

Tyagi, N., & Bhushan, B. (2023). Demystifying the role of natural language processing (NLP) in smart city applications: Background, motivation, recent advances, and future research directions. *Wireless Personal Communications*, 130(2), 857–908. DOI: 10.1007/s11277-023-10312-8 PMID: 37168438

UNISA. (2018). Belt & Road Initiative (BRI), Three Days Work –27-28-29 March. https://web.unisa.it/unisa-rescue-page/dettaglio/id/202/module/87/row/1993

United Nations. (2023). Water management in the 21st century: Leveraging IoT for sustainable development. Retrieved from https://www.un.org/watermanagement

Ushakov, D., Dudukalov, E., Shmatko, L., & Shatila, K. (2022). Artificial Intelligence as a factor of public transportations system development. *Transportation Research Procedia*, 63, 2401–2408. DOI: 10.1016/j.trpro.2022.06.276

Utomo, S. H., Narmaditya, B. S., Wibowo, A., Ali, A., & Sahid, S. (2022). SOCIAL CAPITAL AND ENTREPRENEURIAL INTENTIONS IN RURAL COMMUNITIES OF INDONESIA. *Journal of Eastern European and Central Asian Research*, 9(4), 665–679. DOI: 10.15549/jeecar.v9i4.927

Vallejo, B., Oyelaran-Oyeyinka, B., Ozor, N., & Bolo, M. (2019). Open innovation and innovation intermediaries in sub-Saharan Africa. *Sustainability (Basel)*, 11(2), 392. DOI: 10.3390/su11020392

Van Den Heuvel, F. P., De Langen, P. W., van Donselaar, K. H., & Fransoo, J. C. (2013). Spatial concentration and location dynamics in logistics: The case of a Dutch province. *Journal of Transport Geography*, 28, 39–48. DOI: 10.1016/j.jtrangeo.2012.10.001

Van der Voet, J. (2016). The role of leadership in the implementation of public sector innovation. *Public Management Review*, 18(2), 209–227.

Van Eck, N., & Waltman, L. (2010). Software survey : VOSviewer, a computer program for bibliometric mapping. *scientometrics, 84*(2), 523-538.

Van Hoang, T. (2024). Impact of integrated artificial intelligence and Internet of Things technologies on smart city transformation. *Journal of Technical Education Science*, 19(1), 64–73. DOI: 10.54644/jte.2024.1532

Vanijjirattikhan, R., Khomsay, S., Kitbutrawat, N., Khomsay, K., Supakchukul, U., Udomsuk, S., Suwatthikul, J., Oumtrakul, N., & Anusart, K. (2022). AI-based acoustic leak detection in water distribution systems. *Results in Engineering*, 15, 100557. DOI: 10.1016/j.rineng.2022.100557

Varone, A., Heilmann, Z., Porruvecchio, G., & Romanino, A. (2024). Solar parking lot management: An IoT platform for smart charging EV fleets, using real-time data and production forecasts. *Renewable and Sustainable Energy Reviews*, 189(Part A), 113845. https://doi.org/DOI: 10.1016/j.rser.2023.113845

Vasconcelos, C., Silva, J., Calheiros, C. S. C., Mikusiński, G., Iwińska, K., Skaltsa, I. G., & Krakowska, K. (2022). Teaching sustainable development goals to university students: A cross-country case-based study. *Sustainability (Basel)*, 14(3), 1593. DOI: 10.3390/su14031593

Vázquez-López, A., & Marey-Perez, M. (2021). Factors affecting e-government adoption by dairy farmers: A case study in the north-west of Spain. *Future Internet*, 13(8), 206. Advance online publication. DOI: 10.3390/fi13080206

Venigandla, K., Vemuri, N., & Aneke, E. N. (2024). Empowering Smart Cities with AI and RPA: Strategies for Intelligent Urban Management and Sustainable Development. Valley International Journal Digital Library, 1117-1125.

Vermesan, O., & Friess, P. (Eds.). (2013). *Internet of things: converging technologies for smart environments and integrated ecosystems*. River publishers.

Vermesan, O., John, R., Pype, P., Daalderop, G., Kriegel, K., Mitic, G., Lorentz, V., Bahr, R., Sand, H. E., Bockrath, S., & Waldhör, S. (2021). Automotive intelligence embedded in electric connected autonomous and shared vehicles technology for sustainable green mobility. *Frontiers in Future Transportation*, 2, 688482. DOI: 10.3389/ffutr.2021.688482

Vijayan, D. S., Rose, A. L., Arvindan, S., Revathy, J., & Amuthadevi, C. (2020). Automation systems in smart buildings: A review. *Journal of Ambient Intelligence and Humanized Computing*, •••, 1–13. DOI: 10.1007/s12652-020-02666-9

Vinod Joon, V. J., & Vaishali Jaiswal, V. J. (2012). Impact of climate change on human health in India: an overview.

Vitetta, A. (2022). Sustainable mobility as a service: Framework and transport system models. *Information (Basel)*, 13(7), 346. DOI: 10.3390/info13070346

Von Zedtwitz, M., & Gassmann, O. (2002). Market versus technology drive in R&D internationalization: Four different patterns of managing research and development. *Research Policy*, 31(4), 569–588. DOI: 10.1016/S0048-7333(01)00125-1

Wahyunengseh, R. D., & Hastjarjo, S. (2021). Big Data Analysis of Disaster Communication Policy: Mapping communication issues and public responses on government social media. *10th International Conference on Public Organizations, ICONPO 2020*, 717(1). DOI: 10.1088/1755-1315/717/1/012004

Waldheim, C., & Berger, A. (2008). Logistics landscape. *Landscape Journal*, 27(2), 219–246. DOI: 10.3368/lj.27.2.219

Walldén, S., & Mäkinen, E. (2013). On accepting smart environments at user and societal levels. *Universal Access in the Information Society*, 13(4), 449–469. DOI: 10.1007/s10209-013-0327-y

Walle, Y. M. (2020). The impact of digital government on whistleblowing and whistle-blower protection: Explanatory study. *Journal of Information Technology Management*, 12(1), 1–26. DOI: 10.22059/JITM.2019.291003.2409

Wamba, S. F., Akter, S., Edwards, A., Chopin, G., & Gnanzou, D. (2015). How 'big data'can make big impact: Findings from a systematic review and a longitudinal case study. *International Journal of Production Economics*, 165, 234–246. DOI: 10.1016/j.ijpe.2014.12.031

Wang, B., Xing, D., Zhu, Y., Dong, S., & Zhao, B. (2019). The state of exosomes research: A global visualized analysis. *BioMed Research International*, 2019, 1–10. Advance online publication. DOI: 10.1155/2019/1495130 PMID: 31073519

Wang, D., Zhou, L., Zhang, H., & Liang, X. (2021). A Bi-Level Model for Green Freight Transportation Pricing Strategy Considering Enterprise Profit and Carbon Emissions. *Sustainability (Basel)*, 13(12), 6514. DOI: 10.3390/su13126514

Wang, J., & Deng, K. (2022). Impact and mechanism analysis of smart city policy on urban innovation: Evidence from China. *Economic Analysis and Policy*, 73, 574–587. DOI: 10.1016/j.eap.2021.12.006

Wang, K., Zhao, Y., Gangadhari, R. K., & Li, Z. (2021). Analyzing the Adoption Challenges of the Internet of Things (IoT) and Artificial Intelligence (AI) for Smart Cities in China. *Sustainability (Basel)*, 13(19), 19. Advance online publication. DOI: 10.3390/su131910983

Wang, X. (2022). *AI and IoT in modern irrigation.* Agricultural IoT Journal.

Wan, X., Kuhanestani, P. K., Farmani, R., & Keedwell, E. (2022). Literature review of data analytics for leak detection in water distribution networks: A focus on pressure and flow smart sensors. *Journal of Water Resources Planning and Management*, 148(10), 03122002. DOI: 10.1061/(ASCE)WR.1943-5452.0001597

Wehn, U., Vallejo, B., Seijger, C., Tlhagale, M., Amorsi, N., Sossou, S. K., Genthe, B., & Kileshye Onema, J. M. (2021). Strengthening the knowledge base to face the impacts of climate change on water resources in Africa: A social innovation perspective. *Environmental Science & Policy*, 116, 292–300. DOI: 10.1016/j.envsci.2020.09.026

Wich, S. A., & Koh, L. P. (2018). *Conservation drones: Mapping and monitoring biodiversity*. Oxford University Press. DOI: 10.1093/oso/9780198787617.001.0001

Wiiava, S. W., & Handoko, I. (2021). Researching Covid-19 Twitter Hashtag Conversations in Indonesia: An Approach to Social Network Analysis. In LS, CH, & IR (Eds.), 15th International Conference on Information Management and Ubiquitous Communication, IMCOM 2021. Institute of Electrical and Electronics Engineers Inc. DOI: 10.1109/IMCOM51814.2021.9377382

Williams, M. D., Rana, N. P., & Dwivedi, Y. K. (2015). The unified theory of acceptance and use of technology (UTAUT): A literature review. *Journal of Enterprise Information Management*, 28(3), 443–488. DOI: 10.1108/JEIM-09-2014-0088

Wilson, C., & Mergel, I. (2022). Overcoming barriers to digital government: Mapping the strategies of digital champions. *Government Information Quarterly*, 39(2), 101681. Advance online publication. DOI: 10.1016/j.giq.2022.101681

Winkelhaus, S., & Grosse, E. H. (2020). Logistics 4.0: A systematic review towards a new logistics system. *International Journal of Production Research*, 58(1), 18–43. DOI: 10.1080/00207543.2019.1612964

Wirawan, V. (2020). Application of E-Government in Welcoming the Contemporary Industrial Revolution 4.0 Era in Indonesia. *Journal of Law Enforcement and Justice*, 1(1), 1–16.

Wirtz, B. W., & Göttel, V. (2016). *Smart service systems: Theory and practice*. Springer.

Wirtz, B. W., Langer, P. F., & Schmidt, F. W. (2021). Digital Government: Business Model Development For Public Value Creation-A Dynamic Capabilities Based Framework. *Public Administration Quarterly*, 45(3), 232–255. DOI: 10.37808/paq.45.3.2

Wodnicka, M., & Szukalski, S. M. (2023). Investments in the Industrial and Logistics Real Estate Sector in Poland Compared to the CEE Countries. *Optimum.Economic Studies*, 3(113), 116–136. DOI: 10.15290/oes.2023.03.113.07

Wong, C., & Liew, A. (2015). Challenges in the integration of emerging technologies in public management. *Public Administration Quarterly*, 39(1), 100–117.

Wong, L. W., Tan, G. W. H., Ooi, K. B., & Dwivedi, Y. (2024). The role of institutional and self in the formation of trust in artificial intelligence technologies. *Internet Research*, 34(2), 343–370. DOI: 10.1108/INTR-07-2021-0446

World Health Organization. (2023). Harnessing AI for rural healthcare in Sub-Saharan Africa. Retrieved from https://www.who.int/news-room/feature-stories/detail/harnessing-ai-for-rural-healthcare-in-sub-saharan-africa

Xiang, X., Wang, J., Long, Z., & Huang, Y. (2023). Improving the Entrepreneurial Competence of College Social Entrepreneurs: Digital Government Building, Entrepreneurship Education, and Entrepreneurial Cognition. *Sustainability (Basel)*, 15(1), 69. Advance online publication. DOI: 10.3390/su15010069

Yampolskiy, R. (2020, July). On controllability of artificial intelligence. In *IJCAI-21 Workshop on Artificial Intelligence Safety (AISafety2021)*.

Yang, C., & Suto, H. (2018). Data-Driven Urban Planning: Integrating Big Data and Geographic Information Systems. *Journal of Urban Planning and Development*, 144(3), 1–10.

Yang, J., Zhang, H., & Chen, L. (2023). Ethical considerations in AI decision-making: Fairness, transparency, and accountability. *Journal of Business Ethics*, 145(2), 321–335.

Yang, Y., Shi, Y., & Wang, T. (2022). Blockchain Technology Application Maturity Assessment Model for Digital Government Public Service Projects. *International Journal of Crowd Science*, 6(4), 184–194. DOI: 10.26599/IJCS.2022.9100025

Yavuz, N. (2022). Gender differences in perception and usage of public transit technologies: Implications for digital government. *Information Polity*, 27(1), 97–113. DOI: 10.3233/IP-200305

Yigitcanlar, T., Kankanamge, N., Regona, M., Ruiz Maldonado, A., Rowan, B., Ryu, A., Desouza, K. C., Corchado, J. M., Mehmood, R., & Li, R. Y. M. (2020). Artificial intelligence technologies and related urban planning and development concepts: How are they perceived and utilized in Australia? *Journal of Open Innovation*, 6(4), 187. DOI: 10.3390/joitmc6040187

Yigitcanlar, T., Mehmood, R., & Corchado, J. M. (2021). Green artificial intelligence: Towards an efficient, sustainable and equitable technology for smart cities and futures. *Sustainability (Basel)*, 13(16), 8952. DOI: 10.3390/su13168952

Young, M. M., Bullock, J. B., & Lecy, J. D. (2019). Artificial discretion as a tool of governance: A framework for understanding the impact of artificial intelligence on public administration. *Perspectives on Public Management and Governance*, 2(4), 301–313. DOI: 10.1093/ppmgov/gvz014

Yousaf, A., Kayvanfar, V., Mazzoni, A., & Elomri, A. (2023). Artificial intelligence-based decision support systems in smart agriculture: Bibliometric analysis for operational insights and future directions. *Frontiers in Sustainable Food Systems*, 6, 1053921. DOI: 10.3389/fsufs.2022.1053921

Yu, P., & Zhang, Y. (2019). *The future of smart cities: Emerging trends and applications*. Springer.

Zeman, J. (1965). *Le concept d'information dans la science contemporaine*. Compterendu du Colloque de Royaumont, Paris, Éditions de Minuit.

Zeryouh, A., & Daabaji, A. (2022). Les enjeux de l'intelligence économique dans le développement territorial: Vers une approche de mise en œuvre de l'intelligence territoriale. Alternatives Managériales Economiques, 4(3), Article 3.

Zhang, C., & Kovacs, J. M. (2012). The application of small unmanned aerial systems for precision agriculture: A review. *Precision Agriculture*, 13(6), 693–712. DOI: 10.1007/s11119-012-9274-5

Zhang, H., Lv, Y., & Guo, J. (2022). New Development Direction of Underground Logistics from the Perspective of Public Transport: A Systematic Review Based on Scientometrics. *Sustainability (Basel)*, 14(6), 3179. DOI: 10.3390/su14063179

Zhang, H., Song, X., Long, Y., Xia, T., Fang, K., Zheng, J., Huang, D., Shibasaki, R., & Liang, Y. (2019). Mobile phone GPS data in urban bicycle-sharing: Layout optimization and emissions reduction analysis. *Applied Energy*, 242, 138–147. DOI: 10.1016/j.apenergy.2019.03.119

Zhang, Q., Liu, Y., & Wu, S. (2023). Green technologies for sustainable deployment of IoT in territorial management. *Sustainable Development*, 31(2), 198–210.

Zhang, Q., Liu, Y., & Wu, S. (2023). Integrated AI, IoT, and Big Data platforms for territorial management: Opportunities and challenges. *Journal of Governance and Regulation*, 12(3), 98–110.

Zhang, Q., Liu, Y., & Wu, S. (2023). Regulatory compliance in AI, IoT, and Big Data integration: Challenges and solutions. *Journal of Governance and Regulation*, 12(3), 98–110.

Zhang, Y., Wang, Z., & Huang, J. (2020). Big Data Analytics in Urban Management: Benefits, Challenges, and Future Directions. *Urban Management Journal*, 6(2), 45–67.

Zhang, Y., & Zhou, Y. (2023). Artificial intelligence in urban planning: Current trends and future directions. *Urban Studies (Edinburgh, Scotland)*, 60(4), 801–822.

Zhu, X., & Zhang, K. (2018). Smart technologies and urban governance: A critical review. *Urban Studies (Edinburgh, Scotland)*, 55(4), 1–15.

Ziemba, P., & Gago, I. (2022). Compromise multi-criteria selection of e-scooters for the vehicle sharing system in Poland. *Energies*, 15(14), 5048. DOI: 10.3390/en15145048

Аранчій, В., Ганущак-Єфіменко, Л., Христенко, Л., Шкода, М., Гнатенко, І., & Фастовець, Н. (2022). Моделювання інтегральної оцінки ефективності менеджменту фінансового стану суб'єктів підприємництва. Financial and credit activity problems of theory and practice, 1(42), 259-270.

# About the Contributors

**Lhoussaine Alla** is a professor in Management Sciences at the National School of Applied Sciences, researcher at the LAREMEF Laboratory, Sidi Mohamed Ben Abdellah University, Fez, Morocco. He is a permanent teacher of various marketing management modules at Sidi Mohamed Ben Abdellah University in Fez (Morocco) and in several public and private business graduate schools. He is an accredited professional expert in training engineering, professional coaching and mentoring junior entrepreneurs. After a PhD thesis on creating value for the customer and its impact on the overall performance of companies, Prof. Lhoussaine ALLA invested more in scientific research in marketing, through various scientific contributions in the form of participation in international symposiums and workshops and scientific publications, for various themes inherent to e-marketing, customer experience, commercial performance, Big Data Analytics Marketing, territorial marketing, territorial economic intelligence, etc. Prof. Lhoussaine ALLA is (co)editor of the e-book "Integrating Intelligence and Sustainability in Supply Chains. IGI Global. DOI: 10.4018/979-8-3693-0225-5" and Dirceteur de publication of the scientific journal "Alternatives Managériales et Economiques - AME", indexed on the IMIST portal, https://revues.imist.ma/index.php/AME. Prof. Lhoussaine ALLA is also (co)coordinator of many scientific events devoted to marketing research. As much scientific and educational accumulation that the publisher aims to mobilize as potential to bring together imminent researchers and experts to share the fruits of their relevant and innovative research work in implementation, supervision, evaluation, control and reinvention of innovative solutions developed via Data Engineering and AI in Marketing.

**Bouchra Alj** is a professor and researcher in management sciences, with more than 22 years of experience, having gained international recognition through her contributions to the management of organizations, public finances and taxation. After obtaining her PhD at the Mohammed V University, Faculty of Legal,

Economic and Social Sciences (FSJES) in Rabat-Agdal, she joined the Cadi Ayyad University in Marrakech before joining the Hassan II University in Casablanca, where she is currently working for the FSJES in Mohammedia. She coordinates the Accounting – Finance – Taxation course and teaches specialized modules covering bachelor's, master's and doctoral degrees, such as management of organizations, corporate taxation, tax audit, entrepreneurship and management science research methodology. Prof. Bouchra ALJ is also the head of a research team within the Research Laboratory in Economics, Management and Strategies of Organizations (LAREMSO), where she leads innovative research projects and supervises doctoral theses as well as graduate and master's degree projects. Under his direction, the team explores a variety of topics related to finance, economics, management and econometrics, focusing on an interdisciplinary approach to address concrete and current issues. In addition to her academic responsibilities, Prof. Bouchra ALJ is the author of several books, including on income taxation in Morocco and management of organizations. As the Director of Publication for The Economics & Management Review (https://revues.imist.ma/index.php/EMR/), a journal indexed on IMIST, she is actively contributing to the dissemination of original research, Strengthening links between Moroccan researchers and the international scientific community. She is also a member of several scientific and editorial committees for renowned academic journals. Her work as a private sector consultant allows her to integrate the latest developments in management and taxation into an international context, bridging the gap between theory and practice. Prof. Bouchra ALJ regularly publishes in national and international academic journals, and her research is presented at renowned conferences around the world. His research is oriented towards management, public finance and taxation, with a particular interest in tax psychology and tax justice. She is also co-author of articles published in English and French, thus broadening the scope of her contributions. Very active on the national and international academic scene, Prof. Bouchra ALJ is frequently invited to sit on juries and panels of national and international conferences and plays a key role in organizing and hosting seminars, seminars and study days for committed researchers. She frequently participates in scientific and project evaluation committees, thus strengthening her influence in the field of management sciences.

**Badr Bentalha** teaches Supply Chain and Operations Management at National School Of Business and Management – Fez, Sidi Mohamed Ben Abdellah University – Morocco. Dr. Bentalha investigates the structural dynamics and control of complex networks, applying his findings to supply chain management, Industry 4.0, risk analysis, and digital supply chains. His pioneering research has established seminal academic and practical approaches for sustainable and intelligent supply chain optimization. Using optimization, simulation, control theory, and AI, he tackles real-world supply chain and operations challenges. His work emphasizes the intersection of supply chain management, operations research, industrial engineering, and digital technology. As a professor, he teaches undergraduate, graduate, and, doctoral courses in operations management, supply chain management, logistics, management information systems, and strategic management. Through guest lectures, webinars, and scholarly presentations, he engages students and fosters an active learning environment. He aims to equip future industry leaders with the management knowledge and technological skills to build more resilient, adaptable, and sustainable supply chain operations. Dr. Bentalha's academic background includes management and economics, operations research, and supply chain management. He studied management operations and supply chain management, graduating with honors. He earned PhD degrees and completed an aggregation in economics and management. Before entering academia, he primarily worked in industry and consulting, focusing on process optimization in manufacturing, logistics, and ERP systems. His practical experience includes numerous operations research and process optimization projects for operations design, logistics, scheduling, and supply chain management. Before joining the Fez National School of Business and Management, he was a professor of economics and management preparatory classes since 2009. Dr. Bentalha's influential research is cited in supply chain management and logistics. His publication record includes over 60 papers in prestigious academic journals such as the International Journal of Logistics Systems and Management, International Journal of Business Performance Management, International Journal of Business and Technology Studies, Journal of Environmental Issues and Climate Change, and Economical Managerial Alternatives. He is also the author of three books: Netnography: Principles, Method, and Ethics, Internal Audit of Treasury and Cash Management: Report on the Audit of Treasury and Integrating Intelligence and Sustainability in Supply Chains. Professor Bentalha specializes in supply chain and operations management, operations research, and service management. He is passionate about integrating knowledge across disciplines to solve real-world problems. He has delivered numerous invited plenary talks, keynotes, and panel discussions at conferences and global webinars. He serves as Associate Editor of the Economical Managerial Alternatives journal and is on the editorial boards and advisory committees of several other publications. He regularly presents his research and has chaired organized program committees, and served on advisory boards for over 60 international conferences in supply chain management, operations, management studies, control theory, and information science. He is a member of numerous scientific committees of international journals and conferences. Since 2009, Mr. Bentalha has helped sundry companies implement an audit system, resolve issues, and improve performance.

***

**Mourad Aarabe** is a PhD student at the National School of Business and Management of Fez, Sidi Mohamed de Ben Abdellah University. His research focuses on tourism, marketing, digital marketing, and management

**Ahmed Aftiss** is a professor of higher education in management authors of various books and articles in management

**Nilesh Anand** is an undergraduate student at KIIT University.

**Rajat Kumar Baliarsingh** is currently pursuing Ph D in Marketing from Sri Sri University. His research areas are consumer Behaviour, Sustainability, AI in Marketing, and Neuro marketing. He is currently working as a Faculty Associate in the faculty of management, at Sri Sri University.

**Sana Ben Ghodbane** is an Associate professor at IHEC Carthage, Tunisia. His research topics mainly focus on accounting standardization, CSR, AI, and auditing.

**Naoual Bouhtati** is a PhD student at the National School of Business and Management of Fez, University Sidi Mohamed de Ben Abdellah (Morocco). His research focuses on marketing, logistics and performance management.

**Hicham Eddahmouny** is a Lecturer-Researcher at Sidi Mohammed Ben Abdellah University, where I also serve as the Coordinator of the Entrepreneurship and Innovation Management program. I'm an Associate Researcher at the Interdisciplinary Laboratory of Research in Economics, Finance, and Organizational Management (LIREFIMO). My research focuses on environmental economics, territorial development, and inclusive entrepreneurship

**Younes El Maaqili** is a PhD candidate at ENCG Fès, USMBA Fès, where he specialises in entrepreneurship, social entrepreneurship, development, social innovation, financial inclusion and finance. In parallel with his research, he holds the position of Financial Coordinator at the Ministry of the Interior in Morocco, where he manages Human and Territorial Development projects. Passionate about finance and sustainability, he is committed to promoting positive change and creating meaningful impact through his professional and academic initiatives.

**Youssef Yaccoubi**, professor at the National School of Business and Management of Fez, researcher at the LAREMEF laboratory, Sidi Mohamed Ben Abdellah University, Fez, Morocco.

**Vishal Jain** is presently working as an Associate Professor at Department of Computer Science and Engineering, School of Engineering and Technology, Sharda University, Greater Noida, U. P. India. Before that, he has worked for several years as an Associate Professor at Bharati Vidyapeeth's Institute of Computer Applications and Management (BVICAM), New Delhi. He has more than 14 years of experience in the academics. He obtained Ph.D (CSE), M.Tech (CSE), MBA (HR), MCA, MCP and CCNA. He has authored more than 90 research papers in reputed conferences and journals, including Web of Science and Scopus. He has authored and edited more than 30 books with various reputed publishers, including Elsevier, Springer, Apple Academic Press, CRC, Taylor and Francis Group, Scrivener, Wiley, Emerald, NOVA Science and IGI-Global. His research areas include information retrieval, semantic web, ontology engineering, data mining, ad hoc networks, and sensor networks. He received a Young Active Member Award for the year 2012–13 from the Computer Society of India, Best Faculty Award for the year 2017 and Best Researcher Award for the year 2019 from BVICAM, New Delhi.

**Maha Kareem Abuyabes** is a PhD student at University of Manouba, Tunisia. His current research deal with IFRS and AI.

**Shubham Kumar** is an undergraduate student at KIIT University.

**Somesh Kumar** is an undergraduate student at KIIT University.

**Fatima Zahra Madhat** is a Professor whose research focus is Human Resources, Innovation Strategies, Entrepreneurship. Sidi Mohamed Ben Abdellah University, superior School of Technology (EST), Fez, Morocco.

**Badre Meziane** is an Agrégé Professor specializing in the fields of economic intelligence and territorial development. Holding a master's degree in information systems management, he dedicates his research to crucial themes for strategic development and knowledge management at the territorial level. His research work primarily focuses on economic intelligence, a key domain for the competitiveness of organizations and territories. Prof. Meziane is particularly interested in applying these concepts in the context of territorial development, exploring synergies between economic, institutional, and academic actors to promote growth and innovation at local and regional scales. Territorial intelligence constitutes another major axis of his research, where he studies the processes of collecting, analyzing, and disseminating strategic information to support decision-making and territorial planning. In this framework, Prof. Meziane relies on his expertise in geographic information systems (GIS) to integrate the spatial dimension into the analysis and visualization of territorial data. Knowledge management also occupies an important place in his work. Prof. Meziane explores methods and tools for capitalizing, sharing, and valorizing knowledge within organizations and networks of territorial actors, thus contributing to strengthening their capacity for innovation and adaptation. Through his teaching and research, Prof. Badre Meziane strives to create bridges between theory and practice, developing innovative approaches to address the complex challenges of territorial development in the era of the knowledge and information economy.

**Hitesh Mohapatra** received the B.E. degree in Information Technology from Biju Patnaik University of Technology (BPUT), Odisha in 2006, and the MTech. Degree in CSE from Odisha University of Technology and Research (OUTR) University, Odisha in 2009. He received his Ph.D. in Computer Science & Engineering in 2021 from Veer Surendra Sai University of Technology (VSSUT), Burla, India. He has contributed 30 SCI and Scopus indexed research papers, 21 international/national conferences and books on Software Engineering and C Programming respectively. He has 15 years of teaching experience both in industry and academia. He has served the research community with various capacities like session chair, technical chair, keynote speaker etc. His research interests include wireless sensor network, smart city, smart grid and smart water. Currently he is working as Associate professor at School of Computer Engineering, KIIT DU, Bhubaneswar, and Odisha.

**Samyantak Mukherjee** is an undergraduate student at KIIT University.

**Dyah Mutiarin** research interest is human resources management in public sector

**Achmad Nurmandi** is a Professor at the Department of Government Affairs and Administration, Jusuf Kalla School of Government, Universitas Muhammadiyah Yogyakarta, Indonesia. His research interests are on e-government, urban governance and strategic management in the public sector and published in many international journal and Book Chapter, such as International Journal of Public Sector Management, Transforming Government: People, Policy and Process, Jamba Journal of Disaster Studies, Asian Review of Political Science, Journal of Human Behavior in the Social Environment, Public Policy and Administration, Global Encyclopedia of Public Administration, Public Policy, and Governance, Springer. He is currently the Secretary of the Asia Pacific Society for Public Affairs (APSPA). He is also the Editor-in-Chief of Jurnal Studi Pemerintahan (Journal of Government and Politics) and a Guest Editor of International Journal of Public Sector Performance Management and International Journal of Sustainable Society.

**Abdessamaed Ouchen** is a teacher-researcher at ENCG Fès, USMBA Fès, where he holds the position of Professor Habilitated. His areas of specialisation include Financial Economics and Econometrics. With in-depth expertise in Financial Econometrics, Financial Modelling and Portfolio Management, he contributes significantly to the understanding of empirical finance. His research incorporates advanced econometric techniques to tackle complex financial problems, enriching both theoretical knowledge and practical applications in the field of finance.

**Biswajeet Patnaik** is working as an assistant professor in KIIT School of Management, Kiit University. He has fifteen years of total working experience including academics and corporates. His interest areas are consumer behaviour and sustainability

**Hicham Saidi** is a PhD Student whose research focus is Open Innovation, Human Practices, Social Innovation, Entrepreneurship. Sidi Mohamed Ben Abdellah University, Superior School of Technology (EST), Fez, Morocco.

**Ipseeta Satpathy** is a senior professor at KIIT University. Specializes in Psychology, Behavioral Science, and Organisational Behaviour.

**Aditya Sharma** is an undergraduate student at KIIT University.

**Muhammad Younus** graduated in 2019 from the Karachi Institute of Economics and Technology University in Karachi, Pakistan, and got a Bachelor's degree in Computer Science. The four-year undergraduate program in Computer Science formed the basis of my perseverance towards achieving an in-depth knowledge in the field. After graduation, I worked for the past few years as a business IT analyst in the product and research development of a logistics startup in Pakistan called TPL Logistics. We aim to Digitize Logistics Operations in Pakistan from the First Mile to the Last Mile. After this, I graduated in 2024 from the Universitas Muhammadiyah Yogyakarta in Yogyakarta, Indonesia, and got a Master's Degree in Government Science. My research interest is transforming governance and the public sector through technology. This Experience has given me the confidence and also kindled a desire to do research. The interdisciplinary nature has convinced me in taking this decision as it is the ideal choice for an exciting research career. At the same time, I am confident of contributing originally to the ongoing work. By working under the guidance of distinguished Team, I shall certainly be able to exploit my pote

# Index

## A



## B



## C



## D



## E

## G



## H



## I



## L



## M



## N



## O



## P



## R



## S

## T



## U



## X

www.ingramcontent.com/pod-product-compliance
Lightning Source LLC
LaVergne TN
LVHW080354011026
849161LV00009B/2306
* 9 7 9 8 3 6 9 3 6 8 5 4 1 *